HOWARD
FAST

The Modern Jewish Experience

PAULA HYMAN AND DEBORAH DASH MOORE, EDITORS

HOWARD FAST

For Carol +
Don —
Thank you
for many
wonderful
years of
friendship +
support
Gerry
2/12/13

Life and Literature in the Left Lane

GERALD SORIN

Gerald Sorin

INDIANA UNIVERSITY PRESS   BLOOMINGTON AND INDIANAPOLIS

This book is a publication of

Indiana University Press
601 North Morton Street
Bloomington, Indiana 47404-3797 USA

iupress.indiana.edu

Telephone orders   800-842-6796
Fax orders   812-855-7931

♾ The paper used in this publication meets the minimum requirements
of the American National Standard for Information Sciences—
Permanence of Paper for Printed Library Materials, ANSI Z39.48-1992.

Manufactured in the United States of America

LIBRARY OF CONGRESS CATALOGING-IN-PUBLICATION DATA
Sorin, Gerald [date].
Howard Fast : life and literature in the left lane / Gerald Sorin.
p. cm. — (The modern Jewish experience)
Includes bibliographical references and index.
ISBN 978-0-253-00727-8 (cl : alk. paper) — ISBN 978-0-253-00732-2 (eb)
1. Fast, Howard, 1914-2003. 2. Authors, American—20th century—Biography. 3. Jewish
authors—United States—Biography. 4. Communists—United States— Biography. I. Title.
PS3511.A784Z86 2012
813'.52—dc23
[B]
2012021224

1 2 3 4 5 17 16 15 14 13 12

In memory of my cousin
MARVIN MALKIN,
who introduced me to the writings of Howard Fast

CONTENTS

ACKNOWLEDGMENTS *ix*

Introduction ∞ 1

1 Paradise Postponed ∞ 11
Publish or Perish
Politics Delayed

2 The War against Fascism ∞ 44
The Fatal Embrace
The Reds and the Blacks

3 The Life of the Party ∞ 72
Innocent Abroad
The Road Not Taken
The Politics of Literature

4 Cold War, Hot Seat ∞ 107
The Discouraged American
Down and Out in the USA

5 Banned, Barred, and Besieged ∞ 130
It Can't Happen Here
War and Peace

6 The Myopia of American Communism ∞ 162
Foley Square Follies
Waltzing at the Waldorf
April in Paris
The Poison of Peekskill

7 Literature and Reality ∞ 189
Howard Fast: Prisoner
Great Expectations

8 Free! But Not at Last ∞ 216

9 Trials and Tribulations ∞ 244
    Despair, Distraction, and Defeat
    The Push and Pull of Politics
    Confrontations Left and Right

10 McCarthyism, Stalinism, and the World according to Fast ∞ 269

11 Culture and the Cold War ∞ 284
    Portrait of the Artist as a Captive Man
    To Flee or Not to Flee
    An Ever Brighter Star in the USSR
    Signs of Thaw in the Cold War?

12 Things Fall Apart; the Left Cannot Hold ∞ 307

13 Fast Forward ∞ 335

14 Life in the Fast Lane ∞ 364
    California to the New York Island
    Looking Backward, Seeing Red

15 Fast and Loose ∞ 386
    Disappointment and Despair
    Fast in Pursuit

16 Fall and Decline ∞ 400

NOTES *407*
BIBLIOGRAPHIC NOTE *479*
INDEX *481*

ACKNOWLEDGMENTS

Portions of this biography are based on transcripts of a series of long interviews of Howard Fast done by the late Professor Frank Campenni over a period of twelve years (1965–77). I am grateful to him for his diligence and to his widow, Jeanine, who in November 2003 donated to the University Manuscript Archives of the University of Wisconsin-Milwaukee the transcribed interviews and other materials and letters Professor Campenni had collected in the course of his research.

I garnered a great deal of additional material during seven years of interviews and e-mail exchanges with Howard's daughter, Rachel Fast Ben-Avi, and his son, Jonathan Fast. I cannot thank either of them enough for their cooperation, openness, and willingness to put up with my questions and my constant probing for more detailed information. Rachel was especially forthcoming, kind, generous, and particularly perspicacious in her responses. I have also collected invaluable memories and facts about Fast's domestic life through a series of interviews with Howard's widow, Mimi O'Connor Fast, whose frankness and generosity were essential. In addition I spoke at length with Fast's long-time agent Sterling Lord, Fast's granddaughter Molly Jong-Fast, his daughter-in-law, Erica Jong, and many of Fast's relatives, including Barry Fast, Judith Zander, Susan Shapiro, and Mickey Shapiro.

I am also grateful to staff at the library of the State University of New York at New Paltz, especially those in the Interlibrary Loan Office; Donna L. Davey, Tamiment Library; Gail Malmgreen, Associate Head for Archival Collections, Tamiment Library/ Robert F. Wagner Labor Archives, New

York University; Nancy Shawcross and other curators and archivists at the University of Pennsylvania Library; and Meghan Jensen at the library at the University of Wisconsin-Milwaukee. Most of Howard Fast's rich and immense collection of personal and political correspondence now resides in these last two libraries.

Other archivists who supplied excellent service are David Lowe, head of European Collections and Cataloguing at Cambridge University Library; Michaela Ullmann, Feuchtwanger Curator, University of Southern California; Jacque Roethler, Special Collections, University of Iowa; Patrizia Sione, Kheel Center, Cornell University; Sarah Hutcheon, reference librarian, Schlesinger Library on the History of Women in America, Radcliffe Institute for Advanced Study, Harvard University; Mary Beth Brown, manuscript specialist, Western Historical Manuscript Collection, University of Missouri-Columbia; Harry Miller, reference archivist, Wisconsin State Historical Society, Madison, Wisconsin; Cynthia Ostroff, manager, Public Services, Manuscripts and Archives, Yale University Library; and staff at the University of Tulsa, McFarlin Library, Department of Special Collections, and at the University of Illinois, Russian and East European Center. All helped me find materials related to Howard Fast and his associates that I would not have found otherwise.

In this last regard, I must again thank Mimi Fast for her indispensable help. She was extraordinarily generous with her time and in welcoming my wife, Myra, and me into her home in Old Greenwich, Connecticut, and giving us free rein in Howard Fast's office. We were permitted to go through his files, which measured more than 50 cubic feet, as well as through huge piles of his daybooks and scrapbooks. Without Mimi's cooperation the construction of this book would have been immensely more difficult if not impossible. It is probably not the book she would have written. (For Mimi, Howard, understandably, was "the man," her man, her hero.) Nonetheless, in a special way this is Mimi's book too. The long frank talks we had about Howard Fast contributed her important voice. Her commitment to left progressivism, never absent from our conversations, or, quite apparently, from hers with her husband, gave me a better sense of the life and values she shared with Howard Fast. And, last, but hardly least, Mimi's attachment to the life of the open mind, and the trust she demonstrated in granting freedom to the author, created an atmosphere that allowed my work, my interpretations, and my conclusions to go wherever the evidence led.

I owe too many other people too much to name them all here, but suffice it to say that those listed either have read and responded to the manuscript or at least to substantial parts of it in its various stages and manifestations, or have talked with me about its themes and interpretations. These include Lee Bernstein, Laurence Carr, Robert Polito, Lawrence Bush, and David Krikun. I am especially indebted to Deborah Dash Moore, friend, colleague, and mentor for thirty-five years, who has a sharp eye for lacunae and lets nothing unclear in meaning, direction, or relevance get by her vigilant intelligence, erudition, and professionalism; Lewis Brownstein, who, though troubled by going over again some of the less glorious moments of the Communist history he himself lived through, gave me his time, as well as his firsthand and professionally acquired knowledge and insight in a series of uncountable and vital lunch conversations; and Derek Rubin, who mostly by way of many international phone calls, but also in occasional warm and caring face-to-face talks over coffee or a meal, supplied encouragement and literary insight.

The staff at Indiana University Press could not have been more helpful, including director Janet Rabinowitch, series editor Deborah Dash Moore, project editor Nancy Lightfoot, assistant to the director Peter Froehlich, and freelance copy editor Carol Kennedy, who caught mistakes and omissions, and had incisive and intelligent suggestions for fixing the occasional awkward sentence. Whatever errors or ambiguities remain are entirely my responsibility.

The greatest portion of my appreciation by far goes to my extraordinary wife of fifty years, Myra Sorin, for her patience and unflagging support, and for her keen editorial eye and insistence on choosing clarity over cleverness whenever the two were in conflict. Most of all I am thankful for her unconditional love, which still fills me with wonder.

HOWARD
FAST

Introduction

$\mathcal{H}$oward Fast went from being a badly neglected, rough-and-tumble street kid in tattered clothes to a world-renowned writer worth many millions of dollars. In the midst of this remarkable journey, Fast, to the surprise of many, not only became a Marxist, but by the late 1940s had become the public face of the Communist Party in America.

His commitment to the Party was powerful and had momentous consequences for his life, his writing, and his sense of identity. A biography of so active and influential a cultural and political figure as Fast can't help but add to our understanding of him and his generation, especially the lives and significance of his immediate cohort—Communists, writers, and Jews—as they matured in postwar America.

One of five children born to East European Jewish immigrants, Howie, as he was called well into adulthood, lost his mother in 1923 when he almost nine, and was left with a less-than-ambitious father who was poorly paid or unemployed for most of his life. In order to subsist, Howie started working at odd jobs when he was ten years old. Not earning nearly enough, however, he often resorted to swiping bread and milk from the front steps of brownstones and shirts and pants from backyard clotheslines, and even, along with his older brother Jerry, to begging unabashedly in front of the Polo Grounds, the home of the New York Giants baseball team.

In this way, Howie endured his unpromising beginnings as a poor orphan. But he more than survived; through his fierce dedication to writing he managed to escape from the abject poverty of Jewish immigrant New York to become rich and famous. Though a poor student who skipped school often to go to work, Fast was a voracious reader and an ambitious and inexhaustible writer. Between 1932, when he was eighteen, and 2000, he produced a massive body of work: uncountable newspaper and magazine articles, more than 150 short stories, 20 screenplays, and nearly 100 books, several selling tens of millions of copies. His first published novel appeared in 1933 when he was a mere nineteen, and his last, a literary skewering of the rich and powerful involved in murder, corruption, and infidelity, was published in 2000 when he was eighty-six. By the 1990s sales of his books, several of which have won prestigious awards and gone through multiple editions, and many of which remain in print after more than six decades, topped a hundred million, making him, arguably, the most widely read writer of the twentieth century. His ground-breaking novel *Freedom Road* (1944), which deals with former slaves during the Reconstruction period in South Carolina, alone sold nearly thirty million copies in ten years and was translated into eighty-two languages.

Other multimillion sellers include such minor classics as *The Last Frontier*, a 1941 novel about the Cheyenne Indians' horrific, yet determined and dignified, trek away from their reservation in Oklahoma to their homelands in Montana and Wyoming; *The Unvanquished* (1942), a reverential but humanizing look at George Washington during the American Revolution; *Citizen Tom Paine* (1943), a fictionalized biography of the most radical of the founding fathers; *My Glorious Brothers* (1948), a novelized history of the Maccabean revolt in ancient Israel; *Spartacus* (1951), an epic retelling of a legendary slave uprising; and *The Immigrants*, a series of six novels (1977–1985, 1997) tracing the trials, tribulations, and triumphs of three California families over the course of several generations, which together sold over ten million copies.

Fast was several steps up the ladder to renown in 1943 when, for seemingly inexplicable reasons, he joined the American Communist Party (CP or CPUSA). This decisive and consequential step, explored at great length in *Life and Literature in the Left Lane*, was motivated in part by a quest for social justice engendered by Fast's own impoverished beginnings, which were exacerbated by the Great Depression, and in part by his subsequent saturation in the secular Jewish tradition of "repairing the world." But after reading his private correspondence, transcribed interviews, notes, and unpublished manuscripts, and after interviewing members of his family, I have concluded that the most important ingredient in Fast's decision to join the Party was his fierce desire for fame, fortune, and friends. He believed he could achieve these multiple goals via the CP because almost all the Communists he met had already done so. He wanted desperately to be part of the supportive coterie of highly regarded Communist intellectuals with whom he worked at the Office of War Information (OWI) in 1942, and to live the opulent, glamorous, and sexually exciting life of the Communist screenwriters, directors, and actors he met and befriended in Hollywood in 1943.

Before Fast attached himself to the CP, he and many in the literate world were well aware of the Moscow Show Trials, the murderous behavior of Communists toward Trotskyists and anarchists during the Spanish Civil War (1936–39), and Stalin's Great Terror purges of 1937 and 1938. The Hitler-Stalin nonaggression pact of 1939, in reality a military alliance, was also, of course, no secret. Moreover, refugees from the USSR had made known the existence of the Soviet gulag, in which of tens of thousands were incarcerated as slave laborers; and other credible observers testified to the murder of countless "dissenters," as well as the imprisonment, torture, and execution of writers, a group that would become increasingly Jewish over time. Because these brutalities continued with frightening consistency, and because the leadership of the CP in the United States almost always obeyed the Moscow-defined Party line, including the Stalinist position on art and politics, hundreds of American writers, artists, and intellectuals had fled the CPUSA by the time Fast came aboard.

His choice of ideological commitment raises, not for the first time, a stark and unavoidable question. How could Fast and so many other intelligent people buy into or support Communism, especially during its Stalinist period, when it perpetrated one of the greatest intellectual sins of the twentieth century? Communists worldwide passed judgment on the fate of others in the name of an envisioned utopia about which they claimed a monopoly of "perfect information." Along the way, many radical leftist intellectuals and even "fellow travelers" acted as "true believers." They failed to acknowledge the human inclination to abuse power, ignored horrific consequences, and often rationalized Soviet barbarities as historically necessary. One of the benefits of examining the life of Howard Fast is that it enables us to make yet one more exploration into the hoary question of how this could have happened.[1]

An especially deprived child of the Depression and an emotionally needy orphan, Howard Fast grew enthralled with the Soviet Union's socialist model at an early age, and as he grew older he became a champion of its ferocious antifascist military success, which he consistently confused and conflated with Stalinism. Blinding himself to continuing Soviet atrocities by dismissing them as bourgeois propaganda, or accepting them as the price to be paid for the construction of a "better world," Fast became a Party member in 1943. He adopted its outlook relatively quickly, justifying what he knew of the Stalinist regime's behavior as a revolutionary stage in the building of socialism, while at the same time denouncing American wrongs and injustices as indicative of an increasingly incorrigible fascist state. With so few writers and intellectuals left in the CP, Fast, almost by default, became the most prominent cultural spokesman in, and for, the American Communist Party well into the 1950s.

During his Communist years Fast's writing was either critically panned or ignored in the United States even as he was consistently and automatically praised by critics in the Soviet Union, which by 1948 was reprinting hundreds of thousands of his books, almost all of which became required reading in Russian schools. Fast's positive relationship with the Soviet Union, his pronounced Marxism, and his radical politics in the midst of the Cold War no doubt prejudiced and alienated many readers in the United States. But as I try to demonstrate in this biography, the political bias of American readers was less important a factor in Fast's fading reputation than was the degeneration in the quality of his writing after he joined the CP.

That decline was not the result of Fast's adopted Marxist worldview. Though fuzzy and inadequate, his Marxism, as with the proletarian writers of the 1930s, actually helped free up Fast's creative imagination, moving him away from the sentimental "romance" model of his first two published book-length works, *Two Valleys* (1933) and *Strange Yesterday* (1934), and toward tough-minded fiction, including five important and enduring historical novels, published between 1939 and 1944. It was only after Fast became a full-fledged member of the Communist Party, within which his Marxist perspective morphed into Party orthodoxy, apologetics for the Soviet Union, and anti-American radical activism, that his literary slide began.

From the very beginning of Fast's association with the CPUSA, he had some knowledge of the power of the Party's Cultural Section to intimidate artists. But despite the experience of others, Fast thought he'd be able to remain a free man and autonomous writer in the CP. He believed that by literary sleight of hand, he could maintain control over the quality and content of his work without incurring the wrath of the Party's literary commissars. He was wrong. With his moral integrity already severely damaged by his abject Party loyalty, Fast's creativity and independence as a writer would also be seriously compromised. He made no Faustian bargain: he did not have to submit his writing to the CP for authorization. No artist had to. But on occasion, however reluctantly, Fast consciously agreed to take substantive and stylistic instruction from the Party, which at no time trusted writers. Much later, Fast admitted that soon after joining the CP, he began to feel as if at his typewriter he was encircled by a group of sharp-eyed censors on the lookout for "political incorrectness."

The Party's negative reaction to *Freedom Road*, completed in 1944 near the beginning of Fast's tenure in the CP, and his pliant response to the criticisms of the Party's Cultural Section, was the start of a relationship that soon became codependent. The "literary commissars" determined that some of the content and entire interpretive thrust of *Freedom Road* were in conflict with several Party policies. These "deviations," especially Fast's "error" in using the word "nigger" throughout the novel, "presented problems" in principle and were grave enough, it was thought, to necessitate "disciplinary action." When Fast argued that the "N" word had been used pervasively in American history not only by whites, but by blacks themselves, he was accused of engaging in "bourgeois premises" and missing the whole point of "socialist realism," which was to use art only in the service of the exploited classes. Informed that using the "N" word was in itself grounds for expulsion from the Party, Fast promised to mend his ways in the future and to work on divesting himself of any bourgeois residue. There was no expulsion. Party leaders believed that their withering criticism was enough to keep their new pup in line.

And it was. But it was also "necessary" to repeat the ritual of humiliation from time to time. After having taken flak over *Freedom Road*, Fast suffered a furious tongue-lashing for writing *Clarkton* (1947), his first "proletarian novel." He was not confronted and berated by comrades because the book was bad—which it was; instead, he was lambasted because even in this novel about a labor strike in New England, which depicts Communists in a very positive light, Fast had engaged in yet another deviation. He had drawn the boss, the owner of the mill, as a human being, a capitalist with feelings.

Fast was severely criticized again in 1948 for *My Glorious Brothers*, a fictionalized version of the struggle of the ancient Maccabees against their Greek and Roman overlords. According to several CP watchdogs the novel deserved the strictest condemnation for promoting the reactionary notion of Jewish nationalism. The Party stopped short of expelling Fast, nor did he quit, even in the face of lacerating disapproval. One of the very few known writers remaining in the CPUSA by 1948, Fast had become too important to the Party, and the leadership thought it had no choice but to keep him. And after five years of saturation in the American Communist world, Fast had adopted the Party as his family, religion, and identity. He could not readily abandon it without suffering significant emotional consequences.

Too deeply rooted and entrapped psychologically in the CP, and too profoundly inseparable from his Communist associates, Fast simply would not face down the cultural commissars. By agreeing to each new requirement of the Party rulers, while at the same time thinking he had preserved within himself the autonomy of a free thinker, Fast had become someone who, like "true believers" in virtually any cause in any era, had subordinated himself to and finally internalized the ideas and dictates of others. In the process his creative life had been severely compromised, if not completely degraded.

With the exception of some sections of *My Glorious Brothers* (1948) and *Spartacus* (1951), the books Fast wrote while in the Party, constituting the bulk of his literary output for more than a decade and including *The American* (1946), *Clarkton* (1947), *The Passion of Sacco and Vanzetti* (1953), *Silas Timberman* (1954), and *Lola Gregg* (1955), were, by his own much later admission, sophomoric and unwieldy. Indeed, in the late 1940s and 1950s, Fast's work was mostly flat, one-dimensional, distorted by ideology, and simply uninteresting to those outside leftist circles. Little of it equaled the literary quality or popular appeal of the four or five minor classics Fast had written in his pre-Party period, strongly suggesting that his art—any art—suffers irreparable harm when burdened by ideological obligations.

Between 1943 and 1957, Fast stood virtually alone among American artists as both a full-time writer and a full-time political activist. Even abroad, there were only a handful of writers, such as Arthur Koestler, George Orwell,

George Konrad, and Ignazio Silone, who split their time equally between writing and active politics. Although Fast managed the dual roles physically, his imagination froze, his ideas rigidified, and his place as a writer in the United States declined precipitously.

Within the CP, however, he maintained a rich and complex relationship with leaders and members, as he did with "fellow travelers," or pro-Communists, those women and men who shared many of the values of the Party but never joined. He had correspondence and was friends with major Soviet writers, as well as with singers Pete Seeger and Paul Robeson. He maintained close ties to the African American scholar and activist W. E. B. Du Bois; the Spanish Civil War hero and radical labor leader, Steve Nelson; artist Rockwell Kent; writer-economist Scott Nearing; and Chilean poet Pablo Neruda. He was also closely in touch with Boris Polevoy, an influential member of the Soviet Communist Party and an officer in the Soviet Writers Union, and he communicated with many European Communists, including Jean-Paul Sartre, Pablo Picasso, and Sean O'Casey. Fast also maintained a friendship and a vast correspondence over many years with the East German Communist Jewish writer Stefan Heym.

These robust and varied relationships helped sustain Fast even if they did not quite make up for the fact that, except for *My Glorious Brothers* in 1948 and the self-published *Spartacus* in 1951, his Communist-period writings were mostly disregarded in the United States. In any case, having made his reputation almost as much by his pro-Communism as by his novels, Fast himself, unlike his books, did not drop from public notice. He was, for example, subpoenaed to appear before the House Committee on Un-American Activities (HUAC) in 1946, not for anything he had written or said, but because of his membership on the executive board of the Joint Anti-Fascist Refugee Committee (JAFRC) which was considered to be, not unreasonably, a Communist front organization. For refusing to "name names"—actually for failing to turn over the account books of JAFRC—Fast, along with sixteen others on the executive board, was cited for contempt of Congress, convicted in 1947, and imprisoned for three months in 1950. He also gained attention and loads of press coverage when *Citizen Tom Paine* was banned in the New York City public school system in 1947 and when Fast himself was barred from speaking on college campuses in the late 1940s and 50s. He was also at the very center of the infamous Peekskill, New York, anti-Communist riots in 1949, and instrumental in drumming up support for alleged conspirators

Julius and Ethel Rosenberg. His name stayed in the news too when he made a quixotic run for Congress in 1952 and had a televised shouting match with Joe McCarthy's Senate subcommittee in 1953.

Fast was always troubled at being seen as more a political figure than a writer. After Khrushchev's "secret" denunciation of Stalin in March 1956, and the brutal suppression of the Hungarian uprising by the Soviet Union later that year, Fast finally and loudly renounced his membership in the Party, and in 1957 publicly denounced Communism. Having freed himself from the influence of the Communist cultural commissars to whom he had felt compelled to defer while in the Party, Fast eventually managed to break back into the cultural mainstream. Between 1959 and 1960 he worked behind the scenes on the screenplay for the commercially successful film version of *Spartacus*, as did the blacklisted Dalton Trumbo. After Trumbo's name appeared on-screen among the credits, and it became known that Fast had contributed nearly one-third of the dialogue for the movie, the Hollywood blacklist was broken.

Still, Fast thought he might have some difficulty publishing under his own name, and he began in 1960 to produce mysteries—ultimately major best-sellers at home and abroad—under the pseudonym E. V. Cunningham. His literary reputation wasn't revived, however, until he had been out from under the sway of the CP for some time. Two tepid novels Fast wrote almost immediately after leaving the Party, *Moses* (1958) and *The Winston Affair* (1959), went unheralded and mostly unread. But with *April Morning* in 1961 and *The Hessian* in 1972, two critically admired Revolutionary War novels, Fast reestablished his standing as a writer of serious historical fiction. He also became an increasingly wealthy man from sales of his Cunningham books, twenty in all through 1986, as well as through a host of other popular novels, novellas, short-story collections, and TV screenplays.

In the late 1970s and 1980s, however, those who read *The Immigrants*, Fast's extraordinarily successful six-book California series, while sunning on the beaches of Santa Monica or Provincetown, were unlikely to know that they were reading the author of *Citizen Tom Paine* or even *April Morning*. No matter. The *Immigrants* books themselves were immensely popular and launched Fast into a "second career" and vast riches—proving that F. Scott Fitzgerald was wrong when he said, "There are no second acts in American lives."

During his "first life," and immediately after joining the CPUSA, Fast staunchly denied any strong sense of Jewishness. But before joining the Party he had strongly identified as a Jew and had already written more than one book about the Jewish people and had featured Jewish protagonists in several of his novels and stories. Indeed, throughout Fast's life, as will be seen in these chapters, there continued to be a significant connection between his identity as a Jew, complex as it was, and many of his works, as well as between his second-generation "Jewishness" and his left-wing politics.

After his long stint as a Communist (which I try to show never really ended for him as a state of mind), Fast also discovered that his Jewishness was compatible with other worldviews. He committed himself to pacifism in the 1960s, for example, as well as to the practice of Zen meditation (even as he became a multimillionaire). Possession of a Jewishness informed by other than only Judaic cultural sources was not so unusual among Jewish Americans of the second generation. It was also not unusual that Fast, having become rich and famous again, ventured, like many other successful men, into repeated infidelities. At 5'10", round-cheeked, prematurely balding, and bespectacled—not what we would ordinarily call physically handsome—Howard parleyed his cachet as a known writer into a half-dozen sexual liaisons outside his marriage, including several with Hollywood actresses when he worked as a screenwriter in Los Angeles in the 1970s. His marriage to Bette Cohen, a sculptor and painter who often suppressed both her own talents in support of her husband, and her indignation over his continuing unfaithfulness, was shaky at times, but lasted fifty-seven years until her death in 1994. In 1999 at the age of eighty-five, Fast married Mercedes (Mimi) O'Connor, thirty-five years his junior, a woman with whom he had been living since 1996 and who had become his valued editorial assistant and infatuated admirer.

Elsa Morante, the Italian writer and wife of Alberto Moravia, left a warning for biographers: "The private life of a writer is gossip, and gossip no matter about whom offends me."[2] Such daunting advice gives one pause. But there is no escape from the "private" for anyone involved in the biographical process, which by necessity is an act of conscious psychological intrusion. Still, even as biographer and subject move over the same ground, it is not possible to know fully the "real life," the one led in the subject's head. And perhaps, "biographical truth," as Freud said, "is not to be had" at all.[3]

But looking at Fast's words and actions may at least move us in the direction of illuminating his fiction, its place in the American literary pantheon, and its connection to a private and public life full of adventure and risk, love and pain, confusion and misdirection, struggle, failure, and success. As importantly, Fast lived directly and emblematically at the storm centers of the twentieth century. This crucial circumstance allows us to address questions about the wages of political myopia and single-mindedness; the nature of the CPUSA and its place in American life; the relationship between modern Jewish identity and radical movements; and the complex interaction between art, popular culture, and politics in an evolving America.

1

Paradise Postponed

*O*n July 20, 1948, a month after the United States Supreme Court refused to review Howard Fast's conviction for contempt of Congress,
he wrote to screenwriter Albert Maltz in California complaining about the
"cold fear" sweeping America. Those "bastards in Washington," Fast said,
had purposefully "singled out" and "attacked" leftist writers such as him and
Maltz and the Hollywood Ten. But "once we do go to prison," Fast said, "I
think the whole nature of the campaign will . . . change." He and the other
writers, Fast believed, would then have an "extraordinary distinction" and
"a responsibility we cannot fail."[1]

Despite Fast's belief, neither he nor the Hollywood Ten were going to
prison for what they had written. They had been called to testify by HUAC in
1946 and 1947 for what they had allegedly done, or had seen done by others,
that could be considered "subversive." Their refusal to answer potentially
incriminating questions or to "name names" earned them their contempt
citations and convictions. HUAC did not ask or say *anything* about Fast's
books, which numbered nine in 1946. The congressmen focused instead on
the account books of the Joint Anti-Fascist Refugee Committee (JAFRC), an
allegedly pro-Communist organization to which Fast belonged and which
had founded and continued to support a hospital in France for wounded
antifascist veterans of the Spanish Civil War. Fast ended up in prison not

because he *wrote* books, but because he refused to *turn over* books that contained the names of donors supportive of the work of JAFRC.

As with HUAC, so with the FBI: books were not what brought Fast to the agency's attention. Although J. Edgar Hoover and his agents trusted writers as little as the Communist Party (CP) did, they did not initiate a dossier on Fast in 1932 because of what he had published up to that point: one short story of science fiction not remotely related to politics. Instead, an FBI file on the seventeen-year-old Fast was initiated with astonishing speed after he attended a meeting of the John Reed Club, a literary organization associated with the CP.[2]

Still, it was writing and not politics with which Fast most closely identified in 1932. It was of utmost importance to him—not "all his life," as he told a high school audience in 2000, but "only since [he] was twelve."[3] The students didn't get the joke, but Fast wasn't kidding about his very early interest in writing stories and getting them published. He had submitted his first effort to *Cosmopolitan* magazine at the age of fourteen.[4]

The odds of Fast becoming a writer had not been in his favor. He was the fourth child born to Ida (Miller) Fast and Barnett Fastov, poor Jewish immigrants from Eastern Europe, she via England, who lived on 159th Street near Amsterdam Avenue in a deteriorating section of Manhattan. For the first eleven months of Howard's life he suffered from an infection of the temporal bone behind his left ear, which he barely survived. Howie, as he was called by family and friends, remained small throughout his boyhood, but by the time he was two, he had regained his health and could interact with his three-year-old brother Jerome (Jerry) and his twelve-year-old sister Rena. One brother, Arthur, the Fasts' second child, had died of diphtheria in 1912, two years before Howard was born.

Howie's father, who changed his own name to Barney and the family's to Fast, was something of a romantic. He fell in love with Ida, a sister of one of his fellow workers, after seeing only her photograph. A correspondence followed, and Barney sent Ida the money to travel to America from London, where she had been living with her Lithuanian family. They married with great enthusiasm in 1899. But by the time Howie was born fifteen years later, the atmosphere in the Fast household had descended into general lassitude. Barney, who worked very long hours for very low pay, came home late and exhausted from his job as a wrought-iron worker, didn't talk much, and would generally fall asleep while reading the Yiddish papers. He had little time or energy to spend with Howie and his siblings, and even less to demonstrate affection or intimacy. Ida thought him "dull" and kept comparing him to other men she knew who were "entertaining . . . amusing, and jolly."[5] By doing so, her daughter said, Ida "became more and more unhappy." She took care of the children, cooked, cleaned, and did "a great deal of washing at night," hoping, Rena recalled, to scrub "her unhappiness away." As soon and as often as she could, Rena fled the family's gloomy apartment to visit friends in more "cheerful surroundings."[6]

After Julius (Julie), the family's fifth child, was born in 1918, the Fast household grew even bleaker. Ida failed to regain her strength after giving birth and was increasingly neglectful when she wasn't impatient. Four-year-old Howie, apparently feeling displaced by the newcomer and unsettled by the change the baby seemed to have caused in his mother, began to engage in more and more serious misconduct. Jerry, however, to the disadvantage of Howie, continued to be a "model child." Howie's behavior brought insidious comparison and derision from Rena, and physical punishment from Barney. Though rare, the beatings increased the distance between father and son.[7]

For more than three years before her death in 1923 when Howie was only eight, Ida was intermittently hospitalized. A quarter of a century later Fast, who had suffered what he called instant "infantile amnesia" so as to forget the ordeal of his painful childhood, chose to emphasize only the years of nurture and attention. His mother was "wasting away from a disease [pernicious anemia] which at the time was . . . incurable. The implacable approach of death," Fast wrote, "had a devastating effect on all of us. . . . The end came . . . brutally and abruptly—a coffin standing in the tiny room of a slum apartment, a hideous journey to a cemetery, and then the disappearance of my protector, my love, my total connection with the thing called life."[8]

Although Barney virtually ignored Jewish commandment and entered synagogue only on Yom Kippur, he made Howie and Jerry say Kaddish after their mother died. Their father's insistence "meant rising every morning just before sunrise," Fast remembered, "trudging three blocks to the ancient Orthodox synagogue . . . then going to school, six blocks more in another direction . . . and doing this for twelve long months." At synagogue the service consisted of a dozen or more old, white-bearded men who spoke only Yiddish, not a word of which Jerry or Howie understood. For their ignorance, Fast said, the two motherless boys were held in contempt, never hearing a word of sympathy. "This period of mourning . . . and my experience with these old men" embarrassed and angered Fast, and led, he said, "to my avoidance of Hebrew instruction," and "drove me and my brother away from any connection with Jewish religious practice for years to come." Each had a "perfunctory Bar Mitzvah," but it would take many more decades before Fast could sit without unease in a synagogue.[9]

With the virtually absent Barney working long hours, Rena fully employed, and three-year-old Julius sent to live with his maternal grandmother, Jerry and Howie were effectively abandoned. When Rena finally left the household forever to get married less than two years after Ida died, the boys had no choice but to make their own way. And they were resourceful. Each day they took the nickel Barney gave them to drop into the poor box at the synagogue, changed it into pennies, put in only one coin, and kept the rest for themselves.[10] This was just the beginning of a series of thefts, of milk and bread from front stoops and of shirts and pants from clotheslines, that helped keep the boys fed and fully dressed. Nor were the two street urchins above begging.

"Work as he would, twelve and fourteen hours a day," Fast wrote years later, Barney, "still could not feed and clothe us." Unorganized workers did not benefit much from the economic boom of the 1920s, and Barney's income remained well below average, ranging between only $15 and $30 per week until 1928.[11] Pressed by poverty, Howie at ten and Jerry at eleven began working daily as newspaper delivery boys for the *Bronx Home News,* which was also delivered in their uptown Manhattan neighborhood. By working on Sundays, when they had to rise at three in the morning and drag themselves to the newspaper collating station, they could each earn up to eight dollars a week.

Summer supplied something of a reprieve for the boys, but even this experience had its dark side. From the time Howie was seven and Jerry eight they spent July and August in Kaaterskill, New York, at Camp Jened for boys, owned by their cousin Sam, and named for Sam's mother Jenny and father, Edward, Barney's wealthy older brother. The rich relatives showed "two poverty-stricken slum children . . . some of the most beautiful mountain areas up around Hunter and Tannersville that exist in the East. But they were not kind to us," Fast told an interviewer in 1968; "they were right out of Dickens. . . . We were mistreated and pushed around and given no sustenance of love or compassion or even human decency."[12]

His aunt Jenny, Fast remembered, was "destined to move through the early years of my life as if cast for the role of the cruel and avaricious step-mother so beloved of the Brothers Grimm." The forest, which Howie learned to love, was his refuge "from this half-mad, malignant old woman . . . who ruled this summer kingdom and who regarded my older brother and myself with implacable hatred."[13] Jerry as usual "tried to be deserving of praise," but Howie true to form "went the other way and allowed myself to sink into a deep and unremitting anger—directed in part at my aunt and my cousin, but for the most part directed against myself and this so-called childhood that I was cursed with."[14]

Back home in September, work competed with school, which for Howie was another sorrowful experience. P.S. 46 on 156th Street was a crumbling, dreary pre–Civil War building where, because of overcrowding, what should have been eight years of education were for Howie and some others compressed into five. Moreover, "we had terrible teachers," Fast later complained, "bigoted" and "racist."[15] This was an era of especially strong anti-immigrant sentiment, during which the Johnson-Reed Act (1924) severely restricted immigration from Southern and Eastern Europe. Still, more than half the students were Jewish, with a sprinkling of Catholics, but as Fast wrote, "99% of the teachers were Protestant." They mocked us, he said, "called us names, made fun of us." Fast also had the misfortune of having been born left-handed. In school he was forced to write with his right hand, and the result, he complained, was that his handwriting never became totally legible. Public school in general, he said, "was a nightmare."[16]

Street life was worse. Howie occasionally had time for shooting marbles or playing stickball. More memorable, however, was the degradation, Fast said, and the violence. There were gang fights, especially on Halloween, involving hundreds of kids, black, Italian, Jewish, and Irish boys, wielding knives and broken bottles, leaving more than a few dead. In the 1920s, when the Ku Klux Klan had reached a peak in its membership and notoriety, and lynchings in the South had risen to record numbers, a black boy was hanged by a mob of youngsters at McComb's Bluff over the Polo Grounds, an event Fast witnessed and wrote about later in his novella *The Children* (1937).[17]

In addition to the racism there was, Fast said, a "maniacal" antisemitism that often plunged him, as well as his brothers, into combat. "Until my mother died," he wrote in his memoir, "I had no sense of being Jewish." Being labeled the son of a whore or a son of a bitch was one thing, but being accused of having killed the God of practically every kid in the neighborhood, or being called a Jew bastard or a kike, was thoroughly confusing to Fast. His was the only Jewish family on his block, and to ward off physical attacks by the Irish and Italian kids, which were frequent, Howie had brass knuckles in his pocket and wore a butcher knife, purchased for sixty cents, which he threatened to use. It worked. He, as well as Jerry and Julie, survived the name-calling and the violence, at least physically. "I was the product of the gutter and the gang," Fast said, "the lousy bedbugridden railroad tenement, the burning streets and empty lots. I carried brass knucks and used them, and in my animal way, I was beaten and I beat others."[18] Antisemitism made the Fast brothers bond even more closely as they held off superior forces and endured. But until a very angry Howard Fast had a framework in which to try to understand these experiences, it is probable that they tested his nascent commitment to a more diverse brotherhood, and whatever belief may have been gestating in him about the possibility of solidarity among the poor.

Having been "skipped" too rapidly in public school, Howie found himself at George Washington High School in the Fort George section of upper Manhattan at the age of eleven and a half instead of fourteen. He tried the ninth grade for two or three weeks and "just gave up." Jerry wrote phony illness notes for Howie claiming that his absent brother suffered everything from pneumonia to tuberculosis to yellow fever.[19] After a year or more of "a series of dismal and underpaid jobs," Howie was convinced by Jerry to give high school another try. But then with "going to high school until three o'clock in the afternoon, working from three to seven, coming home [and with his] two brothers putting together some sort of catch-as-catch-can meal," Fast's life was an endless battle against fatigue. "I had no time to study," he complained, "and little time to think."[20]

It is difficult to imagine the frenzied quality of Howie's day. Awake at seven, their father already off to work, Howie and Jerry slapped together a cold breakfast for the three boys, got Julie off to P.S. 46, made peanut butter or cheese sandwiches for lunch, took the streetcar to George Washington, hurried to their newspaper jobs after school, leaving seven-year-old Julie to do his best with his own door key, and then came home hoping to find their little brother there, and not at the police station, and finally somehow got a late meal together. Between them, Jerry and Howie could usually put enough money together for a tin of sardines, bread, tomatoes, and even cake on rare occasions. Jerry, as compulsively neat as he was well-behaved, would take the time to lay a newspaper on the table before the brothers ate, so that when they finished he could just roll it up, food wrappers and packaging encased—there were never leftovers—and throw it all out.[21]

In saying he had little time to think, however, Fast was uncharacteristically too modest. By age twelve Howie was taking batches of books from the public library at St. Nicholas Avenue between 160th and 161st Street and reading prodigiously. He read without discrimination—novels, adventure fiction, psychology, politics, and lots of history. Howie understood only some of what he read, but every book he opened, especially those by Mark Twain and Jack London, was "a treasure," he said, "a new world, a region of hopes and dreams and promise." At fourteen he was writing stories long into the evening. On those extremely rare occasions when Howie's father could spare the time, Barney "sat and watched." Forty years later Fast remembered "the simple joy of the man, his whole life had been his two hands and his strong back, but now he had a son who actually wrote stories. So he sat there in that wretched . . . slum kitchen and watched," and in this way expressed the "love and faith that made any of it possible."[22] It would be four more years before Howie had a story published, but his father, if only infrequently, and his brothers, too, provided the few positive things he could remember about his "so-called childhood": encouragement and cooperation; and with these precious gifts, and by his own voracious reading, Howie widened the world of his imagination.

The material condition of the Fasts improved near the end of 1927. Barney, now employed as a pattern maker, was bringing home fifty dollars a week, the most he had ever earned in his life. Howie and Jerry were working at the Harlem Branch of the New York Public Library and between them were paid another twenty dollars. These previously unimagined riches lasted just long enough to allow the Fast family to leave their cramped and dingy thirty-dollar-a-month railroad flat on 159th Street for a larger, newer apartment in Inwood at the northern tip of Manhattan.

The bubble that was the economy of the 1920s burst with the stock market crash of October 1929. Barney's company folded, he was unemployed for some time, and of the few jobs he was ever to have again, none paid well. The Fasts were poor once more. The boys continued to work and scrimp and were able to keep the family in the apartment, and to keep food, such as it was—beans and water, or spaghetti and ketchup—on the table.[23] Howie had

several odd jobs and occasionally went to the movies between them, skipping
school often. Between 1929 and 1932 *Anna Christie*, *Arrowsmith*, and *Farewell to Arms*, socially conscious films derived from works of Eugene O'Neill,
Sinclair Lewis, and Ernest Hemingway, were the movies he was most likely
to have seen. He may also have been moved by *All Quiet on the Western Front*,
based on Erich Maria Remarque's antiwar novel. And it is quite possible that
he saw Joan Crawford in *Possessed*, an up-from-poverty film that dramatized
the ruthless and seamy struggles of the Depression years.

Since he had always been intrigued by cowboy stories, Howie probably
also saw *The Virginian*, an adaptation of a pulp novel about cattle rustlers.
Scandal Sheet, *Mouthpiece*, and *Dark Horse*, illustrations of corruption in
journalism, law, and politics, may also have been choices. No doubt he was
entertained by the Marx brothers, those anarchic puncturers of pomposity
and class snobbery, perhaps even inspired by the cheerful, plucky Mickey
Mouse, popular during the Depression for representing "a little fellow trying
to do the best he could," but often getting into trouble and out again. He may
even have seen Walt Disney's "Three Little Pigs," a cartoon that debuted in
1933 to extraordinary enthusiasm, perhaps because it seemed to represent
America's predicament: regret for the recklessness of the 1920s, rediscovery
of the virtue of frugality, and determination to take on "the big bad wolf,"
the financial oligarchs who had brought the country to ruin.[24]

Poverty was Howie's primary problem. But he was also on the cusp of
expulsion from high school several times because he was an indifferent student who preferred to read books he chose at the library rather than assigned texts, and to write stories and novels instead of doing homework.
Fortunately his English teacher, Hallie Jamison, who thought Howie had
an "unusual gift for writing," took him under her wing, tutored him, and
got him through to graduation. Long bouts of writing every day and school
attendance, sporadic though it was, in addition to Howie's bread-winning
work, demonstrated his nearly inexhaustible store of energy, including an
everlasting sexual vitality

He "lived in a state as horny as a large toad . . . feeling utterly deprived
every time I encountered a pair of mammary glands [satisfying] myself with
. . . dreams that included women between fifteen and sixty and even my
beloved Hallie Jamison." Howie didn't only dream. The "gentle and wise"
librarian to whom Fast refers in *The Naked God* and other writings was
apparently sleeping with him. Affairs with librarians seem to have run in

the family. Jerry, too, had had "librarian lovers." And when Howie learned that his younger brother Julie was also working in libraries, he said to him, remembering his own experiences, "You must be getting laid a lot."[25]

After Howie showed some of his "adventure" stories to his "gentle and wise" librarian lover, she asked him why he didn't write about things closer to his own experience. His life was just "drudgery," Fast said, and ultimately "meaningless."[26] She handed him George Bernard Shaw's *The Intelligent Woman's Guide to Socialism and Capitalism*. Howie read it through in one night, and Shaw became his "idol and teacher forever afterward." It wasn't his first taste of socialism; he had read Jack London's *Iron Heel*, and he soon became familiar with Dreiser and Farrell. But Shaw gave him a vision of order and hope, and in the long run led him further to the left.[27]

In the meantime, Jerry, who was sixteen months older than Howie, graduated from high school and enrolled for business courses at New York University, a private institution costing $600 a year. Opting for this major expense nearly equal to the amount of rent they had been paying yearly on their old apartment required a family decision. Two boys in college at the same time would have been impossible to afford given the Fast family income; nor had Howie or Jerry done well enough in school to go to tuition-free City College of New York (CCNY), and Julie still had four years of high school to finish. So, the $600 was borrowed at a very high rate of interest from "the Morris Plan, a private bank and usury machine," and it was Jerry who went to college.[28] When he went off to NYU each day he left a quarter on top of the refrigerator. Perhaps in this way Jerry was expiating some small sense of guilt, but he also believed he was helping his younger brother stay away from menial work for an additional hour or two in order to write just a little longer.[29]

Howie graduated from George Washington High in 1931, and on the strength of drawings he had made to accompany his stories in the manner of N. C. Wyeth, the great magazine illustrator and one of Fast's idols, he was admitted on scholarship to the prestigious National Academy of Design at 116th Street, just east of the Cathedral of Saint John the Divine.[30] Howie would wake at six, write, and leave at eight for the academy, a group of ancient barracks-like buildings in the old European style, with skylights in the roofs. After several hours in art classes, it was back to work at the library and then home to more writing. He completed a story every few days, promptly dispatching handwritten manuscripts to one magazine or another. When the academy librarian informed him that no publisher would bother looking at a submission that was not typewritten, he rented an Olympia for $1.75 a month. He tried to teach himself to type, but settled for the two-finger method, which he continued to use to the end of his writing life.

And then, finally, a sale; not of a story about things close to his life, but a piece of science fiction bought by *Amazing Stories* in 1931. He was paid thirty-seven dollars, a grand sum for a seventeen-year-old earning only nine dollars a week at the library. He left that job, which had in any case turned into collecting fines for overdue books mostly from prostitutes in a brothel close to the library who somehow found time between "Johns" for reading. He went to work for a ladies' hat maker for fourteen dollars a week. But even the indefatigable Howie found work, writing, and training to be an artist impossibly time-consuming. Having sold a story, he decided to leave the art academy and devote himself to writing as much as possible.[31]

He continued to be interested in the opposite sex, however, and fell in and out of love with at least three young women over a period of several months. His dating usually consisted of strolls through Central Park. Jerry, on the other hand, was earning enough money in two part-time jobs, even while attending classes at NYU, to do more socializing than mere walks in the park. Early in 1932 he invited his younger brother to dinner at the Russian Bear, a restaurant in downtown Manhattan, where Howie met Sarah Kunitz. Seven years Howie's senior, Sarah was a member of the Communist Party who, with her brother Joshua, the author and translator of several books on Marxism and Russia, had visited the Soviet Union several times.

"Sarah was wonderful," Fast said, "I fell in love with her immediately."[32] At the same table sat literary critic Philip Rahv and writer James T. Farrell, among other notables. Howie, saying little himself, was enchanted by the brilliant discussions, mostly about left philosophy and politics. He had earlier been attracted to the left by many things he had heard and read, including writings by Farrell, who now sat only feet from him at the Russian Bear. And in the light of his own impoverished beginnings and now in the midst of America's disastrous Depression, Howie, like thousands of others, saw the Soviet experiment in socialism as a beacon of hope for the world. Arthur Koestler may have said best what Fast was thinking: "The contrast between the downward trend of capitalism and the simultaneous steep rise of a planned Soviet economy was so striking and obvious that it led to the equally obvious conclusion: They are the future—we, the past."[33]

At the end of the evening, impressionable Howie was determined to join the Party. Days later, with visions of "a romantic liaison with this wise older woman" dancing in his head, he took Sarah to lunch to inform her of his decision. She firmly resisted his ardor, telling him he was too young for her or revolution, and that one book by George Bernard Shaw and even a handful by other leftist writers was hardly enough upon which to base his life. She told him not to join the Party and instead steered him to the John Reed Club, a literary association close to the Party, but not officially in it. But even after going to a half dozen meetings—which got him his FBI file—Howie was unable to connect with the other members. They were left-wing, some were Communists, most were "college people," products of CCNY and NYU. Their thinking was shaped by a culture alien to Howie, who was a self-taught product of the working class. "Their intellectualism awed and astonished me." Feeling inadequate, he never dared open his mouth. "I grew up in the gutter," he said, and "I thought in direct action terms," not in abstractions.[34] The intellectuals had their theories of proletarian literature and culture, Howie thought, but they didn't have any notion of what was down there in what Jack London called "the abyss." Howie, however, had been in the abyss, he thought, or at least at its precipice, and he believed attempts to embrace esoteric Marxist theories were useless.[35]

With no Communist Party, no John Reed Club, no Sarah Kunitz, no novels published despite three written, eighteen-year-old Howie was angry with himself and restless. He had to get out of New York or "burst." He talked it over with Devery Freeman, a friend he had made working as a counselor at Camp Jened in 1931. They took off for "the South," neither sure what they were searching for. The pair did a lot of hitchhiking, looking not very different from half a million other kids on the road in 1932. They rode from Philadelphia to Richmond, Virginia, in a fertilizer truck. In South Carolina, they were given a ride by two boys in a horse-drawn wagon, and for three hours argued the "causes and consequences" of the Civil War. They also walked for miles, sometimes in the rain, slept in shelters or under staircases, and were chased or pointed out of towns in Georgia and Florida by cops, not always gently. They fed themselves on fallen or rejected fruit and loaves of bread purchased for eight cents, until they reached Miami, only to discover that there was no more joy in that city than in New York.[36]

Devery, years later a TV writer and Hollywood executive, who was from an upper-middle-class family, apparently had bus fare enough for one tucked away, and he abruptly parted company with Howie, who tried to make his way home by riding the freight cars. On this return trip he saw many instances of blatant antiblack racism, and he met other boys, unemployed men, drifters, people on the run from the police or families they could no longer support. He got only as far as Savannah, Georgia, before he was arrested and kept overnight in a cell. The next morning, after a court hearing with a friendly judge, Howie was permitted to make a collect call to ask Barney for bus fare. "The only time I saw a real uninhibited display of affection from my father," Fast said, "was when I walked into our New York apartment two days later."[37]

PUBLISH OR PERISH

Back from his southern sojourn, Howie went to work as a shipping clerk in a dress factory in lower Manhattan and somehow found six to eight hours a day for writing. He had finished three long but unpublishable novels before his trip and at least two, but perhaps as many as six or more, in the months after his return, each best left "unremembered."[38] In the summer of 1933 when Howie was at camp there was a "nibble" from Dial Press about a manuscript entitled "Old Johnny Preswick." Howie's older brother, Jerry, forwarded the publisher's letter to Camp Jened, attaching his own note. "Congratulations kid," he wrote, "I told you it was a swell book. I want to leave the house early so . . . I can go down and tell Pa."[39]

The book, to Howie's great disappointment, was never published, but later that year Dial Press did bite. Grenville Vernon was impressed by Fast's *Two Valleys*, a melodramatic love story set in the colonial era in the mountains of western Virginia. And even before that novel was between hard covers, Vernon again responded positively to Fast's *Strange Yesterday*, a bloated narrative filled with daring deeds and adventures, including piracy, fisticuffs, murder, lust, and incest in five generations of the Preswick family. Despite the action, the story is tedious and often confusing, and later Fast rightly called *Strange Yesterday* "a half-assed, hysterical novel."[40] In 1933 and 1934 *Two Valleys* received little critical praise, and *Strange Yesterday* got even less.[41] Fast was devastated because some critics said that "I had [no] business writing at all. They tore down all my hopes, and for [almost two] years afterwards, I wrote nothing that mattered a great deal."[42] Neither *Two*

Valleys nor *Strange Yesterday*, far removed from Fast's real-world experience, sold well. Both books disappeared into deserved obscurity and by 1941 had vanished from Fast's listing of published works.

Disappointing sales forced Howie to continue to do the odd jobs he so longed to escape. He worked for a cigar maker on Avenue B in lower Manhattan, followed by six months at a kosher butcher shop, and then a full-time job at a factory in the garment center on a finishing machine, hemming women's dresses. He also continued to work every summer at Camp Jened until he was almost twenty-two. Having, over an eight-year period, graduated from waiter to counselor and all-around repairman, Howie learned to work with concrete, cut lumber, and do primitive plumbing. He grew taller, nearly reaching his full height of 5'10", and stronger, which gave him the confidence to fend off any physical threats from his employer cousin Sam. Eventually he designed and built sets for plays he wrote, casted, and directed. Playwriting would remain an important pursuit for Howie, but one at which, to his continuing dismay, he rarely succeeded.[43]

Late in 1934, Fast experienced another kind of dismay, when his old friend Sarah Kunitz sent him a stinging critique of his first two books. She pointed out, though not quite accurately, that Fast was the first self-educated, working-class writer, and that he had "sold out," betraying his own rough-and-tumble experience by producing two "fairy tales." Middle-class authors were writing proletarian literature, Sarah said, while Fast, a genuine product of the working class, was cranking out entertainments. She named no non-working-class authors, but she was no doubt referring to Erskine Caldwell, James Agee, John Steinbeck, Josephine Herbst, and James T. Farrell, among others on the left, who were producing timely and exciting novels, short stories, and plays about the oppressions of capitalism, the suffering of the poor and minorities, and in some cases about the hope held out only by Communism. The pro-Communist cultural front also attracted others in the arts besides writers, including many of whom Fast was well aware, such as dancer/choreographer Martha Graham, composers Aaron Copland and Marc Blitzstein, singers Louis Armstrong, Lena Horne, and Frank Sinatra, and artists Rockwell Kent, William Gropper, and Ben Shahn.[44]

Along with writers of proletarian-protest novels in the 1930s, these creative men and women were responding to the hunger marches, the homelessness, and the anger of workers and farmers that marked the era of the Great Depression. Those who painted, drew, danced, sang, and wrote about

breadlines and evictions, and depicted joyless youth, bankrupt entrepreneurs, and the economic and moral breakdown of middle-class families in
their novels, poems, and plays, were responding to what they saw and to the
complexity of their own inventive drives. As John Dos Passos put it, creative
artists, and especially writers, needed no "imported systems" nor phrases,
badges, or banners "from Russia or anywhere else" to describe with passion, even if not always with the most felicitous style, an undeniable reality.
And the best of these works, which went beyond agit-prop or poster art,
succeeded in portraying vividly the social forces that influenced the lives of
real people.[45]

Fast, however, still depressed by Sarah Kunitz's scolding and by his apparent inability to deal with "real life" in his fiction, stopped writing for
months. At the same time in 1934, Henry Roth, a member of the Communist
Party, had published *Call It Sleep*, an extraordinary and enduringly influential novel about immigrant childhood in the Jewish ghetto. The Party's
negative reaction to *Call It Sleep*, a Freudian, non-Marxist aesthetic achievement in the style of James Joyce, hit Roth hard and kept him from writing
anything substantial for decades.[46] But nothing, not even a tongue-lashing
from his beloved Sarah, could discourage the tireless and ambitious Howie
for very long. Indeed, after some defensive fuming, Fast decided that there
was something essentially true about what Sarah had said, and he began to
write about the darker side of his own gritty childhood.

He woke early, drank three cups of strong coffee and smoked while sitting
at the kitchen table with pen and paper for two hours before going off to a
twelve-hour day at the garment factory. Cigarettes cost twelve cents a pack,
and Howie limited himself to one pack a week; he managed, however, to
bum many smokes from the all-Jewish labor force at the factory—Yiddish-
speaking cutters and machine operators. As Howie knew no Yiddish, the
workers good-naturedly nicknamed him "the goy," and demanded that his
questions be asked in Yiddish. "Freg mir in Yiddish," they would say over
and over again. In this way Howie learned about thirty Yiddish words, starting with *pappyrus* (cigarette).[47]

Cigarettes and coffee served Howie well as stimulants, allowing him, he
said, to write a page or two each day of what would become *The Children*.
Creating this long story "was like pulling teeth," Fast remembered, "or like
performing a series of small painful cuts on my own flesh."[48] But he kept
going even in the face of several rejections of novels he had submitted to

publishers earlier. At the beginning of 1935 he received a letter from Pearl Buck, the advisory editor at John Day, who thought his unnamed "modern manuscript" was an improvement, but that his "characters are not [fully] realized" and "emotional moments are too thin." She even went so far as to recommend Fast for a job on a newspaper (which never materialized) in order to broaden his experience.[49]

Two months later, he heard from Richard Walsh, editor-in-chief at John Day, who told Fast that he had "the same experience with 'Free,'" a manuscript subsequently lost, that he had had with Fast's "other manuscripts— starting off with great enthusiasm, feeling halfway through the book we certainly must publish it, and then being let down throughout the last half." "Your trouble," Walsh wrote, is "your detachment from active life." Walsh had his finger on something; by force of circumstance Fast had been a loner. "Perhaps you . . . are not mingling enough with people to have [a] . . . feeling for human motives," Walsh concluded, "and are forced to rely too much upon imagination."[50]

The news for Fast in 1935 wasn't all bad. In May, he received notice of having won a fellowship to the prestigious Bread Loaf Writer's Conference in Vermont. Howie was tickled. He had been nominated by Richard Walsh, the same editor who had returned and continued afterward to reject several of Fast's manuscripts. Walsh, not having seen a draft of *The Children*, was disappointed that Fast was not doing books "arising out of your own experience," but he saw the young author's promise.[51] Fast himself said later that he was undaunted by rejections, claiming that they helped him "to be a better writer than I [ever] conceived of being." Putting himself in some rather distinguished company, Fast said, if he "had gotten the kind of [early] adulation that a Truman Capote or a Norman Mailer, or a Faulkner got," he might have been "destroy[ed]."[52]

At Bread Loaf in the Green Mountains of Vermont for two weeks at the end of August, Fast met the esteemed drama critic John Mason Brown and Robert Frost, among other writers and poets. He learned the finer points in the use of knives and forks, watched Brown consume more martinis than he thought humanly possible, and immediately "fell in love" with Gladys Hasty Carroll, ten years older than Howie and " a very popular and beautiful writer of the time," whose *As the Earth Turns* was a best-selling novel in 1933.[53]

What Fast calls the most important event in his life also took place in 1935. He met Bette Cohen. Devery Freeman telephoned sometime in November wanting a favor. Bea, a distant cousin of Freeman's, was in New York to study art at Pratt Institute. He was determined to sleep with her, and he wanted Howie to be a blind date for Bea's roommate, Bette, a student at the Parson School of Design. The plan was to have dinner at Anselmo's, an Italian restaurant on 72nd Street between Amsterdam and Broadway where two could eat for eighty cents. Then Howie was to take Bette to a movie, while Devery seduced Bea back at her basement apartment. Howie, once again, fell in love at first sight. And Bette did, too, apparently. They skipped the movie and instead talked for hours in Central Park. Bette, who had "wonderful" blue eyes and flaxen hair, was not only "good-looking"; she also shared Howie's political and social views. Having sold a number of stories to pulp magazines at fifty dollars a pop, and working on several other writing projects, including *The Children*, as well as at the garment factory, Howie felt confident enough to ask Bette to marry him—on the second date.[54]

His devotion to Bette was no mere infatuation on Howie's part. All through the summer of 1936 he wrote to her, sometimes two and three times a day, from his job at Camp Jened. Only hours after his arrival at the camp, Howie, already sorely missing Bette, wrote, "The hills are beautiful [but] I'm a lonely and miserable boy." By his second day he seemed ready to come home to be with Bette, a desire he continued to express well into the summer. "I'm a sullen, useless brat without the Bette I love," Howie wrote; but he was tanning himself and building his muscles, he said, in order to "come home good" for his girl.[55]

In the meantime he occasionally expressed a happy, unself-conscious egotism in his letters that would remain with him throughout his long life. "I swim a lot," he wrote, and "I tell stories and jokes, and . . . the kids are crazy about me." In several letters Howie, displaying a tendency that would also endure, addressed Bette as "baby," "child," or "lassie." After taking his boys to visit Stony Clove, a girls camp in Hunter, New York, about fifteen miles north of Kingston, Howie wrote, "I know one thing and strangely it makes me feel terribly happy. I want no other women. I shall never want one. . . . My life is all you, only you." Bette would come to see this declaration in the not too distant future as just the first of a long series of broken promises.

But in early August, Howie was yearning even more for Bette and home. "I still count the days. How I do want to be back with you, baby," he wrote, but "I must work so that we [can] get married." He was happy, however, to report that the "money is in the bank" for "Stockade," a story he sold to *Ladies'*

Home Journal for $500, an amount signaling a new potential level of success. He was even happier when Jerry came up to visit from the city on August 10th with the news that *Story*, a prominent "little" magazine, was going to publish *The Children*. It would fill more than half of the spring 1937 issue, and would come to 190 pages when reprinted ten years later as a novella.[56]

Apparently this success inspired Howie to return to New York for a few days to do some more writing. But he soon told Bette about his lack of progress. "I never knew . . . it could be so miserably difficult to write. I try . . . but I get nowhere. . . . I want to write something awfully good," but "I only succeed in tearing up everything." By August 17th, Howie was back at camp, where his writing was reduced to whatever he could squeeze on postcards for Bette.[57]

Back home in the fall there was some bitter negotiation with *Story* magazine, which had offered only fifty dollars for *The Children*.[58] Fast finally got one hundred. One hundred dollars for "a thousand hours of work" drove Fast to the determination "to dig ditches, to operate a machine, to ride the freights, but to write no more."[59] Of course, Fast did not keep to that decision, but he never again wrote for the prestigious magazines. *The Children*, however, released in 1937, gained unexpected attention when the police commissioner of Lynn, Massachusetts, seized as obscene a copy of *Story* magazine that included Fast's novella, thereby setting off censorship issues in other cities. This kind of repression was nothing new for New England, which had been sensitive about "salacious" language and material ever since Massachusetts threatened Nathaniel Hawthorne with imprisonment, public lashing, and banishment for writing *The Scarlet Letter*. The ban on *Story* spread across the entire region, which, not surprisingly, rapidly stimulated sales. Unfortunately, Fast had sold *The Children* for a flat fee and was quickly and firmly turned down when he asked for a share of the windfall.[60]

A tale about some of the toughest streets of the slums of New York and the kids who spend more time in them than in their impoverished and congested homes, *The Children* depicts a world apart from the world of adults. Yet it is a world not of their making. The pressure of poverty creates resentments among the children and destroys their hope. It sucks the parents as well as Ollie and Ishky and Marie and Shomake, and all the other children, Jewish, Italian, Irish, Polish, and black, into a vortex of primitive values of force and domination. To the confusions and insecurities of ordinary childhood is added a dimension of evil. The lives of the children are filled with both horror and innocence, with both tragedy and guilt. The lynching of a black boy is the focus of it all, the murder of a child by other children, with no one acting to prevent it. But there are also "little murders" that the kids commit among themselves. Ishky, for example, is sympathetically drawn, but out of frustration, resentment, and ennui, none of which he understands, he breaks his friend Shomake's treasured violin. All seems hopeless. Yet Fast's apparent faith in human resilience, while it does not relieve the story of its terror, is expressed in an ambivalent, yet moderately hopeful ending: Ishky, on the edge of introspection, sits on the stoop with Shomake. "We look at each other," Ishky thinks. "Our world is gone, but we have found something. We both sigh. Shomake moves closer to me."[61]

The Children, influenced heavily by Henry Roth's *Call It Sleep*, especially in its use of Jewish immigrant street dialect, and marked by a large degree of social degradation and literary realism, sold well but did not attract a great deal of critical attention. When it was reprinted ten years later, however, Fast got an admiring letter from John Houseman, and one from Albert Maltz, who upon reading *The Children* for the first time, thought it "magnificent," especially in the way it utilized an "extraordinary . . . blend of poetry and terror."[62] Many on the left, however, had read *The Children* in 1937 and were immediately exuberant about it. Sarah Kunitz welcomed Fast "back into the progressive fold," and former members of the radical John Reed Club, which had been disbanded by the Party in 1934 as the CP moved into its nonrevolutionary Popular Front period, saluted Howie, whom they had not seen in four years.

Fast, however, was not eager for the attention of political activists at this time. He was about to be married, and as he explained thirty years later, "there are [several] things a writer wants": To "earn a living" so that he can "go on writing." And he wants to be "famous," to "feel . . . the admiration and plaudits of . . . the people of [his] city or country . . . and the intellectual establishment [in] which he works. . . . I think a third thing . . . is that he wants to create fine works of art."[63] The desire to use art primarily as a weapon in class warfare, so important to Fast between 1944 and 1956, is in this 1967 statement conspicuous by its absence, replaced by a return to the more mundane and moderately aesthetic goals of his youth.

After getting only $100 for *The Children*, Fast said, "society . . . can offer the artist only . . . an occasional crumb of sustenance." It "drives him to prostitution as certainly as it drives the poor women who walk the streets." The artist in him would take a back seat then while Fast kept writing romantic or heroic stories set in the distant past for the popular magazines such as *Ladies' Home Journal,* now at $600 each. "They were not good stories," he said; "they were not stories I was proud of, . . . but they represented mountains of hamburger . . . and bread and butter."[64]

Romances were not the only things Fast wrote; he did not give up entirely on writing about the "reality" of contemporary urban life. *Place in the City,* for example, the story of a Jewish storekeeper, his two daughters, and their lovers in the crowded neighborhoods of lower Manhattan, was published in 1937 after several rejections. It had been taken in hand by Sam Sloan, with whom Fast developed one of the most important relationships in his literary life. And the bond lasted until Sloan's death in 1945. "I loved him," Fast said, "the first gentleman . . . to enter my life. He taught me more, I think, than any other person."[65] Still, *Place in the City,* despite its vivid descriptions of politics, prostitution, and complex family dynamics, is not illuminating or compelling reading, and it failed to garner critical admiration. It was seen, not unfairly, as an attempt to portray the world of *The Children* on an adult stage, "pretentious . . . melodramatic," and full of "garlands and tears and sighs."[66]

After writing *Place in the City* and *The Children,* Fast decided there would be "no more about me and my childhood. It was too close, too confusing, and too filled with pain." It was easier, he said, "and to me, more natural to reassemble the material of my reading and create the kind of entertainments I so loved to read."[67] Occasionally, however, he did again try his hand at fictionalized "autobiography." But in his twenties he burned a lot of manu-scripts, including "Dying Mother and Lost Son," "Ten Lives in Manhattan," "Son of Man," and "Sunshine Tomorrow," a novel about working-class life in Bayonne that he and Sam Sloan together decided to abandon.[68]

Fast also wrote a very small number of stories for the popular magazines about the underside of life, in the dark naturalistic style of Theodore Drei-ser and Stephen Crane. But the high-paying "slicks" were not interested in depressing, deterministic tales.[69] They seemed to require what was best in Fast's style, good, rapidly moving narration, and what was not so good, over-simplification, idealization, and stereotypical characterization. Fast was trying to write fiction he could sell and to free himself from the "torture" of writing about his own experience and from the drudgery of manual labor. The short stories he published during the middle and late 1930s in *Romance,*

Ladies' Home Journal, and *Liberty* magazine were historical or pseudo-historical love tales of the American Revolution or the Civil War, featuring "great" men or the women behind them. They often contained the same unflattering pictures of frightened, wide-eyed, and obsequious blacks—with faces that "recalled [the] proboscis monkey"—that were presented in *Strange Yesterday,* and the same portrayal of Indians as murderous savages "rotten with rum," who "calmly stripped off the scalps" of women and children, that had appeared in *Two Valleys.* To anyone who has read only what Fast wrote after 1939, the racism in these works will come as a shock. But it is indicative of the bigotry, conscious or not, of the xenophobic 1930s that no one, neither reviewers nor publishers, and not even Sarah Kunitz, seems to have raised an alarm.[70]

Howard Fast wrote approximately fifteen novels between 1931 and 1939. Of the five published, only *The Children* and *Place in the City* come close to what students of literary history and theory have classified as "proletarian literature"—fiction, mostly written in the 1930s, dealing with: the underclasses, or racism and prostitution; the awakening of class-consciousness; strikes and labor violence; or conversion to Communism.[71] While Fast's two novels in 1937 involved the degradation of life at the bottom, including prostitution, racism, and violence, he never referred to any of his work as proletarian, nor did *Place in the City* or *The Children* explore the exploitative nature of the capitalist social system. When *The Children* was reprinted in 1947 with an introduction by Fast, he said that if he were writing it now (four years after having joined the Communist Party), he would deal much more explicitly with the causes of racism and poverty.[72] It is difficult to see how that would have improved *The Children.* Readers in 1937 and 1947 had one of Fast's best books in hand; it summons powerful emotions, and it pointedly disconcerts. Indeed, the realism of *The Children* disturbs in a way that social science writing often fails to, and it spares readers a dry programmatic "lesson." As Fast himself said later, he was "a story teller," and despite his several efforts, the ability to write proletarian novels eluded him.[73]

POLITICS DELAYED

When Howard Fast was congratulated by Sarah Kunitz and other members of the Communist Party on the publication of *The Children,* he showed no interest in Communism or, for that matter, politics of any kind. More than a half-century later, Fast claimed that he had been put off by the barbaric Moscow Show Trials, which began in 1936. A stunningly effective form of state terrorism, the trials, prompted by Stalin's murderous paranoia, targeted old Bolsheviks as Trotskyist counterrevolutionaries.[74] Even though the court cases ended most often with forced confessions and death sentences, they were given "the benefit of the doubt" by liberal journals, including the *Nation* and the *New Republic* and unstinted support by the American Communist Party.[75] Albert Maltz, for example, confessed later that "when the trials came along, there were many like myself who believed that these [accused] people must be guilty, because we couldn't conceive that Bolsheviks who had fought together against the tsars and through civil wars would turn on each other and frame each other. . . . We were starry-eyed and innocent."[76] As were some of the non-Communist literary and intellectual progressives in the Popular Front coalition of liberals and Communists who believed that Communism in the Soviet Union was just another version of the New Deal, merely an advanced form of liberalism, rather than one of liberalism's greatest enemies.

It is probable that Fast was as "starry-eyed" about all this as Maltz; in any case, there is no evidence at all in the mountains of material Fast left behind that Moscow had been on his mind in 1937. Instead, everything points to his thoughts having been on his upcoming marriage and his struggle to remain a "professional writer or . . . die in the attempt."[77] That Fast's decision not to participate actively in politics in the late 1930s was made in the context of portentous domestic and international developments raises questions about the strength of his commitment to fighting fascism other than rhetorically. Hard times continued at home, allowing racist opportunists to build more than a hundred proto-Nazi associations. And the continuing Depression provided an audience for the likes of Charles Coughlin, a Roman Catholic priest who, beginning in 1936, in his journal *Social Justice* and on his nationwide radio broadcasts to some 25 million listeners, argued that European fascism was a legitimate reaction to the more serious threat of Communism, a "Jewish" invention.

Abroad, between 1935 and 1939, the Axis nations of Germany, Italy, and Japan were extending fascism's reach in Europe, Asia, and Africa; and in Spain, beginning in 1936, a civil war that had resonance across the entire Western world pitted the Loyalists—the duly elected Republicans, liberals,

Socialists, anarchists, and Communists, against the fascist forces of General Francisco Franco.

Although the Loyalist government was unstable and wracked by violent, often murderous, divisions, many American liberals and professed radicals saw the Spanish Civil War as an uncomplicated, defining fight between fascism and progressivism; a crisis that would either bring the world a new dark age of fascist authoritarianism or usher in the anticipated democratic socialist future. Yet Howard Fast expressed no opinion on any of these developments, foreign or domestic, and he certainly had no interest in joining the Loyalists battling the fascists in Spain. So caught up was he in his attempt to win "fame and fortune" through writing that all else was secondary.[78]

But for thousands, perhaps tens of thousands, of left-liberals, Spain mattered. There were approximately three thousand Americans, including doctors, nurses, and drivers, who volunteered for the Abraham Lincoln Battalion (later frequently referred to incorrectly as the Abraham Lincoln Brigade). Nearly a thousand of these volunteers died, mostly in battles against the better-trained and better-armed forces of the Nationalist Spanish army. The drama, sacrifice, and "romance" of the war inspired many writers on the left, who though failing to acknowledge the atrocities Stalinists were committing in Spain, created poems, plays, stories, and novels portraying the evil of the fascists and what they saw as the dedicated heroic deeds of the Loyalists and their supporters. The war was also covered brilliantly by talented writers including Ring Lardner, John Dos Passos, Ernest Hemingway, and John Gates, the future editor of the *Daily Worker* who fought in the war and wrote about it later.

In the United States there were innumerable fundraising events, and speeches by artists, intellectuals, and writers.[79] Although he claimed that "Bette and I had been deeply and emotionally involved in the Spanish Civil War," the twenty-three-year-old Howard Fast took no part in the rallies and demonstrations. He attended no meetings on the war, delivered no speeches, and wrote no articles or letters, public or private, on Spain. Instead, in 1937, he was writing fiction, working, and thinking about getting married to Bette by midyear.[80]

Late in the summer of 1936, however, a problem had emerged that seemed to threaten the match. Apparently, at the end of August, just as Howie was getting ready to return home from Camp Jened, Bette sent him a letter her father, Isaac Cohen, a wholesale newspaper distributor, had written, critical of her fiancé. "You must realize how your dad's letter affected me," Howie wrote back. "I've tried so hard to like your folks, and all along they've tried harder to make me dislike them—as I would have, were they any [parents] but yours." Most of "my life . . . has been a long lesson in . . . misery. I grew up too quickly, and perhaps I knew too much. But I did keep my senses. I have a lot to be proud of—more than I'm ashamed of—and I am proud. I don't want anyone to pity me, or to pity you for loving me. . . . When I showed [the] letter" to Jerry he said, "'To hell with them—all of them!' I agree. I want you—nothing of your family. . . . I [hope] you are big enough to want me that way."[81]

Bette's parents, Orthodox Jews, regarded Howie, despite his intelligence and drive, as some strange, "feckless creature; hardly Jewish." Out of his hearing, they, like the garment workers from whom Howie had bummed cigarettes, referred to him, but now not as good-naturedly, as "the goy."[82] None of this, however, prevented Howie and Bette from getting married in June 1937 as planned, in the modest home of her parents in Bayonne. Bette's father, whose newspaper business would soon make him quite rich, continued to have little affection for Howie, who he believed was dragging his daughter into a life of poverty. At times, Howie thought the same.

The couple's indigence was relieved by moments of relative affluence. Wedding gifts helped and enabled them to buy a typewriter for seventy-nine dollars that Fast continued to use for decades. And there had been an advance of five hundred dollars for *Place in the City*, followed by payments in 1937 and 1938 of five or six hundred dollars for stories in the *Ladies' Home Journal*, the *Saturday Evening Post*, *Liberty* magazine, *Romance,* and the *Elks* magazine. Affluent "moments," however, did not pay the rent. Potboiler stories for pulp magazines at fifty dollars each and term papers (some written by Bette) sold to college students with money but "no brains" helped fill in the low spaces.[83]

Having given up his factory job to devote himself to writing full time, Howie thought he would "write my books and earn fame and fortune"—an ambition that would remain a leitmotif throughout his life. But Bette, who got mixed signals from her husband about "going professional" with her own artwork, limited herself, not without some resentment, to painting only in their cramped apartment on Pinehurst Avenue, not far from Fort Washington Park in upper Manhattan, and did not exhibit her canvases until many decades later. She did, however, devotedly read all of Howie's work and encouraged him to keep at it. She also suffered through Howie's frustrations, depressions, and explosions of temper, and although most of his infidelities would come later, Bette, as Fast admitted, "endured my propensity for finding too many women too wonderful."[84]

The sixty-five dollars a month they paid for rent proved a challenge for the Fast budget, and over the next three years they had to "retrench," moving to apartments that averaged about forty dollars a month. Nevertheless, they did take occasional day trips in their used 1931 two-seater Ford rattletrap, which, because of a problem with the clutch, only they knew how to start. On one of their outings in 1938, Howie and Bette drove to Pennsylvania to visit Valley Forge. Moved deeply, he claimed, by the crude reconstruction of the Revolutionary War encampment, Fast decided to write about the Continental Army's dreadful winter of 1777–78 at Valley Forge under George Washington's command. For the next several months, Fast read works in late-eighteenth-century American history and wrote the critically acclaimed, best-selling novel *Conceived in Liberty*, his first real breakthrough as a serious writer.[85]

The *New York Times* characterized Fast as "a steadily growing talent" whose "approach is fresh and bold," and whose "writing is genuinely effective." Howard was delighted, but nonetheless chagrined that he was charged with failing to "get the feeling of cold into the reader's bones, as for instance the tougher and more circumstantial description of Kenneth Roberts is able to do."[86] Roberts had written several very well received novels, several of which became films, about the American Revolution, including *Arundel* (1929), *Rabble in Arms* (1933), and *Northwest Passage*, which became the second-best-selling novel in America in 1937, trailing only Margaret Mitchell's *Gone with the Wind*. As a commercially successful writer of historical fiction, Roberts may have been a model for Fast and an inspiration to move away from his unmarketable confectionary romances, as well as from the brutal reality of *The Children*, for which he had earned all of $100.

Hervey Allen, the author of *Anthony Adverse* (1936), may have been an inspiration as well. Allen's massive 1,224-page picaresque-historical novel, stuffed with enough people, action, bloodshed, love, and death to fill a half-dozen books, was marketed as a historical romance. But within the novel lay a searing critique of commercial civilization, the rise of international capitalism, industrialization, and competitive nationalism. It was received by critics as a triumph of writing skill, and became a huge commercial success in America and Europe. *Anthony Adverse* was almost immediately turned into a motion picture, which did very well at the box office and won several Academy Awards. Fast could hardly have avoided some envy as he watched Allen achieve the goals he had set for himself: to write meaningful fiction, to make films, and to become rich.

The *Times* also compared Fast's *Conceived in Liberty* unfavorably to novels by Stephen Crane and Erich Maria Remarque, who were said to have accomplished the necessary identification of reader and narrator in their writing about war. "Able though he is," the reviewer wrote, Fast "falls . . . somewhat short of this distinction." But still, in *Conceived in Liberty*, despite his quest for fame and fortune, Fast transcended the appetite for fantasist historical romance that blossomed and was fed during the Depression by the likes of Mitchell, Roberts, and Allen. Instead of a massive, escapist tome, Fast, in *Conceived in Liberty*, gives us a sharply focused narrative emphasizing the suffering of the common soldier, underfed, underpaid, poorly clothed, and meagerly supplied by an irresponsible Continental Congress.

From the first, Fast indicates that some of his farmers and workingmen at Valley Forge sense that driving the British out may be "only the beginning" of something larger: a battle not only about home rule or independence, but also possibly about who should rule at home. This important question was raised by Fast in all four of the books he would write about the American Revolution between 1939 and 1950. He had not given up his desire for mass sales; the novels were full of violence, derring-do, and other excitements for the commercial market. Still, each book included some serious consideration of the class nature of the American Revolution.[87]

In the end, however, the Revolutionary War in *Conceived in Liberty* looks like one fight, not one embedded in another. In the book's final pages, Allen Hale, a common American soldier recently promoted to captain, says to himself, as if having experienced an epiphany, that the enemy is not only England, but "all of Europe." This is "what we are fighting, this crass contempt of man, this laughing contempt of the life of man . . . of man's right to live, to know simple things . . . to have no man over him."[88]

The novel's primary theme is that history, in the long journey to human freedom, requires the surrender of the individual to the larger goal. If this motif was a conscious application of Marxism on Fast's part, it is abstract and half-formed; moreover, self-imposed restraint of the individual is relevant to many non-Marxist philosophical traditions, including most religions.

In *Conceived in Liberty* itself, a religious sensibility is introduced that centers around brotherhood and Christian sacrifice for the larger revolutionary cause.

Fast may also have been trying to mirror through common soldier Aaron Levy's experience yet another religious and historical theme: the deliverance of the Jews from bondage. At Valley Forge, Levy's mate catches a glimpse of Aaron "sitting by the fire" and sees a universal figure, "a figure out of time," with a "face full of the pain of the world." Levy himself says that all his life he "dreamed of a day when I'd come to this land . . . of milk and honey," a "place for all men." And Allen Hale, taken with Levy, returns to the religious theme of sacrifice. He thinks of Aaron as the "Jew who had come five thousand miles [from Poland] to die with a dream that some day men might be free," while Jacob Eagen musingly recalls that "Christ was a Jew."[89]

Marxism, with its emphasis on universalism and historical materialism, and religion with its emphasis on particularism and spiritualism, are generally thought difficult to reconcile. But Marxism itself has often been recognized as a form of religious thinking. Its abstract ideology and its faith in an inevitable future of justice and brotherhood, challenge, if not undermine entirely, Marxism's own vaunted idea of materialism. In addition, internalized religious ethics and obligations have often served as the basis for worldly reform and even revolutionary movements in modern history. It was not, therefore, an unrealistic intellectual project for Fast to attempt a secular synthesis between Christianity, as Social Gospel theology, and Judaism's injunction to promote justice and "repair the world."[90]

The confluence of religious impulse and love on the one hand, and violence and revolution on the other, and the fit between Judaism and Christianity were themes Fast would wrestle with often. Sometime in the late 1940s he would come to think that his radicalism was informed, if not shaped, by Jewish teachings, particularly those of Isaiah, who railed against selfishness, exploitation, and insensitivity to the poor, sick, and suffering; and the teachings of Jesus, who for Fast was not only a prophet, but the ultimate Jew, a *lamed vovnik,* one of the truly righteous thirty-six people alive at any one time on Earth, on whom the continued existence of the world is said to depend.

Yet in 1940, when Fast was asked by Isadore Werbel of the Hebrew Publishing Company to write a short history of the Jewish people for young adults, he protested, saying he "knew nothing of Jewish history and almost nothing of Jewish culture." Werbel explained, with no intended irony, that Fast's relative ignorance of the subject would give the study a fresh approach. "My wife and I were very hungry then," Fast wrote, and when Werbel offered "$500 to write the book . . . I was delighted because that kept us alive for half a year."

Money wasn't the only incentive. Bette, having been raised in a household of practicing Jews, brought to their marriage a Jewish sensibility that was also an influential factor, just as it must have been for Howard when he introduced Jewish characters in his historical novels. Almost as important, Fast said, was Werbel's promise of a special bonus. "I could go down to the Hebrew Publishing Company on Delancey Street and select all the books I needed for my research." This invitation sealed the deal and "gave me . . . [an] enormously valuable library of Judaica which I have had reference to ever since."[91]

Among the titles Fast chose were the sixteen-volume *Encyclopedia Judaica* (*EJ*) and Solomon Graetz's six-volume *History of the Jews*. After bringing home a carload of books, Fast hungrily plunged in. "My reading," Fast remembered, "was in concert with the . . . stories of Nazi atrocities that [were in some] . . . newspapers of the time." This confluence of events "converted [me] to Judaism," Fast said, "not as a religion, but as an incredible heritage that moved through time and history almost like a measuring gauge of man's civilization."[92]

Reading in his newly acquired books, especially in the nine-thousand-page *EJ*, not only enabled Fast to write *The Romance of a People*, it also helped him "begin an investigation," he said, "into my own heritage and being" that long continued. Indeed, Fast was still reading in the *EJ* and was working on a manuscript tentatively entitled "The Singularity of Being Jewish" months before he died in 2003.[93]

Living in their tiny apartment on West 84th Street and dreaming of making enough money to move to larger quarters and even to build a small house in the country, Bette painted and Howie wrote. "Day and night I worked at the job of learning to write," mostly by putting together "the book which . . . Werbel had contracted for."[94] In that book, *Romance of a People*, Fast stressed the centuries-long Jewish search for a personal yet universal God, as well as the Jewish desire for sovereignty and a homeland. Ever the secularist, Fast minimized greatly the direct presence of the supernatural, so that it only "seems" to Abraham that he hears God's promise and command; it only "seems" to Jacob that he has wrestled with an angel. But the stories and legends are told with deference and pride. They include no divine intervention but are filled with faith in the existence of a transcendental, benevolent God who appears to have given a special role in history to a remarkable people. Fast shows the Jews gradually developing their modern character, emerging from desert tribalism to become a people of learning and peace, all the while retaining a national identity and an insistence on justice and personal freedom.

The Romance of a People was dedicated to Bette's mother and father, who had by this time grown substantially less cool toward Howie. The book remained in print for some time, but in 1941 it had brought Fast only the $500 he had settled for. Still hungry, Fast wrote Werbel asking him for more money. He reminded the publisher of the amount of work done on the manuscript after it was "completed." It had been returned for revision several times, and Fast had also spent at least a dozen full days at the Hebrew Publishing Company, tinkering and rewriting. None of this was specified in the original contract. "Since I am a writer of some standing," Fast told Werbel, "I do not think that $500.00 is too high a price [for] this [extra] work." Fast went on to say that he was certain Werbel would "see the logic and justice of my claims." And then, in an all-too-typical style he would generally regret using afterward, Fast wrote, "I am sure you would not want to give me or anyone else the impression that [your company] demands work from writers without compensation."[95]

The extra five hundred did not materialize, but Fast had the promise of an advance from Simon and Schuster of close to a thousand dollars for work on a novel about the Cheyenne Indians. Of central interest to publisher and author was the thousand-mile trek the Cheyenne made in 1878 from their reservation in Oklahoma to their homelands in Wyoming and Montana. In order to write what became *The Last Frontier* Fast had some traveling to do himself. In 1939, he wrote to Professor Stanley Vestal at the University of Oklahoma in Norman, a specialist in Indian history and lore, and in return received a five-page single-spaced letter full of information and leads about Indian anthropology, ritual, history, and language, with specific material on the Cheyenne.

Vestal added a handwritten note: "p.s. I am an historian. Since your book is fiction, I prefer that you do not mention me in your acknowledgements. You see how that is." This postscript apparently wounded Fast's easily bruised ego, because in a later letter from Vestal, the professor had to assure Fast that he was "quite *wrong*" in his "interpretation of my request. I made it as I should of any fiction writer and not at all in derogation of the quality and authenticity of your work."[96] The two eventually came to an understanding, and Vestal was of great help to Fast when he drove out to Norman in 1940.

From the initial advance provided by his publisher, Howie and Bette bought an ancient but reliable Pontiac to replace their undependable Ford and went west. They were awed by the Great Plains, the Rockies, Arizona, and New Mexico. Then it was north to Powder River country and back east to Norman, Oklahoma. Here Fast interviewed Vestal and survivors of the Cheyenne's bitter zigzag winter flight in the nineteenth century. He did intensive research at the university and at the State Historical Society. And on the way home he and Bette stopped in Washington, D.C., where they pored over records of the Bureau of Indian Affairs in the Library of Congress.[97]

Fast's first complete manuscript was written in the first-person voice of a Cheyenne Indian chief. Editors at Simon and Schuster did not like it at all, and "they made me pay back every dollar of the . . . advance" over time, Fast said. Howie and Bette were living out of their meager savings, withdrawing about six or seven dollars a week. So the return of the advance "was pain . . . squeezed out in droplets of blood."[98] Perhaps because of Fast's relationship with Sam Sloan, the publishers Duell, Sloan, and Pearce took on the manuscript. But Sam told his friend Howie that the editors at Simon and Schuster had been right to reject it. Perhaps it was not possible for *any* Caucasian man to enter the mind of an American Indian, Sloan said, but Fast certainly had not succeeded in doing it. With great help from Sam, Howard diligently reworked his manuscript from the viewpoint of a sympathetic white army officer.[99]

The Last Frontier was well received by most major reviewers. The *New York Herald Tribune* said Fast may be "the next really important American historical novelist." And the *New York Times* went one step further, saying Fast "has already arrived." Although Oliver La Farge, the novelist and anthropologist specializing in Indian life, regretted some of Fast's "anachronistic" parallels to the present, he admired the author's accomplishment in setting "the Indian record straight."[100] The success of the book, which the *New York Times* later called "little short of a masterpiece," rests not upon Fast's having told the "whole history" of the Cheyenne travail, but on its deliberate incompleteness and Fast's creative reshaping of historical facts.[101]

Although Fast, anxious to tell his version of the story, could write too rapidly, he was also capable of producing moving, even lyrical, passages: "They
walked slowly because it was the only mode of progress left to them, and they
walked because there was no place to rest in that sandy, cold expanse from
which escape was hopeless. Their mute tale was of hunger, privation, thirst,
suffering, but their tale was without boast; and the pride of their hopeless,
shattered selves communicated itself to the troops." Fast would get in some
difficulty later when he claimed both the license of a historical novelist *and*
the accuracy of a scholar. But this was not the case with *The Last Frontier*,
which historian Carl Van Doren called subtle in its mythic significance and
literary critic Granville Hicks called "the most nearly perfect and in many
ways the most impressive of Fast's [half-dozen] novels."[102]

The Reader's Club, whose editorial committee included Van Doren and
Sinclair Lewis, the Nobel laureate and popular novelist, chose to produce
its own edition of *The Last Frontier*. With the Second World War well underway nearly all the members of the committee had commented on the
timeliness of the book, seeing parallels to the present not in the tribulations
of nonwhite minorities—120,000 Japanese, two-thirds of them American-
born, were incarcerated on the West Coast in 1942, and Native Americans
were mostly languishing on reservations—but rather in the resistance to
aggressive invasion of homelands and the defense of personal freedoms in
Europe and Asia. Fast was genuinely concerned about telling a good story
and about the human dimensions of the Cheyenne ordeal, but he too recognized a "parallel" to the Second World War as "all over the earth people
begin the long trek to freedom." Not until today, Van Doren said, "could the
story have had the powerful impact it has in the light of daily happenings in
occupied countries."[103]

When asked years later why he wrote *The Last Frontier*, Fast made no
connection to WWII. The "Indian was oppressed [and] abused," he said,
but "I did not write the book because I was pro-Indian. . . . I felt I had hit on
a marvelous unknown story, and I think that if you are a story-teller, [the pro-
Indian politics] had to come secondarily to it."[104] Fast's inclination toward
telling a story first and worrying about politics second would get him into
occasional trouble after he joined the Communist Party, which had those pri-
orities reversed. In the meantime, sales of *The Last Frontier*, mostly spurred
by positive reviews, were good. Large four-figure royalty payments enabled
the Fasts to disentangle themselves from their unstable cycle of poverty and

intermittent small riches. They were even able to buy an acre of land on Old Stony Hollow Road in Tarrytown, New York, where in 1942 they finished building their "dream house in the country."[105]

While Fast was revising *The Last Frontier*, his father, Barney, who had been sick on and off since 1938, died. Howie and his older brother, Jerry, had watched Barney become as helpless as a child, and over the course of many stressful weeks they cared for their "Pa" as best they could.[106] Then only months after Barney's death, Bette experienced a miscarriage fairly late in her pregnancy, and entered a period of enduring gloom. Nothing, however, interrupted Fast's writing, and well before *The Last Frontier* was published he was working on *The Unvanquished*, a second book on the American Revolution, featuring George Washington.

Between 1941 and 1942, older manuscripts Fast had submitted were also finding their way into print. With Bette he had done an illustrated history of the Jews. Alone he did a booklet about the history of the Jewish people in the United States for Jews serving in the American armed forces. During the same period Fast wrote five short stories about the fighting men and women in WWII, and four books for young adults: a biography of Haym Solomon, a Jewish financier of the American Revolution; *The Tall Hunter*, centering on the legendary Johnny Appleseed; *Lord Baden-Powell of the Boy Scouts;* and *Goethals and the Panama Canal*.[107]

The Lord Baden-Powell and Goethals books are novelized biographies of military heroes in which Fast wrote approvingly of the imperialist enterprises that made up the lives of his subjects. That Fast was writing on Goethals, an imperialist adventurer, and George Washington, the leader of an anti-imperialist revolution, at the same time is comprehensible if we remember that before *The Last Frontier* had begun to sell well, Fast was still struggling to make a living. He did the Goethals and Baden-Powell books, Fast said, "on assignment to eat. We were very broke indeed. Of course, the Party would have bounced me for writing [those books] if I had written them while in."[108]

The Unvanquished, also published in 1942, is Fast's version of the most critical moments of the Revolutionary War—the summer and fall of 1776 in New York and New Jersey- when Washington's undisciplined army was most in danger of total collapse. The novel received generally good reviews and sold briskly from the very beginning. There were a few reservations among scholars and literary critics, some of whom, such as Alan Nevins, one of the more prominent U.S. historians at that time, commented on Fast's penchant for melodrama. And Malcolm Cowley, the book editor of the *New Republic*, complained about stock characters, but most of his review praised Fast for humanizing Washington even while "reconsecrating a somewhat neglected shrine."[109]

When *The Unvanquished* was reissued as a Modern Library edition in 1945, Fast wrote a new foreword saying that it was the December 1941 attack on Pearl Harbor that had inspired the form and story of the book. "Things were very black," Fast wrote, "not only for us, but for all of the civilized world; high wide and ugly, the fascist walked across the stage," the Japanese in Manchuria and China, the Germans in much of Europe, "and for the moment, it seemed to many that all of the earth would be his."

By the summer of 1941, Japanese military expansion in the Asia-Pacific region had made confrontation and war with the United States increasingly certain; and by the time Pearl Harbor was attacked, ten countries in central and western Europe were already overrun by the Nazis. On June 22, 1941, Germany launched the largest invasion in modern history up to that point. The Reich's armed forces crossed into the eastern European countries occupied by the Soviet Union, and within a few months were approaching the gates of Moscow itself. Caught geographically between two warring states trying to impose competing ideologies, and in a whirlwind of occupation and reoccupation, many millions of civilians were killed. And for the almost three million Jews who lived in the areas temporarily conquered by the Germans there was a special fate. Killing squads of black-shirted ss and regular army were systematically scouring the countryside, shooting Jews by the thousands. Areas for mass gassings were constructed to speed up the process. Eventually 90 percent of the Jews in German- and Russian-occupied eastern Europe were exterminated.[110]

Although he had not yet moved toward political activism in late 1941, Fast had always been ideologically antifascist; he also knew that Jews were concentrated in the areas the Nazis had conquered. In *The Unvanquished*, as in *Conceived in Liberty*, Fast included material about Jews that appeared to be connected to the Jewish dilemma in mid-twentieth-century Europe. After the British had taken New York City in 1776 (which could be read as the Germans taking the eastern half of Poland in 1941), the Jewish residents, Fast wrote, "saw their hopes and dreams flee with the tattered Yankees" (or the retreating Red Army). "They had cast their whole fortune with the revolution. Every Jew able to bear arms had joined the insurgent army," leaving them vulnerable to the Tories (or to the anti-Communist Poles). "This was not a new situation for them," Fast wrote; "it echoed and reechoed back through all the long, dusty halls of history. The women sat in their houses, behind locked doors and barred shutters, shedding the only tears . . . shed in New York for the defeated [Yankees]. . . . Old men gathered in the synagogue to pray that this, the last retreat of the exiled, might still retain some hope for a promised land."[111]

In *The Unvanquished*, Fast also touched, as in *Conceived in Liberty*, on the question of whether the common soldiers, if and when they finished their war with the British, would turn in solidarity against the Continental Congress. But in several parts of the book, the soldiers and other commoners seem incapable of such a feat. They are shown as bumpkins, stragglers, and deserters. On the other hand, Fast, demonstrating faith in the professional soldier, has Washington, the aristocratic slaveholder, setting "out across the Delaware as a Virginia farmer" to become "on the other shore something else, a man of incredible stature, a human being in some ways more godly and wonderful than any other who has walked on this earth."[112]

Clearly, *The Unvanquished* is connected only remotely to class-consciousness or to veneration of the masses. Indeed, Fast seems to support a view similar to conclusions reached by conservative scholars who saw workers and farmers as virtually apolitical and no better than "fair-weather soldiers." Between 1939 and 1942, then, before he joined the Communist Party, not only did Fast grapple with the nature of his Jewish identity and struggle to earn a living while remaining true to his art, but he had the desire and the ability to use sources broadly and to respect the scholarship of historians with viewpoints different from his own.[110] Later, as his ideological attitude narrowed, Fast, as we shall see, tended to disparage his ethno-religious origins as well as to infuse his stories and novels with propaganda, essentially, and unfortunately, badly impairing his work.

2

The War against Fascism

*F*our days before the attack on Pearl Harbor, Howard Fast spoke at the annual book fair in Scarborough, Maine, where he was introduced as the "next really important historical novelist."[1] But only a short time after the entrance of the United States into WWII, Fast claimed to have "dismissed" the writing period of his life and to have "moved into the anti-fascist effort with all [his] being."[2] From mid-1942 to early 1944, Fast was certainly more active politically, and even expressed a desire to fight fascism physically; but in that same period, unable to put an "abrupt end" to his enduring ambition to become a successful writer of meaningful and marketable fiction, he also produced two of his most substantial novels, *Citizen Tom Paine* and *Freedom Road*.

Howard's younger brother, Julie, had already enlisted in the armed forces, and Fast, with a very low draft number, waited, thinking he'd be conscripted soon. In the meantime, mainly because of Bette's anxiety over Howie's impending military future, the Fasts put the two-bedroom cottage they had built and furnished into the hands of a real-estate agent, and moved back to New York. They never returned to Old Stony Hollow Road in Tarrytown. They searched for a new apartment in the city while they lived in a cheap hotel room, which only added to Bette's gloom over the loss of her baby. Assuming that Howie would soon be away "for the duration" (a phrase heard often during WWII) and fearing the possibility of years home alone, Bette joined the Signal Corps as a civilian artist making animated training films.[3]

Bored, discontented, and expecting to be drafted soon, Fast felt restless even as he worked on *Citizen Tom Paine*. That he didn't simply volunteer, which would have given him the right to choose his branch of service, is curious. Whatever the reason, however, he chose to wait, with growing impatience, he says, to be called up. In the meantime he walked endlessly; and near the end of 1942 he had a chance meeting on Broadway in midtown with the nationally known poet and anthologist Louis Untermeyer. They recognized one another from a conversation they had had the year before in Philadelphia, where Fast had given a talk about the historical novel. Now, over lunch, they had a more consequential discussion.

Untermeyer, a former editor of the Marxist journal *The Masses,* who was writing propaganda pamphlets for the Office of War Information (owi), suggested that Howard, instead of aimlessly wandering the streets, apply for the same sort of position. Fast was reluctant, never having done that kind of work before. But during his visit to the owi building on Broadway and 57th Street, he was impressed with the people he met, especially Elmer Davis, the well-known writer and news reporter who directed the owi; Joseph Barnes, veteran editor and foreign correspondent for the *Herald Tribune,* who (along with Walter Duranty of the *New York Times*), did much to put a veil of ignorance over the worst of Stalin's crimes; and John Houseman, the Academy Award–winning actor and filmmaker, who worked at the owi for the Voice of America (voa).

In December, Fast accepted a job at the owi, and was assigned to the voa division to write fifteen-minute programs produced from the mountains of matcrial coming in to thc officc from thc various ncws scrviccs. So that hc could write more realistically about the brutality of the conflict, Fast also watched unedited battlefield footage. The experience was harrowing, yet valuable, not only for Fast's radio programs, but also for his later novels, lending clarity and realism to the scenes of war depicted in so many of them.[4]

Fast wrote concise, dramatic pieces for broadcast, which were read by actors transmitting via bbc into Nazi-dominated Europe. In doing this work, Fast was "thrown headlong," he said, "into the company of a variety of Communists all of whom knew everything about everything of the world in which [he] was interested." Eighteen of the twenty-two actors available for narration were Communists.[5] Fast was not just "impressed" by them, he said, but "overwhelmed" by his associates' "knowledge" and "sensitivity." And since "most of them were either artists or writers," he was also "delighted by them as people." These men (and they were all men) at the OWI were the first to interest Howard in the overall meaning of the war effort, formal politics, and racial justice. Fast soon joined several antifascist organizations, spoke at Communist-sponsored events, and wrote for magazines close to the Communist movement.[6] His new Communist friends, who seemed to him to have an unusual capacity for passion and engagement, and for responding to injustice and the call of "History," had awakened in him a more pronounced social concern and a more vibrant political consciousness, as well as a desire to be part of their elite circle.

Fast's associates were often quite direct in "instructing him." When "it came to anti-fascist ideology," Howie admitted, "the Communist actors were a lot clearer than I was. Or perhaps they functioned with a single directional intensity that I did not [yet] share." Repeatedly when preparing to go on the air, Fast would encounter "a sort of strike or refusal on the part of the actors—they claiming that I had written something that was ideologically incorrect." Fast would be summoned to the broadcast room, where there were stormy arguments, "in the course of which at least twice I had to call the State Department in Washington to resolve the matter."[7]

Through these "astonishing" coworkers Howard also met the politically progressive Orson Welles, a brilliant actor and the groundbreaking director of the recently released film *Citizen Kane*. He also got to know Elia Kazan, another renowned film and theater director, who had been a member of the Communist Party in the 1930s, and Clifford Odets, a playwright whose theater pieces, including *Waiting for Lefty* and *Awake and Sing*, were a cross between "visionary humanist" and Marxist odes critical of capitalism.[8] For Howie his new connections with "the known and the knowledgeable" was very heady stuff.

Finding his work at the OWI exciting and self-affirming, Fast was no longer especially anxious to be more directly involved in the war. In any case, nearly blind in his right eye, a congenital condition he did not find particularly disabling, Fast was classified as 4F in 1943.[9] But, if he could not be in the armed forces with his brother Julie, Howie would do something else, something rare and important—he would project "a voice into the dark, sad land of occupied Europe"; and each day as he typed out, "Good Morning, this is the Voice of America," Fast's skin would prickle.[10]

Staying on at the OWI surrounded by creative artists and "wise, patriotic intellectuals" who were dedicated to the antifascist cause, Fast completed *Citizen Tom Paine.* Published in 1943, the book received positive reviews, one of which appeared on the front page of the *New York Herald Tribune*'s *Weekly Book Review.* "Once again," the reviewer wrote, "Howard Fast has taken a figure out of American history and by the intensity of his emotional sympathy and intellectual response" has written "a brilliant piece of fictional biography." The *New York Times Book Review* also featured Fast's new novel on page one, where the playwright Elmer Rice wrote a highly favorable piece, calling *Citizen Tom Paine* a "vivid portrait of one of the most extraordinary figures of the eighteenth century."[11]

Fast was delighted. Immediately, he had a copy of Rice's *New York Times* review framed, and, though yellowing, it was still on the wall of his Greenwich, Connecticut, study at least until 2009, when I visited, six years after his death. *Citizen Tom Paine* was one of Fast's favorite creations, and more than sixty-five years later it is still one of his best selling, best remembered and most respected novels. Impressed with the good reviews, the State Department published the book in pocket size in Serbo-Croatian, Slovene, Greek, Polish, Czech, and four other languages. Fast was also flooded with requests for interviews, and Dore Schary, the motion-picture writer and producer, came out from California to talk about film rights. Fast's ego "enlarged itself dangerously," he said, but Bette and his good friend Sam Sloan brought him down to earth.[12]

Part of the book's success was good timing. The Great Depression was over, and the war was moving in a positive direction for the Allies. The enemy fascist states had had only scorn for nations that made "mediocrities" into heroes. But the "common man" was a well-honored ideal in democratic America's culture, literature, and politics; and here was *Citizen Tom Paine,* a book with a hero who, like Fast, had pulled himself out of poverty by the sheer strength of his will.

Paine joined Washington's army not as an officer or even a common soldier, but more as a kind of cheerleader and spiritual advisor for the troops; his love of America and visionary pursuit of global liberation was nicely captured by Fast. "We have it in our power," Paine memorably pronounces, "to begin the world over again," a sentiment that fit well with the propaganda work Fast was doing at OWI.[13] The book also suggests that while ethnic origin, family, and social class were never unimportant in America, talent and innovation in what would become the United States were valued more highly. Fast even has Paine saying, "Here was a land of no one people, of no one prejudice, of no one thought . . . a country so youthful that half the people one met were foreigners or the first generation of foreigners . . . and the promise . . . was freedom . . . no more and no less than that."[14]

In America, Fast said, relative to Europe, there was comparatively little class differentiation. Under pressure from England, free farmers and artisans were united with merchants and planters; and real property, he argued, was so abundant that there was virtually no landless class. Here Fast, surprisingly, given his growing racial sensitivity, appears to have forgotten about the slaves, one million landless souls. But he has drawn in his fictionalized biography of Paine a picture of relative class harmony, not conflict. Fast does imply that ruling-class hegemony emerged after the Revolution, but he seems to have given up temporarily on explicitly portraying the War for Independence as one that was also a battle over who should rule at home.[15]

Fast's "message," however, is not at all that clear. He continues to imply that a "real" American Revolution may have been about to emerge in the course of the War for Independence against England, before it was co-opted by men of money who initiated a "counter-revolution."[16] He also took great pains to depict the troops—the farmers and laborers—as central to the victory over Great Britain. And he implied, inaccurately, that the professional officers, including Fast's admired George Washington, had only minimal influence.[17]

Fast also made Paine more "common" than he actually was. The "first professional revolutionary," as Fast called his protagonist, is presented as a dirty, slovenly, habitual drunkard, afflicted with homeliness and squinty eyes. But one of Paine's respected biographers, W. E. Woodward, the author of *Tom Paine: America's Godfather, 1737–1789,* called Fast's portrait of Paine "grievously" incorrect, and argued persuasively that Paine probably drank no more than his contemporaries; that he was "clean" enough to be the welcome house guest of lords, ambassadors, and presidents; and that he was, despite his bulbous nose, unusually handsome.[18]

In his attempt to paint the revolutionaries as more ordinary and raffish, and much more important to the success of the Revolutionary War than the bewigged professionals, Fast overstated his case. Indeed, by purposefully using concepts and terms loaded with modern connotations, such as "guerilla warfare" and "common front" or "comrades" and "the proletariat," he seems to have recast the American revolution as a fight for classlessness by the "awkward, stumbling, self-conscious, first citizen army the world had ever known." And he even depicts a microcosm of achieved classlessness in the Rumples, a fictitious family, living in a rural setting based on communal economic relationships.[19]

Although Fast was already working on the book before he joined the OWI, it seems as if the Communist colleagues he held in such awe had had, in their many political discussions with him about revolution, global liberation, and the abolition of poverty, some influence on the thrust, and certainly the vocabulary, of *Citizen Tom Paine.* Paine was more radical than most of the "founding fathers." He neither owned slaves nor profited from the trade, and in 1774 he had written at least one impassioned antislavery letter, which called for the immediate abolition of slavery in all the colonies. He also proposed the framework for a proto–welfare state and developed a meticulous tax system that would support it. And although not an atheist, he was a critic of all institutionalized religions and their sacred books. But he was a man of his age, of the eighteenth-century Enlightenment, and no communist.[20] In 1800, after his fellow citizens voted the Federalists out of office, Paine proudly said, "There is too much common sense and independence in America to be long the dupe of any faction, foreign or domestic."[21] Had this quote been included in *Citizen Tom Paine,* it would have resonated with even more irony in the face of Howard Fast's growing relationships with Communists.

Howard was not only getting closer to his revered Communist associates, he was also getting very familiar with his secretary, "a good-looking Bennington graduate." Both of them were often at the office well into the evening, and after work they'd top off the day with dinner and drinks. Fast's secretary did not know how to type; and although she knew Joyce and Proust, she had never heard of Jack London. This ignorance did not please Howard, but it hardly stopped him from sleeping with her. "We were ripe for an affair," Fast said later. "When you're thrown together with a beautiful woman day after day, things happen."[22]

He was after all spending much more time with "Miss Bennington" than with Mrs. Fast. Bette and Howie had moved out of their hotel room into a small studio apartment; but Howie "began to lose sight of [his wife] completely." Bette worked long hours at the Signal Corps. She left for work early every morning, and when Howie returned to their place well after midnight, she was long asleep; and when Fast dragged himself out of bed at eight-thirty in the morning, Bette was already at work. Occasionally they managed to meet for lunch in order to catch up with one another. But "our hours and our work," Fast confided in notes he made later, "[just] continued the process of turning us into strangers to one another." And "suddenly," he said, "I had the feeling that our marriage was breaking up."[23]

Apparently Fast failed to recognize his own responsibility in this development. His already sizable ego was further enlarged by the recent success of *The Last Frontier,* which was in its fourth edition by 1943, and by the positive reception accorded *Citizen Tom Paine,* and he may have been bitten by the bug of entitlement. Whatever the case, he thought he deserved more than what his current domestic life offered. And he seriously contemplated divorcing Bette and marrying his secretary, this "tall, dark, beautiful and rich" new lover. He poured his heart out to Louis Untermeyer (thirty years Fast's senior), with whom he had developed a warm avuncular relationship that would endure until Untermeyer's death in 1977. Married five times, twice to the same woman, Untermeyer virtually instructed Howard not to leave Bette. "If you left your lovely wife," he said, "and married this lady, you might have a daughter and send her to Bennington, and then she wouldn't know who her father was, and the main point is that you're not Proust or Joyce and never will be, if you get my meaning?"[24]

There may have been more than one meaning in this advice. Was Untermeyer merely telling Fast that his interests would not be the same as those of his potential new family, and that the imagined daughter would have no respect for her father? Perhaps. But it is legitimate to ask whether Untermeyer was also suggesting in this way that Howie's talent would never reach the level of genius and that marrying into the Bennington circle would not help.

Whatever he meant precisely, Untermeyer appears to have saved Fast from becoming just one more successful man who dumped the wife of his impoverished years, in favor a younger, sexier, trophy bride. Eventually Fast "returned to [his] senses" and "worked things out" with Bette. But that took several months. In the meantime, in June 1943, Howard was invited out to Hollywood to explore the possibility of making *Citizen Tom Paine* into a film. With his marriage now unstable, filled with mutual anger and recrimination, Howard thought a temporary separation might help. Bette agreed, and with Vivian Shaw, her coworker at the Signal Corps, whose husband, the writer David Shaw, brother of Irwin Shaw, was then in the army overseas, went off to Cape Cod while Howard left for the West Coast.[25]

Fast, along with Frank Tuttle, a Hollywood writer, director, and producer, and John Bright, a member of the Hollywood section of the CPUSA, who had been chosen to write the screenplay for *Citizen Tom Paine,* traveled by train to California. Tuttle had directed the film noir *This Gun for Hire* (screenwriter, Albert Maltz, Communist and Jewish) and *Hostages* (screenwriter, Lester Cole, Communist and Jewish). Bright in 1933 had helped establish the Screen Writers Guild, which after WWII made it onto the Attorney General's List of Subversive Organizations (AGLOSO). In the late forties when HUAC was investigating what it called Communist subversion of the movie industry, Bright moved to Mexico to avoid congressional scrutiny and was subsequently blacklisted. But in 1943, Bright was in no "trouble," and he and Fast, and Tuttle, too, became friends on their ride west.[26]

In California, Fast visited John Howard Lawson, another screenwriter, Jew, and Communist destined to become one of the Hollywood Ten. With Bright and Tuttle, Fast drove over the Laurel Canyon and into the San Fernando Valley, where the orange and almond orchards moved him to think he was in "paradise." At Lawson's spectacular home, situated on a fifty-acre spread, he "was introduced to a great many Hollywood left-wingers" and concluded that "all of the bright and fascinating people . . . were Communists." Fast was "astonished at the way they lived," he told his old friend Devery Freeman in 1943. And he said the same to an interviewer in 1977 when he was living in California opulence himself. "Their living had a quality . . . of upper-class luxury taken for granted" that Fast "had never encountered before."[27]

"It was . . . strange [for] such young people," Fast thought, to live with such lavishness at a time when the American people "were just [coming] out of the Depression," and when the war was still raging. "The amounts of money that they earned, was, to me, fantastic—$1000 and $2000 dollars a week." These were "people filled with goodwill," Fast admitted, but also "with *guilt*." They "wanted desperately to do good, to make their weight felt in this struggle against fascism, to do *something* that would tell themselves, if not the world, that they were *not* what they appeared to be to themselves, that they were not parasites on the body of the country." Here Fast anticipated the formulation of Arthur Schlesinger Jr., who six years later in 1949, said,

"The Hollywood writer feels he has sold himself out; he has abandoned his serious work in exchange for large weekly paychecks; and he resents a society which corrupts him . . . . He has qualms of conscience, however, for making so much while others make so little. So he believes that he can buy indulgences by participating in the Communist movement, just as men in the Middle Ages bought remission of sins from wandering monks."[28] This psychological interpretation contains an important truth, but it takes into account neither that before coming to Hollywood and into money, writers such as Maltz, Lawson, Odets, and Kazan were early participants in the theater of social protest nor that they had joined the Party before they became part of the affluent life of California.

But most of the people Fast met on his trip "had no understanding," he thought, "of what it meant to be poor, to be hungry, or to be oppressed, or to be without an opportunity." This difference between him and them, however, did not tarnish Fast's admiration for his new Communist friends, nor did it diminish what appeared to be his envy.[29] Even if he changed his fellow-traveler status and became a full-fledged member of the Communist Party, Fast saw that he could continue to write, be successful, and become famous and very rich. Perhaps it was here that Fast more fully recognized his true ambition. He told an interviewer in 1967 that he thought "the plans of any truthful writer is to stop writing, get enough money so he won't have to write anymore. This was Mark Twain's dream. To only stop writing and stop the torture. So that's my plan, but it won't work. *I will never get enough money.* And I'll never be able to stop writing." Fast never did stop writing, but after 1946, and until the mid-1970s, a major portion of his income would come from the film industry.[30]

Thinking on and off about the potential filming of *Citizen Tom Paine,* Fast had long talks throughout the evening at Lawson's home—several with Lawson himself. Howard listened while the screenwriter and several other Hollywood Communists pressed Fast to join the Party. Lawson talked to Howard "at great length," arguing that "the only truly conscious anti-fascist force" in these "war years was the Communist Party." Fast had to admit, he said, that Lawson and "these guests of his, movie stars, film writers, directors," almost all of them Jewish, had a greater aptitude for sniffing out injustice, and "were clearer and more informed in their thinking than [he] had anticipated."[31]

At yet another festive dinner at the home of film director Herbert Biberman, also Jewish, a Communist Party leader, and probably the most rigid Stalinist among the Hollywood Ten, Fast for the first time met Paul Robeson, the great African American singer and pro-Communist. Born in 1898, Robeson by accidents of geography, family, talent, and sheer will had overcome the daily brutalities commonplace for black Americans in the 1910s. Resilient, even in the face of indignities and slights, Robeson won a scholarship to Rutgers, where he earned accolades as a brilliant student, debater, singer, and athlete. After Rutgers, Robeson began work toward a law degree at Columbia University, but in the end became convinced that discrimination would limit his possibilities in the legal profession. Not so in the world of entertainment. Robeson's astounding voice and artistic genius led to extraordinary success in the concert halls, as well as on stage and screen; and before he got himself into deep political trouble for his progressive activism in the late 1940s, he had come to be known in the mainstream media as "America's most well-known Negro."[32]

Fast, like so many others encountering Robeson for the first time, "was immediately impressed by his bearing, his gentleness . . . and of course his incredible voice." Fast was well aware of Robeson's "dedication to the antifascist struggle," and during their chance meeting at Biberman's that day, the two men "sat and talked at great length," especially about the Soviet Union. Ever since the "model socialist state" had been attacked by Germany in 1941, Fast had grown increasingly interested in the USSR, and he asked Robeson about his 1934 trip to Russia.[33]

We have no record of Robeson's response, but suffice it to say that since his visit nine years earlier he had become an ardent lover of Russian culture and history and an enthusiastic admirer of the Soviet Union's socialist experiment. Robeson had already swung, rather suddenly, to the political left in the 1930s even before his trip to the USSR. Once there, he was treated to carefully planned evenings "at the theater and opera, long talks with [the director Sergei] Eisenstein, gala banquets, private screenings, trips to hospitals, [and] children's centers."

Events in Russia "tumbled one after another, a heady mix of new confirming experiences, all in the context of a warm embrace," and Robeson, as his biographer, Martin Duberman, puts it, "was smitten." Somewhere along the line, the man who had angrily pronounced the "modern white American" a "member of the lowest form of civilization in the world today" was convinced that the Soviet Union had abolished racial prejudice. Robeson said that in Russia he felt "like a human being for the first time."[34] While it was clear that Robeson, like most on the Communist left, expressed a "realism" in regard to the racial and economic inequality inherent in American capitalism and a prescience about the rise of fascism abroad, these insights were offset by illusions about the Soviet Union that can at best be designated as "romantic idealism."

Fast, a captive of the same illusions, told Robeson that he was tempted by the "coaxing" of Biberman's dinner guests to join the CP. Robeson confessed, truthfully, that despite his own virulent antifascism and political progressivism, he himself had never been a member of the Party. He had some guilt about not joining, Robeson said, but he did not discourage Fast from doing so. No doubt in this first set of encounters with the Hollywood Communists and with the pro-Communist Robeson, Fast was also "smitten."[35]

Nothing came of the plan to film *Citizen Tom Paine*. But the loneliness and despair generated in Fast by disconnection from his wife was softened some by the new relationships he developed in California. The "writers, actors and directors I met, most of them part of the left-wing movement so powerful in Hollywood in those days overwhelmed me with kindness and praise," Fast said, and he gloried in the attention and admiration heaped upon him.[36]

Still, the separation from Bette had been "no easy matter. We [had] both . . . [been] thinking that it might very likely be the end of our relationship. We were both . . . damaged and mystified by the forces that had hurt us." And after Bette returned from Cape Cod, the Fasts "spent two days talking [their] hearts out, and . . . decided to give the marriage another try." They "worked things out," and then when "[Bette] was pregnant again," Howard said, "I realized that we were married and intended to stay married."[37] In the fall of 1943, the Fasts looked forward to a new baby, which they prayed would come to term on this second try. Bette took leave of the Signal Corps, and the couple traded their "miserable one-room studio" for a three-room apartment on the tenth floor at 100 W. 59th Street. It had "a great view of Central Park," and they paid more rent for that apartment than they had ever thought they could afford.[38] But with money flowing in from sales of Howard's last three books, their financial problems had become a thing of the past. For a time.

Still basking in the glow of his Hollywood experience, which came on top of the earlier priming he received from his creative Communist colleagues at the OWI, and with memories of his own impoverished childhood still sharp, Fast began to think about making a formal commitment to the CPUSA. Second-generation Jews such as Fast had long been disproportionately attracted to progressive politics. Socialism had a solid foundation in many Eastern European Jewish immigrant families who had brought with them to America working-class loyalties as well as a hatred of autocracy.

Though the Communist movement did not always live up to its own exhortations, its progressive ideology and its celebration of universalism were attractive to Jews who were moving away from the faith of their more traditional parents, even as the injunctions of the Hebrew prophets continued to inform their changing belief-systems. Communist organizations also afforded Jews an opportunity to teach and write, and to interact generally with non-Jews. This openness contrasted sharply in the 1930s with Jewish exclusion from many professions in an economically depressed and increasingly antisemitic American society.

Jews were also disproportionately attracted to the culture of writers, artists, composers, actors, directors, screenwriters and the like. And as the sociologist Nathan Glazer has shown, they could be strongly influenced by successful people in these fields. The large number of Communists, and Jewish Communists at that, in these areas often played an important role for young aspiring Jews, especially those like twenty-nine-year-old Fast, already possessed of left-leanings. They helped make Communism respectable, acceptable, certainly something to be taken seriously, and as Fast had witnessed, even glamorous.[39]

Fast was "ready." And the Communists knew it. In New York, back at the OWI, the pressure on him to join the CPUSA and the kind of wooing he had experienced in California continued. Joe North, one of the editors of *New Masses,* a magazine closely associated with the CPUSA, was part of "a calculated effort to bring me into the party," Fast said. "Their first move was to reprint a chapter from *The Unvanquished,* for which they had only praise. Then came an invitation to be part of a symposium, then another symposium." Lionel Berman, the CPUSA functionary in charge of the Cultural Section of the Party, met with Howard and Bette in the fall of 1943, and spent hours trying to seduce them. "I learned in time," Fast recalled, "that the people in the leadership of both the [Party] and its Cultural section," among whom were a half-dozen of the actors who worked with him at the OWI, "considered bringing me into the party one of their prime tasks. The effort was headed up by Lionel Berman," identified in Fast's memoir as a very "persuasive man."[40]

THE FATAL EMBRACE

Though his dear friend, Sam Sloan, tried to talk him out of it, Howard Fast, near the very end of 1943 and at a high point in his career as a historical novelist, joined the American Communist Party. Where was Sarah Kunitz when Fast really needed her? Long gone from the CPUSA. She had for too many years suffered the dogmatism, divisiveness, and isolating blindness of the CP leadership, which Howard would now experience for the next fourteen.

Relatively positive views of the Soviet Union were apparent in the United States in 1943, especially in Jewish New York, particularly after the visit of Russia's brilliant actor and artistic director of the Moscow State Jewish Theatre, Solomon Mikhoels, and the great Yiddish poet and Communist Party stalwart Itzak Feffer. Both were in the United States as officers of the Jewish Anti-Fascist Committee to bolster support for the USSR, and they generated enormous enthusiasm. Still, it doesn't seem particularly opportunistic on Fast's part to have become a member of the Communist Party at this point. Even if there was between Russia and the United States an "era of good feelings," there was certainly no love for Communism in America. On the contrary, anti-Communist sentiment had been growing in the Untied States from as early as 1919, a sentiment that had become hardened and institutionalized by 1938 in the House Committee on Un-American Activities (HUAC). Indeed, it seems that opportunism, in its narrowest sense, should have had Fast continuing to shy away from any kind of political activism and instead, concentrating on writing—which he was doing anyway: *Freedom Road* was nearly complete when he joined the Party.

But two powerful forces came together for Fast in 1943: his growing desire to be part of the glamorous world of the Hollywood Communists and to join the coterie of the impressive intellectuals he'd met at OWI, and his expressed conviction that the Soviet Union had from 1941 forward demonstrated its greatness as an antifascist force and as a model for the future. Fast was no longer interested, if he had ever been, in the Moscow trials of the 1930s. He did not justify those atrocious episodes, Fast insisted, but the trials, he said, "were part of the past, as was the [1939] pact between Hitler and Stalin."[41]

When he was asked during a TV interview in 1957 why he had joined the CPUSA in 1943, even after so many writers and intellectuals had left the Party earlier, Fast said, "Well, in 1943 we were in a war against Fascism [and] I didn't come to Communism in 1943 as a stranger. I had been close to this, known Communists, been affected by Communists, read Communist literature and believed it, ever since 1933." In 1941, "I saw the whole world joining with Russia in an antifascist struggle. By 1943, I felt the next step here [was] to effectively . . . struggle, as well as write against this monster that was threatening to consume the earth [and] *the only way* was to join the Communist Party."[42]

One could still reasonably ask, as the interviewer, Martin Agronsky, did not, why, if Fast's motive for joining the Party was antifascism, he joined in late 1943 when the United States, as well as Russia, was moving ever closer to winning the war against fascism. Or why Fast conflated his admiration for Russia's military success with the Stalinist rationale; or why Fast did not commit himself to a more independent American left-liberal antifascist cause, such as the anti-Stalinist Socialists—Irving Howe and his circle, for example; or to a much more organized and powerful group, the left wing of the New Deal Democratic Party, which, recognizing the contradictions inherent in capitalism, had by 1943 introduced many of the reforms that Fast once called for.

Something more than antifascism had moved Fast to join the CPUSA. His desire for even more attention than he was getting from readers and reviewers, and his aspirations for fame, reinforced by his visits to Hollywood with its many rich and famous Jewish Communists living in cheerful luxury and surrounded by beautiful women, surely played a role. This is not to say that Fast's admiration for the socialist experiment in Russia, with which he was first taken at the age of seventeen, and his hope that the Soviet Union would serve as a model for the rest of the world, were not important to his momentous choice. His decision, however, meant not only that Fast had relegated the *past* sins of the Soviet Union to the dustbin of history, but also that he was turning a blind eye, or the unspoken rationale of "historical necessity," to more recent horrors, including a fierce reemergence of antisemitism in the USSR.

Once the Soviet Union, after the signing of the nonaggression pact with
Nazi Germany, was assured of its immediate survival, Stalin not only engaged in imperialist expansionism, annexing Latvia, Lithuania, and Estonia,
and occupying Finland, he also decided to eliminate the Jewish Socialist
Bund in Russian-held Poland. Two Polish-Jewish Socialists, Victor Alter
and Henryk Erlich, had been organizing anti-German resistance in Nazi-
held Poland, but then fled to the eastern territories, where, under the terms
of the pact with the Nazis, they were arrested by Soviet forces.[43]

Several months after the German invasion of the Soviet Union in June
1941, the Russians, no longer beholden to the Nazis, released Alter and
Erlich from prison. The two men immediately got involved in organizing the
Moscow-based Jewish Anti-Fascist Committee. A Jewish committee against
Hitler was acceptable to Stalin when it was expedient, and didn't have an
aroma of Jewish bourgeois nationalism. But the temporary success of the
Red Army in December 1941 in its first full-scale offensive, which drove
the Germans out of Rostov, restored Stalin's confidence; in days, Alter and
Erlich were arrested again on the utterly implausible charge of having urged
Red Army soldiers to stop the bloodshed and immediately conclude peace
with Germany. Erlich and Alter were kept in solitary confinement. Henryk
committed suicide in his cell in May 1942; Victor was executed in February
1943.[44]

These events shocked even ordinarily pro-Soviet commentators. Editors
and writers for the *New Republic,* the *Nation,* and *PM,* a newly launched left-
liberal daily whose board members were mostly pro-Communist, strongly
condemned the executions in their respective periodicals in March 1943.[45]
About six months later, and three months after he had spent time with the
Jewish Hollywood Communists during which he apparently asked no questions about the Erlich-Alter affair, Howard Fast, a believer "in the goodness
and greatness of the Soviet system," but now almost certainly conscious of
its ruthlessness, joined the American Communist Party.[46]

Was Fast's antifascism and his faith in the Soviet system so strong that
Stalin's behavior escaped his close scrutiny? No doubt. He had heard "stories," Fast later explained "about the gigantic horror" unfolding in the Soviet
Union. He rejected these, he said, as did most of the left, but "not without
reason." So "intermingled were the lies and the truths in the charges hurled
at the Soviet Union," Fast argued, "and so pressing was the double advent
of fascism abroad and social failure in the United States, that belief in the

goodness and the greatness of the Soviet system was something we on the left clung to with *religious blindness and ferocity.*"[47] Might Fast have "known" about the Soviet Union's "faults" or "mistakes," but still believed the USSR stood for a better world? Might he have known even of its evils and considered them historical necessities? Very possibly. After all, Fast himself said later that in 1943, he felt that no "decent person had the right to *exist* in this society if he were not a member of the Communist Party."[48]

Only if we see Fast as a figure who, consciously or not, had allowed himself to reach the extreme position of murder as a "historical necessity" can we understand, if only partially, Fast's enthusiasm for Communism, especially its Soviet version; this holds true as well for the enthusiasm of many other writers and intellectuals in the Western world that survived even at some of the worst moments of the Stalinist regime.

Approximately twenty-five thousand people joined the CPUSA between 1943 and 1944 out of a cluster of motives including antifascism and a discomfort with capitalist society. Most of these new recruits, appalled by Soviet behavior and the obsequiousness of the Communist Party's leadership, would leave in three years or less. Fast, however, stayed for another thirteen. It was not because he believed, not yet anyway, that he had to turn his antifascism toward the United States, pitting himself against his own government. He stayed, he said, mostly because to him the Soviet Union and the American Communist Party together constituted "an edifice dedicated singularly and irrevocably to the ending of all war, injustice, hunger and suffering—and to the goal of the brotherhood of man."[49]

Fast's pronouncement typifies the psychology of the "true believer." It contains a Utopian vision of the future and the possibility of human perfectibility and harmony—a sentimental and heroic unity that will dissolve all conflict, social and political. If the drive to fulfill this vision leads inescapably to the eradication of particular sets of individuals and their less than neat, incorrigible characteristics, so be it.

Fast's yearning for social justice was authentic. Although a latecomer to the activist antifascist movement and to the Party, Fast had, like the pioneers, witnessed or directly experienced social injustice and degradation. "No one with a brain in his head or a shred of social conscience," Fast claimed, "could have matured during the two decades following [his birth in 1914] without being well aware of the Communists and the Communist Party."[50]

This last contention leaves out many thousands of ordinary people who went on with their lives during bad times, frustrated, poorer, perhaps even destitute, but without much knowledge of the Communist Party. In the 1930s, however, the Communists were indeed visible in Fast's New York City, where about 40 percent of the membership of the national Party resided. And when in the 1930s, the violent revolution predicted by the Comintern did not take place in the United States, Communists, together with liberals in a Popular Front, responded to the Depression with concrete action for incremental change.[51] They fought for much that was honorable and achievable in numerous arenas of American life, including the rights of farm workers, immigrants, industrial laborers, women, and with the important and troubling exception of the period after the Soviet Union was attacked, blacks. All these things Fast, and his wife Bette, too, supported even before they became Communists. And after the war, the CPUSA, and Howard Fast in particular, as we shall see, began again to battle discrimination and pursue racial justice openly.[52]

Whatever else may be said of ordinary Communists and the goals they pursued and how they pursued them, most of those who joined the Party in the 1930s and early 1940s were animated by a sincere, if hurried and sometimes ruthless, desire to change the world and make it better. Whatever other motives Howard Fast had for joining the CPUSA, including the pursuit of fellowship, fame, and fortune, and no matter what we may think of the revolutionary means he might have had in mind for the future or the brutally inhuman means he tolerated in the Soviet Union, his expressed desire to "repair and improve the world" was not disingenuous. What he didn't count on is that the world of American Communism, and the astounding power of the CPUSA to intimidate, would change him more than he and his comrades were able to change America or the Party.

In November 1943, after Fast had been a Communist for a month or more, the OWI had constructed a medium-wave broadcast system in North Africa and was planning to move the VOA closer to occupied Europe. Fast assumed he was going too, and would finally be "in the heart of the struggle." Bette, though pregnant, could come with him, Howard thought, as an artist for the OWI. His boss, Louis Cowan, however, told him he could not send Fast to North Africa, or anywhere outside the United States, for that matter, but would give him another position at the OWI, writing propaganda pamphlets. Fast was stunned, or so he says, when Cowan told him that "to go overseas as a civilian employee of this department, you need a passport." The FBI, however, had instructed the State Department not to issue a passport for Fast on the grounds that he was either a Communist or a Communist sympathizer with strong connections to the Party.[53] Unbeknownst to Fast, his FBI file contained a statement signed by him in October 1942 "issued by the 'Communist-controlled League of American Writers' calling for a second front." The record also showed that Fast had spoken at an antifascist rally at Carnegie Hall in December 1942 on the anniversary of the Reichstag fire of 1933, which the Nazis had blamed on the German Communists before rounding up their leaders. The FBI also knew that Fast had met and had had correspondence with Paul Robeson, a suspected Communist; that he was on the advisory board of *New Currents,* a magazine close to the Communist movement; and that he was a member of Jewish Writers and Artists, a "Communist front" organization.[54]

The FBI did get things wrong occasionally. With *Citizen Tom Paine* on their minds apparently, the Bureau in 1943, while updating Fast's file, refers to his attendance in 1932–33 not at meetings of the John Reed Club, but at a nonexistent "Tom Paine Club of the Communist Party"! Correct and incorrect, however, Fast's FBI file was growing; but he also had top clearance, about which Cowan was well aware, from the U.S. Civil Service Commission dated May 19, 1943, before he had joined the CPUSA. And so, Howard asked his boss, disingenuously, "How the hell could I be a Communist?"[55] Cowan was entirely sympathetic. But he read the names of four of the actors in the VOA pool and three more from the various foreign desks. According to J. Edgar Hoover, all the men named were members of the American Communist Party.

Fast told Cowan that writing pamphlets was "not my thing. If I can't go overseas for OWI, I'll find another way. I have to." Howard would go overseas, but not for another year and a half, by which time, in late June 1945, the war was over everywhere but in Asia.

THE REDS AND THE BLACKS

During the eighteen months before Howard Fast would finally go abroad as a "war correspondent" for *Coronet* and *Esquire* magazines, he had for about five weeks edited *Scope,* a left-wing periodical founded by the American

Communist Party. He had also, through the intervention of Vice President Henry Wallace, secured the passport denied him the year before; had become a father in May 1944 when Rachel Ann Fast was born; and had finished writing *Freedom Road,* which was published in April.[56]

Howard Fast seemed destined to write this novel. At the OWI in 1943, Fast had been looking at materials about the possibility of integrating blacks into the American armed forces. Several of his Communist colleagues, perhaps thinking about the failure of integration after the Civil War, when the moment might have been plastic enough for so radical a social change, suggested that Fast, having finished *Citizen Tom Paine,* do a novel on Reconstruction.

On Fast's return train trip from Hollywood, in the summer of 1943, Frank Tuttle had been raving about *Black Reconstruction in America,* a book he'd just read, by the African American scholar and activist W. E. B. Du Bois. Tuttle's comments resonated immediately in Fast's mind with the conversation he had had with Paul Robeson only days earlier. At that moment on the train, the image of the black singer-activist became for Fast, "the catalyzing center" of the book he would write about a large and powerful former slave and Union soldier, Gideon Jackson. In fact, Fast thought, the "story of a black man after the Civil War who leads his people through the first years of freedom," if made into a film starring Paul Robeson, might establish the Hollywood connection he so desired, and commercially do just as well as or better than Hemingway's recently released multiple-award-winning *For Whom the Bell Tolls,* which grossed $11 million.[57]

When Fast got home he read Du Bois's eight-hundred-page book. "The thing burned a hole in me," he said.[58] First published in 1935, *Black Reconstruction* completely overturned the anecdotal, racist notions that were the foundation of the "scholarship" of the Reconstruction period up to 1935. Du Bois's research completely discredited, even if it did not fully destroy, the myth that the post-emancipation South had degenerated, because of "negro incapacity," into economic and political anarchy and that it had been kept in a state of chaos by the Union forces during their military occupation.

The kernel of Du Bois's argument was that black and white laborers were divided after the Civil War and so were unable to present a solid front against the white propertied class. The racial split in the working class ensured the failure of Reconstruction and was the fundamental reason for the rise of Jim Crow laws between 1865 and 1890, as well as the perpetration of other serious, indeed deadly, racial injustices. Du Bois's sociological analysis of

Reconstruction was clearly rooted in his Marxist ideology; but his meticulous historical scholarship and use of primary source data on the postwar political economy of the South were groundbreaking.[59]

Back at the OWI, Fast's Communist friends continued to encourage him to write the book on Reconstruction. At about the same time, Fast recalled, reports "were beginning to filter in about the German destruction of Jews."[60] Although the mainstream press failed to give these events the space and place they deserved, the left-leaning *PM* had published an extensive summary of Rabbi Stephen S. Wise's account of the Nazi atrocities in December 1942, including facts about "extermination centers" and "giant crematoriums."[61] A month later, the *Nation* began a series on "The Jews of Europe" aiming to "impress on the conscience of freemen the vastness and the ghastliness of the Jewish tragedy in Europe."[62] And in August 1943, *PM* published a chart to demonstrate that some 1.7 million European Jews had already been murdered.[63] While reading these accounts, Fast claimed, "all the notes and thinking I had done for a novel about Reconstruction came together" with the news about the Jews of Europe, "and every moment I could steal from my work at the OWI was put to writing the new book."[64]

Fast's antiracist radicalism, to which large numbers of Jewish Americans were drawn, was home-grown. It grew out of heartfelt conviction about the circumstances of racial segregation and injustice in the United States. It was not something imposed by Moscow; even if the rhetoric and behavior of American Communists flip-flopped dramatically on signals from the USSR about various other issues, changes in Soviet politics did not markedly influence the attitudes or behavior of Jewish American Communists about racial justice. Most, including Fast, were "anti-religious," but not necessarily without religious sensibility. The alternative moral principles they adopted and developed out of their immigrant family backgrounds, their familiarity with radical ideas, and their political struggles often resembled the prophetic ethics of the Hebrew scriptures. They may have jettisoned Jewish religious institutional forms, as Howie had as early as age eight, but many reshaped for themselves the moral content of Judaism and retained its communal or collective consciousness. Fast, like other stalwarts of the CP, was often stiflingly straight-laced. His Communism, however, was mediated by New York Jewish radicalism, which was profoundly committed to racial equality.[65]

Blacks and Jews, who lived in their own separate, though not quite equal, ghettoes in the 1930s and 1940s, had had occasional but important interactions: in secret meetings between black sharecroppers and Jewish union and Party organizers in the Deep South, for example; or on the picket lines of industrial labor struggles in the North. In addition, Jewish and other white field secretaries and labor organizers, along with rank-and-file Communists, often paid in jail time or blood for their aid to black workers, when other liberal sympathizers paid mainly lip service.[66]

But the broadest and brightest vision of a black-Jewish world, a white-black world, was found in these decades in the creative narratives of left-wing poetry, plays, and novels. Indeed, the "great theme" of the U.S. literary left in these decades was antiracism: Benjamin Appel's *The Dark Stain* (1943), John Sanford's *The People from Heaven* (1943), Henrietta Buckmaster's *Deep River* (1944), Lillian E. Smith's *Strange Fruit* (1944), and David Alman's *The Hourglass* (1947) constitute a very small sample.[67] Howard Fast would add *Freedom Road* (1944) to the list.

At a party at the home of Charles Duell, one of Fast's publishers, Howard spoke with Duell's wife, Jo Pringle-Smith, about his new project. Taken with Fast's idea, Jo told him that he *must* spend some time with her parents in their old plantation house in South Carolina. Her mother and father were truly delightful people, Jo said, but they are full of biases about class and race. And she sent Fast off saying, "Don't tell them you're Jewish."

While living in the Pringle-Smith mansion for several days, Fast, surrounded by the trappings of the rich, listened to the stories Jo's parents told. He was shocked, he said, by the antiblack racism and antisemitism of such "cultured" people. But, now able to add "genteel" bias to the vulgar and violent forms he had earlier witnessed, Fast was again reinforced in his conviction that antiblack prejudice and antisemitism were cut from the same cloth.[68]

It was no accident that in *Freedom Road* Gideon Jackson's first mentor, Francis Cardozo, is part Jewish and part black. Cardozo was not a protagonist drawn from Fast's imagination. He had been a free black man educated at the University of Glasco, who returned from the North to his native South Carolina in 1865 to organize schools for black children. And he was a major figure in Reconstruction politics. In *Freedom Road,* Fast has Cardozo trying, successfully, to educate Gideon about his political role and his obligation as an elected delegate to the constitutional convention in South Carolina, and then encouraging him to run for the state senate. Fast's Cardozo also says that the great problem upon which the future rests is black access to property—an opinion with which most modern historians agree. As one of Fast's black delegates at the convention put it, "How about land? What good are schools and voting, if you ain't got the means to take out a crop."[69]

Jackson, together with many more blacks who returned from the war, lives with his family on the abandoned land of his former master. He and his black compatriots, along with a handful of poor whites, determine to buy the old neglected plantation, and like some actual former slaves, they borrow money, pool resources, and purchase the property for their own. No non-fictional examples can be found in the Reconstruction South of Fast's freed blacks and poor whites cooperating in an interracial enterprise of any kind. Indeed, poor whites were among the more racist constituencies in the former Confederate states, as elsewhere. *Freedom Road* then is a creative imagining of what a postracial world might look like if successfully instituted.

But the novel ends darkly. The entire experiment in black self-determination, and in a much smaller way, black-white cooperation in day-to-day living and working, is wiped out by the firepower of an army of Ku Klux Klan nightriders in the 1870s. The ugly violence of this episode, which results in the deaths of all the noble protagonists, however, does not appear to mean that Fast was ready to give up entirely on force—especially if the use of force were not repressive, but a means to achieve higher ends, as in the American Revolution and the American Civil War. In an important segment of *Freedom Road,* Gideon argues about the need for violence with Brother Peter, a man of God who will not bear arms. Gideon says, "I see men in bondage, and not God broke the bonds but men. I seen bad men and I seen indifferent men take up guns in a good cause, because good men had their way, and out of blood and the suffering there came something."[70]

Nor was the conclusion of *Freedom Road* meant to induce only despair. Indeed, Gideon Jackson appears to be one of Fast's models for the socialist ideal of human perfectibility. At age thirty-six, Gideon, illiterate, is a tabula rasa. But as the socialist ideal requires, an ordinary man, indeed a damaged man, is transformed into a responsible, self-controlling, and even renunciative person. He will live, suffer, and die with and for his people and his class. Introduced to middle-class black delegates who had been freemen before the Civil War, Gideon Jackson is embarrassed by his ignorance. But Cardozo lends him a speller, a grammar book, and less credibly a copy of Shakespeare's *Othello.* The emphasis subtly shifts away from land as the only salvation for ex-slaves, to education "as the only route to change."

Gideon learns much and goes on to become a U.S. congressman. Some critics thought that this part of the story strained credulity, but sixteen blacks did serve in Congress in the era of Reconstruction, and like the vast majority of black officials in South Carolina, they were literate.[71]

Although, or perhaps because, its denouement is failure, *Freedom Road* works as a "protest novel"; and Fast makes a valuable contribution by bringing W. E. B. Du Bois's scholarship to a wider audience, one mostly fed on blatantly racist films and on history written by authors intent on showing that black suffrage was the greatest error of the Civil War era. A consideration of other popular works of fiction about Reconstruction reveals some of the conventional styles and notions that Fast was trying to destroy as part of what he called his "one-man reformation of the historical novel."[72]

Thomas Dixon Jr.'s *The Clansman* (1905), for example, subtitled an "Historical Romance," recounted with naked approval the rise of the Ku Klux Klan. The novel and the play on which it was based inspired D. W. Griffith's famous 1913 film, *Birth of a Nation,* which depicted the evils heaped upon the white South by Reconstruction. *The Clansman,* which Dixon said he wrote as a warning to Northerners to maintain racial segregation, because blacks— uncontrolled—ultimately turn savage, was popular for several generations.[73] In Fast's era other influential treatments of the Civil War and Reconstruction were found in Stark Young's *So Red the Rose* (1934) and Margaret Mitchell's *Gone with the Wind* (1936), each of which focused on the tragedy of ruined plantations and the South's wistful yearning for its "gracious slave culture." Both historical novels were admired nationally; and Mitchell's classic, released as a major motion picture in 1939, eventually sold more than 30 million copies, making it one of the most popular books of all time.[74]

Fast's *Freedom Road,* on the other hand, shows that "negro incapacity" was a tale whites liked to tell themselves. Black-dominated constitutional conventions produced modern documents including equal voting rights, desegregation of public facilities, compulsory education, and abolition of imprisonment for debt. Much, if not all, of this history had been erased as black gains were sacrificed on the altar of North-South reunification. Fast admirably reminded an America in which segregation was ubiquitous in the South, and widespread in the North, that there was a history of Reconstruction they weren't being taught in school.[75]

But as literature, *Freedom Road* fails. Dashiell Hammett got it just right when he told playwright Lillian Hellman that *Freedom Road* is "pretty much like [Fast's] other works with the exception of *The Last Frontier*—on the right side, but over-simplified to death."[76] Fast's depiction of life on the Carwell plantation is romanticism in full bloom. Gideon and his neighbors are so noble, so persistently high-minded, that they demand the reader's suspension of disbelief. Several reviewers retreated in the face of such over-simplification. The literary critic and public intellectual Diana Trilling, for example, wrote, "Having written several times in praise of the historical novels of Howard Fast, I regret having to report, now, my deep distaste for his latest book, 'Freedom Road' . . . even if all Mr. Fast's historical facts can be documented, the novel strikes me as profoundly untrue because it bears no resemblance to human life under any circumstances. I am quite certain that no group of people—black, white or mixed—could behave with the unmitigated virtue of Mr. Fast's Negroes." And Orville Prescott at the *New York Times* worried that *Freedom Road* "mark[ed] a dangerous turning point in a notable career . . . so much inferior to [Fast's] other work it must be judged either as a temporary lapse from creative fiction or as a definite departure from the realms of literature into those of partisan political pamphleteering."[77]

Critics who made judgments such as Prescott's—and there were several who saw *Freedom Road* as little more than a "democratic tract," or Fast as a novelist turned "moralist"—did not know that Fast had joined the CPUSA in 1943; and they were unlikely to know much about his antifascist activities, which were in any case not all that frequent in 1944. But *Freedom Road* was the first book Fast had completed while in the Communist Party, and several astute critics were aware of a change in direction in his writing, not for the better.[78]

Howard Fast could, and did, ignore these reviewers because "never in my life," he said, "has a book of mine been accorded the avalanche of unrestrained praise that greeted *Freedom Road*." The novel won the prestigious Schomburg Award in Race Relations for 1944, and positive responses appeared in the *New York Herald Tribune,* the *Boston Herald,* the *Chicago Defender,* a leading black newspaper, and *Newsweek,* which praised *Freedom Road* extravagantly: "No other novel about race relations carries the strength of . . . historical sting . . . and moving honesty of *Freedom Road*. Howard Fast has written a terrifying book, as timely as headlines describing our latter-day battle for freedom."[79]

Again it appears that Fast's timing was good. The Second World War, characterized by the Allied Forces as a war against racism, was drawing to a

successful conclusion, and black soldiers would be returning from the battle-
fields in 1945 reinvigorated in their quest for racial justice. Black labor leader
A. Philip Randolph had initiated the militant "March on Washington Movement" in 1943; and sociologist Gunnar Myrdal's *An American Dilemma: The
Negro Problem and Modern Democracy* appeared in 1944 at nearly the same
moment as *Freedom Road*. Fast's new book eventually sold many millions of
copies and was translated into more than eighty languages.

Freedom Road had its critics in the mainstream media. But it also had severe critics on the extreme left. When Howard Fast volunteered a completed
and bound prepublication edition of *Freedom Road* to his section organizer
as a gesture of pride in his accomplishment and a desire for approval from
his Party representative, he stepped into what became his first, but not last,
wrestling match with "the Red tar baby."

The Party representative asked for six more copies to distribute to members of the Cultural Section. Although some of the very few writers still in the
Party in 1943–44 submitted manuscripts to Communist leaders, the CPUSA
rarely required such an act. The Party had other instruments of control,
a dressing-down for example, or charges of "deviant" opinion or behavior, which could lead to expulsion; but these depended on the cooperation
of the writer. An author feeling put-upon could, after all, resign from the
Party, as many did. Novelist and screenwriter Budd Schulberg, for one, left
because the Party criticized his work as decadent and tried to make him
rewrite his first book *What Makes Sammy Run?* (1939) into a proletarian
novel that would satisfy the reigning cultural czars, John Howard Lawson
and V. J. Jerome. The African American author Richard Wright, who was
told repeatedly in response to his probing questions, "Comrade, you don't
understand," and more ominously by a Party leader frustrated by the writer's
independence, "The Soviet Union has had to shoot a lot of intellectuals,"
was leaving the Party just as Fast was joining.[80]

It was determined that *Freedom Road* "presented problems . . . difficult
problems" and that the Party might have to take an "action" against Fast for
his "errors," especially on the question of "self-determination" for blacks.
On this issue, Fast's timing was bad. Communist Party policy toward "the
Negro" was in flux. In 1928, the Comintern, following Stalin's model of
dealing with the diverse ethnic and language groups in the USSR, had adopted a policy calling for a separate black nation in sections of the American
South heavily populated by African Americans. While the policy focused

attention on what was by far the worst social problem in the United States, it was completely out of touch with American realities and with most blacks themselves, who wanted most of all an end to poverty and discrimination.

In the mid-1930s, during the period of the Popular Front, the policy of black self-determination was dropped, only to be adopted again after the Nazi-Soviet pact of 1939 as a way of rallying blacks in opposition to entering the "imperialist war." When Germany attacked Russia in 1941, however, the program for self-determination was no longer seriously advanced. The war was now perceived by the CPUSA as a "correct" battle against racism as well as fascism, and after 1943, the policy of self-determination was virtually abandoned.

Independent of Moscow, a new American Communist policy of integration was announced. In January 1944 General-Secretary Earl Browder claimed that blacks had by now exercised their self-determination by choosing to integrate. This, he said, proved that racial justice was achievable even in capitalist America. Now here came Fast with his new novel not only depicting an example of black self-determination in South Carolina, but also showing that the experiment ended in failure because the ruling classes would never tolerate its success.

It looked to some Party leaders as if Fast might be giving up on the reformability of the United States in its current stage of socioeconomic development just as the CPUSA was exploring the possibility of significant social progress within capitalist America. In fact, although it would not last, the American Communist Party was soon to dissolve itself to become the Communist Political Association (CPA), a kind of left-wing lobby rather than a party competing for votes in the political arena. In the meantime, only months after joining the CPUSA, Fast stood accused of deviancy by Party leaders.

Ironically, the FBI seconded the Party's opinion that Fast had prematurely lost faith in the United States. A memo in Fast's file states that his "main aim in writing is to use American history to denounce America." The Bureau referred to "the warped world of Howard Fast," considering him a writer haunted by hatred for his country, a hatred out of which he wrote his books.[81] But Fast's quarrel with his society and his inclination to point up important problems through the vehicle of popular literature came as much or even more from his identity with American ideals as from his alienation or any hatred. It is clear in *Conceived in Liberty, The Unvanquished,* and *Citizen Tom Paine* that Fast loved his country. Fast certainly hated slavery, however; and in *Freedom Road* there is a hint of despair. But, unlike what the FBI and the Party thought, he had not yet given up, not fully anyway, on the American promise.

Deviancy, however, wasn't Fast's only crime according to the CPUSA. Although the Party failed to question Fast's use of "black dialect," the cultural commissars did object to his use of the word "nigger" throughout *Freedom Road* at a time when the American Communist Party was on a campaign (more like a witch hunt) against "white chauvinism." The search for racial prejudice within the Party began in earnest shortly after Russia was attacked in 1941. The CPUSA, which now devoted most of its time and energy to the war effort, virtually dropped the cause of racial justice. Perhaps to hide the fact that the strength of its new commitment to the defense of the Soviet Union was greater than its commitment to equality for black Americans, or perhaps out of guilt, the Party went on the warpath against what it saw as racism in its own ranks. Members were apparently expelled from the Party for using expressions such as "black sheep" or "white wash."[82]

The Party seemed to be imitating the Soviet technique of public-shame trials, which the American CP had employed and then abandoned in the 1930s. The charges then were mostly absurd, as were the charges against Fast and *Freedom Road*. Fast tried to argue that the word "nigger" was used not only by whites, but by blacks themselves. For this contention he was accused of "engaging in bourgeois premises and missing the whole point of 'socialist realism,'" which was to use art in service of the proletariat. In itself, Fast wrote later, this kind of thinking "constituted grounds for expulsion from the Party."[83]

But all was not lost. The section organizer gave the advance copies of the book to "certain 'powerful and reasonable' friends who were high in the Party apparatus." Fast, though mystified, hoped an exception might be made. And it was. Now that the Party believed it had disciplined its novitiate, *Freedom Road* was reviewed well in the CPUSA press. "I had *crawled* through the first barrier," Fast confessed.[84]

He was angry, Fast said later, but did not show it. He would not let himself be expelled from the party of his idols William Foster and Elizabeth Gurley Flynn, the party that had created the Abraham Lincoln Brigade, had organized the resistance in France, and fought the Nazis to the death. Instead, he promised to work on his "problem" in order, finally, to see the "error of his ways."[85]

He "had watched many other writers join the Communist Party and then leave it in bitterness and disillusionment," Fast said more than a decade later; "I had witnessed their affection for the Party turn into hatred. Yet I was able to tell myself that . . . was the past—and that I must make my own decision out of the present."[86] When Fast joined the Party he was determined not to become its instrument. Instead, he aimed to find within the CP camaraderie, high status, and fame, and believed that he and the Party together would become conductors on the locomotive of history, riding inexorably toward a future in which people would be free and equal.

Fast did not, however, see that those elements in his own personality which attracted him to the Party in the first place could lead him over the long haul to become its tool: his need to be part of an outstanding group; his penchant for oversimplification; his tendency to commit himself too quickly and completely; his energetic drive to achieve a great deal in a short time—as in, for example, his publicly announced egotistical promise to accomplish a "one-man reformation of the historical novel"; his emotionalism; and his inclination, perhaps rooted in his lack of a formal education, to be influenced by the subtleties and sophistries of Marxist theorists.[87]

3

The Life of the Party

After less than a year in the Party, Fast had encapsulated himself in a new world that would become increasingly difficult to leave without disruptive psychological consequences. As time went on, he would continue to obey the Party line, although his own instincts sometimes said otherwise. In yielding to Communist "political necessity," Fast also would give up part of his American idealism, including the defense of civil liberties, and he would drop his idea of an exceptionalist American socialism in favor of a Soviet-type revolutionary model.

By admitting to the "error" of his ways as a writer, Fast was able to get *Freedom Road* past the CP's "gatekeepers"—narrowly. Others in the Party were more enthusiastic about the book, and not only because it finally got the Cultural Section's reluctant imprimatur. Even Dashiell Hammett, who hadn't liked *Freedom Road*, told Lillian Hellman that Fast's "sort of stuff does have a place. . . . I know at least a couple of readers whose . . . eyes were opened by the book, and who at least think they'd like to know more about what actually went on down there in the old South."[1]

Albert Maltz wrote Fast that he was "astonished to see the unstinted praise for *Freedom Road*" in such mainstream magazines as *Newsweek* and the *Saturday Review*. "In the left-wing, of course," Maltz went on, "you are being worshipped for it."[2] In the mid-1940s, admiration for Fast continued in both worlds—the mainstream and the CPUSA; but being "worshipped" kept Fast firmly planted in the life of the Party.

His writings circulated widely, especially among young adults. Between 1942 and 1944, textbook publishers reprinted excerpts of Fast's work in editions for high-school courses in literature and history. And in October 1944, Fast received an award for a series of six inspirational stories on wartime heroism written for the monthly *Young America*.[3] Over the next two years he had more than two dozen articles published in popular journals reminding Americans of their heritage, urging patriotic feeling and action, and promoting racial tolerance. Fast's genuine concern for, and activism in the cause of, civil rights, manifest even during WWII when the CP had put racial justice on a back burner, continued unabated throughout his life.[4]

At the same time, Fast paid tribute to the Soviet Union, reminding readers that it was "together [as] allies" that America and Russia "preserved civilization."[5] Fast's first appearance in an openly left-wing journal, *New Masses*, was in November 1943, not long after he had joined the CPUSA; and he continued a close relationship with Communist causes thereafter, without either professing or denying Party membership. In November 1943 as well, Fast gave the first of many speeches he would deliver to Communist-affiliated organizations and at Communist-arranged functions.

Still, because Fast's rhetoric continued to be filled with words like "democracy," "liberty," and "justice," and because he was contributing to magazines of every persuasion including the *Christian Register, Harper's Bazaar, Woman's Day,* and *Mademoiselle,* it wasn't yet clear to the general reader how deep a commitment Fast had made to the Party and the Soviet Union, or how in *Freedom Road,* for example, he had distanced himself, even if only slightly, from the hope that America was still the promised land.

One thing that close readers may have noticed, however, was Fast's changed relationship to Jewishness, which shifted sharply after he joined the CPUSA. In February 1943, less than three years after writing his well-received Jewish history, *Romance of a People,* and several months before his becoming a Communist officially, Fast had reviewed *Memoirs of My People,* an anthology of writing by Jews of a dozen different nationalities. He wrote that "Jews are curiously of a piece. . . . People who were always a little ahead of the world, so far as civilization goes."[6]

Murray Gitlin, managing editor of *New Currents* and general secretary of the committee of Jewish Writers and Artists, impressed by Fast's apparent Jewish bona fides, asked Howard to add his prestigious name to the masthead of *Einikeit,* a biweekly Yiddish newspaper designed "to interpret Jewish life in a progressive militant way to many thousands of American Jews who do not belong to Jewish organizations, who do not read the Jewish press, yet who want to get closer to Jewish life."[7]

But in 1944, several months after joining the American Communist Party, Fast contributed an essay for a symposium in *Contemporary Jewish Record,* the forerunner of *Commentary* magazine, responding to the question of how being Jewish affected his work. With a tone very different from his earlier work about Jews, Fast now wrote as if his Jewish identity were an obstacle to overcome rather than an inheritance to be cherished. "If I understand a Jewish heritage to be cultural in value and historical in content, then . . . my work bears no relationship to it. . . . It seems to me that too many Jews fall into a sort of soul-sickness, whereby they become the center of a universe—a dark universe, where forces are pro-Jewish or anti-Jewish, where Jews are hated or persecuted or tolerated or loved—and so on ad infinitum."[8]

Fast wrote these words at the same time Muriel Rukeyser, the Jewish American pro-Communist poet, was writing one of her most well-known poems, "Letter to the Front," the seventh sequence of which begins, "To be a Jew in the twentieth century/is to be offered a gift. If you refuse/Wishing to be invisible, you choose/Death of the spirit, the stone insanity."[9] In contradistinction to Rukeyser, and in an ironic, obverse echoing of Shylock in *The Merchant of Venice,* Fast wrote, "For me, a Jew is a man. He is persecuted; so are other minorities. He is libeled; so are others. There is discrimination against him; is there none against the Negroes? He has been murdered, tortured, driven across the face of the earth; but isn't that the fate of millions who are not Jewish?" And like his soon-to-be friend Jean-Paul Sartre, Fast defined Jews as people who identify as such, primarily because of antisemitism, and thought that in the end Jews make antisemitism worse by withdrawing behind self-erected walls, thereby intensifying their status as "the other."

As "anti-Semitism went to work upon me, as it does upon all Jews," Fast wrote, he, presumably unlike most other Jews, "was able to see the machine objectively. I could not, nor did I desire to, go groping back into a Jewish past. . . . For me, that past did not exist—and as I found it, through reading or hearsay, it held nothing attractive, nothing that I wanted." Not quite as pithy or chilling as Karl Marx's infamous conclusion that "the emancipation of the

Jews is the emancipation of mankind from Judaism," but perhaps influenced by it, Fast's disdainful pronouncement could not have been more different from what he had said before joining the Communist Party.[10]

Another change in Fast after he joined the CP was his denial of the absolute right of free speech. In his general attempt to recast his past in his 1990 memoir *Being Red,* Fast claims that he had always agreed with the martyred leader of the abortive German socialist revolution of 1918, Rosa Luxemburg, who said "freedom is only freedom for the man who disagrees with you."[11] Fast's rhetoric and behavior as a Communist, however, utterly belies his assertion.

Near the end of 1943, *New Masses* published a discussion between Alexander Meiklejohn, the dean of civil libertarians, and Earl Browder, general secretary of the American Communist Party, on "Free Speech for Fascists?" Browder, turning Meiklejohn on his head, wrote, "We demand the suppression of American fascists! We fight for complete, *merciless, and systematic destruction of fascism* in all its aspects, everywhere."[12]

New Masses sent the exchange to a number of "leading Americans" and asked the following questions: "1) Do you believe that individuals or organizations that disseminate fascist propaganda and incite hatred of Negroes, Jews, and other minority groups should be accorded freedom of speech, press, and assemblage? 2) What measures if any should be taken against such individuals or organizations?" Leaving aside the failure of *New Masses* to distinguish between disseminating and inciting, here is Howard Fast's response:

"In answer to question one, my answer is flatly—no." Fascists have no right to free speech. Fast thought that Voltaire's epigram, "I do not agree with what he says, but I will defend to the death his right to say it," was "arrant nonsense." Are we to follow Voltaire's example to its logical extreme and "defend to the death Adolf Hitler's right to promulgate his vicious race theories?" or the "right of all other fascists, native or foreign, to mouth their lies, their attacks upon democracy? Is it inherent in democracy that it must, for the sake of a vague and mystical ideal [of free speech], give its enemies a legal opportunity to destroy it?"[13]

Not only was this exactly the same line of argument used by the anti-Communist McCarthyites beginning in 1950, when Fast was imprisoned for three months for refusing to name names, but it ran directly against the philosophy of Fast's hero, Thomas Paine, who was as ready as anyone to test the limits of free speech. Civil liberties issues were not a primary concern of even the most seemingly sensitive artists and writers on the extreme left, including the usually gentle Albert Maltz. In another *New Masses* symposium, the magazine posed the question: "Should Ezra Pound Be Shot?" for broadcasting fascist propaganda from Rome during wartime. None of the five writers surveyed, including pro-Communist Arthur Miller, said no. Indeed, Maltz went so far as to argue that "because he is a poet . . . he should be hanged . . . twice—for treason as a citizen, and for his poet's betrayal of all that is decent in civilization."[14] Fascists were not the only group that ought to be silenced. As enemies, Trotskyists, too, according to the Communists were to be gagged and imprisoned, and worse if possible: Trotsky himself had been fatally attacked at his desk in Mexico City in 1940 by a Stalinist henchman using an ice axe.[15]

As part of the Alien Registration Act of 1940, the Smith Act had made it a crime for anyone "to knowingly or willfully advocate or teach the duty, necessity, desirability or propriety of overthrowing or destroying any government in the United States by force or violence." The very first enforcement of this law occurred in 1941 against the Socialist Workers Party (SWP), a Trotskyist group that had adopted a Declaration of Principles explicitly advocating the overthrow of capitalism by force and violence "if necessary."[16]

After the passage of the Smith Act, the SWP suspended its declaration. But the U.S. government argued that the change was cosmetic and that the SWP was still a threat, especially in Minnesota, where the group was tied to labor activists in the Teamsters Union; but as the radical journalist I. F. Stone put it correctly, the Trotskyists could "hardly have mustered sufficient force to seize the dog pound in Minneapolis," let alone overthrow the U.S. government.[17] The prosecution of the SWP went ahead nevertheless, and was enthusiastically supported by the CPUSA, which aided the Justice Department in its successful effort.[18]

The actions of the CP would come back to haunt it as early as 1946, when HUAC began a series of sweeping investigatory hearings aimed at exposing and intimidating alleged Communists. But in 1948, when Communist Party leaders were prosecuted under the same Smith Act whose use they had encouraged against the Trotskyists, the Party, in a blatantly cynical turnaround, made civil liberties into an issue of paramount importance. One of the most outspoken on this question was Howard Fast.

Actually Fast's shift toward the defense of civil liberties began even earlier, when he discovered, about six months after the publication of his January

1944 essay promoting the gagging of fascists, that he was being "tailed" by the FBI, and that his mail was being monitored. As a result of the information gathered by the FBI, Fast was fired on June 24, 1944, from a job he had taken in April as an "Expert Consultant" for the U.S. Army Signal Corps, because his "services were no longer required." On June 25th, Walter Winchell announced on his widely followed radio broadcast that "someone was tapping the phone of Howard Fast."[19] On the 26th, Fast "in a great rage," complained to the FBI. A Bureau memorandum followed, which stated that "if Fast recontacts [us] and requests . . . an investigation," tell him that the attorney general will be consulted for his "advice and decision." Clearly trying to avoid publicly tangling with either Fast or Winchell, the FBI reported on June 27 that although Fast had been working for the U.S. Army as a consultant, he was really a "civilian employee," and therefore his case was being closed.[20]

This official decision doesn't seem to have mattered much. The tap on Fast's phone was not turned off; reports on his activities continued to be inserted into his file. In June 1945, less than a year after his case was "closed," it was "reopened" because "the subject is active in Communist matters." This much at least was certainly true: in the summer of 1944, Fast helped other members of the Cultural Section of the Communist Political Association, which in May had replaced the CPUSA, to organize the Committee of the Arts and Sciences for the Re-election of FDR; as a direct service to the Party, Fast wrote *Tito and His People,* a forty-page propaganda booklet glamorizing the life and politics of the Yugoslavian partisan; and he wrote short articles for the *Independent,* an election-year journal, claiming nonpartisanship, but actually produced under Communist auspices, strongly endorsing FDR.[21]

He also spoke often to American Youth for Democracy, a "Communist front" organization, and was in close and constant contact with Alexander Trachtenberg, part owner and operator of International Publishers, which specialized in Marxist-Leninist books and pamphlets. He had in addition become friendly with "other known Communists," including Samuel Sillen, a major correspondent and critic for the *Daily Worker,* and William Patterson, the vice president of the Communist Party's New York district eight.[22]

Although Fast continued to publish a handful of articles in popular magazines, especially *Coronet,* the vast majority of his dozens of pieces between 1944 and 1945 appeared in left-wing journals, including *New Masses, Scope,* and *PM.* These articles revealed Fast's increasing conviction that literature and life are so inextricably intertwined that the writer must produce his art in relation to political and social ideology. Fast did not mean merely that no author writes in a value-free zone and that no human life or relationship is untouched by the political and socioeconomic structure of the community in which it resides. Fast meant, and would continue to argue for the next twelve years, that the strength of American literature lay in its clear and direct commitment to the working class. In his essay "The New American Scholar" (February 1945), Fast urged researchers and writers to observe their "social duties," in effect counseling authors to use their art as a weapon in defense of labor and "true democracy."[23]

By the end of 1945, Fast was spelling out even more explicitly his narrowing position on the relationship between art and politics. "If the approach of a writer—that is, a novelist—is anything but dialectic, his work will be completely stagnant." The American writer, Fast argued, alluding indirectly to Hemingway, Steinbeck, and Dos Passos, sees the world through a romanticized dialectic, while the Soviet writer sees it through "the realistic logic of dialectical materialism." The Russian, therefore, "is armed far better than we are" with "tools for understanding society." The Soviet writer, Fast claimed, would see a strike, for example, as "an effort on the part of labor to advance the cause of mankind." In the United States, this issue, Fast wrote, would be subject to a furious and interminable debate; but any interpretation of the labor struggle different from the Soviet's, he insisted, "would be . . . falsehood."[24] These political arguments had sharp aesthetic implications. As Fast became increasingly embedded in the CPUSA and its single-mindedness, he grew more directly explicit in his attacks on complexity in literature.

INNOCENT ABROAD

In June 1945, Fast finally got his opportunity to go overseas. Although he was cleared by the Bureau of Public Relations of the War Department, and permitted by his draft board to leave for China, there was a delay again, as in 1943, in getting the State Department to issue a passport. But this time Fast appealed directly to left-leaning Henry Wallace, and secured a passport through the intervention of the former vice president.[25]

The FBI saw Wallace, not entirely incorrectly, as a "dupe" of the Communists, especially after he had begun to criticize Truman and praise Stalin; and Fast's association with Wallace increased the Bureau's "reasonable suspicion of [Howard's] left leanings." His politics did not prevent him from traveling as a war correspondent for *Esquire* and *Coronet* magazines, but Fast was assigned to North Africa and India rather than to the more tumultuous China, where the Communist Eighth Route Army, later called the People's Liberation Army, was resurgent. As Edward Stanley, the editor of *Esquire,* explained it, the War Department "refused to allow [Fast] to go to Europe or China," because of "his known leftist tendencies."[26]

Before he left the United States Fast found a new apartment where Bette and year-old Rachel could live while he was away. It was "a huge barn of a place," an enormous thirteen-room duplex on Central Park West that he was able to rent for only $154 a month. Bette, with Rachel in her arms, walked through the apartment's "barnlike vastness" and burst into tears. "'You mean you're going away and leav[ing] me *here*?'" But "it's a nice apartment," Howard argued feebly. "'For an army, for a barracks,'" Bette complained, "'How can I live here alone with an infant?'"[27]

The Fasts put an ad in the *New York Times* and the following day "a sweet young Nisei woman" named Hannah Masudo arrived. She had been recently released from a concentration camp in Colorado where she and her family had been unjustly incarcerated along with ninety thousand other Japanese Americans on the West Coast. "We hired her immediately," Fast remembered, "as our own tiny gesture of atonement." And a few days later Fast presented himself at Fort Totten in Long Island for transportation overseas.[28]

Fast's plane touched down in Gander, Newfoundland, then flew across the Atlantic to the Azores, and finally into the Air Transport Corps (ATC) at Casablanca in North Africa. Here he immediately encountered a group of black troops from Senegal, "handsome fellows who plied me with a hundred questions about Harlem. . . . When I told them that I knew Paul Robeson, they fought to buy me beer." Used to neither traveling nor heavy drinking, Fast "staggered back to [his] hotel, very drunk."[29]

After he sobered up, Fast wrote to Bette about Casablanca. "Butchkie, this is a city for you and me together, the old and the new, mixed the way we like them, barefooted Arabs, right out of the Bible and modern cars and apartment houses, donkeys, Arab carts, veiled women, modern French people." And the next day he wrote, "This will amuse you. . . . [Two] Howard Fast fans turn up, one the editor of the local divisional newspaper. . . . [They are] going to have lunch with me. . . . What a nice feeling it is.

Just as soon as I get home, you slap me into a chair and have me do another book."[30]

From Casablanca Fast was off to Tripoli, where the public relations officer at the air base, who had read armed services editions of four of Fast's books, entertained the idea that Howard was an expert on proposals for the planned United Nations! And he had him address two thousand GIs on the subject. By cramming information from *Yank, Stars and Stripes,* and a three-day-old copy of the *New York Times,* and putting facts and figures together with his own belief in the possibility of a peaceful future, Fast became an "expert" on the UN in three hours. Fast thought the forum was a great success; so did his orientation officer—so much so that he insisted Fast repeat his presentation at Tunis and Cairo. "You know," he told Bette, "I can't get over it; I'm not getting a swelled head, believe me, but it's such a good feeling to know you're doing a good job." Fast's good feeling increased when after the talk, he was "introduced to dozens of guys, all of whom had read my books and liked them."[31]

Actually beginning to feel like an expert, Fast confidently made his presentation in Tunis, where he also had time to unwind and exercise. He went on to Cairo, where he found a "big sprawling dirty city . . . illustrative of the viler tendencies and tactics of British empire building." Fast's research and writing on the American War for Independence had left him with an aversion for the British that was reinforced by his experiences in North Africa. He was especially shaken by his interaction with his British guide in Egypt, Captain Woodhill. Riding through Cairo, Fast said he'd never seen such human misery. The Brit replied that the natives were "hopeless; it didn't matter what you did for Wogs, they'd soon as rot than lift a finger to help themselves." Fast, taken aback, did not bother to do battle over this remark, but told Woodhill that he'd like to get to Palestine. Impossible, the Captain said; the British had closed the borders because too many GIs had been wangling passes into Palestine in order to get ice cream sodas in Tel Aviv, the closest to the genuine sodas they'd experienced in New York. In this way, Woodhill said, a lot of war material was being smuggled into Palestine. "Jews," Woodhill complained, staying very much in character, "they're everywhere, and they're all trying to push something into Palestine; they sell guns. . . . Trust a Jew to make a dollar out of anything." Although ambivalent about the degree of his own Jewishness since joining the Communist Party, Fast had not yet slipped entirely into the Marxist category of "universal man." He told the British Captain he was Jewish, "and that ended any more talk of Palestine."[32]

Fast's next stop was Karachi, the largest city and main seaport of Pakistan. Most people, he told Bette, take the trip in plush passenger ships. "But not Fast!" he exclaimed. "Fast had to have experience." So the ATC "encouraged" him to take the run in a C46 cargo carrier, a plane with no seats that stopped at every desert station. The trip took almost two days through Palestine, the Sinai, Iraq, Iran, and Saudi Arabia. "All of that in forty hours," Fast said, "lost desert cities, hot sands, oases, old British forts—and heat, such heat as you don't dream of at home, [one] hundred and twenty five in the shade is a regular thing."[33]

In his notes, however, Fast admitted to moments of delight in the air: "We flew from Cairo across the Suez Canal, and then over the Wilderness of Sinai, where the Jews wandered for 40 years." He "got a strong thrill out of seeing Palestine from the air, the Dead Sea, the Jordan Valley, the wild, lonely, arid hills, with here and there a patch of green to mark a Jewish irrigation project." On the other hand, he wrote, "The Arabian and Syrian desert is terrible and boundless, and this whole part of the world is like something out of hell."[34]

At "each station," Howard told Bette, "there's a few dozen men," who had the "toughest deal" in the U.S. Army, and "I want to write about them."[35] The story he produced reads like fiction, but Fast swore to its authenticity. One morning on a flight into Saudi Arabia, Fast's transport plane, to his great surprise, stopped to pick up thousands of empty Coca-Cola bottles. The C46 was filled from floor to ceiling with this odd cargo, and soon enough into the air, the weight of the load convinced the pilot he couldn't make proper altitude. Fast was instructed to crawl back to the tail of the plane, to change the "balance." The situation continued to worsen and Fast suggested that the crew start dumping the Coke bottles. "No Way!" he was told, "you don't fuck with Coca-Cola." In landing, the plane miraculously missed hitting the jutting sand hills, but in their desperation the crew had failed to drop the wheels. "No wheels!" Fast screamed. Too late. The C46 hit the landing strip on its belly and screeched along. No one was hurt; and the crew assured Fast that all was well. "Not a single bottle broken."[36] Perhaps because Fast was emphasizing the power of one of the icons of corporate America and its dedication to the maximization of profit, neither *Coronet* nor *Esquire* would print what the editors said was an unbelievable story.

In India, Fast wrote another story he was anxious to tell concerning the performance of the British during the famine of 1943–44 in Bengal.[37] Perhaps because it was a very controversial piece about the behavior of an American ally in WWII, he could not get it into print for more than forty years. But in *Being Red* he told the dark story, classifying it as one of his most important encounters in traveling from Delhi to Calcutta. After attending a general meeting of the Indian Communist Party, Fast spoke with several comrades, including Bandar Sharim, the secretary of the Delhi section. Fast was told that the lingering hunger he saw around him in his travels in India was the result of British manipulation. In the face of an imminent Japanese invasion of India through Burma, the British in 1942–43 allegedly determined, in league with Muslim rice merchants, to withhold food to weaken the will of Indians who might support the Japanese.[38]

There is no substantial evidence for such a motive; nor was there any significant threat of mass Indian collusion with the Japanese. Gross mismanagement and deliberate profiteering did aggravate the food crisis unnecessarily. The British overlords and the Indian civil service in the Bengal government reacted too slowly and incompetently, neither stopping the export of food from Bengal nor intervening to control the price of rice, which soon exceeded the means of ordinary people. Many migrated to the cities to find food and employment; finding neither, some 2 million starved. Fast, many years later, falsely claimed not only that there were 6 million victims, but that it was the "deliberate intent of the British colonial administration" to commit "a crime so terrible that it rivaled Hitler's Holocaust."[39]

The British military, contrary to Fast's one-sided story, did act eventually to combat the famine, providing sustenance to the suffering and organizing relief efforts. Some 110 million free meals were provided. But these measures, unlike the British response to starvation in Europe, were extremely belated and far too few to cope with the scale of the disaster.[40] Given his animus toward the British, his increasing willingness to accept the word of Communist comrades, and his understandably growing cynicism about all things imperial, Fast bought whole the half-true story told by the Indian Communists of a purely callous, purely English, manmade famine.

No doubt the sights Fast saw on his thirty-seven-hour local train ride from Delhi to Calcutta, including uncollected bodies dead from plague or starvation on the railsides, made the story easier to believe. On a portable typewriter he had dragged with him from the States, Fast wrote: "The old, dirty train stops every few miles, rattles on, stops again. . . . At each station [are] crowds of Indians, begging, hoping for a chance to get on the train, hoping for a little job or errand to earn a little. At one station, a tribe, down from the hills, small people, half naked, carrying possessions, pots, wooden spears, babies. They hoped to board the train, although where they were going or hoped to go, God only knows. But the train pulled out without them."[41]

The next day, as he did every day, Fast wrote again. "The same miserable, hopeless Indian villages sit in each environment—but Calcutta is a huge city, one of the great cities of the world, although not one of the clean ones. The streets are a maze of cabs, carriages, bullock carts and rickshaws. Do you remember that I wanted to ride in a rickshaw; I don't now. It's bad enough to see a man made into a beast of burden without contributing to it yourself. They say the life of a rickshaw driver is ten years or less after he comes [off] his trade, and that's understandable."[42] Bette, who shared her husband's political sympathies, especially about the exploitation of workers, wrote back telling Howie that she had recently "given it to" one of their friends who was "hopping mad" over waiting so long for a bus during the "slowdown" led by pro-Communist Mike Quill's Transportation Workers Union in June 1945.[43]

Near the end of his journey, Fast caught a glimpse of Gandhi, but he could get no closer than fifty yards from him. And "the few words . . . the small slender, figure . . . spoke were blown away by the wind." But the ever impressionable and sentimental Fast "was left with a deep feeling that something wonderful had happened."[44] Fast confided to his notes that he was "struck by the difference between the Hindu and the Arab. The one is gentle, wise, with a soft ancient wisdom. The other is fierce and hard."[45]

Fast's facile generalization was reinforced for him when he was taken by "a PFC from New York by the name of Lefkowitz" to meet a Hindu professor. "We had a very interesting talk," Fast said. "Then we took a tram to the . . . Indian bookshops. *What a hunger for knowledge there is in this land!* Now listen to this—I'm letting my eyes roam over the shelves, and what do I see but the UNVANQUISHED, a novel by Howard Fast, Indian edition, and a very nice edition too. So I bought a copy . . . and had quite a talk with the book clerk there. He was most impressed by meeting me, and showed me his choice books. . . . On the back of this edition, there was a blurb for 'Tom Paine,' which I found . . . in another shop. It made me feel good to know that my books are published and read in India. I'll bring both books home with me, of course." Fast was in his element. "Last night, baby," he wrote Bette, "this same PFC took me to a Hindu home, wealthy and educated Bengali people, supporters of the Congress movement here. They were very nice to me—and they actually had a copy of FREEDOM ROAD there, which they brought out for me to autograph. How's that? Indians who read *Freedom Road* like it immensely; I guess you can understand why."[46]

Fast also met an English soldier, "a Jewish boy" with whom he went to a restaurant operated by Baghdadi Jews. "They are Indians to all outward appearances," Fast told Bette, "but they don't wear saris, and they keep a form of Judaism. They have no Talmud, but they celebrate the Passover, and last [year] they had a gang of GIs in to eat with them." Fast further revealed his divided identity in 1945—one public and Communist, the other private and at least residually Jewish—by going to the synagogue to "hear the ancient Hebrew prayers from the lips of these gentle brown people."[47]

Fast's letters mainly detailed his daily experiences, but he also wrote about his feelings: "It took this trip to . . . tell me what a deep and abiding love I have for you. Many of the guys out here are married, but so few of them seem to have anything which even approaches what we have. Our ten years together were certainly a rare and wonderful thing; even the one time I seemed to go off"—with the Bennington woman—"that meant nothing, although now I hate myself a thousand times, for now I realize the misery I must have caused you then, the suffering; and I will make up for it, believe me my sweet Betsy."[48]

Fast thought that in the long run the trip would prove immensely valuable for him; it already "teaches me so much," and all at once it seems "I am learning about life, love, my wife, and my child. I have values that I certainly never had before, and I do not intend to lose them."[49] A few days later he added, "For ten years now, I've come as close to worshipping you as a man can worship a woman. When I come back things will be as you say, always, and I will do only as you wish me to do. . . . There is so much to tell you that I can't put into letters, but that will make it all the better when I come home, won't it?"[50] Bette, who thought it "so wonderful to have letters like these from [Howie] again," also wanted things to be "better" upon his return. "Once you get home again," Bette said pointedly, "nobody else, nobody." She also said she loved raising Rachel, whose "learning curve" and physical growth Bette detailed in almost every letter. "I want another baby soon," she wrote; but in the meantime was "resting as well as I can so that I will look good to you when you come home" and when we go out "and drink martinis . . . at the King Cole Bar" or to "spend a silly day in town and the zoo and museums."[51]

THE ROAD NOT TAKEN

On his return to the United States in early August 1945, Fast learned that Earl Browder and those close to him had been ousted from leadership in the Communist movement and were replaced by William Foster as chair, and Eugene Dennis as general secretary. Dennis had been more of a Browderite and had been a severe critic of Foster, but he caved under pressure from Moscow. That decision, Fast wrote, killed "the Communist Political Association and all of Browder's dreams of a Marxist movement [made] out of American roots and out of the mainspring of American life." Instead, the CPUSA was "reconstituted" to be more in line with Moscow's "revolutionary" outlook. "All of this trickled through to me . . . while I was in India," and "I had a deep inner feeling that the whole thing was wrong and that Browder's instinct was correct." Fast, however, added this striking passage: "At the same time, my circumstances in India and the things I witnessed there made me wonder whether the horror and poverty that existed in the world could ever be done away with by good will or reason," rather than by revolution.[52] Whatever Fast said aloud or put into print, these thoughts, confided to his private notes, foreshadowed his ultimate loyalty to Foster, the man he judged over the course of the next decade to be the greatest and bravest labor leader in history.[53]

The CPA had been formed in May 1944 while Howard was still more than a year away from going overseas. And the arguments against Browder, which had been brewing for many months, started in earnest after the famous "Letter to American Communists," an article by the French Stalinist Jacques Duclos that appeared in a theoretical journal of the French Communist Party. Published in April 1945, while Fast was still home, it criticized Browder's nonrevolutionary deviancy. It was clearly a message from Moscow. The French had never before shown much interest in the CPUSA. And in fact, the article, before being translated into French, was written by Russians in Russian and originally appeared in a classified Soviet publication.[54]

Duclos argued that the "achievement of socialism [is] impossible to imagine without a preliminary conquest of power." This was a straightforward restatement of the orthodox Leninist position. It may even have constituted Stalin's first step in preparing American Communists for the Cold War and could well have been a signal to Western European Communist parties of the coming shift to a more "confrontational" style in the USSR's international policies.[55] Although the Duclos letter, published in English in July, was hardly summoning the comrades immediately to the barricades, it did reject "the concept of a long-term class peace in the United States."[56] And while Foster, too, soon made it clear that the reconstituted Party did not expect to be leading a revolution in the near future, he did look to political and economic cataclysm—depression, war, fascism—not reform within capitalism, as the motor for revolutionary social change.[57]

Foster had struggled a good part of his life over whether to embrace an indigenous radicalism more in line with American realities or to accept a foreign import. Over time, as Foster's biographer argues, he "became fixed on the Soviet line and more rigid in his understanding and appreciation of Marxism-Leninism." In the postwar period Foster, despite the reforms of the New Deal and the internationalist spirit of the Teheran conference, looked forward to renewed class conflict in which Communists would continue to advocate socialism as the "only final solution for our nation's troubles."[58]

Fast, who liked to compare Foster favorably to other "so-called labor leaders," such as Sidney Hillman, David Dubinsky, and Philip Murray, and to the "dirty conscienceless sell-out artists, the sniveling Social Democrats," wrote privately that Browder's philosophical orientation and political goals may have had merit for the current moment; but *"I accepted my position as a member of the reconstituted Communist Party,"* under the leadership of Foster and Dennis.[59] Indicating just how important the CPUSA had become to Fast's understanding of his general public role and to his self-image, he wrote, "I was much too valuable an acquisition to the Communist movement for them to let go of me or neglect me, and my recent experiences abroad made me all the more convinced that whatever small part I might myself play in making the world a more decent residence for the human race would be worthwhile regardless of the sacrifice it entailed."[60]

By referring to "sacrifice," Fast was demonstrating a sense of the risks he was taking by lining up with the "class-warriors" rather than the "American exceptionalists," those who believed that socialism in the United States would look nothing like socialism in Russia. But several of the Party leaders and even many of the long-term rank-and-file members, though grumbling about foreign interference and policy flip-flops, were happy to get back to the class war again after years of the Popular Front and what they saw as the deplorably optimistic policies of Browderism. The road to American socialism may not have been viable under Browder, but by rejecting him, the flexibility of his policies, and the whole idea of reform, the CPUSA took a fatal detour, distancing itself further from the path of building a stable, authentically democratic socialist movement with the American working class. Howard Fast, with private misgivings, went right along for the ride, while those who continued to side openly with Browder were subject to and most often victims of expulsion from the Party.[61]

Years later, Fast acknowledged that while he knew that the ousting of Browder had come as an order from Moscow, he had a strong sense that the rejection of Browderist gradualism was *ultimately* the right thing to do. Perhaps the horrors he had been witness to in India moved Fast away from a commitment to American exceptionalism, from a socialism rooted in particular American realities, and toward one wedded to a Soviet revolutionary blueprint. Whatever the cause, it certainly looked as though Fast, who had once believed Communism to be the natural and inevitable fulfillment of American democracy, now in 1945 thought that revolution, if only in the distant future, was the best course for the CPUSA to pursue.

Fast did publish a fawning obituary for FDR, who died in April 1945, but it is far from clear that he was writing only or even primarily about Roosevelt. The president, Fast said, had been like "a barometer," sensitive "to the wishes, the needs, and the hopes of [his] people . . . for while he led, the curious contradiction was that he also followed, making no step that the people were not ready for, taking no action until the people had given him their mandate. That was his . . . splendid role . . . and that was what those who called him a dictator were incapable of understanding."

At the very start of FDR's presidency, Fast went on, "the people knew he was their man. They didn't question; when this sort of a leader comes, once in two or five generations, the people don't have to question, draw diagrams, or go to Gallup Polls." Or vote? Is this obituary just Popular Front political pabulum redux? Or is there something more sinister going on between these lines? It's not likely that Fast had read Hegel, but he seems to be invoking, wittingly or not, the German philosopher's idea of "world-historical men," those beings with a critical role to play in the development of "Spirit," those visionary agents of "History" who are followed by ordinary men, and who "feel the irresistible power of their own inner Spirit thus embodied." Is Fast alluding here to Stalin? After all, from his metaphysical-authoritarian premise, Hegel had concluded that the ordinary rules of ethics were not applicable to great men. "Heroic coercion," Hegel wrote, "is justified coercion." In any case, paraphrasing Stalin, Fast also wrote that against fascism, wherever it might manifest itself, our reaction ought to be "clean, angry and unabated." And soon thereafter, Fast began to see fascism wherever he looked in America.[62]

While Fast was abroad one of the leaders of the Indian CP had extracted a promise from him to bring the news of the country's dire problems—disease, poverty, famine—to the leaders of the CPUSA. Joe North who had two years earlier helped recruit Howard for the Party, set up a meeting with General Secretary Dennis. On the appointed day Fast came to the nine-story building on East 12th Street between University Place and Broadway that housed the offices of *New Masses,* the *Daily Worker, Morgen Freiheit,* the Yiddish Communist paper, *Jewish Life,* the Worker's Bookshop, the CPUSA, and the CPs of New York State and of New York County.

Dennis and the National Committee's offices were on the top floor—"the ninth floor," which came to be shorthand for CPUSA bigwigs. Fast got to see the general secretary but was bitterly disappointed in their face-to-face meeting. "Here I am, one of the leading and . . . most honored writers in the country," whom The Party "busted its ass" to recruit. It had "showered me with praise, lured me with its most winning people . . . and embraced me." But Dennis, "the national leader of the Communist Party of the United States," if Fast is to be believed, never once asked to meet him; and now when Howard was finally on the ninth floor telling the story of the Indian crises, the general secretary hardly looked at him. When Fast complained to North about the lack of response, Joe admitted that Dennis was "not the greatest." Having failed to move Dennis, Fast asked North himself to print the story of the "British-made famine" in *New Masses.* North refused, saying the story was "too hot," or perhaps too incredible. Fast got the same answer at the *Daily Worker.*[63]

Discouraged, Fast returned to writing fiction about the past. Yet despite what he called the stupidity and indifference of the Communist leadership, Fast continued to see the Party as a context within which, and through which, he could increase his celebrity and his contacts with the rich and famous, including the OWI intellectuals and the Hollywood writers, even as he fulfilled his strongly felt political obligations. And so he stayed active in CPUSA affairs. He worked hard, for example, in behalf of Benjamin Davis Jr.'s campaign for New York City Councilman. Davis, an African American, had been elected on the Communist Party ticket in 1943. By 1945 he was so entrenched in his post that he even got the endorsement of the Democratic Party, and needed no help from Fast. Aspiring to remain in the limelight, however, and in close touch with other notable authors and screenwriters, Fast formed, along with Paul Robeson, with whom he was now a close friend, the Artists, Writers, and Professionals Group to back the black CP incumbent. In October, Fast was elected as one of the vice chairs of the New York State Division of Independent Citizens of the Arts, Sciences, and Professions. And in November, along with important figures in the American cultural world such as Lillian Hellman and Marc Blitzstein, he addressed a meeting of the National Council of American-Soviet Friendship to make a plea for understanding through the arts.[64]

During this same period Fast had a call from an old friend who had been his liaison with Naval Intelligence at the Office of War Information. He told Fast that Jean-Paul Sartre had come to America and that, among other things, he was representing the French publisher Gallimard. Sartre "had read an English-language copy of *Freedom Road*," and was anxious to meet the author to talk about a French translation. Fast confessed in unpublished notes written a decade later that before that phone call he "had never heard Sartre's name."[65] During dinner at the Fasts' apartment neither Howard nor Bette "was impressed by the small, near-sighted Frenchman." Things changed after Bette went to bed. The two men talked till four in the morning. Sartre apparently went on a lot about his role in the Resistance, which in reality was tenuous at best.[66] But Fast, all too ready to believe, was impressed.

But embarrassed for not having known Sartre in 1945, Fast changed the story of their first meeting for his 1990 memoir *Being Red*. In this version, Bette never got to meet Sartre. She had been at a Communist Party meeting when the guests arrived at her home and did not get back until very late. Irritated by having had to endure the endless and all-too-familiar arguments among her comrades, she stormed off to bed. "The following day," Fast wrote, "when I told [Bette] that I had sat until two o'clock in the morning talking to Sartre, she almost burst into tears. Why hadn't I told her? I don't think she ever completely forgave me."[67]

Whichever rendition of the story one chooses to believe, in both accounts the two men had apparently "talked about the Party, about the Soviet Union, and what the future might bring." Sartre "rejected the horror stories that were told against Russia, the stories of imprisonment and injustice and total disregard for the rights of anyone who opposed Stalin."[68] Fast was delighted to hear this from Sartre, a man of such stature, and was reinforced in his pro-Soviet bias. He remained a friend of the Frenchman, mostly through correspondence, for many years thereafter. And, like almost everyone else, he remained forever bedazzled and bamboozled by Jean-Paul Sartre's constructed image and French fellow-traveling apologetics.

The actualities of Sartre's life were far less heroic than his romanticized self-projections. He did participate in a short-lived underground group, but soon decided to write rather than be involved in active resistance. Sartre never actually collaborated with the German authorities, but the philosopher lived a relatively comfortable wartime existence, about which Fast was completely unaware. After largely acquiescing in the German occupation of France, Sartre retroactively tied himself to the Resistance by becoming a leader of the "post-liberation witch-hunt" that called "down vengeance" on French people whose behavior had not really been so different from his own. In the postwar period Sartre became a model of the committed leftist intellectual, and he embellished and mythologized his role in the Resistance in the widely reprinted 1944 article "La republique du silence."[69]

In January 1945, Sartre was sent to the United States by the newspaper *Le Figaro* and was greeted as a hero of the Resistance. He did nothing to deny the claim. That Sartre, within the psychological dynamics of this process, may have been transformed into his own self- image of a genuine rebel who later denounced injustice in support of the wretched of the earth does not excuse his failure to admit the truth about his past or about his on and off blindness to the horrors occurring in the USSR. In this failure he and Fast were identical twins.[70]

Sartre and Fast and many of their intellectual contemporaries needed an ideal to set against Western and especially American society, and this led them to ignore or rationalize horrendous problems in the Soviet Union. For Fast, any disavowal of the radical left was de facto support of the U.S. capitalist system against which he had wholeheartedly pledged to fight. The class and racial injustices inherent in the socioeconomic system of mostly unregulated capitalism were indeed stubborn and deeply rooted. But Fast and Sartre, like many intellectuals, American and European, were guilty of what historian Tony Judt called moral "double-entry bookkeeping." When "they looked West they saw repression, exploitation, and the inexcusable violation of inalienable rights; but when they looked East they saw only the collateral damage of Historical Necessity."[71]

THE POLITICS OF LITERATURE

Fast's compartmentalization of the world and his insistence on seeing it only through the wrong end of a Communist telescope applied to literature as well as international politics. In the summer of 1947 Fast was invited to teach a writing workshop at Indiana University (IU).[72] Ten years later in 1956 in the *Daily Worker,* and again in 1990 in *Being Red,* Fast claimed that some members of the English department at IU wondered whether their new colleague was a Communist. At a small welcoming party one professor supposedly asked Fast what he thought of James T. Farrell's *Studs Lonigan* trilogy. Howard allegedly replied that "it was important . . . a profound and pertinent tragedy, and one of the unique products of American literature." Farrell, Fast continued, was a man of "great skill, insight and discipline" and "one of the finest social realists of our time." The professor, Fast claims, clapped his hands, suggested drinks all around, and announced to the assembled guests that Fast was not a Communist, since any Party member would face expulsion if he dared to praise a Trotskyist like Farrell.

Fast called such a notion "arrant nonsense." And he insisted that his IU story was "absolutely true."[73] In telling and retelling this improbable but elaborately constructed tale, which appeared to serve no practical purpose, Fast seemed compelled to demonstrate that he was above the petty fray of pseudo-sophisticated academics and smarter and more erudite than any college professors. If the Indiana anecdote is a faithful rendering, it was Fast, not the professor or his colleagues, who was guilty of "arrant nonsense." Fast could not, after all, have "forgotten," in 1947, that as recently as 1946 he himself had lambasted the Communist writer Albert Maltz—virtually reading him out of the Party—because he had praised the ideologically incorrect "Trotskyist" James Farrell as a great writer.[74] Although never even attempting anywhere to explain what he meant by "Trotskyist" (except insofar as it was anti-Stalinist and critical of the Soviet system), and unlikely to have ever

read much of Trotsky's work, Fast knew at least that unlike Stalin, Trotsky
had argued vehemently against a strictly "proletarian culture" and had said
that "art must make its own way and by its own means."[75]

Perhaps he did not know, however, that Marx himself, and Engels even
more so, had contended that some of the greatest moments in the history of
artistic creativity corresponded neither to the general development of society
nor to its material substructure. While Marx and Engels insisted, of course,
that no art was created in a social vacuum, neither man subscribed to a
vulgar economic determinism, or championed the use of art or literature in
the service of any class. As Engels put it, "the author does not have to serve
the reader on a platter the future historical resolution of the social conflicts
. . . he describes."[76] Maltz agreed. He knew that novels and plays (and music
and paintings too) had the power to inspire social concern without being
simplistic or didactic.

Maltz even went so far as to repeat Engels's proposition that a writer may
be confused, or even stupid and reactionary in his thinking, and still be
able to do good, even great, work as an artist. The cultural leadership of the
American Party was embarrassed by Maltz's use of Engels to bolster his case.
So furious was Fast, and apparently jealous, too, of the well-known novelist
and award-winning screenwriter, that he seemed to relish the role of "enforcer" against Maltz. Fast was so obsessed with carrying out his perceived
task as a patrolman for political correctness that he either willfully ignored
or remained arrogantly unresponsive to the nuances and appeals to the rich
leftist tradition in Maltz's essay.[77]

Even worse, as far as Fast and the Party were concerned, was Maltz's
contention that if an artist, consciously or otherwise, were to "use his talent
for an immediate political end," he *might* turn his work into a "form of leaflet
writing." Maltz did not say that from such effort no art was possible, but he
did think that "the failure of much left-wing talent to mature [was] a comment on how restricting" socialist realism and the Communist canon were.[78]

Fast, however, swallowed whole the Soviet theory of "socialist realism,"
which burdened writers with obligations often inconsistent with their immediate experience, personal vision, and instincts of literary honesty. Socialist realism meant that a writer was allowed on the one hand to depart
from accuracy and psychological credibility to preach Party doctrine; but
on the other hand, he was not to treat his imaginative world as a separate
entity with its own possibilities. Communist writers, at least the most or-

thodox among them, knew that their function was to serve society not as individuals with creative vision, but rather, as artists expressing the social will as defined by the Communist Party. As Fast put it to Maltz, "Left-wing art is the result of a conscious use by the artist of a scientific understanding of society, of an identification with the working class . . . and of a sharing of the vital ideology of that class." Such art, Fast said, channeling Stalin, "is always a weapon—a weapon in the struggle for a better world."[79] One of the very few authors who could pass muster with Fast in this regard was Theodore Dreiser, who, though not a Communist until literally his dying day, had great sympathy for the working class, and therefore, according to Fast, had "no peer in the American short story," and no equal either "in the field of the novel."[80]

Fast's long written rant, full of envy toward writers with more talent, and dripping with malice toward Maltz, Richard Wright, Koestler, Dos Passos, and Steinbeck, was followed by a "special" meeting of the Hollywood Communist Party at actor Morris Carnovsky's home in the predominantly wealthy neighborhood of Beverly Glen. Here dozens of Maltz's close comrades denounced him. Some of his critics, such as John Howard Lawson, who had organized the meeting, were genuinely grappling with the peculiar task of writing the "truth" in a restricting class context; but most, more sensitive to the Party line, were trying, like Fast, to enhance their Stalinist bona fides and self-esteem by attacking Maltz.[81] In doing so, they once more illustrated, not for the last time, the astounding power of the Communist machine to intimidate members, including writers reputedly independent.

Following the general critique that Fast had laid out, Herbert Biberman, Alvah Bessie, an author and screenwriter and a veteran of the Spanish Civil War, and some dozen others performed what one of the few Maltz supporters, screenwriter Leopold Atlas, called an "utterly ruthless, unprincipled, cutthroat act of character assassination." Maltz, who never argued for the total separation of literature from politics, and knew that novels had the power to inspire social concern, was "literally shouted down," Atlas said, when he tried to explain his thoughts.[82]

The meeting was followed by a slew of articles in the left-wing press further eviscerating Maltz and his argument. There were, however, a handful of supporters who thought of themselves as Communists, but also as independent writers. The psychologist Bernhard J. Stern, editor of the Marxist journal *Science and Society,* for example, found the attack by Fast and others "shockingly doctrinaire." They are more like "commissars" than "critics," he wrote to Maltz privately, "and you're an innocent victim."[83]

Some of Maltz's supporters were so angry about what had been done to him by the "Fast mob" that they left the Party altogether, and others seriously considered doing the same.[84] Shepard Traube, who had directed the Broadway hit *Angel Street* in 1940, and had then gone to Hollywood, where he did *Street of Memories,* was beside himself after he read the screeds by Howard Fast and *New Masses* editor Joe North and the "tripe" by Mike Gold. "I haven't been as angry in years," Traube wrote Maltz; but he also told him that not all the writers in the Party were as "stupid and mechanical" as Fast. As a matter of fact, Traube said, Fast "is the man who could most profit from your piece. For it is Fast, in his anxiety to be a pamphleteer, who writes slovenly and unevenly, when he could be a *good writer,* and as a good writer even more successful in winning a wide audience for the social-political themes he espouses!" What appalled Traube most "is that Fast, North, Sillen, Gold" go back to a Stalinist "position of 15 years ago! Nothing has been learned."[85]

The respected director was right. Stalinism was back in full force, and Traube wondered what could be done about the culturally narrow-minded such as Fast and Mike Gold. "The first instinctive reaction" that came to mind "is fuck it, let's quit these fools." But, Traube said, "one stays on and fights against them," or else these contemptible "sectarian" Fast-North-Gold-Sillen "boys will drive the middle-class further and further away." In concluding his letter, Traube told Maltz a cautionary tale: he had seen too many "decent people, honest, open-minded non-Party people, being alienated" by the inordinate power of "Communist blocs within what have been united front organizations" such as the Independent Citizens Committee of Artists, Writers and Professionals (ICC).[86]

Unfortunately Maltz's attackers outnumbered his supporters by far, and two months after his original piece, Maltz wrote "Moving Forward," piteously retracting his first article. Directly illustrating the hold the Party had over those who wanted to remain loyal to it, Maltz now agreed that he had written "a one-sided, non-dialectical treatment," and he pleaded guilty to separating "the organic connection" between art and ideology."[87]

The criticism against him had been "so enormous," Maltz said, that he "was in a kind of shell-shocked state" afterward. And then he started to ask himself precisely what the Party stalwarts had intended him to ask: "Well, now, who am *I*?" Actually, Maltz had literary credentials as good as or better than any of the Hollywood Ten, with the possible exception of John Howard Lawson.[88] But despite, or perhaps because of, his success and reputation, "Nobody stood up for [him]." Maltz thought, "Well, Jesus Christ, I must be wrong. I must be mistaken." He wanted to remain a Communist, he said; "I didn't want to become a renegade." So, instead, of quitting or fighting back he crawled and recanted.[89] The Maltz case clearly demonstrates the audacity of far less talented men to humiliate those more gifted, and once more gives us a chilling sense of the power of the Party to extract obedience.

It gets worse. After Maltz was put on the rack in 1946, he in turn was one of the gang of inquisitors who harshly interrogated Robert Rossen in 1949 because of the director's Academy Award–winning film *All the King's Men*. The movie was an assault on the virtual dictatorship of Huey Long's one-man rule as governor of Louisiana, but was viewed by some of the CP cultural commissars as a covert attack on Stalin. The Party decreed that a Rossen "trial" take place—in Maltz's own Beverly Hills home, a sharply pointed message both to Maltz and to other writers and filmmakers tempted to drift from the Party's dictates. When Rossen was summoned he said, "Stick the whole party up your ass," a much more reasonable response than Maltz's obsequious apology and behavior. Unlike Rossen, however, most of the Hollywood Communists submitted to the Party's power. This included the venerable John Howard Lawson, who before he joined the Party had said that "it is not the business of a theater to be controlled by any class or theory," and later, after he had departed, argued that "Marxism has never dealt effectively with aesthetic questions."[90] Attacked, however, while in the Party for being too complex, too subtle, Lawson then went on to attack Alvah Bessie on the same grounds. This chain of shaming was a process by which the Communist screenwriters could pass on their own deep humiliation by inflicting it on others, and a way of demonstrating that they had regained their ideological purity.[91]

Howard Fast, ever vigilant in his search for targets, stayed on the hunt, but Maltz remained his favorite victim for months. Speaking in April 1946 on "Art as a Weapon," with 3,500 in attendance at the Manhattan Center, Fast said that "books have always been the strongest medium through which ideas can be presented to the masses." And he quoted Stalin to drive home the point that "all art must be directed towards attaining socialism." The "failure to understand dialectics," Fast said, "accounts for such errors as

Albert Maltz made. Armed with the weapon of Marxism the people understand the degenerate and corporate nature of capitalism and know how to combat it. Artists who are in the vanguard recognize that *only in the Soviet Union are artists and writers truly free because they operate on the highest level of culture.*"[92]

Fast's behavior in the Maltz case, and his follow-up, with this astonishingly false contention about the USSR and art, shows just how terribly narrow the views of the author of *The Last Frontier* and *Citizen Tom Paine* had become, just how deeply Fast had descended into rigid, stifling Communist orthodoxy, and just how tightly attached he had become to a group that gave him the comprehensive worldview and ego nourishment he desperately needed.

Howard Fast, second from left, with
friends at an outing, c. 1933–34.

Unless otherwise indicated, all
photographs are courtesy of
Rachel Fast Ben-Avi.

Howard Fast, top row right,
counselor at Camp Jened, 1934.

Howard Fast, most likely late 1943,
after publication of *Citizen Tom Paine.*
One of Bette's drawings is on the wall.

Above. Howard and Bette in backyard of home
on West 94th Street, New York, 1948.

Facing. Howard, Bette, and Rachel in backyard
of home on West 94th Street, New York, 1948.

Howard receiving Stalin Peace Prize, 1954. W. E. B. Du Bois is seated
to his left. Rachel and Bette are standing at right. Shirley Graham,
clapping, is at left. *Photograph by Julius Lazarus. By permission of the
Special Collections and University Archives, Rutgers University Libraries.*

Right. Howard with
Rena Fast, his older sister
by ten years, c. 1974.

Below. Howard and
his swimming pool,
Beverly Hills, c. 1975.

Howard, c. 1980 and
below, Howard and
Bette in the 1980s.

Bette Fast, in Greenwich, Connecticut, c. 1981.

Below. Jonathan Fast, wife Erica Jong, daughter, Molly, 1982.

Howard at 75th birthday party, 1989.

Below. Howard at 80th birthday party, 1994, soon after Bette's death. Rachel is looking over his shoulder. Lee Fountain is at left, facing the camera.

4

Cold War, Hot Seat

$\mathcal{T}$he uneasy wartime alliance between the United States and the Soviet
Union dissolved in 1945 with the coming of peace, exposing long-
standing hostilities between the two new superpowers. Dangerous confrontations, especially over the division of Germany and the future of Eastern
Europe, intensified the hostilities and morphed into the "Cold War." American Communists, including Howard Fast, and hundreds of fellow travelers—
those on the periphery of a Party so closely associated with the USSR—found
themselves subject to increased suspicion, investigation, and harassment.[1]

In the face of amplified anti-Communism, Fast began losing faith in the
United States as a natural home for socialism. Moving faster and further away
from American mainstream left-liberalism, he concluded, as did the CPUSA
generally, that trying to reform capitalism would only sustain the system
and bring defeat for Communism. While still not publicly acknowledging
his membership in the Party, Fast recommitted himself as an openly leftist
writer and a radically partisan citizen to the political conflicts of his times.[2]

The most important of these conflicts, Fast thought, was between "the
conscienceless lords of the atom bomb" in the Truman administration and
the Russians, who will use "atomic energy to make the deserts [into] blooming gardens."[3] Exaggerated fear of the Soviet Union in the United States, he
predicted, would allow ever more reactionary forces to gain power. With a

monopoly of atomic weapons in the hands of these forces, America, which had demonstrated its willingness to deploy its nuclear arsenal in Hiroshima and Nagasaki, could, Fast thought, annihilate the Soviet Union. The CPUSA regrouped around this issue, and in line with Moscow, turned its rhetorical fury away from the defeated Axis powers and toward what it saw as "an emerging fascism" in the United States.[4]

That Communists and pro-Communists were the most active and outspoken enemies of fascism, moved many politicians, entrepreneurs, and religious leaders to make a simplistic, opportunistic, and erroneous equation: anti-fascist sentiment equals support for Communism. Given the many anti-fascists who were neither members of the CP nor fellow travelers, and given the fear among conservative, and even some liberal elites of the "Red Menace," the reductionist conflation of anti-fascism with Communism became extremely dangerous to the civil liberties of Americans generally. And it promoted a growing sense within the establishment that First Amendment freedoms might have to be compromised in the context of national security concerns; this unease set the stage for the McCarthyism that sullied American political life in the 1950s.

Beginning in 1946, a broad coalition of American conservatives led by the Catholic Church, the FBI, the Republican Party, and men of influence in the world of commerce and industry, effectively promoted an anti-Communist crusade. There were persistent allegations that spies for the Soviet Union had infiltrated the U.S. government. More troubling still, unreasonable pressure was brought on federal and state employees, and sometimes on private citizens, too, to affirm loyalty to the United States by demonstrating that they had no connection, no matter how oblique, to the Communist movement.[5]

Fast continued to invite suspicion. In January 1946, he not only became a contributing editor of the pro-Communist *New Masses,* he was also employed by the *Daily Worker* for its special series, "Coverage of America's Strike Front." Wartime "no-strike" pledges were no longer relevant, and the pent-up needs and wants of workers exploded in 1946 into a record-setting number of strikes.[6]

In a singular effort to immerse himself in working-class life and battles, Fast went to strike-ridden Chicago for nearly the whole month of January. "I saw the [meat-packers] strike on the first day," Fast wrote, "and for the five days which followed, I watched the picket lines, spoke to the workers, prowled through the soup kitchens, and sat in on strike meetings. It was something to see and something to remember." He delivered a number of strongly pro-labor pieces to the *Daily Worker,* at least two of which criticized the police who had provoked violence in connection with the strike of United Packinghouse Workers. Fast admiringly emphasized the multiracial makeup of the picketers and pointedly identified the positive role of blacks in the work stoppage.[7]

His commitment to racial equality, as we have seen, had grown over time and was entirely genuine. In February, soon after Fast returned from Chicago to his Central Park West apartment, the FBI reported that the "Subject has caused some disturbance . . . by inviting negroes in as his guests." That Fast was "looked on as a Communist" by the doorman and other "persons who are acquainted with him in the building" is illustrative of the widespread assumption in the 1940s that all those who supported integration, including socialists, liberals, and northern New Deal Democrats, were "Reds," dangerous radicals out to destabilize race relations in the United States.[8]

Fast reinforced his imputed Communist identity when in March, about two weeks before he was summoned to HUAC, he addressed a meeting of 1,700 Columbia University students who had been picketing Winston Churchill during his visit to the United States. The students, disturbed about what they saw as the Cold War foreign-policy implications in the "Iron Curtain" speech that the prime minister had delivered a month earlier, were gathered at McMillan Hall as Churchill was about to receive an honorary degree from the university. The students voted to approve awarding the degree to Churchill in recognition of his work as a leader in the war against fascism; but they condemned his newly intensified anti-Communist world outlook. A resolution favored by Howard Fast, for whom the students "vigorously applauded," was approved. It said in part, that the students, rather than relying on American or Western unilateralism, "place our trust for world peace in the United Nations Organization."[9]

Soon after his speech at the university, Fast became a student himself. Determined that he not go "soft" or be corrupted by the trappings of his success—four well-received novels published between 1941 and 1944, all selling briskly—the CPUSA sent Fast to a Communist Party Training School in Beacon, New York. Located in a small hotel on the shore of the Hudson, this ominously titled educational institution hosted ten students for two weeks of saturation in lectures and seminars. Fast went home on weekends, but was otherwise occupied for ten hours a day studying history, philosophy, political science, and economics. Although he claims in *Being Red* that there was nothing secretive about the place, most of the students, some of whom were veterans of the Abraham Lincoln Brigade, used aliases.[10]

The weeks spent at school "were interesting and instructive." Fast listened to lectures and engaged in seminars in Marxism. But he admitted, "We were not educated to an open mind . . . we were drilled in facts as the party saw such facts." This confession is followed by one of the more candid passages in *Being Red:* "[An] ironclad obedience to the party position wreaked havoc in circles where the party had been respected and honored. I had become a sort of priest, and it would take a great deal of pain and suffering and some time in prison before I learned that . . . freedom [cannot be bought] by constricting freedom. *My writing would suffer,* but this party to which I had pledged my wits and energy would suffer even more, and throughout the world, millions more would suffer."[11] It would take another decade before Fast, even if not as strongly as he states it in *Being Red,* came to this recognition. In the meantime, he remained a one-dimensional man of the extreme left.

Fresh from school in April 1946, Fast moved up from "contributing editor" to "editorial board member" of *New Masses;* at the same time he was subpoenaed to testify at HUAC hearings about the Joint Anti-Fascist Refugee Committee (JAFRC), on whose board he also now sat. In 1939, after Franco's victory in Spain, JAFRC had been created to raise funds to establish a hospital just north of the Spanish border in Toulouse to provide medical aid to some 200,000 survivors of the Republican Army who had fled across the Pyrenees.[12] In 1944 JAFRC was licensed by President Roosevelt's War Relief Control Board and granted tax exemption, both of which HUAC now sought to have revoked. But the congressional committee never initiated discussion with Fast or any of the other fifteen subpoenaed board members about what JAFRC had done, or what HUAC claimed this "Communist-front" organization had tried to do. It was enough for Congressman John Rankin, HUAC's chair John Wood, and the committee's chief counsel, Ernest Adamson, that JAFRC was anti-Franco. This position they saw as a symptom of anti-Americanism, and they charged JAFRC with being "engaged in political activity in behalf of Communists" and with promoting propaganda of a "subversive character."[13]

Ed Barsky, the chair of JAFRC board, was a Communist, as were several others, but Fast was certainly the most prominent among them. He, like the rest of the officers at the hearings, was not permitted to question the legitimacy of the investigation, despite its lack of specificity. Congress has only two recognized reasons for subpoenaing witnesses: to inform itself as to the need for legislation and to engage in its supervisory function over activities of the executive branch. The JAFRC investigation met neither of these tests.[14]

That did not stop HUAC's chair, John Wood, from proceeding. "In the interests of saving time," he immediately demanded JAFRC's donor records. The committee's first witness, Edward Barsky, and later all members of the organization's executive board, including Fast, claimed, upon advice of their attorney, that the authority to produce records was in the hands of Helen Bryan, the executive secretary. Here is part of the puerile exchange between Wood and Fast:

> CHAIR: Now, you know what you have got with you here, don't you? You can tell this committee what's in your pockets, can't you?
> FAST: I certainly can.
> CHAIR: Have you got the books that are called for in that subpoena? . . .
> FAST: I will answer that question by—
> CHAIR: (interposing): No; just answer it yes or no. Have you got them here or not?
> FAST: I will have to answer it in this fashion—
> CHAIR: No; I am not concerned about your reading your statement. . . .
> FAST (reading): Mr. Chairman, I have been served—
> CHAIR: No; I just told you we don't want to hear your written statement. We have got the statement . . .
> FAST: You are asking me a question. I want to answer . . . in this way.
> CHAIR: We want you to answer it yes or no. . . . Have you got them? . . .
> FAST: . . . I have the right to answer that question, as I see fit. . . .
> CHAIR: . . . You are a man of average intelligence at least. Let us not try to evade or hedge.

Part of the statement, unanimously agreed upon by the JARFC board, that Fast was trying to get into the record read: "I individually do not have possession, custody or control over any of the material requested. . . . The books, records, and correspondence are in the custody and control of Miss Helen R. Bryan, the executive secretary of our organization. . . . Since I do not have either in my possession . . . or control the books . . . I am unable to comply with your order to produce them."[15] Turning over the records would have amounted to "naming names," including Mark Van Doren, Jose

Ferrer, Ruth Gordon, Van Wyck Brooks, Leonard Bernstein, and Eleanor
Roosevelt. No one complied.

Helen Bryan, a courageous and resourceful woman was, of course, in on
this ploy to establish a legal defense; and in her turn she claimed that the
subpoena was invalid because it was not pertinent to congressional investigations. She also said, correctly, that the constitutionality of HUAC itself was
in doubt. The committee was not interested in collecting information for
legislative purposes, nor was it fulfilling its watchdog role over the executive branch, and therefore its hearings were of dubious legitimacy at best.[16]

Having been advised of their constitutional rights, the board members did
not invoke the Fifth Amendment, which would have precluded a contempt
citation; but they did refuse to turn over records or answer any questions
about JAFRC, implicitly relying on the First Amendment's guarantee of freedom of speech. HUAC for the first time was introduced to the problem of
"recalcitrant witnesses." Frustrated, the committee cited "*collusion* to defy
a congressional subpoena," and recommended contempt citations.[17]

Most astute observers recognized that Howard Fast and the other Communists on the JAFRC board, or anywhere else in the United States in 1946
for that matter, were not a serious threat to the safety and security of the
American Republic. Indeed, it could be argued that Communists with their
resurrected class-war rhetoric, their apparent attachment to Stalin and the
Soviet Union, and their postwar refusal to ally with other liberal groups
including Social Democrats, were more of a threat to a viable and effective
American left than to anything else. Arthur Schlesinger, for example, no
admirer of the CPUSA and a scholar dedicated to preserving what he called
the "vital center" of American culture and politics, rejected the notion that
the CPUSA posed a significant risk to the United States. Communism, he said,
correctly, in 1946, is actually "a great help to the right because of its success
in dividing and neutralizing the left." It is only to the mostly anti-Stalinist
American left, Schlesinger wisely wrote, "that Communism presents the
most serious danger."[18]

Nonetheless, fear, political expediency, and opportunism won the day.
Ed Barsky was cited for contempt by the House at the end of March. Some
weeks later an acrimonious debate erupted among the congressmen. The
argument led by Vito Marcantonio, elected as the candidate of the American
Labor Party but essentially faithful to CP policies, pitted the racist Southern
Democrat John Rankin (an equal-opportunity bigot who did not hesitate to

use the words "nigger" and "kike" on the floor of the House), and Republicans Karl Mundt and J. Parnell Thomas (later to be indicted, convicted, and imprisoned himself for an actual crime: fraud) against Emanuel Celler, a veteran liberal Democrat from Brooklyn, and Helen Gahagan Douglas, the first Democratic woman from California to be elected to Congress, later to be beaten in the 1950 race for the U.S. Senate by Richard Nixon, who mounted a vicious "anti-Red" smear campaign against her.[19]

Celler argued that if Congress voted for the contempt resolution, "we pass up the American way of fair play and embrace the way of unconstitutional procedure." He went on to predict that "our action will come back to haunt us," and, perhaps thinking of Howard Fast's historical novels, added pointedly that if Paine and Jefferson and Lincoln "were alive today, they would . . . run afoul of this . . . Committee. The radicalism of these patriots would not . . . sit well upon [your] stomachs."[20]

The House's answer to Celler's eloquence was a vote of 262 to 56 for the contempt resolution. The representatives set a new record by issuing seventeen simultaneous citations for contempt of Congress: one for Helen Bryan and sixteen for the executive board of JAFRC. Fast wrote that his "cocky and romantic radicalism," and he might have added, his insatiable desire for celebrity, "had now reared up and kicked me in the face."[21]

Fast's colleagues on the JAFRC executive board, which included three physicians, a university professor, a lawyer, and several labor leaders, never thought they would go to jail. Ten of seventeen did, one of whom was Howard Fast. But that didn't happen until 1950, when all appeals had failed. In the meantime, Fast continued writing fiction and stayed active in Party work.

In May, about a month after his HUAC hearing, Fast spoke at the Hotel Concourse Plaza on 161st Street in the Bronx, announcing the formation of a committee to condemn HUAC as unconstitutional. "You can bet," he said, that "the Rankin Committee did not get the right answers from me." Later in the month Fast spoke at a farewell dinner for Ilya Ehrenburg, the Soviet Jewish journalist who in 1946 was about to enter the most morally compromising period of his tangled relationship to Stalin and Stalinism.[22] Fast was asked to speak because of his "standing in the literary world and your feeling about the need to maintain the most cordial relations between America and the Soviet Union." The event was held under the auspices of the American Committee of Jewish Writers, Artists and Scientists (ACJWAS), a group listed by the FBI, the attorney general, and HUAC as a Communist front organization.[23]

The ACJWAS was, like the vast majority of other so-called Communist fronts, strongly influenced by Communists, but it was neither established nor controlled by the Communist Party.[24] Indeed, the CPUSA was not the founding entity in most cases of alleged fronts, including the dozen or more in which Howard Fast was a member or with which he had significant contact; nor did the Party *directly* control these organizations. Still, while many fronts had only modest minorities of Communist members, those members frequently exerted disproportionately significant influence because they were more committed, better organized, and more ideologically focused than most other members.

Less than 10 percent of the 8,500 active members of American League for Peace and Democracy, for example, were Communists; but their energy and concentrated activity made them powerful, and often the most dominant group in this and many other organizations, including the Civil Rights Congress (CRC), Veterans of the Abraham Lincoln Brigade (VALB), and the Authors Guild. The focused behavior of the Communists meant that although there were never more than 80,000 members of American Communist Party at any given time, labor unions, youth groups, antiwar organizations, civil rights bodies, and a plethora of various clubs and assemblies quite often followed the Communist Party's line on domestic as well as international affairs.[25]

THE DISCOURAGED AMERICAN

Throughout his ordeal with HUAC, Fast was putting the finishing touches on *The American: A Middle Western Legend.* A biographical novel about John Peter Altgeld, the governor of Illinois from 1893 to 1897, who pardoned three "anarchist bombers" convicted of the murder of seven policeman in the Haymarket Riot of 1886, *The American* reveals Fast's nearly complete disillusionment with American society. He was trying in a single novel, he said, to embrace both the life of Altgeld and the struggle, futile though it was, to create a truly revolutionary trade union movement in the United States.[26]

Altgeld is portrayed as having full faith in the American political system even as he fights corruption, monopoly, and the power of money in politics—

all of which he sees not as systemic, but as evil aberrations, the product of "greedy men" such as railroad magnates George Pullman and Jay Gould, and financiers Jim Fisk and J. P. Morgan. He understands that there is little difference between presidents Grover Cleveland and William McKinley, and that "there's no more two-party system," only the one party of big business. But Altgeld believes that "while our institutions are not free from injustice" or the maldistribution of power, "they are still the best . . . and therefore must be maintained."[27]

Altgeld, Fast tells us, was a democratic politician, possibly the best America had ever produced. But this is Fast's way of damning with faint praise. The governor, Fast complains, unlike socialist Eugene V. Debs, depicted as flawless, fails to look outside the established system for new ideas and weapons to make the good fight. Instead, he uses his own power and money to do battle, only to lose because his oligarchic adversaries have more of both, and as Fast strongly suggests, always would.

Altgeld's failure in the novel to look toward socialism signaled the unraveling of one of Fast's dreams. Fast had equated a Communist utopia, which he never fully explained or portrayed, with his vision of the fulfillment of American ideals, which he only half understood. In *The American,* Fast is telling us that what he had begun to believe by 1944 was thoroughly convincing to him by 1946: the United States, past and present, was so compromised, so polluted by the industrialization of the nineteenth century and its consequent concentration of wealth and power, that its founding principles had been erased. To become anything resembling a socialist society, America would have to look outside of, rather than build on, its original system for inspiration and guidance.[28]

James Oliver Brown, an editor at Little, Brown, sent Fast a copy of a letter quoting a perceptive friend's take on Howard's shift in mood:

> During the past week, I've been feeding myself a concentrated literary diet of your friend, Howard Fast—reading for the first time his FREEDOM ROAD and CONCEIVED IN LIBERTY, re-reading THE UNVANQUISHED and CITIZEN TOM PAINE—I don't know whether Fast is a great writer—who am I to say?—but I know he . . . makes me feel a very real and honest emotion. And a faith is restored to me . . . in the essential dignity and integrity of man, a faith I thought I'd lost. I wish Fast could find it in him to write a novel about [contemporary] America—so that he might perhaps persuade me that

the purpose of America, in which he so obviously believe[d], has not died, sometime between this present and the past he recreates. Or does he write of the past only because he can find no glory in the present?[29]

Despite his denigration of Altgeld's approach to change, Fast was concerned about workers and the underprivileged and didn't sneer at practical reforms to alleviate their suffering. But neither he nor his comrades in the CPUSA connected such reforms to long-term goals. Instead, they saw progressive legislation as merely ameliorative, capable perhaps of easing distress, while people waited around for cataclysm—war, depression, or economic catastrophe—to bring down capitalism. On the other hand, left-liberal New Dealers, liberal anti-Communists, and Social Democrats, whom Communists in their reckless shortsightedness saw as worse than fascists, were trying to solidify and advance the progressive changes wrought by the New Deal. Rather than seeking to restore a Marxist vocabulary of inevitable progress toward Utopia, they looked to join theory and practice in order to construct a more open, egalitarian society out of materials and conditions already extant.

Several of Fast's liberal contemporaries, including political liberals Hubert Humphrey, Paul Douglas, and Chester Bowles, sociologist Daniel Bell, editor of the democratic socialist journal *The New Leader,* and social critic Dwight Macdonald, editor of the radical journal *Politics,* represented in their own ways those who came to see that in one form or another a modified capitalism was really the only game in town, the only economic system that could create enough wealth to alleviate poverty through redistributive social welfare reform, even as it preserved, with sporadic damaging lapses, precious American freedoms. If there was to be a redemptive power in politics one had to deal, they argued, with the political landscape as it actually existed. They urged that the left-liberal's intellectual and practical energies be dedicated to integrating reform into a larger economic and political strategy, a strategy the American mainstream and working classes could appreciate: the taming and radical restructuring of capitalism over time through the democratic process.[30]

But by 1946, Fast had rejected all versions of social democracy. His association with the Communist movement may have moved some American critics to infer connections between his political views and the substance, or lack thereof, in *The American.* Esteemed historians Henry Steele Commager and Oscar Handlin and the well-known literary critic Diana Trilling, for example, accused Fast of distorting the past to write propaganda.[31]

No doubt sales of *The American* suffered from these reviews and from Fast's contempt citation. But lack of success in the market was not due, as Fast would have it, to any anti-Communist conspiracy or to a reading public alienated by Fast's apparent Communist affiliation. The weakness of *The American* lay at Fast's door. The novel lacks a clear focus. Even more deadly, there is no insight into what motivated Altgeld, a successful lawyer, business-man, and politician, to support unconventional and unpopular causes. And once again the "enemy," the monopolists in this instance, are depicted as one-dimensionally demonic.

The same pattern of reductionism and name-calling seen in Fast's fiction was evident in his political speech as well. In September 1946 at a meeting sponsored by Contemporary Writers, a front organization, he denounced the rival American Writers Association as a "nest of Fascists, Social Democrats, and Trotskyites."[32] Fast continued to drift into the more extreme left-wing parochialism of Communist sectarianism, even as he continued to remain mum about his membership in the CPUSA. At the beginning of September he had an interesting and revealing exchange of letters in this regard with an admiring reader, Clarence W. Donnelly, who had read *Citizen Tom Paine* straight through with only a break for lunch, and did the same thing again, he said, the very next day!

Donnelly wrote that lately he had been reading disturbing things about Fast in the newspapers, such as "'Howard Fast, Communist writer for the *Daily Worker*'" and "'Howard Fast identifies with various Communist Front organizations and committees.'" Donnelly wanted to know if it was true that Fast was "a Communist or a Communist sympathizer." If so, he wrote,

you must want to see our democratic form of government uprooted and Communism take its place. . . . You have as much right to embrace Communism as I have to despise it. But what I cannot understand is how so ardent an admirer of Thomas Paine—who probably had an influence greater than any other human being in bringing freedom to our country and in unshackling the truth—can reconcile getting into bed with a har-lot ideology which, as practiced in Russia and preached in this country and elsewhere, everlastingly perverts, distorts and suppresses the truth . . . and in which freedom of the individual—for which Paine fought right down to his last gasp—is reviled and spat upon as an outworn notion of the bourgeoisie. I should certainly appreciate any comment you might care to make on what strikes me as a curious anomaly.[33]

Fast responded with a single-spaced two-page letter in which he failed, understandably, to answer Donnelly's questions directly. Instead, Howard wanted to know if an organization is a Communist front "because it stands for mercy and peace and the right of human beings to civil liberties? . . . If such work is Communist, then perhaps I am one, and you too." Fast had cleverly taken the patently false assumption that all who work for social justice are Communists, turned it inside out, and used it to his own advantage.

Fast also complained that he had been attacked for his association with the Independent Citizens Committee of the Arts, Sciences and Professions. "Only a madman or a fascist," Fast declared, "would accuse the ICC of being Communist. There are 15,000 of the most prominent people in America in our organization. We believe in peace and democracy," a phrase parroted by Communists with irritating persistency, and "we do not believe in war with the Soviet Union." Fast's description of the ICC is literally true, but greatly misleading. The ICC was one of those organizations in which only a minority were Communists, but an entrenched and disproportionately influential group. As Shepard Traube, a Communist himself, had written to his comrade Albert Maltz only months earlier, he had "watched . . . open-minded non-Party people" become alienated by the Communist control of what had been Popular Front–type "organizations like the I.C.C."[34]

Fast insisted that he would not retreat from the "word" Communism "like a cowed dog; for it seems to me that these . . . gangster tactics which threaten a person with ruin because he writes as he wishes . . . are a more basic threat to our freedom [in America] than Communism." Nothing could be truer. But Fast, who was no champion of civil liberties, has attempted here to don the mantle of the First Amendment in order to pose as a democrat victimized by a government intent on violating its own ideals. And he followed this exploitation of a truth in which he did not believe by writing something that could not be less true. "Communists *everywhere*," Fast claimed, "fight for the rights of the individual."[35]

Understandably confused by Fast's indirectness, Donnelly said, "I take it that you are not yourself a Communist, but that you are sympathetic to some . . . of what you regard as the aim of the Communists—particularly their fight against Fascism." Donnelly, however, voiced a powerful demurrer to Fast's defense of Communism: "You say that . . . everywhere Communists were in the forefront of the struggle against Fascism. I know better. Let some Communist try to explain away the ghoulish partnership of Stalin with Hitler that preceded the rape of Poland and ushered in the Second World War. Were Communists fighting Fascism when they hamstrung our defense program and parroted their cries of 'Imperialistic War' as long as that obscene partnership was in effect? They dropped the humbug quickly enough when Russia was attacked."

Moreover, Donnelly said, in an almost perfectly irrefutable flourish, "The hideous mask of Fascism is not difficult to penetrate, whether it hides behind the Ku Klux Klan, the Christian Front, some corrupt business cartel, or some private exploiter of labor. But Communism, smarter, more subtle and more plausible, is infinitely more dangerous to our institutions [because] it masquerades as democracy. . . . It is . . . political tyranny. . . . [I]t is the [disguised] twin brother of Fascism."[36]

The virtues of the Communists were many, including their struggle against racial injustice, support for unionism, and periodic hostility to fascism. But the American Communist Party's professed commitment to democracy was a sham, belied by its unwavering support of Stalin, one of the most murderous dictators in history, and by its terribly inconsistent and purely self-interested support of civil liberties at home. Donnelly's second letter had it right. Fast did not respond.[37]

He did respond, however, to a second summons to Washington in October. HUAC had discovered that Fast wrote a booklet about Tito in 1943 that seemed to suggest that JAFRC had aided the Yugoslavian financially. Forgetting perhaps that Tito and his partisans had rendered invaluable assistance to the United States by fighting several German divisions to a standstill, and thinking only about the fact that Tito was a Communist, HUAC subpoenaed Fast at 7 PM on October 22, ordering him to appear at 3 PM on October 23.

Only John Wood, the chair, Adamson, the legal counsel, and a stenographer were present when Fast appeared. Howard blew his top and apparently called Wood a number of scatological names that were stricken from the record. Wood and Adamson simply went on and asked him whether he had written *The Incredible Tito,* to which Fast responded affirmatively. Once again, however, the exchange of remarks degenerated into absurdity:

ADAMSON: On page 14, you say that [JAFRC] supplied funds for Tito to
   return to Yugoslavia. Is that so?
FAST: It is more than three years since I wrote the book. I don't recall
   what was on page 14. . . . Do you have a copy?
ADAMSON: I just told you what was on page 14.
FAST: I would rather look at what I wrote than rely on you. . . . I didn't
   even know that you or [Wood] knew how to read.

Wood apparently reacted to this insult with fury, matching Fast in the use
of four-letter words, but these too failed to appear in the record. What did appear was much more disturbing: "There's a hotel strike on in Washington,"
Wood said. "No room[s]. . . . It means you'd have to go back to New York and
come down here again. How would you like that?" Ultimately, either Fast
somehow explained away the sentence, "An agent of the Anti-Fascist Refugee
Committee contacted Tito in Paris and provided him with funds and means
to return to Yugoslavia," or convinced Wood that further questioning would
be futile. Howard was dismissed.[38]

Five months later on March 31 1947, Howard Fast and the other members
of the JAFRC executive board who had refused to name names a year earlier
were indicted by a Washington grand jury for contempt of Congress, rare in
American history up to this point, and for conspiracy, a more serious charge.
All were arraigned in federal court, waived hearings, and were released on
$500 bail.[39] Still, because of their faith in the advice of their new lawyer,
O. John Rogge, formerly of the Justice Department, and a prosecutor at
the post-Holocaust Nuremburg trials, Fast and the others continued to feel
confident that they would do no jail time. Between the indictment and the
trial set for June 13, Fast was busy with making public appearances, giving
speeches, and completing a new novel.

He also wrote several articles for *New Masses* during this period, including "A Reveille For Writers," urging the literary community to speak out
on the ills of postwar America. He went through a long litany of America's
new crimes, including the unprosecuted murders of blacks in the South, the
homelessness of veterans, the emasculation of trade unions, and the murder
by "imperialists" of "men fighting for democracy" all over the world. And
what about Washington, Fast asked, where "a group of native fascists, styling
themselves a 'Committee on Un-American Activities,' traduce democracy
. . . and lead an all-out attack on the constitutional rights of Americans?"

"What has happened in this land of ours?" Fast wondered. "What dry terror has muted [the] voices [and] paralyzed the pens of Ernest Hemingway, John Steinbeck, Erskine Caldwell, Clifford Odets . . . and Sinclair Lewis [who have] allowed wrong to be added to wrong and shame to shame—with only silence as commentary?" There were "giants in the land once," Fast insisted; "there can be giants again. But, as always before, they must [emerge] out of the people's struggle for a better world."[40]

Fast also addressed large crowds on several occasions between April and June, including a Civil Rights Congress (CRC) rally, an emergency meeting to save *New Masses,* which was in dire financial straits, an outdoor rally for American Relief for Greek Democracy, the New York City May Day parade, and a meeting of the John Reed Club at Yale University, where he spoke on "Marxism and Literature."[41]

At Strathcona Hall, in an impressive Gothic building on the Yale campus, Fast addressed an audience of two hundred. In an attempt to show how important left-wing writing could be, Fast pointed out that Karl Marx wrote for Horace Greeley's *Herald* during the Civil War and claimed that it was through Marx's direct pressure on the American president that Lincoln wrote the Emancipation Proclamation! There is no knowing the reaction of the audience to this astounding statement, but Lincoln had issued the proclamation in September 1862, to become effective on January 1, 1863. The only known letter from Marx to Lincoln was received by the president in February 1865.[42]

Fast went on to explain that "the true novel" must depict the class struggle and that no great novel could be written without adhering to "Marxist ideologies." One would hope that, at Yale at least, the audience might note that the speaker had by his remarks swept into the "dustbin of history" such writers as Conrad, Dostoevsky, Joyce, Tolstoy, James, Faulkner, and many others. Fast specifically condemned James T. Farrell and John Dos Passos, both of whom wrote about the proletariat, but as Trotskyists could not create anything worthy. They were not only without imagination, they were reactionary and destructive because they attacked the Soviet Union—where, Fast claimed, there was no censorship of writers.[43]

DOWN AND OUT IN THE U.S.A.

About five weeks after his Yale talk, on June 13, Fast and the other JAFRC board members were tried in federal court for contempt of Congress, and two weeks later they were found guilty. The implications were immense. The JAFRC case, known as *Barsky vs. U.S.,* was a landmark decision that helped free congressional investigators from having to worry about infringing their witnesses constitutional rights.[44]

The general atmosphere of government crackdowns on Communists at home and abroad did not help the defendants. The trouble, however, was not so much with the public's attitude as with opinion at the top. Political leaders and other elected officials, judges, social scientists, and the media were the main shapers of, and participants in, the public discourse, while most citizens structured their lives around personal issues. After WWII only 7 percent of the American people judged "foreign problems" a top priority for the United States. "Fear of war" with the Soviet Union did rank high, but unemployment and the high cost of living came very close, while worry about domestic Communist subversion lagged far behind.[45]

And if movies are any indication of the public mood, anti-Communism was not very important in the popular culture of the late 1940s when Fast and his JAFRC associates were being tried. Hollywood made as many as fifty anti-Communist films from the late forties to the mid-fifties, but nearly all were second features and financial flops. Movies such as *Iron Curtain* (1948), *The Red Menace* (1949), and *I Married a Communist* (1949) were so heavy-handed and stereotyped that their "message" was lost in "incredulity and even hilarity."[46] Even more important, box office receipts indicated that audiences preferred well-made movies and family films by far and were alienated or at best bemused by propaganda.

The point is not weakened but strengthened by our awareness that Communists were well entrenched in the Hollywood studio system and were highly regarded for their craftsmanship by their employers. It was very difficult to slip any pro-Communist—as distinct from socially liberal—messages or ideas into films given the many hands involved in what came to be the final cut of any movie. Despite thoughtful movies that addressed social issues, such as *The Best Years of Our Lives* (1946), *Gentleman's Agreement* (1947), and *Crossfire* (1947), each tagged "Red" and called "deliberately inflammatory" by anti-Communists, Dalton Trumbo's quip that getting *any* idea into a film would have been an accomplishment, essentially defined the general circumstances of Hollywood in the forties. Moreover, despite the FBI's investigation of *It's A Wonderful Life* (1946) because it allegedly used the "common Communist trick" of portraying "bankers as villains," the economic populism in the film bothered hardly anyone, because it dovetailed neatly with American ideals about fairness. Nor does it seem to have made any difference at all in the Cold War at home or abroad that Communists wrote almost all the scripts for the Abbott and Costello comedies, or that many movies whose screenplays were written by Party members received glowing reviews from the ultra-conservative Daughters of the American Revolution.[47]

The domestic Cold War, evidently, was being fought less within the popular culture than at elite levels. Within the political elite, President Truman was pushed by the extreme right as well as by members of both major parties to take espionage seriously and to stand tough against the Soviets. Hoping for reelection in order to carry the New Deal forward, Truman felt that he had to disassociate the Democratic Party and progressive reform from Communism, a label consistently pinned on liberal Democrats since 1933. Less than a month before Howard Fast's trial in June 1947, the president signed an executive order creating loyalty boards in some two hundred government agencies and in fourteen regional Civil Service Commissions. Lying about belonging to the CPUSA or a Communist "front," of which there were seventy-eight and growing on the Attorney General's List of Subversive Organizations (AGLOSO) carried a perjury penalty. But employees were also asked questions regarding their views on socialism, the Marshall Plan, the UN, race relations, government ownership of utilities, and religious education of their children; they were also asked whether they listened to the records of Paul Robeson or read certain authors, such as Howard Fast! Refusal to answer was often sufficient grounds for dismissal.[48]

The vast majority of government employees went through the screening without difficulty, but many thousands lost their jobs. Of these, several hundreds were fired, resigned in the face of charges, or were not hired on loyalty grounds; but people rejected as risks—alcoholics, homosexuals, and gamblers, for example—were also often unfairly tainted with suspicions of disloyalty.[49] Although only a relatively small minority of citizens were *directly* affected by legislation, congressional hearings, or blacklists, the boards and commissions did create a sense of fear and general distrust in many institutions and at many levels of American society and did serious damage to the quality of freedom in the United States. Put in place only weeks before the trial of Fast and the other JAFRC defendants, the new institutions reinforced an atmosphere of anti-Communist bias where it counted, in the media and in the jury box.

That Eugene Dennis, the general secretary of the CP, was convicted of contempt of Congress for failing to appear before that body in April 1947 while Fast's trial was in process contributed to the anti-Communist bias. And just as Fast's trial was coming to an end on June 27, 1947, ten employees of the State Department were fired as security risks under the new provision permitting the government to release employees without the usual right of appeal. On the same day, film producer and writer Carl Marzani, a close friend of the Fasts, was sentenced to one to three years in prison because he had hidden his Communist Party connections when applying for a government job. An ex-officer in the Office of Strategic Services (OSS—a forerunner of the CIA), which had collaborated with Communists in covert antifascist action during the war, Marzani had already left government service and the CP. He admitted lying, but said quite truthfully that his superiors had been well aware of his past.[50] That Marzani could hardly have posed a threat to American security did not stop the government from imprisoning him for perjury.

None of this helped the case for Fast and the other JAFRC defendants, but neither did their lawyer, O. John Rogge, who, instead of concentrating on the question of guilt or innocence in terms of the contempt charge, attacked HUAC as illegitimate, even fascist. Perhaps Rogge could not forget his role as a prosecutor at the Nuremburg Trials, but Fast and the other sixteen defendants were bewildered by Rogge's behavior. The jury, which was instructed by the judge to dismiss the conspiracy charge, which could have carried a sentence of five years, deliberated for all of forty-nine minutes before they brought back a verdict of guilty for all those charged with contempt of Congress.

Edward Barsky, as chair, was sentenced to a six-month jail term and a $500 fine; nine others including Fast got three-month terms and $500 fines. After Fast was sentenced, he like the others was released on a $1,000 bond.[51] The remaining defendants "purged" themselves of the contempt charge by answering "Yes, I would" to the question: "If you had the power, would you present these [JAFRC] books and records to the House Committee on Un-

American Activities?" The "honorable thing, as we understood it," Fast said later, "was not to purge yourself. . . . It was as simple as that." It was a "very peculiar point of honor, and you'd think," Fast said, "that in terms of simple sanity we would've *all* purged ourselves!"[52] Professor Lyman Bradley, who did not purge himself, was sentenced, like Fast, to three months, and he lost his job as chair of NYU's German Department. When in 1948 the Supreme Court refused to hear his appeal he was dismissed from his faculty position. He never got another teaching job.[53]

More than twenty years later, Fast said, "it's hard to reconstruct the emotional atmosphere at the time, where if you were to [purge yourself] could you live with yourself? You said, 'My God, I've backed out on these people,' and so forth and so on. Also [there was] the knowledge that, if a majority purged themselves" thereby making a "friendly" executive board decision, "the books would have to be turned over."[54]

In response to what he saw as the operation of a police state, Albert Maltz delivered an address in Los Angeles in July on "The Writer as the Conscience of the People." Maltz was furious. "Emerson, Thoreau, Longfellow . . . Their names stank in good society once!" he cried out. "We [too] are writers . . . we cherish the arts; we cherish our freedom. What shall we say then of this": Professor Bradley and nine others, doctors, lawyers, housewives, and trade-union leaders have "been declared guilty of contempt of Congress and that they are now under sentence to jail?"

"And what shall we say of the fact," Maltz asked only eighteen months after Fast had tried to eviscerate him for "political incorrectness," that Howard Fast is also "liable to . . . imprisonment?" Fast, Maltz claimed, "more than any other writer in the history of our nation, has sung a hymn to democracy in his novels. What shall we say when the prison gates close on him." Fast and the other ten men and women who refused "to turn the names of anti-fascists over to the mercies of those who would reduce America to one vast concentration camp," were guilty of no more than trying to "save human decency."[55]

In Maltz's statement before HUAC on October 28, 1947, he went even further. Americans, he said, are "groveling before men [who] now carry out activities in [the U.S.] like those carried out in Germany by Goebbels and Himmler."[56] It was remarks like these that were likely to alienate mainstream Americans, who knew that in Nazi Germany there were no hearings, no trials, no defense attorneys, no appeals.

A month before Maltz's testimony, *Clarkton,* the novel Fast was working on all through his legal ordeal, was published. Fast had had a falling out with Duell, Sloan, and Pearce over the failure of *The American* to sell well. The publishing firm, minus Fast's friend Sam Sloan, who had died in 1945, was unable to unload an optimistically large first edition of 100,000 copies. "I had . . . bitter words with them," Fast said, but in September 1947, "they [did] publish . . . *Clarkton.*"[57] Fast's first truly proletarian novel, *Clarkton* centers on a strike at a New England factory, the union that called it, and the Communists who tried to turn the walkout into a mass event that would "make the workers aware of themselves."[58]

But a "true novel," to use Fast's own term, it wasn't. In 1967, Fast himself called *Clarkton* "terribly tendentious . . . nothing I'm satisfied with today."[59] Not counting the two novels Fast had written when he was nineteen, *Clarkton* was his first genuine failure. Not only didn't the critics like it, libraries and the reading public virtually ignored it. The *New York Times* titled its review, "Mr. Fast's Defense of the Communists," and called *Clarkton* a "tract" whose featured Marxists are portrayed as "demigods."[60]

This criticism was minor compared to the beating Fast took from leftists. His French friend and comrade, Renaud de Jouvenal, in a letter to Howard, asked, "Don't you think [*Clarkton*] stops a little short?" Worse than leaving the reader without "an ending," Jouvenal wrote, was that Fast portrayed his capitalist boss George Lowell as a human being, possessed of feelings, a sense of fairness, and a capacity for "making love, and how!" The boss is just too human, the Frenchman complained, and as important, "he's not . . . anti-communist [enough]." We in France, Jouvenal said, *"do not . . . want to see that human side in our worst enemies. . . .* That human side belongs to our 19th century literature, to liberalism, not to our present struggle which is very rough and pre-revolutionary. Our capitalists (and yours) are cold blooded fighters not afraid [of] murder nor war." And then following the common Communist practice of labeling all who disagreed with them as fascists, Jouvenal said that the capitalists "will be worse than Nazis." They *"should not be shown otherwise* in this Kerensky [pre-Bolshevik] period of our history."[61]

Fast responded about three weeks later. "You must remember that [*Clarkton*] is one of the only two novels that exist in all our literature that portrays Communists, or the Communist Party." Fast neither names the other novel nor explains what he means by "our literature." But he is no doubt referring to American literature rather than the writing of the international left, for surely, even if he did not know the novels of Ignazio Silone, he knew Andre Malraux's *Man's Fate* (1934); Arthur Koestler's *Darkness at Noon* (1940), an enormous best seller about the fatal self-deceptions of Communist dialectics, which never went out of print; and George Orwell's chartbuster *Animal Farm* (1945).[62] "You must realize," he told Jouvenal, "that the . . . philosophical concept of the book is to give the reader the understanding that, notwithstanding whether the boss is a good or a bad man, a weak or a strong man, he must play a reactionary and a terrible role, since he belongs to something that is dying and since he opposes something that is growing and coming into new life."[63]

Clarkton features working-class figures from several ethnic groups: blacks, Italians, Irishmen, Greeks, and Hungarians. It also has an important role for a Jewish Communist lawyer, Max Goldstein, the son of Lithuanian immigrants who lives by the Torah teaching *Tzedek, tzedek tirdof* (Justice, justice, shall ye pursue). But when it seems that a confrontation between the union and the management's hirelings might turn violent, Max is fearful. He girds his loins, however, by remembering that "it was my own ancestor Bar Kochba, who said, 'Gather around me the young men, those of bold mien and brave countenance and I will forge them into a mighty sword for freedom.'"[64]

Of course, Max, *Clarkton*'s lone Jew, is one of only two people killed in the ensuing melee, the eternal victim sacrificed like the figure of the "gentle Jew nailed unto a cross and dying" alluded to in Fast's *Citizen Tom Paine*. Once again Fast was attempting to suggest a synthesis between prophetic Judaism and Christianity, and a fit between Marxism and religious sensibility, as in several of his other novels and stories. He was also in this way revealing again an ambivalence about whether man's suffering is best relieved by love or violence.[65]

Fast also has trouble recognizing the significance of some of his own invented dialogue. Bill Noska, a non-Communist union leader, says to Tim Sawyer, a section organizer for the CPUSA, "If I could figure out what the hell you guys are after, I could figure out a way to handle you. But I never seen a Communist who could give me a straightforward answer." Sawyer, with no hesitation, says, "We're after the same things you are." But Noska scoffs, "I want eighteen and a half cents and hour and not pipe dreams. Also, I think we can get it without any strategy from Moscow." This critical exchange, pregnant with meaning, occurs fairly early in the novel, but Fast fails to deal with any of its powerful implications, especially those having to do with the Communist Party's misreading of the goals of the American working class or of labor's general desire to dissociate itself from a socialism tied to the Soviet Union.[66]

Although Fast was completely defensive about *Clarkton* when it was first published, fifty years later he told his editorial assistant and future wife, Mimi O'Connor, "not to read *Clarkton*, because I was too much under the influence of the Party at the time, and it isn't worth the paper it's written on."[67] Fast thought in 1947 that *Clarkton* "was the end of the gravy train . . . the death knell." But still needing to see himself as a victim of the Cold War rather than as a writer who wrote a flop, he insisted that *Clarkton* failed because he was "making a lot of public statements . . . after the war. I shot my mouth off a great deal against the Marshall Plan, [and the North Atlantic Treaty], and . . . was tagged a Red." Even "if *Clarkton* had been a better book," Fast believed, "it would not have sold."[68] As with *The American*, however, *Clarkton*'s sales were hurt very little by Fast's pro-Communism. *Clarkton* was simply a bad book, as Fast readily admitted some dozen years after he left the Party.

This was not the way *Clarkton* was seen in the USSR, however. How- ard Fast had been praised by Soviet critics in the mid-forties, but had not yet been translated until he came out with *Clarkton* in 1947. Recognized in America as flimsy and propagandistic, *Clarkton* in the USSR seemed to herald Fast as "the great Soviet hope" for American literature. Pleased with an American novelist who showed "Communists in action," the foremost Soviet critics began to favor Fast over Albert Maltz, who by 1954 had had 750,000 copies of his various works of fiction published in Russia. Maltz, despite his impeccable Communist credentials, was seen to have had made "ideological errors" and had failed to produce "Communist heroes" in his novels. Fast, the Soviets felt, showed the activity of Communists favorably within the context of a broader workers' movement. Under the stimulus of official praise and massive government printing, Fast's reputation in the Soviet Union expanded rapidly.[69]

In America, the negative responses to *Clarkton* only added to Fast's tribu- lations, including a serious bit of legal trouble that had been brewing for about a year. Not long after the publication of *The American* in July 1946, Harry Elmer Barnard had written to Fast complaining of Howard's failure to mention, as an important source of material for his biographical novel on Altgeld, Barnard's own nonfiction biography, *Eagle Forgotten* (1938). Fast had failed to acknowledge receiving a complimentary copy of the biography even after Barnard wrote reminding him of the gift. He also failed to respond to Barnard's letters of complaint in 1946 and 1947, and ignored a subsequent letter from Barnard's lawyer. The author of *Eagle Forgotten* had no choice but to file a federal court suit in New York, charging infringement of literary property. He specifically accused Fast of following *Eagle Forgotten* in organization and interpretation and of having "largely copied" from his book, "lifting" pertinent paragraphs and phrases. Fast was able to negotiate a settlement in January 1948 that allowed him to deny plagiarism in return for paying Barnard $7,500, with a promise from Fast's publisher to print and distribute a minimum of 2,000 copies of *Eagle Forgotten*.[70]

Several book reviewers had earlier noted similarities between the two works, and the critic for the *New York World Telegram* had gone so far as to conclude that "in all justice," Fast "should have given Harry Barnard's big biography a credit line."[71] This omission on Fast's part appears consistent with an unseemly practice of his. Writers of historical novels must, of course, rely on the research and published works of historians, even as they insert their own characters and apply their own creative imaginations. A problem arises, however, when a novelist fails to acknowledge sources on which he or she has in large part depended.

It is clear from reading his 1941 fictionalized biography of Haym Solomon, for example, that Fast had cribbed heavily with no attribution from Charles Edward Russell's inaccurate and myth-laden *Haym Solomon and the Revolution*, published in 1930. Perhaps the impecunious Fast was overly eager to fulfill his contractual commitment to write the Solomon book or was overly excited to share with young adult readers the real accomplishments of a fellow Jew. Either way, with his carelessly inexact portrayal, Fast broke his own promise of performing "a one-man reformation of the historical novel" in two ways: by not adhering as closely to the facts as art would allow, and more importantly, by violating his professional obligation to assign credit.[72]

From 1948 forward, Fast, less than credibly, maintained his innocence of deliberate or accidental infringement of Barnard's rights, but said he had neither the funds to fight nor the desire or energy for another trial.[73] Howard Fast would have to summon reserves of all of the above for what was yet to come.

5

Banned, Barred, and Besieged

*I*n the year between Howard Fast's citation for contempt of Congress in April 1946 and his conviction in June 1947, he had faced not only a plagiarism suit, but incessant harassment by the FBI and the beginning of a series of attempts to ban his books. And by late 1947, after the publication of *Clarkton,* he would be embattled with college administrators who tried to keep him from speaking on their campuses.

J. Edgar Hoover never ordered the tap removed from Fast's phone. It made little difference in any case, Fast said. After all, "what could we have talked about" that would interest the FBI. "We never did anything illegal, we never *considered* [doing] anything illegal." To give a sense of it all, Fast told a story about two men, one a "spy" and the other a self-identified "Party member," who had come to his home to sell him a map of "the newest battleship in the American fleet." This foolishness, Fast insisted, was an attempt by the FBI to entrap him. "I immediately called the cops," Fast said, but by the time they came, "both men were gone." But at the World Peace Conference in Paris in 1949, Fast "saw the same FBI agent who brought the spy to me." Howard had real enemies, of course, but with more than a touch of paranoia he added, "I knew his mission was to get me—to kill me, and I let everyone know. I accused him to his face."[1]

Fast's daughter, Rachel, a clinical psychologist, and his son, Jonathan, a teacher of psychiatric social work, believe that their father "was loony" and that the attempted assassination story "is a . . . great example of PARANOIAC grandiosity." But, Rachel said, the FBI did consistently "hound" the family. Federal agents followed her parents everywhere. By the time she was six or seven she "was aware of the constant surveillance," and was "enough the eavesdropper to hear conversation about it." One night, "when my parents returned home from an evening out," Rachel remembered, "Father sensing something was amiss, stepped onto the coffee table in the living room, reached over his head, searched inside the top of the chandelier. He stepped down, a 'bug' in hand." The babysitter had been working as an FBI informant. "I can [still] see . . . the look of astonishment on [my father's] face," Rachel said. It was unforgettable, "the three of us staring at each other in mute horror."[2]

The invasion of privacy was constant. In addition to his being "tailed," as he put it, and bugged, Fast's mail was monitored and read. Everything he wrote was scrutinized. Even his essays on "peace and democracy" for foreign periodicals were translated, so that they could be compared with the originals. "Think of the endless thousands of dollars" wasted, Fast said, and "they did this for years and years."[3]

Perhaps as much taxpayer money was spent having agents browse through "leftist" bookstores. In 1947, a typical report by the FBI Boston office noted that pamphlets and books published by the CPUSA and other radical presses were sold at the Progressive Bookshop on Beach Street, and that some, including Howard Fast's *The American,* warranted a security check.[4] A note in the FBI file on Alfred Knopf Inc. brought the bureau's attention to Communist writers included in a children's book entitled *Yankee Doodle Stories of the Brave and the Free.* The source was *Counterattack,* a four-page, fiercely anti-Communist magazine founded in 1947 and published by American Business Consultants (ABC) in New York. ABC also published *Red Channels,* which "exposed" alleged Communists in radio and television. The citation in the FBI file from *Counterattack* names Howard Fast as one of the authors in *Yankee Doodle,* and goes on to ask, "Would you want your children . . . or any children . . . to learn about American history from a Communist Party member whose writing is featured in a recent issue of the Moscow-published *New Times*?"[5]

Organizations in the private sector anxious to cleanse the culture of Communists not only were allowed to operate freely, but were encouraged by the government. ABC, for example, was helped by the FBI, and the American Legion had ties to the Pentagon. Not bound by the limitations of the Constitution, these groups maintained an unofficial "blacklist" in an attempt to punish citizens who were thought to have affiliation with the CPUSA. Names of suspected Communists and fellow travelers were mailed out regularly to subscribers, many of whom were corporations with hundreds of employees. Appearing on the blacklist could have disastrous consequences, most frequently the loss of a job; and those named had limited recourse, even less than those on government lists. One could write to the American Legion, for example, professing "innocence," and appear before the Legion's anti-subversion office in D.C. But no lawyer could be brought along, nor were there any rules of procedure or recourse to appeal.[6]

Because the free-lance anti-Communist vigilantes, like other Cold Warriors, sometimes linked New Deal liberals to Communist fronts, the blacklist occasionally extended beyond those with connections, direct or indirect, past or present, to the Communist Party. But most participants in the New Deal were not, after all, Communists or naïve victims or "dupes" of the CPUSA. The great majority were idealistic radicals, independents, and socialists.[7] Many Cold Warriors, however, like many Communists, lived in a world of fantasy and paranoia, believing that direct and strong ties linked the Comintern, the American Communist Party, Communist fronts, and New Deal liberals to one another, and that these connections extended even to nonaffiliated individuals involved in social justice activism. Progressive political actors were often as vulnerable as Communists to harassment and worse.[8]

Government agencies such as loyalty boards, civil service commissions, and the FBI, and congressional committees such as the Internal Security Subcommittee, and especially HUAC, felt free to insinuate themselves into areas where they did not belong, thereby seriously corrupting the arena of open expression that the First Amendment was designed to protect. That the efforts of these agencies and boards were often disorganized and incompetent and that some citizens were resilient and lucky enough to defend themselves successfully may have indicated that an authentic totalitarian impulse could not readily root itself in American soil. But real damage was done.[9]

Jobs were lost, careers destroyed, friendships and marriages broken, and the germ of suspicion, mistrust, and betrayal was injected into the community of the left. Premature strokes and heart attacks were not that unusual among blacklistees, nor was heavy drinking as a form of "suicide on the installment plan."[10] Little has blackened the reputation of Congress more than the activities of HUAC. Even the historian Arthur Schlesinger Jr., an anti-Communist liberal, who had equated American Communists with the KKK and the Mafia, eventually came to think that the idea that a handful of Stalinists and fellow travelers in the film industry were a grave threat to the republic rated "high in the annals of Congressional asininity." Given his reputation as a civil libertarian, Schlesinger logically ought to have been intensely engaged in the fight to protect the free speech of Communists in the 1950s. Yet he approved of the Attorney General's List, and did not refrain from praising some of those who named names before the congressional committees he later thought fatuous. After fifty years of reflection, Schlesinger at last came to say, quite rightly, that the inquiries of the Internal Security Subcommittee and of HUAC were amongst "the most indefensible, scandalous and cruel episodes in the entire history of legislative investigations."[11] The diminishment of privacy, personal security, moral integrity, liberty, and justice in the United States, by government intrusion and persecution, should not be minimized. And in the private sector results were dishearteningly similar.

Fast, of course, had no job to lose by his being blacklisted, but being targeted in such fashion, could, and sometimes did, make acquiring a publisher, gaining readers, and selling his books more difficult. In February 1947, the Board of Superintendents of the New York City School System decided that *Citizen Tom Paine* was undesirable as reading matter for children and recommended that the Board of Education have it removed from the New York City school libraries. The book, a spokesman for the board said, contained passages "too purple to be read by children," and stressed that the recommended ban had no relation to Fast's reputed connection to the CPUSA, or to Thomas Paine's controversial religious views. Fast complained that the action was "unspeakable" and that it constituted "a form of book burning." The passage thought most offensive, no more than a half-page long, was Fast's description, through Paine's eyes, of the method by which a slave auctioneer generated interest in the sale of a young black female. He emphasized the girl's virginity, and likened her breasts to "two Concord grapes, her behind [to] the succulent hams of a suckling pig." The bidding began at fifty pounds, but when the price reached eighty, the auctioneer tore the blanket off the "frightened and shivering" slave, revealing her full nakedness. It did not matter to the board censors that the passage was carefully contextualized and was important to the strengthening of Paine's antislavery views; it was sexually explicit and inappropriate for secondary school students. By 1947, however, 3 to 4 million people had read *Citizen Tom Paine,* Fast said, with no issue of inappropriate language ever having been brought to anyone's attention.[12]

Whether he was a Communist or not, Fast said, was his own business. In response a school spokesperson repeated the point that the ban had nothing to do with the Communist Party, but only with the book's "vulgar passages."[13] Benjamin Davis, CP member of the city council, sent a telegram to the president of the Board of Education, calling the proposed ban a "witch-burning" and a "disgrace to the city," a "cheap insult to one of America's greatest novelists." Nevertheless, on February 19 the Board of Education voted to support the ban; and despite their initial complaint about vulgarity, did so by a vote of 6 to 1 on the grounds that it was written by "a public representative of Communist totalitarianism" *and* that it contained graphic expressions that were "lewd and lascivious."[14] The lone dissenter, unlike the other board members, had read the book in its entirety. The so-called objectionable passages, he said, are "quickly forgotten in the overall portrait of Paine as a tireless defender of the dignity of man."[15]

Despite sales of millions of copies of *Citizen Tom Paine* and the printing of a government-sponsored overseas edition for the armed forces, the ban stood. Even Rupert Hughes, president of the American Writers Association (AWA), supported it[16] More curious still was a letter responding to Louis Untermeyer's criticism of the Board of Education's censorship of *Citizen Tom Paine* from the executive secretary of the AWA, on whose stationery appeared the names of Norman Thomas, Zora Neale Hurston, John Dos Passos, Margaret Mitchell, Fulton Lewis Jr., Ayn Rand, Dorothy Thompson, and other such worthies. Nowhere in the letter from the author's group was there any substantive or comprehensible discussion of censorship. Instead there was this complaint: "The sale of Fast's book has been built up by a powerful political apparat [*sic*] using all the techniques which could be used to slant the sale of books in his favor." Not only is there no evidence at all to support this accusation, but one wonders, even if it were true, what logic allowed the association to say "this is unfair competition with other, and perhaps better writers on Tom Paine." And more nonsensical still, "It certainly is an interference with free choice by the reader in accordance with his private preferences. Any interference with the free movement of books to readers is in itself a form of censorship."[17] Are we to understand from the virulently anti-Communist, and presumably pro-capitalist, American Writers Association that a government agency's banning Fast's book is not censorship, but that aggressive marketing is?

There was also important and outspoken opposition to the proposed ban, mostly from journals closely associated with the Communist Party. *New Masses* and *Mainstream,* for example, sponsored a protest meeting in October, at the Manhattan Center. Speaker after speaker repeated Albert Maltz's claim that fascism, witch hunts, book burnings and thought control were "being put to work in America NOW," even though, despite Fast's reported claim that "thousands" of his volumes had been set afire "at some place in New York," no books were actually burned.[18]

Representatives of eleven publishing companies also opposed the Board of Education's interdiction. They signed a resolution protesting book banning as a violation of free press and free speech, while at the same time the left-led Teachers Union assailed the proposed removal of *Citizen Tom Paine* from school libraries. The Board of Education, nonetheless, pulled copies of Fast's novel from the shelves. It was then faced with the problem of what to do with them! Outworn textbooks were ordinarily either sold as wastepaper or burned. But for a banned novel there was no precedent. To avoid the charge of book-burning, school officials placed copies of *Citizen Tom Paine* in libraries used solely by teachers.[19]

There were other, more healthy reactions to the ban, which was extended in 1949, when the FBI, going beyond the Board of Education in New York City, ordered *Citizen Tom Paine* removed from all school and public libraries in dozens of American cities. Sales of the book skyrocketed, as did Fast's royalties. Lewis Gannett, who wrote the daily book review column for the *New York Herald Tribune* in the 1940s, talked with a group of high-school newspaper editors and discovered that one after another, they had reviewed and promoted *Citizen Tom Paine* in their papers precisely because they had read about the censorship.[20]

Private publishers, however, began to excise Fast's materials from school textbooks, and they reissued anthologies that were conspicuously free of his stories and the excerpts from his novels that had been included in editions published only two or three years before.[21] Fast was no longer heard on the radio, nor was he welcome any longer in the glossy magazines. In the political and social climate of the late 1940s and early '50s, Fast's two legal setbacks, the indictment for contempt, and the plagiarism suit over *The American,* followed by the banning of *Citizen Tom Paine,* all but destroyed Fast's appeal for publishers trying to stay profitable and steer clear of the FBI. Even Columbia Pictures, which had purchased the rights to *The Last Frontier* for $35,000 in 1947, decided they couldn't risk doing a film based on a book by Howard Fast, and they dropped the project.[22]

Radical writers could still find major publishing houses for their works in the mid-to-late forties. Communist Barbara Giles, for example, wrote about the decaying middle class and the rising power of workers in *The Gentle Bush* (1947) for Harcourt Brace; Alexander Saxton produced a compelling and sympathetic portrait of the lives of American Communist activists for Appleton-Century Crofts in *The Great Midland* (1948), which Howard Fast thought "the finest and most important novel done by any American writer in the past several years";[23] Progressive African American writers Chester Himes, Ann Petry, and Willard Motley also wrote books with pronounced left-wing themes for major houses, and the Jewish American poet and activist Muriel Rukeyser, who was also pro-Communist, continued to publish under her own name in the 1930s, '40s and '50s.[24]

Himes, however, though attracted to the Communist movement in the late 1930s and 1940s, was disaffected by the time he wrote *The Lonely Crusade* (1947), which while left-wing in its sympathies, was strongly anti-Communist. Moreover, neither Petry nor Motley was a Communist. Rukeyser, too, was adamant about her independence from the CPUSA. She told fellow poet Louis Untermeyer that while she was a committed antifascist, "I do not belong to any party or organizations." Most important, none of these writers were as well known as Howard Fast, who had become "more or less the public face of the Communist Party in the United States."[25]

In the midst of his besiegement, however, and very soon after his having been sentenced to three months' imprisonment, Fast could take some solace in finding that, if not to publishers, he was still attractive to women. In July 1947 during a week-long workshop in creative writing at Indiana University, Fast, living alone in the Union Building on campus, away from Bette and three-year-old Rachel, seems to have had a fling with someone in his class, or with one of the young women who came to hear his all-campus lecture on "Marxism and Literature." This adventure was likely the basis for his short story "The Gentle Virtue," originally published in *Departure and Other Stories* in 1949. Sarah, twenty-nine, the key female protagonist of the story, is described as beautiful and long-limbed six times within the course of fourteen pages. The visiting professor is immediately struck by her loveliness, intelligence, and animation, but it is she, of course, who comes on strong. In the story, for reasons best left untold here, but which work as literature, there is no consummation of the mutual desire. One would have to be naïve, however, to think, that Fast, given his history and his confessed voraciousness for women, did not bring home with him the memory of a sexual liaison along with his two-hundred-dollar honorarium.[26]

Fast's general situation continued to deteriorate, however, and it was not improved when in December 1947 a series of newspaper articles in many of the major dailies treated him primarily as a controversial political figure and only incidentally as a writer. Fast got as much media attention as he did because he was the victim of more academic boycotting than any other figure of the time. And with only a rare breakthrough, Fast continued to be beleaguered by these campus bans right through 1953.[27]

In December 1947 the *New York Times* reported that Columbia had barred Howard Fast from speaking at a meeting of the university chapter of the Progressive Citizens of America. The provost explained that barring Fast was in compliance with Columbia's policy of prohibiting anyone "under jail sentence" to speak on campus. The editors of the Columbia *Daily Spectator,* the college newspaper, accused the university of caving in to threats made by HUAC to launch investigations of higher education. Controversy intensified when a few days later faculty committees at both CCNY and Brooklyn College voted to bar Fast from addressing previously scheduled meetings. On that same day, however, student chapters of liberal organizations, including the American Veterans Committee and Americans for Democratic Action, called for administrators at Columbia to repeal the ban on Fast.[28]

As the arguments began to intensify and to involve an increasing number of campuses, as well as the American Civil Liberties Union and the Board of Education, one thing became clear: colleges had no consistent policies for dealing with proposed campus speakers who were alleged subversives, indicted or not. A CCNY student-faculty committee finally voted to uphold the barring of Fast from campus, but suggested that in the future, student clubs be allowed to invite whomever they wanted to hear as long as

the meetings were not open to the public. This bizarre compromise, typical of resolutions issued at other institutions, seemed to recognize the right
of the people, but apparently not too many people, to hear controversial
speakers.

The day after Brooklyn College (BC) banned Fast, he addressed a rally
near the adjacent Midwood High School. Three hundred CCNY students
joined with students from BC to protest the bans. The initial response of
City College was to reopen the campus to Fast; but a last-minute order by
the dean reversed that decision, which Fast called a "craven submission to
the most ignorant and miserable elements in American life." But then, in a
move that surprised both supporters and opponents of Fast, Thomas Pollock, the dean of Washington Square College of Arts and Science, granted
Fast permission to address the Young Progressive Citizens of America at
NYU's School of Education. Pollock deplored the Communists who attacked
democracy while seeking the shelter of democratic institutions such as the
American tradition of free speech. But, he said, NYU faculty member Lyman
Bradley, convicted like Fast of contempt of Congress, was being afforded full
academic freedom on campus while appealing his case. Therefore, Pollock
would give his approval "for this one meeting."[29]

Fast was disappointed to learn that several campus organizations had
actually denounced the dean for granting even this restricted opportunity.
Finally on a campus, however, he praised Pollock for having "struck a blow
for Academic Freedom"; and he spoke at two meetings, the first jammed
with a total of eight hundred students, the second with the overflow of five
hundred more. Like the editors of Columbia's *Daily Spectator,* Fast charged
that the administrations of Columbia, CCNY, and Brooklyn and Hunter Colleges, both of which followed CCNY's lead, were fearful of HUAC's threat "to
carry on an extensive investigation of higher education," and had given "an
endorsement" to "the black ignorance of fascism."[30]

In the midst of all the controversy, Fast joined Congressman Vito Marcantonio, singer Paul Robeson, and legislative director of the Communist Party
Arno Johnson, at a December 1947 rally in the St. Nicholas Arena in New
York City, where they endorsed Henry Wallace as an independent candidate
for president of the United States. In the early months of 1948, in addition to
campaigning for Wallace, Fast spoke several dozen times to left-wing and labor union groups.[31] In March, Fast began to think that all this public activity,
on top of his indictment for contempt, was holding up a decision from Sidney

Buchman, a screenwriter at Columbia Pictures who had been considering *Citizen Tom Paine* and *Freedom Road* as material for films.

Buchman had written the Frank Capra–directed film, *Mr. Smith Goes to Washington* in 1939 while he was a member of the CPUSA. The movie was widely attacked in D.C. and in the press as pro-Communist. Buchman, investigated in 1951, admitted his past membership in the Party, but he refused to name names, and was, like Fast, cited for contempt. Still, he had had Fast's books since late 1945, the year Buchman had resigned from the Party, and Howard was understandably suspicious.

In a hostile letter, he accused Buchman of bailing out on his books for political reasons. Buchman pleaded financial exigencies. "Columbia has been hysterical about box office and the loss of foreign markets," he wrote; and "I can assure you that no part of the resistance" to your books "ever related to the subject matter." Buchman told Fast, "You are a fine . . . man, whose work I respect, and whose present personal trials I am acutely aware of. I would not add to that burden."[32]

Fast replied saying, "Your letter made me deeply ashamed . . . and made me promise myself *once again* that I would be . . . less quick about jumping to conclusions. Please forgive what was rather hasty and thoughtless anger, and be assured I understand quite well [your] predicament."[33] Still, political content may have had something to do with the delay in dealing with Fast's best-selling but controversial novels. After all, RKO, in the same year 1948, produced, from "Rachel," Fast's apolitical little love story, the film *Rachel and the Stranger*.[34]

Whatever the case, the movie became one of the studio's biggest hits that year, earning nearly $400,000, a piece of which was pocketed by Fast. This money, along with the many royalty checks he received regularly, especially for the millions of copies of *Citizen Tom Paine* and *Freedom Road* being reprinted and sold all over the world, moved Fast closer to his continuing goal of becoming wealthy. When Joe North, a leading member of the CP, discovered that the Fasts had savings in the many thousands of dollars, he persuaded them to invest $10,000 in IBM and 3M stock. Fast, however, later claimed that he felt uncomfortable as a Communist, owning shares in capitalism. This, despite the fact that a significant number of his comrades, including many wealthy people like North, knew how to play a system that they alone, they claimed, *really* understood. In 1990, Fast said that if he had held his stock certificates, they would have been worth $250,000.[35] No

doubt. But by then, for Fast, as we shall see, a quarter of a million dollars
would have amounted to only a fraction of his total wealth.

In the meantime, in April 1948, Fast, though still under indictment, was
granted the "privilege" of speaking at Columbia, where he addressed more
than a thousand members of the Students for Wallace chapter. Fast took the
opportunity to denounce President Truman, Secretary of Defense James
Forrestal, and Secretary of State John Foster Dulles as "obscene hideous
people who can sign a death warrant that will murder 500,000 people without a thought. . . . [They] are no longer of the same species as you and I."
Fast's remarks not only put a set of human beings outside the "universe of
moral obligation," his words were in themselves a kind of unwitting warrant
for murder. That Fast may have been genuine in his fear that America was
"turning into a new anti-democratic imperialistic nation that in time will rule
the world" does not diminish the sorry quality of his rhetoric.[36]

During this period, Fast also wrote many articles for Communist periodicals and taught at the Jefferson School of Social Science (JSSS), a
Communist-run center of adult education in New York City. The JSSS at
6th Avenue and 16th Street flourished during the 1940s and early '50s, offering a wide array of courses, lectures, and cultural programs mostly on
Marxism, trade union issues, and related topics, along with classes about
practical applications to the day's political struggles. Art, music, dance,
and literature were also featured, and in the Division of Jewish Studies,
Yiddish language, literature, and culture were taught. Each semester some
nine thousand students, at five or six dollars a class, were enrolled in hundreds of courses. The faculty, Communists all, and mostly Jewish, included
Philip Foner, Herbert Aptheker, Dashiell Hammett, Eleanor Flexner, the
preeminent feminist historian of her generation, and Marc Blitzstein, the
radical composer.[37] Howard Fast offered courses and lectures with such
themes as "Fascism and the Novel," "Terror against the Intellectual." and
"Literature and Reality."

It may have been at the JSSS that Howard first laid eyes on Isabel Johnson,
who taught a course for women on "Beauty and Appearance." Much later
the wife of Alger Hiss, Johnson was consistently described as a "tall, good-
looking blonde." Her class might seem inappropriate at a Marxist institution,
but Johnson, the beauty editor of the leading fashion magazine, *Glamour,*
and a model in Paris and New York, who had been photographed by Edward Steichen and Alfred Stieglitz among others, focused primarily on how

women could improve their chances of getting jobs in bourgeois society. It is also possible that Fast and Johnson first met as colleagues on the National Council of the Arts, Sciences and Professions. Either way, sometime in 1948 they found themselves in bed together, initiating an affair that lasted on and off through the 1950s.[38]

Fast lauded JSSS as a place where "academic freedom still burns bright and clear," and where he could say what he pleased without fear or restraint.[39] He knew that student applicants were screened, but was likely unaware that more often than not, agents of the FBI were able to enroll; and information about JSSS gathered by the Bureau was passed on to friendly journalists. *The Saturday Evening Post* in 1949, for example, carried a piece entitled "Here's Where Our Commies Are Trained." The writer admitted that while the school adhered fairly strictly to the line out of Moscow, students appeared to be independent and willing to challenge teachers. But he misleadingly reduced the JSSS, which motivated individuals to involve themselves in the social struggles of the day, to a place where "discontented youth get transformed into 'tireless mischief-makers.'"[40]

IT CAN'T HAPPEN HERE

In May 1948, Fast again found himself at the center of media attention. The *New York Daily News* carried an editorial at the beginning of the month entitled "32 'Artists' Vs. Uncle Sam." Readers were informed that the *Moscow Literary Gazette* in its May 2 issue printed "a curious document," an open letter from twelve leading Russian artists and writers "demanding to know whether U.S. intellectuals favored America or Russia in the 'cold war.'" According to the *News*, more than two dozen artists and intellectuals, at least twenty of whom were Jewish, including V. J. Jerome, a major cultural spokesman for the CPUSA; Herbert Aptheker, historian; Raphael Soyer, artist; and Nelson Algren and Howard Fast, novelists, "favored the Russians in the 'cold war,' and accused U.S. capitalists of killing off our intelligentsia's freedom of speech." Where, the *News* asked, "do you suppose" Howard Fast and the others "would line up in case the 'cold war' turned hot?"

The *News* editorial was not only snarky but terribly misleading. The *New York Times*, however, had it about right: the writers and artists did not choose the "Soviet side"; they were in a struggle to prevent their own country from going fascist.[41] On the other hand, the response of the American artists, writers, and intellectuals, which was printed in full in the *Daily Worker* on May 10, was fuzzy. The signatories strangely attested to somehow knowing "how differently artists are looked upon" in the USSR, which "provides them the means to carry out their social responsibility" instead of using them as pawns in a capitalist game, as in the United States.[42]

The letter reads, on the whole, not as if the American intellectuals were taking sides in any war, whatever its temperature, but as if they favored "Communism" partly because they thought that in such a system they would not have to compete in the marketplace. In this perception they were correct. They would have had to compete for the favor of the regime. Book publishing in the USSR was completely controlled by government agencies and looked upon as part of "national security."

And after WWII, the Soviet government as part of its "cultural rebuilding" began to publish hundreds of millions of books in Russian, and many in foreign languages as well. Because of Cold War strategy major novelists such as Richard Wright, Dos Passos, Hemingway, Faulkner, and Steinbeck were prohibited, as were most upcoming American writers of the postwar years, including Bellow, Salinger, Mailer, and Styron, all of whom were seen as politically incorrect. Howard Fast, however, after 1947, became the "fair-haired boy" of the USSR, which promoted his fame through the accolades of cultural bureaucrats and huge printings of his books by the government. And from 1948 to 1956, official pageants made from Fast's historical novels (*The Last Frontier* was a favorite), stories, poems, and plays brought him to the attention of virtually every adult throughout the Soviet Union as well as in several satellite countries. In East Germany, Fast's framed portrait, along with Paul Robeson's, was hung in almost every bookshop and in many offices, the only two Americans so honored.[43]

As the media continued to pay close attention to Fast's cozy association with the Soviet Union and his profound connections to the American Communist Party, the writer's fear of imprisonment and separation from his family increased, and his appeals for support from friends grew more desperate. His cause was championed by radicals at home from as early as the fall of 1947. William Gropper, for example, the extraordinary social-realist artist and staff cartoonist for the Communist *Freiheit,* agreed with Fast that the "reactionaries have gone beyond the book-burning stage. . . . They are imprisoning and attempting to destroy . . . creative people" like those who write books. Progressives need to unite on an international basis, he said, "to put an end to this witch-hunt and persecution of anti-fascists."[44]

Fast followed suit with letters abroad filled with similar hyperbole. To Gwyn Thomas, the leftist Welsh novelist, with whom Fast corresponded for more than twenty years, he wrote, "we have already begun our own brand of fascism which, [although] cloaked in The Star Spangled Banner is as frightening as Adolf Hitler ever cooked up. . . . Secret arrests are a daily occurrence." Secret arrests? Fast, like Gropper, never "named names" in his letters of appeal other than those of his JAFRC colleagues and the Hollywood Ten, none of whom from either group was yet imprisoned. A month later, still consciously following the Party line and deliberately disseminating misinformation, he told Gwyn Thomas that "storm troopers" were being organized in "a hundred cities," and that "there is no such thing . . . in America . . . today as a free trial by jury."[45]

Fast was a master at exaggeration, but he knew that even with his inflated "facts," he could not get much mileage out of Gwyn Thomas, who was committed enough, but was hardly well known or well placed enough to rally the European left. For significant impact, Fast counted on the French intellectuals, who were as devoted to Stalin's "experiment" as he was. He reminded Renaud de Jouvenal that he and his JAFRC colleagues were going to prison, but so was "John Howard Lawson, [the] anti-fascist writer of great talent . . . with a long history of courageous struggle . . . and along with him, Dalton Trumbo, a brilliant screen writer. . . . We are being punished for the crime of anti-fascism."[46]

The United States, Fast told Jouvenal, "has turned itself" into a powerhouse of "such concentrated propaganda" as never before seen in any nation, and this had produced "a cold terror . . . in intellectual circles."[47] His exaggerations aside, Fast was right in saying that in American political and cultural circles, fear of being tarred with the brush of Communism was palpable. This "terror," Fast said, must be seen in the context of "the Mundt Bill which has just passed our House of Representatives." The Smith-Mundt Act, engineered by Republican representatives Richard Nixon (Calif.) and Karl Mundt (S.D.), and passed by the House on May 21, 1948, by a vote of 319 to 58, required that members of the Communist Party of the United States register with the attorney general. In addition, federal employees were prohibited from participating in the CPUSA and could not "knowingly hire" any Communist Party members. Finally, the bill denied passports to Party

members. As there was no benefit to registering with the government, many
Communists remained "underground" or anonymous.

The Mundt bill, Fast wrote, "is an open, unashamed and brazen law for
a fascist America. It goes much further than . . . Hitler or Mussolini dared
to go. It makes the act of *thinking* any sort of dangerous thought punishable
by 10 years imprisonment and $10,000 fine, and loss of citizenship."[48] There
was nothing in the Mundt bill in any of its versions about "thinking" or loss
of citizenship; yet Fast's saying that the Mundt bill goes further than Hitler
ever dared to did not decrease his credibility with his European friends, even
those who had seen the Nazis up close. Communist intellectuals, especially
in France, were easily reinforced in an anti-Americanism that was rooted in
resentment of a United States emergent after WWII as a successful democratic capitalist world power.

The National Committee to Defeat the Mundt Bill, of which Fast was a
leading member, also argued that if the bill were put into effect, it would create legal fascism and pave the way for the restriction of civil liberties of *any*
group the government considered a threat. The legislation, however, in no
way implied an attack on any group other than Communists. They were the
perceived enemy. Without the Communists there would have been no bill.
Nevertheless, Fast was on the mark about how bad a moment this was for civil
liberties in America. Mundt, arguing in support of the Subversive Activities
Control Bill, is quoted as saying, with no substantiation whatsoever, that
"communists in this country are guilty of sabotage, propaganda against the
interests of the United States in time of war, physical abuse during elections
(and murder) plus hundreds of crimes such as draft dodging, passport fak-
ing, perjury and lesser crimes."[49]

Throughout the congressional battles over internal security, during which
the Mundt bill died because the Senate took no action, Fast continued his
own battle against the contempt convictions imposed on him and his cohort
even though the convictions were affirmed by the Court of Appeals in March,
and by the U.S. Supreme Court on June 14, 1948, when the justices declined
to review the lower court decision.[50] The next day, Fast wrote "An Open
Letter to the American People," which was published on the inside covers of
the July 1948 issue of *Masses and Mainstream.*[51] In an understandably bitter
outline of the case, Fast wrote that with the impending imprisonment of the
JAFRC board, "anti-fascism becomes a crime under the law of the land." This
is not "a time for silence and forbearance," Fast proclaimed, but "almost all

of our newspapers have been closed to me." And "the magazines too," he said, "and the radio as well. To slander a man; then to permit him no answer, no defense . . ."[52]

Fast had had a trial, of course, and he continued to publish in the *Daily Worker* where in August he had become a coeditor and the writer of a column called, with no intended irony, "I Write What I Please." His pieces were carried in other Communist papers as well, including the *Seattle New World*, the *Chicago Star*, and the *San Francisco People's World*. He also continued to write essays for *New Masses* and later for *Masses and Mainstream*. But in all these periodicals and elsewhere, Fast implied that it was "the beginning of Fascism in America" and "the end of the free press in the U.S."[53] Still, he fought on in the press and elsewhere. He even wrote to Eleanor Roosevelt in her role as head of the UN's Human Rights Commission. "Our going to prison," Fast told the former first lady, "will make the Government of the United States party to one of the *grossest and most unbelievable violations of human rights ever witnessed. . . .* I request that you open the . . . the testimony on our case to the United Nations . . . in the interests of international understanding."[54]

Yet even as he pleaded for help in stirring up a worldwide outcry against jailing antifascist writers like himself, Fast took time to answer his correspondents' questions about U.S. literature. In this way he was able to reveal the Party's list of which American writers were to be read and which shunned. In response to Jouvenal's request for information about progressive and talented American writers, for example, Fast wrote that he could see where "such information would be very valuable in France, for again and again it has come to our attention that the French left embraced American writers who were not only not progressive, but avowed enemies of the working class." Fast complained that *Les Lettres Francaises,* initiated as a publication of the French resistance, and edited by his friend Louis Aragon, had featured stories about Richard Wright, for example, and had reviewed his *Black Boy* (1945) favorably. Wright, Fast falsely claimed, "rode to fame on the support and training" that the CPUSA gave him, and betrayed all of us "in a series of the most vicious lies and fabrications against the Party."[55]

Wright's grievances against the American Communist Party actually mirrored Fast's own when he himself finally broke with the Party in 1957, yet Fast goes on to tell Jouvenal that the "harm" Wright did to "the progressive movement in America" by his negative observations "is incalculable." And how is it, Fast asked, that Faulkner, too, "is a favorite with the French left?" In the United States "we look upon Faulkner as completely decadent, as an enemy of all the forward looking forces in American life." John Steinbeck also made Fast's "to be avoided" list. The author of *Cannery Row* (1945), Fast complained, "rates very well in France. Yet Steinbeck has never taken a position in this country on any subject." Fast, and the American Communists generally, seem to have missed a central feature of *Cannery Row,* in which a racially mixed group of friends, because of their honesty and kindness and their generosity of feeling, fail in an impersonal, cash-nexus capitalist system.[56]

Fast's problem with Steinbeck, as with almost all non-Communist writers, was twofold: he despised him for the more nuanced anti-Stalinist socialism that made Steinbeck politically unacceptable to the CPUSA, and he envied the Pulitzer Prize–winning author of *The Grapes of Wrath* for his wide recognition as an artist and a popular writer whose books became films. By 1947, nine of Steinbeck's novels had led to films, including *Of Mice and Men, Grapes of Wrath,* and *Tortilla Flat.* Fast, on the other hand, who had been trying to get his books to the big screen since 1943, was unsuccessful until his *Spartacus* was turned into a major motion picture in 1960.

After Howard wrote to Renaud de Jouvenal, the French writer in turn contacted François Mauriac, Leon Blum, Louis Aragon, and Sartre about Fast's predicament. Sartre failed to respond, but Louis Aragon, a radical intellectual and fierce supporter of Stalin until the very end, took Fast's letter "immediately to my fellow writers. It made a great impression on them, and it has been decided to support [with] all our forces the cause of American writers."[57]

Fast told Maltz that there was still hope that the two of them and the other writers convicted on contempt charges could avoid prison. But none of our cases, he added, "can be won on a narrow legalistic basis." Victory is possible for us, Fast said, only by raising enormous mass pressure throughout the world. He told Maltz that European writers were "tremendously interested," and assured him that the issue was receiving more publicity in Europe than in America.[58]

WAR AND PEACE

Even after the birth of Fast's second child, Jonathan, on April 13, 1948, Howard was still hunting and pecking out his columns for the *Daily Worker* and other Communist papers, or walking a picket line, or addressing different rallies several times a week between April and December. And not only in New York City, but also in Philadelphia, Cleveland, and Chicago. Often he had to leave Bette alone with Jon and Rachel, because Hannah Masudo, the Japanese nanny whom the Fasts had hired in 1945, had been let go. Though she had become "part of the family," Hannah was dismissed after a bizarre incident. Bette and Howie, returning from an evening out in August or September 1948, found Hannah "holding Jon in her arms and singing to him." But he was naked and "covered in a thick layer of baby powder, white as a ghost . . . a little Kabuki-like." Bette, who recognized that Hannah had "clearly gone . . . around the bend," washed Jon, fired the nanny, and for years afterward "wailed about [how] the talcum clogging all his pores," could have "killed her son."[59]

Several months passed before a new nanny, Juliette, a black woman, was hired. This new arrangement allowed Howard Fast to feel less guilty about being away from home so often, and to intensify the pace of his activism. Many of the issues that Fast wrote, marched, and spoke about dealt directly with questions of war and peace. The fledgling state of Israel, for example, at war in defense of its tenuous independence in May 1948, had been on Fast's mind since early in the year. At a January meeting of the Communist front group Progressive Citizens of America, Fast, in the face of a shortsighted UN arms embargo slapped on all of the Middle East, proposed lifting "the embargo on the sale and shipment of arms to the Jews in Palestine until such time as the UN implements the peaceful partition of Palestine."[60] Fast clearly recognized the special needs of the Jews in what was to become Israel, as well as the unfairness of an arms embargo when imposed "even-handedly" upon a proto-state embattled against several well-established and well-armed nations. At the same time, in campaigning to help elect Henry Wallace president, Fast gave innumerable speeches emphasizing the prevention of war—nonproliferation of nuclear weapons, peaceful coexistence with the Soviet Union, and nonintervention against "independence movements abroad."[61]

Even in the midst of all these political activities, Fast somehow found the time and energy to write another substantive novel. After having written eleven novels about the American experience from the colonial era through the mid-twentieth century, Fast for the first time chose a context not only outside the United States, but one set in pre-modern times. *My Glorious Brothers,* about the uprising of the Maccabees, in ancient Israel was related to Fast's direct concerns in 1948: modern Israel and independence movements. In his proposal for *My Glorious Brothers,* Fast, toning down the Jewish particularism a degree, told his publisher Little, Brown that he was attempting "to set down the parable of *all* struggles for national freedom of all partisan movements." And in the end he dedicated the book to "*all* men Jew and Gentile," and called the Maccabean story "the first modern struggle for freedom, and . . . a pattern for many movements that followed."[62]

Fast's twelfth novel clearly has an important anticolonial, antislavery, universalist dimension. But the story, recounted by Simon, the eldest of five Maccabee brothers, is also very much a Jewish story. A Jewish rebel army led by the Maccabees liberates Judea from the Selucid Empire, the Greek dynasties ruling Syria from the fourth to the first century BCE. In the process, the rebels establish the Hasmonean or Maccabean dynasty, which while reigning from 164 to 63 BCE reasserts the Jewish religion, expands Judea, and reduces the influence of Greek thought, customs, and styles collectively known as Hellenism.

Fast's history consciously paralleled the very recent past. His ancient Greeks, evoking images of Hitler's Nuremberg laws and the Nazi program of extermination, had closed down Jewish schools in Judea and ordered an end to Jewish religious practices—not in order to make Jews Greek, but ultimately to wipe them "from the face of the earth forever." And when Fast wrote that Jews all over the ancient world "lifted their heads [over] the rumor that Judea might be free again," he must have known how that would resonate with those who had witnessed the establishment of the State of Israel only a few months before his book was published.[63]

Success of the revolt itself required great and bloody violence in many individual battles, including those against Jewish Hellenists and collaborators, and the Maccabean forces grew infamous, if not respected, even among the Syrians for their fierceness and their use of guerilla tactics. Fast supplies abundant scenes of the type he did so well: armies clashing in merciless combat, thousands of arrows piercing the skies, bloody executions. After their victory the Maccabees entered Jerusalem in triumph, cleansed the Temple of all traces of alien idolatry, and reestablished traditional Jewish worship.[64]

Fast was writing *My Glorious Brothers* in 1948 at just that moment in history when the Soviet Union and the American Communist Party were in favor of a Jewish state as the inevitable outcome of an anticolonial liberation movement by the Jews of Palestine. He was feeling particularly and proudly Jewish when he received a "Dear Friend" letter from the American Jewish League Against Communism (AJLAC), signed by Rabbi Benjamin Schultz, who was soon to become well known as an accessory who could influence blacklisting decisions in the entertainment industry.[65] How Fast got on AJLAC's mailing list is a mystery, and why Fast bothered responding is also a puzzle unless we remember his self-confessed hair-trigger temper.

The League's letter indicated that it was as much against fascism as Communism, but wanted to serve as "a standing refutation of the stupid libel that Communism is a 'Jewish movement.'"[66] It asked for Fast's moral support in order to strengthen the cause of America and Israel. Fast responded to "Mr. Schultz," refusing to use the title "rabbi" because for "many years now a sincere scholar" of Jewish history, "I cannot . . . couple your name with the term 'Rabbi'" without profaning "all that is honorable and decent in Jewish life." Schultz's plan, Fast charged, "is a new step in the old and rather shameful tradition of those Jews who have contributed so readily to fascism."[67]

That most of Fast's Communist friends—and the only friends he had were Communists—were Jewish, and that Jews continued to identify disproportionately with Communism, allowed Fast to believe incorrectly that "millions of American Jews" would disown Schultz and his "kind," and consign his "miserable little organization" to "the silence and the obscurity it deserves." Fast's personal synthesis of Jewishness and Communism was even more powerfully expressed when he concluded his letter by saying, "what will remain with me as a burning shame which I must carry to my grave is the fact that you, and the people around you"—including two former Communists, Benjamin Gitlow and Eugene Lyons—"are Jews."[68]

Fast represented for Schultz precisely what the rabbi and his conservative cohort feared: Jews, even those who were pro-Israel, who identified as Jews mainly by being Communists, and loyal to the Soviet Union, which Fast claimed in his letter to Schultz was "the one country on the face of the earth that makes anti-Semitism a crime."[69] Schultz's American Jewish League Against Communism was representative of an important position held by many post-Holocaust Zionist Jews, emphasizing Americanization, anti-Communism, and pro-Israelism, even while remaining antifascist.[70]

Fast and his comrades represented another position, seeing no conflict in their loyalty to radicalism, devotion to America, and the values of their Jewish heritage.

Opposing versions of American Jewish identity competing for ascendancy in this era of immense political complexity aroused powerful emotions, partly explaining Fast's passionate letter and Schultz's response, telling Fast, in effect, to drop dead: "I read your letter of March 19th, for purposes of relaxation, to our Board of Directors, who were greatly amused by it. You speak of a 'burning shame which I must carry to my grave.' I assume that this sets a limit to the period of time during which the American people must tolerate your antics. But must they?"[71] With this exchange the correspondence mercifully ended, and Fast went on to complete one of his better novels.

One of the earliest reviews of *My Glorious Brothers* was in the *New York Times,* which, despite Fast's contention, was not ignoring him because of his politics or his pending jail sentence. Indeed, the review was quite positive, calling *My Glorious Brothers* "an absorbing and moving chronicle throughout," which should, along with *The Last Frontier,* "rank with [Fast's] finest work." The *Boston Globe* also liked *My Glorious Brothers,* as did the *Chicago Tribune.*[72] Perhaps because of his identification with Israel's struggle for statehood, and the reinvigoration of his Jewishness which that connection provided, Fast had transcended the need to write a political tract. Whatever the reason, he delivered in *My Glorious Brothers* a complex, multilayered, and credible story. Edmund Fuller, a reviewer for the *Saturday Review,* who generally found Fast guilty of "oversimplification," wrote that *My Glorious Brothers* in its "style, characterization and . . . searching presentation . . . outstrips anything Fast has ever done."[73]

In Mattathias Maccabee, the father, and his sons, the well-known Judas and Simon, the eldest, Fast drew three larger than life, yet believable, portraits. *My Glorious Brothers* can be read as an epic: a fight for freedom from oppression, filled with heroes and bloody battles; but it can also be read, especially in its lengthy coda, as an exploration of the healthy as well as unhealthy tensions between the religious and the secular, between particularism and universalism, the traditional and the modern, and nationalism and internationalism.

Most criticism of *My Glorious Brothers* did not come from the mainstream press, but from journals on the right and the left. Milton Himmelfarb, an accomplished conservative intellectual and contributing editor of *Commen-*

tary magazine, wrote a vicious and ultimately absurd response to *My Glorious Brothers.* "On the surface the book is a tract to arouse admiration for a great national resistance to a foreign oppressor intent on wiping out the national culture." But, "its real purpose," Himmelfarb wrote, "is to make this respectable sentiment a vehicle of propaganda against American policy toward the Soviet Union." Himmelfarb also accused Fast not only of writing a Communist political pamphlet in disguise, but of displaying "his love of violence," which the reviewer, in an extraordinary and illogical stretch, related to the "Stern Gang," a term coined by the British authorities to describe an armed underground *right-wing* Zionist faction in Mandate Palestine.[74]

The attack on *My Glorious Brothers* from the left was a bit milder, but nonetheless stringent. It came from those in the Party who thought the novel was a deviation into "Jewish nationalism" or Zionism. Morris Schappes, the editor of *Jewish Life* and one of the Party's experts on Jewish affairs, wrote that Simon Maccabee seems infected with and blinded by the concept that Jews were "chosen" by God to carry his message, to be a light unto the nations. For Simon, and for Fast, too, Schappes writes, "Judea is the center of the universe, geographically, politically and even morally. This emphasis is one of the unfortunate nationalistic elements running through the heart of the . . . book."[75]

Schappes admits that Fast does not entirely share Simon's nationalistic views. When the Roman legate in the coda of *My Glorious Brothers* talks about "international relations," those forces that allowed for Judea's relative autonomy, he also says, "I will not believe that a Jew is so different from all others."[76] Of course, this view is not so far from what Fast also believed. But Schappes thought that because Fast put this phrase into the mouth of a Jew-hater, the reader "is *impelled to discount it.*"[77] Schappes sees absolute nationalism, where Fast, precisely because he introduces a complex tapestry of uncertainty, has produced a scene of genuine tension between particularism and universalism.

In an interview in 1968 and again in his 1990 memoir *Being Red,* Fast claimed that Morris Schappes followed up his negative review by bringing a charge of "Jewish nationalism" against him and calling for his expulsion from the Party.[78] No charges were brought. The USSR was supporting a Jewish state in 1948, as were most Communists, even those—the vast majority—who, following the Party line, considered Zionists to be fascists before and after 1948. Fast himself said later that there were enough in the leadership of the CPUSA who said "any Jew here in 1948 who is *not* a Jewish nationalist is an idiot."[79]

One of Fast's most loyal supporters in the Party, Robert Hall, thought it not incidental that Howard, "both as a Jew and as a people's historian, would want to deal with the saga of Judea. For the battle of Israel, from the wilderness of Ephraim to the embattled kibbutz in the Negev, symbolizes the struggle of all men . . . Jews and non-Jews . . . for a just and decent world."[80] Hall was undoubtedly correct. Fast did not choose to write a book about Jews casually, but he was also persuasive in saying that his story "might simply be described as the struggle of a small people to liberate their land, obtain their freedom, and discover in so doing, the essence of the dignity of man."[81]

Jewishness as part of Fast's identity, despite his distancing disclaimers when he first became a member of the CPUSA, was in tension with, but hardly a contradiction of, his internationalism or his progressivism. Indeed, Fast believed, and rightly so, that his Jewish values, rooted as they were in the prophetic idealism of the Hebrew scriptures, fed his universalistic radicalism. This is not to say that Fast completely avoided confusion about these connections. He generally claimed that his "religion" was strictly cultural, but at times he would espouse a faith in the power of love and pacifism—values with religious dimensions that he clearly linked to Jesus, whom Fast saw as the ultimate Jew.[82] Just as often, however, Fast, perhaps with the whip-wielding Jesus in mind, would promote revolutionary violence in the cause of liberation, and *My Glorious Brothers,* though it also paid attention to Jewish religiosity, was just such a promotion.

The violence employed by Jews in *My Glorious Brothers* may have been part of the reason for the novel's success. Between 1947 and 1950, when Jews were fighting vigorously in a life-or-death struggle in the Middle East, the image of the "tough Jew" was not unusual in popular American fiction or film. In 1947, Laura Hobson, for example, the daughter of Jewish socialist immigrants, wrote *Gentleman's Agreement,* a powerful best-selling novel about antisemitism that featured several strong Jewish characters. In a film of the same name, also produced in 1947, two of those characters were played by John Garfield and Dean Stockwell, both of whom were seen by American moviegoers as handsome and masculine.[83]

Through Norman Mailer's *The Naked and the Dead* (1948), a hugely successful novel based on Mailer's fighting with the 112th Cavalry Regiment during the Philippines Campaign (1944–45), and Irwin Shaw's *The Young*

Lions (1948), a monumental best seller based on the author's wartime experiences, hard-hitting yet honorable Jewish soldiers had become familiar types to American readers. Jews displayed even greater physical prowess in John Hersey's *The Wall* (1950), a fictionalized yet searing version of resistance to Nazi genocide by Jews in the Warsaw ghetto.

My Glorious Brothers then, was another of Fast's books that had timing on its side. What it also suggests, however, is that Fast in 1948 was still where he was in 1943, struggling, consciously or otherwise, to maintain in his work, if not in his life, a synthesis between religious sensibility or love on the one side, and violence on the other. He was also still struggling to maintain a degree of independence as a writer while remaining a member of the American Communist Party. After all the irritations, including the recent charge of "Jewish nationalism" suffered at the hands of "arrogant, thickheaded people" who were in "the cultural bureaucracy" and national leadership of the CPUSA, Fast had reached a point where he had begun to take an impish pride in the fact that he "could not be broken." The strength he exhibited, however, Fast wrote later, "is nothing to be proud of, and the fact that I was reduced to a point where I scanned each manuscript microscopically in hope that I could frustrate the end critique is utterly contemptible as I look back at it. My only virtue lies in that I continued to sin," that is, to leave some "politically incorrect" material in his books, knowing, perhaps even hoping, he would be called on it, and dressed down.[84]

Staying with the Communists was also made easier for Fast by a slew of friends and admirers who either were inside the Party like Albert Maltz, Joe North, Robert Hall, Carl Marzani, Louis Weinstock, Pete Seeger, and Philip Foner, or were fellow travelers like Mary Dreier, Shirley Graham, W. E. B. Du Bois, Louis Untermeyer, Scott and Helen Nearing, and Paul Robeson. The Grand Old Dame of American Communism, Ella Reeve Bloor, aka "Mother Bloor," was a frequent and often fawning correspondent. One of the last letters she wrote to Howard, before she died in 1951 at the age of eighty-nine, concerned *My Glorious Brothers*. Addressing Fast as "My Dear 'Simon' [Maccabee]," she told him she knew of "no greater book published in our time."

Interestingly, Bloor also tied Fast's radicalism to his Jewishness. She thought he "could not have written that book if [he] hadn't been a *real Bolshevik*," and unlike the more conservative Jews who were Fast's adversaries, including Rabbi Benjamin Schultz, Bloor believed that Howard was "a better Communist because you are an *understanding* Jew." As she read *My Glorious Brothers,* Mother Bloor came to understand for the first time, she said, that "it was not alone 'to win *power* and the right' to rule" that the Maccabees fought for so bitterly, and so long—they were really "fighting against *Slavery* and *For Freedom.*"[85]

Fast also heard the same kind of unqualified praise for almost all of his work from Communist correspondents overseas, including Louis Aragon and the French physicist Frederic Joliot-Curie, and especially from his Welsh friend Gwyn Thomas and from the East German writer Stefan Heym. Heym told Fast that he was a "household name" in Germany and that in the USSR, "You are a very big man. . . . When they speak of American literature, they speak of you, and if you could only go there, they'd fete you until the caviar and vodka come out of your ears. I would suggest you keep your stomach in shape for that time."[86] Heym was certainly right about Fast's status in the USSR, but *My Glorious Brothers* was not welcome there. Indeed, the Soviet Union, despite its support for the creation of Israel in 1948, solved the problem of Fast's "Jewish nationalism" by ignoring *My Glorious Brothers* altogether—just as it had ignored all of Fast's books dealing significantly with Jews or Jewish themes.[87]

Fast failed to mention that none of his "Jewish" books were ever reprinted or reviewed in the USSR, perhaps because praise flowed in from almost everywhere else, including Israel itself. From Wales, Gwyn Thomas wrote Fast, congratulating him on his accomplishments in *My Glorious Brothers*. The theme of the book "and the way of its telling," Thomas said, "will have a deep interest for the people of these mining valleys." The Hebrew scriptures, Thomas said, had been injected into the marrow of the workers' tradition as deeply as the writings of Marx. The Jew, in Fast's pages, Thomas wrote, inspires every worker in Europe by reinvigorating the "creative legends of the people that first made Socialism." And to that end, Thomas said, "*your books have a force and a fitness that cannot too often be praised.*" This was especially true Thomas thought of "this latest book of yours [which] a lot of my friends have read . . . and feel about it as I do."[88]

Praise like this from comrades in America and from all over the world easily made up for the silence of the Soviet Union and the "nonsense" Fast had to put up with from the leadership of the CPUSA; and it worked like a powerful glue to keep him in the movement. And, of course, untoward and troublesome events occurred often enough outside of the American CP to reinforce Fast's idea that he could make "the good fight" only within the Party. In January 1949, for example, after the Jewish Book Council (JBC) of the Jewish Welfare Board unanimously bestowed upon Howard Fast's *My Glorious Brothers* its newly minted "Annual Award for the Best Novel of the Year," there was a delay in making a public announcement about the award. Howard told his friend and neighbor on Central Park West, Rabbi Lewis I. Newman, he had heard from "a completely reliable source," that "enormous pressure" was being exerted on the JBC by "certain people" who associated Fast with Communism to reverse its decision.[89]

Fast asked Newman to see if he could do something "to halt this unbelievable business." The moral implications of the pressures being brought were thoroughly deplorable, Fast rightly thought; he also believed that "since the prizes were awarded in Washington with a good deal of attendant publicity," his receiving it might become an important, if not the "determining factor . . . in the question of whether or not I am to go to prison."[90] Two weeks later Fast received a letter of congratulations from the JBC and a $250 check. He responded graciously, but with a hint that he knew that there had been resistance: "I cannot think otherwise than that the granting of this award represents an act of real independence and courage in the best tradition of Judaism. Let me say that I will try, in my future work, to be worthy of it."[91]

Unfortunately, this was not the end of the story. In 1950, in the publications of the JBC, it was stated, falsely, that the book prize for novels was initiated in 1949. As *My Glorious Brothers* was published in 1948, the council had deliberately wiped Fast's name from the very top of its subsequent published lists of book awards. There was not a peep of complaint from any quarter until Morris Schappes in 1955 noticed that Fast's award, even though not revoked by the JBC, had been erased. "Such tampering with historical data is less than honorable," Schappes told the council. It was also ironic, Schappes said, that in order to expunge the name of Howard Fast, the editors also had to delete Dr. Harry A. Wolfson's award for the best work in nonfiction. "As usual, the attempt to suppress the left . . . is harmful to circles distant from [it]."[92]

Fast thanked Schappes for his letter, but in late 1955, Howard confessed that "the whole incident fills me with such disgust that I hardly know whether to give it publicity or not." Reflecting some of the complexities existing between the majority of American Jews, who were not Communists, and the minority, even if a disproportionate one, who were, Fast wrote, "It is such a cheap, petty, and distasteful affair that it can only fill a . . . Jew with a sense of shame." If something were to be written about it, Fast thought that it should come from Schappes rather than from himself. Schappes agreed and printed a copy of his letter to the JBC in a conspicuously large, bold-lettered box in *Jewish Life*.[93] There was no response from the council.

It was in 1948, while Fast was working on *My Glorious Brothers,* that he began to suffer from chronic "cluster" headaches. "Cluster" refers to the tendency of these headaches to occur in sustained stages, over a period of three or four consecutive hours a day, potentially for several days running. "The suicide headache," a common nickname for the malady, is a neurological disease that involves, as its central feature, an intense degree of pain, almost always thoroughly debilitating. The only reason Fast could write as much as he did in 1948 and thereafter was that active periods of the ailment were interrupted by spontaneous remissions—sometimes sustained for weeks. But because cluster headaches were often confused with migraine, Fast's condition went undiagnosed for nearly fifty years.[94]

Fast, who along with his doctors was basically mystified, looked for relief through "home remedies" and found that he could make his symptoms a touch less severe by the application of ice packs, for example, or wrapping his head with towels soaked in cold water, or by drinking more coffee. Later, he learned that increasing his level of oxygen would also reduce the pain. Some researchers have pointed to low testosterone levels as a possible cause of cluster headaches. Without trivializing his unenviable physical burden, it could be said that for Fast, who was as "horny as a large toad," this was an unlikely trigger.[95]

Fast's headaches affected his family in myriad ways. Rachel Fast Ben-Avi remembered that when an attack came, her father had "excruciating pain, and there were times when he just sat and cried and times when he screamed and screamed." Fast would have to stop driving if a headache hit, park, and sit "eyes closed, head in hands . . . weeping, sometimes for as long as an hour or even more." Rachel said that at these times she and her mother and younger brother Jon would remain in the car "silent, scarcely daring to breathe."[96]

It is impossible to know for certain what set off Fast's first set of sieges, but they came during an extremely stressful period from March 1948 to July 1948, when Howard and his colleagues on the JAFRC lost their contempt appeal and had to confront the refusal of the U.S. Supreme Court to review their case. It was in these months as well that Eugene Dennis, William Z. Foster, Benjamin Davis Jr., and nine other Communist Party leaders were arrested and charged under the Alien Registration Act, or Smith Act as it was more commonly known. In the same period the Hollywood Ten were indicted for contempt of Congress. It was also at this time that Morton Wishengrad, a liberal anti-Communist and radio playwright, advised the staff at the Jewish Theological Seminary (JTS) that it ought not submit to WABC a script proposed by Fast for the radio station's weekly broadcast *Eternal Light*. The play, based on Fast's short story "The Price of Liberty," presented Johnnie Ordroneux, a highly successful privateer in the War of 1812, as a Jewish American—for which there is no hard evidence. Wishengrad represented, wittingly or otherwise, the post-Holocaust liberal but acculturationist Jewish community, as against those Jews who held fast to the crucial connection between their radicalism and their Jewishness. He told the JTS that Howard Fast's turning Ordroneux into a Jew was "a CP tactic. . . . If you do such a script," Wishengrad warned, "you become allied to a communist interpretation of American Jewish History. And you will open the Seminary to attack from an entire political spectrum that will begin on the anti-CP liberal left and go [all the way] to the Catholic right." The Catholic Church, Wishengrad reminded the executives at JTS, was already gunning for Fast. He thought the Church's crusade against Fast's books disgraceful. But it seemed to him "that if you're going to pick a fight with the Church on the issue of academic freedom, the fight should be on an issue where truth is on our side."[97]

Despite these kind of frustrations, as well as internal Party hassles over political correctness, and the unimaginably painful headaches, Fast felt he could not possibly leave the CPUSA at its greatest moment of crisis. On the contrary, he dedicated himself to the Party's causes with renewed fierceness. For Fast, as for much of the CPUSA, America had become a society "very much like the Germany of '33"—fascist, and at the core of its ideology and of its political and social life, incorrigibly racist. Communists were sustained in their beliefs and in their opportunities for anti-American propaganda by the disproportionate political strength of a segregationist faction of the Democratic Party. The Dixiecrats, as they would later be called, bolted from the Democratic nominating convention in 1948, in response to President Truman's pro-integration positions, and went on to run the virulent racist Strom Thurmond as an independent candidate.

Much earlier, the Communists, too, had backed an independent nominee. They had decided as early as October 1947 that the only defense against what they saw as an ever-deepening American fascism was the mobilization of electoral support for Henry Wallace as a third-party candidate for the presidency. This was a radical turn away from the Popular Front political course American Communism had run from 1935 to 1939 and from 1941 to 1945, when the Party fielded a pro-forma candidate of its own while supporting FDR and progressives in the Democratic Party. Wallace, the former vice president, unceremoniously dumped as FDR's running mate in 1944 and also ousted from Truman's cabinet as secretary of commerce in September 1946 because he opposed the president's Cold War policies, founded the New Party, renamed the Progressive Party in 1948.

By August 1948, Fast and many other CP activists were ever more deeply involved in the growing Progressive movement to elect Henry Wallace president. Fast told Gwyn Thomas, however, that "it would surprise no one of us if the Government in its bestial and reactionary desperation, attempted to destroy this movement with physical force." The "framed arrests of the 12 CP leaders" a few days before the opening of the founding convention of the Progressive Party, Fast said, was "good evidence" of what the government would do. These "baboons," Fast told his friend, "seem ready to stop at nothing." Hitler, Fast's favorite point of negative reference, "may have thought that he had a propaganda machine," Howard wrote, but it was only "a tiny tin trumpet compared to the blast the American press, with its ten thousand controlled newspapers, is letting loose today."[98]

Lacking the support of labor, however, the Progressive Party movement was doomed to failure, and for a time the American Communist Party seemed to know it. John Gates, editor of the *Daily Worker*, had presented a report to the national committee of the CPUSA in June 1947 that strongly favored a third party, but insisted that any such move would be an exercise in futility unless backed by the United Auto Workers, the Amalgamated Clothing Workers, the United Mine Workers, the International Ladies Garment Workers Union, and other important segments of the labor movement. The Party unanimously approved this precondition, but only months later "recklessly reversed" itself. Enthralled with the possibility of a name as well known as Wallace at the head of an independent ticket, the Communists told themselves that masses of ordinary laboring women and men would rebel against their union leadership to vote for the former VP.[99]

This delusion was a terrible misreading of American workers, who were in no mood to chase elusive butterflies, nor to be so closely associated with the Communist Party. The working class, in the main, unlike the CPUSA, which presumed to speak in its name, did not see fascism rampant in the United States. For them, America, though far from having fulfilled completely its pronounced ideals, did not resemble the authoritarian societies of wartime Italy and Germany. In the United States, workers did not see, as they had in the recent history of the Axis powers, a government driven by ultra-nationalistic imperatives or by racialist ideologies; nor was there in America an exaltation of an absolute leader or celebration of brute force. For all the chilling effects of anti-Communism, the extralegal operations of the FBI, the unconstitutional behavior of HUAC, and the existence of blacklists, there were no black shirts seriously contending for power. Wage-earners generally perceived America as fundamentally liberal in its culture and democratic in its politics.

Fast and his Communist comrades simply failed to understand, in any nuanced way, the American working class. In some unions, there was great admiration for Communists who were devoted to driving out corrupt and undemocratic labor leadership and to raising consciousness about larger political, social, and cultural questions. Still, as Fast once knew in his bones, most working men and women, trying to feed their families, were more interested in bread and butter issues. In 1948, post–Popular Front and postwar workers correctly saw close identification with Communism as a political kiss of death.

Dwight Macdonald, writer, editor, social critic, philosopher, and a political radical representative of the anti-Stalinist left, said in 1948 of the Progressive Party and its candidate "It is not true that Henry Wallace is an agent of Moscow. But it is true that he behaves like one."[100] Whether Wallace was a witting actor or the dupe of the American Communist Party is less important than the fact that he consistently gave Stalin the benefit of the doubt. He advocated abandoning Berlin when Stalin imposed the Soviet blockade, and he characterized the coup Stalin ordered in Czechoslovakia in 1948, accompanied by the crushing of dissident Czech leftists, as a necessary and just response to the Truman Doctrine, "the policy of the United States to support free peoples who are resisting attempted subjugation by armed minorities or by outside pressures."[101] Wallace not only strenuously resisted Truman's decision to oppose Stalin's expansionist ambitions in eastern Europe and elsewhere, he saw Stalin as the exemplary man of peace and Truman as the dangerous militarist. Perhaps trying to transcend his reputation for cheerlessness, Wallace, "the most boring humorless egomaniac on the American political scene," according to socialist Irving Howe, described the Marshall Plan for the reconstruction of Europe as the "Martial Plan."[102]

Fast agreed with Wallace in every instance. In October 1947, for example, Fast was among the one hundred Americans who signed a statement sharply attacking U.S. foreign policy and urging an emergency meeting between Stalin and Truman. The statement, which contains no word about Stalinist expansionism, reads as if Fast, along with W. E. B. Du Bois, artist Rockwell Kent, and scores of other left notables, thought that bringing the "big two" together might mean the American president would drop the Marshall Plan and the Truman Doctrine in return for a promise from the Soviets not to issue "bitter broadsides" or to employ the veto so often at the UN![103]

Fast also agreed with Wallace that there ought to be no peacetime military conscription and that Stalin's Soviet Union, more than any other nation, would lead humanity to a world without war. Addressing an audience of ten thousand at Madison Square Garden in late 1949, Fast, echoing Wallace's earlier statements, said, "that if we have to have an atomic bomb, thank God the Russians have it too." Russia, Fast said, retailing the ridiculous and fatuous Party line, "will use atomic energy to make the deserts [into] blooming gardens." He followed this foolishness by saying something only someone fully wedded to Communist Party humbug could say: "Russia is the hope of mankind today and of humanity tomorrow."[104]

There was no question that the dominant force in the new party was the CPUSA. At the Progressive Party's presidential nominating convention in Philadelphia, in the summer of 1948, H. L. Mencken, the acerbic critic of American life and culture, who was covering the event for the *Baltimore Sun,* saw clearly the inordinate influence the Communist Party had over Wallace. Spotting Fast on the floor of the Philadelphia Convention Center, Mencken, who may not have been aware that Howard was so stellar a figure in the CPUSA, warned him to break away from the Progressives. Fast simply said, "I can't put politics aside." Mencken, in response, seems to have exploded. "'You *don't* put politics aside"; he said, "you state it, smell it, listen to it, and *write it.* You *don't join it.* If you do, these clowns will destroy you as surely as the sun rises and sets.'"[105]

One wonders why Fast includes this self-deprecating episode in his 1990 memoir *Being Red,* unless he hoped to blame his own lack of judgment about the electoral chances of the Progressive Party on those "clowns." But no conspiracy of muddle-brained manipulators was needed to keep Fast among his worshipful Communist friends or to keep him doing the Party's bidding. Despite its periodic harassment of the writer for his "errors," the CPUSA desperately wanted Fast to stay. Moreover, by late 1948 Fast was so closely connected to the Party in the public eye that he may have believed that his writing would no longer find an audience in the American mainstream. His oversized ambition would have to be fulfilled more or less within the world-wide Communist community.

Howard Fast, banned, barred, and besieged in the broader American world and in some trouble with the conventional Jewish community, was well aware that as a Communist he retained the status of being a big fish in a small pond; and in any case, he was as committed as ever to seeing socialism take root in the United States and everywhere else in the world. The problem was that the pond within which Fast was swimming had shrunk to a puddle after the Communists went with the Progressive Party candidate, rendering themselves historically irrelevant and politically impotent. Wallace, who had served as secretary of agriculture from 1933 to 1940, had been FDR's vice president from 1941 to 1945, and had been secretary of commerce in Truman's cabinet for over a year, received barely one million votes of 47 million cast, won not a single state or electoral vote, and came in fourth behind the rabid racist, Dixiecrat Strom Thurmond.

6

The Myopia of American Communism

With the disastrous Wallace campaign behind him, and imprisonment ahead of him, Howard Fast spent less time writing fiction and more time writing columns, pro bono, for various Communist periodicals.[1] His pieces were often a running commentary, mostly ironic, on issues of immediate interest in the news: the firing of college professors accused of Communist affiliations; Red-baiting in the union movement; the imprisonment of HUAC chair J. Parnell Thomas for fraud; lynching in the American South and racial injustice in every region; biting ad homonym essays eviscerating Louis Budenz, Fast's favorite professional ex-Communist informer; attacks on Paul Gallico, award-winning writer of the novella *The Snow Goose,* but also an antisemite and virulent anti-Communist; and fierce criticism of New York's Francis Cardinal Spellman, whose hatred of Communism was boundless. Fast's targets were most often well chosen, but his language was venomous, riddled with words like "filth," "swine," "lunatic," "monstrous," and of course "fascist." There were also a small number of tributes to fellow Communists and friends such as the writer and film director Carl Marzani.

In addition to his column, Fast in 1948 and 1949 covered special news stories for the *Daily Worker,* in particular the trial in New York City's Foley Square courthouse of the twelve top leaders of the CPUSA, who had been detained in July 1948. That the arrests occurred when they did was no accident.

Despite the president's proactive foreign policy, especially the interventionist Truman Doctrine designed to prevent Communist expansion outside of Eastern Europe, he was characterized by Republicans as weak. And his administration's reluctant and sometimes bumbled handling of espionage cases increased doubt about Truman's anti-Communist bona fides. The growing suspicion was inflamed in 1948 when the testimony of Elizabeth Bentley, a defector from the CPUSA and from Soviet intelligence, became public. Ultimately she named more than eighty Americans, including Alger Hiss and more than a dozen others, who worked or had worked for the U.S. government as spies for the Soviet Union.[2] The revelations of Whittaker Chambers, another former Communist spy, who in August also named names including Hiss, added grist to the mill. For some time, indeed through all of the second half of 1948, Bentley's and Chambers's exposures, which Howard Fast dismissed as the malicious rantings of "renegades," were a media sensation and one of the more powerful stimulants of political anti-Communism prior to the Korean War and the concomitant rise in popularity and power of Senator Joseph McCarthy in 1950.[3]

An apparent presumption of espionage lay behind the decision of the Truman administration to prosecute the top CP leaders. Fast was carefully covering the case, and intimated that the timing of the arrests on July 20, 1948, of General Secretary Eugene Dennis, Chairman William Foster, *Daily Worker* editor John Gates, long-time Party leaders Benjamin Davis and Gil Green, and eight other major Communists, was connected to the looming presidential election, and was partly motivated by a desire to neutralize Truman's mounting reputation as being "soft on Communism."[4]

FOLEY SQUARE FOLLIES

The CPUSA leaders, joined by Howard Fast and Dashiell Hammett, and by the even more renowned Paul Robeson and dozens of other sympathizers, apparently having learned little from the debacle of the Wallace campaign, attempted to get a postponement of the trial so that a "mass movement" could be organized to protest the indictments. They launched a challenge to the court's system of jury selection and succeeded in demonstrating that jury pools were not constructed, nor jurors picked, in a way that would guarantee a trial by one's peers. But Harold Medina, the judge sitting on the case, whom

Fast described as unctuous and closed-minded, ruled that the defense had
not demonstrated the *deliberate* exclusion of minorities, the poor, or women.
Still, after months of skirmishing, the jury that was finally selected included
seven women and three blacks.[5]

Medina was confronted by another twenty or more defense motions for
adjournment and even dismissal on the grounds that prejudicial statements
by Truman, Cardinal Spellman, and Attorney General Tom Clark had promoted "public hysteria" and made a fair trial impossible, that no "clear and
present danger" existed, and that police presence outside the courtroom
constituted an "armed force" that intimidated jurors and defendants and
their lawyers.[6] Clearly irritated by the "profuse and prolix" and repetitive
arguments of the defense, Medina, alternatively facetious and brusque, rejected all further motions for postponement, and ordered "*the* symbolic trial
of the Cold War" to begin on March 7, 1949, at Foley Square in downtown
Manhattan.[7]

The government did not try to prove that the American Communist Party
actually committed overt revolutionary acts, which would have been virtually impossible since no investigation, including government monitored
phone calls of Fast and other Communists and left-wing radicals by the FBI
or congressional and state committees had produced a single instance of
"force and violence" or planned "force and violence" against any agency of
the U.S. government. Nor did the innumerable searches, many illegal, produce anything more "dangerous" than books, articles, and pamphlets.[8] In a
more rational universe, one less governed by political opportunism, a sound
governmental policy might have been to protect the right of Communists
to advocate force and violence on every street corner. No better way could
have been designed to guarantee the failure of the CPUSA to engage, no less
capture, American opinion.

Instead the Justice Department argued that the *advocacy* of the overthrow
of the political system through Marxist-Leninist "teachings" constituted a
crime under the Smith Act. One might have thought that the CPUSA could
(should?) have employed a First Amendment defense, a strategy Fast himself
had suggested and encouraged. General Secretary Eugene Dennis seemed to
move in this direction when on the very first day of the court case he maintained correctly that the judicial procedures amounted to the trial of a political party, not for its actions, but for its ideas, and were in themselves "a grave
blow to the people's constitutional right." Fast and other leading figures in

the CPUSA called the trial a fight for "freedom of speech" and for "the enforcement of constitutional liberties."[9] Communist Chairman Foster, however,
though never himself brought to trial because of ill health, insisted that the
Communist leaders forgo the civil liberties approach. He dismissed the idea
of making the plausible claim that no matter what the Party advocated, it was
speech protected by the Bill of Rights. Instead, Foster called for making an
assertive defense of the Party's theoretical and political positions.[10]

Dennis and the other ten defendants, in obedience to Foster, claimed that
since the mid-1930s the CPUSA had not been a revolutionary organization, but
a democratic socialist movement that had adhered to a constitutional path to
power. The defense went so far as to argue that the American Communist
Party was not even *theoretically* revolutionary, a problematic position at best,
given the writings of Browder and Foster, no less those of Marx, Lenin, and
Stalin.[11] The Justice Department responded by showing that during that
same period, the CPUSA, despite flip-flops on tactics, had continued to "employ" Leninist texts supporting violent revolution.[12]

As a result of these strategic legal choices by the CPUSA and the government, the eleven accused men and their lawyers wound up in long, fruitless
exchanges with the prosecution over the "true meaning" of passages in the
classic works of Communist theoreticians, dead or alive—a strategy that
brought neither legal nor political benefit to Dennis and his codefendants.[13]
It may, however, have brought moments of hilarity. Fast, in his coverage of
the trial, never mentions laughter; indeed his articles are striking for their
darkness and abstraction to the point of obfuscation. They rank among Fast's
worst journalism.[14] But it is hard to imagine there having been no expressions
of mirth when Louis Budenz, former editor of the *Daily Worker,* and now a
key witness for the prosecution, introduced the "Aesopian language thesis."

Insisting that CPUSA leaders were communicating in metaphors and codes
(which Russian Bolsheviks had been doing ever since the beginning of the
twentieth century), often writing things that were the opposite of, or at least
radically different from what they really meant, Budenz testified that in
Communist Party correspondence and publications, "nonviolence" meant
"violence," and "peace" meant "war." And when Lenin in exile in Germany
wrote "Japan," Budenz said, he meant "Russia."[15]

In response to questions about this kind of veiled communication, Fast
said that in 1944 the FBI had thought that even his novel *Freedom Road* was
a variation of an Aesopian "code book." Spies, Fast said, sometimes devised

codes keyed to certain pages and lines of a previously agreed-upon publication. "*Any* book could become a code book. There's a pattern to the use of certain words. Suppose you want a word that's on page thirty-one, fifth line. So your code for that word can be 31–5." Not particularly sophisticated, Fast implied, but a code based on a book, he said, "cannot be broken" unless the decoder can decide "which of the million books that exist *is* the code book." This shows, Fast insisted, that the Justice Department was " totally crazy! Who are we having codes with?" Fast asked facetiously, "Russia?"[16] Well, yes. Fast was not himself involved, of course, but as we have learned from the opening of the Soviet archives in 1991, coded information was exchanged between leaders of the CPUSA and Soviet intelligence.[17]

Crazy or not, the prosecution seized on the fact that in his preface to *Imperialism,* Lenin had written that in order to get past the Russian censors he would have to use "that cursed Aesopian language." The U.S. government's strategy, then, was not only to convince Judge Medina to allow the introduction of Lenin's writings as evidence, in the hope of proving that whatever Vladimir Ilyich Ulyanov wrote or did, all Communists do or planned to do, but also that innocent-sounding words in the texts had veiled and often malicious meaning. Whether anyone on either side in this legal battle was reading George Orwell's just-published dystopian novel about language and thought control is impossible to know, but it was a fitting moment for *1984* to have appeared.[18]

The gap, however, between the Party's use of "subversive language" and the possibility that a party as weak and depleted as the CPUSA was after the war could use violence to bring down the American government was so enormous as to make that danger neither clear nor present. The "clear and present danger" argument had been enunciated by Justice Oliver Wendell Holmes Jr. in 1919 concerning the right of the government to regulate speech in emergencies, such as war. With no emergency in sight, however, the Justice Department, the lower court, and eventually the higher court succeeded in shifting the focus away from the clear-and-present-danger argument to the *intention* of the language itself, which they insisted "meant" that the CPUSA had "plans" for illegal, violent action in the future. But 90 percent of the evidence presented by the prosecution had no direct connection to the CPUSA, to Dennis, or to any of the other defendants.[19]

Courtroom outbursts by CPUSA leaders and their lawyers led Judge Medina to jail three of the defendants for contempt *during* the trial, and when proceedings ended after nine months, he briefly jailed all six defense attorneys for contemptuous conduct.

The heavy-handed style and tactical manipulations used by the government and the raucousness and disrespect evidenced by the CP leaders and their lawyers contributed to the general chaos of the whole affair. What was in form a criminal trial was in fact from the start a propaganda battle in which neither side earned much glory. The prosecution, however, won. All the defendants were convicted. All but one were sentenced to five years in prison and a $10,000 fine.[20] In response to the long-term sentencing of defendants John Gates, Harry Winston, and Gus Hall, 2,500 people attended a protest rally organized by the Civil Rights Congress, where they heard Howard Fast and more than a dozen others attack Medina and his ruling.[21]

Although apparently pleased with the result, the press demonstrated little evidence of understanding it. In addition to erroneously reporting that the CPUSA was found guilty of criminal conspiracy against the United States, most editors, even of liberal journals such as the *Nation,* thought that the Truman administration was right to refuse, as the *Washington Post* put it, "to permit a tightly organized and conspiratorial agency, drawing its inspiration and a large measure of its strength from the Soviet Union, to operate freely within our 'market-place of ideas.'" The *St. Louis Post-Dispatch,* however, raised a lonely cry of protest. While declaring that there was no excuse for the unruly behavior of the Communist defense in the courtroom, the paper correctly warned that the verdict had established a new and repressive limitation on the freedom of speech.[22]

Of course, most criticism of the convictions came from Stalinists such as Fast, and habitual fellow travelers. Ironically, however, they were joined in protest by the Trotskyists, those men and women of the left despised by the Communists, whose own convictions under the Smith Act in 1941 the CPUSA had abetted and celebrated—convictions Howard Fast continued to defend.[23] As late as the final days of June 1949, an emergency meeting of the New York State Civil Rights Congress (CRC) was held to condemn the Foley Square trial as a "fantastic witch-hunt." Farrell Dobbs, the national chairman of the Trotskyist Socialist Workers Party asked the Communist-dominated CRC to "clean" the record of the Communists by condemning the convictions imposed on the Trotskyists for their political activities eight years earlier. In response to Dobbs's reasonable request, Fast joined the audience in a boisterous hissing and booing session clearly intended to silence dissent, indicating once again that the Communists favored civil liberties only for their own party.[24]

This was further illustrated a few days after the CRC emergency meeting by an interesting exchange that took place in the *Daily Compass* between Fast and the radical journalist I. F. Stone. Civil liberties were by definition "indivisible," Stone wrote, and Communists ought to have supported Trotskyists when they were prosecuted under the Smith Act. Fast whipped off a letter to the editor that was an exercise in leftist apologetics and Communist logic-chopping, disputing Stone's argument. The Communists, Fast maintained unpersuasively, were "correct" in not having supported the fascist "Trotskyists" in 1941, and he continued to insist that they were justified in aiding the government in its prosecution of the anti-Stalinist group.[25]

Of course, when their own sentences were announced the Communists talked bravely of fighting back, using the protection of the First Amendment. They began making speeches and disseminating leaflets almost immediately. On October 17, as the *Daily Worker* announced that a "great campaign" was underway, Howard Fast and Paul Robeson revealed plans to take the case of the "Communist Eleven" to the UN Commission on Human Rights. Nothing came of this effort. The defendants, except for Dennis who was already serving a year's sentence for contempt of Congress in 1947, remained out of prison, on bail, until the Supreme Court upheld the Foley Square verdict in 1951.

Feeling besieged, the CP, in the name of defying the "witch hunt" against its leaders, apparently thought it was appropriate to compensate with a "witch hunt" of its own. Clearly desperate, and unable to beat the "fascist system," the Party, starting in 1949 and running through 1953, reopened its earlier wartime campaign against the "white chauvinist" enemy within. Here was a battle it could win, even if at great cost to its enrollment and credibility. And this was not the end of the foolishness or self-deception of the CPUSA.[26]

WALTZING AT THE WALDORF

Part of the reason Fast's coverage of the Foley Square trial was so spotty and poorly presented was that his time and attention were divided among several additional extraordinary events in 1949. One was the Cultural and Scientific Conference for World Peace held over a period of several days in late March at the Waldorf-Astoria hotel in New York City. "I was the major stimulating force for the Waldorf Conference," Fast boastfully told an interviewer twenty years later. Indeed, he claimed that he "literally forced the Conference down the throat of the left wing." Evidence of Fast's responsibility for the Waldorf Conference exists only in his own notebooks. Whether or not his leadership in generating the conference was as vigorous as he claims, he *was* subsequently chosen as one of the Communist Party's delegates to go to Paris in April for the founding of the World Congress of Peace.[27]

In his 1990 memoir *Being Red,* Fast continued to insist that the Waldorf Conference was his creation. "Subsequent histories and newspapers of the time indicate that [the conference] was Soviet-inspired and backed with Soviet money. Let me put that to rest," Fast wrote. "It was my idea." Yet only pages later in the same memoir, Fast wrote more truthfully that "Over 500 of the nation's leading intellectuals were willing to put their careers and names on the lines for a conference created by the Communist party . . . . The lines were clearly drawn, and no one at the conference had any illusions as to who the organizers were."[28]

Whomever the idea came from, the conference was mainly supported by the USSR and had, in addition to Fast, dozens of other nominal sponsors associated with the CPUSA, including Dashiell Hammett, Lillian Hellman, and Clifford Odets, as well as some non-Communists such as Berenice Abbott, Leonard Bernstein, Marlon Brando, Aaron Copland, Jose Limon, Norman Mailer, Arthur Miller, and Isaac Stern. At least one initial sponsor, Rabbi Mordecai M. Kaplan, less naïve, or perhaps simply more honest, than some of the others, publicly withdrew his support when he became "convinced that the symposium had 'become other than representative.'"[29]

Kaplan's phrasing was an exercise in understatement. Everything at the Waldorf conference was one-sided, and any dissent from the line laid down by the Russians was deftly brushed aside or masterfully evaded. The conference took place only months after the Stalinist takeover in Czechoslovakia, and the Communist Party, Russian and American, kept discreetly in the background, knowing any open defense of Soviet foreign policy would alienate many long-term fellow travelers. But as Fast had put it, no one at the conference was deluded about who was in charge.

Norman Mailer, whose first novel, *The Naked and the Dead,* had been published months earlier, though no Communist, was invited as a sponsor of the conference because he had supported Henry Wallace in the 1948

election. He surprised almost everyone in the Waldorf's luxurious Starlight
Roof conference room when he got up on Saturday night to declare that he
considered Russia an example of "state capitalism" and to express doubt that
any such gathering as the conference could contribute to world peace. Up to
this point, the audience had been clamoring for the young novelist to take the
floor. But, according to several in attendance, Mailer's three-minute speech
brought loud gasps of dismay and a number of public attempts to persuade
him of his mistakes.[30]

Mailer disturbed the conference's sense of unanimity, but so did the presence of several hundred anti-Stalinist intellectuals of various left persua-
sions. Many of them demanded a disclosure of the true sponsorship of the
conference; challenged the intellectual independence of the Soviet representatives; and denounced the organizers' failure to include leftist anti-Stalinists
among its speakers. Two seasoned leftist anti-Stalinists, democratic socialist
Irving Howe, and the editor of *Partisan Review,* William Barrett, were per-
plexed neither by the predictable absence of anti-Stalinists such as James T.
Farrell and John Dos Passos, nor by the roles played by Alexander Fadeyev,
the head of the Soviet Writers Union, and Howard Fast, both of whom Howe
and Barrett saw as "commissars of literature."[31]

It was "inevitable," Barrett thought, given the way the sessions were organized, and by whom, that Fast should emerge as the American counterpart to the Russian delegate Fadeyev. As with all of the Russian speakers,
Fadeyev never deviated from the Communist Party line, while Fast, like most
of the Americans who spoke, assailed his government and praised the Soviet
Union. Indeed, Fast even took a short break from the conference to criticize
the United States at a meeting of the Hellenic American Brotherhood of
the International Workers Order (a Communist Party–affiliated insurance,
mutual benefit, and fraternal organization), which was celebrating the 128th
anniversary of Greece's independence from Turkey.

Fast told the assembled Greeks that he had to hurry back to the Waldorf
Astoria, New York's Art Deco symbol of opulence and splendor, to be "in the
company of outstanding writers and scientists who came from many countries
to work out a people's platform for peace." Yet he took the time to falsely characterize armed bands of foreign and foreign-sponsored Communist guerillas
as "a "force" representing freedom-loving Greek people "successfully fighting
against the armed might of the United States." He added that "if our American
imperialists want to go to war with the Soviet Union, they will have to defeat

Greece first." Rushing to return to the hotel to help make "world peace," Fast left his audience with one last question: "What chance," then, "have [the Americans] got in a war against the Soviet Union?"[32]

Back at the writer's panel, as Fast remembers it in *The Naked God,* the left-liberal literary critic Mary McCarthy and "some of her friends," most likely Dwight Macdonald, the editor of *Politics,* an independent radical magazine, and the pacifist poet Robert Lowell, asked Fadeyev to explain dark rumors about what happened to a number of Soviet writers, most of them Jewish, including Itzak Feffer, David Bergelson, Layb Kvitko, and Peretz Markish. The Socialist-Zionist Nachman Meisel, editor of the left-wing monthly *Yiddishe Kultur,* also asked Fadeyev why communication from the Yiddish writers in Russia had come to an abrupt end. As chair of the panel, Fast "was quite naturally provoked," that McCarthy and the others should be so disruptive and "should so embarrass" Fadeyev, "this fine and distinguished guest."[33]

Fadeyev may have been distinguished, but certainly not for telling the truth. The Russian writer looked, according to Irving Howe, "as if he'd like to get these American wiseguys back home [where] he'd teach them to ask questions!" Fadeyev nonetheless quickly named a number of Yiddish writers, gave the titles of their books, and talked about their works in progress. He even spoke about when and where he had seen them last, all the while knowing that each one was already in a Soviet prison or dead. Characterizing the asking of these questions as "disruptive," as Fast and Fadeyev did, might be expected, Howe wrote, from someone taught in a school for the GPU, the Soviet State Secret Police—or at a Communist Party Training School in Beacon, New York.[34]

In *Being Red,* written forty-one years after the conference, Fast remembered the incident differently. "Mary McCarthy anti Communist was neither a supporter nor was she invited, but she appeared, umbrella in hand, striding fiercely down the center aisle of the room where the literary panel was in session, accompanied by three friends, right up to the platform, where she declared loudly, 'You wouldn't dare let me speak.' 'Why not?' I wanted to know. 'Because I'll tell the truth.' I reached down and helped her up the platform. 'Go ahead, tell us the truth.' I think the unexpectedness of my action took a bit of the wind out of her sails, and nothing she said," Fast wants us to believe, "was very upsetting."[35]

McCarthy, along with Macdonald and Lowell, also asked questions of the famed composer Dmitri Shostakovich, who, according to several witnesses, looked as if he wanted to be anywhere but at the conference.[36] Lowell was particularly interested in the fate of conscientious objectors in the Soviet Union. Nicolas Nabokov, cousin of Vladimir, and writer and composer in his own right, asked if Shostakovich agreed with *Pravda,* the leading newspaper of the USSR and the official organ of the Central Committee of the Communist Party, that "such lackeys of imperialism" as the distinguished modernist composers Hindemith, Schoenberg, and Stravinsky "should be banned in the Soviet Union." Shostakovich, visibly trembling, said "Yes." Unsure as to whether his response would be seen in the USSR as resolute enough, he thought, "When I get back, it's over for me."[37]

A lifelong philo-semite in a society drenched in antisemitism, Shostakovich, only months before the Waldorf Conference, had written a song cycle called "From Jewish Folk Poetry." Afraid of the consequences, however, conductors refused to mount a premiere until after Stalin's death. Shostakovich himself thought his life in danger at least twice during his career under Stalin. The day after his relatively weak condemnation of the modernist musicians he tried to improve matters for himself by delivering a bitter diatribe in which he apologized for his own music's failure "to meet with approval among the broad masses of listeners." At the same time he accused the United States of "preparing world opinion for the transition from the cold war to 'outright aggression,'" of perfecting new kinds of weapons of mass destruction, and of engaging in the resurrection of "the theory and practice of fascism."[38]

Fadeyev, unlike Shostakovich, never trembled, and was much too slick and arrogant to worry about his fate back home, where he was a powerful figure. When he was confronted by several indignant young women about the absence of females in the delegation from the Soviet Union, a socialist state "dedicated to a solution of the 'woman question,'" Fadeyev responded that "we have solved the woman question, so you see, for us it no longer presents a problem." Howard Fast witnessed this exchange and much later, after he had left the Party, said bitterly, and finally with some honesty, "This same combination of stupidity, contempt and arrogance marked the answer to every question of propriety of socialist action that we put to the Russians through the years that I was a Party member."[39]

But at this time in 1949, for Fast to break with the Party would have meant finding himself outside a sustaining "family," feeling as if he were on the mere periphery of history itself, or indeed, banished from it altogether, and suffering a kind of symbolic death. It was to take almost a decade more before Fast decided that he had had enough of inanity, derision, and cover-up. In the meantime, as far as the Party's sins went, Fast operated mostly with eyes closed, or when open, mouth shut.

APRIL IN PARIS

Just prior to the Waldorf Conference, Fast, without much hope, had applied for a passport to go to Paris as a delegate to the World Congress of Peace. Because his conviction for contempt of Congress was still in the appeals process, the sentencing judge, despite Fast's pessimism, approved his obtaining a passport good for thirty days.[40]

If Fast were not already glued tightly to the CPUSA, within which he was, as Albert Maltz put it, "worshipped," the Paris experience by itself might have supplied enough adhesive to do the job. Kissed on the lips by Pablo Picasso, seated next to Louis Aragon, poet, novelist, and cochair of the conference, and not far from Paul Robeson, Fast was "transported into another world . . . where Communists were honored, not hunted down and imprisoned." Indeed, for all the days he was in Paris, Fast felt warmly welcomed, "loved," his feet rarely touching the ground.[41]

The love fest continued throughout. Fast had affectionate conversations and "a wonderful meal" with Renaud de Jouvenal, in the Frenchman's old Paris mansion, was toasted at a "splendid dinner" that the Russians gave for the Americans, and met with many other demonstrative delegates, including Pablo Neruda. Fast soon after would write an article published in Spanish for the Chilean magazine *Pro Arte* in which he said, "I think that it was the day that Pablo Neruda entered the floor of the Congress that the magnitude of the forces of genius, talent and intellect on our side became clearer than ever to me."[42] And when it was Fast's turn to speak at the culmination of the conference in a huge soccer stadium on the outskirts of Paris, he "was introduced as one of the greatest writers of the U.S." Fast felt he had become "a hero to some of the leading minds on earth."[43]

In a speech he had written out for him phonetically in French, he told the crowd of twenty thousand people assembled "shoulder to shoulder in ranks," about the many positive things groups of progressives working together could accomplish for mankind. But he concluded on a more ominous

note, declaring that Americans were being deceived daily into thinking that
the Soviet Union was a threat to their freedom, and that every voice in the
United States raised against war was being gagged. This "terror" in America, he said, was "only the beginning."[44]

On the last day of the conference, a mass rally for peace mobilized in Paris.
Even if not meant to be facetious or cute, the *New York Times* sub-headline
for the story had its humorous side: "Big 'Peace' Rally Staged in Paris . . .
Martial Music Featured." In the same vein, when it was earlier announced
at the conference that Nanjing had fallen to the People's Liberation Army,
the "peace" delegates cheered wildly.[45] Peace, it was clear, simply meant
victory for Communists, and if war was necessary to achieve that victory,
then war was peace.

After the closing rally, Fast visited the Walter B. Cannon Memorial Hospital in Toulouse, which was created and maintained in the main by funds
supplied by the Joint Anti-Fascist Refugee Committee. In this "old and
lovely city" nestled under the slopes of the Pyrenees, Fast was impressed by
what volunteers and Spanish physicians had done in converting a broken-
down chateau into a modern medical facility. He took justifiable joy in this
accomplishment, and was equally pleased by the book signing that followed
his hospital visit. At an event in a Toulouse bookstore, jammed with men
and women, apparently prepared in advance by Fast's French hosts, he spent
three hours inscribing French translations of *Freedom Road* and *The American.* "Nothing," he said, "warms a writer's heart more than autographing
his books."[46]

What ought to have been the most consequential event for Howard Fast
between the opening of the conference on April 20 and its closing on April
25 was his meeting with Alexander Fadeyev, the Russian writer and head of
the Soviet delegation to the Paris Peace Congress. Fast had interacted with
Fadeyev, who was also the American contact for the Union of Soviet Writers,
at the Waldorf Conference in March, and had been, since the beginning of
1949, corresponding with him regularly.[47]

Of all the claims made in *Being Red,* yet never mentioned in *The Naked
God,* the most astonishing and controversial is that Fast brought to this "secret" meeting a formal charge of antisemitism made by the CPUSA against the
Soviet Central Committee of the Communist Party of the USSR.[48] Nowhere
else in the archives available to researchers or in any of the oral history collections, biographies, or in the many memoirs of American Communist Party

leaders or former leaders, is there even a hint of such an extraordinary event as the CPUSA criticizing the CPSU about anything ever, much less bringing charges against it. And the idea that the Party in the United States, which in 1949 was absorbed from January to October by the trial of eleven of its most important leaders charged under the Smith Act, was even thinking about, no less making formal charges of, antisemitism against the Soviet Union, is preposterous.

But that Fast had a meeting with Fadeyev in Paris about antisemitism is virtually certain. It was held in a small basement room in the Salle Pleyel, a great music hall in the Rue Mirabeau, where most of the peace conference events were taking place. The appointment was arranged under the auspices of Laurent Casanova, a leading French Communist, and Renaud de Jouvenal, Fast's friend and correspondent. Fadeyev, representing the Central Committee of the CPSU, brought with him two Russian translators.[49]

Fast insists that he began the meeting by telling Fadeyev he had been instructed by the National Committee of the CPUSA to bring formal charges of antisemitism against the CPSU. But it was actually at the urging of Paul Novick, the editor of the Communist Yiddish paper *Morgen Freiheit*, and Chaim Suller, secretary of the Jewish Commission of the CP, that Fast had asked for the get-together. Fast was carrying with him the concerns raised with Fadeyev at the Waldorf Conference about the fate of Solomon Mikhoels, the great Russian actor-director, and of the Jewish writers Itzak Feffer, David Bergelson, Layb Kvitko, Peretz Markish, and others. Fast had also been briefed by Suller and the Jewish Commission in New York to ask about leading Jewish figures in the Red Army and in government who had been arrested on what appeared to be trumped-up charges, and to inquire about the Yiddish newspapers that had been shut down, and the Hebrew schools unceremoniously closed.[50]

Fadeyev, a "large and very handsome man" with piercing blue eyes, responded, humming softly to himself, "There is no anti-Semitism in the Soviet Union." Taken aback, Fast asked, "No more than that?" To which, like "the creature of a slave state" that he was, Fadeyev simply repeated, "There is no anti-Semitism in the Soviet Union."[51] What is to be done? Fast wanted to know. "Am I supposed to go back and say there is no anti-Semitism in the Soviet Union?" Fast spelled out more details of the "rumors," saying that perhaps some were untrue, but "we know that the closing of the schools is true. . . . Why can't you discuss these things?" Fast was bewildered, even angered, by Fadeyev's saying yet again, this time with more than a touch of irritation at Fast's persistence, "Because there is no anti-Semitism in the Soviet Union."[52]

In *Being Red,* Fast says he could not get Fadeyev to say anything more. "Also," Fast adds, almost as a throwaway line, *"it might well be true that Fadeev knew nothing about anti-Semitism in Russia."* Fast in 1990 had once again failed to tell us the truth. For in actuality, Fadeyev finally lost control over Fast's persistent pestering and said two shocking things that not only belied the Russian writer's prior denials, but also clearly indicated that Fadeyev fully justified the actions taken against Jews and was willing to retail Soviet-style antisemitism.

Fadeyev told Fast "confidentially" that when Itzak Feffer had been with Solomon Mikhoels in the United States in 1943 as leaders of the Jewish Anti-Fascist Committee (JAFC), drumming up support for the Soviet Union, Feffer had been hired by the "Zionists of the United Jewish Appeal" to be their chief spy in the USSR. When he was back in Moscow, Mikhoels, Fadeyev said, discovered Feffer's treachery, and planned to inform the Soviet authorities. Feffer, learning of Mikhoels's intention, murdered him. And that's why Feffer and the other writers were arrested! As if this ridiculous tale were not enough, Fadeyev added "that there existed in Russia a vast . . . plot against socialism," a conspiracy between Zionists and the American-based Joint Distribution Committee (the "Joint") to launch a counterrevolution in the Soviet Union.[53]

As with many conspiracy theories, so with Fadeyev's: there were tiny fragments of truth available for exploitation. The JAFC *had* helped Holocaust survivors and displaced Jews in the Soviet Union. It had even tried to make contact with the Joint in an effort to send humanitarian supplies on a nonsectarian basis to regions of the USSR with large concentrations of Jews. Although this activity generated suspicion about "Jewish nationalism" in the Kremlin, it was reluctantly allowed while the war continued. With the end of hostilities and the beginnings of the Cold War, however, everything the JAFC had done was held against it.[54]

The situation grew immeasurably worse for the JAFC with the founding of Israel in 1948. Golda Meir, carrying the first ever issued Israeli passport, and serving as ambassador to the Soviet Union, was greeted by cheering crowds when she arrived in Moscow. Thousands "followed her on her first Shabbat" in September 1948 "as she walked from the Hotel Metropole, next to the Bolshoi Theatre, to the Central Synagogue on Arkhipova Street." This scene was repeated on Rosh Hashanah and Yom Kippur when tens of thousands of Jews poured into the streets in celebration and, as correctly perceived by the authorities, defiance.[55]

The Soviet Union officially dissolved the JAFC in November 1948, and over the winter of 1948–49, hundreds of Jews associated with the committee were arrested, among them the fifteen eventually put on trial in 1952. In the meantime, several prominent Jews were tortured and forced to confess to "nationalist errors." Itzak Feffer, like many other Jewish antifascists who by their revolutionary commitment and naïve idealism were tied to a system they could not renounce, was compelled to say—putting meat on the bones of Fadeyev's elaborate lie—that JAFC was conspiring with the Joint to establish a Jewish "republic" in Crimea as a base from which to dismember the Soviet Union.[56]

None of what Fadeyev told Howard Fast is mentioned in *The Naked God* or in *Being Red*. But in private letters written after Fast left the Party in 1957, he claimed that upon his return from Paris at the end of April 1949, he told Paul Novick the whole truth about the Fadeyev episode and its implications for Jews in Stalinist Russia. Fast also "reminded" Novick of the story that Leonovich Gordon, representative of the Polish government, had told him in 1949: "'Itzik Feffer had been imprisoned for the murder of Mikhoels.'" Fast also claimed that he had had a two-hour conversation with Chaim Suller about his meeting with Fadeyev and about his conversation with Gordon, and even "told the full story to V. J. Jerome," cultural czar of the American Communist Party, "asking him to pass it on."[57]

It may indeed be, despite Novick's furious denials, that Fast shared the information about Fadeyev's revelatory statements with two or three comrades. Whatever the case, and whatever private fears Fast, Novick, and Suller may have had about the fate of the Jews in the USSR, they were not psychologically prepared or courageous enough to go public with this information so vital to understanding the nature of Stalinism and Jewish life in the Soviet Union. They continued to believe the USSR "to be the bastion of world socialism" and that virtually nothing else mattered.[58] Fast, post-Paris, chose not to speak about Jews in Russia. He said only that "this thing in Paris was not a league of nations or parties or even of organizations, but the beginnings of a league of the human race . . . promulgated for the survival of the human race"; minus apparently a sizable portion of Fast's own people.[59]

Four years later in 1953, when antisemitism reached another of its many peaks in Soviet history, Fast, according to his account in *Being Red,* felt compelled to tell Jacob Auslander, one of the convicted members of the JAFRC, in confidence, about his talk with Fadeyev in Paris in 1949. What he actually told Auslander, Fast does not reveal. But Auslander was shocked that Howard had never written about the Fadeyev episode. The "party asked me not to," Fast said. "My God, Howard," Auslander exclaimed, "what are you saying to me?" He couldn't have written about the encounter with Fadeyev, Fast explained, unless the Party agreed. Remember, he told Auslander, "I spoke to Fadeev as a disciplined party member."[60] Fast, until late into 1956, remained "a disciplined Party member." He continued to dismiss publicly all criticism of the Soviet Union as the "lies and slanders" of the bourgeoisie, and suppressed any temptation to reveal openly what he knew about the antisemitism and barbaric inhumanity of Russian Communism.

Unfortunately, Fast, Novick, Suller, and V. J. Jerome, Jews all, were not the only ones who failed to disclose what they knew about the status of Jewish notables and of Jewish culture generally in the Soviet Union. Fast's good friend and confidante Paul Robeson was also guilty of hiding the truth about antisemitism in the USSR and about the "mysterious" death of Mikhoels. Robeson, who was on tour in the Soviet Union in 1949, may have believed the story that the actor-director had been accidently hit and killed by a truck; but he had heard new dark stories circulating in the USSR about antisemitism, particularly about the fate of Mikhoels's comrade Feffer and the other missing Yiddish writers. It was partly to quell these disturbing rumors that Robeson, still touring, undertook his "mission to Moscow."[61]

As soon as the great singer and progressive activist arrived, he was struck by the campaign in the press against "Zionists" and "Cosmopolitans." Robeson was also distressed to learn that Feffer had been in prison for a year and that his plan to visit him had to be delayed while the incarcerated poet was being prettied-up for an elaborately arranged meeting. The hotel room in which Robeson and Feffer finally talked was bugged, and the prisoner had to communicate through written notes and gestures. Feffer did make it clear, however, that he faced imminent execution and that other prominent Jewish writers and poets and members of the Jewish Anti-Fascist Committee were under arrest. Robeson also learned that a massive purge was underway of the Leningrad and Moscow Communist parties, purposely singling out their large Jewish memberships for persecution. Before leaving the hotel room, Robeson tore up the little note papers Feffer had handed him and flushed them down the toilet.[62]

Robeson did not confront his Soviet friends over the horrors he had come to know firsthand, nor did he, in protest, cancel further singing engagements in Moscow. Instead, at a farewell concert, Robeson proclaimed his friendship for Mikhoels, who he now suspected had been brutally murdered on Stalin's command, and for Feffer, who languished in Lubyanka Prison awaiting execution. As a finale, Robeson sang in Yiddish the resistance song of the Warsaw Ghetto uprising, "Zog nit keynmohl" (Never say you have reached the end). The audience, Jews and non-Jews, rose as one in sustained applause. The recording of the performance, which had been broadcast live throughout the USSR, was quickly destroyed by government authorities.

After Robeson returned to the United States, he denied the rumors of antisemitism, announcing to a reporter from *Soviet Russia Today* that he "had met Jewish people all over the place . . . . I heard no word about it." And as Robeson's biographer, Martin Duberman, demonstrates, he went to great lengths to instruct doubters that the Stalin regime "had done everything" for its minorities, including the Jews. Robeson told the true story only to his son, but made him vow not to make any of it public until well after his death because, though not a CP member, "he had promised himself that he would never publicly criticize the USSR," where he had been treated royally and where he believed blacks were "raised to the full dignity of mankind."[63] Duberman argues that the singer could not really have done much more, and may even have hastened Feffer's execution had he spoken out. But this misses a larger point. Beginning in the late 1930s and for many years thereafter, Robeson explicitly defended Stalinist purges even when they swallowed some of his own friends. It was right, he said, for the Soviets to "destroy anybody who seeks to harm that great country."[64]

Fast's silence in 1949 looks slightly less outrageous only in contrast. It took eight more years from this point, and about ten months after Khrushchev's speech in 1956 "revealing" Stalin's cruelties and crimes, before Fast left the CPUSA. He did finally leave, however, and soon thereafter wrote a blisteringly critical book about the Party and about antisemitism in Russia. Robeson, on the other hand, not only maintained his silence about the murder of Jews and the obliteration of Jewish culture in the Soviet Union, he continued to be a staunch supporter of Stalinism for the rest of his life.

Howard's daughter, Rachel, remembers that at the Fast house "Paul Robeson was a frequent guest. When he visited, he held me in his lap, sang to me." Paul, she wrote "was . . . a great gorgeous man with a deep voice, a gentle manner [and] . . . intelligence." She also wrote that he was "perfect" and possessed of "prodigious . . . courage." Well . . . as we have seen, not always; and as Rachel herself realized, "I have, I imagine," like so many others, "idealized memories of Paul."[65]

Neither Robeson nor Fast was anything approximating perfect, and both were capable of betrayals other than political. The singer, like Fast, was frequently unfaithful to his wife. When asked about why he slept around, Robeson said that men, especially creative men, had great needs, emotional and physical, and that if his family was hurt in the process of his fulfilling those needs, so be it. In any conflict between "art" and the family, Robeson maintained, "my family must suffer . . . the artist gives joy to hundreds of thousands, perhaps to millions . . . . He must consider his responsibilities to this multitude rather than to those few."[66] Fast was never so blatant in justifying his infidelities, but as his son, Jonathan, told me, his "father always wanted to have his cake and eat it too." Howard wanted Bette "to be his and also to have mistresses, one after another . . . about whom he confessed," or bragged, and "for whom he expected to be forgiven."[67]

Occasionally, Fast actually brought his lovers home when the kids were in school or at camp and Bette out. From as early as 1948 or 1949, before Fast went to Paris, he and the famous model Isabel Johnson initiated a sexual relationship that continued steadily until 1951, and that may have picked up again in 1956. "I was making my bed yesterday," Howard wrote to Isabel in 1950, "and I found your lovely gift. I just can't tell you how touched I was. I felt as if I wanted to cry, and all of a sudden I felt as lonely as a person ever can feel and wanting above everything else for you to be here in town . . . and such a long two weeks ahead. But I swallow as I write that, for you know only too well how idiotically I act when you are here."[68]

Rachel was well aware that her father "was 'in love' with Isabel for many years." Fast's younger brother, "Julie, the warm, supportive, and all-accepting one," for whatever perverse reasons, "used to tell [Rachel] about it every chance he got." Her father, Rachel said, liked to see himself as the "embodiment of *a passion more intense than any the planet had yet produced.*" Indeed, she believed that sexual exploits were "central to [his] character." Whenever an infidelity was discovered or suspected, Bette "would look pissed, grit her teeth, then make excuses for [her husband] because 'he's an artist.'" Fast was actually "tickled" at "being AKA Don Juan," and he pursued this strategy of self-presentation by proudly appearing at family dinners with Isabel in tow while he and Bette were temporarily separated.[69]

Bette was not always forgiving, however. In 1949, just prior to or just after Howard's adventures in Paris, the couple separated, "possibly about to be divorced."[70] Bette stayed in the apartment on 94th Street, and Howard moved in with Isabel, though he did spend time with the children at home. In late August, Bette left sixteen-month-old Jonathan and five-year old Rachel in the good care of Juliette, their "fat, soft, and huggy" black nanny, and took off for Europe on her own. She visited Amsterdam and Venice, but spent the greater part of her time in Paris. She saw some of her French Jewish relatives, and befriended Irene Joliot-Curie, the wife of the prominent physicist and Communist activist Frederic Joliot-Curie.[71] Although she missed her children, and Howard too, Bette had a grand time in Paris and "positively glowed" whenever she reminisced about her time there.[72]

Escape wasn't Bette's only response to Howard's dalliances. She tried therapy, and even returning to school. But Howard "made her stop" both; he simply refused to pay.[73] Apparently, perhaps in retaliation for Howard's intransigent need to control, Bette had a few flings of her own. She also "fell seriously in love" with Robert (Bobby) Goodman, a socially progressive intellectual and father of Andrew Goodman of Schwerner, Chaney, and Goodman renown. So serious was their relationship that Bobby and Bette considered leaving their respective spouses and marrying one another.[74] Rumor had it that Bette also had an affair with Dashiell Hammett in the early fifties. Hammett, according to Fast's granddaughter, Molly Jong-Fast, offered Bette "an escape from all the chaos and philandering." Although Molly thinks Bette resisted Hammett's entreaties because he "was a horrible drunk and probably wouldn't have been a better [choice] than Grandpa," Molly's mother, Erica Jong, for a short time in the 1970s the wife of Jonathan Fast, isn't so sure. When I asked the author of *Fear of Flying* whether Bette had had an affair with Hammett, she said, "I certainly hope so!" Erica also had come across a copy of Hammett's *The Maltese Falcon,* inscribed to "Howard and Bette, but to Bette really."[75]

THE POISON OF PEEKSKILL

Even in the face of Howard's infidelities, which continued until at least 1980, Bette stuck by him. In September 1949, while she was in Paris, Bette's letters and phone calls were supportive, and sometimes even loving. After reading accounts in *Le Figaro* and *Le Monde* describing the anti-Communist riot in Peekskill, New York, initiated by people angry over a planned concert featuring Paul Robeson, Bette, knowing Howard was to serve as master of ceremonies, did some "high-grade worrying over it." After a phone call home she was relieved to discover that the children were safe. "It was wonderful talking to you last night," Bette wrote the next day. "You don't know how worried I was about the children," she said, and added, "I hope nothing happened to you."[76] Fortunately, the children had been in the protecting hands of their nanny Juliette, who, certain there'd be trouble, had warned Howard—to no avail—to stay away from the Robeson concert.[77]

Bette also wrote about her pleasure in seeing Venice, but said, "The only trouble with it is that it's wasted unless you're in love." Yet in her next letter, two weeks later, Bette wrote, "Strange business Howie. I miss you a hell of a lot more than I miss the kids. This I never dreamed could be—but it is." And soon thereafter, Bette wrote, "Your letter yesterday was very sweet. Everything is fine now. "[78]

The Peekskill riot did more than help Howie and Bette get back together (though despite his promises he continued to see Isabel). Peekskill injected poison into Fast's political veins by intensifying his conviction that America had become an irredeemably fascist country, not by accident or increment, but by conscious design. What we know about the Peekskill riots comes to us from looking through a glass darkly. That the concertgoers were the victims of anti-Communist mobs during the first attempt at holding the event on August 27 as well as after the end of the "second" concert on September 4 is certain. Beyond that everything else turns into a murky swill of conflicting stories, guesswork, contradictory official testimony, and political hyperbole from all sides.[79]

The Civil Rights Congress (CRC) had scheduled a concert in Peekskill for the end of August. Most of the proceeds were to go to the legal defense of the eleven Communist leaders on trial at Foley Square, and a much smaller amount to championing the cause of the "Trenton 6"—six black youths who had been convicted of murder and sentenced to die in the electric chair in New Jersey, but who by the efforts of CRC had had their convictions overturned and were scheduled to be retried.[80]

Paul Robeson, the featured attraction, had performed in Peekskill in 1946, '47, and '48 with no serious resistance from resentful residents. In 1949, however, Robeson had been quoted as saying in Paris in April, and then two days later in Stockholm, "It is unthinkable that American Negroes would go to war on behalf of those who have oppressed us for generations against a country [the Soviet Union] which in one generation has raised our people to the full dignity of mankind."[81] According to Martin Duberman, Robeson's biographer, the performer-activist was misquoted. Unlikely. But even if the papers had it right, Robeson's words were relatively mild and not without precedent. During World War II, A. Phillip Randolph, the black labor and civil rights leader, had said something similar: The wealth of America had been built "on the backs of millions of blacks," Randolph proclaimed. "And we are resolved to share it equally . . . . And we shall not put up with any hysterical ravings that urges us to make war on anyone . . . . We shall not make war on the Soviet Union."[82]

Those remarks were made, however, before the 1948 testimonies of Elizabeth Bentley and Whittaker Chambers, and prior to the disclosures of Judith Coplon, who had been recruited as a spy by the Soviet secret police in 1944 and was one of the more important figures tried for espionage in the United States. Randolph's statements also preceded the victory of Mao's Communist forces in Nanjing in April 1949. With Robeson's failure, however, in the same month, to disavow his "anti-American" remarks, indeed, with his having repeated them at his homecoming from the Soviet Union, which got front-page coverage in the *Peekskill Evening Star* as well as in articles in the *New York Times*, Communism and the black singer had become much more controversial, at least in Peekskill.[83]

A public opinion poll in 1949 indicated that only 3 percent of the American public placed Communism first as the most serious problem facing the nation.[84] But Peekskill was different, especially during the summer. By 1949, summer residents, mostly middle-class Jews with a distinctly left-wing political culture, outnumbered the local population. The Jews had brought some prosperity to the area through land purchases and the building of more than a dozen camps and colonies within fifty miles of Peekskill, but whatever small amount of cultural or social interaction there was with the natives generated resentments: Jews had more money and free time, they produced crowds and traffic, and they enjoyed public services without having to pay taxes. They were also much more liberal, politically and socially, and dressed more casually, especially the women.[85] One could detect a distinct atmosphere of antisemitism, antiblack racism, and class antipathy to "summer folk" in the Hudson Valley town; but what distinguished Peekskill was not its prejudices so much, nor even its anti-Communism, but that its people in August 1949 thought that they were facing down the "Red menace" in their own backyards.

In the summer of 1948, two young men, who were easily dispatched, threw apples at the stage on which Robeson performed. In August 1949, however, the veterans' organization in Peekskill called for a "patriotic parade" outside the Lakelands Acres picnic grounds where Robeson was to sing, along with Pete Seeger, Woody Guthrie, and others, and where Howard Fast was to serve as MC. Although the *Peekskill Star* carried a number of inflammatory editorials on Robeson and Communism, it joined the mayor of the town and the district attorney in entreating the veterans to move their protest further from the concert grounds—to no avail. There were voices of restraint, but few were loud or clear. Ultimately, by blocking the highway with their parade, the veterans and others who joined them closed the only means of access to the grounds by car, in effect preventing the concert.[86]

Howard Fast was the only one to get into the area where the stage had been set up. But he soon joined several scheduled entertainers and members of the disappointed audience outside the concert grounds, where they stood in a tight circle singing "The Star-Spangled Banner," "God Bless America," and "Solidarity Forever." The rowdy and mostly inebriated crowd of Peekskill protesters, which included some veterans, made a bonfire of the chairs that had been set up for the performance and tossed into it pamphlets, books, and music they had gathered from the concert area. Fast, worried that the concertgoers themselves would be targeted, took charge of what remained of the audience, organized the men into seven squads of six, and dispatched them to different defensive posts around Lakeland Acres.[87]

Fast claimed that the protesters, who numbered "about 300 . . . against our handful," started throwing a barrage of rocks, some the size of grapefruits. Whatever sparked it directly, the concertgoers by all accounts did not initiate the violence, and in the melee that ensued they suffered the worst of it by far.[88] But, among other injuries, a twenty-four-year-old veteran was stabbed, an act Fast a few days later claimed was performed by a protester "in a plot to accuse [the Communists] of murder." Photographs, however, show the knife in the hand of a concert usher who was standing no more than fifteen feet from Howard Fast.

The CRC also charged that the cops had abetted the rioters. Given the heated rhetoric surrounding the planned concert, there ought to have been many more officers in uniform in the area, but there is no evidence that the authorities helped to initiate or perpetuate the violence; and the rioting, which lasted nearly two hours, ceased immediately upon the arrival of a larger police force.[89] Whatever Fast's exaggerations, however, he did take the lead in physically defending the concertgoers, and he battled hard. In an interview of an elderly woman present at the event, Gerald Meyers, a journalist and historian, was told with great vehemence, "Don't you go and say anything bad about Howard Fast. I saw him . . . with a Coke bottle in each hand fighting back."[90]

The CRC was determined to have its concert, so it announced a meeting at Harlem's Golden Gate Ballroom for the 30th of August to mobilize support. Its flyers were not designed to pacify: "People of Harlem, the Ku Klux Klan held a Lynching party in Peekskill Yesterday. Let the Klan Know That Harlem Will Fight Back." The KKK was not even indirectly involved, nor was a lynching attempted. More than one hundred people were injured, some seriously, but no one was killed.[91]

At the meeting, after Pete Seeger sang some of the songs he had intended to perform at Lakeland Acres, Howard Fast gave a vivid account of his experience at the picnic grounds, describing how twenty concertgoers held one thousand Peekskill natives at bay. And almost as if inviting more violence, he said, "The thousand . . . Americans, for all their big talk, were not very brave hand-to-hand in the dark." Outside the ballroom Robeson addressed an overflow crowd that had waited for him to emerge. "From now on out," Robeson said, "we take the offensive. I want my friends to know in the South, . . . all over the United States, that I'll be there with my concerts, and I'll be in Peekskill too."[92]

Although it was assumed that the local veterans, who were treated to a fierce dressing-down by their national organizations and a significant tongue-lashing by many in the national media, would not want another riot, the CRC came to Peekskill on September 4th better prepared to defend the concertgoers against other protesters. Thousands of members of militant unions and the Communist Party arrived by busses. Carrying chains and baseball bats, about 2,500 men formed a human barrier that prevented any troublemakers from even approaching the concert grounds. Moreover, significantly more police were provided, including a very large contingent of state troopers.

It was rumored that two, perhaps as many as four, men were spotted atop a hill with high-powered rifles. For years there was only Fast's testimony to corroborate this, but Helen and Sam Rosen, who had hosted Robeson at their home in Katonah, New York, told Martin Duberman more than thirty years later that they had seen several men with guns on the ridge surrounding the hollow that day. Although the men were flushed from the site by the CRC security force, Fast, fearing for Robeson's life, considered canceling the concert. But fifteen men, including Fast himself, volunteered to provide a shield around the black singer as he performed. That some people wanted Robeson dead seems real enough. Fast, however, continued to insist even fifty years later that there had been a conspiracy among fascists, in the government and out, from the very start. It was the fascists who "wanted to kill Paul," Fast said; about this "there is no question in my mind."[93]

The concert went on without incident, but leaving the grounds was a nightmare. Young men and women who had gathered stones and had hidden on the borders of the exit road poured out of the woods, creating a blockade within which they smashed cars, badly damaged buses, and bloodied concertgoers. The rock-throwing continued for six miles south of Peekskill, through the towns of Buchanan, Montrose, and Croton along Route 9, as cars and buses with smashed windows and dented fenders headed back to New York City. More than 150 people were injured, some seriously. There is documentary evidence, including photographs, showing that many policemen tried to protect the concertgoers, but also that about as many stood by.[94]

Fast, from the stage, in his role as MC had called the protestors fascists, and "un-American filth," among other insulting epithets. This, along with Fast's fiery language preceding the second concert, moved some, including the novelist T. C. Boyle, to imply that in insisting on a second attempt at a concert, the CRC, Paul Robeson, and Howard Fast were trying to provoke a politically exploitable incident. Perhaps. But Boyle's fictive Sasha Freeman, a character modeled on Fast, seems drawn too cynically. Freeman, Boyle wrote, wanted "to stir things up till they were good and hot, work in a little slaughter of the innocents with some broken bones thrown in for good measure. . . . And if some poor coon got lynched, so much the better. A peaceful sing along? What the hell good was that?"[95]

Whatever the motives of the concert organizers, they gained little for their cause. Condemnation of the Peekskill rioters came from many quarters, including the capitals of Europe. Even those who felt that the Communists had exploited the concert as an opportunity to elicit violence and cloak themselves in the mantle of martyrdom had to confess that the right to defend oneself against assault at an open public event was thoroughly "American."

But most Americans saw the incident as aberrant, and Peekskill as a delin-
quent among American cities, not a representative case.[96]

For Howard Fast, however, the violence in Peekskill was blatant evidence
that all of America had been poisoned by fascism. The Peekskill incidents,
Fast insisted, were not only proof of what he called the process of "fascization" of the United States but also a step in the preparation of America
for "the promulgation of World War III." The *Daily Worker* immediately
warned Americans not to delude themselves that Peekskill was a local affair,
with local significance only. Peekskill, the editors maintained, "marks the
carefully organized effort to impose police state terrorism in the U.S.A."[97]

Fast agreed that "the whole matter was by no means a spontaneous outbreak of local filth." Not only was the murder of Paul Robeson part "of the
official program of American reaction," Fast said, but the "unreasonable
facsimiles of human beings who were bent, with such intentness, upon our
death" were recruited by neo-fascists in Peekskill, who were part of a larger
"plan for the imposition of a police state in America."[98] That there were
fascist groups in the U.S. is undeniable. Unquestionably, there were also
important vestiges of antisemitism, and persistent, seemingly intractable
antiblack racism. After all, well over one million people voted for Strom
Thurmond in the 1948 presidential election. But that the government was
planning to mobilize support among reactionary portions of the American
population for the imposition of a police state was hardly credible.

Pete Seeger was less concerned about the "fascization" of America. "It
may sound silly," he said in an interview in 1999, "but we were confident law
and order would prevail." Seeger had been hit with eggs in North Carolina,
Alabama, and Mississippi, but the riots in New York State surprised him and
temporarily shook his faith in the resilience of American ideals. Ultimately,
however, sanity, regret, and even shame did return, when about five days
after the riots, signs around Peekskill reading "Wake Up America: Peekskill
Did!" came down. The powerful American ideas of free speech and dissent,
Seeger said, were too deeply rooted to be completely overcome even in this
era of anti-Communism and political conformity. Fast also expressed some
optimism for the long term, but with distinctly less enthusiasm and with
much more of a sense of embattlement. Indeed, Fast, seemingly unhinged,
wrote an article for *Masses and Mainstream* saying, "We saw the sub-human
frenzy of the union of police and storm troopers, Ku Klux Klan and Legion,"
while the "governor in Albany," not only "welcomed the storm troopers" but

"aided them and put his cheap stamp of white washing approval on their work." There is, however, "a people in our state who do not want Fascism and are willing to pay a price to halt it. Halt it we shall!"[99]

Fast's article was eventually expanded into *Peekskill, USA,* a book reprinted in the Soviet Union as the definitive account of the rise of fascism in America. Only true believers like Fast could characterize Peekskill as the beginning of fascism in the United States, while championing as a flourishing socialist state the USSR, which, among its other crimes against humanity, was closing Jewish schools and newspapers and arresting and torturing Jewish writers and "nationalists." Fast's reaction to Peekskill was another unfortunate example of the double-standard morality of many Communists.

Except for Communists and a small number of others on the radical left, Fast's book *Peekskill, USA* was all but ignored in the United States.[100] All the more ironic then is Fast's post-Peekskill proclamation: "I am different [now], and I am not just a writer anymore, and this is something writers who read this must understand, that from here on, we must make of our writing a sword that will cut this monster of fascism to pieces or we will make no more literature."[101] Fast cast his pen into a long jousting spear with which he continued to tilt at the windmill of American fascism, but for nearly a decade he neither accomplished anything of significance politically nor made much in the way of literature.

7

Literature and Reality

A prisoner of his own ambition and of his unwavering loyalty to Communist orthodoxy, Fast on June 7, 1950, became a prisoner of the state. The U.S. Supreme Court, on May 29 had dashed Fast's last chance at reprieve by denying for a second time in two years a review of his appeal lost at lower levels. Fast and the other convicted members of the Joint Anti-Fascist Refugee Committee had known for many months that their chances were exceedingly slim, and this last attempt at a review by the highest court was little more than a formality on their part.[1]

But in the months preceding what Fast now saw as his inevitable imprisonment, he continued to speak, write, and correspond with supporters. In October 1949, in a letter to his Welsh friend, novelist Gwyn Thomas, Fast said he was convinced that the Truman government had "gone truly berserk," and that "gibbering idiots" were running the nation. He went on in a bizarre non sequitur to say that the atom bomb "which the Russians so innocently exploded has shown up the utter insanity and bankruptcy" of Washington, "a city sick with terror and paralyzed with fear." Fast, who hadn't been in D.C. since October 1947, told Thomas that "there are spies, informers, and various kinds of touts at every street corner" of the capital. And although he had never been to Germany, Fast told Thomas that he agreed with a Czech associate who had recently remarked that "Berlin at its worst was not quite as bad" as Washington. Fascism, Fast concluded, has come to America as anti-Communism "in the name of democracy."[2]

Thomas, who had never been to America, responded in terms mimicking Fast's. It is necessary, he wrote, to go beyond "the simple setting down of words" to defend those who are being silenced by "the bigots who have restored the Inquisition in America. . . . When artists in their thousands [!] can be bludgeoned into flight and shameful silence by the repressive phobias of sick-minded fanatics and rogues, the community deals itself a mortal wound."[3] Fast's public statements were just as inflammatory as his private letters, and no public event, even if only obliquely related to politics, would go unexploited by him—including F. O. Matthiessen's 1950 plunge from a twelfth-story window of a Boston hotel. Despite Matthiessen's other "problems," including a nervous breakdown, closeted homosexuality, and deep depression after the death of his partner, and despite a suicide note that read in part, "How much the state of the world has to do with my state of mind I do not know," Fast insisted that the American "witch-hunt . . . destroyed Professor Matthiessen," as American fascism "would . . . destroy all he stood for, Christianity, free inquiry, and a democratic way of life."[4]

Nor during the months preceding his imprisonment would Fast let the sleeping dogs of Peekskill lie. He, Paul Robeson, the Civil Rights Congress, and twenty-five others sued the Westchester County district attorney, the mayor of Peekskill, the captain of Troop K of the state police, the Associated Veterans Council, and several other organizations for trying to prevent the concerts and for neglecting or refusing to give protection to concertgoers on August 27 and September 4, 1949. The plaintiffs asked for over $2 million and announced their intention to sue for an additional $10 million on behalf of injured individuals. The court, however, restrained the civil action pending a report by the grand jury investigating the case. Fast placed great importance on the outcome. A verdict for the Peekskill victims, Fast said, would be a victory for justice and "a setback for fascism."[5]

The plaintiffs, as most interested people expected, lost their suit, but hoped that they had kept alive the issue of impending, or as they sometimes said, already implanted American fascism. Few outside of their immediate left circles, however, were thinking about Peekskill six months after the riots. Even Fast himself, though worried about being indicted for incitement to riot, spent much of his time writing about other things. Early in 1950 he completed a book, or more precisely a one-hundred-page broadside, called

Literature and Reality. Fast's white-hot anger and intense frustration were on display in this poorly written, disorganized work, as he laid out the role of the writer and the artist in society, once again devaluing literature by trying to transform it into nothing more than a weapon in the "good fight."

He drowned the reader in the crude rhetoric of Marxist-Leninism about objective reality, socialist realism, dialectical materialism, and something Fast called "super-truth." All truths are equal, but some are more equal than others? Whatever he might have meant by this, those writers who failed to create "super-truth," according to Fast, included Franz Kafka, "a petty-bourgeois German fascist" and an exponent of "helplessness, disgust, and self-loathing"; T. S. Eliot, the "voodoo" master of "art for art's sake"; Alfred Lord Tennyson and Rudyard Kipling, pompous pimps for imperialism; of course, Trotskyists and renegades such as John Steinbeck and Richard Wright, capable only of "adolescent pessimism" or "cheap maudlin sentimentality," were relegated to the "cultural dung-heap of reaction."[6] Like St. Augustine, Fast, just as ruthlessly, though with far less understanding and intelligence or success, tried to turn intellectual persecution into an art form. He wielded words like an ice pick, slashing away at the enemies of the One True Church, with pages of invective and ideological quibbling, pages as ugly and dreary as anything to be found in the work of Lenin.

So who had gotten hold of super-truth? In every land, Fast said, it was the Communists: O'Casey in Ireland, Aragon in France, Neruda in Chile, and Gwyn Thomas in Wales. And the Soviet writers, too, of course: N. A. Ostrovsky, Fadeyev (yes, the very same), P. Pavlenko, and Leonid Sobolev had grasped the essence of literature and sounded a new note, which Fast paraphrases for us, using, perhaps unwittingly, the cadence and vocabulary of fascist rhetoric: "I am the citizen of the future, the narrator of the future of mankind which is already here. We are indestructible because we bear the hope and aspiration of mankind, and hundreds of millions follow us."[7]

Sean O'Casey, flattered perhaps, wrote to Fast about *Literature and Reality:* "I think it is most reasonable" and "the clearest and by far the best essay on that subject which has ever come my way." A less predictable and more extraordinary letter came from P. Pavlenko, the Soviet author of a novel called *Happiness.* He "liked" *Literature and Reality* but took issue with Fast's contention that "the literature, creative and critical, of America is sick, deeply sick," and that "only a great progressive upsurge can cure it." Pavlenko also disagreed with Fast's conclusion that "American literature is dominated by writers distinguished for the love of the almighty buck and their compassion for their own skins." It seemed to Pavlenko, who had visited with Fast in the United States in January 1950, that Howard was being "too pessimistic." In addition to "the reading public of the USSR and the People's Democracies," Pavlenko argued, "there is a substantial number of readers of American books in France, England, Belgium, Italy and elsewhere . . . and that is why I believe that you are inclined to underestimate . . . the influence of progressive American literature as a whole." After all, Pavlenko said, undermining Fast's thesis in its entirety, "books on critical realism appearing in the capitalist countries, books written not altogether from the correct position, can, it seems to me, also be on our side of the barricade along with works of Socialist realism."[8]

Criticism from the left did not come only from the Soviet Union. *The Daily Worker* gave *Literature and Reality* a generally favorable review and a large layout of pictures, including a photo of Fast displaying international editions of his books. But the reviewer thought Fast was superficial in his research and documentation. He praised Fast for his persistent use of the term "socialist realism," but was thoroughly annoyed that Howard had failed to condemn the bête noir of most Marxists, Freudian psychoanalysis and its influence on contemporary writers. *Masses and Mainstream,* too, although praising the book, referred pointedly to its limitations, especially Fast's unreflective denigration of recent European and American literature as decadent.[9] Fast, it seems, had grown more intolerant, dogmatic, and doctrinaire than his comrades abroad as well as at home.

Albert Maltz, after retreating four years earlier in the face of Fast's vicious critique of his theories on art and politics, now advanced aggressively against Howard's. Maltz wrote that *Literature and Reality* was filled with mistaken propositions that assume that America would make "automatic the censorship of any [progressive] work of art. . . . This just does not happen to be true of the United States today," he told Fast. "You are" incorrectly "assuming a class conscious, absolute fascist censorship in all aspects of our society," Maltz wrote. He asked Fast if it wasn't true that the two of them would celebrate the appearance of new authors, with new books of "progressive social content." What if, Maltz asked, the new author were Maltz himself, under a pseudonym, freed to reach a broader audience with what he had to say "—then what is unsound about that?" If, however, Fast was proposing that any book published and in the United States today was by definition a reactionary book, precisely what he *was* doing, "then," said Maltz, "we really have no common language on the subject."[10]

In effect, but with less fury, Fast and Maltz were having the same argument about art and politics they had had in 1946. But in the four years since then, Fast had managed to become more rigidly orthodox in his demand for political correctness. In referring to distinguished writers of his era as "belly-crawlers" and "literary degenerates," Fast was using epithets standard among Communist critics. But the frequency and bitterness with which he used them indicated his desperation about standing virtually alone at the barricades, isolated from other writers whom he once had admired and likely still envied.

After Fast left the Party in 1957, he said *Literature and Reality* "was not an act of sensible criticism." It was an attack on "the literary establishment," which Fast apparently hungered to belong to even while stubbornly keeping to his own inimitable style. In 1967, he told an interviewer that *Literature and Reality* was the one book of which he was "ashamed," and that he had in the late fifties dropped it permanently from lists of his published works.[11]

In 1950, however, Fast still saw himself in the tradition of dissent, not so much in line with the proletarian writers of the 1930s as with writers such as Whitman, Twain, London, and Dreiser. He was completely dismissive of contemporary America's "miserable literary output" as merely more "evidence of a dying culture." But this was nothing new according to Fast, who thought there had always been an "enormously static quality" in early American literature. And in several essays he named Poe, Hawthorne, and Melville as prime examples of writers living in a "changeless world." Fast missed the significance of these nineteenth-century writers completely. Although marked by vestiges of Romanticism, their works were elevating such popular modes as the magazine "prose tale" into the modern short story; as importantly, they were harbingers of Freudianism and modern psychology generally.[12]

Fast went on to compound his seriously mistaken assessment, particularly of Melville, by saying that even the "tale of *Moby Dick*, the white whale, was of no special American condition." Melville ought not to be ignored, Fast thought, but added that the novelist dwindles into practical insignificance in the face of Whitman the poet. Fast quite accurately said that Whitman burst "like a thunderbolt" upon the American scene, abandoning Greek urns for "the seething caldron of millions of human souls"; but Fast's relative dismissal of Melville, arguably America's greatest writer, was an error of gargantuan proportion.[13]

Mark Twain was also superior to Melville, Fast believed, and more authentically American, especially in his "protest novel," *Huckleberry Finn*. Not altogether persuasively, Fast said, *Huck Finn* was something entirely new in America, something that went beyond the dark strains evident in Hawthorne and Melville. Fast basically argued that Twain was "a writer who draws his content and strength out of man's struggle for social and economic freedom."[14] In this way, he took what he needed ideologically from Twain, and magically transformed *Huckleberry Finn* into a story more about class than about slavery and race.

Yet even here Fast failed to see that *Huck Finn* transcends questions of both class *and* race. Twain's novel is an attack on "conscience"—the veneer of civilization propped up by Christian propriety, inertia, and hypocrisy—and a staunch defense of direct, intimate human connections over the "conventional wisdom" of society. Fast also fails to talk about Twain's remarkable ability to capture speech or even to mention that *Huck Finn* contains some of the greatest passages of prose ever written by an American.[15] For Fast, it was, as usual, politics over aesthetics, and the social question over the more immediately human.

After Twain came Fast's "hero," Jack London, who persisted in "shocking the world awake" on the social question. He was followed by Dreiser, to whom Fast was in thrall, because "filled with an aching love and hurt," Dreiser wrote out his saga of disappointment in twentieth-century America's failure to live up to its ideals.[16] But since then? Writing to Pavlenko, and later to Boris Polevoy, Fast claimed—using no examples—that contemporary mainstream authors and critics "hate" the older American tradition of indigenous skepticism and non-conformity and "they hate us." He wished that more traditional "good left-wing writing" were being done in America. Instead, Fast said, we have "the terror" that is "mounting very rapidly" and intimidating our writers. He found, to his "constant disappointment, that writers are not the most courageous of people."[17]

Perhaps so, and perhaps there is something to the conventional wisdom that insists that fiction writing and literary criticism in the 1940s became more introspective, shifting toward poetic and personal expression and away from Dreiserian or Craneian naturalism and social concerns. If aesthetic standards during the hot war and the Cold War that followed moved away from an emphasis on social engagement and toward skepticism and relativism, this was not merely a conscious or concerted role to promote and celebrate irony, ambiguity, and alienation; it was also a relatively autonomous phenomenon partly influenced by what Isaac Rosenfeld called "an age of enormity," in which mass murderous regimes were built by Hitler and Stalin on a foundation of "big ideas," charisma, emotional chaos, and mob psychology.[18]

Moreover, Fast was writing his critical words about a decade that saw important publications by writers once in or strongly influenced by the Communist movement: Hellman's *Watch on the Rhine* (1940); Richard Wright's *Native Son* (1940); Saul Bellow's *The Dangling Man* (1944) and *The Victim* (1947); Muriel Rukeyser's *Beast in View* (1944), which contains her justly famous "Letter to the Front"; Robert Penn Warren's *All the King's Men* (1946); MacKinlay Kantor's *Glory for Me*, which became the film *The Best Years of Our Lives* (1946); Langston Hughes's four volumes of intense and biting poetry (1942–49); Eugene O'Neill's *The Iceman Cometh* (1946).

Also appearing were several pro-Communist African American novelists, including Ann Petry (*The Street*, 1946) and Willard Motley (*Knock on Any Door*, 1947). Poet Robert Lowell published *Lord Weary's Castle* in 1947; Novelist Mailer wrote *The Naked and the Dead* in 1948, and playwright Miller delivered *All My Sons* in 1946 and *Death of a Salesman* in 1949. These were works that, although so different from one another, and from earlier proletarian novels and other works of "left-wing writing," were hardly without social critique and courage. The irony in these works was frequently separate from apathy and despair and often served as an indispensable tool of resistance.

None of this was enough for Fast or his Communist comrades at the *Daily Worker* and *New Masses,* who were distressed about the failure of modern artists to expose in explicit detail the underlying social and economic reasons for the pathologies and disaffections inherent in contemporary America. Ann Petry, Chester Himes (*The Lonely Crusade,* 1947), Dan Levin (*Mask of Glory,* 1949), and Jo Sinclair (*Wasteland,* 1946), for example, African American and Jewish left-wing writers of whom Fast was only vaguely aware, were dismissed because they failed to mention directly, or pay enough attention to, the specific "progressive" struggles being waged to overcome exploitation and suffering.[19] Petry, for example, a writer far superior to Fast, "failed," according to his tone-deaf reading, "to represent the truth" or to create "an artistic product of real stature" because "she was unable to extract from the lives of her characters any shred of hope or meaning."[20]

But the pro-Communist writers, left-liberal artists, and other social realists aimed to do something more important than provide prescription. For them literature's greatness and practical usefulness lay in the unremitting work of exacting painful confrontations with the reader's own thoughts and intentions. The novels, especially those by Petry, Sinclair, and Himes, were certainly not "fictionalized sociology" or handbooks for radicals, but nor were they "mere" aesthetic exercises. They were written in part to promote an empathy with the struggles of ordinary people—an identification powerful enough, it was hoped, to inspire the kind of social consciousness that would lead to a politics of transformation.[21]

Fast, more interested in the directly political, ignored most of these works, or dismissed them as without courage. He was also reinforced in his opinion about writers and their lack of courage when his pleas to mount a protest movement against his jailing and the imprisonment of the JAFRC board and the Hollywood Ten fell mostly on deaf ears.[22] Little was heard from Hemingway, for example, or from Farrell, Sinclair Lewis, John Hersey, or Carl Sandburg.[23] And in response to a letter from Fast asking Sean O'Casey to sign a petition in his support, the playwright wrote that the imprisonment of writers was of course "a most unjust act." But to send "a letter to the head of a foreign state would be the essence of impudence," especially "seeing that H. Truman has millions of Americans behind him." It is "probable," O'Casey thought, "that [the president] has never even heard my name mentioned." To write a letter or sign a petition then "would be foolish," O'Casey concluded, "and, in my opinion, do harm to whatever influence I have in the U.S.A."[24]

Many American writers, however, did issue a protest statement. Pro-Communists, ex-Communists, and non-Communists such as Carson Mc-Cullers and William Carlos Williams, for example, signed on as did Marc Blitzstein, Budd Schulberg, Louis Untermeyer, Muriel Rukeyser, and Clifford Odets.[25] This was no mean list of names, though just as likely to be unknown to Truman as Sean O'Casey's. In any event, by mid-1950 the Republican "soft-on-Communism" rap on the president, no matter how undeserved, had more resonance with the general public than ever, and it was absurd to think Truman would intervene in Fast's case.

HOWARD FAST: PRISONER

On the fifth of June 1950, Fast's lawyers informed him by phone that he had to be in Washington two days later to surrender to the authorities. What to tell the children? Jonathan, only two, could do without much explanation. But Rachel was just past six, and the Fasts thought they needed a way to explain Howard's absence without telling the truth about his forthcoming incarceration. Although Rachel would later resent having been lied to, it is difficult to judge whether Howard and Bette made an appropriate choice in hiding the truth from their daughter, who was already a troubled little girl.

"The events of the time," Rachel wrote in her adulthood, "terrible enough intrinsically but exaggerated by my father's fiery rhetoric, his aggressive suffering and theatrical outbursts, frightened me into silent, sometimes sycophantic submission and a stance of peace-and-harmony-at-any-price in almost any threatening situation."[26] Fast had been anxious to "educate" Rachel, to teach her enough about "objective reality" to prevent in her the development of any kind of "false consciousness."[27] Bette hated Howard's "politicizing me so young, his demanding that I respond as if I were forty when I was only four."[28] So Rachel spent her early years at home "living in an atmosphere of tension and anxiety; dread, unspoken fears, resentments of all sorts, and secretiveness . . . not to mention the FBI banging on the doors" and all the other "stuff" her parents "couldn't hide."[29]

Rachel didn't know "if other Communist Party members were as fanatically certain they had a corner on the absolute and pure truth or whether that conviction was peculiar to my father." But if *Red Diapers,* Judith Kaplan and Linn Shapiro's anthology of memoirs by those who grew up in the Communist left, is at all representative, Rachel was not alone. Jeffrey Lawson, for example, resented his parents for "indulging their Utopian views" and "fell apart psychologically" under the pressure. Bettina Aptheker, too, the daughter of the leading Communist Party theoretician, Herbert Aptheker, though remaining in the Communist movement into her early adulthood, admits to growing up in a family in which "Marxism was all-consuming," and where the "terrible violence of her parents' frequent outbursts" forced her into her "own private gulag."[30] And in *Red Diaper Baby,* Josh Kornbluth tells us his Communist father believed "there was going to be a Communist revolution" in America "and that I was going to lead it." Paul Kornbluth used to wake Josh every morning at 5 AM by running up to his bed, looming over him and singing, "Arise, ye prisoners of starvation/Arise, ye wretched of the earth."[31] According to his daughter, Howard Fast was not *that* loony. But her father "always insisted my mother and my brother and I (*everyone* come to think of it) believe *him*, whatever the subject," especially politics. By the time she was six or seven, Rachel said, "I was clinically depressed. There are photographs of me that were taken then. In them I look sad, beaten, angry."[32]

A trip to Paris was invented. Rachel had heard her father speak positively of the great city where Fast had been lauded only a year earlier, and she had already survived, in the warm and protective hands of the family's nanny, Juliette, the absence of her mother, who for many weeks had been in Paris in the summer of 1949. Rachel remembers that her father "wrote postcards to me from prison, sent them to a friend in France, and the friend sent them on to me so that they would have French stamps and postmarks." Years later, when Rachel's parents told her the truth, she was enraged. "They had betrayed me," she thought at seventeen. "Why couldn't they have trusted me to have the maturity . . . at six! . . . the strength to know the truth and to cope with it? I could have helped, somehow." Rachel, in many ways her father's daughter, "was sure of it."[33]

And Fast was "sure" that he and his JAFRC colleagues were "being sent to prison primarily to help clear the ground for a new world war. In all actuality," Fast said, this is "the last moment before fascism."[34] Howard's paranoia had him convinced that he might never be released from jail if war with Korea were to break out, which it did ten days after he reached the federal penitentiary in Mill Point, West Virginia; so Bette and the kids were instructed to retreat immediately after his incarceration to a little cottage owned by her parents right next door to their summer beach home in Bellmore, New Jersey. And on the morning of June 7, while Jonathan and Rachel slept, Howard kissed Bette goodbye, slipped from their soon-to-be-vacated apartment, taxied to Pennsylvania Station, and took a train to Washington.[35]

Once in D.C., Fast learned that a last-minute plea for clemency had been turned down. "What now?" Howard asked his attorney. "You go to jail." Indeed, he was soon in handcuffs, as were ten other members of the JAFRC board, including Dr. Jacob Auslander, Dr. Louis Miller, and Professor Lyman "Dick" Bradley, to whom Fast was cuffed. The courts, Fast said, "have become open and unashamed instruments of fascism, and the very word 'justice' rings hollow in today's America." After telling reporters that the meaning of their "imprisonment can be found only in the United States' attempt, for purposes of war, to shore up the tottering structure of Fascism in Spain," all the prisoners were marched by marshals two flights down from the courtroom to the basement cell block.[36]

From his twenty-by-twenty-foot holding pen, where Fast spent about two hours with his JAFRC colleagues and a dozen other prisoners, he was taken, handcuffed yet again, to the D.C. district prison, which he found surprisingly large, with high red-brick walls, a series of electric gates, towering cell blocks, and armed guards who, he said, "never look at you as . . . if they considered you human." One of the most vivid memories Fast recounted was the sight of long benches on which sat a hundred men, black and white, all naked, hunched over, heads bent despondently, "evoking pictures of the extermination camps of World War Two." Fast, too, sat naked, waiting for his antiseptic shower, blue uniform, and the five-by-seven-foot cell he'd share with another inmate.[37]

He spent more than a week in this cramped space with an eighteen-year-old who, Howard claims, had already been through years of prisons and reformatories. Apparently locked up this time for "carnal knowledge," a charge brought by the father of the girl with whom the boy had "petted," the "slender, blue-eyed handsome kid with cornsilk hair" had been held for fifty-eight days without indictment. After he finally began to open up to Howard, he told him he had been raped by fellow prisoners over one hundred times.[38]

For nine days, Fast says in *Being Red*, he listened to this boy "whose soul had been crushed" before he had had a chance to grow. For nine nights he listened to inmates two rows beneath him who were being held in D.C. before being sent to another prison for execution. He was awakened, he said, from time to time, by "their anguish, their sobbing, pleading . . . that they . . . not be put to death." Fast, who even before his imprisonment was an opponent of capital punishment, "swore an oath" to himself to see that this "barbarism was done away with."[39] And in the course of eating three meals every day with hundreds of convicted men, Fast listened to the conversations of many ordinary thieves and hoodlums. His conclusion, after a week and a half of paying attention to murderers, rapists, crooks, and gangsters, was that "hate and bruises and mistakes and cruelties" were inflicted on these prisoners by others, "so that their path to hell was laid out for them before they took their first step." In his brief stay, Fast said, he learned all he needed to know about prison and about the "human condition," things, he insisted, that could not be taught in any other way.[40]

A day or two before Fast was to turn himself in, he ran into Dashiell
Hammett near Central Park and told him about his about-to-be served jail
sentence. The hard-boiled mystery writer said, "It will be easier for you"
in prison, "Howard, if you first take off the crown of thorns."[41] But Fast
intended to make the most of his "martyrdom." In this he was encouraged
by fan mail he began to receive immediately upon his incarceration. A letter
from the novelist and Party member David Alman was already waiting for
Fast in Washington when he arrived. Alman wanted Howard to know that
"at the meetings and coffee klotches I've been to recently, we've talked a good
deal about Howard Fast. Everyone feels badly, in a deeply personal way, at
your going to prison. But above and beyond that, there is a sense of great
pride that one of our own has become such a giant." Alman promised that
"we—all of us—will continue and increase our fight for your freedom and
vindication." He assured Howard that "at every gathering of any sort—people ask 'Is it true that [Fast is] going to prison?' And they feel badly, in that
simple and profound way . . . and they feel proud. To that I add my own feelings, as a class-conscious worker and writer, as a Jew, as a human being."[42]

During his first week in jail Fast also heard from Shirley Graham, the African American activist and soon-to-be wife of W. E. B. Du Bois, whom Fast
had helped on her way to recognition and modest financial success as a writer
of biography and historical fiction.[43] "Dear Comrade-for-Peace, That's what
I called you Thursday night at our marvelously successful Peace Rally" in
New York City, Graham wrote. "And you [must] have heard the people shout
all the way down in Washington." Fast no doubt had told Graham earlier,
with what would have been false modesty, that he was not interested in hero-
ics, because she wrote, "So you don't want to be a hero! Well you are one.
Within the past week mass demonstrations [were] held all over the world.
. . .Thousands of people [even] in Berlin shouting for the freeing of political
prisoners in the United States! . . . Now your books will sell all over the world
like hotcakes. Such publicity publishers should have to pay for—*your face
and name pasted in windows and on banners*—people making up songs about
you. . . . [C]ouldn't you maybe find a nice, empty cell for me. *I'd like* to be
a world-wide hero."[44] Shirley Graham's letter reveals the desire she shared
with Fast to be celebrated as a person in the thick of the action. "Shirley,"
Fast was fond of saying, could "never stop . . . talking," about left politics,
or anything else for that matter. Neither could he, it was generally agreed,
and neither of them, as David Levering Lewis, the biographer of Shirley's

renowned husband, Du Bois, put it, "would be libeled by the claim that both possessed outsized egos."[45]

On the same day, Fast, still in the D.C. district prison, received a telegram expressing sympathy from fifteen Soviet writers who, though they had much better examples at home, likened the activities of HUAC to the Spanish Inquisition, saying Howard's jail sentence illustrated the "total terror" in the U.S.[46] And not too long after Fast was transferred to the federal penitentiary at Mill Point in West Virginia, he received a packet from a member of the Israeli parliament containing an article from the left-oriented Israeli newspaper *Al HaMishmar* (On guard) explaining that a group of Knesset members of various parties, including Mapam, General Zionists, Religious Front, and Communist, as well as authors and artists of the Center of Progressive Culture, sent a cable to Truman expressing, "together with the democratic public opinion of the world . . . shock . . . at the imprisonment of the well-known writer, Howard Fast, and his [JAFRC] colleagues. . . . We urge you," the Israelis wrote, "to use your powers to release them from prison immediately."[47]

In one of Fast's early letters to Bette from prison he wrote, "I'm glad people are upset by this. To be thrust away for no crime, for being a . . . decent human being . . . is an awful thing. People should . . . be angry."[48] Fast felt, and believed the government knew, that if he were interned in Danbury, Connecticut, instead of isolated at Mill Point, "there would be endless demonstrations and delegations and vigils."[49] But Fast was also thinking specifically about the silence of John Steinbeck, Sinclair Lewis, Erskine Caldwell, Hemingway, and the rest. "How do *they* feel, I wonder, snug as each one is in his little hole of safety. . . . Have they no soul, no conscience, no sincere awareness?" It was Hemingway, after all, Fast wrote, "who repeated John Donne's wonderful line, 'No man is to himself an island entire.' I'm learning that, in here as well as outside—but what does it mean [now] to Hemingway? I've become very proud of my writing while [thinking about it] in here. Whether I've written well or badly," Fast said with some defensiveness, "I've written of America with love and honor."[50] Bette herself was moved in late June to speak at a rally of nine thousand in Madison Square Garden, defending her husband and assailing President Truman for the Korean War.[51]

Fast wrote to Bette immediately after his transfer to Mill Point, which, as he discovered, was one of FDR's favorite New Deal projects, constructed in 1938 as "the model penal institution in America." Fast raved about the place.

"We're 3,800 feet high. The country is like Greene County at home, and the place is an honor camp—no walls, no bars, no cells." Inmates knew to stay within an area marked by small white signposts spaced every forty feet around their "legal perimeter."[52] Fast was also more than impressed with the "good food," eaten by inmates and staff alike, " a decent respect for human beings," and "work to do, a fine library, and an opportunity to put the time to good use. Can you imagine how I feel?"[53]

Two weeks later, in early July, Fast learned that Pablo Neruda had written a poem, unpublished, about him, and he immediately wrote Bette asking to see it. Titled "Ode to Howard Fast," it reads in part:

"I speak to you, Howard Fast. You who are jailed/I embrace you, my comrade; and I bid you good morning my brother/I saw Spain's doors close, and I saw a poet's head rolling in the shadows/. . . . I am not of this country. I am from Chile./My comrades are there, and my books and my house that/gazes upon the cold Pacific's gigantic waves/. . . . We march toward peace with you and your people./Your face is a banner that we see from your prison,/and we follow the steps of each jailer." Perhaps it reads better in Spanish, but the poem does not seem anything like Neruda's best work. Fast's granddaughter, the writer Molly Jong-Fast, thinks in fact that it is his worst poem by far, and concludes that "Communism does not translate into good poetry, though it does translate into a good backdrop for James Bond movies." This doesn't mean that Communists couldn't write good poetry. The lyrical work of the Turkish poet Nazim Hikmet, the proto-surrealist work of Peruvian Cesar Vallejo, and the love poems of Berthold Brecht attest to this; but the most explicitly political poems by Communists, including Neruda and Aragon in the forties and fifties, were ponderously didactic.[54]

Fast recognized Neruda's good intentions, but said nothing about the quality of the poem. Nonetheless, he was glad to have support among writers such as Neruda, McCullers, William Carlos Williams, Rukeyser, and Odets; he told Bette "My state of mind is not bad." In light of his recent affair with the model Isabel Johnson, however, Fast also needed to assure his wife that he loved only her. "I seem to understand and love you . . . only when I'm separated from you," he wrote. "More and more I've been thinking of . . . the troubles we've had, the happiness we've had." All in all, he thought "the good outweighs the bad. And I think there can be many good years for us . . . ahead." We "will work that out," he wrote, and then less than resoundingly, he added, "I think we will perhaps have much more happiness together after this than we ever had before. That, of course, remains to be seen, but I shall certainly try."[55]

There wasn't much more Fast could write and remain within prison regulations, but he told Bette that he was reading *Northanger Abbey,* the first novel he'd ever read by Jane Austen, and that he found her perspective on the tedium of high society and the loss of innocence and good faith "charming and delightful." Perhaps perusing Austen reminded Howard to get back to writing to Bette about their own relationship. "Let me continue with what I spoke of before, the stuff of us. How small how petty, how inconsequential it now seems!" Thinking no doubt, about his affair with the "Bennington girl" at owi in 1943, his fling with his student at Indiana in 1947, and still fresh from his love-fest with Isabel Johnson, Fast said, "I always learn the hard way, don't I?" Two days later Howard told Bette, "for the first time, I understand the deep bonds— . . . unbreakable—between us." And a week after that he asked Bette to "believe that the things I have felt . . . and written you about are very deep-seated . . . and permanent too. That is a security which you must not doubt."[56] Embedded in Fast's expressions of love in these letters, and in his confessions—and the many more to come—was an implicit promise, one Howard would not keep.

Most of the jobs in the prison were in the lumber mill, laundry, or kitchen, but Fast was assigned to the "education department," where his work consisted mainly of putting together the prison's quarterly periodical. The authorities may have hoped that Fast, as a "well-known author" and political critic of the United States, might write something positive about Mill Point. Except for a few lines in the *Daily Worker* upon his release, however, and several paragraphs much later in *Being Red,* Fast, who was cultivating a public image of sacrifice, wrote nothing about the prison.

When there were signs to paint for the education department, Fast put his youthful National Art Institute training to good use, laying out designs in pencil. He told Bette, "I am also doing 4 covers for the . . . magazine here, of which I am official artist." Except for those horrific ten days in D.C., prison for Howard was more like summer camp, and superior to Jened, where he had had to work very hard and was closely supervised by his oppressive cousin and aunt. None of Fast's European correspondents, including Gwyn Thomas, who expressed outrage and sympathy at Fast's imprisonment, or Pablo Neruda, were aware that Howard was in a model prison where he suffered little, except for the not so trivial experience of forced separation from his family. He told Bette to tell Rachel "that her daddy will soon be with her, and will always be with her then, and she must never be allowed to be sad over the fact that I am here. Someday, I think, she will be proud of what brought me here."[57]

In the same letter he told Bette he was eating well, saw a ballgame, got his hair cut, and was getting tan from working outside designing and helping to construct a large decorative fountain. Near the end of that job, he amused his fellow workers, who were by then "devoted" to him, Fast says, by completing the structure in such a way that the water flowed out of the copper penis of a replica of the *Pissing Prince of Essen* borrowed from the warden. There is an inescapable indignity in imprisonment; but Fast clearly enjoyed his stay at Mill Point and did nothing to disabuse his European friends of their darker view of his captivity.[58]

As good as it was, Fast said two months after his release, Mill Point prison still suffered "the ills of the whole system." Blacks were segregated in their sleeping quarters and in the dining room. The educational program was insufficient, as Fast had reason to know, for both he and Dick Bradley had served in the "night school" as volunteers. Fast admitted that "for the political prisoner, jail is part of the struggle for a better world." But for the criminal, Fast said, imprisonment is "a senseless oppression." Indeed, Fast added, imprisonment is the most revealing aspect of the dark side of class society. In five thousand years of operation, Fast claimed, "its method of dealing with law breakers has not progressed one inch."[59]

Fast knew better. From his research for the Spartacus book, which he continued in earnest upon his release at the end of August, and for his novel *The Proud and the Free,* completed just before he entered prison in June, Fast had learned a great deal about savage prison conditions. He knew of the colonial-era punishments of the stock, pillory, and whipping post, the medieval practices of drawing and quartering and amputation, and the ancient horror of crucifixion. But his penchant for polemic and exaggeration and his quest for martyrdom survived even his own cushy prison experience. Indeed, in Fast's introduction to the Yiddish edition of *Spartacus,* he wrote that he "had already composed long parts of [the book] in my mind during the hours of hard labor as a political prisoner." And he could not pass up the opportunity to say, even as late as 1990, that "there is no way of understanding prison without experiencing it; it is a stupid and barbaric institution," once again giving the false impression that his own experience was brutal.[60]

It wasn't until 1998 that Fast went so far as to admit that he "enjoyed the experience," and that he'd "always had the feeling that a writer should be in prison for some time at least."[61] Still, Fast had no desire to stay too long even at Mill Point; just long enough to gain some stature as a victim and to add an experience he could use as a pamphleteer and novelist. As early as June 16, Howard wrote to Bette with "the specific purpose" of tendering his "resignation from the Board of the Joint Anti-Fascist Committee," adding that his "resignation should take place immediately." In jail, Fast explained, "I can no longer fulfill the functions of a board member." It appears, however, that he was looking, understandably, for ways to shorten his sentence, and thought that leaving the board might in the eyes of the authorities constitute "good behavior." He also told Bette, "You know, a special illustrated edition of MY GLORIOUS BROTHERS, announced while I am in here, might have a profound effect." And he encouraged Bette to talk to Angus Cameron, his editor at Little, Brown, about producing it.[62]

In the meantime, Fast had his own drawing and painting to do, and for the occasional prison play, sets to design, a skill he had taught himself years before at Camp Jened. He told Bette how proud he was about "getting to the point where I can mix just about anything out of the primaries" for painting. Fast was even more delighted with work he was doing on a flagstone walk. "You should see it!" he told Bette. "It's quite a production, and would grace any country place. Nor do I have regular flagstone," Fast bragged, "but plain rock which is dug out of the hillside. I break it and shape it myself—with goggles over my glasses—and lay it myself. . . . You know, there's a certain joy and pride in work that is completely apart from pay. I see it all the time here, where men with one trade or another take such a real pride in doing a fine job. I look at this flagstone thing, and I see it as something permanent and lasting, which I made."[63]

Fast also took pleasure in teaching at Mill Point, and claimed that he developed a new method of reaching illiterates by combining sounds and ideographs. Sometimes "at the end of the hour [of class], my head is reeling," he told Bette. But, despite Fast's claim in *Being Red* (1990) that it was in prison that his cluster headaches intensified and became more frequent, in no mail home from Mill Point, nor in any of Fast's other letters and papers in 1950, did he mention the headaches that had plagued him sporadically since 1948. Indeed, at Mill Point he said he was getting a full eight hours of sleep, hadn't touched a drop of liquor for two months, and was feeling healthy, in fact "fine and dandy."[64] Even after a whole day of hauling, cutting, and fitting stone, "down on [his] hands and knees," Fast would have "a hot shower, put on clean clothes," read, and feel "pretty darn good."[65]

About his teaching the prisoners, Fast admitted that Bette was right. "It's quite true what you say about adults learning much more slowly than children." But he wasn't complaining. "It's [an] experience," he said, "and worth something." Fast's time in the classroom, however, was cut short by an order from the federal prison system. Communists, perhaps because of the outbreak of the Korean War, were no longer allowed to teach in the jails.[66]

But Fast found one or two literate inmates outside of class who seemed eager to learn. Arthur, an African American veteran of WWII (whose name we know only because of a letter Maltz sent later to Fast), with a high-school diploma and some college experience, was at Mill Point serving a term for forgery. When questioned by the FBI, Arthur apparently informed the agents that Fast, and Maltz, too, who had arrived at the West Virginia "prison paradise" at the end of June 1950, had been attempting to interest him in Communism, as well as in joining the Party. Fast even offered to get Arthur a job in New York City when he got out on parole.

Arthur told the FBI that he liked the idea of eventually becoming a professional informant for Hoover and company, and perhaps, therefore, what he told the bureau agents was spiced up some. But there is enough in the way of detail and logic in the handwritten reports he made for the FBI after Fast's departure to suggest a high degree of credibility. Fast "constantly sought me out," Arthur wrote, "so that we might 'converse.' . . . Although he thought me an intelligent person, he sought me out for a far greater reason. . . . No matter what our conversation was about at the time, he invariably turned it" into a lesson about "Communist theory."

"This was immensely interesting to me, especially so since he constantly hammered at . . . my being a Negro, and the disadvantages and oppression I am made to suffer because of this. . . . I have been exposed to college professors, but . . . Howard Fast was much more THOROUGH in his 'lectures.'" He had "me look up in every available book in the camp Library, all the information on Marx . . . and the government of Russia . . . which [Fast] termed, 'The greatest form of government man has ever known.'"[67]

In the evenings, Arthur said, Fast "insisted that we go through a question and answer period" about the books Arthur was reading. It was "my duty . . . in the interest of [my] race," Fast told Arthur, to join "an organization which offered me and my race freedom for the first time. He said that my people needed me and I only needed to be taught how to best serve them. ... I ... never completely accepted his offer, although he has renewed it twice since he left, through the visit[s] of Albert Maltz's wife." Both she and Albert tried "to convince me to go to New York, where I could "do the most good in the struggle of my people. Maltz has religiously continued my lessons."[68]

GREAT EXPECTATIONS

Fast, of course, wrote nothing of this to Bette, nor, for obvious reasons, did he write anything at all about politics in his prison letters. He mostly wrote about missing Bette and the kids, telling her that the only drawback of Mill Point was that she could not visit him easily. Still, he said, "I would rather be here than in Danbury," which was no model prison. Distance, Fast hinted again, may even have helped their relationship. "It's quite true that [here] I feel very close to you," Fast wrote to his wife of thirteen years, "and very good being married to you." And echoing the very sentiments he had written to Bette in 1945 when he was away from her during his journalistic sojourn in North Africa and India, Fast said, "why one has to go through something like this"—separation, prison—"to understand the depth and warmth of a relationship is something I'll have to figure out here ... so that when we are together again, there will be rich years, not lean ones." It ought not to have taken too long for Fast to "figure out, his yearning." As sung in *Finian's Rainbow,* a Broadway musical that opened in 1947, the year Fast was indicted for contempt, and closed shortly before he was incarcerated, the answer was clear: when Howard was not near the girl he loved, he loved the girl he was near; and at Mill Point there were no "girls."

Fast apparently did break off his relationship, at least temporarily, with Isabel Johnson, either before he was incarcerated in 1950 or through an intermediary during his stay at Mill Point,. He did the same, apparently, with another woman he had been seeing. Early in his confinement in West Virginia, Howard heard from his younger brother, Julie, that he had "called the redhead and she took your message. We haven't seen her since."[69]

Howard still wanted his Bette, and once out of prison, he wanted her within reach. As far as her going to work was concerned, he told Bette, "I would just as soon that you didn't, but I realize ... there are very few deci-

sions I can make for you while I am here," and almost as an afterthought
he added, "which again is perhaps as well, since you are quite capable of
making them yourself. That too is something that I've learned." Still, Bette
told Howard she wanted him to help her make a bunch of decisions about
the household and the family when he returned. "After having Jonny [more]
to myself," she wrote, "I think he's outgrown Julie[tte]," the nanny, who is
a "retarding influence." In the confines of the house with Julie, Bette said,
"Life . . . will not be stimulating enough" for their son. And somewhat unrealistically, perhaps desperately, Bette believed that the two-year-old might
be ready for school. She wrote with some anxiety, that no matter what, "we
must find . . . a [more] responsible person" for Jonny at home.[70]

Rachel Fast wrote later that her "parents' marriage was in tumult" during
the late forties and early fifties, and "I have no doubt that the terrors of the
time contributed to their troubles [and] exacerbated [the] tension, anger
and resentment already present."[71] Without question the personal and the
political were a combustible combination for the Fasts. Bette's personal bitterness was not only understandable, it came boiling to the surface within the
context of what was happening all at once politically: Howard's imprisonment from June 7 to August 29, the outbreak of the Korean War on June 25,
the ongoing FBI watch, and the continuing deliberations of the Westchester
County Grand Jury over Howard's role and fate in the Peekskill case.

There's lots to worry about and "lots to decide," Bette wrote in July, especially about "what you [Howie] will do." She wanted "to start fresh," Bette
said, "because the remnants of the mud we've been wading through still
cling. When you wrote that you had two letters [in prison] from a woman you
were exceedingly fond of . . . I wondered who it was." The blonde, the redhead, someone else altogether? Fast's letter about the mystery woman does
not survive, no doubt torn to shreds by Bette in anger. "I did a real double
take," Bette wrote, no longer calling him Howie, but Howard. "You see, I've
read what you've written and reacted to it immediately." Though Bette said
there was still "a real fear clinging" to her, she insisted, "No more '*what was.*'
I've no use for chewing the cud any longer. I want to look ahead."[72]

In the meantime, Fast, who simply could never accept things the way
they were, in small matters or large, tried to make his life in prison as easy
as possible. He said that because he grew up motherless and impoverished
he had become someone who "shamelessly" throughout his life "worked the
angles."[73] In prison he was no different. For example, Fast loved reading his

New York Times on the toilet in the morning, but even at comfy Mill Point the there were no toilet seats. In the small prison infirmary, however, which was almost always empty, there were two toilets with seats, and the convict in charge of the infirmary was bribable. Each day after handing the "hospital guard" a candy bar, Fast was privileged to read his paper while relaxed on a wooden toilet seat.

Less than a month after Fast arrived, the infirmary inmate was due for release, and Howard feared the loss of his special perk. But when he heard that Albert Maltz would be at Mill Point soon, he began concocting a scheme to get the infirmary job for the Hollywood writer. Fast was able to convince the trusting warden that Albert had always wanted to be a doctor, and in due time Maltz was made hospital orderly. On Albert's first day on the job, when Fast came sauntering up to the infirmary with his *Times,* Maltz, in what can only be described as poetic justice, barred his way, saying the toilets were only for the sick. That there were no sick didn't matter, Albert simply would not extend the privilege to Howard. Fast chalks this up to Maltz's being "the most principled person" he ever knew. But it could also be that Albert was giving a little payback for the nastiness heaped upon him by Fast in 1946.[74]

Still, the two men remained close as fellow inmates and had many conversations at Mill Point regarding the quality of the leadership of the CPUSA. They expressed a host of doubts, but their loyalty to the Party remained unwavering. Indeed, Maltz "wrote a ream of material about the prison," some of it apparently critical, that he wanted to deliver to the Communist press. One day in answer to Albert's question, "How do I get it out of here?" Fast said "keep it and take it with you" or "mail it to your wife." Maltz believed the authorities who censored the mail would never let it pass, and so Howard thought he'd humor Albert's alleged penchant for the "cloak and dagger" role. He told Maltz to "roll each onionskin sheet up to the size of a cigarette, take the tobacco out and insert each page in. . . . Ask your wife for a cigarette, . . . exchange packages, and she'll take it out." Although the story sounds apocryphal, Fast claims that Maltz "was so enchanted" with this kind of secret agent stuff, "that he did it!"[75]

Though he was also supplied with paper and typewriter, Fast, unlike Maltz, wrote nothing at Mill Point but letters. He had, however, been thinking about a novel on Sam Adams, tentatively entitled *The Seldom Yankee,* and one on Jesus, about whom Fast believed "every serious novelist should do a book." And he read prodigiously. Over the course of only eighty-three

days he finished Tolstoy's *War and Peace,* Austen's *Northanger Abbey,* and
Conrad's *Lord Jim,* with which he was apparently bored. He also read three
hundred pages of Samuel Putnam's new translation of *Don Quixote,* which
he had specifically requested but could not bring himself to finish, and Rafael Sabatini's swashbuckling high-seas adventure *Captain Blood,* which
he devoured with "great relish." In addition, Fast read whatever he could
from the prison library on the history of Christianity. And near the end of
his sentence he asked Bette to send him Karl Kautsky's *The Foundations of
Christianity,* which he studied closely.[76]

Kautsky was one of the first modern radical leftists interested in the ideas
and enigmatic personality of Jesus. And like other socialist militants who
retained some religious sensibility, Fast was taken with Kautsky's appropria-
tion of Jesus as a leader and martyr for the "proletarian cause," and his use
of Marxist methodology to interpret a religious phenomenon in terms of the
class struggle. Howard went so far as to tell Bette that he was very excited
about doing the novel about Jesus, that it had "taken shape wonderfully" in
his mind, and that after his release he'd "probably spend the next six months
doing little else."[77]

Fast wrote no book on Christ, as he preferred to call the man from Naza-
reth. But after reading Kautsky, who dealt in great detail with the Roman
Empire and the slave economy, he went through works by and about Rosa
Luxemburg, who like Kautsky insisted that the first Christian apostles were
Communists. A Polish Jew, admired by Lenin and Trotsky for her revolutionary élan, Luxemburg had led the abortive German Socialist uprising
in 1918, and named her group the Spartacus Bund. Fast, disturbed by her
murder by right-wing paramilitary proto-Nazis, thought he might do a book
on her. He claimed, however, that going to Germany to do the research so
soon after the Holocaust made him uncomfortable. Besides, Fast knew no
German. But in August 1950, during his last month in prison, he began to
think about why Luxemburg chose the name Spartacus for her league of
revolutionaries, and to read for himself about Spartacus, the putative leader
of a slave rebellion in the first century BCE.[78]

Fast did not begin writing *Spartacus* until he was out of prison, but in
his reading toward it, he had added much to his earlier knowledge about
scripture. Learning this, many of the white inmates, mostly deeply religious
moonshiners from the mountains of Kentucky and West Virginia, called
upon Howard, whom they took to calling "Reverend," to interpret portions

of the Bible.[79] But nowhere in Fast's memoirs or in his unpublished manuscripts is there any hint that at Mill Point he ever identified himself (or Jesus for that matter) as a Jew. Indeed, when an opportunity arose to do so, he seems to have avoided it.

Fast was the only Jew in the place until Albert Maltz arrived at Mill Point in the summer of 1950. There was among the prisoners, however, a petty thief named Kline, not Jewish, but thought so by the others. During an after dinner softball game, a passion at Mill Point, Kline, umpiring, angered one team by an "out" call. The players came at him roaring "get that Jew-bastard." He was beaten badly. A guard immediately elevated the event to a timeless and international level by saying, "Jews are trouble makers. Look at what's happening in Israel."[80] Unlike in the interchange Fast had had with British Captain Woodhill in 1945 in Egypt, when Howard defiantly announced his Jewish identity, here Fast remained silent. He says he "brooded over" the situation, but, perhaps thinking about reduced jail time for "good behavior," he neither argued with the guard nor revealed his Jewishness, thus continuing the balancing act of maintaining a public identity as a radical and an intellectual, and a private one, in this case more like a secret one, as a Jew.[81]

Toward the end of Fast's sentence, which was in fact shortened by 10 percent for "good behavior," he was visited by his editor at Little, Brown, Angus Cameron, who brought with him the book jacket for Howard's new novel, *The Proud and the Free.* "Isn't it funny," he told Bette, "I preserve the same childish excitement I had when my first book was published. How many have there been since then? Too many to count," Fast said. In fact, there had been fourteen including his nonfiction *Literature and Reality* and his collection of short fiction, *The Departure and Other Stories.* "Yet here I am just as excited about the birth of another."[82]

Fast was also excited about his play, *The Hammer,* which was tentatively scheduled to open after his release. Fast knew late in June that "some of the best actors in town [had] been contacted," that a "top-flight" scenic designer was donating the drawing for the set, and that Clifford Odets had agreed to help in case changes had to be made during rehearsal. Fast was delighted that "there [was] so much enthusiasm."[83] By August, his "tongue [was] hanging out with curiosity," and he was anxious to know who was in the cast, playing which parts, and what the exact date of the opening would be. He asked Bette to gather a little more "dope" about the play, "and pass it on" to him as soon as possible.[84]

About a week before he got out of Mill Point, nine days early, on August 29, 1950, Fast told Bette that Ben Rubin, one of the literary mavens of the CP and editor of the *Sunday Worker* book review section, "is really excited about the play" and "seems full of hope and confidence in its success." Rubin had informed Fast that a number of benefit performances had already been booked. This "may just be . . . the thing," Howard wrote Bette, "that will be a tremendous success."[85] It might even lead to a film.

Bette was happy and hopeful too, but more so that Howie was finally coming home after three months. She and the children, Rachel and Jonny, had spent the summer of Fast's incarceration at the Jersey shore near her parents, and Bette felt isolated and lonely—partly because Howard's family had remained somewhat distant. Although Howie's brother Julie, a fellow traveler, had written several supportive letters to Howard while he was in prison, the two appear to have had a fiercely competitive love-hate relationship. "The sentence you are serving," Julie wrote, "is not yours alone, but the sentence of every decent American. I'm proud of you as one of our best patriots, but I'm also proud of you as my brother. The love and pride I have always felt is more than doubled now, and it serves as a force to help me in the same fight."[86]

Julie's devotion is evident, but it was always compromised by envy and resentment. With the exception of his first novel, *Watchful at Night*, which in 1945 won the Edgar Allen Poe Award for best first detective fiction, Julie's works (two novels in 1946 and 1947, and four in the 1950s), unlike Howard's, sold no more than a few thousand copies each. As Julie grew older, the odds of his ever having a "breakthrough" book grew slimmer, and advances from publishers dwindled. This was only one of several reasons that, as time went on, Julie grew more aggrieved at his older brother.

Howard told his adult son, Jonathan, over dinner one night in the 1970s, that he didn't understand why Julie had always "hated" him. "I did everything for him," Fast said plaintively.[87] "Everything" included Fast's taking credit for practically rewriting Julie's first prize-winning book in 1945. "It was an interesting book," Fast admitted to Jonathan, "but it had no sense of structure." Howard claimed to have stayed up with Julie all night, and to have taken "the damn thing apart and put it back together again so that it had a shape to it and the action made sense." And Bette, who had helped edit Julie's book right up to and through page proofs, added "he never even thanked your father [or me]."[88] When Julie finally did have another successful book,

Body Language (1970), which analyzed the "unconscious messages" sent by the human body, Howard dismissed it out of hand, calling it, unjustly, a mere self-help book.[89]

Bette also pointedly reminded her husband that he had helped Julie pay most of his college tuition, and that when his books were not selling, Howard was always there with a helping hand. Bette also brought up the time in the late 1940s when Howard had bumped into Julie on his way to a job interview. "He was dressed like a bum," Fast told Jonathan. "So I took him into Brooks Brothers and bought him a suit; I shouldn't have done it, it must have been very humiliating, but I couldn't let him go to a job interview looking like that."[90]

Compounding the humiliation, Howard, not long after his release from prison, initiated an affair with Julie's wife, Barbara. It didn't last long, and Julie learned about it only much later. Rachel Fast heard all of this at a family event in the sixties, when Julie, perhaps to hurt Howard, let his niece know that her father "had made it" with Barbara a decade earlier. Having begun to overhear Julie's "little gossip," Barbara, livid and embarrassed, tried to shut her husband up, but it was too late, and "the words were out of his mouth, to hang there forever."[91] Fast's failure to understand why his brother "hated" him, especially after Julie discovered that Howard had cuckolded him, was either another exercise in denial or a façade behind which Howie could hide his several sins.

Jerry, Howie's older brother, unlike Julie, had not had any communication with Fast while he was in prison. A liberal in the classical mode with a New Deal overlay, Jerry wasn't particularly "keen on" having, through his brother, a "very out-of-the-closet affiliation" with the Communist Party, and was probably, as Rachel Fast put it, "pissed at Pop."[92] Although Jerry and Howie maintained a strong brotherly bond, it was tested over the years by what Jerry's son Barry calls "Howie's narcissism and dogmatism." They would argue on and off, and most of the time it took Jerry's wife, Dotty, to heal the wounds. No doubt there had been some such falling out just before Howie entered prison. He told Bette that after his release they ought to have his whole family, including Julie and Barbara, over to the beach house to "make peace right down the line."[93]

Adding to the sense of isolation Bette suffered, only "one friend" had called, "and only once," during the entire three months that she and the children were in New Jersey. Later, when Rachel asked her mother why she thought that there was such neglect, Bette said, "They didn't give a shit." After a short pause she added, "They were afraid. Everyone was afraid." Paul Stewart, a tough-talking character actor who had appeared in *Citizen Kane* (1941) and *Twelve O'Clock High* (1949), and his wife, Peggy, "walked right by us in Sardi's one day, pretended not to see us. You remember how dear [Paul] was, how affectionate? They were afraid," Bette said. "There were agents watching, everywhere, noting who knew whom, who talked to whom." Stewart's careful behavior kept him out of the crosshairs of the "Red-hunters" and allowed him to continue his lengthy career throughout the blacklist period, during which he appeared in seventeen films including such classics as *The Bad and the Beautiful* (1952) and *Kiss Me Deadly* (1955). "We understood it," Bette told Rachel. "You can't imagine how it was. It was a terrible time. Terrible."[94]

So terrible, in fact, that Bette had intensified her identification with Howard's victimization and came to believe more deeply in his overblown self-image. "Since you've been 'in,'" Bette wrote in one of her last letters to Howard at Mill Point, "I've been reading of protests from every corner of the globe. *Your name is a household word in every language amongst hundreds of millions of people.* The protests are usually coupled with astronomical figures on the sale of your books. Since truth is on your side your ability to fight back has increased immeasurably in spite of "—more likely because of—"bars and prison walls."[95]

Bette also seemed to have internalized and begun to articulate some of her husband's more extreme political positions. "Knowing you to be a prolific writer," Bette wrote, "all your friends are looking forward to a novel that will send your jailers and their spiritual leaders reeling." She told Howard that she had met the screenwriter Alvah Bessie "before he went 'in' and his only regret was that you would beat him to the punch on the great American anti-fascist prison story." Bessie may not have known, but Bette surely did, that Mill Point was no setting for an antifascist prison story. No matter. "There's one good feature about your present situation," Bette wrote. "It demonstrates to the entire world the abject desperation of those who jailed you and *who would like to jail every decent American.*"[96] Bette wanted Howard, as she put it, to "fight back"; yet when only a week later he told her of the all the activities and speaking engagements the CPUSA had planned for him upon his homecoming, she was irritated: "What the hell is this overwhelming urge [by the Party] to start tearing you to pieces again?"[97] Bette was wary, but even she had no idea just how much tearing up by the Party Howard would experience.

The *Daily Worker* announced Fast's release from prison, emphasizing that he was "twenty-eight pounds lighter than when he entered," omitting to say, of course, that Howard was now the fittest he'd ever been in his entire life. The paper was happier to say that Fast was returning to New York "practically on the eve of the opening of his play—'The Hammer,'" which was to have its premier September 8, 1950, at the Czech Workers House on East 72nd Street. "I keep thinking," Howard wrote Bette, "about what an exciting evening the opening night of the play will be. Perhaps we'll go in to see one of the rehearsals." In any case, he said, "You and I will be able to attend the opening together, which will be a real treat, won't it?" Unfortunately, there was nothing remotely like a treat in store for the Fasts, not at the rehearsal nor on opening night nor for the next six years.[98]

8

Free! But Not at Last

$\mathcal{A}$t the end of August 1950, Howard Fast was out of jail but not out of the clutches of the CPUSA or free of his own inclination to obey the Party line. That he could still be intimidated into acquiescence by the power of the American Communist Party was demonstrated in the first week of September when Howard and Bette attended a rehearsal of *The Hammer* several days before its official opening.[1]

In the audience with the Fasts for the run-through were Howard's friends Barney Rubin, a Spanish Civil War veteran, a machine-gunner in WWII, and a columnist for *Stars and Stripes;* and Herb Tank, a merchant seaman turned writer. Both men, along with Fast and a handful of other writers and actors, had recently formed New Playwrights, a progressive theater group, and *The Hammer* was Fast's contribution to the endeavor. Also in attendance were Al Saxe, the notable People's Theatre director whose works included productions of Odets's *Waiting for Lefty,* and Sean O'Casey's *The Plough and the Stars.* Lionel Berman, who had been instrumental in recruiting the Fasts for the Party, was there along with a half-dozen other members of the Cultural Section.

The actor Michael Lewin, described by Fast as "a skinny little guy with thin red hair and one of those pasty white skins," played the father. An even smaller actress, Nina Normani, played the mother. No performer on the stage was taller than 5'8", until the youngest son, played by none other than an eighteen-year-old black actor named James Earl Jones walked on. A "magnificent physical specimen" at 6'4", "built like a mountain," with shoulders "as wide as any three men," and with a voice that shook the place to its foundations, Jones dwarfed the other actors. "God help us," Howard said to Bette. She whispered back that Jones must only be a stand-in. Howard, incredulous moaned, "The muses hate me. I'm doomed."[2]

In a story he repeated with unvarying consistency from the 1960s through the 1990s, Fast claims that after the first act he turned to Barney Rubin and said, "Jimmy was a stand-in, wasn't he?" Even before Rubin could stop shaking his head no, Lionel Berman apparently boomed, "What do you mean stand-in. . . . Jimmy's been cast for the part." Fast's question, Berman added, was "a chauvinist reaction." Fast, remembering that "this little commissar was the voice and power of the party, and that *every friend I had in the world was in the party*," tried to restrain himself. He turned to Herb Tank, the producer, saying, "What the hell are you doing? This is a Jewish family. The father is a skinny, little redheaded Jew. What are you doing?" "We are carrying out the decision of the Party," Tank replied, which was that blacks, denied roles as actors, ought not to play in whiteface, and that by the sheer force of skill as actors, black men or women should be able to convince audiences to suspend disbelief and see white people.[3]

The technique is used in some modern theater productions where sophisticated audiences are prepared for it. But casting James Earl Jones as the child of "this little Jewish father" was preposterous, and Fast knew it. "Every one is going to see Jimmy Jones," he said. "They will not see the suspension of disbelief." Fast liked "Jimmy," but he thought, quite rightly as it turned out, that if Jones performed this impossible role, the play would become a joke. Howard continued to resist for a time as Rubin and Tank listened in silence. Like Fast, they had invested their lives in the Party; like him they had seen people expelled from the Party, isolated from friends of a lifetime, and unable to return to an anti-Party world. Fast said in 1990 that at the theater that evening, he was *"almost ready"* to face expulsion on charges of white chauvinism. But in 1957, after finally leaving the Party, Fast, without further exploration or elaboration, admitted that for years preceding his resignation, "the more troubled, the more hurt, the more sickened, I became by [Party] procedure, the more I committed myself."[4] And so, Fast in the fall of 1950, fearing the loss of a world in which he was obviously deeply rooted and emotionally entangled, gave in to the demands of the cultural commissars.

Opening night was a benefit performance for the socialist Jewish Workmen's Circle. Yiddish-speaking garment workers in their fifties and sixties filled every seat. Things went nicely for a time. The audience was engaged, absorbed—and then along came Jones, a black man "towering over the rest of the cast" and "trying desperately to control the rich vibrancy of his voice." Bette and Howard shrank in their seats as all over the hall they heard members of the audience whispering—*"Ver is er?"* (Who is he?), *"Fun vonent cumpt er?"* (Where does he come from?), and *"Vas tut zey mit der shvartze?"* (What are they doing with the black man?) As the spectators realized that Jones *was* actually playing the younger son, the whispering stopped—and the uncomfortable laughter began.

The theater critic from the *Herald Tribune* came up to Fast after the performance and told him he was going to do Howard a favor by not reviewing the play.[5] No other major paper reviewed it either. The *Daily Worker,* of course, took it on, saying that *The Hammer* had "serious weaknesses as a play," and that "one is often aware that Howard Fast, the novelist, is not on familiar grounds in writing for the stage." But for all the play's weaknesses, the reviewer Bob Lauter claimed, against all evidence to the contrary, that "no one leaves the theatre . . . resentful of a wasted evening." Members of the audience "see an attempt to deal with ideas and concepts of importance . . . and find themselves stimulated to applause because [the play] is, for all its faults, living theatre."

Lauter, who either failed to attend the play or sat through it with eyes and ears closed, slipped deeper into unreliability by writing, along Party lines, that *The Hammer* "proves again, with the performance of the Negro actor Earl Jones as the Jewish Jerome Green, that the excuses for jimcrow [*sic*] in the theatre are absolutely baseless." Those who thought it would "seem strange," Lauter wrote, "will discover how completely wrong they have been" about "this eminently sensible method of casting."[6]

In his 1990 memoir *Being Red,* Fast wrote that "in a microscopic form," the incident over *The Hammer* defined the leadership of the Communist Party. They were "cut off from the rank and file, and most important, they were absolutely rigid, in their preference for theory over reality." In the case of Fast's tendentious and preachy play this failure and stubbornness of the leadership was a small matter, but in the larger arenas of art and politics it was more often than not self-destructive, and finally harmful to the formation of a viable and credible left with a mass following in the United States.

By this point a naïf might wonder why Fast, like Robert Rossen before him, didn't simply say "Stick the whole Party up your ass." But by the time *The Hammer* was staged, Fast apparently suffered few if any of the moral conundrums that regularly perplex non-ideologues. Perhaps even more important, the CPUSA had become too important to Howard's self-definition. He was widely admired by the Party's cadre, if not by a handful of leaders at the pinnacle. He had become an internal as well as a public Communist spokesperson on every issue from civil rights to socialist realism. He headed innumerable committees and ad hoc pro-Communist associations, and he lost no opportunity to take the floor at every conceivable meeting, even if only to deliver the usual Party blather. He took his turn in prison and became ever more heavily invested in heroic martyrdom. Despite the irritating critiques by the literary commissars, the imposition of artistic restraints by the Culture Section, and an occasional slap on the wrist, Fast could not and would not leave the Party that had become his life.

Joseph Starobin, the foreign editor of the *Daily Worker* from 1945 to 1954, who knew Fast well, was perceptive about his comrade and friend and is worth quoting at length: "Throughout it all he neither grew as a writer nor gained wisdom as a man. . . . The Soviet leaders needed a mythological Howard Fast and they invented him even at the cost of damaging the real one. . . . Fast thus became the vehicle for a deception of which he was also the first victim. Instead of asking himself if it was wholesome that his world audience increased while his [American readers] found each of his successive books less important, he rode the gap. He won the prizes, was photographed with the happy children of beaming . . . consular officials at the UN," and at Soviet embassy cocktail parties, and he "accepted the invitations to write on every conceivable subject for distant magazines whose editors" and writer-intellectuals "cabled him as though he were a world power."[7]

In such a heavy fog of flattery and fame, Fast could not abandon his Party post, even as petty bureaucrats continued to nitpick at his work. This became even clearer when two weeks after *The Hammer* opened on September 8, 1950, *The Proud and the Free,* Fast's novel about a mutiny of foreign-born common soldiers in revolutionary Pennsylvania, was published.[8] Almost immediately Fast was "brought up on charges" by a special meeting of the Party secretariat. The committee, with V. J. Jerome serving temporarily as "special cultural consultant," accused Fast of "white chauvinism" for using the word "nayger" throughout his new book.[9]

Fast argued that American soldiers used the objectionable word with some frequency during the Revolutionary War. Six years earlier he had made a similar defense for "politically incorrect" language employed in *Freedom Road*. New to the Party in 1944, Fast was only reprimanded; but now he was given to understand that unless a public apology was forthcoming he would be expelled. Once again Fast went through the apparently therapeutic and transformative process of "confession" and absolution by writing about his error for the pages of *Political Affairs* (*PA*). But soon after Fast completed his essay, it was rumored that the U.S. government was about to take action against the journal and its editors; it was decided that Fast's appearance in the journal with an admission of this sort would not be politic, and the piece was killed.[10]

The Proud and the Free created the usual stir among the leftist critics. It was reviewed positively in the *Daily Worker*, but negatively in *Masses and Mainstream*.[11] Fast had argued that in the aftermath of their mutiny, the common soldiers of the Pennsylvania Line came to see that going beyond the bourgeois democratic revolution would put them in uncharted territory; therefore the workers and farmers backed away from their efforts to take the revolutionary process further, and united with the merchant and planter classes to preserve what had already been won. Critics at *Masses and Mainstream*, including Herbert Aptheker, contended that Fast had failed to grasp the revolutionary fervor of the soldiers or their commitment to the creation of a truly egalitarian society. He had not understood, Aptheker said, that in revolutions made by the bourgeoisie, true democracy is extended to workers and farmers only to the degree that these lower classes demonstrate extraordinary strength and conscious revolutionary activity.

Within the struggle for independence from Great Britain, it was argued, contra Fast, that a class struggle *was* waged, one that not only overcame the vacillations of the merchants and landowners and forced the issue of independence, but aimed at capturing the Revolution for the masses, and failed, only because of bloody repression by the exploiting classes.[12] Fast in his guarded response to his critics argued, as he had tried to show in the novel, that the mutineers surrendered not so much because they were overpowered, but because of the historical necessity they recognized.[13]

The intra-Party tempest in a teapot over *The Proud and the Free*, however, was far less important than Fast's conscious distortion of the historical sources in order to model the "foreign brigades" of the Pennsylvania Line after the foreign battalions of the Spanish Civil War. For starters there were no purely foreign brigades of common soldiers on the Pennsylvania Line. All units were of mixed ethnicity and included many indigenous Americans.[14] Fast was clearly aware of the available facts: seven years earlier he had reviewed favorably and at some length his friend Carl Van Doren's *Mutiny in January,* the definitive historical work on the subject.[15] As Fast himself admitted, Van Doren's book, which became the main source for *The Proud and the Free,* included "detailed accounts of the actions of the officers as well as an extraordinary description of intelligence and counter-intelligence; but of what went on among the men of the Line," what they said and what their goals were, "there is almost nothing at all." Van Doren himself had quite frankly confessed the difficulties of obtaining such data.[16]

Nor did Van Doren claim as Fast did that the Pennsylvania mutiny was a class-conscious attempt at revolution within the Revolution. The mutineers, Van Doren showed persuasively, dismissed the superior officers of the Pennsylvania Line and created their own Committee of Sergeants in order to seek remedy of their grievances—deficiencies and inequalities in pay, lack of supplies, inadequate food and clothing, and confusion regarding terms of enlistment. When material conditions improved, more than half the two thousand soldiers involved immediately withdrew from the revolt, and the entire mutiny ceased very soon thereafter.[17]

In his reply to his critics, left and right, Fast put himself in an almost indefensible position by claiming, rather oddly, that "the strange and little-known narrative I have told through the person of one Jamie Stuart, soldier in the Continental Army, would be neither justified nor tolerable if it were an invention." But the quality of novels, including historical novels, inheres precisely in their authors' ability to invent, to exercise their creative imaginations, and to build alternative stories on a nucleus of actual incident. Fast insisted that in *The Proud and the Free,* as in most of his other historical novels, he had adhered closely to the facts, and invented people and events only when necessary to present a coherent narrative. It is in Fast's desire to be taken seriously both as a novelist *and* as a historian (not an impossible synthesis) that one of his problems as a writer lies. Had he believed along with André Gide that "fiction is history that might have taken place" and made clear, even if only implicitly, that Jamie Stuart's recounting of the mutiny in Pennsylvania was an exercise in literary license to stimulate thinking about what might be possible in human affairs, Fast would have been on safer ground. But he opened himself to attack by refusing to say, as many other fiction writers do, that it is necessary to "lie" in order to tell a "larger truth." And so he was forced to defend himself by flailing around in the historical literature and resorting to the polemics of victimization and martyrdom. Fast complained without substantiation that "the only novels published in America over the past decade . . . challenged as to historical content are my own. Most bitterly resented was and is my partisan position—in defense of the working class. . . . This is the position I have chosen," Fast concluded, "and on this ground I stand."[18] That ground, however, did not meet his own minimal standard for novelized history. Apparently Carl Van Doren agreed. Too scrupulous to promote his erstwhile friend Howard's novel as credible history, Van Doren, when asked to write an introduction to *The Proud and The Free,* turned down the opportunity, twice.[19]

The American reading public and the mainstream media mostly ignored Fast's flawed works.[20] The CP, however, paid attention. It praised Fast's books publicly, but in its journals and in private, many Party leaders and cultural commissars resented Fast's fame and were critical of his work. Similarly, Fast publicly lauded the CP, but kept his complaints mostly to himself or shared them with Bette and a small number of close friends. In this way, the American Communist Party and Howard Fast maintained an unhealthy but symbiotic relationship, like a codependent marriage troubled from the start. It was a bitter ritual dance they performed with one another, in which neither partner could really let go.

Still restrained by his fear of expulsion from the CPUSA and by his own delusional but deeply internalized Manichean worldview—Communism is democracy, capitalism is fascism—Fast also continued to have constraints imposed on him. The FBI, for example, reinstituted Fast's status as a "security risk," and he was literally locked within the United States by his own government. In the fall of 1950, even after he had "paid his debt to society," Howard Fast was refused a passport by the State Department to attend, as an invited delegate, the Second World Peace Conference to be held in Warsaw, Poland in November. The State Department "denied my request," Fast said, because "I stated that my intention was to go abroad to speak of peace!" He challenged the department's opinion that his travel would not serve "the best interests of the U.S.," and labeled the government's decision "a despicable fraud." There is no higher loyalty to America today, Fast said, "than to speak of peace, fight for peace—anywhere" and everywhere. "I have already been in one of Truman's prisons," Fast said; "now my whole country is a prison."[21]

Hyperbole aside, Fast was rightly angry.[22] The denial of passports to politically suspect writers and artists was completely unjustified. But, entirely ignoring the long-standing Soviet policy of restricting travel and forbidding emigration for anyone, Fast insisted that such a degrading and despicable situation as existed in America in terms of the right to travel was never witnessed before in the history of modern man. Invoking his favorite point of negative reference, Fast said "Adolph Hitler at least had the forthrightness to say that he was denying rights to those who espoused democracy because he himself despised democracy." But the State Department commits "this vilest of all crimes against democracy in the name of democracy." The denial of a passport, Fast said, is in effect "imprisonment without trial, or due process, or benefit of judge or jury. It is not simply a figure of speech to say that these antics of the State Department turn the United States of America into a concentration camp."[23]

Much of Fast's rhetoric was out of bounds, but in 1950, the politics of the Cold War did put additional chill into the civil liberties climate. Some of the saber-rattling between the United States and the USSR had quieted, but anti-Communism, at least at elite levels, appeared to intensify at home.[24] In February, Republican Senator Joseph McCarthy of Wisconsin made his demagogic speech falsely claiming he had a list of 205 Communists working in the State Department. The Korean War broke out in full force at the end of June 1950, and the Chinese would enter the conflict in November. In July, J. Edgar Hoover personally announced the arrest of Julius Rosenberg, describing him as a leading wartime spy; less than a month later, Ethel Rosenberg was arrested, and like her husband was charged with conspiracy to commit espionage for the Soviet Union; twelve days after the start of the Korean War, Hoover sent to the White House a secret plan to suspend habeas corpus, "apprehend all individuals potentially dangerous" to national security, and institute the "permanent detention" of twelve thousand suspects at military bases and federal prisons; the U.S. Chamber of Commerce recommended expunging liberals of every stripe from positions in schools, libraries, newspapers, and the entertainment industry; and in September 1950, the U.S. Congress passed the Internal Security Act.[25]

One of the most controversial laws in the history of the republic, it was popularly named for Nevada's Senator Pat McCarran, an aging political hack, who resurrected the legislation from an earlier version drafted by congressmen Karl Mundt and Richard Nixon. The McCarran Act required the fingerprinting and registration of all "subversives" at large in the United States, and added a section that came to be called the "concentration camp clause." In vague and clumsy language, the act called for the detention of persons likely to commit or conspire to commit espionage or sabotage in a time of internal security emergency.[26] A large margin in both houses of Congress voted for the bill.

As a Jew, surrounded by other Jews in New York, Fast, who had written a long prose poem about the Warsaw ghetto as early as 1946, was agonizingly aware of the Holocaust; and his deep fears of a fascist dictatorship in America, even if unwarranted, were intensified by the "concentration camp clause."[27] Indeed, the McCarran Act was so sweeping and so severe that it made credible to others Fast's expressed terror that any group considered a "threat" could be restricted in its civil liberties in "emergency situations" by government fiat. The radical journalist I. F. Stone told his daughter he feared "American intellectuals were going to be put in concentration camps."[28] President Truman challenged the constitutionality of McCarran's Internal Security Act, calling it "the greatest danger to freedom of speech, press, and assembly since the Alien and Sedition Laws of 1798." His veto, however, was overridden in September 1950 by a majority vote approaching 90 percent.[29]

Although virtually unenforceable, the Internal Security Act frightened many people, Howard Fast among them. Banned from traveling, he feared re-arrest.[30] Nonetheless, he refused to remain quiet. In a variety of venues Fast continued to say that America had become a fascist state, and that "we have the lesson of Germany staring us in the face."[31] James Reston of the *New York Times* discovered in a cross-country pre-election survey that many on the liberal-left, including militant crusaders and philosophical mentors of the New Deal, afraid of being smeared as Reds, and college professors worried about losing their jobs, were conspicuously silent.[32] But Fast continued to speak out against the American government, even on the most controversial issues. During the Korean War he called for the wholesale withdrawal of American troops and UN recognition of the Chinese People's Republic as a member state. "Were [the American people] consulted," Fast asked, "when Harry Truman and the miserable men who surround him plunged us into the war with Korea?" Of course not, he wrote, because "never before in all our history has there been such a gang of evil, disloyal and un-American men in power!" According to *Time* magazine, he also conveyed the following message to the leaders of Red China who were battling U.S. troops: "My heart is with you in the mighty struggle."[33]

Fast was certainly having his say, but he was once again barred from speaking at Columbia, NYU, and other universities, despite the policy several of these institutions of higher learning had adopted in the late forties that Fast, and others like him, would be permitted to appear on campus after they had served their sentence.[34] Columbia barred Fast from addressing the campus chapter of Young Progressive Citizens of America in November 1950. University officials declined to discuss the decision, but Grayson Kirk, the provost, said that "automatic approval" of invited speakers would be "a complete abdication of educational responsibility." Despite the fact that Columbia had broken a promise made to its students and the public, the *New York World-Telegram* supported Kirk and went on to attack Fast in language bordering on hysteria: "Mr. Fast is not merely a member of the Communist party. . . . He has sought to foment prejudices and hatreds among classes, races and religious groups." Therefore, his "presence could contribute scant element of truth either on or off a college campus."[35]

That the protection of the freedom of speech was not high on the agenda of a major newspaper or a prestigious university is indicative of the continuing threat to civil liberties in America in 1950. After NYU also banned Fast, in this case with the support of the Student Affairs Committee, representatives of student clubs at Fordham and Brooklyn College claimed, irrelevantly even if correctly, that Fast "has consistently in his recent writings and speeches espoused the propaganda lines of our enemy." But strangely, even those taking courses at Brooklyn Law School joined the other student groups in commending the administrations of Columbia and NYU for "terming speech-making . . . a privilege and not a right."[36]

At Brooklyn College, administrators demonstrated just what that concept might look like, if put into practice. The Karl Marx Society at BC, which had invited Fast to speak, was summarily banned from the campus, and the college newspaper that dared to defend the student organization was promptly closed down. Six of its editors were suspended from school, which resulted in a demonstration for free speech by several student groups. Demonstrations went on for days. But in the end, fifty-six students were suspended and Fast was barred from speaking.[37]

Because he could speak on college campuses neither at home nor anywhere abroad, Fast devoted himself for several weeks in 1950–51 to the work
of the Chicago Peace Conference. It was a "wonderful experience," he wrote
to Albert Maltz, now released from Mill Point and permanently living in
Mexico, "and a real affirmation of the sources of strength in grass roots
America." For myself, Fast said, "I am trying to overcome whatever nervous-
ness accompanies life in this society and to prepare myself for another stretch
in jail if that becomes necessary."[38]

During this period, Fast continued to be deeply committed to racial justice, and was directly involved in three particularly distressing cases: the
"Martinsville Seven," seven black men convicted of rape in Virginia in 1949,
sentenced to death, and electrocuted in February 1951; the "Trenton Six,"
a half-dozen black men arrested in 1948 for the murder of a seventy-three-
year-old shopkeeper in New Jersey, convicted, and sentenced to death, but
released in 1951; and the case of Willie McGee, found guilty of the rape of
a white woman in Mississippi in 1945 and executed in May 1951, notwithstanding the extraordinary efforts of Howard Fast and other Communists.[39]

It was demonstrated beyond reasonable doubt that the Martinsville Seven
had been involved in the gang rape; but as many as four men had done nothing but watch, and at least one failed to achieve penetration. Yet all seven
blacks were executed in a state in which no white man, between 1908 and
1948, had been sentenced to death for rape of a black or white woman.

The Trenton Six may or may not have been involved in a botched robbery
that ended in murder, but the evidence on which they were convicted was
entirely circumstantial, and in a series of trials, attorneys for the Communist-
affiliated Civil Rights Congress succeeded in demonstrating that police had
extracted confessions from the men using opiates and threats of violence.

It is possible that Willie McGee had had consensual sex with a white
woman, but in Mississippi such a thing was thought impossible by most, and
certainly by the judge, who said such a claim was a "revolting insinuation."
Needless to say, after a series of appeals during which Communist defense
lawyers unfortunately persuaded McGee and several witnesses to change
their stories—more than once—McGee was found guilty and put to death.

Several historians and journalists, including the African American writer
and newspaperman Carl Rowan, and even the former first lady Eleanor
Roosevelt, now chair of the United Nations Commission on Human Rights,
thought that had the Civil Rights Congress, and Bella Abzug, one of the

few independent attorneys willing to take "Communist cases," not thrust themselves to the forefront of the defense, McGee might have been spared the death penalty.[40] Perhaps. But no matter who the defense would have been in the McGee case, as with the Martinsville Seven and the Trenton Six, cases lasting from 1945 to 1951, rampant, virulent racism clearly played the more critical role.[41]

Moreover, the CPUSA and the CRC were spending far more attention, time, and money to defend the top Party leaders during the Foley Square trials in the late 1940s and again in 1951 than to any of the "race" cases, including McGee's. In the final quarter of 1948, for example, the CRC allotted only sixty-seven dollars for McGee's legal defense, but spent over twenty-six thousand on the Communist defendants. Fascism and anti-Communism then, not racism, continued to be the Party's primary concern.[42]

Howard Fast agreed with the Party that the defeat of fascism would mean that racism along with all the other ills of capitalist society would be vanquished. He never tired of bringing this message to audiences at home and to friends abroad. On January 25, 1951, he sent telegrams to the Union of Soviet Writers in Moscow and to *La nouvelle critique,* the journal of the Communist Party of France, conflating American antiblack racism and fascism by saying that unless mass international protests against American fascist infamy were mounted, "seven innocent. . . . Negroes will be executed Friday, February second."[43] By fusing (indeed, purposely confusing) undeniable American racism with the phantom of American fascism, Fast and his comrades thought they could more easily make the case for the reactionary nature of the United States.

As we have seen, Fast did not have to prove his antiracism bona fides, and for several consecutive nights before the Martinsville Seven were to be put to death, he even turned up in the February snow before the White House for long vigils in a last-ditch effort to save the men.[44] In addition to getting the attention of the national media, Fast's action was noticed in as remote a place as Mill Point prison in West Virginia. Albert Maltz, still serving out his sentence at the prison, wrote Fast that while "other inmates leave and are forgotten . . . you remain . . . present in the life of Mill Point." The officers, all white, Maltz said, "read of your doings and buzz with wonder and disdain." But when Maltz took the newspaper account of Fast's White House picketing into "A" Barracks, where black prisoners were housed, the buzz was of a different sort. Blacks who were angry that many of the white prisoners were "celebrating" the imminent executions, were made to "pause and think and wonder . . . that you should be picketing." And one African American inmate said "with admiration and respect, 'That Howard.'"[45]

As admirable as Fast's work was on behalf of the Martinsville Seven, "that Howard" apparently could not resist demagoguery. In addressing a demonstration sponsored by the CRC in Harlem for the condemned men two days after the executions began on February 2, Fast declared that it was "time to rise," not against racism per se, which was only a product of an evil system, but "against Fascism in America, the Fascism that was taking over this country as it had in Germany." The Communists were first to be prosecuted, now it's the Negroes, Fast said, and soon "Jews and other minorities will face the same burden." Today, he went on, in his inimitable style, we are talking about seven Negroes, but if fascism is not challenged and defeated, "there will be a thousand and then millions." He told the crowd, "Go out and rouse your neighbors, bring them out." Otherwise, Fast insisted, once again exploiting the Holocaust, "you will go down like the Jews of Germany."[46]

Jews and blacks were very much on Fast's mind during this period. Even as he devoted a great deal of his time to the "Martinsville Negroes," and was putting the finishing touches on *Peekskill, USA,* a book in which Jews and blacks were featured as both victims and antifascist radicals, Fast was also doing his annual organizing and arranging for the upcoming May Day celebrations. Desirous of emphasizing a strong connection between being Jewish and being radical, so as to distinguish his brand of Jew from the competing identity of acculturated, post-Holocaust, anti-Communist Jew, Fast asked artist William Gropper to design a May Day pamphlet centered around "the theme of the Jewish worker and May Day." Gropper, although pro-Communist and Jewish himself, had some difficulty with Fast's request. "What is there that I can portray" as particularly Jewish, the artist asked. "I have always thought . . . May Day . . . a workers' day regardless of race . . . or religion." If "something new has been added," Gropper wrote, "let me in on it." But ever creative, Gropper finally told Fast, "The only idea that comes to mind for a picture" is a group of Jewish workers at the head of a May Day parade wielding Yiddish signs that read *in dreard mit di basses,* literally, into the earth with (or death to) the bosses.[47]

At the same time that Fast was trying to connect the dots between Jews and Leftism, and Jews and blacks, and to equate antisemitism and antiblack racism with fascism, he wrote to the Jewish antifascist writer and literary scholar Alfred Kantorowicz in Berlin, asking "whether you and your friends have heard of the latest series of Hitler like crimes on the part of the Truman-Acheson gang." Fumbling for a connection between the Martinsville Seven and alleged American suppression of genuine peace movements, Fast told Kantorowicz, "We have execution of hostages now. . . . Seven innocent Negroes" were put to death by the state of Virginia "with the approval of the Truman government." Without ever linking the Martinsville Seven in any way to peace movements, Fast, in his desperate attempt to paint America as incorrigibly militaristic and fascistic, insisted that the executions were a warning to all Americans, Negro, Jewish, and white, *"that we can expect death as a reward for engaging in the struggle for peace."*[48]

A little later Fast led a demonstration near New York's city hall protesting the scheduled execution of Willie McGee and again attempted to tie racism to fascism and militarism. He called for all citizens to join the Civil Rights Congress in making a mass protest of "Government legal murder in the United States as well as Korea," where Fast said, "MacArthur abandoned Negro troops to slaughter."[49] Willie McGee's case, partly because of Fast's involvement, became an international cause célèbre. President Truman came under pressure from England, France, Russia, and China to pardon McGee or to grant clemency. Many American notables, including Albert Einstein, Norman Mailer, and Paul Robeson, also spoke out in the convicted black man's defense, and William Faulkner wrote an open letter insisting that the case against McGee had not been proven.[50] The Communist Party in May 1951 asked volunteers to go to Washington to protest, and Howard Fast, covering the event for the *Daily Worker,* joined dozens of men who gathered at the Lincoln Memorial. Half were veterans of the Spanish Civil War, and forty-five of them were courageous enough to chain themselves in a circle around each pillar of the memorial, while Fast stood aside with his notebook, which as he put it later, "is always an advantage a reporter has—to be out of the direct line of fire."[51]

Fast fully expected the Washington police to come out shooting. To his surprise, they used no guns, only tools to cut the chains, and they made no arrests. But Fast told readers of the leftist newspaper *Austrian Voice* that "we could not save the Negro McGee" because the "most infamous kind of fascism [has] gained ground in our country." It has kept the "average American completely ignorant," Fast said. Indeed, he went on to say that the American citizen "is the worst and most falsely informed creature on this earth . . . thanks to the gigantic monopolization" of the press in the United States. McGee's execution, Fast argued, not only was a consequence of the sickness of racism, but was "intended to intimidate and terrorize the Negro population as well as all peace-loving groups."[52]

Only about five weeks after McGee was executed, the government helped reinforce in Fast's mind the link between antiblack racism and American fascism. On the morning of June 20, 1951, one hundred FBI agents in a well-orchestrated operation burst into twenty homes throughout New York City and hauled eighteen Communist Party leaders off to jail. They, like those eleven leaders arrested in 1949, were charged under the Smith Act with conspiring to teach the overthrow of the U.S. government by force. Among those arrested was V. J. Jerome, chairman of the Party Cultural Section. A month later, Jerry, as he was more familiarly known, was released on $10,000 bail posted by six individuals including Alice Jerome, Jerry's wife, Herbert Aptheker, and Howard Fast.[53]

In his efforts to help Jerome and the others, Fast wrote to Max Lerner, who in the forties had served on the editorial boards of left-liberal magazines including the *New Republic,* the *Nation,* and the radical daily *PM.* "I know that you make a practice of not allying yourself with public demonstrations of this sort," Fast said, "but I also know that you as well as anyone realize how terribly, terribly late the hour is, and how desperately [we need] some sort of . . . united front against this creeping fascism." Lerner, who found Jerome's "cultural" leadership offensive, responded quickly. In "the struggle for Civil Liberties," he said, he could work best through his own writings, and added that "the 'United Front' to which you refer . . . would be, after everything that has happened in relations between Communists and Liberals, an ironically hollow gesture." A few days later in answer to a phone message from Fast, Lerner wrote that nothing "will be gained by our talking. . . . There is no common ground between us which could serve as the foundation for any joint action."[54]

Although Lerner could speak and write freely, all on the left who openly defended Jerome had reason to fear that they themselves might be targeted for blacklisting, harassment, and even arrest.[55] Fast was already a victim of FBI harassment. And because of the banning of *Citizen Tom Paine* in public school libraries in 1947 and 1949, the attempt to do the same with all of his books in Scarsdale, New York, in 1950, and his being barred from speaking on college campuses even after having served his sentence, Fast thought it inevitable that he'd end up on the blacklist no matter what he did.[56] It could be said that by continuing to provoke the authorities Fast had little to lose. He did, however, genuinely fear being rearrested, perhaps with detention in a place like the federal penitentiary at Danbury, Connecticut, which unlike Mill Point was no summer camp. Privately, Fast also feared for his life. In a letter to Gwyn Thomas, he enclosed a document about Dashiell Hammett, who had been sentenced to six months in prison for contempt of court in July 1951. He concluded by saying, "some time in the next couple of weeks I will be writing to you. . . . Providing I am at large and alive."[57] Maintaining a high profile in the Communist movement in 1951 by putting up bail for V. J. Jerome demonstrated Fast's continued loyalty to the Party—perhaps a bit of foolishness, but also courage.

He put himself front and center again later in the year when he joined with Civil Rights Congress chief William Patterson, Paul Robeson, and a small team of scholarly writers to create a book-length document entitled *We Charge Genocide: The Historic Petition to the UN for Relief from a Crime of the U.S. Government against the Negro People.* Patterson, although more committed in 1951 to the defense of the new group of Communist leaders arrested in July, was well known for his leadership of the black left. And Robeson was arguably the most famous black man in America.

In June 1950, however, Robeson had repeated the fateful sentiments he had expressed at the Paris Peace Conference in 1949. Speaking against the Korean War in a packed Madison Square Garden, Robeson said, "[If] we don't stop our armed adventure in Korea today—tomorrow it will be Africa. . . . I have said it before and I say it again, that the place for the Negro people to fight for their freedom is here at home."[58] In 1949 his words had opened a national debate. Repeated in 1950, when the political climate had changed for the worse, Robeson's provocative remarks led to the loss of his passport, moving him into the small but growing club of writers and artists—including Charlotta Bass, African American editor and owner of the *California Eagle;* Corliss Lamont, founder of the *Marxist Quarterly;* Rockwell Kent, radical artist and writer; Albert Kahn, leftist author, journalist, and photographer; and Howard Fast—who were forbidden to travel outside the United States. In Fast's case this meant having to turn down, over time, invitations to speak from nine different countries, including Czechoslovakia, the USSR, Spain, Israel, and Germany.[59] Fast ought to have known that his openly pursued Communist activity and his ferociously critical comments about fascism and racism in the United States would win him no points at the State Department, to which he continued to apply for permission to travel. The possibility of incurring even more disfavor did not, however, stop him from participating in the *We Charge Genocide* project.

Fast claims that the idea for the project was his, and that it had been germinating in his brain ever since 1944, when Raphael Lemkin, an attorney who lost forty-nine members of his family in the Nazi Holocaust, coined the word "genocide" after hearing Churchill's radio description of German atrocities as "this crime without a name." Fast told an interviewer in 1994 that in 1951, three years after the UN adopted the Universal Declaration of Human Rights and established the Convention on the Prevention and Punishment of the Crime of Genocide, that he and William Patterson "were discussing the Holocaust." Fast claims to have said at the time, "Bill, if we put together every unjustified murder . . . of a black in the South—you would have a Holocaust." Patterson agreed, and as soon as *We Charge Genocide* was put together, Fast urged the CRC to "take it to the United Nations."[60]

A book-length petition, *We Charge Genocide* postulated that the suffering of black Americans, numbering some 13 million, equaling or exceeding the populations of many individual UN countries, qualified as genocide. The National Association for the Advancement of Colored People had also made a strong case for international condemnation of U.S. racial policy in a statistic-laden booklet edited by W. E. B. Du Bois called *Appeal to the World*. Its tone, however, was amiable compared to the CRC's scathing indictment of American racism and the Communist group's use of the startling new term, "genocide." How much of the CRC's more aggressively explicit and sensationalist approach reflected the influence of Howard Fast is difficult to determine, but he, along with Robeson and Patterson, did indeed present the petition *We Charge Genocide* to the United Nations on December 18, 1951.[61]

Through this action, Fast continued to reach audiences at home and abroad. But constraints on him continued from both left and right. Fast's play *Thirty Pieces of Silver*, for example, based on an earlier short story of the same name, ran into trouble with the Party after its formal world premiere in April 1951 in Prague. A dark story that details the rise of Judas Iscariot, *Thirty Pieces* can be read as a parable about all those who forsake their ideals for material gain. Apparently well received in Prague, the play was performed by sixteen other Czech companies. In addition, *Thirty Pieces* was performed in Vienna and Berlin, and in Poland at the Yiddish Theater and at the Theater of Warsaw. It was even staged in the remote Siberian city of Omsk, from which the theater director wrote Fast that *Thirty Pieces* was "one of the most interesting plays," which will be "long . . . remembered by its performers and its audience. . . . because, we believe in the truth of each line which you have written."[62]

Unfortunately, the manuscript of his play fell into the hands of some Party hack in the United States, who ordered Fast to change the third act. The petty bureaucrat told Fast that he was close to Pettis Perry, the general secretary of the Party, and unless changes were made in the play, he would see to it that Perry, already looking for an excuse, would have Fast expelled. What the Party objected to is impossible to determine as no copy of the original version of *Thirty Pieces of Silver* is available. That, of course, is less important than Fast's continued obedience to the Party line. Less than a year had passed since he had expressed shock over the Party's foolish dictates concerning the casting of his play *The Hammer;* but Fast, dutifully if resentfully, "made very considerable revision of the manuscript" of *Thirty Pieces.*[63]

Even after he quit the Party in 1957, Fast continued to believe that despite the humiliations he had undergone within the CP over the years, he did the right thing each time in refusing to allow himself to be expelled from the Party. If it had come to that, he claimed, in a manner indicative of an overblown sense of his own social clout, he would have "lost all power to influence . . . hundreds of thousands the world over."[64]

At almost exactly the same time that Fast's creative impulses and artistic instincts were being circumscribed by the American Communist Party, he also faced obstacles from the right. Whether the FBI was putting the screws to publishers directly, or editors were simply running scared in a climate of increasing suspicion and guilt by association, Fast found himself blacklisted. *The Proud and the Free,* put out by Little, Brown in 1950, would be the last book under his own name with a mainstream publisher until 1958, a year after he resigned from the CPUSA.

Fast planned to do a series of novels over a twenty-year period, on the class struggle through history. In May 1951 he had already completed a good part of the first book, which focused on the slave rebellion led by Spartacus 73–71 BCE. Fast thought *Spartacus* was developing into his best and most important work to date. But to Bette, Albert Maltz, and a small circle of friends, he expressed his fears about being rejected by the publishing houses. By late 1950, Angus Cameron knew that the executive board at

Little, Brown was nervous about putting out more of Fast's work, and had even earlier suggested that Fast publish under a pseudonym. Maltz, too, thought using a pseudonym a good idea, especially after the intensification of McCarthyism and rumors of a new investigation of Fast by the HUAC.[65]

Fast told Maltz in May 1951 that he was not averse to using a pseudonym to make some money as security against "the future." In fact, with the advice of his agents, Fast had in 1950 already written a money-making short story under the name of Simon Kent, and as Walter Ericson, "an anti-fascist mystery" called *Fallen Angel*. The manuscript was accepted by Little, Brown, but apparently someone in the publishing house tipped off the FBI about Fast's authorship. The FBI, according to Fast, accused Little, Brown of collaborating with Communists, threatened a conspiracy charge, and "forced" the publisher to put Fast's name on the inside jacket-flap of the book.[66]

When it was finally published at the end of 1951, *Fallen Angel* brought other pressures, this time from an infuriated CP leadership, which lambasted Fast for violating Marxist injunctions by writing "bourgeois propaganda." The emphasis in the novel on disguise and the submerged identity of the protagonist may have reflected Fast's own internal conflicts and repressions about his place as a writer in the CPUSA. Whatever the case, the Party's cultural commissars were upset about Fast's liberal allusions in the novel to Freudian concepts of guilt projection, the subjective interpretation of reality, and the unconscious. The reviewer for the *New York Times* liked the book even less. *Fallen Angel,* he said, had a limp, tired plot, heavy prose, and a "general air of never quite making sense." And then the cruelest cut of all: "Fast-Ericson has forgotten most of the requirements of the straight novel without learning the specialized technique of the suspense story."[67]

With all his troubles, however, Fast did not think that he could "surrender the right to have my own work, that is, my important work, appear under my own name."[68] Maltz thought this position wrong-headed. He pointed out that *The Proud and the Free* had sold poorly, only because of Fast's authorship. Why not "reach a wider group of readers" under another name with a socially progressive book, Maltz asked. Fast would have none of it because, unlike his friend Albert, Howard had an ego of inordinate proportion.[69]

At the same time that Fast was rejecting the use of a pseudonym, another pro-Communist writer, Len Zinberg, in response to the arrest of V. J. Jerome and the other Communist Party leaders, took the name Ed Lacy for the publication of his paperback crime novel *The Woman Aroused* (1951).

The Lacy pseudonym protected Zinberg from blacklisting and harassment, and his books became part of the mass culture market. Nonetheless, his books continued to be filled with radical leftist themes. Ultimately, they sold 28 million copies and became the main competition for the ultra-reactionary, anti-Communist productions of Mickey Spillane. Zinberg was somewhat melancholy about his entrapment as a pulp writer, but it fulfilled his powerful need to fight on for the ideals he had been pursuing in the antifascist movement.[70] Fast, on the other hand, felt that the "struggle at this point is for us who are known and symbolized as leaders of the literary movement on the left, to fight an intensive battle to publish our work under our own names."[71] Courageously dedicated to his politics and his art, imprudent, or mostly vain, Fast remained adamantly against using a pseudonym for his major writings. But he did worry about whether he would be able to finish *Spartacus* "before they crack down on me again." If they do, Fast thought, again overestimating his own importance, it will be a "circus," one that would deepen fascism in the United States, but would also in the long term contribute to "a cataclysm that would bring down the American system."[72]

Fast was not subpoenaed again to appear before Congress until 1953, but in the meantime, he encountered significant difficulty getting a publisher for his big new book. Despite his having been able to publish ten novels in the twelve years from 1939 to 1950 with major houses, and to receive relatively wide and often positive attention for these books from the mainstream media, Fast continued to believe that most critics and publishers "are a petty and terror-stricken group of people who never were very long on character or courage."[73] It ought not to have come as much of a surprise to him that a half-dozen major publishers determined not to publish *Spartacus*.

As early as March 1951, Fast thought the book was "shaping up more excitingly than anything I have done in years, and I am really enchanted by the project." By June, feeling that "for the first time in his life" he had mastered his material and "created an enduring book," he submitted a 550-page manuscript to Little, Brown, which had published his previous two novels. Angus Cameron told his editorial board that *Spartacus* was "endlessly engaging, most ingeniously put together, and . . . an entertaining and meaningful novel." The story gives a "feeling of [Roman] times and a profound comment on these times," Cameron wrote. And he added, somewhat defensively, "Fast however, does not draw any analogies."[74]

Cameron sent a copy of the report to Fast, along with a positive personal letter telling Howard that his new work showed "the sure hand of a real artist." Fast was certain the book would be published. On September 1, 1951, however, *Counterattack,* the anti-Communist weekly, devoted its entire six-page issue to an article, "What Has Happened to Little, Brown?" charging that the company which had published Fast, Lillian Hellman, Albert Kahn, and other leftists, had become a Communist front. The smear piece was quoted liberally in the *New York World Telegram and Sun* and other Scripps-Howard newspapers.[75]

Fear among the editors at Little, Brown, already fiercely criticized as pro-Communist by other right-wing periodicals and by the FBI, was great enough to generate a rejection of *Spartacus.* Cameron, who later resigned, wrote a memo of protest, but the directors, without ever discussing his arguments, stated that Little, Brown would no longer "publish Fast under any circumstances."[76]

Fast mistakenly assumed that Cameron had resigned because Little, Brown "refused to undertake publication" of *Spartacus,* and that Hoover was directly behind the firm's decision. Fast was again exaggerating his own importance as well as the role played by the FBI. Indeed, he wondered "what J. Edgar Hoover would have done without [him]." Cameron disputed Fast's version of events, saying his resignation had to do with the "larger issue" of Little, Brown's generally restrictive policies, and that Spartacus "had nothing to do with my leaving." Nor did he ever mention pressure from the FBI.[77]

In any case, more than a little irritated, Fast began sounding out other publishers. Macmillan did not even want to see the manuscript. It *was* read at Random House, but despite Fast's fifteen-year friendship with editor Bennett Cerf, *Spartacus* was found "undesirable." World Publishers, which had been reprinting Fast's titles for a decade, returned his submission after only five days with no comment. An editor at Viking apparently liked the book, but claimed he had to check with two others about "the politics." Fast was finally told that "if all other channels were exhausted . . . the doors of Viking would not be closed to [him]." He did not, however, resubmit the manuscript even after rejections by Doubleday and by the Communist editor at Citadel Press, Phil Foner, who begged Howard "not to put him in the terrible position of having to reject it out of fear."[78]

Simon and Schuster told Fast they would be happy to read *Spartacus,* but because he, a writer of "seven best sellers and some 10 million books," could no longer abide the humiliating experience of rejection, Fast did not send it to them. "I am going ahead with self-publication," Fast told Albert Maltz. *Spartacus,* Fast believed, would be a best-selling money-maker as well as an education for the American public about class war. It "represents something so important in my life," Fast admitted, "that I must . . . achieve its publication."[79]

Enclosing Cameron's favorable reader's report, Fast sent a "Dear Friend" fundraising letter to innumerable institutions and organizations, saying no firm would publish *Spartacus* or any other book written by him.[80] Cameron was apparently put out that he wasn't asked for permission to use his report in this way, and later told an interviewer that he "wasn't quite as enthusiastic over [*Spartacus*] as Howard thinks I was." But Fast was desperate. If he were to submit "to this kind of censorship," Fast wrote, "the harm done to many others beside myself would be by no means inconsiderable."[81]

He also disingenuously told guests at a small private reception at the home of a friend (surreptitiously attended by a bureau informant) that *Spartacus* was initially "received with enthusiasm" by every publisher to whom he had sent the manuscript. But Fast said, continuing the charade, that his work was subsequently rejected by all of them because of intimidation by the FBI.[82] Fast need not have been so deceitful; the blacklist in publishing often functioned in what the French philosopher Jacques Ellul called "the sociological atmosphere," a less immediately menacing, but more subtle and more stealthily treacherous force than direct interference by government agencies.

Because Fast believed that for over two decades enough Americans had "come to know and love the books I write," he also believed he could self-publish profitably if he had some money up front. He asked prospective readers to purchase, by subscription, in advance of publication, a specially bound, numbered, and autographed edition of *Spartacus* for $5.00. He also tried to promote prepublication sales of a regular edition for $2.50. Even though Fast had no experience with self-publishing and was working mostly out of his own home on West 94th Street—seven-year-old Rachel and three-year-old Jonathan being tended to by Bette—he was having significant success. In a letter to his lover Isabel Johnson, who was in San Francisco at the time, but with whom he was to meet again in New York in two weeks, Fast wrote that he was "very busy, working hard on preparing the book and quite dumfounded by the tremendous response from people I've written to. It really begins to look as if I shall hit that thousand mark [of subscriptions] after all."[83]

And after actually putting the book out, Fast sent a mailing to labor organizations promoting a one-dollar special paper edition for unions. "By now,"
he said, "I have received sufficient good comment from trade unionists to feel
that *Spartacus*," a book Angus Cameron had claimed made no analogies to
the present, "can do an important agitational job among workers."[84]

While writing *Spartacus,* Fast was mindful of what he called "a wonderful
continuity between that first class war," the largest slave rebellion in Western
history, "and all the times that followed." Fast's political goal was clear from
his epigraph: "I wrote [*Spartacus*] so that those who read it . . . may take
strength for our own troubled future and that they may struggle against oppression and wrong—so that the dream of Spartacus may come to be in our
own time."[85] For Fast, ancient Rome, with its slaves and factory workers, was
a capitalist society, and like the United States, an unjust imperialist society
in the last stages of decay.

Very little is known about the historical Spartacus or his provenance.
Before he performed as a gladiator, he may have been a deserter from the
Roman army, a mercenary, or a highwayman. Or as Fast preferred, a third-
generation slave—a figure more clearly oppressed. Whatever Spartacus's
background, Fast's version of the mythical rebel has him organizing seventy
thousand runaway slaves in an uprising that holds the mighty military of
Rome at bay for more than three years.[86]

Fast imagines the slave uprising as a war of grossly exploited, but unfailingly heroic, "proletarians," against a decadent, debauched, and brutal
ruling class. The oppressive upper echelon of Roman society, including the
patrician General Crassus and the plebian gangster-politician Gracchus, is
riddled with sadists and immoral sexual deviants of every variety. And they
are in league with men like the lawyer-philosopher Cicero, who come from
the "money-grubbing upper middle-class."[87]

The rebel slaves, in contrast to the perverted patricians who are morbidly
fascinated by mass crucifixions of "enemies of the state," live in an impossibly perfect egalitarian, communal, and heterosexual harmony. In this way,
Fast evokes, through Spartacus, the dream of restoring a mythical golden
age "where all men and women too had been equals . . . and all things had
been held in common."[88]

Spartacus is to his slave army a good, gentle, and lovable hero. Indeed,
Spartacus, the warrior, in his kindness and charisma seems to his troops
nearly divine, and resembles Fast's earlier depictions of Christ. At the same

time, perhaps like the Jesus who said, "I come not to bring peace, but a sword," Spartacus seeks, with the mass of runaway slaves under his leadership, not only liberation, but ultimately, and most unrealistically, the destruction of the whole system of Roman slavery.

In several ways *Spartacus* seems a "substitute" for the book on Christ that Fast had contemplated writing while in prison. This is even more explicit in David, the Jewish gladiator and last survivor of the revolt, who, as he nears death on the cross, recounts episodes of his life. This is one of the longest and most gripping creations in the novel. And when Fast adds an old woman, who has mistaken David for her son, weeping at the foot of the cross, thereby mimicking the scriptural accounts of the crucifixion of Christ, the scene becomes another example of Fast's attempt to link Jesus to the prophetic tradition of Judaism. Even David's final painful question, "Spartacus, Spartacus, why did we fail?" echoes the final words of Jesus; and also, whether Fast knew it or not, the first line of Psalm 22 in the Hebrew scriptures.[89] As imitative as these passages appear, they signify Fast's continuing quest to blend Judaism and Christianity, as well as his struggle to hold on to love *and* violence, the seemingly incongruous pieces that constitute the vehicle through which progressive social change will finally come.

Fast answers David's plaintive cry by implying that even if Spartacus failed, Rome (like the United States, allegedly collapsing under the weight of its own contradictions) was doomed. Moreover, though his rebellion lost its force and will, Spartacus provided an example, Fast thought, that would inspire "faith in the ultimate victory that will be the outcome of *our* struggle."[90]

Spartacus is marred by a simplistic depiction of an utterly unredeemable ruling class and slave rebels who are unfailingly noble and courageous. Fast also introduces clumsy anachronisms—terms such as "proletarian," "upper middle-class," and "enemies of the state," as well as direct allusions to Marx—"To the slaves of the world we will cry out, Rise up and cast off your chains." Yet, *Spartacus* has its forceful moments, which together create an entertaining and often fast-moving narrative: a poignant rendition of David's last recollections; harrowing descriptions of slaves laboring in the gold mines of the Nubian desert; the dramatic struggles of gladiators who fight to the death in the arena at Capua; the extraordinary pitched battles against the Roman legions; the vivid, horrific scenes of crucified slaves lining the Appian Way; and an abundance of sex.

Spartacus was read by millions who could not fail to recognize the misery of chattel slavery, which not only oppressed its victims, but degraded and corrupted its masters by engendering idleness and moral depravity; those readers, however, did not necessarily see the story as a parable "illuminating" the "class struggles" of the mid-twentieth century. Indeed, eight years before it became a film, left-liberal writer and critic Harvey Swados called *Spartacus,* with its spectacular grand-scale entertainments, a popular "epic in technicolor." The behavior of Fast's heroes and heroines, Swados wrote, rather presciently (given the film version made later), are what "we have come to expect from the movie[s]." Fast's conception of history, Swados said, "is not very different from Cecile B. DeMille's."[91]

However the general public felt about Fast's "conception of history," or about his politics, *Spartacus* sold more than forty-five thousand copies in the first three months of publication, and by April 1952, it had been reissued seven times despite a dearth of reviews.[92] There were only nine, three of which were in radical journals, compared to fifteen reviews of *Citizen Tom Paine,* and twenty-three of *Freedom Road.* Critical, as distinct from popular, reception was decidedly mixed. The reviewer for the *New York Times* thought that it was no longer possible "to distinguish the creative writer from the pamphleteer in the works of Howard Fast." And he found *Spartacus* filled with sentimental clichés and histrionics, a "far cry" from Fast's best works, and another "dreary proof that polemics and fiction don't mix."[93]

The Communist critics, though "greatly indebted to Howard Fast for resurrecting and interpreting the significance of this heroic slave war for liberation" in a novel clearly "written to illuminate our times," thought *Spartacus* deeply flawed by its "disturbing liberal, self-negating and incredible finish."[94] Though not entirely beyond belief, the denouement of Fast's novel is certainly peculiar. Crassus, who has destroyed Spartacus and his rebel army, appropriates as his own slave Varinia, the slain hero's wife, and falls in love with her. Even harder to believe, Gracchus, the cynical leader of the Roman Senate, also falls in love with Varinia, sight unseen. He will give up his fortune to have her taken from Crassus, who like Gracchus believes he can redeem himself and the immoral life he has lived through the purity of "true love." Less credible still, Varinia, widow of the crucified Spartacus, after one evening with Gracchus seems willing to share her life with him.

Angus Cameron had seen this ending as a sign of artistic maturity in Fast, because without excusing anyone or anything, the author had demonstrated "that each human being has the capacity for being something other than he is."[95] This judgment was precisely what the radical left found *"absolutely inexcusable!"* on the part of Fast, who with "Freudian mystifications" and sentimental and impossible tripe, fatally damaged his novel and betrayed the cause for which Spartacus fought. Albert Maltz, who also neither liked nor believed the ending of the book, said he understood what Fast was reaching for. Even when "they don't succeed," Maltz wrote, "I am very tolerant of such efforts," and "feel that in [many of your] pages are some of the noblest and most vivid passages in English Literature."[96] Perhaps this praise took some of the sting out of the harsher critiques from the left. But more likely it was the extraordinary success of the book among the reading public that did it.

Spartacus had its own inherent popular appeal, but Fast's relentless marketing also helped. He sold books at receptions in the private homes of friends and associates. He appealed to librarians to challenge the "censorship" imposed on him, and told them dishonestly that, in any case, *"Spartacus* is not a political book. . . . It is a novel of ancient Rome, and it has no line." Fast also sent a form-letter advertisement to many Jewish organizations harking back to *My Glorious Brothers,* the writing of which, he said, "made him understand the hopes and aspirations of an oppressed and persecuted people." And he got several rabbis, including Lewis I. Newman and Robert E. Goldburg, who later presided over the conversion to Judaism of Marilyn Monroe (who could then marry the pro-Communist Arthur Miller), to promote sales and even to distribute return envelopes for orders.[97]

Once the book started to take off, it was reprinted by the Liberty Book Club, placed in bookstores by Doubleday, which had rejected it, and distributed by Citadel Press, which had refused to consider it for publication.[98] In April 1952, Fast founded the Blue Heron Publishing House. Despite good sales of *Spartacus,* now under Blue Heron's imprint, Fast claimed that he was hovering close to "devastating poverty and . . . bankruptcy."[99] This assertion was very far from the truth. Many of Fast's books, especially *Freedom Road* and *Citizen Tom Paine,* were translated into dozens of languages, even if occasionally in pirated editions, and sales abroad were brisk. Most important, Fast's popularity in the USSR and Eastern Europe meant not only sales, but substantial royalties. The Soviet Union paid Fast handsomely, even if irregularly.[100] Moreover, by the time Fast had been "consecrated" in the USSR in 1948, his novels had already become big sellers outside the Soviet bloc, especially in Argentina, France, the Netherlands, Belgium, and Denmark.[101]

Spartacus appeared in more than thirty languages, including French, Russian, Chinese, Bengali, Hungarian, Hebrew, and by 1954 Yiddish. It had become the only self-published best seller in literary history up to that point.[102] While Fast was occasionally strapped for cash because payments from the Soviet Union arrived erratically, he was financially secure.[103] The same could not be said for Blue Heron, but still Fast could afford with the help of contributions and advance subscriptions to publish or reprint, often at a loss to his company, many of his own titles and several books of his left-wing friends, including *The Best Untold: A Book of Paintings* by the blacklisted artist Edward Biberman (brother of Herbert), *Goldsborough,* a novel by Stefan Heym, Walter Lowenfels's *Sonnets of Love and Liberty,* and an exceptionally well-done edition of W. E. B. Du Bois's *The Souls of Black Folk.*[104]

All through 1951, a busy year of Fast's negotiations with publishers, energetic self-marketing, and the financially risky organization of his own press, he continued his many political activities. He wrote "A Dialogue for Unity," a prose poem praising Jewish and black culture, read by James Earl Jones to an audience of fourteen hundred at the annual concert of the Jewish Studies division of the Jefferson School for Social Science; worked on the May Day committee and marched at the head of its parade; addressed peace rallies; stayed extraordinarily active in the pursuit of racial justice; spoke at a fundraising rally of the Civil Rights Congress; helped post bail for Dashiell Hammett and V. J. Jerome; noisily opposed the Supreme Court's rejection of appeals in the Smith Act cases; and protested the indictment of W. E. B. Du Bois under the Foreign Agents Registration Act.[105]

He even took time to lead a protest at the Park Avenue Theatre at 59th Street, which was showing *Oliver Twist,* a film Fast considered "monstrously" antisemitic; and he tried to link the movie to the death sentences imposed in the Rosenberg case, which in 1951 had become a focal point of Cold War passions and a source of competition within the Jewish community for ascendancy between opposing versions of American Jewish identity. Fast, representing the radical tradition, asked the "comfortable" Jews of New York to ponder the fearful "Judenrat role" played in the Rosenberg trial by the "liberal Jews," the "good Jews": Judge Irving Kaufman, prosecutor Irving Saypol, and anti-Communist financier Bernard Baruch, for example.[106]

During this time Fast also covered the longshoremen's strike in New York City, writing in November and December 1951 two substantial pieces for

Masses and Mainstream, the second of which he concluded by saying that the striking workers "had a strength and . . . solidarity that holds a bitter threat for the future of Wall Street." He also sponsored the newly formed American Peace Crusade (denounced immediately by Secretary of State Dean Acheson as a Communist front).[107] Through his persistent activism, journalism, and oratory, Fast demonstrated that he continued to share the long-term revolutionary goals of the CPUSA. And even as he wrote that no press in history had ever been "subject to such strict control as ours," and that America "surround[s] itself with an . . . impenetrable curtain of lies and deceit," Fast remained in awe of the Soviet Union, which, he said at the end of 1951, was "a mighty bulwark of peace" and "the final achievement of mankind is its struggle to end oppression."[108]

Trials and Tribulations

*T*hroughout the mid-fifties Howard Fast, certain he was in possession of the truth, fully supported the USSR and remained genuinely committed to the goals of the Communist Party of the USA. At the same time he persisted in his indefatigable quest for fame and fortune through writing. Fast never stopped working at his craft, even as he continued organizing, traveling, fundraising, and speaking for the Party. Albert Maltz was "constantly astonish[ed]" at Howard's "enormous productivity," and his "great gift of combining solid writing with so many other activities."[1]

In 1952 Fast published *Tony and the Wonderful Door,* a book for school-age children, and in 1953, *The Passion of Sacco and Vanzetti: A New England Legend,* even during a grueling, but unsuccessful, run for Congress in 1952, significant, direct involvement in the Steve Nelson sedition case, a careful following of the trials of the Smith Act defendants, and rapt immersion in the international effort to save Julius and Ethel Rosenberg. Early in 1953, even as he was writing his novel about the Italian immigrant anarchists, he also squared off with Joe McCarthy's Senate subcommittee.

For his loyalty to Communism, the Soviet state in 1953 awarded Fast the "Stalin Prize for Promoting Peace among Nations." This recognition, the international socialist alternative to the Nobel Prize, was deemed by Fast "the highest honor that can be conferred on any person"; and it seemed to spur him to even more furious activity. In 1954 he gave two dozen speeches at pro-Communist events; attended innumerable leftist rallies; participated in forums on a variety of topics including, with V. J. Jerome and Dashiell Hammett, "Fiction Writing as a People's Art"; taught courses at the Jefferson School for Social Science; worked to overturn the conviction under the Smith Act of the poet Walter Lowenfels; tried to get Morton Sobell, who was convicted along with the Rosenbergs for conspiracy to commit espionage, transferred from Alcatraz to a "better prison"; and began work on *Silas Timberman,* his sixteenth novel. Somehow Fast also found time to write more than a dozen shorter pieces of fiction, which were collected in *The Last Supper and Other Stories* and published in 1955.

Throughout U.S. history large segments of the American public have paid close attention to trials. The drama involved in testimony and argument over what was true and what false, and the suspense inherent in the question of guilt or innocence, sustained intense general interest. The public took particular notice of those trials during the Cold War era that seemed to feature confrontations between good and evil, as in the cases of Steve Nelson, the Smith Act defendants, and the Rosenbergs. Howard Fast played a significant role in each instance.

In mid-January 1952 Fast entered the Allegheny County courthouse in Pennsylvania to witness the opening of his friend Steve Nelson's trial. Arrested in 1950, Nelson, a major labor organizer and leading figure in the Communist Party, was charged under a state sedition law with conspiring to overthrow the government of Pennsylvania by force. In the early 1930s, Nelson had studied at the Lenin School in Moscow, and had served the Comintern as an "international agent" in Germany. In 1937, he fought as part of the antifascist forces in Spain, where he played the role of "political commissar" and helped the Communists suppress, sometimes murderously, non-Stalinist radicals who were fighting against Franco. But no evidence was ever presented linking Nelson to conspiratorial or seditious behavior in the United States.[2] Still, Nelson's radical labor-movement activism and his background on the far left made him a good target for anti-Communist opportunist politicians and jurists who hungered for election.

On January 17, 1952, just prior to the proceedings in the Allegheny County court, Fast, as a representative of the Communist-affiliated National Committee of Arts and Sciences, made an unsuccessful attempt to meet with presiding judge Harry Montgomery in Nelson's behalf. A day or two later, at the Ethical Culture Home in Philadelphia, and at the Jewish Cultural Center in Pittsburgh, Fast was the main speaker in support of Nelson. But never missing an opportunity to serve the "larger cause," Fast, with an irrepressible instinct for the impolitic, also praised the "strong points" of Communist nations and the superiority of Chinese troops fighting in Korea.[3] Almost two weeks later, he attended a meeting of the Philadelphia Freedom of the Press Association, where he insisted on the historical importance of the Nelson case. This trial, Fast said, ranks in "grandeur and heroism with the court fights of the greatest working class heroes such as Sacco [and] Vanzetti," about whom Fast was soon to begin writing.[4]

Despite Fast's efforts on Nelson's behalf, the defendant received a twenty-year prison sentence, was fined $10,000, and charged $13,000 in court costs.[5] This was not the end of the battle, however. Fast worked to raise these sums as well as bail money by appealing to comrades at home and abroad, including Louis Aragon and Pablo Picasso. In the summer of 1952 Fast published a poem in the *Daily Worker* promising that the struggle for Nelson's freedom would continue. And he wrote a long letter to the governor of Pennsylvania, representing, he said, "not . . . myself alone, but . . . many, many thousands when I ask you to pardon [Nelson] and restore honor to your office," and to the State of Pennsylvania.[6]

In July, Fast, sponsored by the Veterans of the Abraham Lincoln Brigade spoke to a crowd gathered at the Capitol Hotel in New York City to celebrate the defense of the Republic of Spain. "To anyone who is not completely bamboozled by the press and radio drivel," Fast said, "the thought of keeping Steve Nelson in jail twenty years is laughable." And then somewhat ominously he added, "Steve need not [remain imprisoned]. This is for us to decide. . . . A mighty wave of protest can quickly turn the tide and give the people a great victory."[7]

Later, when Fast got wind of Steve Nelson's commitment to solitary confinement at Blawnox Workhouse, an infamously desolate and oppressive place, he sent a telegram to the warden demanding that Nelson be taken "out of [the] hole." If this were not done, Fast threatened, he would tell the "Entire world" of the "torture of this great American leader." To no effect, he also sent a telegram to Judge Montgomery in Pittsburgh begging for the "transfer [of] Steve Nelson to Allegheny Jail before he is killed by inhuman treatment in Blawnox."[8]

Fast also kept up a steady stream of correspondence with Nelson himself, who was delighted to stay connected in this way. Nelson told Howard that "when others [here in prison] . . . read corny pornography . . . that is, all [of] present-day capitalist 'literature' . . . I pore over [your] letters." He also said that because of Fast's efforts some Allegheny towns previously quiet "are starting to [come to] life on this case." And when Nelson, after eight months, was finally released on bail in February 1953, and began to pursue appeal, he thanked Fast for his persistent and unremitting struggle to garner support. Fast's pleas and petitions to influential people in so "many parts of the world," Nelson wrote, "brought great results."[9]

Having recognized the propaganda value of his campaign to free Nelson, Fast increased and intensified his public role in opposing the Korean War and American intervention in Greece and Turkey, denouncing the intimidation of American citizens by congressional committees, and challenging the Feinberg Law, which in 1949 gave New York State the right to fire, and not to hire, teachers belonging to "subversive" organizations. His many public appearances on these issues led at least one student group, the Yale Political Union, to disinvite Fast as a guest lecturer. The FBI, whose informants believed that Fast endangered the security of the United States by indoctrinating American youth with his subversive speeches at various universities, was delighted.[10]

Only weeks later, however, Fast did appear at Yale by agreeing to debate Arthur Schlesinger Jr. over the proposition that "The United States Safeguards Cultural Freedom." At the New Haven campus, Fast admitted that freedom of speech existed in America, "to a certain extent." But he could not agree with Schlesinger's contention that "More people enjoy freedom under the capitalistic democracy of the West than people ever enjoyed before in human history." Schlesinger, an associate professor at Harvard and leader of the liberal anti-Communist group Americans for Democratic Action, called McCarthyism what it was—an "ugly and sordid phenomenon"; but he saw it as the price paid for political freedom, and something the country would get through eventually, as it had other periods of "hysteria." Fast, on the other hand, pointing to the Smith and McCarran Acts, insisted that people must fight now before the "horror of fascism clamped down [fully] on the United States."[11]

In his attempt to connect what he saw as American fascism with antisemitism and the Holocaust, Fast also pointed to the anti-subversive Feinberg

Law. With no way of knowing the number of teachers dismissed under this fiercely contested law, Fast implied that a great many educators were let go. Furthermore, he claimed that with "one exception, every teacher fired" was Jewish. How many were fired (probably fewer than two dozen up to April 1952), and how many among them were Jewish, is difficult to determine. Still, one can imagine that some, perhaps scores, of left-liberal and Communist teachers in New York City resigned between 1949 and 1952 because the Feinberg Law or refusal to sign loyalty oaths might make them public targets. It is also important to remember that if most of those who were fired or resigned were Jewish, Jewish teachers were heavily represented in New York City schools. In any case, despite the old and continuing claim of Fast and the Party that "under the cloak" of legality "Jewish workers are being deprived of their right to work for their Government," the Feinberg Law was neither promulgated nor passed nor held constitutional because lawmakers and jurists wanted to make life difficult for Jews in particular. Yet, Fast, as was too often his wont, drew an egregiously facile parallel between the Feinberg Law and the "attitudes of Hitler."[12]

Fascism, Fast said, as he had in September 1951 on the Rosenberg case, is inextricably linked to antisemitism and the Holocaust, which, he strongly implied, "could happen here." This is "not to be laughed at," he sternly told his audience, because fascism, which was now waxing in America, had been "responsible for the death of six million Jews in Europe." In response to Fast's tenuous logic and his sensational comparisons, the undergraduate students in attendance at the debate voted 104 to 19 in favor of Schlesinger's defense of the resolution that the United States safeguards cultural freedom.[13]

While Schlesinger had argued reasonably and well, Fast had faced an even more powerful opponent: Jewish-American history since 1945. To convince Jews, or non-Jews for that matter, that they were threatened by anything like genocide in the United States in 1952 was not merely a formidable task, it was impossible. As a result of the destruction of European Jewry, the United States became the most important Jewish community in the world—in numbers, wealth, and intellectual resources. It compared equally or favorably with white Protestant society in education, income, and life style. In 1945, when Bess Myerson, the daughter of a housepainter, became the first Jewish "Miss America," and Detroit Tigers first-baseman Hank Greenberg, the son of Jewish immigrants who had worked their way up into the middle class, became a national hero, "a golden age of American Jewry" had begun.

Greenberg's one-time observance of Yom Kippur after hitting two home runs ten days earlier on Rosh Hashanah in 1934, vicariously certified young people of the second generation as good Jews and "real" Americans. Even more important in this regard, perhaps, was the patriotic luster Hank, and by implication, Jews, accrued when he reenlisted in the military service the day after Pearl Harbor because "My country comes first." And it was Greenberg's ninth-inning, bases-loaded, pennant-winning home run in 1945 after returning from five years of service that fully cemented Jewishness and baseball, that most American of national pastimes.

Meeting the needs of Holocaust survivors and helping in the struggle for Jewish independence in Palestine between 1945 and 1948 greatly revitalized the American Jewish community, as did the return from the war of 550,000 Jewish servicemen, now even more Americanized and self-confident. In 1948 American Jews embraced Jewish statehood in the Middle East with extraordinary alacrity and pride. That same year, Brandeis University was established as the first secular, nonsectarian institution of higher education under Jewish auspices. Some six hundred new synagogues and temples were built in the United States by 1952, while secular Jewish communal institutions assumed a remarkable role in American civic affairs. They lobbied against racial discrimination and in favor of social welfare programs, stronger trade unions, and a foreign policy that emphasized internationalism. By the mid-1950s, antisemitism had undergone a steep decline, and a collective Jewish sense of well-being was palpable.[14]

Jewish writers and critics, including Bernard Malamud, Saul Bellow, Leslie Fiedler, Grace Paley, Norman Mailer, Harold Rosenberg, Muriel Rukeyser, Alfred Kazin, and Karl Shapiro, to name only a small sample, had emerged as figures central to postwar American literature and high culture; and there was a long list of second-generation Jews in the world of entertainment, including Hollywood giants Samuel Goldwyn and Louis Mayer; musical luminaries such as George Gershwin, Beverly Sills, Benny Goodman, Irving Berlin, and Leonard Bernstein; comics and actors such as Milton Berle, Gertrude Berg ("Molly Goldberg"), George Burns, Jerry Lewis, Kirk Douglas, and Edward G. Robinson; and playwrights ranging from Arthur Miller to Neil Simon, all of whom helped shape American popular culture. Indeed, most had become household names in the United States, undoubtedly contributing to the increasing acceptance and admiration of Jews by non-Jews.[15]

Fast failed to notice or chose to ignore these changes. Nor while a Party member did his connection to the larger Jewish community go beyond minimal at best. He almost never participated in Jewish ritual observance; and even when he deigned to attend a family Passover Seder, he'd end up attacking his Orthodox brother-in-law and wind up going home early with a mortified Bette in tow.[16] Ignorant of Jewish-American culture and blinded by Communist ideology, he argued that antisemitism, like antiblack racism, was rife in America, and that the Rosenberg conviction was a direct result. Only days after his debate with Schlesinger, Fast published "Save the Rosenbergs," a manifesto written mostly in reaction to the Federal Circuit Court of Appeals unanimous decision in February 1952 upholding, for the second time, the conviction and death sentence of the hapless couple. Although the presiding judge, Jerome Frank, a Jew and New Deal liberal, had advised Judge Kaufman in March 1951 not to impose the death penalty, and later urged the Supreme Court to hear the case, he rejected the argument to reduce the Rosenbergs' sentence to thirty years or life imprisonment in order to prevent the first-ever execution of civilians for espionage in American history. Clearly, Jewish jurists, like ordinary Americanizing Jews in this second-generation drama, were divided, not only among themselves, but within themselves, on the guilt or innocence of the Rosenbergs and on the severity of the penalty to be paid for conspiracy to commit espionage.[17]

In the anti-Communist climate of the early fifties when Senator Joe McCarthy and his ilk were riding high, explicit identification as a Communist was dangerous. Despite the growing self-confidence of the American Jewish community, many Jewish organizations continued to fear the equation "Jew equals Communist," and purged their left-wing elements. The American Jewish Congress, an association of Jewish Americans organized to defend Jewish interests at home and abroad through public policy advocacy, expelled the pro-Communist Jewish People's Fraternal Order; and the Anti-Defamation League, an international Jewish organization based in the United States, established to fight antisemitism and other forms of bigotry, in its rush to show that Jewishness and Communism were incompatible, shared its files on Communists with HUAC. American Jews, without separating themselves entirely from the prophetic injunction to pursue justice or to be merciful, reduced their commitment to radicalism and dropped their identification with the extreme left.[18]

Still, even before McCarthyism began to diminish in the early fifties, Jews, including Judge Kaufman, remained in the left wing of the Democratic Party. They were supporters of New Deal liberalism and internationalism, and were antiracist. Indeed many Jewish-Americans embraced political liberalism as a civil-religious creed, a secular surrogate for Judaism. Nonetheless, in the process of acculturation to a United States in which anti-Communism had become something of a touchstone of Americanism, the Rosenbergs and their supporters including Fast had to be "excommunicated."[19]

Howard Fast, however, like Julius Rosenberg himself, was one whose Jewish identity inhered in, and depended upon, continued devotion to radical social justice activism. Although such a perspective allowed him to remain an American as well as a Jew, Fast's loyalty to Communism and admiration of the Soviet Union prohibited him from seeing the Rosenbergs as anything but innocent victims of American fascism and antisemitism. Like the CPUSA generally, Fast was quick to see fascism in anything with which he disagreed. In the opening lines of his April 1952 essay on the Rosenbergs, Fast mischievously tied the court of appeals' decision to the strikingly similar timing of "the decision to rearm Western Germany under Nazi generals." This provocative insinuation was followed by two long paragraphs dealing exclusively with the Holocaust. And in the remainder of the piece Fast made yet another fervid attempt to link the Rosenberg case to what he saw as American fascism and to connect it to the Nazi genocide in Europe.

"Are the Jewish people in America so . . . dulled to the meaning of history," Fast asked, "Can they avoid asking why the first peace-time death sentence for espionage in all the history of the United States was reserved for . . . Jews?" Fast not only implied but insisted that the Rosenbergs, after careful deliberation by the Truman administration, were chosen for prosecution precisely because they were Jews. And if American Jews "are willing to accept with all its hideous implications this terrible judicial murder," it means "that the great mass of *the Jewish people in America have chosen supinely to accept the fate which fascism historically reserves for Jewish people everywhere.*"[20]

The Jews were bamboozled, Fast said, by the appointment of Jewish prosecutors, Irving Saypol and Roy Cohn, and by a Jewish judge, Irving Kaufman. They are told "See, it is one of your members who sentences [the Rosenbergs] to death.'" The Jewish judge, Fast claimed, in order to prove his patriotism and anti-Communist bona fides, had charged Julius and Ethel with responsibility for the Korean war! Fast was right to call Kaufman's accusation about a Korea-Rosenberg link preposterous—morally and juridically outrageous. But he argued that it was calculated to make "the compounded insanity" of the case "diabolically sane," and to teach American Jews the implications of "the new order. . . . 'For the Jewish people, as for the Negro people, death will be the penalty for the struggle for peace.'" In a special way, Fast wrote, the Rosenberg prosecution "defines the epoch we live in." Through this case, he said, "the Truman administration squarely and undisguisedly uses the death penalty for those who stand in opposition to it. More subtly, perhaps, than Adolph Hitler proceeded, . . . but with the same tactic, the Truman administration seeks to inflame anti-Semitism. . . . The Rosenbergs have been offered up by the men of war, the men of death." If we let the Rosenbergs burn, Fast argued in a derisory and offensive fashion, "particularly those of us who are Jews [will] have committed the deepest sin, the sin of breaking faith with all of the holy dead who fought against, and who died fighting against, the monster of fascism."[21]

Strong stuff. Yet, although the Rosenbergs had been arrested in the summer of 1950, indicted in January 1951, and tried, convicted, and sentenced to death by April 5, 1951, neither Fast nor the Communist Party had made more than passing reference to the case during that entire period. In the early months of 1951, the *Daily Worker,* for example, carried nothing on the Rosenberg trial. The Communists might very well have maintained their nearly absolute silence had the anti-Communist Yiddish press including *Der Tog* (the Day) and the socialist *Forward* not reacted negatively to the death sentence.[22]

In April 1951, Party journals, including the *Daily Worker,* the *Freiheit,* and *Jewish Life,* though still reluctant to *feature* the Rosenbergs, began gingerly to criticize their death sentence. It wasn't until the beginning of 1952, however, a full nine months after the Rosenberg conviction, and six months after the fellow-traveling *National Guardian* in a series of investigative articles argued that the Rosenbergs were framed, that the Communists began to make the imprisoned couple a cause célèbre.[23]

In February 1952, the *Daily Worker* said, "The Rosenberg case is a ghastly political frame-up. It was arranged to provide blood victims to the witch-hunters, to open the door to new violence, anti-Semitism, and court lynchings of peace advocates and Marxists as 'spies.'"[24] This turnaround and the virulent language employed suggests that the Communist Party now saw an opportunity to persuade the international community that the government of the United States was controlled by an antisemitic conspiracy aiming to exterminate American Jewry and that the conviction of the Rosenbergs was a prelude to that inevitable genocide. Fast, as we have seen, was quick to articulate this new position, as was William Patterson, head of the Civil Rights Congress, who said that the "lynching" of the Rosenbergs "will serve as a signal for a wave of Hitler-like genocidal attacks against the Jewish people throughout the United States."[25] Most Jewish communal leaders, however, even as some invoked the scriptural concept of mercy in resisting the death penalty, stood strongly against the movement to overturn the conviction of the Rosenbergs. But the startling and offensive commentary by Communists connecting the Rosenberg case to an ineluctable genocide against Jewish-Americans continued throughout 1952 and into 1953.

It was no accident that Communist interest in the Rosenbergs went from incidental to fierce beginning in late 1951. At this time, news was leaking out of the Stalinist East about atrocities, particularly against Jews, from which the American Party felt an increasing need to distract the Western world's attention. In November 1951, in Czechoslovakia, for example, Rudolf Slansky, a Jew and once a Communist hero awarded the prestigious Order of Socialism, was arrested along with thirteen others, ten of them Jewish. They were charged as Trotskyists and Zionist spies, part of a Western capitalist conspiracy to undermine socialism. Imprisoned, tortured, and forced to accuse themselves of treason, Slansky and the others were found guilty after an eight-day trial at the end of November 1952. Eleven men, eight of them Jewish, were hanged four days later.[26]

During this period from November 1951 through December 1952 the National Committee to Secure Justice in the Rosenberg Case was "spontaneously" established in the United States, and several international committees to defend the imprisoned pair of convicted conspirators were formed. Fast stood at the center of these activities. He may not have "actually [begun] the Rosenberg movement in the US," as he boasted later, but his November 1952 article on the Rosenbergs in *L'Humanité*, the daily newspaper of the French Communist Party, did help galvanize the movement for clemency in France.[27]

The Communist press in America and Europe began to focus on the Rosenberg trial—admittedly riddled with prosecutorial and judicial misconduct—and to rail against the death sentence, which was indeed obscene and gratuitously cruel.[28] Opposition to the sentence became an international cause, with Jean Cocteau, Frida Kahlo, Diego Rivera, Picasso, Pope Pius XII, and hundreds of scientists, artists, and world leaders urging clemency. But of the Slansky case in Czechoslovakia, or of the rumored execution of the Yiddish writers Itzak Feffer, David Bergelson, Leyb Kvitko, and others in the Soviet Union in 1952, the Communist newspapers said almost nothing. And when they did, it was to counter the "daily hysteria of anti-Soviet propaganda," or to say that Jewish people are "equal in every respect with all other peoples of the Soviet Union" (which wasn't saying much), and to suggest that Stalinist Czechoslovakia was being "slandered" by bourgeois anti-Communists.[29]

Since the defendants in Czechoslovakia "confessed," there were no judicial appeals; and since they were executed virtually overnight, there was no time to form "defense committees" or to organize demonstrations in front of Soviet or Czech embassies. Picasso, with whom Fast had met in 1949, helped immortalize the Rosenbergs in 1952 with his signed lithographs of their faces, but he sketched no portraits of Rudolf Slansky; and while Sartre, who had befriended Fast in 1945, helped create the Rosenberg Defense Committee in France, he remained silent about the Slansky case and other crimes of the Stalinists in the East.[30]

Fast, too, was silent on Czechoslovakia in the early fifties, yet later he had the audacity to tell a friend that one of the reasons he left the Party was the Slansky case. Fast claimed that his "uneasiness" grew "from day to day" after the 1952 hangings and that he was forced to ask himself how antisemites "could hold office in a socialist country?" Simply put, Fast was lying. He may have had a momentary demurrer about the Slansky case, but he remained a fiercely dedicated Communist, finally leaving the CPUSA a long four years and two months after Slansky's execution.[31]

DESPAIR, DISTRACTION, AND DEFEAT

It wasn't until October 1952 that the U.S. Supreme Court announced its refusal to hear the Rosenbergs' appeal on the unconstitutionality of America's conspiracy and espionage laws. In the preceding summer months, however, Fast and his friends were very worried about the outcome. Fast distracted himself in part by writing *Tony and the Wonderful Door*, a young adult fantasy with some resemblances to H. G. Wells's story "The Door in the Wall" (1911).[32] Except for a strong emphasis in the book on independent thought, tolerance, and internationalism, Fast's politics are not noticeable. Eleven-year-old Tony MacTavish Levy, a mix of Indian, Swede, Scot, Italian, Haitian, French, and Jewish, tells his sixth-grade teacher he doesn't really have a "national origin." But in the story there are no evil capitalists, indeed no villains at all, and education, not radical politics, is the vehicle for social change. The plot revolves around Tony's escape from his bleak urban environment through a magic door in his own backyard that leads to a more natural, more harmonious eighteenth-century world—an imagined world in which whites and Native Americans once lived together peacefully. Apparently, many children were drawn to read *Tony* and "re-read it again and again" not merely for its escapist fabulism, but also, interestingly enough given Fast's own pessimism, for the book's hope and reassurance for the future. Even the doomed Ethel Rosenberg decided from prison to ask her lawyer to purchase *Tony and the Wonderful Door* as a holiday gift for her young sons.[33]

While writing the story, Fast was thinking of his own children, especially eight-year-old Rachel, who was herself in need of some confidence-boosting about the future. Sadly, Rachel knew children her own age whose parents had been imprisoned, including her playmate "Riki," the daughter of Carl Marzani. And in 1952, while Julius and Ethel Rosenberg were in jail awaiting execution, Rachel was taken to a Christmas party for their two sons, Michael, nine, and Robert, five. The party was in a dark basement room of the home of W. E. B. Du Bois, "the mood somber despite a lighted tree and gifts." There was "much whispering," Rachel remembered, and she huddled "in a corner somewhere as far from the Rosenberg boys as I could get, afraid even to look at them."[34]

She cried straight through the party because, although still unaware that her own father had been in prison, there was no reason for her to believe that what was happening to the parents of Robert and Michael, and Riki, too, "could not happen to mine." Indeed, after Fast told his daughter that Marzani, who had lied about his Communist past on an application for a government job, was serving a three-year sentence "because he was a good man [who] fought for the rights of the poor, the oppressed, the Negro people and the working people," Rachel wondered why her own father still had his freedom. "'Aren't *you* a good man?'" she asked. As she told me much later, her father had a penchant for twisting the truth about these things to make what he thought was a larger political point. It was the kind of thing, Rachel said, that drove her and her brother "NUTS!"[35]

In June 1952, Fast sent many "Dear Friend" letters in an attempt to raise funds for children "displaced" by the Smith Act. He wanted, he said, to give the seventy children whose fathers or mothers were in or facing prison some time in a summer camp. This, at least, was something, in the face of so many defeats, he thought he could accomplish.[36] Too much else seemed unfinished or ruined. The Rosenberg situation especially troubled him. And the cluster headaches that plagued Fast intermittently for most of his adult life returned with intensity. Brought on most often by defeat, frustration, and depression, the headaches could last hours at a time, for periods of two weeks or more. Over the years Fast would generally hide himself and his suffering in his bedroom at home, or in bathrooms, dark corners of public buildings, and the back pews of cool church interiors until the pain passed.

In August 1952, while the Fasts were staying at a resort frequented by left-wingers in White Lake, New York, the headaches resurfaced. Although on vacation, and at times relaxed, swimming or boating, Fast was still carrying the burden of a series of setbacks, some recent, some less so. He had been indicted in 1947 for contempt of Congress and convicted in 1948. In January of that year, he had been forced to pay a stiff fine to settle a plagiarism suit, and by November he was seriously disappointed and enervated by his failed attempt to get Henry Wallace elected president. He was imprisoned in 1950, blacklisted by 1951, and worried, too, about returning to jail in violation of the McCarran Act. And in the midst of marital difficulties produced by his infidelities and the absences his political activism entailed, Fast failed in his efforts to save Willie McGee and the Martinsville Seven, all of whom were executed in 1951.

Fast and his comrades also failed in April 1952 to get a delay in the trial of sixteen Communist leaders arrested and charged under the Smith Act in 1951. The defendants included Fast's close friend and associate Alexander Trachtenberg, a very able Communist editor and translator, and part owner of International Publishers, which brought out, among other proletarian and revolutionary books, American editions of the works of Marx and Engels and Lenin and Stalin. As busy as he was with the Steve Nelson trial and the Rosenberg case, Fast also served as a vice chair of the Committee to Defend Trachtenberg.[37] But he could not prevent his friend from going to prison.

Gradually, Fast, enervated by increasingly frequent headaches, grew tired of fighting mostly losing battles, especially in securing justice for Smith Act defendants.[38]

Several of the defendants, also tired of fighting losing battles, "jumped bail." Gil Green, Henry Winston, Gus Hall, and Robert Thompson changed their names and went into hiding, prompting a significant part of the Party cadre to go "underground." They knew that it was an awful time for radicals in America, and that reaction was in the saddle. But, like Fast, they mischaracterized the nation as fascist, underestimating its long-term democratic character and the possibilities, small though they were at the time, for success in an open fight against McCarthy. By reinforcing its image as secretive and duplicitous, the Party did considerable damage to itself, alienating many members as well as pro-Communists and undermining whatever sympathy may have still been alive in the general public.

THE PUSH AND PULL OF POLITICS

One very early August morning at White Lake, Fast's physical and emotional suffering drove him to the front steps of his cottage, where he could bear his pain without disturbing Bette and the kids. His good friend and legal adviser, Julie Trupin, unable to sleep, was taking a 3 AM stroll around the grounds and joined Howard when he saw him sitting alone. After hearing the details of his friend's infirmity, Trupin told Fast that to overcome all the frustration bottled up in his head, he needed to fight back more directly. And he stunned Howard by suggesting that he run for Congress. Fast, silent for a time, finally responded, saying that he couldn't get elected dogcatcher of White Lake, no less a congressman; that he had lost interest in electoral politics since his futile campaigning for the Progressive Party in 1948; and that he now shared H. L. Menken's contempt for all political parties.[39]

Trupin, however, persisted, even promising to give up two months of his legal practice to help Howard campaign, and he finally succeeded in breaking Fast's resistance. With strong backing and significant funding from the CPUSA, Fast accepted nomination as the American Labor Party (ALP) candidate to represent New York's 23rd congressional district. The ALP had emerged out of a factional fight in the Socialist Party in the mid-thirties and was formed in 1936 mainly as a vehicle to bolster the electoral chances of

FDR in New York State. It was led mainly by representatives of non-Communist unions and anti-Communist Social Democrats. Fast's agreement to run on an ALP ticket was entirely pragmatic, and partly reinforced by the fact that the Bronx congressional seat he aimed to fill had been held briefly by the ALP in 1948 when Leo Isacson won a special election after the incumbent congressman was named a judge.

Like Fast, Isacson had opposed the Marshall Plan and the peacetime draft, and was a strong supporter of the new state of Israel. Barely a month into his term he was in trouble. After expressing interest in going to Paris for an international congress on the future of Greece, where Communist guerrillas were trying to overthrow the government, Isacson, although he said he had no connection to the Communist Party, became the first congressman ever to be denied a passport by the State Department. He was trounced in the regular election in November 1948 by a Republican-Democratic-Liberal coalition formed to unseat him.[40]

Remembering this setback ought to have given the beleaguered Fast some pause. After returning from White Lake, however, he was infected with "candidatitis"—the conviction that one can win against all odds, including electoral history, media projections, and common sense.[41] Asking for support, he wrote to a large number of notables on the liberal-left, including Albert Einstein, who had earlier argued for socialism over "the economic anarchy of capitalism" and had supported the Progressive Party in 1948. Fast told the eminent, politically outspoken scientist that the 23rd congressional district, which included the South Bronx, had in it a small Puerto Rican and black constituency, but was overwhelmingly Jewish and working-class. This constituency presented an opportunity, Fast said, for the "election of a person like myself" who has battled for workers "my whole life," and who continues to be "a fighter for human rights, rather than a politician." Reflecting some sense of his own self-importance, Fast wrote that his victory in the 23rd would "be a great contribution to the struggle for human freedom and dignity here in America."[42]

There is no evidence of a response from Einstein, but the painter and sculptor Philip Evergood lent his name to the campaign, and the artist Rockwell Kent agreed to serve on the committee to elect Fast, as did W. E. B. Du Bois, Paul Robeson, Yiddish folk-singer Martha Schlamme, and the blacklisted actors Howard Da Silva and Morris Carnovsky. Albert Maltz sent a contribution from Mexico, as did author, literary agent, and putative Soviet spy Maxim Lieber. Gordon Kahn, another Jewish American screenwriter who was blacklisted and had fled to Cuernavaca, Mexico, also sent a check.[43] Support was forthcoming from numerous union leaders, too, many of whom publicly endorsed and campaigned for Fast, as well as from Elmer Benson, the former governor of Minnesota who had been a force in the short-lived Progressive Party.

On September 8, 1952, when Fast officially announced his candidacy, he wrote to Harry Truman asking him to "lift immediately" the passport restrictions imposed upon him by the State Department.[44] But simultaneously Fast issued a press release that attacked the rearming of Germany as an effort by the Truman government to recruit a "new Nazi Army" with which "to plunge mankind into a third World War." He also announced that as a candidate he would "spare no effort in exposing the plans of the Truman Administration to establish a Fascist concentration camp system in the United States."[45]

How Fast thought such statements would help him attract a political following or regain his passport is beyond rational explanation. Under guidelines issued by Secretary of State Dean Acheson in May 1952, a passport could be denied if the applicant was believed to be a member of the CP or if the applicant's conduct abroad was likely to do damage to U.S. interests. From 1951 through 1958, Fast was refused a passport at least eight times, and built up quite a file of correspondence with Ruth Shipley, chief, Passport Division, U.S. Department of State. Shipley consistently replied in general terms such as: "the SD has given careful consideration to your case, but is unable to provide you with passport facilities regardless of the purpose of the trip and the countries to which you desire to travel." Fast persisted, always arguing, quite rightly, that the United States had absolutely nothing to fear from him as a threat to the "security . . . of this country." He also several times made the fully justified, if not entirely sincere case that denial of the freedom to travel "simply pulls out from under us the moral high ground in the battle for friends of freedom and democracy around the world."[46]

Between early September and the beginning of November, Fast made several dozen campaign speeches to a variety of mostly Jewish, mostly left-liberal groups ranging from the Parents' Association of Public School 61 and the Adult Activities Committee of the Bronx River Community Center to a group of prominent members of the American Jewish Congress, the Women's Committee for Peace, and the National Council of Jewish Women, University branch.[47] In the same period, for three nights every week, Fast, ever the tireless campaigner, gave radio talks or sat for interviews over station WMCA.[48]

He also rented a sound truck, which he used for three hours every night, ten on Saturdays, to campaign in the South Bronx neighborhoods of the 23rd congressional district. He was often accompanied by the socialist philosopher and director of the American Civil Liberties Union, Corliss Lamont, who was running for the U.S. Senate. Lamont, like Fast, was a prolific writer, as well as a pro-Communist supporter of Stalin and the USSR; and he, too, had been indicted for contempt of Congress and deprived of a passport. But unlike Fast, Lamont, the son of the chairman of J. P. Morgan and Company, was extraordinarily wealthy, and he contributed generously to the American Labor Party campaign, as did other well-to-do individuals, though, with McCarthy still raging, much more discreetly.

Occasionally, Fast took Jonathan and Rachel along for the ride, partly to demonstrate his status as a "family man," but also to give the kids a thrill. The fun stopped when bottles and rocks began to rain down upon them from rooftops. From there on Rachel was always afraid that someone would attack her father.[49] But nothing could stop Fast's relentless crusade to bring his message to the voters. He billed himself as a "peace candidate," calling for an immediate cease-fire in Korea and the establishment of a civilian commission to effect the exchange of prisoners.[50] Fast also called for an immediate repeal of the Smith Act, but most of his other proposals were in line with the agenda of liberal Democrats, in and outside the ALP, including repeal of the McCarran and Taft-Hartley Laws, the unfreezing of wage controls, state and federal grants for housing projects, and the funding of educational and unemployment opportunities for the Puerto Rican population in New York City.[51]

His foreign policy proposals were few, but emphasized immediate independence for Puerto Rico and a $1 billion credit extension to the State of Israel for peacetime construction, housing, and medical facilities. Now that the USSR had the atomic bomb, there was barely a mention of the Soviet Union, or nuclear power, which Fast had insisted years earlier would be used by the Russians to make gardens bloom. Nor was there much said about the Rosenbergs in this heavily Jewish district whose residents were no doubt as conflicted about the espionage case as were Jews in other American communities.[52]

Given the help Fast got from Trupin and Lamont, and the $8,000 contribution he received from the CP, the endorsements he received from the *Daily Worker, Morgen Freiheit,* and *Masses and Mainstream,* and especially given the ethnic composition of the 23rd congressional district, Fast expected, in a field of four candidates, to do much better than to finish dead last with 6,800 votes—well behind the Republican's 23,000, and the Liberal Party's 15,000 votes. The Liberal Party, formed in New York City in 1944 by a breakaway faction of the ALP, was led by anti-Communist unionists and liberals who hoped to influence the major parties in their choice of candidates by promising to grant or withdraw support. With four parties in contention in 1952, the victory went to the incumbent, Democrat Isidore Dollinger, who was considered by many to be "unswervingly liberal," devoted to the needs of his constituents, and unmatched in his ability to deal with what was then called "melting-pot politics." Without really mounting a campaign, Dollinger, a former state legislator, district attorney, and judge characterized by Fast as "a mindless party hack," received 79,000 votes, about double the number of all the other contestants combined.[53]

The day after the election results were in, Fast took solace, apparently, by attending the thirty-fifth anniversary of the "Great October Revolution" at the Soviet embassy. He also sent a note to Konstantin Siminov, the editor of the Moscow *Literary Gazette,* telling him that although he had lost his bid for a congressional seat, he believed that the majority of people who voted Democratic were expressing a "desperate fear" of fascism, and were protesting the bellicose policies of Eisenhower. In the face, however, of Eisenhower's landslide victory nationally—thirty-nine states, to Adlai Stevenson's nine, almost all of which were in the deep South—Fast seems to have been either obtuse about what had really happened or desperate to believe the confusing, indeed contradictory, things he told Siminov: "Working people," he wrote, really know that "Eisenhower represents fascism." But he also insisted that Eisenhower's victory was merely a result of the general's "demagogic use of the peace issue." Despite Fast's own devastating defeat and ostensible sense that his trusted proletariat had been so easily "taken in," he closed his letter saying, "we are in good heart and spirit, filled with faith and confidence in the future."[54]

CONFRONTATIONS LEFT AND RIGHT

With the election over, Fast turned his attention back to the Rosenbergs. In a talk at Columbia University's School of Public Affairs, he attacked the death sentence imposed by Judge Kaufman, while insisting again that there was a stout link between the looming execution of the couple and antisemitism. Referring to just one case and one extended family, Fast misleadingly asserted that every person convicted of espionage since the war had been Jewish. In response to this attempt by Fast to pin antisemitism on America, Murray Polner, the socialist journalist and freelance editor, who was studying at Columbia's Russian Institute in the early fifties, rose from the audience of some two hundred to ask Fast about the treatment of Jews in the Soviet Union, and about the fate of Yiddish poet Itzak Feffer, not seen or heard from since 1949. Fast, who knew that the USSR was waging a virtual war against what his Russian friend and correspondent Fadeyev called a "Zionist conspiracy to destroy socialism," denied that the Stalinists in Russia were driven by antisemitism. And he falsely claimed that Feffer, who had been executed on August 12, 1952, was alive, well, and writing.[55]

More troubling even than his response to Polner in December 1952 was Fast's take on the anti-Jewish "Doctors' Plot," an infamous episode that ran in the USSR from January through April 1953, the very months in which Fast and friends were fighting to save the Rosenbergs from the "juggernaut" of American antisemitism. The episode speaks volumes about Fast's willful blindness to Stalin's paranoid murderousness and to the continued existence of overt and aggressive antisemitism in the Soviet Union.[56]

On January 13, 1953, *Pravda,* the official newspaper of the USSR, declared that nine of the Kremlin's most eminent doctors not only had murdered two of Stalin's closest associates, but were engaged in a vast plot, instigated and orchestrated by Western imperialists and Zionists, to "eliminate," mainly by poisoning, leading Soviet political and military figures.[57] The government's media saturated the public with stories about a Jewish "fifth column" in the USSR. In an attempt to explain why so many Jewish leaders were being fired, arrested, or executed between 1948 and 1953, the articles were filled with constant references to the disproportionate number of Jews, especially physicians, involved in the conspiracy to bring down international socialism.[58]

That Jewish doctors were poisoners, and that Jews conspired to topple governments and control the world, were not ideas born full-blown from the brain of Stalin. The libelous charge that Jews poisoned the wells of Christians was common among medieval antisemites, and very early in the twentieth century the *Protocols of the Elders of Zion* (a fraudulent text "revealing" a plan to achieve global domination by the Jewish people) was written in Tsarist Russia, and was widely circulated there and elsewhere ever since.[59]

As early as December 1, 1952, two days before Slansky was hanged in Czechoslovakia, Stalin, at a meeting of the Politburo, announced, "Every Jewish nationalist is the agent of the American intelligence service. . . . Among doctors, there are many Jewish nationalists."[60] This fractured syllogism set the stage for a show trial. In addition, a letter appeared in *Pravda*, signed by many terrorized Soviet Jewish leaders, implying that the deportation of Jews to Siberia would protect them from the violence that would inevitably follow revelations about the Jewish doctors' intent to destroy the Soviet regime. Apparently the goal was to provoke widespread pogroms and flood the press with letters demanding deportation as either punishment or a kind of perverse "protective custody" for the Jewish people.[61] No blueprints for the deportation were formally developed, ratified, or implemented, but much speculative talk about the deportations circulated within elite party circles in January and February 1953.[62]

A small number of American notables, including even pro-Communists such as Albert Einstein, demanded that the Soviet Ministry of Foreign Affairs launch a formal investigation after the arrest of the doctors. But from the Communist Party there was not a whisper of protest. In fact, Howard Fast offered a shocking defense of the state terrorism directed against Jews by the Soviet Union. The National Council of the Arts, Sciences, and Professions (NCASP), an organization with a relatively large and influential Communist membership, including Fast, was presented with a resolution written in early February by two non-Communist professors of law who were anxious to bring Soviet antisemitism to public attention. The resolution read in part: "[Russian] anti-Zionism and the subsequent trial and conviction of prominent public officials is so reminiscent of the anti-Semitism of Nazi Germany . . . that we regard, with the gravest apprehension, the present purges in the Soviet Union as the probable prelude to wholesale persecutions of innocent persons."[63] Fast had not attended the NCASP meeting where this issue was raised, so his approval was solicited by mail. He responded almost immediately: "This couplet of anti-Zionism and anti-Semitism is deeply disturbing. I am not a Zionist. I have frequently taken a sharp anti-Zionist position. Nevertheless I am a Jew. . . . I cannot accept an anti-Zionist position as being synonymous with an anti-Semitic position. Nor do I see in this trial of a group of [7] Jewish and [2] non-Jewish doctors in the Soviet

Union resemblances to anything that happened in Germany."[64] Fast, behaving like the most loyal of Stalinist stooges, actually went on to imply that the accused were guilty unless they could prove their innocence: "So far we have a picture of men engaged in espionage through contacts provided by Zionist organizations, and possibly even by the state of Israel. As a Jew thinking in terms of my own people, I would more bitterly protest the use to which the Israeli state is putting Jews, than the inevitable defense of the Soviet Union against saboteurs."

It gets worse. Fast, knowing all about the false charges and execution of Slansky, and since 1949 knowing quite a lot about the oppression of Jews in the Soviet Union, concluded his letter by saying, "If the sponsors of the resolution will clearly and straight-forwardly set down any single act of anti-Semitism which has occurred in any of the socialist nations, I will protest such an act with all my power. But this they have failed to do. So far as I can see, they are advancing hastily a position which was the original intent of those who invented the anti-Semitic slander" of the Soviet Union.[65]

Only two days later, Fast received a letter from journalist Max Frankel making reference to the Doctors' Plot. Frankel thanked Howard for having sent him Robert Boyer's Communist Party pamphlet "Cold War Murder: The Frame-Up against Ethel and Julius Rosenberg." But Frankel was unmoved, "largely," he said, "because the whole literature of the [Rosenberg] defense . . . strikes me as being basically phony. What little charity I ever had for them in the first place has been exhausted by the behavior of your group on the issue of Kremlin anti-semitism." Frankel recognized the skewed game Fast was playing, and was repelled by the reprehensible politics pursued by the Communist Party in regard to Jewish questions. Frankel shrewdly challenged Fast to write a pamphlet similar to "Cold War Murder," defending the "Jewish doctors who are being placed on trial at Moscow." Only then, the liberal journalist said, will I "rethink my judgment of your defense of the Rosenbergs."[66]

Less than a week after Fast's exchange with Frankel, he found himself entangled with Joe McCarthy, the venomous anti-Communist senator from Wisconsin. McCarthy had come into prominence in 1950 with his wild allegations against the State Department, which he said was riddled with Communists and spies. But when the Republicans captured the presidency in 1952 for the first time in over thirty years, they also gained control of Congress, and Joe McCarthy's power and celebrity increased with his assumption of the chair of the Permanent Subcommittee on Investigations of the Senate Government Operations Committee. On February 15, 1953, the McCarthy subcommittee opened public hearings to investigate misman- agement and "subversion" at the Voice of America (VOA), which had been created in the early 1940s as part of the State Department's drive to "pierce the Iron Curtain with the story of American democracy."[67]

McCarthy's initial allegations had been correctly labeled by the Tydings Committee (another Senate subcommittee investigating loyalty) "a fraud and a hoax," and Democratic Senator Millard Tydings himself said that McCarthy's irresponsible actions only served to "confuse and divide the American people . . . to a degree far beyond the hopes of the Communists themselves."[68] The senator from Wisconsin was enraged, and now finally head of his own subcommittee, was on the warpath.

McCarthy knew that the VOA had been part of the defunct Office of War Information (OWI), an agency notorious for the number of pro-Communists employed there. Primarily going after Communist writers and intellectuals who had worked for the VOA or the OWI or whose books were "overrepre- sented" on the shelves of American libraries abroad, McCarthy saw Howard Fast as a key target for investigation.[69]

Fast was among the first five witnesses questioned by McCarthy and Democratic Senator Henry M. Jackson in executive session on February 13, 1953. McCarthy claimed that he wanted to give those called a "chance" to testify "before we do anything public." But he told the press beforehand that Howard Fast was among the witnesses because he had been cited by the State Department as a "Soviet-endorsed" writer whose works, where they celebrated democracy, might be useful in "selected areas" in Stalinist- dominated Eastern Europe. "Soviet-endorsed" was apparently the operative phrase for McCarthy. The senator, who promised that these initial sessions would not be public, also told the press that Fast had refused to answer questions about his affiliation with the Communist Party or to say whether he knew Communists working for the VOA.[70]

Accompanied by his lawyer, Benedict Wolf, Fast appeared in an open tele- vised session of the McCarthy subcommittee five days later, on February 18. Serving as chief legal counsel for the subcommittee was Roy Cohn, who had helped prosecute the Rosenbergs and had urged Judge Kaufman to impose the death sentence on Julius and on Ethel, about whose guilt there was great doubt.[71] Cohn's opening question, "Are you now a member of the Commu-

nist Party?" elicited from Fast a claim of protection under both the First and
Fifth Amendments of the Constitution. Cohn, however, tried to trap Fast by
reframing the question several times, asking, for example, whether he was a
Communist at the time he wrote books such as *Citizen Tom Paine.* "Let me
make my position plain," Fast said, with some irritation, "I will claim [the]
privilege," of these amendments "in terms of any question which makes
reference to the Communist Party or organizations or periodicals cited in,
let us say, [HUAC's] list of so-called subversive organizations."[72]

McCarthy also tried "creative" questioning. "I am not asking you . . .
whether you were a member of the Communist Party [in 1942 or 1943]," the
chairman explained, "but . . . did you have the reputation at that time of being a Communist writer?" The witness thought McCarthy more suited than
he to answer that particular question, but Fast did say that his "reputation"
was "spelled out" in the excellent reviews his books had received, especially
those of *Conceived in Liberty* and *The Unvanquished.* Fast also pointed out
that the U.S. government had seen fit as late as 1944 to issue special editions
of his books, including *Citizen Tom Paine* and *Freedom Road,* for the armed
services.

In an attempt to make light of Fast's genuine accomplishments, McCarthy
said, "I don't happen to be a reader of your books, so when you name them, I
have difficulty." Wolf, Howard's counsel, had the best of this exchange with
his retort: "You missed something good"; Fast followed with, "If you are
interested in the history of [our country] it might be important to read them."
Getting nowhere, indeed getting bested, the committee turned its attention,
oddly it seemed at first, to the income Fast received "directly or indirectly"
from government agencies.

Fast could not possibly remember the exact amount of money he had
earned for the use of his materials at the OWI, the VOA, and the Signal Corps,
where he had worked for a short time in 1944; nor could he be expected to
name precisely his earnings from the armed services editions of his books.
That this approach was an attempt to force the witness into an embarrassing
evasiveness, or even perjury, was made apparent when McCarthy ordered
Fast to produce his "account books" for the years in question.

Wolf successfully pointed out the irrelevance of presenting those ten-
year-old materials, some of which no longer existed, and then went on the
offensive, demanding to know the explicit purpose of the proceedings. At
this point, Fast also assertively launched into a complaint about the way his

subpoena had been served—rudely and with duplicity, he said, and at the inappropriate hour of 1:30 AM. His children, he added, were terrified by these "Gestapo methods." McCarthy, in an unusual display of intelligent irony, asked Fast if he "would . . . say they were . . . [also] NKVD type tactics." Refusing to be drawn into a comparison of Stalin to Hitler, Fast said, "I have read of these tactics in connection with the Gestapo [and], this is my choice of description." In any case, he said, the actions were "offensive and unworthy of any arm of government of the United States."

Fast's complaint was for the most part ignored, but questions about his loyalties and the quality of his Americanism continued. The chairman pointedly told the subcommittee that the former first lady Eleanor Roosevelt, herself tagged by McCarthy as pro-Communist, had helped with the circulation of Fast's books, all of which had been embraced by the Soviet Union for their anti-American content. As usual, McCarthy was exaggerating wildly. In her syndicated newspaper column, "My Day," Mrs. Roosevelt did no more than mention *Freedom Road* as well worth reading for an understanding of race relations in the United States. Later, she said, she had "no idea" what McCarthy was talking about.[73]

Fast continued to refuse to answer any questions about his association with Communism; but he did try to explain the general importance of the Fifth Amendment in the history of the United States, and to make clear why he was invoking its privilege. Several angry senators told him to go home and "write another book" and spare them a "lecture on American history." McCarthy added that he would not permit the subcommittee "to become a transmission belt for the Communist Party," and he shut Fast off repeatedly. This pattern led to angry shouting and gestures, some of it captured on the new medium of television. Nine-year-old Rachel Fast, on the family's recently purchased TV, saw her father "ridicule, sneer at [and] shame Joseph McCarthy." Her "father's eloquence, his nerve," she said later, "awed me."[74]

The points Fast gained with the public for his shouting match with McCarthy may have been lost near the end of his testimony, when Senator Potter, who had lost both his legs in combat in WWII, asked the thirty-nine-year-old writer whether he would serve in the armed forces if that meant he would have to fight Communism in Korea:

HF: I have dedicated my entire life to the service of my country.
SP: Would you serve?

HF: I would serve my country in any capacity which would benefit or advance my country's welfare.

SP: [What are] you saying?

HF: I will serve in any capacity that could benefit my country, that would aid my country.

SP: The question was very simple. Would you serve in the fight against Communism in Korea?

HF: You are asking me would I serve if I were called?

SP: Answer "yes" or "no."

HF: If I were called into the service of my country, the answer is "yes."

SP: You have not answered the question.

CHAIR: Mr. Fast, you are ordered to answer that question unless you want to claim the privilege.

HF: I would like the question to be clarified. What is the question?

SP: If you were drafted to serve to fight the Communists in North Korea, would you do so?

HF: If I were drafted into the service of my country, I would do so. I would accept the service of my country if I were drafted. That answer is plain.

SP: To fight Communism in Korea?

HF: Why don't you ask me what you mean, would I . . .

SP: Why are you so nervous when we say fighting Communists?

HF: I am not nervous; angry but very calm. Don't tell me I am nervous!

SP: If drafted would you fight Communism in Korea?

HF: If you add the last part of that question, I will have to invoke my privilege against self-incrimination. If, however, you ask me whether I would accept service in my country's army, I answer "yes."

In its own inimitable style the *New York Daily News* rendered this as, "'I refuse to answer . . .' mumbled Fast, as spectators gasped."[75]

Gasps or not, Fast's hearing petered out without a clear answer to the hypothetical question of his willingness to "fight Communism." Thus, he remained under subpoena, but was never recalled; his name and his books, however, continued to be important in the ongoing McCarthy investigations and were prominently featured in the news coverage.[76]

10

McCarthyism, Stalinism, and
the World according to Fast

*O*n the day after Fast's session with the subcommittee, G. David
Schine, who was appointed to McCarthy's staff by Roy Cohn and
would later become a central figure in the Army-McCarthy Hearings of 1954,
summarized the novelist's testimony. But he added what he called "new
findings" relevant to Fast, including two memos indicating that the State
Department, on the recommendation of writers, critics, and educators, had
authorized—"in the interests of balance," Schine claimed—the inclusion of
materials and books by leftists in VOA broadcasts and in the overseas libraries
of the United States.[1]

The memos, however, contained nothing about "balance." Instead the
key paragraphs said that the "reputation" of an author as a democrat would
determine the use of his material and pretty much repeated the earlier statement made by the State Department: "If he is widely and favorably known
abroad as a champion of democratic causes, his creditability and utility may
be enhanced," and if "like Howard Fast, he is known as a Soviet-endorsed
author, materials favorable to the United States in some of his works may
thereby be given a special creditability," indeed, would "carry double the
weight" of influence among "selected audiences" behind the Iron Curtain.[2]

On the approved State Department list were nine of Howard Fast's novels.[3] An incensed McCarthy lambasted the department, demanding and

receiving a promise of the "prompt removal" of books by Howard Fast from voa libraries "everywhere in the world." The senator from Wisconsin also said that the State Department's attempt to achieve balance in the overseas libraries (clearly not the goal of the memos) was an "automatic capitulation to the Communists." Indicative of McCarthy's power to intimidate, as well as Secretary of State John Foster Dulles's eagerness to collaborate with the senator, the department issued a new directive, titled "Information Guide 272," banning the use of all materials, books, and paintings by "controversial persons, Communists, fellow travelers, et cetera."[4]

This imprecise directive led to a welter of voa and State Department memos and counter-memos impossible to disentangle, and to a tidal wave of confusion overseas. Who after all was a "controversial person"? and what did "et cetera" mean? The number of authors whose books were to be banned or removed from the shelves ranged in the minds of library staff from under forty to over four hundred. Some reacted with caution, waiting for clarification; other terrified foreign service officers hastily placed hundreds of volumes in storage to await further instruction. But in several instances, including at the U.S. library in Tokyo, books were actually burned.[5] Only one directive, however, specifically named names of authors and books, and Howard Fast's works were especially prominent among them. Seven of his novels led a pack of books by forty authors, including three by Dashiell Hammett and at least one each by Herbert Aptheker, Morris Schappes, Philip Foner, Earl Browder, and William Gropper, Communists all.[6]

Howard told a cousin that this whole library episode "increased my understanding. I would never again fulminate against the German people for not defying Adolf Hitler. He, at least, had firing squads and concentration camps."[7] McCarthy quietly gave up his voa and library-cleansing crusade when it was learned that if the Orwellian sounding "Information G 272" were literally and fully implemented, more than 2 million books might have to be pulled from the shelves, and that a lot of effective broadcast material would have to be discarded.[8] The hearings on library policy evaporated inconclusively in late March 1953. But almost immediately, McCarthy's chief counsel, Roy Cohn, and chief consultant, David Schine, embarked on a seventeenday foray abroad to rummage through card catalogues in U.S. libraries, sniffing and snuffing out books written by authors whom the fanatical twosome deemed Communists or fellow travelers. The actions of Cohn and Schine, dubbed the "junketeering gumshoes" by one wag and lampooned by many, nonetheless disturbed dozens of librarians, writers, educators, and civil libertarians, and generated negative press across Europe.[9]

As ridiculous as this episode appears to have been, in some important ways it epitomizes that piece of the 1950s we've labeled "McCarthyism." About McCarthy's reputation as a serial slanderer who polluted political debate and made America look absurd in the world, there is little debate. The senator made an extraordinary number of mendacious allegations. He used intimidation and guilt by association to repress leftist groups, all in the pursuit of an enemy movement in America already too weakened to do anything like overthrow a local IRS office, no less the United States.[10]

It was clear to some that the "Communist threat" in the postwar period was greatly exaggerated by McCarthy. And it was just as clear that the fear-mongering and paranoia of American elites about the dangers of Communism in the United States did more damage to the nation than the behavior of the CPUSA, including even its espionage. What gave McCarthyites their moment were the grievances, fears, and ambitions of liberal as well as conservative and opportunistic politicians, not only in the context of the Cold War, vis-à-vis the Soviets, but also of a hot one in Korea. It is not a coincidence that the years of the Korean War, 1950–53, match almost exactly the period of McCarthy's political and social influence. But a generalized anti-Communism did not depend on the war or McCarthy. It derived more from a strongly held cluster of values shared by much of American society, a world outlook friendly to private property and political democracy and antithetical to the alien anti-capitalist and anti-democratic doctrines of Communism.[11]

In the excesses of McCarthyism, however, we have a cautionary tale of how a nation's rational concern for security and for its deeply rooted political values can in uncertain times be turned into something repressive and cruelly damaging.[12] Even someone as conservative as Norman Podhoretz, the former editor of *Commentary* magazine, could say about his "liberal anti-Communist" past, "There can be little question that the hard anti-Communists were more concerned with fighting what they took to be misconceptions of the nature of Soviet Communism than with fighting the persecution to which so many people were being subjected in the early fifties; and it shames me to say that I shared fully in their brutal insensitivity on this issue."[13]

Without discounting or denigrating the positive social reform contributions of the Communist movement, however, or the motives and accomplishments of the many tens of thousands who spent some time in the Party, it is necessary to recognize that the CP was derelict, and destructive to its own goals. By failing to admit to, or change the nature of, its authoritarian and secretive leadership, and by failing to acknowledge or cut the Party's powerful ties to Moscow, Communists contributed to the degeneration of American politics. In the heyday of Stalinism, loyalty to an American Communist Party that remained mostly silent, even as great evil was being done in the name of ultimate good, discredited left-liberalism and helped impede a resurgence of serious radicalism in America.[14]

Howard Fast was so deeply entrenched in Communist orthodoxy, however, that he was incapable of seeing that the Party's positions, in the main, were hypocritical, if not immoral, and that its power to influence the political dialogue in any positive way was pathetic. The CPUSA had been sinking throughout the late forties and early fifties for many reasons: the wartime alliance with the Soviets had ended; the Depression receded; espionage was exposed; and the horrors of Stalinism were beginning to be revealed. Repression and harassment of Communists by the government played an important part in weakening the Party, but not the critical one. Indeed, McCarthyism was on the wane, not on the rise, as disintegration of the CPUSA intensified.[15]

The national headquarters of the Party, hardly a match for "the granite and gold opulence of its Moscow counterpart," was housed in a grubby four-story building on Seventh Avenue between 25th and 26th Streets at the south end of New York's lively garment district. The structure was an apt symbol of the poverty of a party that was finding it more and more difficult to keep old members, no less lure new ones. Inside, the dull green walls were decorated with pictures of Stalin, Lenin, and other Soviet heroes. And on the ground floor of the same building, the Workers Bookshop carried thousands of pamphlets and books, most extolling the virtues of the USSR. And as one contemporary journalist put it, "The works of Howard Fast [got] top billing."[16]

This kind of inflated star status kept Fast from seeing how ineffectual the CPUSA really was. And his blindness, or more precisely his rationalizations, about the USSR continued even after the truth about the Soviet Union could no longer be denied by anyone but the most ardent "true believers." Stalin died suddenly in March 1953, and the Doctors' Plot case came to an abrupt halt, followed by an admission in April that it had been an antisemitic frame-up from the start. What Fast made of this additional evidence of Jew-hatred in Stalin's USSR, after swallowing whole the Soviet Union's earlier story of a Zionist-American conspiracy to overthrow socialism, is impossible to know. But despite what was revealed to him in April 1953 and what he had learned from Fadeyev and Leonovich Gordon in 1949, Fast remained a loyal Stalinist.

Soon after Stalin was buried and the first post-Stalin "reforms" were announced in Russia, Howard and Bette had a drink with the Tass correspondent Eugene Lateshkey, who had recently returned to New York from the Soviet Union. "Howard," Lateshkey said, " I walked on the streets of Moscow and for the first time I breathed in freedom." Bette and Howard, apparently aghast, asked Eugene, "[W]hat are you saying? That before this you couldn't walk [in] Moscow and breathe freely?" Lateshkey mumbled something like "you don't understand." But what he had said seemed quite plain. So Fast persisted: "Why don't I understand?" Well, Lateshkey responded, "it's impossible to explain it to you."[17]

Impossible to explain for a loyal Soviet citizen such as Lateshkey perhaps; but why, at this point, so very late in the day, was it impossible for Howard and Bette to understand that their hero Stalin was imprisoning, terrorizing, and murdering his political "enemies" without compunction, and had long ago gone beyond and forfeited anything that looked like an unavoidable "revolutionary stage"? That he was neither an uncompromising visionary nor a consolidator of "gains" made by the Bolsheviks, but a paranoid monster who would, with impunity, do anything to maintain total power? Such an admission would deny everything they had supported for a decade or more and would destroy the rationalizations and defenses, including the case for "historical necessity" they had constructed and internalized over that same period. Also, and of equal weight, critical respect and public admiration of Fast in the Soviet Union, where he was likened to Maxim Gorky, the doyen of socialist realism, was increasing just as his reputation and popularity was plummeting among American readers and writers. And having over the years alienated all of their non-Communist friends, Howard and Bette would lose their only remaining associates if they separated from the movement. The Party had been Howard Fast's life for too long. Only the most shocking public revelations about the Soviet Union, made by officials of the Soviet Union, would enable, indeed force, Fast to make the break, and even then not immediately. In any case, the horrendous "disclosures" would not come until three years later, in 1956.[18]

In the meantime, Howard Fast, with no apparent cracks in his wall of faith, continued to support the Communist Party and to speak and write at a furious pace in its defense. Along with the Party, he persisted in claiming that America was a fascist state. When Fast, after Stalin's death, was invited to City College in mid-March 1953 to participate in a debate on the proposition, "Should Communists be allowed to teach in New York City schools?" he, in what had become general practice for Communist speakers, tried to change the question by twisting it into a loaded proposition: "The charge of Communism used against teachers is a weapon for fascism in America."[19]

In the end, however, Fast agreed to debate on the original question. His opponent, the economist Ernest van den Haag, like Fast, had worked at the Office of War Information in 1942, and had been a Communist. Unlike Fast, he was now a staunch conservative commentator on social issues, a foremost proponent of the death penalty, and a leading anti-Communist.[20] Before 250 CCNY students, Fast argued, with little success, that the drive against teachers was not merely against Communist teachers, but rather against all teachers who at any time dared question the policies of the American government.[21] He continued in April and May to speak at a number of colleges, including Hunter, whose president was afterward criticized by McCarthy for allowing Fast on campus and for his "failure to join along with millions of Americans in fighting communism in our great public education system."[22]

Fast also continued to campaign for mercy for the Rosenbergs right up to the fatal day of June 19, 1953. Once started, he was unrelenting and unforgiving. Despite *Nation* magazine's having made more than one plea to postpone the execution of Ethel and Julius, and having wired the president urging that the death sentence be commuted, Fast accused the editor, Freda Kirchwey, of remaining silent "while Julius and Ethel Rosenberg go their graves."[23] Five days before they were executed, Fast published a poem honoring and glorifying the Rosenbergs. On Friday, June 19th, he participated in a deathwatch vigil along with thousands of other New Yorkers gathered on East 17th Street off Union Square. Standing there in eerie silence since late afternoon, the people were hoping against all odds that their mass demonstration might elicit a last-minute grant of executive clemency. But only a few minutes after 8 PM, just before sunset ushered in the Jewish Sabbath, Howard Fast got word and took the microphone to announce to the crowd that Julius Rosenberg was dead. Ethel, who lived through the first attempt to kill her, died soon after.[24]

Fast told the East German writer Stefan Heym, one among many international supporters of the Rosenbergs, that although he hadn't met the Rosenbergs, he had "never identified so closely with two people. When they died a part of me died with them. . . . I don't think one ever gets used to fascism and what a dirty unspeakable business it is." In a letter to Renaud de Jouvenal, a member of the Rosenberg Defense Committee in France, Fast wrote that the Rosenbergs could be alive today had they signed "false confessions prepared for them" stating "that the progressive movement in America and the Communist Party of the United States were tools of the Kremlin." The government did want the Rosenbergs to talk, and no doubt would have cut some kind of deal if they had, but nothing like the papers Fast describes existed. Had the Rosenbergs signed, and named names, Fast went on, "the evil and murderous men who rule this country" would have been provided "a public excuse to smash . . . democracy" by a process of "merciless repression and mass imprisonment." The Rosenbergs "understood this," Fast insisted, and "instead, chose to die."[25]

Fast pledged to the Rosenberg children "a bright . . . glorious . . . new world in which such things will never happen again." To "the people of Europe" he said, "Know how well and nobly" the Rosenbergs fought "in this land which is ruled by the wicked and conscienceless lords of the atom bomb. . . . Some day build monuments so that your children will know their story." The Europeans needed no prodding. On the very day Fast's letter to Jouvenal was written, Jean Paul Sartre published an article in *Liberation* calling American authorities "Animals with Rabies." "Don't be surprised," he wrote, "if from one end of Europe to the other we cry 'watch out, America is rabid! We should sever our ties or risk being bit and made rabid in turn.'"

This hyperbolic rhetoric, this labeling of human beings as poisonous animals, especially in the aftermath of the Holocaust, was ghastly. It reflected in part the postwar European left's guilt, resentment, envy, and frustration over America's success as a thriving capitalist democracy. Sartre went on to insist that the Rosenberg execution was evidence that the United States was heading for war. "We didn't want your dollars or your army," he said, "we only asked for two lives, and you answered to hell with [us]. Don't talk to us of alliances. We are not your allies. Our governments are your servants, soon our peoples will be your victims." Killing innocents, Sartre wrote, is "criminal folly," and in this execution, the leaders of the United States had chosen to be beasts. "You pulled the same on us," he said, "with Sacco and Vanzetti."[26]

Sartre was referring to Nicola Sacco and Bartolomeo Vanzetti, convicted in 1921 for the murder of two payroll guards in South Braintree, Massachusetts, in 1920, and executed in 1927 after a trial infamous for its juridical irregularities and innumerable, but unsuccessful, motions, appeals, and clemency pleas that followed. During the 1920s, an era of great political turmoil and reaction in America, many liberals and intellectuals came to think that the foreign-born anarchists had been "railroaded" for reasons of state, and killed because of who they were and not for what they had allegedly done.[27]

Sartre, of course, was not the only one to make the connection between the Italian immigrant anarchists and the Rosenbergs. Fast had begun working on *The Passion of Sacco and Vanzetti* in mid-1952, just as he was picking up the cudgels for Ethel and Julius. And in June 1953, a week before the Rosenbergs died, he wrote that he had "finished writing [his] new novel" about Sacco and Vanzetti, which he hoped "would prove to be an important factor" in the Rosenberg case. "Twenty-five years after the fact," Fast said, "it is so easy to see the unjustness of the verdict against [Sacco and Vanzetti]— and now twenty-five years later, we [should] also understand full well" the injustice being done to the Rosenbergs.[28]

There were some important differences between the Rosenberg "conspiracy to commit espionage" trial and the Sacco and Vanzetti robbery-murder trial. But for Fast as for Sartre and many others, the parallels between the cases were more obvious and significant. Indeed, Fast's sense of the similarities led him to hope that his novel about Sacco and Vanzetti would get significant attention and help in the Rosenberg defense.[29] Both cases involved the conviction and death sentence for two members of minority groups suspected of disloyalty. Evidence presented by the respective prosecutors was tainted or questionable, and there were many judicial improprieties during the two trials. Neither the Rosenberg nor the oft-changing Sacco and Vanzetti defense team was particularly strong. In the 1950s as in the 1920s, a political atmosphere unfavorable to the defendants was palpable: anti-Communism and concern for national security in the case of the Rosenbergs, and xenophobia and anti-radicalism in the case of Sacco and Vanzetti. The Rosenbergs had been arrested in the summer of 1950 when McCarthyism was riding high; Sacco and Vanzetti were arrested on suspicion of murder during the "Red Scare" of 1919–20, which intensified after a number of bombings and bomb plots were directed at U.S. Attorney General A. Mitchell

Palmer and other American leaders. These attacks and schemes led to the most extreme period of anti-radical repression in American history.[30]

Although both trials attracted worldwide attention and became international crusades for justice, especially on the left, there were few non-Communists, including American liberals, intellectuals, and journalists, in the 1950s who thought the Rosenbergs innocent. Yet, even in the repressive and xenophobic 1920s, many liberal notables, including Walter Lippman, John Dewey, H. L. Mencken, Bennett Cerf, Edmund Wilson, Upton Sinclair, and Justices Louis Brandeis and William O. Douglas, thought Sacco, a shoemaker, and Vanzetti, a fishmonger, blameless targets of a frame-up. Fast, however, thought both cases were "frame-ups"—of progressive Jews in the one instance, and detested foreign radicals in the other. Fast also believed that Judge Irving Kaufman of the Rosenberg case and Webster Thayer, the presiding judge in the Sacco and Vanzetti trial, were corrupted—Kaufman by his desperate need to dissociate Jews from Communism, and Thayer by his deep prejudice against "aliens," especially Italian radicals.

While, outside of Communist circles, Kaufman emerged from the trial relatively unscathed, Thayer's integrity was the target of a major attack by Felix Frankfurter, then a professor of law at Harvard, and in 1953 a Supreme Court justice and potential protagonist in the Rosenberg case. Fast was so taken with Frankfurter's book *The Case of Sacco and Vanzetti* (1927), and an article that preceded it in the *Atlantic Monthly,* that he made these the chief source of his novel—unfortunately with no attribution to Frankfurter, even though several sections of *The Passion of Sacco and Vanzetti* were plagiarized.[31] Fast either thought he was doing nothing wrong or justified his illicit behavior in his rush to help the Rosenbergs avoid execution. In any case, he was too late. "The animals here who decide such things," Fast wrote to Jouvenal, "were too impatient for blood, and before the book was ever published, I lived tragically through its closing episode."[32]

Fast had tried to bring to the new book a sense of tragedy, fed by his belief in the innocence of all four defendants, his death-row visits while covering the case of the Trenton Six, his deathwatch vigil for Willie McGee, and his own brief but harrowing incarceration in a Washington, D.C., prison among men facing execution. It was also fed by his deeply felt connection to Jesus Christ as a martyred revolutionary, hence the word "Passion" in the title of his novel.[33]

Fast, following his worst literary inclinations, swallowed whole the patently spurious confession of Celestino Medeiros, and portrayed Sacco and Vanzetti not merely as innocents, but as saints, despite their possessing pistols and bullets when arrested. Vanzetti, in actuality probably innocent of murder, announces several times in Fast's version of the fisherman's story a compassion for all humanity. This feeling is combined, however, with a deeply held and bitter conviction that the "oppressors" of the working class must be "destroyed" before men can love one another. Fast has Vanzetti alluding to Lenin, hankering for a gun, and promising not to go quietly, turning him into a Communist revolutionary rather than the anarchist he was in reality.[34] For Fast, who throughout *The Passion* makes direct connections between Vanzetti and Jesus, the important thing was to get readers to see Vanzetti as a loving yet fierce Christ, capable of lashing the money-changers in the temple.[35]

Sacco, in real life probably guilty of the murders, writes a letter to his young son in the novel—and in actuality—saying, "They can crucify us today, but they cannot destroy our ideas." And, according to Fast, he tells Medeiros, who is to die that same night along with Nicola and Bartolomeo—in rhetoric resonant of the Talmud and the preaching Jesus—"every human life in the whole world is connected to every other human life. It is just like there were threads that you can't see from every one of us to every other one of us."[36]

Even Medeiros, a twenty-five-year-old hoodlum, "hophead," and convicted murderer, is turned into a Christ-like figure by Fast. Apparently, having seen the light through Sacco and Vanzetti's preaching, Celestino says that even though he has "sinned all the sins a man can sin," he was driven to his nasty deeds by the miserable and inexorable logic of his experience. None of it is his fault, Medeiros says, and he "want[s] to be forgiven." He did not, after all "ask to be a companion to sin," and he now understands that "from the beginning I never had a chance."[37] Here, and throughout the novel, Fast goes beyond the social determinism of the naturalists such as Crane and Dreiser, and moves into a kind of secular fatalism.

To complete the Christ-story to which Fast was so attracted, not only in this book, but also in *Conceived in Liberty, Citizen Tom Paine, Clarkton,* and several short stories, Vanzetti says, "What is there more that a human being can do than to lay down his life for another. That is why we are perishing. We give our lives as hostages for the working class."[38]

If Fast's heroes are Christ-like, his other characters, complex enough in reality, are here reduced to caricatures of indifferent, fearful, or evil men, and are referred to only as the "President of the University" [A. Lawrence Lowell]; "the Governor" [Alvin T. Fuller]; "the President of the US" [Calvin Coolidge]; "the Justice" [Oliver Wendell Holmes]; and "the Law Professor" [Felix Frankfurter]. Once again, as in *Freedom Road, The American, Clarkton,* and *Spartacus,* Fast constructs a story of good, brave men and villains. What are we to make of *The Passion of Sacco and Vanzetti?* Is it a history, a novel, or an oversized political pamphlet? In some bibliographies *The Passion* is listed as nonfiction.[39] If we take the book as such, it is an abject failure, full of speculation, error, and even theft of intellectual property.

The book does maintain a consistent tone of sorrow and lamentation for something irrevocably lost. It also elicits and illuminates a sensitivity to the final agonies of men facing death. *The Passion* may therefore have some claim on us as literature. But in the end we are left with a political pamphlet, consciously written in good part to serve a political goal—clemency for the Rosenbergs. Fast apparently sent to Supreme Court Justice Felix Frankfurter a pre-publication copy of *The Passion* that carried an inscription saying, "if only it were possible because of [your] brilliant work on Sacco and Vanzetti, where [you] stood up against a whole nation as a Jew at a time of great anti-Semitism" and defended the Italian immigrants, that Frankfurter "might remember those days and be . . . inspired by this book into doing something of the same today." The justice did not respond. He "never acknowledged the book or what I had written," Fast said, "nor did his position [on the Rosenbergs] change."[40] If Frankfurter had actually read the book, he might have taken great umbrage, not only at what looked like plagiarism in places, but also at the radical rhetoric, wholly alien to his own, that Fast puts in the mouth of the thinly disguised "Law Professor."

Self-published and distributed by Citadel Press, *The Passion* sold 17,000 copies in six months, but with virtually no reviews outside the left press, it did not take off to become a book widely read. Fast, disappointed, concocted a story for his Soviet friend Boris Izakov that because of "fear and trepidation" *The Passion* had to be "sold in many commercial book stores from under the counter."[41]

In the weeks and months following the Rosenberg executions, Fast's anti-American rhetoric increased in intensity. In July he wrote five pieces for the *People's Voice,* the daily paper of the Communist Party of Austria, under the heading "American Diary." The people of America, Fast said, "are the loneliest and unhappiest people of this world." They "would like to talk," Fast wrote, but are afraid to do so; they "are lost in a labyrinth of incomprehensible lies and contortions. . . . They live in a mixed up state of mind, half in ignorance, half in suppressed fear." He had learned all of this, Fast said, on train rides to and from Boston to give a talk at Harvard Law School about HUAC and Hollywood.

After the House committee started investigating the university, however, the "intimated students," Fast said, canceled the invitation. They told him that "putting on such a program at this time," would "embarrass [and] hurt several people" connected with Harvard. The only opposition to disinviting Fast, futile as it turned out, came from Arthur Schlesinger Jr. and several dozen other faculty members. Two days later, however, Fast came back to Boston to take part in a debate at Boston University about "Freedom of Culture." His opponents were James T. Farrell, described by Fast as a "corrupt Trotzkyite," and Ludwig Lewisohn, a professor of English at Brandeis, a Zionist and anti-assimilationist, but in Fast's eyes, "an old clerical fascist."[42]

Fast consistently argued in Boston and elsewhere that there was little, if any, freedom of any kind in America. Indeed, he said, a growing fascism was more prevalent. Of course, in the United States, Fast explained, the fascists "try not to make the same mistakes as Hitler and Mussolini." Instead, immediately after the election in 1948, Fast said, Truman and the "gang of unscrupulous and unmoral people" around the president "carefully and cautiously [laid] the foundation of a police state in the United States." They "built several concentration camps which are kept in ready reserve" to terrorize the American people. Like the blacklists, he insisted, the camps are part of the planned "systematic destruction," the complete "annihilation of human personality and individuality." Fast claims that he won the debate and that six of Lewisohn's students came to him at the end of the discussion, thanking him for his participation.[43]

All through July, Fast was also writing relatively long letters, about twelve in all, to his children, Rachel and Jonathan, at Lilliput, a summer camp in upstate New York. The letters, almost always typed, contained mostly quotidian details, sometimes even about Fast's writing and publishing, along with expressions of concern for the welfare of the kids. Children, his own and those of others, were very much on Fast's mind in July, and by the end of the month he wrote a piece for the *People's Voice,* beginning with a quote from Stalin: "'Our children are our greatest and most precious possession.'" Yet, here in the United States, "we are told on every possible occasion that Stalin has been an enemy of mankind . . . and that the sacred duty of each American is to fight communism." Therefore, Fast concluded peculiarly, and with no specificity or any attempt at explanation, "as a result of the cold war, the children of our country have suffered more than anywhere else."[44]

Although possibly only a degree more detached from logic and reality than usual, Fast's rhetoric throughout the summer and into the fall of 1953 seemed more inchoate than ever. Intermittently, but powerfully, his cluster headaches were back. Whether these contributed to Fast's confusion or were caused by his political frustration (including the arrest in July of his friend poet Walter Lowenfels), his repressed knowledge of the evil being committed in the USSR, the trauma of the Rosenberg executions, or all of these, is hard to say. But that he suffered excruciating pain was obvious. In October, Fast took nine-year-old Rachel and her "boyfriend" Buzzy to the sixth game of the World Series between the Brooklyn Dodgers and the New York Yankees. Fast was struck with a headache midway, and he sat with his head in his hands, moaning, "oh, oy, oh" quietly, but steadily. Buzzy was frightened; Rachel, who had witnessed her father's painful episodes many times in the past was worried, but also embarrassed.[45]

Humiliation for Rachel was unfortunately no stranger. Her father's behavior unrelated to his headaches had also discomfited her in various other situations, mostly having to do with family interactions. When the Fasts visited Howard's older brother, Jerry, and his family, for example, which they did almost every other weekend, there were consistently mortifying incidents. According to Jerry's son, Barry, "Uncle Howie" was always favorably comparing Rachel, a "good girl, thin, and smart," to Barry's sister, Judith, who "always cried after Howard left." When Judy complained to her mother and father about all the insults she suffered, they would say, "imagine if you had them for parents, and imagine what Rachel and Jonathan are going through." After one particularly nasty visit, Jerry actually said, "No More!" The relationship between Jerry and Howie was so strong, however, so "psychologically necessary," Judy said, that she told her father not to say anything to Uncle Howie that might endanger it.

Until he was about twenty, Barry "idolized" his "infinitely interesting" uncle; but in 1953, at twelve years old, he began to be put off by Howard's increasingly hurtful behavior. At times Howard "seemed crazy," Barry said, and he could be a "mean son of a bitch, not only to Judith, but to his own kids as well." Indeed, Bette and Howard often bragged about Rachel and Jon in public; but as both Fast children have confirmed, they were not treated quite as nicely at home.[46]

Fast's contemptuousness, insensitivity, pettiness, self-centeredness, and blindness to the damage he was doing were all traits that fit Howard's role as a Communist Party hack, and reflected the possibility of hypomania or narcissism: "inflated self-esteem . . . a certainty of conviction about the correctness and importance" of his ideas; "chaotic patterns of personal . . . relationships, impulsive involvements in questionable endeavors, . . . extreme impatience, intense and impulsive . . . sexual relations," disproportionate need for admiration, lack of empathy—and reckless driving.[47] "Nobody wanted to drive with him—he was out to lunch at the wheel," Erica Jong told me. "Amazing he never got killed. Not to mention Jon and daughter Molly. I am grateful," Erica said, "that they remained healthy and sane." Molly also said she was never so scared as when she rode in a car with her grandfather driving.[48]

Bette, as committed a Communist as her husband, was under pressures similar to Howard's. Barry thought she "was even worse" in her arrogance—perhaps because she was suffering from the added strain of her husband's continued cheating with Isabel Johnson, and her own retaliatory affair with Bobby Goodman, with whom she had fallen in love. Bette was very often "glib and sarcastic to her children," Judith said, and Barry added that "she may have instilled at least a temporary sense of worthlessness in both their kids."[49] Rachel agreed, saying that her mother's several worries, including contemplating leaving Howard, and her father's "aggressive outbursts" often drove her into silent submission.[50]

Through it all, Fast continued his "normal" activities. He wrote several short stories, including "Christ in Cuernavaca," "The Holy Child," and "The Last Supper," all attesting to his continuing tension-ridden interest in Jesus as a representative of revolutionary potential as well as of peace.[51] Fast also continued to do his work for the Party. He made speeches and wrote articles slamming all anti-Communists as fascists. That distortion appears even in *Silas Timberman,* a new novel Fast was writing, a chapter of which was published in the pro-Communist magazine *Masses and Mainstream.*[52] He taught "Literature and Reality" at the Communist-affiliated Jefferson School for Social Science in the fall semester; attended the thirty-sixth anniversary of the Bolshevik Revolution at the Soviet embassy in November 1953;

and in the same month was the featured speaker at a Civil Rights Congress (CRC) meeting in Philadelphia.

Here, in what can only be regarded as a bizarre presentation, Fast predicted that after Attorney General Herbert Brownell "and his gang have run wild terrorizing America," the Democrats would win the November 1954 elections; unemployment would be sky-high, and six congressmen would advocate trade with the Soviet Union and Communist China. These six would immediately be brought to trial—and acquitted. Then McCarthy would be tried for treason! President Eisenhower in order to divert attention from turmoil at home would send the marines to Guatemala (not all that unlikely), but France and England, countries in which "Americans were afraid to walk the streets or ride the busses," would join Mexico in a stand against the United States. Fast made similarly outlandish remarks at another CRC meeting at the Jewish Cultural Center in Detroit in December.[53]

Two weeks later he received the "Stalin Prize for Promoting Peace among Nations," the greatest reward, Fast wrote, that "the human race can bestow on any one of its members." And if he had "no other cause for honoring the Soviet Union," he said, "I would honor it greatly and profoundly for giving prizes for peace."[54] Like Paul Robeson, who in 1952 was the first American to win the Stalin Prize, Fast, the second American winner, had no passport. He could not travel to Moscow to claim the awards he would eventually receive in New York: a gold medal and $25,000.[55]

That Fast, deprived of a passport by the State Department, could not go to Moscow was disturbing to many on the left. On the other hand, the Brooklyn Council of the Veterans of Foreign Wars, wanting never again to see this outspoken defender of such "communists" as the "seditious" Steve Nelson, the "disloyal" Rosenbergs, and the many violators of the Smith Act, and tired of seeing the writer's face and his outright lies about Communism and the Soviet Union in the newspapers, offered to buy Fast a one-way ticket to Moscow, provided he renounce his American citizenship![56] The veterans may not have understood much about civil liberties, but they were clear-eyed enough about Fast's duplicity, approval of Stalinism, persistent and irksome apologetics for the tyrannical Soviet Union, and willingness to be a lapdog for the CPUSA.

11

Culture and the Cold War

hat the VFW wanted to pack Fast off to the Soviet Union was symptomatic of the anti-Communist mood of some Americans in the postwar period; but whether the Cold War between the United States and the USSR and the anti-Communist and conformist attitudes it helped reinforce were the main ingredients of the American cultural stew of the 1950s is an open question. Fast, however, was convinced that the repressive anti-Communism of the McCarthy period had a powerful chilling effect that kept novelists in line and "kill[ed] social writing in America."[1]

Certainly McCarthyism continued at important levels throughout the decade. The Smith Act cases in which Fast was directly involved as a journalist and an unofficial advisor to the defense were ongoing; and the Communist Control Act of 1954, incorporating President Eisenhower's call for outlawing the Communist Party altogether, was signed in August, instilling worry in many, including Fast, who feared being imprisoned a second time.

Still, to contend, as many historians have, that the country was steeped in a nationwide "paranoia over Communism" that led to rigid conformity not only in politics, but also in lifestyle and culture, high and low, does not seem true in any absolute sense. McCarthyism and anti-Communism, particularly among political elites, union leaders, professional groups, and nongovernmental organizations, had significant effect on domestic politics and social attitudes, and negative impact on the lives of many Americans, including the Fasts, who would flee to Mexico in 1954. But in that same year, McCarthy himself finally had his feet cut out from under him by Edward R. Murrow on a half-hour *See It Now* TV special in March. The broadcast helped speed up a nationwide backlash against the senator from Wisconsin, which intensified after McCarthy picked a fight with the U.S. Army in the spring, charging lax security at a top-secret facility. Censured by Congress and ostracized by members of his own party, McCarthy saw his career as a politician and media star finally collapse.[2] In the end, despite a decidedly rightward turn of the American political axis in the fifties, and Howard Fast's observations about "creeping fascism" in America, Democrats continued to win elections, as did Republicans who promised not to dismantle New Deal reforms.

That many Americans sought stability, security, and "normalcy," and constructed a postwar world marked by tradition, conventionality, and homogeneity, may have had less to do with the Cold War or McCarthyism than with the end of ten years of the Great Depression and four of the Second World War. Similarly, unease over Communism and political repression may have been less responsible for an alleged decline of the "social" dimension in the world of creative imagination than WWII itself—its coming, conduct, and consequences. Genocide, slave labor camps, and the use of atomic weapons may have been quite enough to move writers and artists into the more personal and the less broadly and aggressively political.[3]

Many literary critics and authors in the postwar period, including Howard Fast, thought that introspective writers such as Saul Bellow and abstract artists such as Mark Rothko, whatever the cause, were representative of those who were giving up on politics and slipping into a new "genteel uninvolvement." Alfred Kazin, Lionel Trilling, and Irving Howe, for example, worried that writers and artists enjoying the "cozy prosperity of post-Communist America" would not want to be reminded, or to remind readers, that there were deep and wide pockets of social and economic inequality in the success-oriented, chillingly smug America of the 1950s.[4]

They criticized fifties writers not only for what they saw as their alienation from the larger world, but for making the alienation that haunted their fictional protagonists attractive, even aesthetically and psychologically necessary. Kazin, Trilling, and Howe, among others, feared that the novel of social inquiry was in retreat, yielding to novels of estrangement, where individual experience and self-contemplation, not politics or the pursuit of social

justice, provided the only source of illumination and human fulfillment.[5]
Though not engaged so much in literary criticism, Fast expressed great
disdain for what seemed to him a withdrawal of literature from political
commitment and social conscience, a slide into the literature of solipsism
and disaffection.

"I am not a writer like Bellow," Fast told an interviewer in 1968. There is
no irony, myth, or alienation in "my books," Fast said. "I am an old-fashioned
writer who primarily tells stories." These stories, however, as we know,
did not just materialize; they came out of a Communist consciousness and
agenda. Fast was after a directness and simplicity that would make clear
where the real battle lay. It was not "the major duty of a writer," simply "to
write," he said in 1955. The major duty of any human being, not just writers, "was to engage in the struggle for the advancement and the betterment
of mankind." In the world we live in today, he said, *"greatness of literature
can only be the result of particular participation in this struggle."* But in the
aesthetics of modernism, Fast complained bitterly, "obscurity is raised to
the level of a virtue," and therefore "action," especially political action, "is
logically shunned."[6]

Fast thought that the obliteration of politics in the novel was the direct
result of repressive anti-Communism. He went so far as to say that one of the
most "terrible thing[s] the FBI did was to destroy social writing in America."[7]
Indeed, he thought the whole government apparatus, including the CIA,
along with big business and the new "purveyors of culture" such as the
Rockefeller Foundation and the Cultural Committee for Freedom, not only
had driven the political dimension from the writing of fiction, but also had
co-opted New Criticism in literature, and Abstract Expressionism in art.
Both schools, Fast thought, not only steered clear of social context, but did so
as *a conscious move to silence leftist artists and writers.* The modernists and
especially the New Critics, who treated literature as if it were hermetically
self-contained, Fast argued, were not apolitical—they were "anti-progres-
sive," purposefully focusing on individualism and ambiguity, and taking us
away from the communal.[8]

Fast and many of his comrades believed that the workers, the common
people, would not read or look at, no less understand, modernist works.
Art, Fast predicted, would no longer be what it was once thought to be in
the 1930s, a weapon in a political struggle. Interestingly, this attitude un-
derestimated those classes who were to serve as the base of any progressive

movement, and it neglected some of the experimental writing done by the "proletarians" themselves in the thirties. Mike Gold's *Jews without Money,* Jack London's *Iron Heel,* and Jack Conroy's *The Disinherited,* as well as the stories Conroy published in H. L. Mencken's *American Mercury* magazine, are all examples of another kind of modernism, not so much in its aesthetic as in its having synthesized naturalism and realism with the world of labor.[9]

There may well have been, as Fast believed, a conscious drive by pro-capitalist and anti-Communist forces to inhibit art and thought critical of American culture; but if so, despite motion picture production codes and congressional investigatory committees, much was left untouched. Resistance to conformity remained resonant in postwar America in film noir, for example, and in comic books, rock and roll, and science fiction, as well as in the powerful beginnings of movements for racial and gender equality.[10] Moreover, major innovative works by critical thinkers in sociology, psychology, philosophy, and economics were written and published during the so-called sleepy nonpolitical fifties: David Reisman's *The Lonely Crowd* (1950), Erik Erikson's *Childhood and Society* (1950), Herbert Marcuse's *Eros and Civilization* (1955), C. Wright Mills's *White Collar* (1956), John Kenneth Galbraith's *The Affluent Society* (1958), and Philip Rieff's *Freud: The Mind of the Moralist* (1959) are a small sample.

"Social writing" in fiction and poetry also survived, indeed thrived, in the fifties. There were even books with proletarian themes: Lloyd Brown's *Iron City* (1952), a novel about men behind bars, which focused on race, class, and ethnicity, and Harvey Swados's novels, *Out Went the Candle* (1955) and *On the Line* (1957), which gave us the first literary expressions of American worker discontent in the affluent 1950s, are only three among many instances. And Howard Fast himself continued to remind readers that despite the much celebrated rise of workers to the material level of the bourgeoisie, class conflict was not only a critical part of the American past, but still alive in the present, not very far below the surface of what looked like harmony and consensus.

The much more numerous non-proletarian writers about whom some critics were fretting included, among many others, Saul Bellow, especially for *Seize the Day* (1956); J. D. Salinger for *Catcher in the Rye* (1951); Flannery O'Connor for *Wise Blood* (1952); Ralph Ellison for *Invisible Man* (1952); and Carson McCullers for *The Ballad of the Sad Café* (1951). But why classify as neither social nor political these and dozens of other novels by lesser-known authors when all of them, even if sometimes only indirectly, explicate the "shadow narrative," the larger public story within the smaller "private" one, as well as the other way around; when all, or almost all, observe the sadness, anxieties, frustration, and anger lying just beneath the seemingly smooth veneer of middle-class American life.

Even the Beats, those drug- and alcohol-besotted writers and poets, some of whom valued spontaneity over careful crafting, included artists such as Alan Ginsberg, whose modernist "Howl" not only opposes sexual repression but excoriates the destructive forces of capitalism and conformity in the United States; and Lawrence Ferlinghetti, who admired abstract expressionism, yet urged poets to be engaged in the political and cultural life of the nation. Poetry, Ferlinghetti wrote, "should transport the public/to higher places/than other wheels can carry it."[11] This too was the fifties. Works produced in that decade dealt with alienation, but also morality, ethics, race, gender, class, and social conflict. They cannot, as Fast would have it, be dismissed as part of a culture of "genteel uninvolvement" and "conformity and homogeneity" simply because they contain no explicit political inquiry, message, or agenda.

It is true that after a period of varied and innovative programming in the late 1940s and early 1950s, television broadcasting, for example, surrendered to its own economic imperatives, offering little more than variety shows, "horse operas," and family serials full of bland, safe images of American middle-class life.[12] But if the new medium eventually became socially isolating, in its early days it also brought people, most of whom were watching the same programs, together. And those without TV were often invited into the living rooms of those with it.

The area around the television became something of a shrine, the set itself an icon, touchable only by its owner. Although her extended family often gathered together to watch television, Rachel Fast, for example, remembers getting smacked hard on the hand after reaching to turn on her uncle Jerry's new color TV. Her father was less horrified by this action than by his brother's "possession of such a thing." Of course, it wasn't long before Howard, too, had a color TV. Fast actually grew to love television and watched a lot of it in the evening. His son Jonathan said that viewing *The Lone Ranger* with his father allowed for "the few moments of intimacy we ever had." These moments weren't perfect. While watching, the elder Fast would provide a critical narrative, pointing out the clichés, and then, annoyingly, would anticipate the ending.[13]

Rachel Fast also watched TV with her father. She was even occasionally inveigled into watching wrestling with him, Bette in the background shaking her head in a combination of bewilderment and disgust. But the whole family got together for *I Remember Mama,* Sid Caesar, Groucho Marx, *Father Knows Best,* and Fast's absolute favorite, *I Love Lucy.* On one occasion he told Rachel, falsely, that Lucille Ball was the head of the Cultural Division of the Communist Party!

Fast despised the increasingly ubiquitous drama series, and verboten in the household was the explicitly anti-Communist *I Led Three Lives.* Very loosely based on the life of Herbert Philbrick, a business executive who infiltrated the American Communist Party as an FBI informant in the 1940s, the show originated in 1953 when McCarthyism was still powerful. Although all scripts required the approval of J. Edgar Hoover, the story lines became more and more bizarre, and the series was canceled in 1956.

TV wasn't all pap even in the mid to late fifties. The Fasts watched memorable television dramas presented on *Kraft Television Theatre, Studio One,* and *Playhouse 90,* including Paddy Chayefsky's *Marty* (1955) and Reginald Rose's *Twelve Angry Men* (1954). There was also serious journalism, including Edward R. Murrow's investigative *See It Now* and Dave Garroway's *Today,* show on which Fast himself was incisively interviewed in 1957 after he left the Communist Party.[14]

That TV, given its vast educational potential, became an instrument that aimed to please the lowest common denominator was unfortunate, even tragic. It was no accident, of course; but it was also no conspiracy of Cold War champions to fragment or erode collective consciousness or social content in art in order to foster conformity and homogeneity. The same could be said of the so-called Red Scare science-fiction films, which most often featured, as alleged stand-ins for foreign Communists, dangerous aliens and enormous monsters of one sort or another, such as *The Blob* (1958), a huge amoeba-like creature that ravenously sucks up the residents of a small town in Pennsylvania. The Blob can be defeated only by freezing it, which convinced at least one media specialist that the film was about stopping *cold* "the creeping horrors of communism." There it is, he wrote confidently, but unpersuasively, "the Cold War writ small and literal." Whether audiences saw any of these films this way is questionable. As film producer Walter Mirisch wrote, some critics have "read meanings into pictures that were never intended." *The Invasion of the Body Snatchers,* which Mirisch helped create, was not, according to him or the director or the scriptwriter, "an allegory about the communist infiltration of America."[15]

Just as we have seen with high-brow literary development, so with popular filmmaking: no conspiracy theory is necessary to trace its contours. Writers, painters, musicians, moviemakers, and artists of all kinds would likely have moved into abstraction, and pursued private worlds and subjective accounts of consciousness, with or without the Cold War or Cold War schemers. Auschwitz, the Gulag, and Hiroshima were more than enough to promote a retreat from the grand, overarching ideas, which when implemented with fanatical passion exposed not only the "dark side of reform," but the very depth of the abyss.[16]

PORTRAIT OF THE ARTIST AS A CAPTIVE MAN

Fast had always preferred the noncircuitous and the unambiguous in his writing. But after he got close to and then joined the CP in the mid-1940s, his proclivity to abstain from exploring the natural complexity of lived experience in favor of "moral fables" intensified, as shown only too well in *Freedom Road, The American,* and *Clarkton.* In the fifties this inclination toward telling stories packed with propaganda deepened. Fast's novels *The Proud and the Free* (1950), *Spartacus* (1951), *The Passion of Sacco and Vanzetti* (1953), *Silas Timberman* (1954), and *Lola Gregg* (1956) are filled with obvious and heavy-handed political messages. But except for *Spartacus,* these books are ignored and long out of print, unlike the poems of Ferlinghetti and Ginsberg, and the novels of Salinger, Ellison, and Bellow. And who in the twenty-first century has even heard of *Silas Timberman* and *Lola Gregg?* Fast himself came to think little of these two books, and by the mid-sixties he stopped including them in the lists of novels he'd published.

Fast's writing was marked not only by political polemic in the fifties; there is also in his work a pervasive tone of despair. With *Silas Timberman* and *Lola Gregg,* as with *Sacco and Vanzetti,* two men waiting for their inevitable execution, Fast seemed to have lost some of his faith in the power of dissent and resistance, and had turned fully to writing about victims. Timberman, a liberal college professor suspected of "Communist associations," is hounded by the government, betrayed by colleagues, framed, and unjustly sentenced to three years in prison for perjury. Lola Gregg's husband, Roger, is a machinist and a union leader, a "good man" and a proud Communist on the run from an FBI dragnet slowly closing in on him. His wife waits helplessly at home. Lola and Roger, neither of whom is fully fleshed out, survive an ordeal full of action and melodrama, but nothing really changes.[17] And in the end, in both books, unlike in his political writings and speeches, Fast seems to pull back just a little, perhaps with an eye toward sales, focusing only on "excesses" and abuses of the system, and not on the inability of the system itself to produce a just and equal society.

Yet the Soviet Union had high praise for the new novels, especially for *Lola Gregg*. Boris Izakov and long-term CP powerhouse Boris Polevoy, both influential members of the Soviet Writers Union, wrote at different times to say they liked the book quite a lot, and Russian theatrical producer and editor Alexander Shubin agreed. In addition to the rapturous acclaim, Fast was happy to receive a royalty check of nearly $1,500 from A. Chakovsky, the editor of *Inostrannaja literatura,* which had run pre-publication excerpts of *Lola Gregg* in Moscow.[18]

Only Albert Maltz was willing to tell Fast the truth. "I wish I could be . . . enthusiastic," about *Lola Gregg,* Maltz wrote, but "I cannot, and I have too much admiration for the body of your work to go in for polite deception. . . . It felt to me," Maltz said, "as though it were written off the surface of your mind without any pause for reflection. . . . The great gift of enormous fertility, which you have, would sometimes seem to carry pitfalls within it. . . . And then again perhaps I am wrong."[19] Maltz was not wrong.

Fast's work tended to succeed or fail as art to the extent that he distanced himself from rigid ideology. *Silas Timberman* (compared in the Soviet Union to Maxim Gorky's *Mother,* arguably one of the classics of world literature) and *Lola Gregg* amounted to little more than polemical sentimentality, demonstrating the logical end point of the artist turned propagandist. And not too long after he wrote these books, the last he would write while in the Communist Party, Fast admitted, "I was not objective. I had lost my distance." He had "obeyed the writ of the [Party] priesthood," Fast said, and his work suffered, bearing the "trademarks of the same frigid and deadly narrowness and intolerance that other Party material contained."[20]

In one thing at least, Fast did resist the dictation of the "priesthood." Unlike what he did with his plays *The Hammer* and *Thirty Pieces of Silver*—and who knows how many other pieces of writing—Fast, in regard to *Silas Timberman,* ignored an influential Party member's "suggestion" of a small change in the text. Even in this tiny defiance, however, Fast reveals his penchant for self-serving rationalization or an extraordinary talent for denial. Ted Baer, the American Communist Party's expert on Soviet affairs, advised Fast to change the name of one of the key figures in *Silas Timberman* from Isaac Amsterdam, to something that "sounded less Jewish." The Soviets, Baer said, "don't like . . . to read [or] publish things about Jews." But Amsterdam, Fast said, "is *not* Jewish." The Russians, however, will "think he's Jewish," Baer predicted, "because his name is Isaac." Fast, knowing full well the details of Soviet behavior toward the Jews in the USSR and its Stalinist puppet-states, beginning with the arrest and murder of the Yiddish poets, the incarceration and execution of Rudolf Slansky on completely concocted charges, and the potentially genocidal consequences of the invented "Doctors' Plot," said, with what one hopes was mock astonishment, "Ted, are you telling me the Russians are antisemitic?" "No, not at all," Baer replied, apparently without facetiousness; "they do, however, have problems about Jews." But "*I'm* Jewish!" Fast said. "Don't they know that?" "Of course," Baer answered, "but they don't *consider* you Jewish." Fast finished recounting this ridiculous tale to an interviewer in 1977 by saying what could more truly, and sadly, be said of himself: the Soviets "had a kind of schizophrenic attitude," vis-à-vis Jews "that was impossible to analyze or to understand!"[21] In any case, in *Silas Timberman,* Isaac Amsterdam, Fast was proud to say, remained Isaac Amsterdam.

Fast used novels such as *Silas Timberman* as well as his journalism to deliver his political message. Oddly, however, in 1954 and 1955 his target audience seemed to be Russians rather than Americans. In an article in the *New Times,* a weekly journal published in Moscow, Fast told readers this is "What I Want for My Country in 1954": the repeal of the Smith Act; the release of "political prisoners"; and the destruction of "five concentration camps," which in Fast's fevered imagination not only existed but had been "built . . . strongly and carefully." He also wanted an end to the ban on travel for those on the left, so that they could see for themselves the wonders of the Soviet Union and the People's Republic of China and report on these to the American people.[22]

Fast also kept up a friendly correspondence with Russian writers Izakov and Polevoy, and with Fadeyev, the powerful head of the Soviet Writers Union. "What a joy it would be," Fadeyev wrote, "to sit with you in a peaceful circle here in Moscow at a tea-table to talk of your . . . fresh, exciting book[s]."

Until that time comes, Fadeyev said, he wished Fast "all the big successes in your struggle and in your creative work."[23]

TO FLEE OR NOT TO FLEE

Fast also continued to correspond with Albert Maltz in Mexico and to keep in touch with a small number of comrades in the United States, including Shirley Graham, Scott Nearing, and Herbert Biberman; but his American world was narrowing. It was a world, he told Maltz, in which he faced a "day to day struggle" to *live* rather than simply exist. Upset by the "stupid persecution" he experienced at the hands of J. Edgar Hoover's "goons," and fearful of being recalled by HUAC and ultimately re-imprisoned on a second contempt conviction, Fast, in the early spring of 1954, suffered a particularly intense run of cluster headaches.[24]

In April, Fast's reception for having won the Stalin Prize, attended by a thousand people at the Hotel McAlpin in New York, and presided over by W. E. B. Du Bois and Paul Robeson, permitted no relief from the novelist's pain or his fear of re-arrest. Though reportedly "deeply moved as he came to the mike and faced his many friends," Fast could shake neither his worry nor his headaches.[25] And in late May, according to Fast's unpublished manuscript "The Singularity of Being Jewish," he learned directly of an incident he considered "the last straw." A "friend of ours," Fast claimed, "a brilliant composer and a Communist," possibly the blacklisted Marc Blitzstein, "had just been visited by three FBI agents, all of them homosexual," as was Blitzstein, and they "raped him again and again in a scene that Nazis might envy, and one the media avoided mentioning."[26]

Fast's recollection, written in 2002 or 2003, when he was ill and close to death, reveals little more than the homophobia he suffered for most of his life; and according to his daughter, Rachel, was likely hallucinatory. Whatever the truth of the matter, the Fast family, like Communists John Bright, Dalton Trumbo, Albert Maltz, Gordon Kahn, and Maxim Lieber before them, headed south of the border in 1954 with one-way tickets. In Mexico City, where Howard was reportedly recuperating from a "nervous disorder" (actually a severe bout of cluster headaches) the Fasts were the guests of Dr. Ernesto Amann, a political exile from the Spanish Civil War, who inadvertently told an undercover FBI informant that the family had no intention of returning to the United States any time soon and that Fast had mentioned the possibility of establishing permanent residence in Mexico. Not likely. The Israeli ambassador, with whom Howard lunched one afternoon in Mexico City, offered to get him a passport to the Jewish state under "the right of return." But giving up "my American citizenship and raising my children anywhere but in the United States," Fast said, "was out of the question."[27]

Whatever his plan, at Amann's home, Fast's headaches worsened. Rachel, who wrapped a pillow around her head in a futile attempt to muffle the sound, says she "will never forget the weeping and screaming." Bette finally called her cousin, a doctor who lived in Mexico City, and in the middle of the night a temporarily ameliorating injection was administered. The Fasts then moved to Cuernavaca, where they stayed in the hotel Latino Americano. "A wonderful housekeeper" named Raquel, whom Rachel and six-year-old Jonathan loved, cooked and cared for the family. When Fast discovered that he and the other Americans at the hotel were paying the help the equivalent of forty cents a day, he was outraged and doubled Raquel's wages. Instead of simply relieving Fast's sense of guilt, this gesture increased his misery because the American friends he had made in Cuernavaca were furious at him. Fast stuck to his decision, but grew increasingly uncomfortable in Mexico.[28]

There were visits to Albert Maltz and the social realist muralists Diego Rivera and David Siqueiros, both active Communists with hazy links to the assassination of Trotsky in Mexico in 1940. This was not a subject for discussion over café con leche or tequila, or in front of Fast's children. But Rachel, who, in several interviews and innumerable e-mail exchanges with me, supplied "snapshots" of the family's life in Mexico, remembered enjoying the trips to Taxco to look at silver, as well as her climb, Jonathan in hand, to the top of the Pyramid of the Sun in Teotihuacan. Cathedral tours, however, were always followed by a "passionate lecture" from her father about the "wickedness" of a religious system that extracted pesos from the poor.[29]

During her Sundays out in Cuernavaca, Rachel saw the crippled beggars who every week "crawled the streets with their legs all twisted under them," and she "went on strike." She would not leave the hotel on Sundays; and soon, despite Raquel's delicious tortillas and frijoles, Rachel developed a strong dislike of Mexico. Her parents, too, had become more and more ill at ease there. And they missed New York. Bette ached for the ballet, the museums, the symphony, Howard for the theater. Ironically, the Fasts returned to the States in late September 1954 just before President Eisenhower signed the Communist Control Act (CCA).[30]

Officially designating the CPUSA "an instrumentality of a conspiracy to overthrow the Government of the United States," the act suspended the citizenship of CP members and made them, as well as members of "Communist-infiltrated" organizations such as labor unions and civil rights groups, liable to fine and imprisonment. Despite the egregious attack on civil liberties represented by the CCA, liberals, with the exception of the American Civil Liberties Union, failed to offer any real opposition to the legislation. Instead, Hubert Humphrey, supported by twenty other liberal Democratic Senators, including Paul Douglas, Wayne Morse, and John F. Kennedy, offered an amendment guaranteeing that any person prosecuted under the CCA would be protected by the Bill of Rights and all other procedural safeguards, including the presumption of innocence.

Humphrey and the others hoped the amendment would discourage attempts at character defamation and protect the reputations of the innocent. Clearly, however, the goal of the liberals was to dissociate the Democrats, charged by McCarthy as the party of "betrayal and treason," from Communism. Humphrey himself said it was politically necessary "to remove any doubt" as to where the Democrats and liberals stood on the question. The CCA, with Humphrey's amendment attached, which passed by a vote of 85–0, was more a grand political gesture than a genuine attempt to kill American Communism, which for all intents and purposes was already dead, if not fully buried. Moreover, the act was plagued by constitutional problems, especially because it used overly broad and unspecific language. No administration ever tried to enforce it.[31]

Of course, Howard Fast had no way of knowing that he would not be targeted. He and Bette talked about returning to Mexico or leaving New York City for the anonymity of the "country." Worried about drowning in the dreariness of suburbia, but more worried about going to prison again, Fast in October moved his family to a house in Teaneck, New Jersey, very near the home of Bette's parents. Oddly, given Fast's fears, he was soon encouraging ten-year-old Rachel to hang a framed picture of Stalin in her new bedroom. A gift to Howard from the Russian consulate, the photograph showed "Stalin standing in Red Square holding pink-cheeked children in his arms, surrounded by thousands of smiling admirers, flowers everywhere. He appeared [to be] the soul of kindness." Rachel remembered thinking that

Stalin looked "like God, Goodness incarnate" and that she "desperately" wanted to have the picture in her room.[32]

Bette objected strenuously. Howard objected to her objections, and the debate grew red-hot. Bette, as she commonly did when Howard yelled at her, displayed "gritted teeth" and a deeply "furrowed brow." But despite her mother's obvious distress, Rachel, "daddy's girl," as she put it, sided with her father. Her mother, however, was clearly the sensible one, Rachel confessed; Bette knew how "INSANELY INAPPROPRIATE it would have been to have that picture on [the] wall of my bedroom" in suburban New Jersey in 1954. Finally, Howard, too, recognized that in addition to the pain on Bette's face, there was in her voice "an edge of panic." He wisely backed off, and the picture of Stalin remained face down on a shelf in Rachel's closet.[33]

Despite Fast's continued immersion in the Communist movement, and his admiration for Stalin, he refused to admit—indeed, he tried, understandably, to hide—his membership in the CPUSA. In response to a review of *Silas Timberman* written by Philip Toynbee, the British novelist and editor, and son of the renowned historian Arnold Toynbee, Fast objected to being called a Communist. He issued no denial, but insisted that Toynbee had no evidence for such labeling. There "has never been," Fast wrote, "a public statement made by myself which designated me as a Communist." Since the CP was now illegal in the US, and Party members faced imprisonment, Toynbee's language, Fast argued, "is to put it mildly, unfortunate."[34]

AN EVER BRIGHTER STAR IN THE USSR

Fast's objections to being labeled a Communist notwithstanding, he continued to be involved in the activities of the CPUSA, mainly through his work for the *Daily Worker* as a permanent staff member and regular columnist, and he maintained his many connections to the Soviet Union. He had been well known as a novelist in America before he joined the Communist Party, but Howard Fast's radical activities and writings, and his public political appearances, gave him a cachet and a notoriety greater than he could have achieved by his fiction alone. By 1955, however, those rewards, as well as material recompense, became far less available to Fast in America. From the Soviet Union and its East European satellites, on the other hand, there was not only a continual, if erratic, flow of substantial royalties from Fast's twenty-five books in more than a dozen languages and 2 million copies, but payment in critical respect and public admiration. These two things, which he could no longer count on from American critics or even CPUSA leaders, were far more important even than cash in keeping Fast tightly within the Soviet orbit.

All the same the cash was welcome, allowing the Fasts to live "decently" for most of the 1940s and the first half of the '50s in commodious quarters in Manhattan, send their children to summer camp, throw parties, and pay a full-time housekeeper. Even during the family's stay in New Jersey from 1954 to 1960, while Fast was still blacklisted, the family lived a comfortable suburban life. Howard could afford to drive Rachel and Jonathan into New York City every weekday so that they could continue attending the private Walden elementary school until 1956.[35] And he remained financially secure enough to continue to make thousands of dollars in contributions to the Party; give all his royalties from *Peekskill, USA* to the Civil Rights Congress; and, through Blue Heron Press, help subsidize the publication and reprinting of books by other blacklisted Communists, including a novel by Stefan Heym, a short history of the early-nineteenth-century labor movement by Meridel Le Sueur, and a volume of modernist poetry by Walter Lowenfels.[36]

When Fast left prison in 1950 he had enough money to purchase the rights to ten of his novels and short story collections. This investment turned out to be quite profitable. Between 1951 and 1956, Fast received $20,000 in royalties from the Soviet Union for *The Last Frontier* alone, and an equivalent amount from Poland. By 1954, the same year in which Fast collected his $25,000 Stalin Prize, an award equal to more than five times the annual salary of a New York City schoolteacher, *Spartacus* had been translated into a dozen languages, including Bengali and Yiddish, and was being purchased at an extraordinary rate, making it the first self-published best seller in history up to that point.[37] Additional income was also provided by Bette, who worked between 1953 and 1959, not because she had to, but because she enjoyed using her bottled-up talent in sculpting and painting to design blouses as a freelancer.[38]

Fast told an interviewer in 1957 that there were no money difficulties, that his earnings from Russia and Eastern Europe, especially Czechoslovakia, Poland, and Hungary, had always been good. Indeed, he said, "half his income has been from . . . Communist countries," and that in addition he could count on receiving annually a "very considerable income from

France and Italy."[39] He liked to moan and groan about the blacklist reducing him to "devastating poverty" and "near-bankruptcy." But whatever impression he was trying to give, Fast was really talking only about the drastically undercapitalized Blue Heron Press. Personally, Fast said, "I never had a problem" making a very good living "even during the blacklist." As he announced during a TV interview after he left the Party, "I'm the most widely read author of this century. . . . There is no living author in the whole world whose books have sold the quantity that mine have." But "I don't boast about it."[40]

After completing the manuscript for *Lola Gregg* in 1955, Fast, his headaches active almost full-time, had no other book in the hopper. "My health has been miserable," he told Maltz, "to a point where I certainly could not survive even six months in prison, for I live only by oxygen and specific medication." But Fast said he could work a bit "in between the bouts of agony."[41] Sustaining "serious writing," however, was apparently out of the question. When he was asked by the editor of a Soviet magazine to write a piece on the thirty-eighth anniversary of the October Revolution, Fast begged off. "Perhaps with a little more time I could turn out something worthwhile, but . . . I have been very ill and only with the greatest difficulty can I sit down [to write]. This illness . . . is an old chronic thing" and "there seems to be no hope of curing it. . . . And so somehow I manage to accommodate myself to it."[42]

When he could get something on paper, Fast mostly wrote articles and stories for the Communist papers *Masses and Mainstream* (though he thought it a "rather stodgy magazine with a faltering point of view") and *Morgen Freiheit*.[43] He continued his twice-weekly columns in the *Daily Worker* and in addition wrote nearly two dozen feature articles for the paper in 1955 and 1956. Many of the stories Fast wrote for *Masses and Mainstream* during this period were collected along with several others and published under the Blue Heron imprint as *The Last Supper and Other Stories* in 1955.

Several of the sixteen pieces in the anthology show that Fast was still struggling, creatively, to forge a synthesis between Marxism and religion, between love and anger. "Walk Home," in which two FBI agents pressure a factory laborer to betray his Communist coworkers, is directly reflective of the Judas-betrayal theme, as is "The Upraised Pinion," in which Fast creates a backsliding Communist editor, who out of fear and greed becomes a paid government informer. Fast's fascination with Jesus is also evident in a number of these tales, including the allegorical title story, "The Last Supper," and the more direct "Holy Child," a secularized retelling of the birth of Christ.

Several of these stories, especially those marked by religious sensibility, are an improvement over Fast's novels of this period. Perhaps the pain Fast suffered and the periods of rest he required for recovery allowed him to slow down the assembly-line pace of his writing and to be more reflective. Whatever triggered their high quality, the stories elicited much praise from first-rate writers such as Stefan Heym, who thought that "Christ in Cuernavaca," the best story in the anthology by far, was "world [class] literature." "Love shines through these stories beautifully," Heym wrote, and "that's strange insofar as most writers I know (myself included) hate better than they love." The stories that express "your hate," Heym concluded, "come off second best compared to those in which you love."[44] Heym's insight squares with what Fast had been trying to do from as early as 1939 in *Conceived in Liberty:* paint a Christ whose redemptive power resembles a more this-worldly, indeed more Jewish, messianism; a Christ who brings a message of just action born of righteous anger, but also one of love.[45]

Although there was less writing than usual by the generally prolific Fast in the second half of the fifties, he had more interaction with his friends and correspondents in the USSR than ever before. He and Bette attended receptions and celebrations at the Soviet embassy throughout 1955. There were also several letters to and from Boris Polevoy, especially in March and April, in one of which, Fast astoundingly wondered "whether Soviet writers realize the priceless opportunities they have for creation. To one writing here . . . without a publisher, barred from the bookstores, penalized with jail staring one in the face everyday—to such a person the situation of a writer in your country is as inconceivable as some glowing dream."[46] Less than two years later, Fast would admit that the situation of the Soviet writer was more like a fiery nightmare, but in 1955, he was still deluding himself, as he had been since 1943.

In April, exhibiting his robust capacity for fantasy, Fast told Polevoy that writers in the Soviet Union have the "treasure" of "time, peace, and contemplation, and the knowledge that they can write what they please as they please, and the time and money to live while they write." Fast, "a prisoner within the borders of [his own] land," believed he was suffering "a form of minor torture" and yearned for a situation like that of Polevoy and Izakov, who had "the knowledge that no secret police wait outside their home or follow them or plot against them."[47] Two weeks later Fast wrote to A. B. Lakovsky, the editor of *Inostrannja Literatura,* extending the logic in his letters to Polevoy by implying that he'd prefer to be in Moscow or at least to be surrounded by Muscovites. "It is a long and very deep-seated wish of mine," Fast wrote, "that some day I can sit down with you and your colleagues and talk about all . . . things."[48]

Soon, in a small way, Fast got his wish. In November, Polevoy and seven other powerful Russian cultural figures visited the United States and spent some time with the Fast family in New York and New Jersey. Howard, who had through their correspondence come to love and respect Boris, met him in Manhattan and "embraced him as a beloved and old companion." Polevoy's "big . . . open . . . smile [being] a thing of joy to see," Howard and Bette "dragged him home" with them to Teaneck. Rachel remembers Polevoy the same way: "a big ebullient, effusive, passionate Russian," to whom she attached herself "like mad, immediately." What followed were two evenings of "warmth and closeness and drink and food and fellowship" among the Fasts, Polevoy and Izakov, and two or three other Soviet colleagues.[49]

Fast wrote to Polevoy that "those two nights we spent with you and your comrades were two of the warmest and most meaningful nights of our whole lives. We cherish them, and . . . they provide us with sustenance and constant refreshment." For Fast, Polevoy's letters, sent before and after his visit, had "the effect of a . . . hypodermic needle." They leave the whole family "immensely cheered and with more vigor."[50]

Hypodermic needle aside, Fast continued to be burdened by headaches. "It is not merely the pain and the inconvenience which affects me," he told Polevoy, "but the thought that as this thing worsens I may [be] unable to work. . . . Prison will mean a particular kind of agony, but even that is easier to accept than a future in which I could not work."[51] That Fast was fearful was testified to by his smacking eleven-year-old Rachel for only the second time in her life, the first blow having come more than nine years earlier.[52] But what saved Fast from erupting more often, he told Polevoy, was that the Soviet United Nations House gives "a number of parties" in celebration of the opening of the General Assembly and the anniversary of the "Great October Revolution" each year, "so every few weeks, we set foot on Soviet soil and that . . . is enormously helpful."[53]

SIGNS OF THAW IN THE COLD WAR?

Fast told Maltz that just as with his health, so with the United States: he went through "alternate periods of hope and despair." For all his criticism of the American establishment, Fast's posture toward the United States in 1956 was riddled with ambiguity. In a period of five days at the very start of January, he went from saying, "here at home, the frenzied prophets of the Cold War are screaming louder than ever . . . for a new era of hatred and mistrust," to "America is beginning to shake loose of the nightmare of this past decade." A little later Fast told Izakov, "Many interesting things are happening here and it does seem that we have weathered the worst of the storm. These have been a difficult and troubled 10 years that we have lived through. But now there is a real hint of hope and it may just be possible that I will see you one of these days. I look forward to it."[54]

What cracks Fast saw in the ice of the Cold War or diminishment in the anti-Communist pressure at home, he fails to specify. But HUAC and an ailing, powerless McCarthy were no longer constantly in the headlines, and the anti-Communist mood of the late forties and early fifties seemed to have largely dissipated. Racial segregation was ruled unconstitutional in public schools by the U.S. Supreme Court in 1954, and blacks, in the South especially, were organizing a struggle for civil rights across the society that promised a boost not only to racial equality but to the cause of democracy in America generally. After long estrangement the AFL and the CIO joined together in 1955, broadening and deepening the strength of the working class of the United States. In the same year, the four-year-old sedition conviction of Steve Nelson was reversed by the U.S. Court of Appeals.[55]

There was even talk of "detente." Nothing very definite, but enough to allow some hope for peace. Fast even ventured to make a book proposal to a mainstream publisher. He may have thought—may have desperately needed to think—that the world was opening up again, and perhaps there was room for a writer interested in something other than anti-Communism.[56] Fast was prescient here. On February 25, 1956, the last day of the Twentieth Communist Party Congress in Moscow, Nikita Khrushchev delivered, in an unscheduled closed session, an extraordinary "secret" speech that seemed to signal important change in the Soviet Union.

That morning Khrushchev had made oblique references to the damaging results of elevating one leader to so high a level that he took on the "su-

pernatural characteristics akin to those of a god." It was clear to gathered
delegates that Stalin and Stalinism were to be targeted, but the details were
disclosed only that evening in a four-hour harangue. Stalin was accused of
distorting the principles of Marxist-Leninism and was made responsible
for the Great Terror of the 1930s, particularly the destructive purges of the
military and upper Party echelons. The Party, Khrushchev insisted, was a
victim of the "cult of the individual," not an accessory to it. Indeed, he lavished praise on the CPSU and urged a return to the "revolutionary fight for
the transformation of society."

Shocked surprise, disbelief, and then grief, even to the point of open
weeping, was reportedly the general reaction in the room. One would think
that many of the facts disclosed had to have been already known. Yet, most
Soviet Communists claimed that the exposés were "revelations." Objectively, for some few, this claim may have been true; but for many, especially
leaders and those who had swallowed the merciless idea of historical necessity, "revelation" could not have been more than "psychologically" true.
That the word had come finally from an unimpeachable source, and not
from "enemies of the state," pierced the walls of repression and ideological
rationalization. Denying that awful deeds had occurred, or were still occurring, even if thought "necessary" to protect the Revolution, was now more
difficult, if not impossible.

Beyond Khrushchev's obvious desire to consolidate his own power and
garner public support for the arrest and execution of the head of Stalin's
secret police, Lavrenti Beria, which he had ordered after Stalin's death three
years earlier, it was difficult to know whether the speech actually implied
plans for significant reform.[57] Although most Western Communists were
made aware of the details only after the *New York Times* and the *London
Observer* published the text of the speech in June, there were leaks galore
much earlier, and the central ideas and tone of the speech were known by
early March, mere days after the "closed" session.

American Communists, like their Soviet counterparts, and with the same
psychological implications, spoke of "revelations." Yet many of them, including William Foster, Herbert Aptheker, Paul Novick, Herbert Biberman, and
dozens of others also knew of, and even entirely encouraged, the "necessary" actions of the Soviet Union. But now all were forced to admit, face up
to, defend, or explain away the horrors of Stalinism. Still, many, including
Howard Fast, soon consoled themselves with the hope that a therapeutic

self-examination was beginning in the Soviet Union and that healthy change was in the offing. Perhaps Peggy Dennis, the wife of Eugene Dennis, reflected best the reaction of this important segment of American Communists. She remembered that after reading Khrushchev's speech, the last page of it "crumpled in my fist, I lay in the half-darkness and I wept . . . for a thirty-year life's commitment that lay shattered. I lay sobbing low, hiccoughing whimpers." But she recovered her "political bearings," and agreed "with Gene that the exposures and the processes of correction are expressions of the stability of the Soviet Union and the intent of the post-Stalin leadership to rectify these crimes."[58]

As early as March 5th, Fast sent a letter to O. Prudkov, the deputy foreign editor of the *Literary Gazette* in Moscow, indicating his belief not only that reform was possible in Russia, but that Soviet Communism remained the truest hope for the future of the world. He also ridiculed the reactions of the American media to Khrushchev's remarks. Even the "liberal" *Nation,* Fast wrote, "was cynical and suspicious," and of course, "the *New York Times* sported *the insane shrieking of Harry Schwartz*" about "the Soviet trap." The papers shout, "'Nothing has changed, nothing can change, nothing will change.'" But Fast concluded, with decreasing logic, that all the frantic warnings only bore witness to the fact that a great deal had already changed, and that power lay in the USSR where it always did, "with the Soviet people."[59]

Fast's confidence began to waver a little after additional rumors and paraphrases of the "secret" speech drifted his way from across the ocean. But then the U.S. government struck an incomprehensibly clumsy and badly timed blow against the *Daily Worker*. On March 27, the IRS staged a coast-to-coast raid on the paper, padlocked its doors, and seized the *Worker*'s assets, meager though they were, as a lien against alleged unpaid taxes. This action not only moved Fast, editor Johnny Gates, and many others on the paper's board to close ranks and try to keep the *Worker* going, it moved several among the mainstream papers, including the *New York Times,* which contributed reams of newsprint, to join, at Fast's urging, in forming an "Independent Emergency Committee for a Free Press." Using the offices of the Yiddish Communist daily, *Morgen Freiheit,* Fast had made the necessary phone calls to bring together the committee that he went on to chair, and that helped the *Daily Worker* get past its imposed crisis. Not only did the committee recover the paper's assets, the staff moved two stories below into temporary quarters in the offices of the *Freiheit*—and with remarkable diligence and alacrity got out the next day's edition—which sported the headline: "Our Offices Seized—Here We Are." Realizing that the government had committed a colossal blunder, all officials involved denied responsibility.[60]

"One of the most terrifying things about this raid and seizure," Fast wrote his East German friend Stefan Heym, "was the destruction" the government wrought. "Books were torn and scattered about, a handful of pages [ripped] out with the same childish hatred that a sick youngster might evidence." The "useless and senseless destruction of books . . . brought home to us how close in psychology and in action our secret police are to the monsters who served Hitler."[61] Less than two weeks later, however, this newly witnessed evidence of American "fascism" paled when yet more Soviet dreadfulness was confirmed.

On April 10th, the *Freiheit* reprinted an article from the April 4th issue of *Folks-Stimme* (People's voice), the Yiddish Communist paper in Warsaw, disclosing and documenting the Stalin regime's destruction of virtually the entire Jewish cultural community. The article summarized the evidence showing the existence of blanket antisemitism in Russia, pointed to the "disappearance" of Jewish leaders in all fields, and listed the names of many Yiddish writers who were murdered. To measure the magnitude of the literary catastrophe alone, wrote Irving Howe at the time, one "should imagine a situation in which, for political reasons, Faulkner, Hemingway, Auden and Frost are summarily executed."[62]

Worker editor John Gates, born Solomon Regenstreif, pointed out that "for centuries the Jewish question has been the acid test of the democratic-mindedness and humanity of societies and individuals; the failure on this score by the Soviet Union . . . is the most shameful blot on its record."[63] In the meantime, during April, May, and June 1956, he threw open the *Daily Worker* to all opinions and printed one letter after another attacking the leaders of the CPUSA, most often as "apologists" for the Soviet Union. The paper included letters eviscerating William Foster and Eugene Dennis, many demanding the reinstatement of Earl Browder, who had called for an Americanized, de-Sovietized Communist political association. About these particular matters the editors were mostly silent, but they did announce that the transition to socialism in America could be accomplished democratically and that they had been "wrong" about many things, "terribly wrong."

In April, Fast's *Worker* column grew increasingly critical of actions by the Soviet Union, especially on the Jewish question. "No thoughtful or sensitive person can read the accounts of gross injustice perpetrated against Soviet Jews under the authority of Lavrenti Beria . . . without a sense of horror and remorse; and certainly, for one on the left, such horror is personalized and increased."

Yet in the same column, and representative of what became an unwavering pattern in his response to "abuses" in the USSR, Fast switched gears and wrote a virtual apologia: "no one can deny that in its less than four decades of existence, a million contemptible slanders were hurled against the Soviet Union. Men of good will who believe in socialism defended the Soviet Union from those slanders—and will continue to defend the Soviet Union from slanders still to come." American Communists, Fast went on, in sentences that bristled with ambivalence, inconsistency, and outright lies, will not be able to forget "the awful acts against Jewish culture and its leaders," but neither will they "overnight forget the record of the Soviet Union . . . three decades of warfare against chauvinism and anti-Semitism . . . and the unending struggle . . . for the equality of all peoples."[64]

At the end of April and throughout the month of May, Fast, in a series of almost two dozen *Daily Worker* columns, was sharply critical of the Soviet Union and the American Communist Party, and at the same time abysmally illogical and defensive about both. He took the USSR to task for inventing a crime called "cosmopolitanism," a word Soviet cultural commissars used to condemn writers, Jewish writers in particular, as "victims of worldly and international sophistication"; faulted the Soviets for denying citizens the right to free travel; rejected the Communist use of "comparisons" to excuse their actions as the lesser of evils; ridiculed the Party's ban on Freud and psychoanalysis as bigotry and philistinism; and identified a distressing "record of mistakes, large and small, of dead-end roads, of wrong turnings and unhappy waystops."[65]

In almost every case, however, Fast, defended the CPUSA by reciting some variation of the theme: "the role of American communism was never coupled with dishonor." One has to ask here not only about the many Communists, including Howard Fast, who remained silent in the face of dishonorable, indeed horrific, actions, but also about the many who supported these actions, sometimes with great enthusiasm: the Moscow Show Trials, state terrorism in the guise of justice; the Nazi-Soviet nonaggression pact, in reality a Communist military alliance with fascism; and aid rendered in depriving others on the left, such as the Trotskyists, of civil liberties.

And again in almost every article, and despite his alleged contempt for justifying one's own injustices by pointing to the crimes of others, Fast continued to compare American "realities" to Russian "mistakes." Moreover, while saying he shrank from excusing evil in the name of "historical necessity," Fast insisted on telling "the story of [the] proud and happy people" of the Soviet Union, "who have done away with hunger, wretchedness and disease . . . the story of shining railroads built, of mighty grids of electrical power, of vast industries, of new roads and new cities, of great fleets of airplanes, of tractors and penicillin and hospitals, of schools and universities, of rippling wheat fields and herds of cattle." Fast concluded this elegy to Russian socialism in a stunning example of extreme denial: most of all, he wrote, we need to know the Soviet story "of millions of human minds set free," the story of the establishment and protection by Communism of "the holy right of man to knowledge."[66]

The most relevant and basic fact about the Soviet Union, Fast argued throughout, "was never Stalin, and it is not . . . Khrushchev—it is socialism and it is the Soviet people, who have made socialism their way of life. It was the mighty life force of socialism that destroyed Hitler and his irresistible army"—military success as the last refuge of Communist apologists—"and neither the mistakes of Stalin nor the villainy of Beria could alter that process." He had "believed in socialism for a long time," Fast said, and then strangely added, "I believe in it *now*, more firmly than ever."[67]

12

Things Fall Apart; the Left Cannot Hold

*I*n his very last column for the *Daily Worker,* on June 12, 1956, several days after the full text of Khrushchev's speech had been published in English, Fast was still saying he was not an enemy of the Soviet Union. He did finally admit, however, that while "I have written . . . bluntly and consistently of the injustice that exists" in America, "I failed miserably . . . in not exercising the same judgment toward the Soviet Union." He had learned as early as 1949 "that Jewish culture had been wiped out in Russia." This, he confessed, "I did not challenge." He had also known "that artists . . . writers and scientists were intimidated, but [had] accepted this as a necessity of Socialism."[1]

Fast's mea culpa was significantly compromised, however, by his continuing to argue that unlike what the Soviets did, "no similar . . . injustices carried out by capitalist governments . . . have been publicly admitted and corrected."[2] Moreover, he contended that any evils committed in the USSR were to be blamed not on the inherent nature of Marxist-Leninism, Communism, or totalitarianism, but on the "madness and weakness of a handful of Soviet leaders," including Khrushchev, who to Fast's great dismay and disgust continued Stalin's brutal policy of executing his political enemies.

In the spring and summer of 1956, Fast not only worried about the future of the Soviet experiment and the American Communist Party, which he was trying to help salvage after a mass exodus of membership. He was also worried about his own health. Fast had become desperate about "ever getting over" his increasingly immobilizing cluster headaches, and, as he told Polevoy, was "beginning to believe that [the headaches were] in very large measure the result of the past 11 years of unremitting tension and strain." Paul Robeson, Fast said, is also "at the moment very sick with an illness that is . . . the result of [suffering] the same conditions" of oppression, harassment, and humiliation. "The poor man," Fast said, perhaps as a way of "explaining" his own affliction, "has been the victim of severe and terrible depression, a specific result of the insane and murderous attacks against him for so long now." Thinking of how poorly his own work had been faring in the last six years, Fast told Polevoy that the "reaction of an artist to this systematic destruction of any ability on his part to create . . . always has bitter and terrible results." Fast did not think he was on the verge of death, he said, but of the Blue Heron Press's demise he was certain, "a fate shared by all progressive publishers in our country." The left, Fast said is "racked with persecution" and feels entirely "cut off."[3]

Fast recognized, however, that his isolation as well as his incessant pain resulted from living a lie for so long, and in his last *Daily Worker* column made a powerful promise: "Never again will I remain silent when I . . . recognize injustice," even if that injustice may be "wrapped in the dirty linen of expediency." It was this promise that prompted the American journalist Eugene Lyons, who had lived and worked in the USSR for six years, to write Fast an open letter urging him to "throw off the Communist weights from your heart and mind . . . to break out of the closed world of Communist alibis for unlimited horror."[4]

Lyons had caught the undertone of Fast's secret doubts about the true nature and future of the Soviet Union, and sensed the frustration Howard felt over the pettiness and anti-intellectualism of the CPUSA. Lyons was sympathetic, even calling Fast courageous; but he lashed out at Fast for inventing "childish alibis based on transparent falsehoods," and berated him for doing something the novelist had promised not to do: equating flaws in free societies with barbarous crimes in the Soviet Union. Lyons also pointed out that Fast had expressed deep disappointment over the absence in Khrushchev's speech of anything about the atrocities committed against the Jews; but why, Lyons wanted to know, hadn't Khrushchev, or for that matter Fast, made any reference to the brutality of forced collectivization in the Soviet Union; the hundreds of thousands killed as class enemies or enemies of the state; the construction of a system "of slave labor on a chilling scale?"

In the same *Worker* column Fast, contradicting himself, and apparently without compunction, wrote: "It is some comfort to say that I did not know the facts in the Khrushchev report." Lyons did not directly confront the novelist about this lie; instead, he told Howard to ask himself "*why* a man of your intelligence remained ignorant of facts known to the overwhelming majority of civilized men, facts accessible to you in any library." Lyons was asking a question troubling to many. After all, events in the Soviet Union had been reported extensively in innumerable books by scholars and foreign observers and in memoirs by refugee Soviet officials and former inmates of labor camps. Whatever the answer to Lyons's question—selective perception, willful repression, or the rationale of historical necessity—the journalist urged Fast to quit hoping for Soviet reform, to give up on Communism altogether, and not, like some of his comrades, to crawl "back into the fetid womb of the Party for surcease from the pain of thinking and the dread of acting."[5]

With this last point Lyons clearly hit an already throbbing nerve. Fast replied in a rage, accusing the journalist of encouraging him to become a professional informer for the FBI, to purge his "guilt" by committing the worst "infamy"—naming names. "I will never again remain silent while evil . . . men profane . . . man's hope," Fast said, but "[I won't] turn upon . . . those who have stood at my side during the darkest days this country ever knew." Honorable enough. Fast then muddies the waters by saying, "there was evidence . . . I closed my eyes to," while six lines later claiming, "I was never silent where injustice was being done."[6]

In his response to Lyons, Fast also committed two sins he had promised never to commit again: he fell into excusing evil as the cost of historical necessity and into justifying Soviet atrocities by comparing them to the same or "worse" behavior on the part of the United States. On the first score, Fast cited with approval the argument of a professor of economics who had "demonstrated" that a fundamental difference existed between the despotism of a Hitler and the tyranny of a Stalin. Hitler was unleashing one of the most destructive wars in human history, but Stalin was creating all the prerequisites for the development of a prosperous and free society.

Fast let this preposterous and simple-minded proposition stand as self-evidently correct, and then went on to commit sin number two. "Communists may have made . . . *mistakes*," Fast admits, but "it is not the . . . Communists

who are . . . exploding hydrogen bombs in the Pacific [or] the . . . Left who
nourish the . . . dope racket . . . print torrents of vicious comic books and sex
magazines . . .build bombers instead of schools . . . kill children with defec-
tive vaccines . . . [or] nurture hatred of the Negro people."[7] In his attempt to
paint the United States as bad as or worse than the Soviet Union, Fast failed
to say anything in his private correspondence or published articles about
the Supreme Court's 1954 desegregation ruling or about the triumph of Dr.
Martin Luther King Jr. and the civil rights movement in the Montgomery,
Alabama, bus boycott. Nor did he say anything later about the use of troops
to enforce integration in the schools of Little Rock, Arkansas, in 1957 or the
influential March on Washington in 1963.

Instead, Fast confidently asserted that he "know[s] what socialism means,"
and for him it derives not from Stalin but from "a lifetime of thinking" about
the teachings of the "ancient Jewish prophets," and of Jesus Christ, Thomas
Jefferson, and Karl Marx. Socialism is "brotherhood, love, reason, work with
dignity." It means "freedom of religion and speech and thought." And since
the "Soviet Union is a socialist land," Fast said. "it still has in me a friend."[8]
Lyons could hardly have disagreed with the liberal boilerplate prose of Fast's
definition of socialism, but he wrote yet another "open letter" correctly identifying Fast's avoidance of the key question: whether one who sought brotherhood, love, reason, and freedom, would not "more truly devote himself to
[his] ideals . . . even to socialism . . . by ending his subservience to the Soviet
oligarchy, the Communist party and a movement corrupted by power and
diseased by Machiavellian morals."[9] This Fast would indeed do; but not for
another six months.

Two days after reading Eugene Lyons's first "open letter" Fast got a personal one from twelve-year-old Rachel at summer camp. During music appreciation while a boy was putting on a Paul Robeson record, he had asked
the assembled campers if they knew what had "happened" to the singer.
Though no one said anything, Rachel, who knew how close her parents were
to Robeson, and who was herself "madly in love" with Paul, even to the point
of dreaming about him, was worried. The boy had said that "Paul was sent
out of the country for treason," and Rachel wanted to know, "Is that true? Is
it fair?" Write soon, she pleaded, "and give me an answer. I'm miserable."
Though sophisticated and exposed to far more politics than most children
her age, Rachel was still only a preteen. She added a postscript: "Having a
wonderful time. I like Rickey C. But don't tell his parents." She also doesn't

seem to have been bothered by not having had her question about Robeson answered in Howard and Bette's return letters; she did not ask again.[10]

Rachel was, however, worried about her father's headaches. "I haven't said anything about the headaches," Fast wrote back, "because like taxes, they seem always to be with me." Not a surprise given all he was struggling with in the summer of 1956. Even away at camp, Rachel could sense that there were difficulties at home. The political tumult within and around the Communist Party had only added to the enduring tension in her parents' troubled marriage, and Isabel Johnson may also have been back in the picture.[11] When Rachel discovered that her bunkmate was writing to her father at one address and her mother at another, she immediately assumed the girl's parents were separated, as hers had once been, and she wrote home asking about it. "Gee whiz!" her mother wrote back, "you kids are suspicious. Put your mind at ease. Marriage isn't such a tenuous affair."

Howard, however, wrote that because "mommy" had been "feeling a little low," he "bought [her] a scotch and soda at a bar" at three in the afternoon. "It was so sinful to drink in a bar" at that hour that "she immediately felt better." That "demonstrates the virtue of just a little sin," Rachel's father said, if "used properly."[12] An odd piece of advice to a young daughter at camp, but apparently not unusual for Fast. As Rachel put it later, "if only that had been the *strangest* of his fatherly suggestions."[13]

Here, though gauzy, there is a hint of sexual abuse. Rachel's younger brother Jonathan is fairly certain there was molestation. Rachel said she is not sure about this, but told me that her father used to "schlep her into the bathroom to watch him pee," until she was nine. That "I do remember," Rachel said, "and Mother coming into the bathroom and saying, 'Howard, that's enough. She's too old for that now.'" In his letters to his daughter, which were all addressed to Dinklehoffer, Dollink, Rukko, Rachpot, Gedinkus, or some variation thereof (all of which Rachel hated), Fast, though often condescendingly ironic, also demonstrated a feeling of unrequited love, and later jealousy.[14]

When she "noticed boys," her father "ridiculed the competition behind their back, sometimes to their faces. He did what he could to belittle them in my eyes," Rachel said. "Pre-puberty he was my hero. Post, he was not." Little wonder. Whenever Rachel was friendly to people her father thought inappropriate for reasons often mysterious, he called her a "whore." If not directly physically abused, Rachel was, as she put it, "certainly verbally abused."[15] Indeed, she "got the message from Father that [she] deserved to be abused," which is why when the time came she often "chose men who abused [her] psychologically and physically too." Or why for several years in her late twenties and early thirties she "turned away from men altogether."[16]

In the meantime, although the kids were at camp and the house quiet, Fast's early summer continued to be tumultuous. As he followed the first and only open dialogue conducted by the *Daily Worker* in its history, he slowly moved away from defending the Soviet Union and drew increasingly closer to that portion of the Party urging a clean break. But in July, Moscow, irritated by the nature and substance of what was appearing in the leading Communist paper in America, made it clear that the boundaries of permissible dissent had been crossed. In response the *Worker* failed to follow through on its promised editorial analysis of the various opinions that had come its way. Instead it carried an apology from William Foster full of rhetoric and delusionary predictions—based on a resolution issued from the Kremlin—of a new and glorious period of accomplishment in Russia led by the Communist Party of the Soviet Union (CPSU).[17]

Fast himself got a scolding letter from a Soviet editor who knew all "about the repercussions in your country of the events in USSR connected with the liquidation of personality cult that had formerly existed here." These repercussions, B. Leontyev said sternly, "have not always been of a *correct*, wise and sober nature. We [however] are now full of enthusiasm, [and] still convinced in the truth of our ideas, still surer of the great advantages of our Soviet socialist system." A few weeks later the national committee of the American Party (CPUSA) confirmed Foster's position: "We believe that the resolution of the CPSU provides a convincing answer to the Big Business enemies of socialism, who claim that the gross *mistakes* under Stalin's leadership are inherent in socialism. . . . We . . . are convinced that the Soviet Union under the leadership of the CPSU is moving ahead to a new period of unprecedented Socialist progress."[18]

For approximately three months beginning in July (when he stopped paying dues or attending Party meetings) through the end of September, Fast, as part of a reformist faction led by John Gates, sat watching and agonizing. Gates claims that he told Eugene Dennis, the general secretary of the CPUSA, and other Party leaders of Fast's deep personal crisis and begged them to talk to him. Apparently no leader thought it important enough to talk to the one writer of international reputation still loyal to the Communist Party.[19] Fast looked on ruefully as the old guard, led by Party Chairman Foster, resisted de-Sovietization and tried to outmaneuver those who favored an American Communist Party with a more independent flavor.

Dennis and his followers, after a period of hesitation about the Foster position, yielded, and to Fast's dismay, a Dennis-Foster coalition regained control of a Communist Party that for a short time had discussed becoming an indigenous radical party. Those who had written to the *Daily Worker* calling for an end to CPUSA conventions that merely rubber-stamped Soviet policy positions on nearly all matters gave up, and along with thousands of others left what they now saw as an irrevocably disgraced and incorrigibly rigid Communist Party.[20]

Although he had made no official announcement, the rumor that Howard Fast was no longer an active Communist spread quickly within Party circles at home and abroad. At the end of July, Stefan Heym wrote from East Germany to say that he was "disquieted" because "in the last few days, three . . . different people have approached me with the same question: 'What's the matter with Howard Fast?' My . . . answer was: 'What should be the matter with him? What's the matter with you that you ask?'"

Heym guessed correctly that the question stemmed from reports in the Western press concerning Fast's reaction to the Khrushchev speech and its aftermath, and he asked Fast to send him copies of the *Daily Worker* in which his "contributions to the general discussion . . . appeared." Heym who saw the Twentieth Party Congress as "a most interesting and . . . salutary development," suspected that he would take issue with the opinions voiced in Fast's columns. "Things do look a little bit different from Berlin's Eastside than they do from New York's," Heym said, "and so my views might be of . . . interest."[21]

It took three weeks for a troubled Fast to formulate an appropriate response to his friend, who believed that with the Khrushchev speech the Soviet Union had taken a giant step toward reform. "It seems [I] have been misquoted all over the world by [people at] the Voice of America who would like nothing better than to boast that I became anti-Soviet," Fast wrote, but "nothing of the sort is the case!" He went on to say, however, that "the Left in America has done itself irreparable damage by [its] refusal to be in any way critical of the policies of the Communist Party or the Soviet Union. . . . I believe this has done damage as well to the Soviet Union, for a voice of criticism and a voice of protest need not interfere with unity and can also be a source

of strength and health."[22] These statements made to Heym, unaccompanied
by any of the columns the East German had requested, foreshadowed where
Fast would be only months later: openly anti-Communist, loudly anti-Soviet.

Heym told Fast in October that he had "no doubts" about his American
friend personally or his "integrity and . . . sense of balance." But he reminded
Fast that "this thing is much bigger than just one man." It is "a qualitative
change and leap forward in the Socialist half of the world . . . and it's going
to change your corner of the globe, too." Fast was not convinced. He told
Heym that it was "very comforting to hear the kind of hope you express
[because] here at home we have all too little of it." Even those of us who for
a time looked forward to the "'giant strides into the future' that you speak
about," Fast wrote, are now "limited by our own sense of tragedy." Without
being explicit about the victory of the pro-Soviet old guard in the CPUSA,
Fast confessed his fear that "the Communist movement [in the US] had been
struck a mortal blow from which it will never recover."[23]

Fast thought he too might not recover. "Here I sit," he complained, "42
years old, 25 years of literary effort behind me, and apparently at the end of
the road. It would seem that I have no place in my own country, no one to
publish my books, no one to distribute them, no one to read them. What
do I do [now] and how do I start life [again] at 42?" Fast still believed that
socialism was historically inevitable. "We can still see mankind's future very
clearly," he told Heym, but "it is our own that is so difficult to see."[24]

If there is such a thing as a second mortal blow, it came late in October
1956 when Soviet tanks rolled into Hungary to suppress a rebellion against
the country's Stalinist puppets—men who had since the end of WWII participated in the full spectrum of totalitarian methods: forced collectivization,
unwarranted arrests, torture, terrorism by show trials, complete with Zionist
and fascist conspiracies. It took Moscow several weeks to decide upon its
course of action, but when it did, it exposed the Soviet system as imperialist
and antidemocratic, and by shooting down unarmed students in the streets,
fully committed to rule by brute force.[25] Fast was finally convinced that it
mattered little who sat at the top of the system; it was the system itself that
was irredeemably rotten. He told himself he was finished for good as a Party
member. The CPUSA was not finished for good, but it was reduced to sham-
bles. Twenty thousand Party members at the beginning of 1956 became nine
thousand by the summer of 1957, and a mere three thousand by the summer
of 1958. And when the *Daily Worker,* which initially supported the Hungar-

ian rebels, finally, unlike many European Communist journals, supported the suppression of the uprising, the newspaper had to cease publication for lack of subscribers.[26]

What little hope, if any, Fast still had left for the "rehabilitation" of the Soviet Union was drowned in the barbarous behavior of the USSR, which with its invasion of Hungary, a member of the Warsaw Pact, achieved the dubious distinction of becoming the only state in modern history to go to war against a member of its own alliance. Fast openly opposed the attack on Hungary. The American Communist Party, however, under the leadership of Foster and Dennis, could not bring itself to issue an unconditional condemnation of Soviet military intervention. Instead, a watered-down compromise resolution was adopted, satisfying no one.

Fast's friend and correspondent Stefan Heym was unhappy that Howard spoke in opposition to the Soviet action—even if only among his dwindling circle of associates—and he chastised him for failing to see that the rebels in Hungary were not "freedom-fighters"—but counterrevolutionaries, landlords, and antisemites who within a week had "liquidated [the] workers' power" and brought fascism back. It was four more years before Fast and Heym wrote to one another again—one final civil, but quite cool, exchange in 1960 about the defunct Blue Heron Press and Heym's publishing rights.[27]

In late November 1956, Fast accepted an invitation from Brandeis University to share the stage with Irving Howe, who was teaching at the school, for a presentation on politics and the novel. Inexplicably, Fast put himself in the position of defending a proposition he no longer believed in fully: socialist realism, Stalinism straight down the line.[28] According to the student-moderator Jeremy Larner, Fast rambled on forever about "something he called scientific socialism." Howe grew impatient and asked Larner by way of a note how long he was going to "let this thing go on." Moments later, Larner, who was literally dozing, was jolted awake by Howe bellowing at Fast: "You have blood on your hands!" Fast, stunned, stopped speaking; Howe rose, admitted that he had been waiting ten years to eviscerate Fast, and "attacked him hard." Some in the auditorium felt sorry for Fast and accused Howe of having kicked around a helpless man. "They didn't understand the passion," Howe wrote later, "the Moscow trials, the murder of the Jewish poets and writers." Fast professed himself scandalized, and claimed, ironically, given his own caustic rhetoric over the years, that he'd never heard such invective before.[29]

Weeks before Fast appeared at Brandeis, he had in his own mind dis-
sociated himself from the CP. Fast's private decision became public by a
circuitous route. *Fortune* magazine, in preparation for an article about the
Communist movement in America, successfully pressed Fast for an interview. In the article that appeared in January 1957, Fast was featured in only
one short paragraph, but it proved explosive. In response to a question about
"hypocrisy" and "sincerity," Fast recalled with some chagrin that he had
once told a university audience that if Stalin were to take any actions contrary
to the best interest of the Soviet people, he could be immediately removed
from office. At that time, Fast said, "'I firmly believed [it].'" This admission,
as revealing as it was of Fast's naivety or dishonesty, was far less important
than Fast's having been correctly identified in the magazine as "no longer a
member of the party."[30]

On the day the article appeared, Harry Schwartz, a contributing editor at
the *New York Times,* whom Fast had recently characterized as "hysterical,"
phoned Howard wanting to know whether *Fortune* magazine had it right.
Fast's affirmative answer stunned Schwartz. Didn't the novelist know that
this was a story of international significance? Given "all that was happening
in the world," Fast said, it had not really occurred to him; but he agreed to
be interviewed by Schwartz on the condition that he'd have the right to a
final edit.

The story appeared on page one of the *New York Times* under the headline: "REDS RENOUNCED BY HOWARD FAST." Though no longer pro-Soviet or
pro-Communist, Fast also wanted to make it clear that he was not going to
become a professional ex-Communist. He could no longer "work and write
in the Communist movement, " Fast said, or submit to Party discipline; but
"I am neither anti-Soviet nor anti-Communist." Two major things brought
him to his present position he said: "Khrushchev did not end his speech with
a promise of reform," and there were revelations of widespread antisemitism
in the Soviet Union.

He had always known a "little" about antisemitism in the USSR, Fast admitted, but regrettably he had "repressed his doubts." That became less
possible in April 1956 when the Yiddish-language Communist newspaper,
the *Folks-Stimme,* revealed the extent of the murder of Jews and repression
of Jewish culture in the Soviet Union. "It was not an easy thing to live with,"
Fast said. In reality, however, he had lived with knowing *much more* than a
"little" about antisemitism in the USSR for at least eight years. Since 1949 at

the very latest, after his conversation with Alexander Fadeyev in Paris, Fast was aware of the virtual war going on against Jews in Russia. He may have been troubled, but his choice was to keep silent and remain loyal to the Communist Party even as the atrocities were being committed.[31]

Fast told Schwartz, "I am not ashamed of anything I have done. I fought against war, Negro oppression and social injustice." He also said he would neither repudiate nor return the Stalin International Peace Prize awarded him in 1953. He told a second interviewer, even in the face of all that Fast now knew, that to disown the prize would be to reject "the struggle for peace." In any case, Fast said, in a sentence remarkable even for him, "Not only was Stalin dead when the prize was given . . . [but] I knew nothing of the real Stalin as revealed subsequently in the Khrushchev report." Fast not only defended keeping his medal and the $25,000 prize money, he went on, even at this late date, to give his interlocutor a review of Soviet accomplishments, clearly implying that whatever the Stalinists had done might very well have been historically necessary. After all, Fast said, "The very fact that forty years ago there was in Russia a population of the most oppressed and poverty-stricken and backward human beings on earth bears stunning contrast to what we [now] read every day. . . . We read of thousands of doctors graduating yearly—most of them women; we read of thousands of engineers, of a whole literate population, of books published by the millions, of cities built and rebuilt, of ever increasing production. One no longer hear[s] of famine or plague in the Soviet Union."[32]

The reaction to Fast's unburdening himself in the *New York Times,* and directly to a leading Cold Warrior like Schwartz no less, was swift, but mixed. "I've no doubt the furies will descend upon you as a result of your statement . . . this morning," one acquaintance wrote, "I think its publication was unfortunate, and I would not have taken the step you did, [but] I . . . value our friendship and hope it will continue." Edith Marzani also sent a note, saying, "The *Times* article made me feel very sad that I had not contacted you in this period." Her husband Carl had tried, she said, but had found Fast distant. "Remember dear Howie, you are not alone. . . . Call on us if it will help—call on me if you want to."[33]

After reading Fast's interview with the *New York Times,* the editors of *Masses and Mainstream,* to which Fast was a frequent contributor, asked him to state his position more fully, and he agreed. In an essay called "My Decision," Fast emphasized ideas and themes he had been attempting to

bring into confluence with one another for nearly twenty years: Judaism and
Christianity, love and violence, and the religious roots of his progressive vision. As he had done many times before, Fast attributed his commitment to
egalitarianism to the "prophetic teaching of Judaism, the love and brotherhood of man preached by Isaiah, and the morality, in terms of the poor and
oppressed, of Jesus Christ."

He included two examples that he thought would illuminate the Chris-
tian-Jewish synthesis and the love-violence connection: Rabbi Akiva emphasized love as a central principle of the Torah, and yet, Fast writes, "it was this
same gentle Aki[v]a who supported Bar Kochba in his glorious, pre-doomed
revolt against Rome." Fast also argued that Jesus, even as he paraphrased Le-
viticus and other parts of the Torah to preach love, "preached more against
temporal tyranny . . . it was precisely this that made him Christ."

Fast knew that his nonscientific idealism and the transcendental part of
his explanation, which emphasized a mystical bond of love and suffering
between all peoples, would be anathema to a Communist Party steeped
in an incorrigible atheism. So, he said more explicitly that he and others
had realized long before the "secret speech" that "something was tragically
wrong in the world communist movement." Communists knew, he said, that
"Jewish culture had disappeared in the Soviet Union," that horrific crimes
had been committed by the Stalinist regime, "and that capital punishment"
was widely used in the USSR as an instrument of state terror.[34]

But if *they* knew—if *he* knew—the difficult question again raises its ugly
head: why did Fast stay in a movement so closely associated with the Soviet
Union for so long? Any answer would be incomplete, but it would have to
include the fact that in the Party there was just too much for Fast to give up:
the adulation and respect of the Soviet Union and the Eastern Bloc, even as
his stock dropped in his own country; very high regard and status within
the American Communist cadre if not within the leadership at the very top;
his like-minded Communist friends and the exciting social and political life
they shared; and not least, fourteen years of intoxicating ideological and
emotional investment in a cause—one that he kept thinking might even be
rescued with a little more patience. Fast waited in agonized silence, hoping
for reform, he said, only to learn of continued antisemitism and executions,
and of slaughter in Hungary and Poland. Finally, he had come to say, perhaps
even believe, that "within the very structure and historical development of
[all] Communist Parties, as we know them in recent years, there is an almost

incurable antithesis to the socialist democracy which they name as their ultimate goal."[35]

That he was finally able to admit the facts concerning injustice elsewhere, Fast said, "does not close my eyes or my heart. It only opens both more. I intend to continue my solidarity with all people of good will in America, communist and non-communist, who fight injustice and treasure the precious, the infinitely precious, traditions of Jefferson, Franklin, Lincoln and Douglass—to mention only four of the many great who built the foundations of that most splendid thing, American Democracy."[36]

The editors commenting on Fast's essay conceded the justice of his charges against the Soviet Union and the CPUSA on every point, but then wrote something Fast had stopped saying: "contradictions" and "mistakes" were not "inherent" in Communism or the Soviet government; indeed, they were already being repaired through "fundamental and long-awaited criticism."[37] The editors believed that after a period of reflection, Fast would change his mind about leaving the movement, and would be warmly welcomed back into the fold of the Party. But some of the other commentaries on Fast's essay, all by Communists, suggested that the prediction was dead wrong.

Those such as John Gates who were still trying to reconstruct an American-directed party of "social democrats" were sorry to see Fast go. But those who sided with the toe-the-line Foster-Dennis coalition heaped only scorn upon their ex-comrade, mostly for his naively high expectations, but also for his "misunderstanding" of the nature of revolution. Revolutions, several said in their commentaries, take long to complete, are messy things, and only by looking beyond the mistakes and the inhumanity of the still unfolding Bolshevik Revolution could Fast get the bigger picture. There are, said Louis Harap, a literary editor at *Jewish Life,* a Communist magazine, not only atrocities that must be remembered, but "facts" of real accomplishment that "must figure in any overall evaluation." And Herbert Aptheker, a specialist on black and American history and an enthusiastic supporter of the Soviet invasion of Hungary, paraphrased Jefferson, one of Fast's "heroes": There are "difficulties and dangers" in revolution, and one should "not expect to be transported from despotism to liberty in a feather bed."[38]

Joseph Starobin, another respondent to Fast's essay, had worked as Moscow correspondent for the *Daily Worker* in the early fifties, and had no illusions about Stalinism or about the possibilities for reform in a "new" Soviet

Union. As early as 1953, he had urged his American comrades to develop an institutional and ideological identity separate from the Kremlin. Knowing Fast very well, Starobin wrote one of the more insightful responses to his former comrade's resignation and *cri de coeur*. Starobin believed that Fast had "pursued a reckless romance with the bitch-goddess . . . success," which was as alive and well in the Communist Party as it was in mainstream capitalist America. In the Party—the party of the glamorous high-living Hollywood writers, the party of the confident, intellectually sophisticated Communists at the Office of War Information—Fast had been able to rub shoulders with the smart, the famous, the rich—indeed, could pursue his own twin goals of wealth and fame, and at the same time say something serious and politically leftist in his work. In the Communist Party Fast found not only respect and critical admiration, but idolization. And by 1948, more so abroad than at home. But, as Starobin said, the Soviets, after "excommunicating" Farrell, Steinbeck, and Hemingway, made too much of Fast because they needed a writer who would tell the Russian masses what the Party needed them to hear about America, what it was "really like."[39]

Fast heard only wonderful things about his work from the East, and reveled in what he should have resisted, if he were to grow as an artist. And so it took him too long to discover in the American Communist Party its destructive "narrowing of approach and purpose." Nor could Fast accept criticism from any quarter, criticism that might have helped shape him into a better writer, and even a better person. "We all let it happen," Starobin admitted. "But how is a man to be helped who is not listening, and who is not listening because he hasn't stopped talking?" And hasn't stopped talking because he knows the truth about everything and commits to those truths absolutely. "For example," Starobin explained, "when Howard concludes his outcry . . . with a ringing testimonial to 'that most splendid thing, American Democracy,' . . . I feel like shouting: 'Hold it . . . here we go again.'" Yes, Starobin said, democracy *is* very much "the terrain for great battles to come. But let us talk about it with a small 'd.' We do not need anything in capital letters any more."[40]

Fast's decision came as a terrible disappointment to his favorite Soviet correspondents, Izakov and Polevoy, two men Howard considered friends. Boris Izakov, who had translated several of Fast's books and was in possession of a photo of Howard and Bette, inscribed by Howard on the back "To Boris Izakov, my other self," was "hurt . . . deeply." Fast wanted to continue correspondence and friendship with Izakov, but worried that the Russian writer's "fear" might prevent him from responding. "Such a notion . . . offends me," Izakov wrote back. "It shows how little you . . . [in the US] know about what is going on in our country. . . . Pity . . . that you are unable to visit" instead of seeing us "through the eyes of Harry Schwartz."

Stalin is gone, Izakov said, and a "frank recognition of everything unsatisfactory in our past is the best guarantee it won't come back." And then in a pair of statements, one doubtful, the other illogical, Izakov reminded Fast that "Socialism is built in the Soviet Union. . . . That means the Soviet Union is a bearer of progress and progress without the Soviet Union is inconceivable."[41]

Polevoy, too, was hurt and insulted by Howard's desertion under fire, and felt certain that Fast's heroes—Gideon Jackson, Spartacus, or George Washington—would not have quit the way Howard did in the face of setbacks. "The main thing now," Polevoy believed, "is to strengthen ties between writers East and West," which cannot be accomplished by "quibbling and mutual recrimination." Polevoy "firmly believe[d] that . . . both of us . . . have much to do in the precious fight for peace and progress." We both have children, he reminded Fast, and asked him if he didn't think that "in itself," this was "a common platform on which to work together for peace?"[42]

Fast wrote back immediately, assuring Polevoy that he treasured him and Izakov as friends, as Bette did, and that "this must not change." But Fast said plaintively that he had "raised questions" with Polevoy, "points of heart-breaking life and death significance; are there no answers?" Can it "do more harm [now], to tell us why Jewish writers were murdered by your Government?" And why, Fast wanted to know, did *Pravda* try to influence the inner struggle of he CPUSA, supporting Foster and his faction? "These are not good men," Fast said after having fawned over Foster publicly for years. "They are sick, power drunk men," he insisted, "who are divorced from [American] reality." And finally Howard asked, why "did you tell us here in New York that the Yiddish writer Kvitko was alive and well . . . when he was among those executed [in 1952] and long since dead?' Fast pleaded with Polevoy to tell him and the world the "terror" is finished. "Tell me that anti-Semitism is over . . . with. . . . Let the words fly!" Howard thought it not too late to remain Boris's friend. "Can I?" he asked. "It is up to you."[43]

Polevoy, opening with "Well Howard!" rather than his usual "Dear Howard," responded with indignation to the "tone" of Fast's letter and "some of the statements in it." He classified Howard as formerly a "fiery revolutionary," and now "a nervous and panic-stricken man." Polevoy, wittingly or not, admitted that he had known all along of the crimes committed in the USSR, when he blamed all the "hard and tragic" events on Stalin and the "cult of the individual"; pinned antisemitism entirely on Beria; and told Fast that oppression of the Jews was no longer possible in the changed Soviet Union. He reminded Howard that the slandered physicians of the infamous "Doctors' Plot"—two of whom had died in prison!—were, unlike the Rosenbergs in America, "publicly rehabilitated" with all their rights restored.

"It was a blow to me," Polevoy continued, that "you have left the Communist Party." But "is it necessary or dignified," he asked, "to throw stones at a house you just left after [a] quarrel with its hosts?" He wondered if Howard thought it "easy to accept an accusation of being a liar from a man you consider your friend." Think it over, Polevoy said, "Is this OK, old pal? Ask . . . your nice and well-balanced Bette whom I always called your best friend." He had no doubt that she "will confirm that it is no good," and ended by sending "heartfelt greetings" and "Best wishes to the kids." Absent from his sign-off was his usual "Yours sincerely, Boris Polevoy." The correspondence was over between them. But eager to keep himself in the mind of what he hoped would be an increasingly receptive American public, Fast, with no request of permission from Polevoy, had his March exchange with the Soviet writer published in the magazine section of the *New York Times*.[44]

Fast also parted ways with Renaud de Jouvenal, his French friend of fifteen years. "The Khrushchev business," Fast wrote to him "hit us like a bolt out of the blue." What eleven "years of terror and persecution [by the United States] could not do to us, this [speech] seems to have done." Unfortunately, Fast said, we here "are not in the situation of a great movement like yours with its hundreds of thousands of working class supporters." We were only a handful, Fast continued, "who had nothing left but our integrity, and overnight that appears to have been shattered."[45]

Jouvenal, apparently irritated by Fast's whining, asked Howard if he thought that "the K report was swallowed [in France] without difficulty?" Published in the bourgeois paper *Le Monde,* the speech "was exploited by all our enemies: our traitors, the reactionary press and the socialists." But the French Communists are still standing, Jouvenal said, unbowed, and ready to keep struggling. In attempting to clarify the difference between the reactions to the K speech by the Americans, who were "shattered," and the French, "who were not taken off our feet," Jouvenal wrote that the French proletariat was not only quite large, but "the best politically educated working class in a capitalist country." Moreover, Jouvenal added, French proletarians were part of a large self-aware working class culture led by "good Marxist thinkers . . . firm in their beliefs." In the United States, on the other hand, as Howard had admitted, the CP was a tiny fraction of the electorate, mostly made up of middle-class men and women. This is why the politically educated French workers, 20 percent of the electorate, stuck in a class system more rigidly stratified than that in America, cast ballots for the CP throughout the postwar period. And why, Jouvenal said, the Italians for similar reasons had done the same.[46]

Whatever tensions existed between Jouvenal and Fast might have eased had the Frenchman not gone on to tell his Jewish American correspondent that he was "quite shocked" that he had chosen such a time to speak of the "Jewish question" in the Soviet Union. In France, Jouvenal said, we call this "howling with the wolves." He apologized for shocking Fast with such talk, but he said, with some condescension, "I would appreciate your opinion."[47] Many months after Fast failed to respond, Jouvenal, in *Lettres Francaises,* launched a particularly foul attack on Howard for having discovered in America, "Freedom," and "Democracy." M. A. deJong, a friend of Fast's living in France, sent Howard this news with a warning to be careful. "De Jouvenal says he's got a lot of letters you wrote him and that it would be a 'mauvaise blague' [an offensive joke, not at all funny] to publish them." The right thing, if not the best thing to do, deJong wrote, would be to go to Paris, "ask for Mr. de Jouvenal and kick off his balls—although I doubt whether he has any."[48]

Given the many distressing letters Fast received from Europe and the Soviet Union, he was glad to have had a more gentle response to his public statements about the Party and the USSR from his long-term friend and correspondent Albert Maltz. From Mexico, Maltz wrote Fast that he not only agreed with much of what Howard said, he endorsed it. "But so far," wrote Maltz with his usual insight, "I don't think the sum of the parts add up to your total position." Apparently, Maltz was reacting to Fast's switch to an open anti-Soviet and anti-Communist position only six weeks or so after he denied holding such a position.

Perhaps Howard had learned since his interview with Harry Schwartz that even more executions were taking place under Khrushchev or that a general regime of terror was continuing.[49] Perhaps he came to feel that without denouncing the USSR and Communism fully and publicly, he would lose his opportunity to regain an American audience. Whatever it was that did it, the almost forgiving tone toward the Soviet Union in the *Times* interview was entirely missing from Fast's later articles. Now that Fast had left the Party, he was no doubt signaling his desire to get back into the literary mainstream. Only months earlier he had written desperately to Stefan Heym asking, "What do I do [now] and how do I start life [again] at 42?" Fast could not tolerate a future of having "no place in my own country, no one to publish my books, no one to distribute them, no one to read them."[50]

A long and pretentious letter from his friends Scott and Helen Nearing was full of advice for Fast about his future. "An urban industrial . . . society cannot survive," the Nearings wrote, "unless it is collectivized, planned and effectively coordinated." And "if you Howard, are not satisfied with the techniques . . . thus far developed in the Soviet Union," you must "dedicate the remaining years of your life to working out a better alternative than any thus far proposed."[51] Fast ignored the Nearings and instead dedicated his remaining years to doing what he did best, writing. Indeed, already by July he had finished a new novel about Moses, and before the year was out he published a scathing anti-Communist, anti-Soviet memoir.

In the meantime, Fast, in August 1957 was subject to withering criticism from the USSR. In the *Literatnaya Gazeta* (Literary gazette), the organ of the Soviet Writers Union (upon whose board sat Polevoy and Izakov), Fast was denounced as "a deserter under fire," a slanderer, an opportunist, a bourgeois nationalist, and a "bellicose reactionary agent . . . of Zionism." Worse would come later, but to this early name-calling, Fast responded by telling Harry Schwartz that he had "made no statement of fact about Russia which did not come from Communist sources," including material given to him by representatives of East European countries "even more monstrous" than the picture that was painted by Khrushchev.[52]

Despite his being defamed, Fast was glad to be back in the news; and he jumped at a request to be interviewed three days later on Dave Garroway's *Today Show*. In his first appearance on TV in ten years, Fast said he did not believe in "the cult of anti-Communism," but thought that the CPUSA should "go out of business." When Garroway asked if he still considered himself something of a Communist, Fast said, "when you break with the Communist Party it's a terrible and a soul-splitting break, but you break, you break clean, there is no part time after that." In that case, Garroway asked, "Do you feel like a lonesome, disillusioned man?"

FAST: No, not disillusioned. I'm not lonesome, I never felt like a pariah, I never felt like an outcast.

G: And yet, you are, you know, in your own country.

F: No, no, no, no I'm not.

G: Among many millions of Americans.

F: No, no I wouldn't say that.[53]

Fast's anxious protesting suggested doubt about how he stood with the American people. He was struggling, at least privately, not only with the need to come to terms with his loss of faith (the Party as religion), loss of warmth and security (the Party as family), and loss of identity (Party as community). Believing that people who remained loyal to the USSR would spurn them, Bette and Howard preemptively broke many relationships; but inexplicably, they also backed away from all their comrades, many of them close friends who left the Party when they did. Most, they never saw again. Bette, a great cook and entertainer who loved to have "famous people" around, was devastated. Howard muddled through until over the following years, the couple established a new circle of friends and reconnected with others from the past. He picked up again with his old traveling companion and correspondent Devery Freeman, for example; and the actor Paul Stewart and his wife were also back in touch.[54]

On August 30, the very morning after his appearance on TV, Fast was questioned by the FBI, and then several more times through September 16. The Justice Department had been interested in talking with Fast ever since his resignation from the Party was made public on February 1. There was hesitation about interviewing him, however, because the bureau believed he was "still a convinced Communist." It was thought that Fast's "past history of antagonism before Congressional Committees, his outspoken criticism of Government Agencies, particularly the FBI would militate against an interview with him at this time." Hoover also felt that as a writer Fast might turn a contact by the Bureau into "an embarrassing situation." Though no interview was undertaken, a handwritten note at the bottom of the memo, signed by "J. Edgar," advised: "follow this and reconsider when situation appears more likely to be productive."

How "productive" the subsequent interviews with Fast were for the FBI is difficult to judge. Fast said that when he talked with agents at his home in New Jersey for about two hours, there was nothing he "could . . . possibly tell them about the Communist Party that they didn't [already] know." But soon thereafter Fast apparently called the FBI and asked, "Am I in danger?" One agency memo explains that Fast "asked this question" because "he was in the process of writing . . . an 'explosive' book exposing the Communist Party . . . and his friends have advised him to be careful."[55]

Although the FBI told Fast to go to the "local police" about any danger he might be in, they did question him again later, and while he would not name names, he did say that his nearly completed book "will assist the anti-Communist cause." He even invited agents to come to his home to pick up a set of galleys. They interviewed him there in Teaneck and reported that "Fast and his wife were friendly [and] agreeable re future conversations." Fast allegedly told the agents that "the strong grip and reign of terror that Khrushchev is conducting is more terrible than Stalin's" and that he "considers Khrushchev a man who is vain enough to start a world war within the next six months to rally the Russian people to his support. The uprising in Hungary, the strikes in Poland and the discontent expressed in East Germany may influence Khrushchev to make desperate moves for his own benefit."[56] If these agents have reported his remarks accurately, it would appear that Fast had become not only a Cold Warrior, but something of a provocateur, wittingly or otherwise.

Fast also told agents many other interesting things, bits of information that seem designed to curry favor with the bureau or its director. On the Rosenberg case, for example, Fast said he had thought at first that Julius and Ethel were innocent, but now had serious reservations. He suggested that even defense attorney Emanuel Bloch thought the couple was "in some way involved" in spying. And while Fast was diligent in naming no unknown names, it was his opinion, he said, that Benjamin Davis Jr., a leading African American Communist and staunch supporter of the power-hungry Foster, was a "crackpot." He is a man of "violent nature," Fast said, and capable of drastic action, including doing Howard physical harm for his recent denunciations. Fast also admitted that he had always had very little regard for

Eugene Dennis, whom he thought either very stupid—or an undercover FBI agent looking to wreck the Party.[57]

Even though Fast was clearly invested in cleaning his own slate, he bravely suggested dispensing with the pending trials of Communist leaders and granting amnesty to those still in jail. This action, Fast said, would help deflate the propaganda of the Soviets and the American Communist Party. It would also, he thought, make it easier for CP members to resign or drift away from the Party, just as many Jews had done when they "discovered" the extent of antisemitism in the Soviet Union. Indeed, Fast believed that the CP would soon have no influence in American Jewish circles. Already, he said, no Jewish Communist can give a speech before a Jewish audience in the United States without being insulted or severely bombarded with questions regarding antisemitism in Russia. The FBI was apparently delighted with this information, which one report suggested could be used as "an excellent psychological weapon" in connection with wavering Jewish Party members![58]

Although as we have seen, Fast never went so far as to inform, his cooperation with Hoover's agents was a giant step back into acceptability. Merely talking to the FBI, of course, would not complete a process of reintegration, which required a more substantial explanation from Fast of his "mistakes," perhaps even a shaming ritual of the kind he had suffered, and imposed on others, in the Communist Party. He cultivated a friendship throughout 1957 with Schwartz of the *New York Times;* in October, he agreed to another TV interview.[59] NBC host Martin Agronsky immediately wanted to know if Fast had gone through life in the Party "with blinders, self-imposed." "Of course I did," Fast replied; "you begin to believe, you find yourself trapped in believing . . . unable to shake loose from . . . an arrogant, stupid, Victorian, terroristic dictatorship of thought." It works, Fast said, "through the application of censorship by the writer [on] himself, because he knows that punishment will follow his violating the [Party's] decrees of censorship."[60]

Despite having made changes in at least two of his plays at the Party's behest, and having earlier admitted that after *Freedom Road,* cultural commissars were always in his mind as he wrote, Fast told Agronsky that he didn't accept censorship. Apparently Agronsky looked puzzled, because Fast quickly said, "This isn't the place for a detailed story of my struggles . . . within this organization to write as I pleased." But he did explain that while Communist leaders in the United States did not have the power to punish by torture or execution, "as we saw in Russia," it did have the intimidating power of "excommunication." To "a sincere and devoted Communist" like himself, Fast said yet again, "expulsion was almost as bad as death—and sometimes worse." So how did Fast, long since bereft of his non-Communist friends, feel, Agronsky asked, now that the Communists had excommunicated him by calling him a "slanderer" and a "capitalist beast at work?" Fast, either truly dejected or seeking sympathy, answered simply, "I feel rotten."[61]

Soon after this interview, Fast heard from Lee Hays, the folksinger and songwriter best known for his work with Pete Seeger and the Weavers and for cowriting "If I Had a Hammer," the unofficial anthem of the Communist Party. Hays remembered Fast as a practitioner of "Stalin worship," and he berated himself for not having tried to get Howard over that infatuation much earlier. "What troubled me about your [TV] interview," Hays wrote, "was the inwardness—the personal suffering—and sorrow—almost a feeling that the whole thing was a conspiracy aimed at you Howard." He asked Fast if it wasn't better "to rise above the storm" than to "be so completely shattered?" Socialism "*is* the only possible form of decent life," Hays said, but "To hell with parties—parties and politicians the world over are corrupt, absolutely." He advised Howard to start over by getting "out from under yourself, and laugh a little at yourself, as Mark Twain would have done, and figure out what should be done in the future."[62]

What Fast did in the future, without dropping his socialist beliefs entirely, was to turn himself back into a best-selling author and ultimately into a multimillionaire. In the meantime there was a bit more public backpedaling to do. According to his FBI file, Fast had sometime in February 1957 received a call from a "Hollywood friend" about making a film based on *Freedom Road,* something Howard had been longing to do since 1943. Fast reminded the filmmaker that he had been convicted of contempt in 1947 and had "taken the Fifth" six years later. "The chances of making a picture then," his friend predicted, "are slim."[63]

What was to be done? Fast reiterated that under no circumstances would he name names. Hoping, however, after his revelatory interview with the FBI in February 1957, that he could keep his honor and make films, too, he offered to talk to the Senate Internal Security Subcommittee (SISS) "off the record."[64] The counsel for the SISS, Robert Morris, didn't think an informal chat a very satisfactory arrangement. Fast, still under subpoena, was then ordered to appear before HUAC in April; that hearing was soon put off until July, and then postponed indefinitely.[65]

Fast decided that his only way to get a return ticket to an American reader-ship lay in a more public, more explicit anti-Communist, anti-Soviet state-ment. Despite having told Eugene Lyons six months earlier that he would not "write books about the devil that deceived me," Fast proposed to do just that in a letter to Praeger Publishers at the end of February. He told Praeger that he was uniquely qualified to write the book to "bury" the Communist Party because "no other writer in America has been through what I have." Fast pushed his proposal by implying that if we don't put out a message like the one he could write, and if we don't "begin to understand what happened in the Soviet Union and what forces in the communist movement led to this situation, we can very neatly dig our own grave."[66]

Fast got his contract. But even before *The Naked God* was published, a long article appeared in *Prospectus,* a short-lived journal of opinion, which along with the Fast-Polevoy correspondence published earlier in the *Times,* constituted about 70 percent of the forthcoming book. Lengthy "advance" excerpts also appeared in many magazines and newspapers, and the cover of a November issue of the *Saturday Review* displayed the headline, "Notes on Leaving the Communist Party by Howard Fast." *The Naked God,* which appeared only weeks later, was one of the most heralded and anticipated books in many a season.[67]

Alas, most reviewers were disappointed. Instead of delivering a manifesto fulfilling his announced goal of "enlightening others," Fast released a hur-riedly written hodgepodge of a memoir, an episodic and evasive document with which he hoped to reenter the commercial publishing market. It earned little. Fewer than 7,500 copies were sold in the United States and England in the first year, and sales dwindled thereafter.[68] But despite its treatment at the hands of reviewers and the marketplace, *The Naked God* did have something to say—though hardly enough.

Throughout the book Fast demonstrates powerful political commitments informed by a religious sensibility and faith. Indeed, the loss, or what he calls the betrayal, of that faith led Fast to expose in *The Naked God,* over and over, a deep hurt and anguish. These feelings may have been genuine, but they were also connected to histrionic displays of self-pity, defensiveness, and apologia. Fast admitted to having blinded himself to some things, but disingenuously claimed to have been unaware of the worst horrors occurring in the Soviet Union. It was "Stalin and those who share his guilt," not Fast, "who betrayed democracy, betrayed socialism—betrayed the best hopes of mankind, the noblest dreams." We in "the rank and file of the Party," Fast wrote seven times in this short book, in one version or another, "were honorable people; [this] I have always held—and still hold." Unlike the leadership here and in Russia, Fast wrote, citing not a single example of saintliness, we "were gentle, selfless, and endlessly sacrificing men and women." But we were "swindled" into surrendering in the Party, all the "gains and liberties of mankind . . . [indeed], we betrayed mankind."[69]

That the Party *made* Fast part of this horror was in his view "unforgivable"—as was what he said it did to his art. The Communist commissars, the cultural censors, Fast insisted, "took away whatever it was inside of me that had given my work an excitement and passion that people loved." But oddly, only eight pages later Fast writes that "the priest-commissars" failed to destroy him as a writer, "just as they failed with every writer of status and integrity who was ever a member of the Communist Party of the United States."[70] Inconsistencies like this abound. Fast says, for example, "I did not state that I was a Communist, but I did not deny it." True enough. But ten pages later he wants us to believe, "My life as a Communist was very open; I have always detested concealment and conspiracy as unbecoming and degrading."[71]

Especially troubling, however, is Fast's continued insistence that he did not "know." For he and many other American Communists *did* know. Perhaps he did not know the full extent of Stalin's crimes. But surely he knew of the purges, arrests, and expulsions and had read of the public trials. At first in the late 1940s, puzzled and disappointed over accounts of Soviet actions, he finally accepted them as part of the brutal realities of making a revolution, of building an essential island of socialism in an ocean of enemies. He bought fully into the idea of Soviet wisdom and the infallibility of the Communist Party in the USSR, even on the "Jewish Question."[72]

Yet he himself admits in *Naked God*—with the inexcusable qualification, "in a sense"—that Joseph Clark was right when he said to Fast, "If you and Paul Robeson had raised your voices in 1949, Itzak Feffer would have been alive today." Yes. Now take the Feffer case and multiply it thousands of times, and include the names Osip Mandelstam, Isaac Babel, David Bergelson, Peretz Markish, and other lesser-known Jewish writers, artists, generals, scientists, and political figures who were killed during various waves of Stalin's

"Great Terror." And those were only the Jewish victims. As a *Pravda* correspondent in New York asked Fast, "'Howard, why do you make so much of the Jews? Jews? Jews? That is all we hear from you! Do you think Stalin murdered no one but Jews?'"[73]

Obviously Howard Fast wasn't responsible for the murders and other atrocities committed in the name of Marxist-Leninism, but those acts of inhumanity make his silence and apologetics obscene. Fast had knowledge of crimes against humanity being committed in the USSR, and it wasn't sufficient for him to say he couldn't separate the bourgeois slanders from the truth. Others did. Richard Wright, Arthur Koestler, Ignazio Silone, and Stephen Spender, while remaining on the left, retreated from the Communist movement and wrote about their decisions in a widely read book, *The God That Failed* (1949), of which Fast was undoubtedly aware. And if Fast chose to dismiss the revelations, accurate as it turned out, of defectors from the Soviet Union such as Walter Krivitsky (born Samuel Ginsberg), or of home-grown ex-spies such as Elizabeth Bentley or Whittaker Chambers, or of some who moved to the right like Sidney Hook, there were other memoirs by people who lifted the curtain on what was really going on in the Soviet Union, yet stayed true to some form of socialism, including John Dewey and the Gulag-imprisoned Victor Serge.[74]

Fast's own daughter, Rachel, asks, "How could my father not have known . . . ?" Friends of the family, "Russian Jews had . . . disappeared into the Soviet Union never to be heard from again." And "How could it possibly be that none of our comrades knew . . . about the many crimes of the regime: purges, imprisonment, repression of civil liberties and the like?" Fast himself acknowledges that the "sick god," Communism, Stalin, the CPUSA, "was naked from the beginning. There only had to be a voice to proclaim the fact." Reading this, one wants to shout, "And why not yours Howard; why silence and continued loyalty to the Party until the very end, until you really had no choice?"[75]

The central and fatal weakness of *The Naked God* is that it fails to explore the most important question, not "How could you not have known?" but "What was it that held you in 'intellectual bondage' long after the vast majority of writers, artists, and intellectuals had fled?" Fast calls these queries the questions of "simpletons," of those who say they "have always known the truth about the Party," and then ask "Why did it take *you* so long?" He follows this question with an astoundingly dense and morally evasive one of his own: "What truth?" Well, how's this for starters: the Soviet Union is a brutal dictatorship; Stalin's government murdered innocent millions; and the Communist Party in America and elsewhere were dupes of this regime.

Fast actually acknowledged these things in *Naked God,* but said nothing important about his reasons, long years after learning about them, for continuing to hang on to the sinking ship of American Communism. After all, not only he, but *anyone* in the Party, after say three or four or five years, who thought about leaving the CP, faced the charge of "desertion under fire" and several other crushing consequences: the loss of a fictive family and a paradigm for understanding a complex world; indeed, the loss of what had become a way of life. They would also be burdened by the need to return to a place outside the movement where, over time, they had cut all their non-Communist ties. But thousands *did* leave in 1936 and 1939, even before Fast *joined* in 1943. Thousands more left beginning in 1945 with the end of the wartime alliance and in the face of Stalinist oppression at home and expansionism abroad, bringing membership down from a high of 75,000 in 1938 to about 32,000 in 1950. Another exodus, nearly two-thirds of the rank and file, took place in the mid-1950s when it became clearer that Poland, Hungary, and East Germany were captive nations. By the time Khrushchev denounced Stalin and the "cult of the individual" in 1956 there were fewer than 10,000 Party members in America, and about 3,000 stalwarts remained after Fast finally announced his departure in 1957.

Why Fast waited so long is a question he ought not to have avoided in *Naked God,* if self-discovery, or even the enlightenment of others, was really his goal. Yet there is nothing but confusion and evasion in statements such as this: "My learning was hard and slow—too hard and slow for an explanation of why I remained to have any meaning to any but those comrades of mine who also remained."[76] Nor is there any grappling with motivation in questions like these, framed with Eugene Dennis in mind, but equally relevant to Stalin: "What does one do when he is part of a movement the leader of which is either an idiot or a madman? Who knows what we thought? It was not easy to admit to ourselves that we wanted to leave, get out of the nightmare. The nightmare that specified that whosoever left discarded all hopes of salvation." This state of mind, Fast said, "was not easy to live with."[77]

A CPUSA functionary once told Richard Wright, "No one can resign from the Communist Party," meaning that if he tried they would expel him publicly, and assassinate him morally.[78] Is this the threat Fast feared before 1956?

Or were there positive reasons for his sticking with Stalinism? The same reasons that moved him to join the Party in the first place? Certainly anti-fascism and the pursuit of social justice cannot be discounted as a motive for joining, but for staying? More important, as we have seen throughout, was Fast's tendency to oversimplify and to commit himself impulsively and absolutely. His ego and ambition also played critical roles, as did his need, even as he pursued the serious calling of writing, to be part of an outstanding group, especially an artistic, glamorous, and wealthy elite. All of these desires and needs were met and strengthened by the fawning, the adulation, even the worship, he received within the Party; and because he served its purposes so well, from the Soviet Union.

One is left asking, had Khrushchev not delivered his "secret speech" in 1956, might Howard Fast have remained a loyal Stalinist? Several of the reviewers of *The Naked God* seemed to think so, as the titles of their reviews suggest: "Truth Has Not Made Him Free," or "A Captive Not Yet Free." Irving Howe, who had had quite enough of Fast in their debate in 1956, now thought the novelist had finally shaken the substance of Communist belief, but not the style of thought behind it. Howe cites what he calls "an apparently trivial yet very revealing" example in Fast's statement that the writer in America confronts "the Communist Party on his left and the flesh-pots of well-paid mediocrity on his right." As usual, for Fast, there was no "third way."[79]

But were there in 1950s America no writers who pursued their craft seriously, creatively, imaginatively, intelligently, or even simply honestly? Howard Fast seemed to think not, but he also implied a promise to fix all that. He claimed he no longer enjoyed writing. "It is full of pain" because of his experience in the CP. But writing was all he knew, he said, and, in any case, no one ought to weep for writers. And then, no doubt thinking about the manuscript he had "put to bed with the publisher" in July, and another he had already begun working on before completing *The Naked God,* Fast said, writing is "an old and once honorable craft, and perhaps someday it will be that again."[80]

Fast was right to say that the CP did not "destroy" him as a writer, but what he wrote under its influence was seriously flawed, as was his integrity as a man and an artist. Even he admits more than once that he was humiliated over the changes he made or allowed the Party to make in his work. And most of the novels Fast wrote while a Communist—*The American, Clarkton, The*

Proud and the Free, The Passion of Sacco and Vanzetti, Silas Timberman, and Lola Gregg—are simply not worthy of the author of *The Last Frontier, The Unvanquished, and Citizen Tom Paine,* all published before Fast joined the CPUSA. Nor, except for sections of *Spartacus* and *My Glorious Brothers,* are the Communist-period novels comparable in quality and durability to a small number Fast would write after he left the Party, when, as he in his apparent new enthusiasm for the United States put it, he had returned to the land where "the individual in his work and in his rights, is recognized and defended. Sometimes better, sometimes worse—but always defended."[81]

13

Fast Forward

*I*n late 1957, a letter to *Masses and Mainstream* from a loyal American Communist Party official responding to Fast's "My Decision" accused Howard of sins worse even than those attributed to him by his former Soviet admirers. "Continuing his psychotic conduct of wallowing in his own retchings in public print," James Jackson said, Fast "is heard from again." A "chicken-hearted" defiler, wielding a "copiously filled" pen "dripping of his own enormous gall," Fast, according to Jackson, was trying to enter "into the lush 'guts and gore' market" in "which such 'titans' of the moral low-key lumpen literati as Mickey Spillane play it up for bucks." Hysterical and reductionist, Jackson nonetheless had a point.[1]

After leaving the Party Howard Fast lost little time resuming his career writing for the American market. Less than three months after publication of *The Naked God*, he signed a contract with Broadway producer Joe Hyman to deliver a "comedy-drama" based on an extension of his 1942 novel, *The Unvanquished*. Fast had already written a play along these lines called *George Washington and the Water Witch*, which had been performed in the early 1950s in several Communist countries; but the newly liberated, ex-Communist Fast rewrote the entire script in 1958 and again in 1959, as *The Crossing*, completely omitting a crucial scene in which the scheming Revolutionary War general, Horatio Gates, morphs into the villainous Joe McCarthy. Fast was taking no chances that his reentry into the American literary mainstream would be spoiled by a perception that he was still pro-Communist.[2]

Inadvertently, the Soviets helped Fast in this regard. At the beginning of 1958, the *Moscow Literary Gazette,* which had denounced the American novelist in August 1957, returned to the attack with a longer, more scathing denunciation: Fast was savage, dishonest, cowardly, and most distressingly, a "militant Zionist." According to N. Gribachev, the author of the piece, Fast had confused religion with Marxism; thrown Karl Marx and Jesus together in contradictory union,; and made a misguided attempt "to view the struggle of the working class through the smoky incense of Sunday services." Though ironic and snarky, Gribachev had come close to identifying a synthesis Fast had been working on for some time. But the Russian critic left out one crucial ingredient: Fast's enduring attachment to the precepts of the prophet Isaiah. In his rebuttal, Fast made no allusion to his twenty-year struggle to synthesize love and revolution, or his attempt to tie together prophetic Judaism and social-gospel Christianity; instead he called Gribachev's essay a "maniacal castigation," a "hooligan-like obscenity," which employed epithets worse than those used to revile even Hitler. And he referred to the *Literary Gazette,* for which he had written right up until 1956, as "the craven . . . tool of Party leaders in their war against free expression."[3]

Fast's de-radicalized "comedy-drama," *The Crossing,* never reached Broadway, nor—fortunately perhaps—did any of his other attempts to write for the stage. It is difficult to imagine what *The Naked God: A Play in Three Acts,* for example, would have looked like had Fast been successful at getting it published and produced. At his best with the historical novel, Fast had begun to return to it even while he was writing *The Naked God.* And in March 1958, Crown Publishers released *Moses: Son of Egypt,* Fast's first post-Communist novel. The book is well researched and competently written, but despite mildly titillating scenes of sex and violence, rarely compelling.

Moses was a giant-sized subject, and the fictionalized biography was initially proposed as a trilogy. The project was abandoned after the first volume produced lower than expected sales, but *Moses* signaled an attempt by Fast to recapture his own Jewish identity and audience.[4] He hired the well-connected Paul Reynolds as an agent, and felt that he had achieved his "first touch of legitimacy after all those years of blacklisting."[5] As a political actor, signing petitions and broadcasting messages to Russia via Radio Liberation, Fast continued to protest against the Communist government's treatment of

Soviet Jewry.[6] And as a writer, he began again to focus on Jewish themes and characters, and to include Jews in his novels and stories as he had earlier in *My Glorious Brothers* and in a dozen other pre-Communist publications.

If Fast's renewed interest in things Jewish was not obvious enough in *Moses,* he spelled out "what it means to him to be a Jew," in an article for the Jewish quarterly *Midstream* in spring 1958. Fast wrote that others who had left the Communist Party had been criticized by Moscow as traitors, even degenerates; but the basic attack on him, Fast claimed correctly, had been antisemitic. The "filth" directed against Fast was indeed custom-designed for a Jew and a Zionist. Fast was no Zionist, he said, but insisted he had "always respected Zionists," and had supported "every step in the reconstruction of Israel."[7]

Fast had not "always respected Zionists"; indeed, as we have seen, he had accepted as largely true the patently false accusation that Jewish doctors on trial in Moscow in 1953 were Zionist agents bent on murdering the leadership of the Soviet Union. Still, in his *Midstream* essay, Fast explicitly admitted that in 1949 in Paris, he had heard a flustered and irritated Alexander Fadeyev "explain" that the closing of Hebrew schools, and the mass arrests and purges of Jews in the USSR, were a justified response to a plot by a vast espionage network of Zionist organizations and the Jewish Joint Distribution Committee to overthrow socialism in Russia.[8]

Fast insisted that immediately upon his return from Paris, he had informed several members of the CPUSA that Jews in the USSR were in trouble. He also spoke out consistently, he said, against Russian antisemitism and against the "anti-cosmopolitanism" Soviets had constructed to disguise their Jew-hatred. *Midstream*'s readers could not have known that the former Communist, instead of speaking out, had maintained a decade long silence about the war against Jews in the USSR; nor would most of them have known that Fast wrote nothing on "cosmopolitanism" until late April 1956, when the Polish Communist Yiddish-language paper, *Folks-Stimme,* forced his hand by publishing articles about the destruction of Yiddish culture in the Soviet Union.[9]

Whatever else may have mattered to him in the late 1950s and early 1960s, Fast was determined to reestablish his Jewish bona fides. He and Bette joined the Stephen Wise Free Synagogue on 68th Street and Broadway when they returned to New York City in 1960. But it was in his writings, and certainly not in prayer or Jewish observance, that Fast would manifest his secular-historical brand of Jewish identity.[10] *Moses* was almost immediately followed by the *Midstream* piece, and shortly thereafter by *The Winston Affair*, a contemporary novel featuring a number of Jewish and anti-Jewish protagonists involved in and around a military murder trial of a psychotic antisemite and homosexual. Despite its confrontational situations and superficial excitements, the novel is surprisingly light on drama. It is, however, heavy on socially conscious rhetoric, a temporary hangover perhaps from Fast's Party days. Fast is interested in "teaching" two central lessons: no matter how monstrous a man may be, he deserves his day in court; and capital punishment, no matter what the circumstances, is barbaric. But nowhere, as the *New York Times* critic put it, "does the author rise above banality."[11] Nor, the critic might have added, homophobia.

Two subsequent Fast novels were also dense with Jewish characters and themes: *Agrippa's Daughter* (1964) and *Torquemada* (1966). In the first, Berenice, the daughter of King Herod Agrippa, and great-granddaughter of Herod the Great, is drawn by Fast as a woman wrestling with her Jewish "identity" until she is liberated from her crisis by Shimeon, the grandson of Hillel, who "converts" her to the "worship of peace." Following up on the *Winston Affair* and his earlier post-Party pronouncements against capital punishment and violence in general, Fast pitched *Agrippa's Daughter* as "an anti-war" novel. "I took that time in Jewish history," Fast said, when "Judaism put aside war forever as an instrument of change or . . . even survival." Fast not only treats Judaism as if it were some kind of monolithic entity capable of making momentous decisions, he posits a decision made by Berenice as the decision of a whole people. The claim that Jews in the first century CE, or at any point in their six-thousand-year history, became pacifists, especially to the point of giving up their right of self-defense, has no basis in Jewish religious literature or reality.[12]

Nor is such a conversion to pacifism demonstrated in the novel. Indeed, this is a book filled with bloody, sometimes entirely gratuitous violence. Berenice herself says, "How strange that in spite of the fact that I was won over to the House of Hillel, I seem to have lived with nothing but violence, war, and murder and the death of those I loved most."[13] In the last few pages, however, Berenice returns to Tiberius, where Galilean peasants are living in a fruitful and blissfully peaceful manner, with memories of war clouded or gone. This is neither a believable scene nor one logically connected to anything that precedes it.

Like other writers of historical fiction, Fast legitimately uses the power of his creative imagination to invent characters, places, events, and even outcomes radically different from what "really" happened; but he wants us to believe that in the time of Herod Agrippa, the conversion of the Jews to "the worship of peace" was a demonstrably true event. He was after all, he said, writing about "one of the most important moments in the history of mankind."[14] The historical novelist, however, cannot have it both ways. In literature, "lying" can be a powerful way of telling larger truths. But for Fast to claim that a particular creative falsehood is an objective truth suggests that he had not yet escaped the thinking and style of an ideologue, only that he had dropped one absolute enthusiasm, Communism, for another, pacifism.

The critics were correct to see *Agrippa's Daughter* as little more than "ticky tacky."[15] *Torquemada* fared no better with the reviewers or in the marketplace. A graphic portrait of antisemitism in fifteenth-century Spain, the novel appears to have been written as a parable about the dangers of fanaticism. It is possible to see in Fast's version of medieval Catholicism's ethnic cleansing a parallel to the totalitarian oppression of Jews and dissidents in Stalin's Russia. The *Times* critic thought the book was "timely" in this regard, but saw that it failed to grow beyond its single "truism."[16]

In none of these "Jewish" novels is Fast's strength as a dramatic storyteller apparent.[17] It is only when he returned to the familiarity of the Revolutionary War that he matched the narrative drive and complex character portrayals of *The Unvanquished* and *Citizen Tom Paine*. In *April Morning* (1961), for example, Fast portrays in layered and historically credible detail a day in the life of Adam Cooper who, during the Battle of Lexington, gains his independence from his overbearing father; and like Henry Fleming in Stephen Crane's *Red Badge of Courage,* he defines in battle his own "manhood." At first, Adam says that "the most important thing I had learned about war was that you could run away and survive to talk about it"; but ultimately he chooses to fight, perhaps to kill, not in God's name, but as his Reverend says, "in freedom's name," God's forgiveness to be asked for afterward.[18] Obviously, Fast was still some distance from the absolute pacifism he displayed in *Agrippa's Daughter,* but in *April Morning,* the costs of war are readily apparent.

Though not necessarily written as a novel for young adults, the inclusion of a love interest for fifteen-year-old Adam Cooper, and Fast's successful effort to make accessible the complex political currents in colonial America on the eve of the Revolution, brought the book to the attention of school-teachers. When the Board of Education in Bronxville, New York, discussed adopting *April Morning* as part of the school district's curriculum, there was some murmuring about putting their imprimatur on a book by a former Communist. Those in favor of using Fast's novel surprised those who protested by citing J. Edgar Hoover's *Masters of Deceit.* Three years after his agency had done a series of interviews with Fast, the director of the FBI wrote that ex-Communists should not be subject to prejudice because of their former political loyalties, and he mentioned Fast in the text in three separate places.[19] *April Morning* was adopted in Bronxville, and since 1961 has frequently been assigned as required reading in English and social studies classes throughout New York State. The novel sold over 3 million copies, was well received by the critics, and stands on its own merits; but Fast's several interviews with the FBI in 1957 do not seem to have hurt his chances to reenter the literary mainstream.[20]

In 1962, *April Morning* was selected as one of the ten best books of 1961 for the pre-college reader by the Booklist Committee of the Independent Schools Education Board.[21] In the same year a new paperback edition of *Freedom Road* was printed, and over a period of eighteen months, seven of Fast's science fiction stories were published, one of which, "The Large Ant," appeared in a number of anthologies. Textbook publishers began again to use excerpts from Fast's historical novels of the 1940s; and *Spartacus* was reissued in softcover in 1960 to coincide with the release of *Spartacus,* the film.[22] In 1961, Fast was finally successful in his effort to get his passport renewed.[23] The ex-Communist, whose *Citizen Tom Paine* was banned by many boards of education in 1947, who could not travel outside the United States after 1949, and whose work had been banished from schoolbooks in the '50s, appeared to be fully "rehabilitated."

Fast had sold the rights to produce *Spartacus* to Kirk Douglas in 1958. That's about all that can be said with any certainty about how this block-buster movie came to be made. Douglas, who produced and codirected the film; Fast, who wrote a good part of the screenplay; Stanley Kubrick, who became the director after Arthur Mann resigned or was fired; and Dalton Trumbo, who had a major hand in the screenwriting, all had different and frequently contradictory versions of events.

Douglas agreed to have Fast do the script for *Spartacus* reluctantly, because he believed most novelists were failures at transforming their work for the screen. And when Fast's first sixty pages were delivered, Douglas was not pleased. All Fast had given him, the actor-producer complained, was a load of "unusable" material, "characters spouting ideas, speeches on two legs." Douglas turned to Dalton Trumbo, who agreed to "fix" the material despite his intense dislike of Fast. Trumbo and Fast had known about one another, of course, but had met for the first time only when the two were in prison together in 1950. Trumbo thought Fast as narrow-minded in his Marxism as HUAC was in its anti-Communism; and Fast thought Trumbo was extremely "unpleasant, needlessly hostile," possessed of "a kind of 'free floating' anger that he directed at the whole world."[24]

Douglas, knowing Howard hated Dalton as much as Dalton hated him, presented Trumbo's treatment to Fast as the work of producer Eddie Lewis. Fast exploded, saying it was "the worst script" he'd ever read, and wanted out of the project; but after speaking to his agent, he agreed, not without significant resentment, to work on "Eddie's" outline. According to Douglas, Fast's second effort was "still terrible."[25] Howard claimed otherwise. He said Kirk "loved" his first draft, but for some reason had given it to Trumbo to rework. After Trumbo's "treatment" was read by Douglas, Fast said, "I was summoned back to Hollywood" by a "devastated," "pleading," and "weeping" Kirk Douglas, who had already shot ninety minutes of film.[26] Fast agreed to return to LA in late June 1959, this time with the whole family. Jonathan and Rachel, unsurprisingly, had great fun at the studios. Fast's job, however, was no fun at all. He had to write twenty new episodes in order to sew together Trumbo's scenes, which Howard said "had no real continuity and no climax."[27]

When the $12 million picture was completed in February 1960, Fast claimed that he was "directly responsible for at least half of the finished script," but Douglas "used every device to cut me out." Credit went to Trumbo. "I cared and I didn't care," Fast said, and "Trumbo needed the credit more than I did."[28] And besides, a bitter Fast said later, the making of the film involved stupidity and waste; worse, Douglas and Kubrick, and even actors Laurence Olivier and Peter Ustinov, "added things" and "lost the main drive of it. They lost the political message, and . . . the connection [to the] struggle for human . . . freedom."[29]

Fast appears to have admired only those scenes directly "lifted beautifully from my book": the portrayal of the contest between a black and a white gladiator, for example, and the frames showing the defeated black gladiator's body hung from the ceiling of the barracks. This image of modern lynching resonated with audiences in 1960, just as the liberal Douglas hoped it would, and as the radical Fast had wanted it to in 1951.[30] Fast did not, however, admire the added scene in which Spartacus and Antoninus fight to the death. "I wrote the silly scene," Fast said, in a sentence with a familiar ring, "because I was instructed to." Fast seems to have misunderstood that the fight was a love scene, each warrior trying to spare the other a crucifixion. Or as likely, Fast had been bothered by the scene's intimation of homosexuality.[31] But in the end, what Fast seemed to feel most was relief. "Thank God," he said, "the nightmare of working with Kirk Douglas was over."[32]

Near the end of his life, a somewhat more mellow Fast said he admired Kubrick and Douglas for their brilliance, even if "Kirk [was] obstinate and arrogant." He admired Douglas also, Fast said, "for his support of Israel, his openness and pride in being Jewish—rather unusual in Hollywood." Most of all, Fast respected Douglas for "his direct, intractable courage." By allowing Howard to work openly on the set and in the studio, and by insisting, over the resistance of Universal, that Trumbo's name appear on screen as the scriptwriter, "Kirk did more to break the blacklist than anyone else."[33]

With the blacklist gone, Fast's career in the world of film took off. His nearly twenty-year-old dream to be part of the wealth, fame, and glamour of Hollywood seemed to be coming true; and it was magnified by Fast's success with *Spartacus,* for which he received a Screenwriter's Guild Award, and from which he derived substantial income. So substantial was it, in fact, that in combination with royalties pouring in from Bantam's new edition of *Citizen Tom Paine* and the fees paid by Crown for the rights to reprint his other books in paperback, the Fasts were able to move from their modest home in Teaneck and purchase a lavish apartment at 1016 Fifth Avenue, directly across from the Metropolitan Museum of Art, as well as a country home in Westport, Connecticut.[34]

Several critics referred to Fast's books as the stuff not of novels but of movie spectacles. And it is entirely possible that Fast was hoping, even while writing them, that his novels could be turned into screenplays. For many years he had been trying to persuade producers to do films based on *Citizen Tom Paine* and *Freedom Road,* and more than once he had had offers, even sizable advances, from Hollywood studios for rights to use his novels. In 1958, even before the blacklist was broken, Fast had himself written a film script based on *Moses* that went unsold.[35]

His big break came in 1961, when he was asked by Paramount Pictures to write a screenplay for E. V. Cunningham's *Sylvia,* a mystery novel. No one in Hollywood except Paramount knew that Cunningham was actually Fast's pseudonym, adopted in 1960 partly because he was still uncertain about the power of the blacklist. Fast may also have generated this alternate identity in order to write thrillers or "entertainments" as he preferred to call them, while at the same time protecting his reputation as a "serious writer." *Sylvia* "was a book I wrote just for fun. I had wanted to write it for some time," Fast confessed, "but it was just the kind of book"—nonpolitical, bourgeois kitsch—"that, if written within the confines of the Communist Party, would only get a writer into great trouble."[36]

Fast worked on the screenplay for *Sylvia* in Hollywood for several months in return for a weekly pay check from Paramount, as well as a lump sum of $12,000. The studio also gave him a "sumptuous" office and put him up at a fine hotel with a pool, which he used every day. He did as much "goofing" off as possible, Fast wrote home, because *Sylvia* was "so easy to do," and he was "way ahead of [him]self." It was especially easy, he said, because producer Martin Poll, with whom he was working "is human, as contrasted with . . . Kirk Douglas."[37]

Dinner and beach-party invitations came from Devery Freeman, Paul and Peggy Stewart, the formerly blacklisted writer and director Martin Ritt, songwriter Ray Evans, and many others, including screenwriters and directors Mike Kanin and his wife Fay Kanin, whom Fast described as a "tall, lovely brown skinned woman." Apparently, Fast noticed all the "pretty-pretties," as he called them in his letters to Bette. He also told his wife that he was getting lots of calls from the twenty-three-year-old English actress Barbara Steele; a "very disturbed girl" according to Howard, but a woman made famous by playing in horror films such as Mario Bava's *Dark Sunday* (1960), and thought of generally as having "talent, intelligence, and [a] dark, mysterious beauty."[38] He told Bette that although he had invited Steele to lunch, she had not come; and that *he* had not responded to any of her invitations. He did not, however, tell Bette about the rumor, likely true, that he and the statuesque actress were sleeping together. Nor did he tell her that he *was* sleeping with Lori Wynn-Ferber—not an actress, but good-looking, and as Jonathan put it "sort of a personality" known to all the Hollywood makers and shakers. Howard assured Bette that he was "discovering" yet once again, "that I want only one woman." After he returned home, however, he would fly back to California at least once a year to rendezvous with Lori.[39]

Fast wrote often to Rachel and Jonathan as well as to Bette, and he called home, too, from time to time. He genuinely seemed to miss them all and tried to make sure that when Rachel, now seventeen and at Dalton, a private prep school in New York, came out to the coast (to be joined later by Bette and thirteen-year-old Jon) she'd have young male company. Howard also got the studio to agree that Bette could set up an easel for her painting anywhere on the lot. For his science-fiction-loving son Jonathan, who had recently "suffered" through Hebrew lessons in preparation for a bar mitzvah, made "obligatory" because of Bette's Orthodox parents, Fast tried to find prints from the film *When Worlds Collide;* and twice he watched Richard Boone acting on the set of the acclaimed TV series, *Have Gun—Will Travel,* so that he could give Jon lots of details.[40]

Fast looked forward to seeing the family, but was having a grand time on his own. At the many parties he attended, there was not only great food, and too much of it, but also "red hot and lively discussions" about "film and books and writers and [psycho]analysis." The subject of politics seems conspicuous by its absence; but one wonders what Fast talked about with Lee J. Cobb, whom he met for lunch several times. Cobb, because of his involvement in progressive causes in the 1940s and his membership in several organizations named as "fronts," was thought to be a Communist. He was called to testify by HUAC in 1951, but for two years he resisted. In 1953, however, with his career threatened, no work, no money, and his wife institutionalized for alcoholism, he relented, and unlike Fast, "named names." What the two men said to one another eight years later, Fast did not write home about. Nor did he talk about his growing friendship with the Academy Award–winning director Robert Rossen, who after being severely reprimanded by the CPUSA for his "politically incorrect" film *All the King's Men,* turned "friendly witness" at the HUAC hearings in 1951 and named names.[41]

In addition to having meals with the stars, Fast also, at first, enjoyed doing business at the studios. There were several negotiations for *The Crossing* and for a screenplay based on *April Morning.* He eventually complained about too many boring, unnecessary meetings, but believed "this stay of mine will prove very profitable indeed." It did in the long run. *The Crossing* was published as a novel in 1971, and produced as a TV movie in 1999. *April Morning* also became a TV movie in 1988.[42] That several projects would not come to fruition until much later did not matter much to Fast. He was getting paid, and besides, he told Bette, here is what's "really important": Los Angeles "is a big Howard Fast reading town and my paper books are all over the place." And "studio executives," he said, "are particularly nice to me and seek me out to talk."[43]

Hollywood, Howard felt, was in "awe" of him, and it seems that the film world was beginning to fill the deep need he had always had for unqualified admiration and ego-stroking, a need once filled by the Communist Party. In this regard, it didn't hurt that Bette Davis had called Fast "the moment she discovered I was here." It turns out, he told his Bette, "that for years [Davis] has been dying to meet me." And referring to the various pro-Communist organizations to which the Fasts had once belonged, Howard said, "Can you imagine, all those meetings where we sat [only] a few chairs from her!" She has "such vivacity," he added, "such a lust for life! . . . And believe it or not, I am her favorite of all authors. Never did I have to sit and listen to such praise." He needn't have added, "I enjoyed it!" When "you meet these old timers who are like . . . royalty," Fast continued, "they give you such a sense of living at its best. . . . And what a lot of stuff they have!" Although he hastened to add that some "louse up their lives," it was obvious that Fast was still enchanted by glamour and wealth—and by being worshipped.[44]

Fast's physical ailments tainted his joy: the nightly headaches continued to be excruciating, and his stock of honey and apple-cider vinegar, which he took daily as a "tonic," sometimes ran low. But he comforted and amused himself by telling Bette, before she came out to Hollywood at the end of June, that he had let only Paul and Peggy Stewart in on the *Sylvia* secret. "You know," he said, "it's all over the industry, 'Can you imagine,' people say, 'what shmucks they are . . . at Paramount. They got a tough, hard-boiled story about a prostitute called Sylvia . . . and of all people, they bring this Howard Fast out here to write it! . . . He's fine for historical stuff—but you got to be out of your mind to give him a story like *Sylvia*.'"[45]

Sylvia, the film, wasn't produced until 1965, but in the meantime the book sold very well. It was followed rapidly by a series of novels, each with the title of its female protagonist's first name: *Phyllis* (1962), *Alice* (1963), *Lydia* (1964), *Shirley* (1964), and on through 1968, eleven mysteries in all. Fast's women are criminals, abettors, or victims (though much less often), or detectives and co-investigators. They are resourceful, witty, intelligent, courageous, and sometimes hilarious. Away from the watchful eyes of the cultural commissars of the CPUSA, Fast finally revealed a genuine sense of humor in his writing. It may be, too, that in creating women who were better, more capable, and more honest than most men, Fast was trying to overcome his reputation as a "sexist tyrant," a label applied to him in all seriousness by his daughter and wife, and later by his daughter-in-law and granddaughter.[46]

The narratives are as fast-paced as their production, and the plots demand significant "suspension of disbelief." What rescues the often bizarre stories, what keeps them from imploding completely, are the plucky, clever, and occasionally whacky high-heeled heroines who challenge the male domination that held sway in the private-eye tradition of Dashiell Hammett, Rex Stout, and Mickey Spillane. Social criticism, other than the self-conscious anti-misogyny at the center of these novels, is not readily evident. There is an antinuclear "message" in *Phyllis;* a picture of the corrupting power of American materialism in *Helen* (1966); and a portrayal of the decadence and depravity of a Hollywood culture addicted to money and sex (in which Fast would become a player for a few years in the 1970s) in *Samantha* (1967). But, ultimately, as Fast admitted, most of these books were "pure entertainment [and] had no message and no particularly important political point of view."[47]

Not only did the Cunningham books sell extraordinarily well, especially in England and France where they carried Fast's name, six were sold to Hollywood producers, and four became films.[48] In addition, two moving pictures, *Mirage* (1965) and *Jigsaw* (1968), were made out of material in Fast's *Fallen Angel* (1952). During this period, too, *The Winston Affair* served loosely as the basis for *Man in the Middle* (1964). The creativity repressed during Fast's CP days was on full display: six films, including *Spartacus,* between 1960 and 1968, and in the same period, fifteen novels, including the eleven Cunninghams, which would grow to twenty by 1986.[49]

Why Fast, ambitious and committed to accumulating wealth and fame, turned to the practice of Zen Buddhism in his post-Communist years is not entirely clear. Indeed, he told Scott Nearing that "like so many people who practice Zen, I don't know why I do it or what it's all about." But Fast surely knew much more than that. After all, his involvement in the "Zen business" had started in the late fifties, "after everything else fell to pieces." And the practice, he felt, was "an antidote" to the poisons he ingested while "living in this vast asylum called the world."[50] Fast did not name the poisons, but it seems fairly clear that Zen and his growing pacifism, which were compatible and easily synthesized, served him as a substitute for Marxism, providing a new "frame of reference" for understanding the world.

Fast began his formal training with William Segal, a relentless spiritual seeker, artist, and successful entrepreneur in the competitive world of New York publishing. "Before meeting Bill," Fast had "given little thought to Buddhism," which he saw as "one of those arcane religions of the East." Yet his coming to Zen, he said, was "the result of a lifetime of religious thought and questioning," and he insisted that it did not mean abandoning "Jewishness." Fast had asked his teacher early on whether he was a Buddhist or a Jew, and he was satisfied with Segal's response: "Why not both?"[51]

Fast rejected the "free floating fantasy of Transcendental Meditation," which he said supplied a too facile comfort, and opted instead for an eyes-open, head-erect, mindful approach. He meditated every day for about thirty minutes, and by the 1970s he was teaching the practice to a handful of friends, some of whom became what they called his "disciples." In 1977, Fast published a very short pamphlet on the subject (illustrated by nine pictures of himself!), the idea for which may have come from his correspondence with a professor of psychology at Princeton who was writing her own book on Zen and creativity. Fast told the professor he had "lost all desire for fame, notoriety, [and] ego importance," and that he "never used meditation specifically as a device to enhance the creative process." But in the same letter Fast revealed how little he had actually been changed by Zen meditation. Conceivably, he wrote, what is helpful "philosophically," the diligent and creative search for the divine spark in the soul, "might be quite destructive commercially or financially," but he doubted it. Indeed, he said, like Bill Segal, who achieved professional recognition and lasting wealth as a self-made artist and business man, and like his partners in meditation, Arnold Schulman, an award-winning and commercially successful producer, playwright, and songwriter, and Alan Sacks, an Emmy Award–winning executive producer best known for creating tv's *Welcome Back, Kotter* in 1975, Fast "had no problems in this direction."[52]

The adoption of Zen Buddhism did not induce "detachment" in Fast, or keep him from the pursuit of material success; but it did allow him to express openly what he could not as a Communist: his belief in a mystical bond of love and suffering among all people. It meant, too, along with the pacifism that was an integral part of his practice, that the fierce Christ whom Fast had invoked from time to time as a martyred revolutionary was displaced by the loving, nonviolent Christ who had also been ingrained in the writer's imagination from the beginning. And though Fast now saw himself as both Buddhist and Jew, he was hardly through with Jesus; in 1962, he plunged into writing *The Hill,* a modern allegorical screenplay depicting the last three days in the life of Christ, according to the *Gospel of John*—an odd and unexplained choice for Fast, *John* being the most explicitly antisemitic of the four Gospels.

More than once, and very explicitly in prison, Fast had said that no serious author could avoid taking on the story of the Passion, not simply because of its compelling dramatic content, but because, "regardless of religion, each generation relives the mortal dilemma and agony of the man who dies for all other men." It would have helped had Fast expounded on this statement, or at the very least supplied a modern example of this idea in the introduction to *The Hill.* Instead, in answer to an interviewer's question, Fast said simply, "The death of Christ is a permanent condition of the human race." It didn't make things any clearer when Fast, the nonbeliever, wrote, "for this reason the story demands an approach that is holy in its veracity."[53]

Fast had hoped that Sammy Davis Jr. would play the lead role in his projected film, for which Walter Reed Associates had already put up half the money; and he invited the versatile entertainer-actor to dinner with the family. Apparently Davis arrived "completely coked up," to the amusement of fourteen-year-old Jonathan. Fast, however, was not nearly as happy with Davis, who incessantly, but not particularly coherently, pressed the idea that all the followers of Jesus be black, and all the Romans white. Wanting his movie to be framed around the basic theme of universalism, Fast wisely nixed the proposal.[54]

In the end, *The Hill,* originally set in England, was moved to Mt. Morris Park in Harlem, *all* roles to be played by blacks. Sammy Davis Jr. would play the lead, sober it was hoped, as a carpenter named Joshua. "We trust," Fast announced that "while we will make no attempt to explain," *The Hill's* "miracle play aspects will be obvious." He told Rachel, who often served as his editor (her grammar and spelling being far better than his), that "we have a great screenplay here . . . and we are going to open new horizons in motion picture art." Although shooting began in December, the film, for lack of financing, was never completed; but the screenplay was published in 1964 with the subtitle *A Modern Miracle Play,* just in case what was obvious to Fast wasn't so obvious to readers.[55]

Fast's withdrawal from the ideological wars of the 1940s and '50s meant the demise of his political activism. Of the fifteen articles and reviews he wrote between 1957 and 1989, almost all for bourgeois magazines, only five were about politics; but within the Fast family, he did continue to express concern about the political life of his society from time to time. In the fall of 1962, he wrote to Rachel, now in her first semester at Wellesley, curious to know of any reaction on her campus to the race riot sparked by James Meredith's admission to the University of Mississippi. In Oxford, the violence had lasted several days, leaving two dead, seventy-five injured, and many arrested, and Fast wanted to know whether there was among Wellesley students a show of support for Meredith or for the civil rights movement generally. In the same short paragraph, however, he asked his daughter if she had seen the full-page ad in the *Sunday Times* for his recently released novel *Power*, which was also on exhibit in several New York bookstores. Brentano's had a huge display in its window, and Fast confessed to Rachel that he had "just stood" on Fifth Avenue "and gurgled with ill-concealed delight."[56]

Several letters to Rachel in late October allude to the Cuban Missile Crisis and the Kennedy-Khrushchev face-off, but Fast expressed nothing more substantive than hope for a peaceful resolution. Nor did anything political appear in their correspondence again except for one final note in November 1963 that seemed designed as a warning to Rachel to judge people, especially her male friends, not on what they say, but on how they behave. In his years in the Communist Party, Fast said, he "knew many a man who put forth as . . . unchallengeable a set of social ethics as you could find." These were stern, "upright fighters for the new and better world"; but almost as if he were shining a light on his own life, he went on to say that these men, even as they announced their righteous values, "degraded their wives, neglected their children and abused their comrades." Other Communists, equally stern in their progressive political postures, he told his daughter, "were in and out of bed with every woman they could seduce."[57]

Letters to Rachel often included praise but were almost always colored by condescension. "Dollink," Fast wrote in a note all too typical, "we got your marks from college—well, we never claimed our daughter was a genius, but she's sweet." Patronizing advice surfaced often in his correspondence, along with the universal parental plaint: "Why don't you write, why don't you call." After receiving what he called a "precedent-shattering letter" from Rachel, Fast responded by saying it was "astonishingly well-written." He couldn't, however, leave it at that, and went onto say, "I leaped into the air and chortled, 'the old girl is very much a chip off the old block.'"[58]

After a particularly trying "story-conference" with interested filmmakers, about which Fast gave Rachel many humorous details, he added only half-jokingly, "You should know what your poppa goes through to send . . . you to a high-type ladies' seminary." Fast also once apologized for shouting at his daughter during one of her visits home, but asked, "What am I to do?" A parent "is so built constitutionally as to worry. . . . All those years when I used to look in on you each night to see whether you were properly covered . . . sort of set up an action-reaction path."[59] A path not particularly appreciated by Rachel, who thought her father's paternalism was patriarchal and his expressions of love inauthentic or "off " somehow. She did recall, however, one rare, if not unique, moment when her father treated her with "genuine affection." During a trip in the mid-sixties on the Super Chief to California, Fast, out of oxygen, got up in the middle of the night with one of his awful headaches. Rachel got up too and sat with him in the dining car; "and after the pain broke, we watched the sun come up" and the porters prepare the car for breakfast. It was then she said that her father looked at her with real "appreciation." More than ten years later, Howard reminded his daughter of that long ride during which she had stayed "awake with me, keeping me company. . . . It was a strange, wonderful night. I felt so close to you, *so filled with a sense of love that doesn't come too often.*"[60]

Jonathan too experienced only "rare moments of intimacy" with his father. The elder Fast's insistence on being the only "star" in the family permitted little else. His father was extremely competitive, Jonathan said, and while he "encouraged" his son to be a writer, indeed, insisted that there was no other worthy profession, he did not want him "to be a better writer than himself." In the 1970s and '80s, Jonathan did write seven novels, but he showed his father none of his books until they were published. In the meantime, as a teenager, Jonathan, in order to avoid an uncommon amount of criticism from his father (and his mother, too), pursued things that were out of his father's league, music in particular. Fast was tone-deaf and had no appreciation for any of it: jazz, classical, rhythm and blues, or rock. In what he described as a "defense mechanism," a "good escape from the craziness of my family," Jonathan worked hard and long at his music while attending the High School of Music and Art, becoming proficient with the banjo and the piano and at composing; and with three classmates, he formed a band.[61]

Now a tenured associate professor of social psychology at the Wurzweiler School of Social Work at Yeshiva University, Jonathan plays cello with various chamber music groups, mostly for his friends and for his own enjoyment. But as a young man Jonathan liked to play banjo in Washington Square Park on Sundays, and with his three classmates looked for gigs, hoping even to make some extra spending money. Their first invitation came in the spring of 1963 from a small after-hours café on McDougal Street in Greenwich Village. There'd be no pay, but a hat would be passed. Howard Fast, intrigued, even though bewildered by it all, took the four boys downtown on the night of their scheduled performance. His description of the evening, in a letter to Rachel, reveals some of Fast's feelings about the culture of the sixties: "McDougal St.—well, you know what a creepy spot that is of a Friday night. So we look for the *Caliph* . . . the name of this coffee house, which has no telephone number. . . . Down in a cellar, no chairs or tables, cement ledges, dirty pillows, way out, way, way, way out—manager a girl who has plainly not bathed since the end of the Korean War, assisted by creeps in thong sandals and beards, non-bathing *faigeles*." Fast, who consistently used this Yiddish word meaning "little birds" when alluding to homosexuals, found himself the only customer.

The boys were told to play. "For whom?" Just play, the manager said, and the customers will come. And they did—the fathers of two of the other boys in the band! And then finally, after two more hours, come other folk singers. "Over-muscled *faigeles* reciting Shakespeare." Then more folk singers, and "creepy customers enter. Air supply ceases. Smell ripens and ripens. . . . Hat is passed. I put in three dollars, and the rest of the audience puts in about sixty cents more. . . . Weird, incredible night. Boys made about twenty cents each, apart from what fathers and friends put in."[62]

Fast eventually "lightened up about the sixties scene," Jonathan remembers. His father even regretted being too old to let his hair grow long, and demonstrated jealousy over the "apparently free and easy sex, and the drugs, too." In 1964, Rachel bought Howard some pot for his fiftieth birthday. "Over the objections of Mother who ran into the kitchen to have a fit," Jon and Rachel stayed in the living room of their Fifth Avenue apartment, and "gave Father a lesson in smoking dope." Fast, not certain he had gotten high, wanted something stronger; he even talked about trying LSD, but ultimately backed off, believing it would affect his writing ability.[63]

Even though the family was "living on Fifth Avenue and employing a black maid who had to wear a uniform, and respond during dinner to a little gold bell," his father's politics, Jonathan said, "fit the 6os very nicely." Fast never knew the pro-labor lyrics of Bruce Springsteen's or Bob Dylan's antiwar songs, but by the late summer of 1964, Fast was "out there with the students" in his anger against the war in Vietnam.[64] He was apparently very much affected by reading Joseph Heller's *Catch-22* (1961), a book not yet seen as explicitly against the war in Vietnam, of course, but soon to be picked up as one of the "bibles" of the sixties' antiwar movement. Rachel said he "went nuts" with delight after reading Heller. For a change, Fast had not only found a modern writer (and a Jewish one at that) whom he admired, but one he judged the "greatest writer alive today!"

After listening to her father "rave" about Heller "day after day," Rachel persuaded him to have a dinner party in the young author's honor. At first Fast protested, saying, "I don't know the man. I can't do that." "Of course you can," Rachel insisted. "You're famous; no one's ever heard of [Heller]. He'll be flattered, and . . . he'll come." And that Heller did—showing up looking "like a guy ready for work on the railroad" and speaking so deep a Brooklynese, Rachel said, that all of us "were shocked." Heller soon stopped talking and looked extremely uncomfortable, "WAY out of his element" among the chattering classes. Fast "made a little speech" extolling the visiting writer and praising *Catch-22,* but otherwise, "everyone was . . . embarrassed." Of course, if we had had "any class, we'd have made him feel comfortable and welcome," Rachel said, "but Dad, the working man's man, the Commie, was a snob."[65]

Snob or no, embarrassed or not, Fast was probably relieved that he could now continue to think of himself alone as the greatest living American writer. Nor did Heller's lack of social grace change how Howard thought about the war. Not only did he see early and correctly that U.S. military involvement in the Southeast Asian conflict meant engagement in an "unjust war," he had, around the time of reading Heller's book, stopped believing entirely in the possibility of waging a "just war" for any reason. At the height of the antiwar movement, Fast confessed to an interviewer that he had once believed there were such things as "the just war." Now, he said, "I consider [that concept] ridiculous." Fast told Bertrand Russell that he had "come to a pacifist position, totally sharing the belief that since history began, there has been no cause worth the taking of a human life." This was a radical shift for Fast, and meant that he no longer defended the ancient Maccabean revolt in which he had expressed such pride, nor his once beloved American Revolution, or the Civil War, without which, as he once recognized, slavery would not have ended. It meant backing away from his proactive antifascist crusade during WWII, and even temporarily from his staunch defense of Israel's war for independence in 1948.[66]

"I will not defend the process of killing whether by punishment or by war," Fast said, and "I allow no shades, no gradations to my belief." This statement, sent to Rabbi Arthur Gilbert of the Jewish Peace Fellowship (JPF), with which Fast had become affiliated in 1966, indicates Howard's continuing embrace of absolutism, and suggests yet again that though an ideologue may change his views, he rarely changes his temperament, and almost never the conviction that he is "right."[67]

Rabbi Gilbert asked Fast whether he had taken his position "on religious grounds . . . as a Jew." In 1944 when he was a Communist neophyte, Fast said his Jewishness was more of a burden to dispense with than an inheritance to be cherished. But now he answered, "[How] could it be otherwise? I cannot read a book, enter an argument, watch a sunset . . . or breathe in sweet fresh air except as a Jew." Howard's pacifism may have had roots, as he claimed, in his "rediscovery" of Jewishness after he left the Communist Party, but the two constructs, pacifism and Jewishness, were in tension with one another when the subject of Israel was broached. After the Six-Day War in 1967, Fast "got into arguments" with Christian friends about the military behavior of the Jewish state. "There was no alternative," Fast insisted. "This doesn't mean I agree with Israel's position," he said, but "I understand very well, being a Jew, what Israel faces, and I . . . understand their psychology . . . the desperation and the anguish and the anger of people who have come through the Holocaust . . . and who say, even 'if we have to kill everyone who comes near to us, this is not going to happen again.'" His Christian friends, he said, however, "can't understand it, because they don't have the identification as Jews."[68]

In the wake of the war, Fast was asked by the editor of *Fellowship,* the magazine of the JPF, to make a statement about pacifism and the Middle East. Fast thought it unnecessary for the JPF to make any statement at all, but went on to tell the editor that when he himself is "asked . . . what *I* would do if a bandit . . . attacked me or my wife or children . . . I reply that I would resist with all my strength . . . but this is quite different from putting on a uniform that defines a killer and training for the art of killing, and *of course it does not apply to Israel*. . . . Peace in Israel is not by any means to be considered apart from the world's attitude toward the Jews." After all, Fast wrote, "The only time that the Security Council of the United Nations is wholly united is on the condemnation of Israel." He mentioned this, Fast said, because "*Israel is not simply a nation; it is a Jewish nation:* and the whole world must come to understand that we cannot countenance endlessly the murder of Jews."[69]

Here Fast sets aside an absolute pacifism, for an essentialist position as a Jew. But in his futile attempt to make his position clearer, Fast revealingly invoked another absolutism to which he had once subscribed. "In the same way," he said, "if you're a committed socialist, and you believe that the *only* solution for mankind is the socialist order, *you are ready to forgive a thousand things that are done in the heat and fury of revolution,*" and for that matter during the postrevolutionary consolidation, "*providing* that this socialist order will bring peace and a new way of life to mankind."[70] Of course, only the strictest ideologue could possibly "know" that such an outcome was inevitable. In the 1940s and '50s, Fast believed that the only solution for humanity's problems was Communism. In the '60s, he allowed "no shades, no gradations" in his pacifism; and after 1967, more reasonably, but no less absolutely, he brooked no opposition from his pacifist friends to Israel's "right of self-defense."

Like many other Jews on the liberal-left, Fast also faced the challenges presented in the late '60s by an increasingly militant black civil rights movement. For most of the twentieth century, but especially after 1945, there had been in the United States an affinity, even a sense of kinship, between blacks and Jews. Both groups had had rich histories as people apart. Both had suffered, in varying degrees of intensity, from discrimination by the majority Christian society. And Jews had been the white group most deeply committed to racial equality in America. But the "alliance" between blacks and Jews had been unequal and uneasy from the start. When the economic interests of the two groups began to diverge in the 1950s, the inequality and uneasiness grew. Matters worsened with the emergence of postcolonial African states in the 1960s and Israel's triumphal war in 1967. Both Jews and blacks developed a more pronounced ethnic consciousness, and powerful tensions made themselves felt, some of which were expressed as antisemitism among black leaders.

Fast, who all through the 1940s and 1950s was consistently and courageously active in the crusade for black equality, reacted to black antisemitism by proposing an extraordinarily reductionist explanation. "The simple fact is that the Negro, by and large is a Christian, and anti-Semitism is a Christian way of life."[71] Not only is this formulation ahistorical and noncontextual, it deprives blacks of agency and flies in the face of what Fast had been saying for decades. The word "class" seemed to have disappeared from the former Communist's vocabulary, and the synthesis of prophetic Judaism and Social Gospel Christianity seemed to have vanished from his dreams.

Fast had not yet seen the emergence of antisemitism, black and white, within the anticolonialist New Left, nor had he heard the racist rhetoric from both sides in the Ocean Hill–Brownsville school crisis in 1968, when black community leaders in the Brooklyn neighborhood were pitted against the Teachers' Union, many of whose leaders and members were Jewish. But the last thing he ever said publicly about black antisemitism was reasonable and even prescient: the phenomenon was "less important in the human scheme of things, than the enormous over-all fact" of black oppression.[72]

Despite Fast's complaining in the late sixties about his failing eyesight and declining energy, he continued to be an enormously prolific writer. "If I don't write . . . one page a day, which is the minimum," Fast said, "It's a very unhappy day." Fast may have been exaggerating his infirmities; he wrote well more than one page a day for the next thirty years.[73] In 1967, for example, he wrote two more Cunninghams—*Sally* and *Samantha*—as well as two novellas, *The Hunter* and *The Trap*, published as one book. *The Hunter*, featuring a novelist back from a safari, is an antinuclear parable about humans pursued by animals of their own manufacture, and *The Trap*, a surprisingly dark fantasy about children and human potential.

Although there was a liberal dimension to nearly all of Fast's work from the beginning of his writing life to the very end, in the 1960s and for decades thereafter he was writing what he called, à la Graham Greene, "entertainments." Yet, in 1968 he complained about the lack of meaning and substance in American modern writing and said quite directly, and in total contradiction of what he had written in *The Naked God* a decade earlier, that only "the Communist school of writing . . . had as its basis" the "meaning [of] human existence." He proudly named Frank Norris, Sinclair Lewis, Theodore Dreiser, Jack London, and even Edith Wharton as having been "completely influenced by Communist thinking and leadership."[74]

Fast went even further. In a 1968 interview with Frank Campenni, the doctoral student doing a dissertation about him at the University of Wisconsin, he claimed that "people who opposed . . . Communist thinking," especially those Jews who had "grouped around *Partisan Review"* (PR), had given up not only on ideology, but on the quest for "meaning." The anti-Stalinist critics and writers at PR, however, did not conform to Fast's notion of them. Philip Rahv, Irving Howe, Delmore Schwartz, Isaac Rosenfeld, Clement Greenberg, art historian Meyer Shapiro, and many other Jewish writers and critics had been strongly influenced in the incubator of social-ism, which continued to inform their thinking, even as they jettisoned the belief that reality can be fully understood or improved futures fully real-ized. And for some time, these modernist anti-Stalinists remained smit-ten with Joyce and Stravinsky, and Freud and Kandinsky, as well as with Trotsky *and* Marx.[75]

Fast not only neglected or entirely misunderstood the backgrounds, in-terests, and values of the PR writers, he characterized them, out of deep envy and resentment, as "the apostles of confusion, the mindless universe, the mindless people." Even more strangely, Fast added that for them "there is no reason for life." They were, he said, "hysterical," essentially "a group of disoriented, alienated Jews who had utterly lost contact with the concept of Judaism."[76] Fast's take on the PR crowd (Jews, for the most part) during his interview in 1968, the very same year in which Irving Howe had coined the term "New York Intellectual," reveals a celebrity manqué.

Fast's irritation and pique stemmed from his failure in the late 1940s and '50s to be seen as part of the elite circle of Jewish writers and critics who had emerged as prominent shapers of middle- and high-brow American culture. "It's . . . interesting to note," Fast told Campenni, "that in no list of Jewish writers . . . am I . . . included. Have you noticed that?" It's because "my Jews," psychologically healthy, strong, unalienated Jews, Fast explained, are not seen as Jews by other Jewish writers and critics.

In fact, Fast went on, Jewish writers perfectly reflect the "hysterical" so-ciety he had mentioned minutes before. This, of course, he quickly added, wasn't always the case. Fast claimed, quite erroneously, that in the '30s and '40s the Jew was portrayed by Jewish writers as one who "*prevails* over the environment"; but now, in the work, for example, of Bernard Malamud, Saul Bellow, and Philip Roth, the typical Jew is nothing more than "a confusional [*sic*] *victim* of the environment."[77] He especially despised Roth's *Portnoy's Complaint*—"dreadful," he said, and "antisemitic."[78] Leslie Fiedler, too, Fast continued, writes of Jews "who are mortal enemies of themselves, and since self-hatred . . . is a cause of deep depression, sooner or later [this is] suicide, whether physical suicide, mental suicide, or the suicide of the soul." Jewish novelists, Fast complained, take victimization, confusion, and alienation as the primary "emblem . . . of their Jewry," which is why "my Jews," who have conviction and are rooted in progressive political movements, do not strike the Roths and the Bellows as Jews, "they reject my Jews as Jews."[79]

For the many Jewish novelists and critics who dominated postwar American writing, the issue of social conflict did yield significant ground to reflections about the mysteries of the human condition and the incapacities of the human heart. But while Bellow's Jews, and Roth's and Malamud's too, were still subject to, and interested in, the injuries of class and the failures of politics, they were, in contrast to Fast's Jews, subject to many other influences both more particularly personal and more broadly universal. Fast failed to recognize that the "*PR* crowd" rejected not only Stalinism, and in some cases Marxism itself, but all rationalized material "systems," socialism and capitalism alike.[80]

In any case, it is not likely that Bellow or Roth paid any attention at all to Fast's Jews, especially because throughout the '50s and '60s, Fast's Jews were historical figures and very rarely contemporary. Even so, the author of *Haym Solomon, My Glorious Brothers, Moses, Agrippa's Daughter,* and *Torquemada* was annoyed about his exclusion from most "lists of Jewish Writers." He was even more upset, he told Campenni, about a "list," a paragraph really, in which his name *was* included, and he bristled over how his writing was characterized there. In an essay in the prestigious *Harvard Guide to Contemporary American Writing,* the literary historian Mark Shechner wrote, "The emergence of Jews as major contemporary writers had to wait to the 1940s, when a prevailing fiction of documentary realism and proletarian romance, produced by the likes of [Abraham] Cahan, [Mike] Gold, [and] Howard Fast . . . gave way to the subtler and more evocative writing of Delmore Schwartz, Saul Bellow . . . and Norman Mailer, and a significant advance in articulateness, power, and modernity appeared to be at hand."[81]

Fast's resentment was stoked by this kind of dismissal not only because he had already written a substantial number of "Jewish books," and several short stories featuring Jewish characters and themes; he was also, at the time of his interview with Campenni, just completing *The Jews: The Story of a People,* an updated and upgraded version of *Romance of a People,* his 1941 history for young adults. Whether Fast consciously decided to "resign" from the club that would not accept him, it is impossible to know. But for the next three decades, of the more than thirty books and short story collections he wrote, only two or three could be characterized as "Jewish," and then only obliquely.

In the course of the 1968 interview Campenni kept returning to the question of the "alienated Jew" and asked Howard to "comment . . . on the role of the Jew in your novels—as a fighter for freedom . . . a sufferer or . . . revolutionary, the various roles that seem Christ-like?" Fast took this opportunity to insist that he, unlike the postwar Jewish novelists, did not fall victim to the suffering part or to the alienation. He and "a lot of other people," he said, had been rescued from losing their "concept of Judaism" by the Communist Party, which nurtured their Jewish roots. Was Fast saying now, after having said nearly the opposite more than two decades earlier, that the CP had kept him in touch with the Jewishness he thought had eluded the New York Intellectuals? By 1968, through some exercise in selective perception or imaginative self-reconstruction, Fast may have come to think so, but the Party hardly saved him from losing his Jewishness. Quite the contrary.

Making such positive, but patently false statements about the CP, combined with his praise of Communist and Communist-influenced writing, suggests that despite his break with the Party in 1957, Fast, apparently repressing memories of censorship, humiliation, and accusations of "engaging in bourgeois premises," and "Jewish nationalism," needed to believe that there had been something beneficial about his having devoted fourteen years of his life to the CP. Indeed, Fast's son, Jonathan, believes that in the late sixties his father was still, in the deepest part of his consciousness, a Communist, and that he continued to yearn for the connection he once had with the Soviet Union.[82]

The FBI agreed. The agency kept track of Fast until 1971, still referring to him as a "Communist," but no longer a "menace."[83] His father "didn't talk much about Communism after he left the Party," Jonathan said; but after "I visited the USSR" in the winter of 1968, assisting the conductor of the Sarah Lawrence College Chorus, which was performing in Moscow, Leningrad, and Kiev, he "wanted to know whether people had contacted me with questions about *him*." He "seemed very disappointed," Jonathan said, "when I admitted they had not."[84]

Jonathan told his father that one of the worst things he had discovered in the Soviet Union was the continued repression of Jews; but he also told him "about the long lines of people outside of stores waiting for goods that didn't exist, the awful food, the panhandlers, and the black marketers begging us to exchange money, offering us rubles for our blue jeans, our ball point pens—not to use, but to sell." The country, Jonathan said, is "filled with a lot of hungry little capitalists." The elder Fast, who had never stopped singing—literally—the 1944 anthem of the Soviet Union, "expressed a cross between amazement and disbelief" and quickly decided that Jonathan had "misunderstood all that [he] had seen."[85]

What was going on in Fast's mind is hard to pin down exactly, but when we add the romanticized, bordering on hallucinatory, remarks he made to Campenni about the CP and the sustenance it provided for his Jewish identity, and about the positive contribution Communism made to writing in the '30s and '40s, to his inability to accept continuing social and economic failure in the USSR, we see that Fast had apparently retained significant nostalgia for the Communist dream and for an idealized version of his own Party past, and perhaps a deep psychological need, too, for that decade of undiscriminating adulation heaped upon him by the Soviet Union, especially its Russian writers.

Soon after the Campenni interview in 1968, in which Fast expressed exasperation about being overlooked as a Jewish writer, he produced *Cynthia*, another mystery in the Cunningham series. In 1969, apparently tired of his female gumshoes, Fast temporarily broke the pattern and wrote *The Assassin Who Gave Up His Gun*, a Cold-War thriller inspired by and imitative of John Le Carre's 1964 *The Spy Who Came in from the Cold*. He also returned to science fiction in 1970 with *The General Zapped an Angel*, a volume of satirical, ironic, and occasionally humorous short stories, none of them particularly Jewish. And by the mid-seventies, despite his acceptance of several invitations to speak at Jewish institutions about literature, Fast was saying that he had "never looked upon [himself] as a Jewish writer."[86]

Not having had a critically acclaimed or commercially successful book (aside from the Cunningham series) since *April Morning* in 1961, Fast returned to the subject with which he was most comfortable, the American Revolution. In 1970, months after a massive protest in Washington, D.C., calling for U.S. withdrawal from Vietnam, Fast wrote an antiwar screenplay set in colonial America called *The Hessian* and sold it to Canon Productions. Not happy with any of the ten previous films made from material in his books, Fast decided that with *The Hessian* he would make his debut as a director. He had high hopes for the film, and was "certain the movie [would] have great meaning for young people today," especially those in the anti–Vietnam War movement. Shooting was scheduled, but undisclosed problems in production ended the project.[87]

Staying with the American Revolution, Fast in 1971 expanded *The Crossing,* his play about George Washington, into a full-length book. Here, Fast revisited the heroism of Washington, focusing on the general's critical realization that retreat followed swiftly by surprise attack was a spectacularly effective form of warfare against the British-hired Hessians. But *The Crossing* is no mere celebration of the brilliant tactic of recrossing the Delaware. Fast homes in hard on the reality of defeat and death, and helps the reader feel the agonizing experiences of war and what happens to men who fight, even those who "win."[88]

As *The Crossing* showed up in the bookstores in 1971, with the war in Vietnam still raging, Jonathan Fast's number came up for the draft. In 1964, a sixteen-year-old Jonathan had documented his status as "a conscientious objector" with the Fellowship for Reconciliation and the Jewish Peace Fellowship. Seven years later, now a high school teacher, he "was still a determined CO." But "my father," Jonathan said, "forced me into a kind of silly charade involving a false letter" from psychologist Helen Kaplan, a sex therapist and one of Howard's "girl friends." Kaplan's story for the draft board, "completely manufactured," was that Jonathan, like his father, was a "migraine sufferer." Nothing in the letter was true, "but the shrink at the induction center," Jonathan guessed, "must have taken pity on me and rated me 4-F." Jon had "wanted so badly to take a political stand" but was manipulated into a "pointless deception," and for this, he said, "I never forgave my father."[89] To Jonathan the fakery was pointless, but however one judges his father's behavior, Howard, perhaps fearful that CO status might not be granted, was trying to save his son from a war both thought immoral. As Fast had told Rabbi Gilbert of the Jewish Peace Fellowship earlier, "What is [for me] a question of philosophy . . . becomes for my son . . . . a matter of life and death."[90]

Matters of life and death were also at the center of Fast's novel *The Hessian,* adapted from his 1971 screenplay. *The Hessian* was Fast at his very best. At the core of the story stands Evan Feversham, a war-weary army surgeon, loyal to the fight for independence, but appalled by its human cost. He treats the sick and wounded on both sides of the conflict, and is disturbed by the way war reduces complex moral issues to questions of "right" and "wrong." Inspired by real events in Revolutionary-era Connecticut, including the hanging of a deserter in Ridgefield, where Fast had his country home, he created an ingenious plot, in which Dr. Feversham faces particularly tough choices.

In the novel, a contingent of sixteen Hessian soldiers and their drummer boy, on a reconnaissance mission in the Connecticut countryside, stumble on what they can plainly see is a mentally challenged man. Fearing he will give an alarm to the Yankees, they hang him with dispatch. In retaliation, the local militiamen, in a graphic and gripping set of scenes, ambush the Germans. Only the wounded drummer boy escapes. He finds refuge with a Quaker family and is surreptitiously treated by Feversham, even as the townspeople, seething with anger, seek out the escapee.

In the meantime, Fast deftly introduces a love interest, a budding romance between the Hessian boy and the daughter of the Quaker family. Ultimately, the German is captured, hurriedly court-martialed on the charge of murdering the civilian "half-wit," and hanged. Although this outcome, in the context of local fear and vengefulness, is predictable, Fast gives a full and fair account of the prosecution's case. And he keeps our attention throughout with a keen portrayal of Feversham's struggle to stay true to the American cause and yet remain on "the side of mankind." In the end, despite his much earlier books on the heroes of the War for Independence, Fast wants the reader to recognize the dehumanizing consequences, if not the complete futility, of war, even revolutionary war. The book, then, has a "point of view," but it is without the polemics and oversimplifications that marked Fast's Communist period.

As with the proposed film version, Fast, not without cause, was convinced that the novel was a "masterwork." *The Hessian* and *April Morning*, Fast said, "are extraordinary enough to make me wonder how I could have written them." They are "not the sort of books you can plan to write," Fast explained, "and if they happen you're very fortunate. Twice in a lifetime is more than any writer can expect." He told his son, Jonathan, who was beginning to do some writing of his own, that *The Hessian* would finally put the name Fast back on the literary map. It would be to his career, Fast said, what *The Old Man and The Sea* was to Hemingway's. He was terribly disappointed when *The Hessian* was mostly ignored by the critics; nor was he happy about the undeservedly short and lukewarm review it received in the *New York Times*.[91]

Reviews were not Fast's only problem in the early 1970s. He was also filled with "grief and disappointment" over his inability to "reach" his daughter Rachel. After dropping out of Wellesley in her junior year, an "unsuccessful" crack at modeling, a "moderately successful career as an actress," and five years of teaching at the Dalton School in New York City, Rachel had returned to college to complete a B.A. In 1972, at age twenty-eight, she was in a doctoral program in clinical psychology at Long Island University. Her father was very proud, but he had known for some time that Rachel, independent and accomplished, resented frequent get-togethers with her parents. Fast was concerned less about "the number of times we see each other" and more about the "quality of what happens between us." "No matter how hard I try," he said, we miscommunicate and fall into "wretched states of mind."[92]

There was also mutual dissatisfaction in Fast's relationship with his son. There wasn't very much interaction between them, but their conversations were most often marked by tension and irritation. Most of the problem, Jonathan said, was generated by his father's domineering, self-centered personality and intense competitiveness. In any case, the elder Fast was bothered enough by what he saw as Jonathan's distance and impatience to complain about him during a 1973 interview with Campenni.

Fast was explaining why contemporary young novelists could write about their early experiences while he himself could not. He wasn't "detached" enough, he said, to "overcome the successive traumas of my childhood."[93] But today, Fast claimed—giving no examples and ignoring the emotional experience and creative imagination of young writers—these authors come from affluent families and are detached from their experience because they "have the ability to control [it]." Take "a kid like my son" who aspires to be a novelist. He "lives in his pad in New York . . . a little dark apartment, and he lives as miserably as a poor working-class family does. But he wears a hundred dollar leather jacket that Pop bought. He knows all emergencies are surmountable because I'm there." Apparently growing angrier as the interview continued, Fast said, "This kind of freedom from their circumstances is a mark of the youth today. But *we* had no freedom. . . . If [a] day came when we had no money, we did not eat." Then lapsing into a kind of vulgar Marxism, Fast said that unlike his son and his generation, "*we* were totally the prisoners of our circumstances."[94]

Fast may have been puzzled and annoyed by Jonathan's lifestyle, but he continued, as with Rachel, to grasp for, or imagine, a deeper and more durable relationship. And when the Fasts moved to California in 1974, they encouraged Jonathan to do the same. The move west was triggered by Howard's frustration over the reception of *The Hessian,* "as nearly a perfect novel as I ever hope to write," and by the lure of money, sex, and ease. The elder Fast, remembering his many positive experiences in LA in 1961, and his jaunts out to California every year thereafter to be with Lori Wynn-Ferber, moved to Hollywood to do screenwriting full-time, and Jonathan soon followed to do the same.[95]

14

Life in the Fast Lane

$\mathcal{H}$oward and Bette bought a large house in Beverly Hills with a "private pool right outside the bedroom window" and a patio overlooking "the whole city and basin of Los Angeles . . . which is like a sparkling jewel with a million facets." Fast looked upon the pool, he told Rachel, "less as a luxury" than as a "means" of staying alive and healthy "on my own account." Mortality was very much on Howard's mind. His brother Jerry died of a massive heart attack in March 1974, only two weeks after his sixty-first birthday; and Howard was so burdened by cluster headaches at that time, "truly sicker than I have been in many years," he said, that he did not fly east for the funeral. He complained to Rachel that he had had "a desperate necessity" to share his grief with his family; and being "alone out here, three thousand miles away," he said, "was one of the most terrible things I have ever endured."[1]

Fast could make everything, including his brother's death, about himself; but Howard genuinely loved Jerry, and he thanked Rachel effusively for her having "rallied round the family" during the mourning period. "Aside from loving you as much as a father can love a daughter," Fast told thirty-year-old Rachel, as if she were still fourteen, "I am also filled with admiration for your capabilities and your sense of responsibility."[2] Worse, he felt compelled to tell her that he was disappointed that she didn't write to him often enough, and he let her know that in nearly every other letter.

Fast was deeply troubled by "the sense of distance" that separated him from Rachel, "three thousand miles, which is a great deal, but also a distance of time during which I guess we have drifted apart." He tried repeatedly over the years, he said, "to understand . . . what separated us," but to no avail. "I sometimes think," Fast wrote, "that the gulf between father and child is the most unbridgable [*sic*] in the world."[3] Part of the problem in the 1970s was Howard's initial difficulty in accepting the same-sex relationship that Rachel had developed with Carole Losee, an older teacher at the Dalton School in New York.

Soon after arriving in California, the Fasts sent Rachel an invitation to a party and did not include Carole. Rachel wrote a furious response saying she and Carole were a couple, and "if they wanted me, they got both of us, otherwise forget it." In return, she got an "over the top almost smarmy apology," and the distance between Rachel and her father increased. Howard, however, eventually came around, and grew to like Carole, who was a historian and "very political." Thereafter, when Rachel and Carole were invited to the Fasts' Beverly Hills home, it was as a couple, and a guest room was redecorated to accommodate them. Howard insisted that he had understood from the beginning "the direction" Rachel had taken with Carole. "I never spoke of it," he said, because "I saw nothing helpful or constructive coming out of my raising . . . the matter with you." He was writing all this now in the summer of 1974, he said, because he was "filled with nostalgia and love," and perhaps because "my sixtieth birthday is coming up, and . . . I live with an increasing sense of my own mortality."[4]

Despite his attention to his health, and despite the change of scene and climate, Fast continued to suffer cluster headaches almost nightly. Migraines weren't the only thing giving him pain. Frank Campenni, who had in 1971 completed his dissertation on Fast, "the writer," was now working on a comprehensive biography and had come to Beverly Hills in the summer of 1974 to add to "his data" on Howard's life. "Having him around," Fast said, "is like suffering through an all-day psychoanalysis. He drags up things out of the past that I have no memory of . . . things which I desire *to have* no memory of." Fast complained to Rachel that Campenni had been interviewing him since 1965 and had "been working on this damn book for eight years on and off. My . . . opinion is that he will never complete it."[5]

About some of their meetings, Campenni said that Fast had "politely but unmistakably" avoided talking about the details of his years in the CP. Despite Fast's claim that his Communist experience "had been worthwhile" and had even contributed to his literary development, Campenni was left with the impression that Fast was embarrassed about or ashamed of many of the things he said and did in his Party years. After one six-hour conversation, Fast admitted that Campenni's questions about the "distasteful subject-matter had provoked the severest migraine seizure he had suffered in years."[6]

But as usual, neither being dragged through a past some of which he preferred to forget, nor headaches, nor grief over Jerry's passing, nor the emotional distance between him and his daughter stopped Howard from writing. He plunged into work even as he continued to fall in love with Beverly Hills, swim steadily, bike, tend to his pots of succulents—a new hobby—and get used to a Husky, a huge dog given him as a gift by a friend and neighbor. In his first months in California, Fast completed a TV miniseries on Benjamin Franklin, a project that had been initiated in New York. Although CBS promised viewers four parts, only one, *The Ambassador,* was broadcast. One *Times* critic who previewed the show thought it "gently entertaining" and "rewardingly informative," but another thought it the same dull stuff Fast "has been cranking out for decades."[7]

Fast expected this kind of dismissal from the *Times,* which he believed, unjustly, was biased against him. But he, too, could afford to be dismissive. Not only had he been paid well for *The Ambassador,* he won television's coveted Emmy award in 1974 for "Outstanding Writing in a Dramatic Series." After this stunning start, however, things went somewhat more slowly. As E. V. Cunningham, Fast wrote *Green Goods,* a one-hour episode of a thirteen-part teleplay called *Paper Moon,* which was broadcast on ABC in 1974. Under his own name he completed two original screenplays and two TV movie scripts; all were sold but none were published or produced.[8] He also invested more than two months in a struggle to turn his book *Freedom Road* into a film script, but it took five years before his reworked novel became a TV movie in 1979. And although he wrestled for a time with his Revolutionary-era novel *The Proud and the Free,* he never transformed it into a screenplay.

Fast also had some trouble getting started on a new novel. Somewhat shaken apparently by the poor reception of *The Hessian,* he discontinued working on what he had told his daughter would be "an important book on John Quincy Adams"; and three months of "hard work" on a manuscript that was developed later as *The Immigrants* also went "into the waste basket."[9] More surprising, *Amanda,* a Cunningham book Fast had completed after a year of work, was turned down. Howard apparently wrote a strongly worded letter to his publisher, Lawrence Hughes, who responded that he was "stunned." Hughes "had no idea," he said, "how aggrieved you were at our rejection," and he reminded Fast that the "substantial guarantees" to publish his novels were still in place. Moreover, Hughes said, "the fact that none of these" aside from *Amanda* "materialized was . . . because . . . you decided not to proceed."[10]

Writing, Fast said many times, is "something always tried, but never completed . . . the condition of doing it easily somehow never arrives." Yet, while never praising Jonathan or his work directly, Fast did not discourage him from writing. He told his daughter Rachel that Jon had a "tremendous instinct for the dramatic form and for comedy," and his being "out here where all the action is," will be "the best thing in the world for him career-wise."[11] During his time in California, Jonathan submitted several novels to his agent, three of which were published between 1977 and 1979. He also had some success selling ideas and screenplays to movie and television studios, though none were produced. "Occasionally out here," he told Rachel, a movie "*does* actually get made." His father, for example, not long after his first success with *The Ambassador,* cowrote and saw through to production, *21 Hours in Munich,* a TV docudrama about the Israeli athletes taken hostage by Arab terrorists and killed, many in a botched rescue effort by the German police (seriously glossed over in the film), during the 1972 Olympics.[12]

Howard basked in these achievements. Two of his screenplays had been produced, and there was a continual flow of income from other scripts, purchased though never filmed by the studios. Bette, who was still drawing and sculpting, and now finally exhibiting her work, was according to her husband "blooming and happier than I've ever seen her." The Fasts thoroughly enjoyed Hollywood. "The weather is lovely—work, play, good friends. What else can I want," Howard asked. "You can buy tofu and spaghetti squash and tortillas and plantains and sourdough bread in any market," he marveled, and said, "given the choice [I] would live nowhere else."[13]

Bette and Howard also entertained often, surrounding themselves with the "rich and famous," including for dinner one evening Jane Fonda and her activist husband, Tom Hayden. Jane was "absolutely charming and beautiful," Howard thought, but he told Rachel that he saw Tom as "a caricature of a 1930s CP member."[14] The dinner parties to which Bette and Howard were invited were also "filled with all kinds of celebrities, film actors, directors, [and] writers." At one of these galas, Fast met Senator Jack Tunney, a close friend of John Kennedy and son of the famous heavyweight boxing champion Gene Tunney. "Believe it or not," he told Rachel, this "absolutely charming and knowledgeable" man was "overwhelmed to meet me, having grown up on my books as he put it."[15]

In October 1974, almost a year into their California sojourn, the Fasts held a party for Erica Jong, a poet more well known for her sexually explicit and provocative novel, *Fear of Flying.* Jonathan picked up the guest of honor at her hotel in LA, and for both it was love at first sight. "This is the man," Jong thought at the time, that "I want to wake up next to for the rest of my life." And Jonathan had long before fallen for Erica through her poems.[16] The party, Erica remembered, was "full of radiant movie stars, pale hunched over writers, and Zen Buddhist disciples of Howard." Jong, who had become acquainted with Fast back east through their mutual friend, the poet Louis Untermeyer, said that at the party "Howard was madly flirting with me." This surprised her, she said, until she discovered that "he was fucking every actress in sight."[17]

Fast later said that in LA "you work like Hell" on your writing, "because there is nothing else to do, unless you're cheating on your wife."[18] Howard managed both. Barbara Babcock, an actress ranked among the fifty most beautiful women in the world by *People* magazine, and twenty-three years younger than Fast, was one of his conquests. Another, of course was Lori Wynn-Ferber, for whom Howard had shown unusual constancy, flying out to LA to be with her at least once a year for thirteen years. There was also Salome Jens, the award-winning actress with a distinctive sultry voice, most famous for her role as a female changeling on nine episodes of *Star Trek.* Rachel remembers Jens suddenly appearing at a party her parents were giving in LA. The actress flew in the front door, Rachel said, making "the hugest stage entrance" imaginable, and "Father threw his arms around her exuberantly, as if Mom was not there." Bette pointed Jens out to Jonathan, who, ever since he was a teen, had been well aware of his father's dalliances. "Do you know who THAT is?" Bette asked. Many years later Jonathan told me, "I didn't really want to know."[19]

Even though Bette had at times said that artists like her husband were entitled to their infidelities, she resented getting the frayed end of their never openly agreed- to "open marriage." By this time, however, for whatever reasons, she was determined to stay with Howard, though he, as Erica Jong, his daughter-in-law from 1977 to 1981 recognized, was a most "contradictory spirit." He "worshipped Zen Masters," Jong said, because he was their polar opposite, a man who instead of attaining "detachment," wanted "to shackle everything to himself—his children, his wife," eventually his grandchildren. He was "a proponent of freedom who practiced slavery on his family," and "a practitioner of open marriage who couldn't let his wife out of his sight." Bette, on the other hand, Jong said, was "so wonderful, talented, and smart, and loveable," that she "made up for Howard's anger, jealousy, pettiness, and self-centeredness; and if not for Bette, Howard would have no friends." That's right, Jonathan Fast added, especially if you don't count Howard's "sycophants . . . and mistresses!" Rachel shares her brother's opinion, but she also said, "Mom was not just loveable"; she, too, in her arrogance and sarcasm could be "a tough cookie."[20]

Through it all, Howard's work went on. Despite his unsuccessful first attempts at playwriting in California, he devoted himself to trying three more. *The Novelist,* a play about Jane Austen, written in 1976, initially had trouble getting off the ground, and was not produced until 1987. But *David and Paula,* Fast's script centering on David Ben-Gurion and his wife generated some excitement. He acquired a producer who said "money was no problem." And "so it seems," Fast said, "another career starts." Not quite. The play was not finished, cast, or produced until 1982, when it ran for less than a week. Opportunity knocked again, however, in 1976 when Fast was invited by an LA production company to write a one-man play about Tom Paine. "When we called," one of the producers said, "Howard Fast . . . jumped through the phone."[21]

Fast delivered a script in less than three weeks; Kirk Douglas, with whom Howard had made a quick peace in the lobby of the theater, did a reading, and Fast thought it was "magnificent." But he also thought that Douglas kept looking for explicit "admiration" from the producer and director. When he didn't get it, Fast said, Kirk "exploded." The project fell apart, and *Citizen Tom Paine: A Play in Three Acts* was not produced until 1986, with Richard Thomas starring as Paine at the Kennedy Center in Washington, D.C.[22]

In the meantime, Fast learned that his daughter-in-law Erica's agent Sterling Lord had successfully negotiated high six-figure advances for her books. Fast, opulent lifestyle notwithstanding, was envious; and as Lord put it,

"Always hungry for more, Fast came to me wanting 'what Erica gets.'" Fast's first effort for his new agent was a memoir, but even after a rewrite, which Fast had resisted, Lord found it unsatisfactory. He asked Howard "what else he had going," and Fast said, a "dead screenplay" dealing with San Francisco in 1906, "supposedly . . . a history of an American family for the next seventy years."

Lord's "instinct" was to encourage Fast to drop the memoir, and resurrect the San Francisco story. And soon Fast was deeply immersed in what would become *The Immigrants,* a series of five books (with a sixth added much later) that made Howard Fast a multimillionaire.[23] With Lord as his agent, Fast, from 1977 to the end of his life in 2003, sold nearly thirty books, including seven more Cunninghams (six written and published while Fast was working on *The Immigrants* series!). Bette thanked Lord early on. She may have thought that the busier her husband was writing, the less time he'd have for sleeping around. But whatever she was thinking, Bette told Lord, "Howard needs to write; on the days he doesn't he's really cranky."[24]

The $906,000 Fast earned for the first three books of *The Immigrants* series, and the $832,000 he received for the paperback rights, did not exactly make him wallow in guilt, but the money may have made him think again about the vast disparities of wealth in America and the world. Whatever the cause, he "began musing [to Jonathan] about how wonderful it would be to have a Communist revolution." When Jon pointed out the continuing horrors in China, Cuba, and Vietnam, his father said, "Well, that's not real Communism!"[25]

Nothing in any of the volumes of *The Immigrants* could lead readers to believe that Fast in the late 1970s was dreaming about the possibility of a Communist revolution. His talk about such a thing—talk that never went outside the family—was probably another of Fast's ways of hanging on to something in his past in which he had invested so much for so long. In any case, *The Immigrants,* which is peppered with self-referential material, suggests Fast wanted to be seen as a left-liberal and a pacifist, and not a Communist.

Indeed, in the first two volumes—*The Immigrants* and *The Second Generation*—Fast, the aging Marxist, reveals a genuine excitement about the values of rugged individualism. His enthusiasm for laissez-faire entrepreneurialism is evident in his detailed, energetic descriptions of Dan Lavette's rise from San Francisco crab fisherman to business tycoon. Born in a boxcar in the 1880s to an Italian immigrant mother and a French-Italian father, both of whom die in the 1906 earthquake, Dan "had come out of nothing"; but driven, and somehow always in the right place at the right time, makes himself "a veritable Emperor," who rules a great fleet of passenger liners, a giant department store, a luxury resort hotel, an airline, and vast properties; and "he dispense[s] the food of life to hundreds of men and women who labor . . . at his will." But this apparent paean to capitalism, while never entirely dropped by Fast, is soon qualified. Dan, handsome, fair-minded, and industrious, gradually recognizes, as he unselfconsciously climbs up Nob Hill, that his struggle to achieve has eroded his spiritual and moral fiber and has left him feeling drained of meaning.[26]

Dan remains important throughout the series, which is primarily about the extended Lavette family and its connections to the Levy, Cassala, and Feng Wo families through several generations from the 1880s to the 1980s. This structure gives Fast room to deal with the tensions and rewards of assimilation in California, a "state [that] is a nation, a nation of immigrants," as well as with racism, antisemitism, and both the malleability and the divisiveness of class in an industrializing polyglot society topped by a Protestant elite.

Fast sees California as the final chance to set the American Revolution "right," to let everyone, Italians, Asians, Jews, and Chicanos, compete to demonstrate their ability and worth without the influence of established family or inherited wealth. There is no final judgment on whether what can only be called Fast's idealized picture of "pure capitalism" will work. But all along the way there are strenuous reservations expressed about the chronic unleveling of the playing field, the corruption of power, and the rapaciousness of the war machine that keeps the economy afloat.

The struggle for economic survival in *The Immigrants* becomes a struggle for economic ascendency, which in the end is replaced by a state of loneliness so intense and widespread that by the fifth volume it becomes a permanent condition of American life. Idealists like Dan's daughter Barbara Lavette, who by volume two emerges as the key protagonist in this saga, search for personal connection and community, and they display courage and loyalty. They are, however, exceptions in the fragmented, soulless, and finally debased world depicted by Fast.

The sweep of the story through the first five volumes also gives Fast a broad canvas upon which to paint capsule histories of the significant events of the twentieth century—all of which affect his key characters in one way

or another—from the San Francisco earthquake through WWI, the Great
Depression, WWII and the Holocaust, the Korean Conflict, Vietnam, the
antiwar movement, and finally American intervention in El Salvador. The
story soon begins to read like soap opera. There are conveniently timed fatal
car crashes, instances of love at first sight, parent-child alienation, adultery,
divorce, erectile dysfunction, even "cluster headaches." Barbara is unfortunate enough to lose a lover in the Spanish Civil War, a husband in the Israeli
war for independence, and several relatives in Korea and Vietnam, before
narrowly escaping rape and death herself in El Salvador.

Though resourceful, intelligent, and brave, Barbara can sometimes be
judgmental and impatient, often arrogant, and even egotistical. It is almost
as if Fast, in the process of writing *The Immigrants,* had become more conscious of his own flaws. And indeed, the fictional Barbara, born like Fast in
1914, is in many ways his alter ego. Barbara is grilled by HUAC, as Fast had
been, about her politics, is cited for contempt, and serves several months in
prison. Again, much like her creator, Barbara does newspaper work, spends
time in India, and decides to run for Congress, becoming infected beyond all
reason by the siren song of victory. She is also invested with Fast's pacifism,
and as with *his* commitment to peace, hers is not absolute when challenged
by concerns about the safety of Israel.

The most consistent theme in *The Immigrants* series is that war is hell,
unnecessary, and an ugly game played by "men and idiots." In book after
book, sentence after reductionist sentence, women say, it's "the male curse,
the male abomination that has filthied this beautiful world for centuries."
Women (nearly all of whom, as in the Cunningham series, have long legs
and firm breasts), on the other hand, are portrayed by Fast as stronger, wiser,
more resilient, and more sensitive than men. Men *and* women, however, are
merely "impotent specks in a gigantic senseless universe," an idea much
closer to Tolstoy than Marx.[27] Fast underlines this point by having Dan
Lavette read *War and Peace* while serving time in jail for his part in a bar-
room brawl. Out of prison, Dan also reads Thomas Hardy's dark novels and
Dreiser's fatalistic short stories, reinforcing Fast's message that we live in a
universe of chance.

That life and fate are mysterious is also what Rabbi Blum seems to be
trying to tell Sarah Levy, whose daughter has been killed in an automobile
accident. When Sarah inquires where God and fairness lie in such a tragedy,
Blum says, "the idea of justice is something *we* put together, not God." So far

so good, as the rabbi seems to be invoking a divinity that neither "allows" nor "causes." But Sarah, mortified, asks, "And what *does* He put together, a mad house?" That "has occurred to me," Blum replies. "On the other hand," he says, "even a cup of tea has its own good taste."[28] Whatever the rabbi or Fast means by this non sequitur, it certainly seems alien to Judaism, perhaps even to Zen, and in any case is jarringly inappropriate in the circumstance.

Flaws in *The Immigrants* and the four books that followed it, including cryptic or sophomoric philosophical exchanges, significant repetition, and a heavy dependence on coincidence, were apparently overlooked by readers who were intrigued and entertained by the wide variety of characters in domestic as well as exotic settings, the sweep of historical events leading right up to their own time, and the often well written dramatic flashbacks that linked the volumes together. "You can enjoy this book," the *Times* reviewer said of the first volume, "without a thought in your head."[29]

Fast seemed resigned rather than angry that most critics didn't take his work seriously. "I think I function in the direct tradition of the early American novel, as a storyteller rather than a philosopher or a teacher," he said, "so I'm resented by the school of criticism that rejects storytelling as superficial and looks on the novel as basically an examination of the interior life. They automatically see something like [*The Immigrants*] as a soap opera"; indeed, Fast went on, these critics dismiss *anything* "that traces a family history."[30]

With this contention, Fast ignores the critical admiration garnered by the many enduring books centered around family history such as Thomas Mann's *Buddenbrooks*, I. J. Singer's *The Brothers Ashkenazi,* and Joseph Roth's *The Radetzky March.* He compounds his error by saying that critics "don't choose to examine how *well* you tell the story, and that's what I'm interested in." Book reviewers, Fast repeated innumerable times, "are like eunuchs working in a harem. They watch it being done; they want to do it; but, they can't do it!"[31] The bitterness reflected in Fast's remarks was tempered by the success of *The Immigrants* series, which sold more than 10 million copies by the late eighties, earning Fast close to $5 million.[32]

Another $130,000 was added to Fast's income in 1978 when Universal bought the rights to make a four-hour TV miniseries based on *The Immigrants.* Fast had had the opportunity to read the screenplay before the broadcast and thought it was "awful beyond belief." The studios, he said, "have a marvelous touch when it comes to . . . vulgarity." America "rewards brainlessness" and the "networks exalt stupidity."[33] John J. O'Connor of the

New York Times agreed, calling the series "silly and far-fetched," just another adaptation saturated in "stupefying banality." But, he said, the quality of the film was not very different from "the literary and artistic level of Mr. Fast's novel."[34]

Far more unsettling than the production itself, O'Connor said, was an article Fast wrote for *TV Guide,* explaining why he had not done the screenplay himself. He could not "face the prospect," he said, of working with people who had little "possibility of doing anything decent" for what he and writer Irwin Shaw called "the idiot box." In short, the *Times* critic wrote, Fast wanted to keep his virtue and sell it too! And then, as if O'Connor had been privy to the details of Fast's political and literary history in the Communist Party, he said, "to participate in the system and then sit around clacking about its grubby compromises amounts to a tightrope moralizing act that is as dangerous as it is unseemly."[35]

Unseemly or not, the Fasts took the money and went off to vacation in Israel, but also while there to gather material for yet another series of shows for "the idiot box"—this one sponsored by the government of Israel and American Public Television on the history of the Jews. Bette told Rachel that in Israel she and Howard felt like they had come "home after two thousand years" and that they were particularly thrilled when the mayor of Tel Aviv held a lunch in their honor and presented them with a "special medal" of the city.

Howard, who was very well known in Israel for *My Glorious Brothers,* traveled throughout the country with Bette, meeting several important figures he admired, including Yigael Yadin, the renowned archeologist and the second chief of staff of the Israel Defense Forces (IDF), Moshe Dayan, the "symbol" to the world of a fighting Israel, and Yigal Allon, a former general in the IDF and minister of foreign affairs. About his admiration for the IDF, Fast wrote later, "I know that this conflicts with my position as a pacifist, and I do not argue it, but simply accept it as a part of being human."[36]

Upon returning from Israel, after a week of theatergoing in London, Fast discovered that he had been "bumped" as writer and narrator of the Jewish TV series. Orthodox Jews, he claimed, had protested the choice of a "totally secular Jew" like himself. Abba Eban was chosen instead, and he, according to a disappointed Fast, who was not alone in his opinion, "did what no other Jewish historian had ever done. He made the history of the Jews dull."[37] This experience may have pushed Fast into intensifying his fiery critique of TV.

Adaptations for the tube, he said, although "lucrative," are always "artistically disappointing." Indeed, television as a whole, Fast said with venom, can only be described in words that are "unspeakable." And any civilization that "takes its 'art' from TV is doomed to extinction."[38]

None of this stopped Fast, who was always eager for more money and public recognition, from agreeing to do yet another TV series, this one based on *Freedom Road*. The novel had been optioned six times, beginning in 1944, the year of its publication. Although the story never went into production, the dropped options brought Fast $80,000. Finally, in 1979, thirty-five years after the novel was published, a screenplay based on *Freedom Road* was produced and broadcast. Fast had originally wanted Paul Robeson, now dead, for the role of the emancipated slave Gideon Jackson, but instead it went to Muhammad Ali, no actor, notwithstanding his theatrical antics in the boxing ring. Despite direction by Ján Kadar and narration by Ossie Davis, the teleplay was mostly panned. Fast told a reporter who had come to interview him in his opulent Beverly Hills home, with its "marbleized floors and swimming pool," that the TV version of *Freedom Road* would bring him only $75,000 plus a share of the profits. But the novel, he pointed out, had earned tens of thousands of dollars over the years, and his "recent trilogy," *The Immigrants, The Second Generation,* and *The Establishment,* was already bringing him "more money than I've earned in my 46-year writing life."[39]

Fast, the son of poor Jewish immigrants from Eastern Europe, had everything he had always dreamed of: a commercially successful career as a writer, great wealth, and worldwide fame. He had had all of that, too, during much of his time in the Communist Party. Although he did suffer some decline in income and reputation in the United States in the mid-fifties, now in his post-Communist phase Fast was raking in millions in a capitalist universe he had often said he deplored. And he dedicated *The Establishment* to his new granddaughter, born in 1979, when the novel was published—"To Molly, Welcome to this best of all possible worlds."

CALIFORNIA TO THE NEW YORK ISLAND

Bette wanted to leave Beverly Hills for Manhattan in 1980, ostensibly to be closer to Jon and Erica and their newborn Molly, and to be near Rachel, now a senior clinical psychologist at the Rusk Institute and a psychoanalyst in private practice in Greenwich Village. Howard resisted. "LA is the most cosmopolitan city in the world," he said, and "given the choice I would live nowhere else." With no small amount of bitterness, he told a radio host, "I did *not* leave California voluntarily." He did so, he said, only at his wife's "insistence." Bette's maternal "instinct" was no doubt genuine, but perhaps she also thought it best, finally, to remove Howard from so sexually tempting an environment as Hollywood.[40]

Fast, however, still lived *with* California, even if not in it. In 1981, in a "swanky" Fifth Avenue apartment overlooking the Metropolitan Museum of Art, and in Greenwich, Connecticut, in "one of the finest houses in one of the nation's wealthiest suburbs," he completed *The Legacy,* the fourth volume of the San Francisco–Los Angeles based *Immigrants* series. In the same year, he began *Max,* another big book set in the Golden State, and rooted in the history of the film industry.[41]

The Legacy sold 125,000 copies in its first printing, and quickly made the *New York Times* best-seller list, where it remained for many months. Nevertheless, from the comfort of his new country home decorated with Bette's sculptures and drawings and other pieces of original art, including paintings by Benjamin West and Norman Rockwell (which was, he had recently informed a cousin, "now worth one million dollars"), Fast told a journalist he was frustrated at the poor sales of *Time and the Riddle,* his recently published collection of more than thirty "Zen" stories.[42]

In the same conversation, Fast also expressed again his "disgust" at the way TV had adapted his work, transforming his books and screenplays into "monstrosities." He had thought that *The Ambassador* (1974), his teleplay about Benjamin Franklin, was well done, "but . . . was no great success." "When you write something important," he said, "you want people to see it." With no apparent irony, he complained that there were "only 24 million" viewers. No amount of sales or recognition, it seemed, could slake Fast's thirst for wealth and admirers. This appetite may help explain his compulsion to write, which he continued to do at age seventy-three for at least four hours a day. The nonstop writing may also reflect Fast's fear of death, which remained with him despite his daily practice of Zen Buddhist meditation, in which breaking the cycle of death and rebirth is central, as is peace, detachment, and even joy in the present. Fast never achieved detachment and wanted to live forever. As he liked to quip, quoting the 1920s writer of satirical works of fantasy, James Branch Cabell, "An author won't die in the middle of a book."[43]

Soon after the Fasts were resettled in the East, and just as *The Legacy* was being published in 1981, Howard's older sister, Rena, died. Fifty-seven years earlier in 1924, Rena had fled the misery of an impoverished Fast household and rushed into what became, she said, an unhappy marriage to a man "so stupid all his life" that "he never prepared for the future." For years, especially after Rena's health began to deteriorate, Fast, without fanfare, sent monthly checks to his sister, keeping her "solvent and able to live." No doubt remembering that she had abandoned Howie (and Jerry, too) when he was only ten and motherless, Rena thanked her brother for having "done everything in the world for me" even though "I am not worth it." In the end, Howard paid all the expenses of Rena's funeral.[44]

He could be mean-spirited and demeaning at times to members of his family. But Fast also had a quietly generous side. In addition to helping Rena, he sent money to his younger brother, Julie, who was dependent primarily on writing for income and had cash-flow problems from time to time, and he paid for his niece (Julie's daughter) Melissa's surgery.[45] There were also "subsidies" to Rachel and Jonathan when they were just beginning their careers; and when the Fasts moved to Greenwich in 1980, they gave their house in Redding to Rachel, who had separated amicably from her partner Carole, and in 1982 married Avrum Ben-Avi, a cofounder of the postdoctoral program in psychoanalysis at New York University. In addition to the many contributions Fast made during his time in the Party to various pro-Communist organizations, he later made frequent donations to the Jewish Peace Fellowship. He also signed over all his royalties for the Hebrew edition of *My Glorious Brothers* to the Jewish Foundation of Israel.[46]

For an undetermined, but apparently significant, amount of time, Fast also helped pay the health-care expenses of Rabbi Robert E. Goldburg of Congregation Mishkin Israel in New Hamden, Connecticut. Goldburg and Fast had had a relatively steady correspondence since the late 1940s. The two men had also participated together in many of the same liberal causes, including movements for peace, and over the years they became close friends— that is until Fast revealed during a 1984 radio interview that Goldburg was the model for Connecticut Rabbi David Hartman, the chief protagonist in his new novel *The Outsider*.[47] How Goldburg reacted to Fast's depiction of his rabbi friend as "a man who loved women ever since he could remember" and who was unfaithful to his wife is unknown.[48] Nor do we know how Goldburg felt about Fast's unnecessary revelation that the rabbi had fallen in love with Marilyn Monroe in the process of helping her convert to Judaism in 1956. There is no correspondence in the files between the two men after 1984. By his talk-radio sensationalism Fast may have stimulated sales of *The Outsider*. It remained on the *New York Times* hardcover best-seller list for weeks, and on the paperback list for months. But apparently he lost a friend. There is no correspondence in the files between the two men after 1984.[49]

As he was writing *The Outsider*, he was also putting together material for *The Immigrant's Daughter*, the fifth book in his California saga. But *The Outsider*, even though many of its events and themes parallel those in *The Immigrants* series, was the book that finally extricated Fast from the West Coast, and rooted him in Connecticut. And while not "autobiographical," there is much in *The Outsider*, as in *The Immigrants*, that is self-referential. A leftist writer, for example, goes to prison for six months and describes his eleven days in a DC jail exactly as Fast had described his own incarceration in 1950; characters who are the very thinly disguised Rosenbergs, in whose defense Fast was intimately involved, are sentenced to death for conspiracy to commit espionage; and throughout there are sexual temptations and infidelities analogous to Fast's own.[50]

The fictive Rabbi Hartman, a former chaplain in WWII, and like Fast a pacifist, teams up with a like-minded Congregational minister in Connecticut in the broad American struggle for peace. The two religious leaders, both also family men, symbolize Fast's post-Party contention that the antiwar movement in America has been led not by workers, nor by the poor and dispossessed who die disproportionately in U.S. wars, or even by students, but by a coalition of rabbis, ministers, and priests.

More familiar is Fast's old Communist rhetoric. Rabbi Hartman says, for example, that by 1948 America was a fascist state, and equates those "cremated" at Hiroshima and Nagasaki with those cremated in Auschwitz. In a discussion with friends, which concludes by consensus that Hitler's Nazis were responsible for more suffering and death than any group in history, Stalin is never mentioned.[51] There are two Fasts here in one rabbi: the radical Fast, who clings to the rhetoric of the far left, refusing to believe that he had wasted completely his fourteen years in the Communist Party; and the pacifist Fast, who deemphasizes class analysis and leaves the proletariat out of the peace movement, which he judges to be the most "earth-shaking" crusade in history.[52]

The *Times* reviewed *The Outsider* twice, calling it neither "deep" nor "gripping," but at times "thoughtful" and "touching." Fast took this as high praise from the *Times,* which he continued to believe either ignored his books or "hated" *him.* What difference did it make anyway, Fast proclaimed defensively for the tenth time or more since 1944, "I am the most widely read serious novelist in the twentieth century." And in an interesting turn of phrase, added, "I exist in 82 different languages. No other writer of our time has achieved that."[53]

He wasn't so much defensive as disappointed over his meager achievements as a playwright. But he never gave up. In 1985 he wrote a pilot for ABC television featuring the fictional Japanese American detective Masao Masuto, a member of the Beverly Hills police force and a Zen Buddhist who made his first appearance in *Samantha* (1968). As E. V. Cunningham, Fast had already written six Masuto mysteries, but he had no high hopes for the teleplay, because the TV producers (the very same who had helped make him wealthy) "take stupid pills day after day."[54]

No Masuto TV film was broadcast, but in the summer of 1985, a play Fast had been hoping to launch for many years was finally produced. *Citizen Tom Paine* opened at the Williamstown Theater Festival, ran for a week, and then two years later played to packed houses for three weeks in Philadelphia and seven at Washington's Kennedy Center. That the play received mixed reviews, and that it didn't get to Broadway, left Fast frustrated. But just as his play was closing for good, *The Dinner Party,* his big new novel, was published.[55]

Filled with contemporary issues, including AIDS, homosexuality, drug abuse, infidelity, foreign policy intrigue, and political corruption, *The Dinner Party* centers on the controversial sanctuary movement, with which Fast was involved for a time in the 1980s. He had demonstrated for and made donations to American churches and synagogues that were taking in refugees fleeing the death squads in El Salvador and Guatemala and helping them find safe places in the United States and Canada. With memories of the Holocaust, and an admiration, renewed in the 1960s, for the "religious" roots of reform, Fast felt driven to write something connected to the organized rescue effort.[56]

Fast's new story, so unlike the multigenerational chronicle of *The Immigrants,* takes place over the course of just one day. It features a U.S. senator with a conscience—and a mistress. He has invited the American secretary of state and the U.S. assistant secretary for Central America, and his wife's parents, Jenny and Augustus Levi, to his magnificent home for a formal dinner, the motive for which grows clearer as the day goes on.

Mr. Levi is the billionaire head of an engineering firm building a road across Central America to connect the two oceans. But because the United States would have no guaranteed control of the road in so politically unstable a region, the administration wants the project stopped. Augustus Levi, who is in the engineering business "to have fun and make money," is cynical—sympathy and compassion are not his "line," and he "bleeds for no one." Yet his son-in-law, in a less than credible scene, asks the crusty old man to make a deal with the government officials: his company would promise to halt construction in return for a promise from the American administration to halt the pursuit of the Central American refugees and their U.S. sponsors.

Other events and little dramas occur over the course of the day, including rare, passionate lovemaking between the senator and his wife, the discovery that their son is HIV positive, and the news that he has a black boyfriend. But it is the after-dinner face-off that heightens the moral dimensions of Fast's narrative. Levi, one of the few characters not simply a stand-in for a type, is refreshingly imperturbable and fearless. Understanding that all the nefarious wheeling and dealing is a function of Cold War competition, Levi, channeling Fast, tells the secretary of state, "You and your mirror image in the Kremlin could have stopped this lunacy years ago, but neither [side] had the brains or guts. . . . Sure we're enemies. [But] you damn fool, it's not communism that's going to destroy us—it's plain old fashioned ignorance and stupidity."[57]

Well, it's a good bit more complicated than that; but nuance is hardly Fast's strong suit. Indeed, the book seems hurriedly written, even for someone who had published thirty-five novels by the time he was seventy-three, and it is obvious in its didacticism: the Cold War military economy is wasteful and destructive and takes precedence over more humane needs such as rescuing refugees from murderous tyrannies or funding AIDS research. Still, Fast has effectively portrayed protagonists grappling with persistent questions about selfishness and conscience, and the use and abuse of power.

These concerns carry over into Fast's next novel, *The Pledge,* published only a year later. Here, too, the lessons Fast wants to teach, especially about the human costs of the Cold War, are too heavy-handed. But after more than thirty years, Fast has finally dealt again with the subject of McCarthyism in his fiction. The important novelists of the postwar period who had tackled this shameful period were few and far between, and not particularly successful in their efforts: Lionel Trilling's *The Middle of the Journey* (1947) and Norman Mailer's *Barbary Shore* (1951) and *The Deer Park* (1955) were neither critically admired nor widely read. *The Pledge* was no better a book than these, but at least it confronted the Red Scare head on, and Fast wrote the last hundred pages or so, the best in the book, out of his own direct experience with HUAC, the FBI, and imprisonment for contempt of Congress.

Fast's anti-imperialist politics are again on full display. But once more, as in *The Outsider* and *The Dinner Party,* we are left with the sense that Fast wants it both ways. He wants to criticize money and power, and have it, too. He had long since been "rehabilitated" politically, and was no longer thought to be a Communist. But he still seemed desperate to identify with radical-liberalism in order to convince himself and his reading public that he was still on the left; on the other hand, he was so saturated in wealth and fame that he could afford to stick it to the capitalist establishment, and at the same time eat heartily from its trough.[58]

Capitalist imperialism remained the enemy in another of Fast's hastily written novels, published in 1989, less than a year after *The Pledge.* In *The Confession of Joe Cullen,* Fast's criticism of the United States not only becomes more strident, it is unremitting in portraying American foreign policy as the scourge of the earth. Written in the style of a thriller, crammed with murder, manhunts, and police procedurals and to Fast's credit some serious examination of the concept of guilt in Catholicism—the book is little more than a novelization of the conspiracy theory about a "secret team" of high-level politicians, powerful corporate interests, drug runners, gun suppliers, and the CIA in Central America. This clandestine cabal is supporting the Contras and other anti-Communist rebels or dictators against the Marxist Sandinistas, who have gained ascendency or are seeking it in Nicaragua, Honduras, and El Salvador.

Some of what Fast tells us here is undoubtedly true. Although a federal court found the conspiracy charges against the State Department to be without hard proof, there was plenty of circumstantial evidence and solid investigative journalism linking elements in the American government to assassination and the drug and gun trade in Central America.[59]

The problem in the novel, however, is twofold, and it is fatal. Fast gives not even the slightest nod to U.S. efforts, in fits and starts to be sure, to promote democracy in the region; and Communists are conspicuous by their absence. A reader would not know from reading *The Confession of Joe Cullen* that the Sandinistas, for example, were Communists trying to force the Latino peasantry and the indigenous minorities of Nicaragua into the Marxist-Leninist model of agricultural organization and production. Nor would they know that the project was a complete failure, not primarily because of U.S. aid to the Contras, but because, as elsewhere in the world, the experiment, and with it Marxist-Leninism, collapsed under the weight of unworkable Communist dogma.[60]

Writers of fiction are obviously not required to tell the truth, but it would have enriched Fast's narrative and made it more credible had he admitted that there are Communists in Latin America! And that in Cuba, El Salvador, Nicaragua, Honduras, and elsewhere, they too committed atrocities, and were like their opposition saturated in the drug trade. But Marxism is vaguely alluded to only six times in a four-hundred-page book, and Communism is mentioned exactly once, in a clumsily written, cartoon-like exchange between two New York City cops, insulting to policemen and readers alike: "What the hell is a Marxist, Lieutenant?" one cop says to the other. "A Russian, I suppose. A communist—people in Africa. . . . The state owns everything or something like that—how the hell do I know?"[61]

Yes. And how are Fast's readers supposed to know what *he* means by "Marxist"? That seems far less important to the writer than preparing his readers, through novels unrelentingly critical of the U.S. government, such as *The Dinner Party, The Pledge,* and *The Confessions of Joe Cullen,* for his 1990 memoir, *Being Red,* an inelegant exercise in revisionism and creative nonfiction.

LOOKING BACKWARD; SEEING RED

Memoirs are notoriously untrustworthy. Selective perception, embellishment, and simple misremembering play havoc with accuracy. The problem for the biographer is multiplied when the memoirist's reputation for being disingenuous and egotistical precedes him, as with Howard Fast. Important segments of *Being Red* are honestly rendered: Fast's account of his confrontation with HUAC and McCarthy's Senate subcommittee in 1953, for example, and the now almost forgotten 1949 anti-Communist riots in Peekskill, New York, are valuable tales of values in conflict, and examples of the novelist's courage.

There are also some self-deprecating admissions. Fast confesses his weakness for women other than his wife and his inability to escape his acerbic style, or his impetuousness; he is forthright about his willingness to put up with the "inanities that constituted ideological and cultural theory in Communist Party circles," his willingness to be disciplined by the CP and to practice self-censorship, accepting the attendant humiliation of making changes in his work to fit the Party line.[62] Fast even confesses to a Party loyalty so powerful that in many crucial instances it outweighed his loyalty to what he knew as the truth. However, the most important truth at which he only obliquely hints—his failure in 1949 to tell what he knew about the murderous and persistent antisemitism in the USSR—is kept from the reader of the memoir, and thus becomes another lie by omission.[63]

In general, *Being Red,* except for the pun in the title, is a humorless, irritating, and unashamedly egocentric portrait of a man who believes he had made the right choices at the right times, including the fateful one of joining the CP in 1943—in order, as he puts it, to fight for everything good and against everything bad.[64] Moreover, it should have been no surprise to anyone who had read his previous three books that Fast would take a much more benign view of his radical political past in *Being Red* in 1990 than he had in 1957 in *The Naked God.* Of the USSR, for example, which in *Naked God* is described as a "collection of hangmen and murderers" who "were . . . terrible enemies of socialism," Fast says in *Being Red,* as if it is the only thing that counted, "The plain fact of the matter was that Soviet troops, at a cost almost beyond measure, had destroyed Hitlerism and restored hope to mankind."[65]

Fast continues in *Being Red* to say that the rank and file of CPUSA were "the noblest human beings" he had ever known. But he omits anything as explicit as what we find in *Naked God:* "There was evil in what we dreamed of as Communists; we took the noblest . . . hopes of mankind as our credo"; but we did "evil" in our "Party existence" by surrendering "the most precious gains and liberties" of humanity. Because "we did this . . . the Communist Party became a thing of destruction."[66]

Howard Fast openly admitted in *Naked God* that he had long heard rumors of Stalin's homicidal crusades against Jews and writers but had not
believed them. He also confirmed more than once, especially when eviscerating Communism and the Soviet Union, that the American Communist
Party was basically in thrall to Moscow. But in *Being Red,* he wants us to
believe that "Stalin was no great presence in our thoughts." And even if he
were, Fast said, with feigned naïveté, the vast majority "of us had never been
to the Soviet Union" and knew very "little about it and less about Stalin."
Moreover, the lies being told about the Party were so severe, Fast insisted,
yet again, that there was simply no way of "winnowing out the truth about
Russia and Stalin from the mass of manufactured indictments."[67] But what
was said in the 1950s about horrors in the Soviet Union was more often true
than not; Fast knew a good deal about the actual atrocities at the time, and
by 1990, he had to have known even more.

Compounding his delusions, or more likely, continuing his consciously
self-serving reconstruction of the past, he said of an American Communist
Party more dependent on the Kremlin than any other CP in the Western
world, we "had no connection with the Russians. We asked nothing from
them and received nothing from them." Maybe, and only maybe, the CPUSA
did not receive as much financial aid from the USSR as implied in the term
"Moscow Gold," but Howard Fast knew that the American Communist
Party received a steady flow of political directives from the Soviet Union,
which it implemented almost always without question.[68]

That Fast admitted to having written *Being Red* after years of reflection,
unlike *Naked God,* which was written in a fit of anger, underlines the novelist's late-twentieth-century attempt to recapture an idealized version of his
long-term commitment to the Communist Party.[69] Fast did not fully acknowledge the deep corruption within which the Soviet Union was drowning, and
could not admit wholeheartedly even as late as 1990 that a commitment made
in 1943 that lasted fourteen years was at the very least misguided. Nor did he
admit that the inordinate length of his stay, after most writers, performers,
intellectuals, and politicians of any note had left, was as much about ambition, the need for adulation within an elite group, and the quest for wealth
and fame as it was about social justice.

Being Red is episodic and confusing about when events occurred and
in what order; and although small fragments of enlightening personal psychology are scattered throughout, there is more action than introspection

in *Being Red*. It reads like an apology for having written *Naked God,* a more honest, even if an equally disappointing book.

The newer memoir, Fast said, was inspired by his forty-two-year-old son, Jonathan, who wanted something about his father to show his own children—Molly, from his marriage with Erica Jong, and Ben and David, sons he had with his wife Barbara Aileen Grace, an attorney and Unitarian pastor.[70] Jonathan always suspected that his father's political beliefs had not changed dramatically after he left the Communist Party. *Being Red* confirmed Jonathan's suspicion that his father in his "heart of hearts . . . was still a Red."[71]

Jonathan wasn't the only one who thought Howard "was still a Red." Several reviewers were taken aback at Fast's retreat from important anti-Communist, anti-Soviet positions he had taken in *The Naked God.*[72] Perhaps even the USSR saw that Fast was in his "heart of hearts . . . a Red." Vladimir Kirdyanov, the third secretary of the Soviet mission, was a guest at a party in New York City in November 1990 celebrating Fast's seventy-sixth birthday and the publication of *Being Red.* Warren Shaw, another guest, the author of *The Encyclopedia of the Soviet Union,* interpreted the presence of Kirdyanov as "a gesture" indicating that Fast was no longer held in contempt in the Soviet Union.[73]

15

Fast and Loose

$\mathcal{T}$wo months after *Being Red* came out, Howard told an apparently credulous journalist from *People's Weekly*, "Ideally, I would prefer to spend my life on the third floor of a tenement in a run-down neighborhood surrounded by left-wing lunatics." Fast, however, was making this pronouncement from his splendid seven-figure home in Greenwich. And he admitted that his house in that affluent Connecticut suburb was a "form of exile from the gritty life of an urban activist."[1]

In speaking earlier with another journalist from *Bridgeport Newsday*, Fast had begun to contrast the plight of the poor during the Great Depression with what he called the "Easy Street" now provided by public welfare, but then broke off—apparently having realized that he sounded further to the right than he had intended. "I'm not against welfare," he protested mightily.[2] And later with the same degree of defiance he said that the $3 million he was worth was mostly in Treasury bonds. "Not a penny in unearned wealth. Just the sweat of my own labor," Fast said, again missing an opportunity to have a serious discussion in the media about the nature and causes of poverty and the wide gap between rich and poor in post-Reagan America, and perhaps to remind himself and his wealthy Connecticut neighbors that Marx had once said, quite correctly, that poverty was a political condition and not an economic inevitability.[3]

Instead, Fast, who clearly preferred to await the anticipated revolution in the company of the rich rather than that of the poor, mentioned dinners with Bette at the opulent home of their Stamford, Connecticut, neighbor William Buckley Jr., one of the founders of modern American conservatism. It's quite likely that the two men talked about their mutual interest in writing mystery and spy novels "for fun."

More importantly, Howard said, they did get around to discussing socialism and capitalism, but "without venom." He told Bill, "You know my side is going to beat your side because we're open to the future and your side is holding on to the past." In fact, both men were involved in a "search for lost time," a time that, however differently envisioned, never existed. And although Fast had forty years earlier run for Congress, and Buckley thirty years earlier for mayor of New York City, the two were far too comfortable now to make that search in anything more than the context of a dinner conversation, a potboiler novel, or an occasional op-ed piece.

As the visiting correspondent from *People's Weekly* put it, as Fast "strolls along the clipped Connecticut lanes . . . passing the guarded estates of merchant princes, there is no place to find that romantic left turn back to his socialist-activist roots." The old tenements of New York City, Fast said, have degenerated into crack houses, and the left has withered or withdrawn entirely from the struggle; he reminded his visitor that publishers outbid each other for his books, and that Hollywood still beckoned. Besides, Fast went on, only half joking, "'I am beloved.' And rich."[4]

Bette added "scrappy" and "[not] easy to get along with." But, she said, "we have a marriage that endures in spite of everything, because we love each other and we agree about almost everything," perhaps even Howard's infidelities. "I understand about his affairs," Bette said with some resignation. "Creative guys are like that."[5] As her granddaughter Molly put it, "Duty was the defining aspect" of Bette's life. When "Grandpa Howie was fucking every famous actress west of the Mississippi, Grandma just kept baking sourdough bread."[6] Of course, she did a lot more than that, including producing museum-quality sculpture and drawing. But while Bette may have "understood" the "creative guy" rationale, and had had an affair or two of her own, there is no indication in the couple's history that suggests she was forgiving.

As he neared eighty, Howard remained libidinous and aggressively flirtatious. "The day that a beautiful woman walks by and I don't strain my neck," Fast told a radio interviewer in 1990, "I don't want to be here anymore."[7] He also admitted to having a recurrent "dream about being on a bus or train or plane, seated next to a beautiful woman reading one of his books." But, he said wistfully, "Never happened." Still, in 1991, Bette's thirty-seven-year-old cousin Susan Shapiro affirmed Fast's sense of himself as a "sexual magnet." Susan saw herself, she said, as a "hot . . . fellow writer who offered [Fast] . . . confirmation that he was still relevant," a "kissing cousin" with whom Howard "could flirt before an audience."[8] Susan naïvely assumed she was merely the answer to a "fading writer's dream," one who "reflected back his god-like status" as an author and a Don Juan. A relative, forty years Fast's junior, Susan thought she was safe from Howard's desire to "sleep with me." Bette disagreed. "He has the gift of gab," she told Susan. "He can charm the pants off of anybody."[9]

Perhaps Fast was spending an inordinate amount of time charming the ladies in the early nineties, because after the publication of *The Confession of Joe Cullen* in 1989, there was for the first time ever in his fifty-year writing career a four-year gap between published novels. He did, however, revise a play he had written in 1976 about Jane Austen, and in 1991 it was staged in New York. Despite his admiration for her, Fast, apparently taking a step backward in his self-proclaimed feminism, depicted Austen as a woman who seems to believe she has wasted her time writing, and ought to have pursued love instead. The fictive Austen, in the last three months of her life, finally meets Mr. Right, Thomas Croughton, a naval captain, with whom she is smitten. In her "love" for Croughton, Fast's Austen says, "I found a quality that was all I had ever dreamed of."[10]

Whether or not it was Fast's conscious intention to portray Austen in this reductionist fashion, the play received a positive review from Fast's bête noir, the *New York Times,* and ran, after opening in Mamaroneck, for a short time in New York City.[11] Not well known as a playwright, Howard tried to explain his sporadic surrender to the call of the theater by saying, "the novel is like my wife, and that has paid for my existence on this earth. And the theater is my mistress."[12] Nonetheless, Fast at seventy-six, while not yet through with infidelity, gave up on playwriting, and apparently on writing in general other than columns and op-ed pieces for various newspapers. Journalism once again, as in the late forties, became his vehicle for expressing rage at everything wrong in America and the world. From 1989 to 1993 he wrote fairly regularly for the *New York Observer* and contributed occasionally to various newspapers from Rhode Island to California. He was also interviewed about

Being Red several times on TV, where Fast continued to tell his hosts that in the 1950s he had been "the most beloved and most hated writer in America," and claimed that "things were done to [him] that were never done to any other writer."[13]

Encouraged by Bette to vent his anger by doing more writing rather than by "yelling at television newscasts" or newscasters, Fast in 1993 contributed columns each week to local Connecticut papers. His pieces were consistently left-liberal in tone and position. But whether the essays promoted reproductive choice, increased public welfare expenditure, the legalization of drugs, peace in the world, and campaign finance reform, or were against antisemitism and racism, corruption, secrecy in foreign-policy making, and American military intervention anywhere for whatever reason, few of his pieces avoided his inimitable rage, jumbled prose, imprecise arguments, distortions, and errors of fact.[14]

A key issue for Fast was what he called "the war against women." By this shorthand he meant the negative portrayal of women in the media, the pervasiveness of pornography, and especially the politics of anti-abortionists, which, Fast argued persuasively, had less to do with the "lives" of embryos and fetuses and more to do with the control of women by men. When he got back to writing novels in 1993, his first was *The Trial of Abigail Goodman*, a courtroom drama about the reproductive rights of women. There is no pretense in the book to even-handedness. Every "right-to-lifer" is either narrow-minded or misogynistic, and no argument made by any of them about abortion as a moral issue is taken seriously by Fast.

Abigail Goodman, a forty-one-year-old pregnant college professor with two grown children, does suffer her own moral qualms about having an abortion, but for no more than a day or two. Her decision to terminate her pregnancy after ninety-one days leads to her arrest in a nameless Southern state where a recently passed law makes having an abortion after the first trimester a capital offense. The story is clumsily structured, painfully repetitive, and full of contrivances. Except for several pro-choice groups and individuals who praised Fast's work, *The Trial of Abigail Goodman* was almost entirely ignored by the press and the reading public. During his interview on a call-in public radio station about the new novel and its central issue, the phone never rang; and by the summer of 1994, after Fast turned down an offer to purchase thirteen thousand unsold copies of his new book at the price of $1.23 each, the novel was remaindered.[15]

Fast's argument about "the war against women" continued to carry with it a corollary insistence that men were wired to be aggressive and irresponsible. But his seemingly relentless defense of women against men was called into question when he wrote an article supportive of the privacy of Woody Allen (Fast's East Side neighbor in the 1980s), who had been accused by the actor-director's former partner Mia Farrow of making "improper advances" toward her young adopted daughter, Soon-Yi.[16] Allen and Farrow separated in 1992 after Farrow discovered nude photographs that Allen had taken of Soon-Yi. A judge eventually determined that the sex abuse charges were inconclusive, but called Allen's conduct with Soon-Yi "grossly inappropriate."[17] Allen was fifty-six and Soon-Yi twenty-two in 1992, and the filmmaker said in his defense that equality in age is not necessary in a relationship. "The heart wants what it wants. . . . You meet someone and you fall in love and that's that." Which sounds awfully like Fast's defense of his own behavior with his secretary in 1942: "We were ripe for an affair," Fast had said. "[W]hen you're thrown together with a beautiful woman day after day, things happen."[18] Fast's public support of Allen's right to privacy in this instance may have meant that he saw something of himself in Woody's behavior, not only in terms of Howard's own infidelities, but in his relationship to his daughter Rachel, who said, "There were many interactions between him and me that were tinged on his part with something sexual."[19]

DISAPPOINTMENT AND DESPAIR

Throughout 1993 and 1994, almost forty years after he left the Communist Party, Fast continued to express his views and political anger in a variety of media; but these were not good years for him. An American edition of *Sylvia,* published originally as an E. V. Cunningham book in 1960, was finally issued under Fast's own name in 1992, but was remaindered in 1993, as was his novel *The Pledge.* Nor in that time could his manuscript *The Battle* find a publisher, one of whom said, "it's not for us. . . . It seems awfully creaky."[20]

More important, Bette's health began to fail. She contracted pneumonia in the summer of 1993 and was diagnosed soon thereafter with advanced-stage colon cancer. Surgery and seven months of chemotherapy only made her life "a tortuous thing," Howard said, often "close to unbearable."[21] One of the few things that allowed Fast some respite and distraction was a symposium organized at the University of Pennsylvania in the spring of 1994 called "The Politics of Culture in the Cold War Era." The event, preceding Fast's eightieth birthday, marked the opening of a major exhibition, "Being Read: The Career of Howard Fast," which was based on the materials the author had deposited in the university archives.[22]

The symposium featured five leading scholars in American studies whose talks were followed by a "conversation" with Fast, led by professors Alan Filreis and Alan Wald. Three of the more substantive papers argued that the culture of the 1950s was mainly repressive and, with the help of government agencies and private foundations, promoted conformity and homogeneity. They also strongly suggested that radical writing from the thirties to the fifties was for the most part not substantively or aesthetically restrained by membership in the Communist movement.[23] During the exchange with Fast, however, Wald reminded Howard of his 1946 role as cultural commissar and enforcer of political correctness in the case of Albert Maltz, who had written an article on the necessity for artistic freedom. "You and others such as [Samuel] Sillen and [Mike] Gold," Wald said, "jumped on Maltz viciously until he finally capitulated and said he was wrong and that art is a weapon and people have to be judged by their politics."

Fast responded: "Absolutely true." But at that time "I thought Maltz was . . . wrong because . . . I believed . . . in anything that John Howard Lawson or V. J. Jerome would say." Wald, not fully satisfied with Fast's answer, asked if there hadn't been "something more than stupid guys at the top . . . some kind of culture that encouraged the judgment of art by political positions." Fast, contradicting a substantial point made earlier by the academic presenters, said, "It was more than a culture. It was a dogmatic part of the Party's existence." So, at a conference structured around the presentation of Fast's papers to University of Pennsylvania, where several speakers strongly suggested that proletarian literature, with some exceptions, was art freely made, Fast, the guest of honor, said that many novelists and poets, especially in the 1930s, were virtually propelled by the Communist movement into a kind of agit-prop literature, much of which was unreadable. This elicited no comment by the moderators.

Later in the same conversation, Fast, either preoccupied with Bette's condition, tiring, or trying to soften the picture of himself as former culture cop, characterized V. J. Jerome, whom he had moments before said he "believed [in] wholly," as "a horribly rigid little monster who never knew what he was doing." One can only hope that the situation for moderators, speakers, and audience wasn't as embarrassing as it reads on paper.[24]

In any case, Howard had bigger problems. Bette died on November 9, 1994, two days before his eightieth birthday. Rachel phoned in an obituary to the *New York Times,* and Howard, Rachel says, "had a fit," because she had added that "we'd be sitting *shiva* [the week-long period of mourning in Jewish tradition] at my house." Fast wanted no such ritual, and he and his daughter had a long "loud fight about it," ending with Rachel shouting, "Don't come, if you don't want to, but I'm sitting shiva . . . period!" Fast came, but, as Rachel put it, "was pissed." She believed that her father, who had thrown himself upon his wife's coffin during her funeral, did not want to participate in another public display of grief. Or, as Rachel also speculated, Fast did not want a prolonged period of mourning because for nearly a year he had been intimately involved, indeed "madly in love," with Lee Fountain, the daughter of silent film star John Gilbert and Bette's best friend.[25]

Later Fast said his initial "grief was interspersed with indignation. Why had she left me alone, a hapless old man? Why? Why?" On the first night after Bette's death, Fast claims he "sat staring at a bottle of morphine pills" and "was sorely tempted." But then he heard Bette's voice: "Howard, don't be such a horse's ass!" The pills went down the toilet, and the next day Fast had lunch at the home of his "wife's best friend, Lee, a beautiful woman," ten years his junior.[26] Jonathan doesn't count his father's relationship with Fountain, about which lots of people seemed to know, among Fast's infidelities. Bette's decline had made her emotionally and physically "unavailable," and Lee, Jonathan said, was companionable and comforting. In any case, the shiva sitting, Rachel said, was a nightmare. November 8th was the birthday of her husband, Avrum, "November 9th my mother died, November 10th we buried her," and "November 11th was my father's 80th birthday," which Rachel tried to mark "while we were in mourning. . . . It was awful."[27]

His first years "as a widower," Fast said were also awful, "never much better than dismal." Despite his extramarital activities over a fifty-year period, and his love for Lee Fountain, Howard had also loved Bette and was depressed by her conspicuous absence. Half their house had been devoted to Bette's art. The walls were covered with her drawings and paintings, and she had had a separate workshop for her sculpture, much of which was displayed in various rooms.

Howard said he paced the house restlessly, listening to classical music, while wondering how he could continue to live in such a big space alone, especially with so many reminders of Bette. "What does a man of eighty do with himself?" he asked, and he worried about whether he'd "ever write again." He did continue writing columns for *Greenwich Time* through the 1990s, but he had put aside, he said, "any thoughts of books."[28]

Before Bette's death, *Seven Days in June* (likely a rewrite of *The Battle*, rejected in 1993) was published in 1994. It is a detailed and graphic look at the Battle of Bunker Hill, mostly from the perspective of quasi-pacifist American Colonel Evan Feversham, who was also the narrator in *The Hessian* (1972). *Seven Days*, like *The Hessian*, clearly asks whether the lives lost in war are ever worth the effort; but unlike *The Hessian* it is neither subtle nor equal to Fast's other books on the American Revolution, especially his popular masterpiece, *April Morning* (1961).

After Bette died, Fast wrote virtually nothing for months. But near the end of 1995 he put together and published forty photographs of Bette's sculptures, including "Banjo Player," done in 1961, and "Crucifixion," left unfinished in 1994 after Bette grew too ill to work.[29] He also published *The Bridge Builder's Story* (1995), a novel about an American couple who tour Berlin on their honeymoon in 1939, and after a series of less than credible events and coincidences, fall into the clutches of the Gestapo. Why anyone, especially as in this case a woman with Jewish ancestry no matter how far removed, would want to be in Nazi Germany after the passage of the Nuremberg Laws in 1935 and Kristallnacht in 1938 is never addressed. In the end the husband escapes, but the wife is tortured and killed.[30]

"In its way," Fast told a gathering of two hundred people at a Jewish community center in New Jersey, *The Bridge Builder's Story* "is my best work yet." More important, he said, the novel allowed him to deal with "the whole mystery of the meaning of being Jewish." In response to a question from the audience about whether Fast's work on the book had in fact helped him "define" that mystery, he said with a smile, "I answer that in the last ten pages of the book. You wouldn't want me to spoil that surprise, would you?" A straighter, less disingenuous answer would have been a simple "no." Because addressing the "meaning" of being Jewish is nowhere evident in *The Bridge Builder's Story*.[31]

Fast's response to a phone interviewer was far more honest. He told her that the book "sprang out of my own agony. . . . It's . . . about WWII, the horror of the Holocaust," he said, but mainly "it's a story about a man unable to work out a way to survive the death of a woman he loved."[32] He told the interviewer that he, himself, had found a way to survive: "hard work and the support of his wife's closest friend," Lee Fountain. Today, Fast said, "I live from day to day because life is a wonderful thing."[33]

Howard's sunny outlook dissolved, however, after Lee, wisely according to Fast's children, turned down his proposal of marriage. He lost weight, he said, becoming "a skinny old man," who "for a month . . . had eaten alone" and slept alone. There would be no book in 1996, and Fast continued to battle loneliness. He found a smaller house in Old Greenwich, sold the big one, and distributed half his furniture to his children. "All this," he said, "was a diversion of sorts. I packed my thousands of books, tapes and records, gave a library of Bette's large art books and a fat check [$1,000] to the local arts center, and settled in to live the rest of my life in lonely isolation." His friends advised travel, but Fast, though always full of curiosity even at the worst times, hated traveling alone. He did visit London again, but cut the trip short. Even when he went to Helsinki with its "thousands of beautiful blond women," he wanted "only to go home" immediately after arriving.[34]

He did go out from time to time, but at the wedding reception of Bette's cousin Susan Shapiro, for example, the widower "looked gaunt." Indeed, Susan thought that "everything," for Howard "was off balance without Bette." Still, the bride was amused that a photographer from the *Times,* which was covering the wedding, snapped a picture of a "bald, bow-tied Howard" chatting up Susan's twenty-nine-year-old personal trainer, "the hottest female in the joint."[35]

FAST IN PURSUIT

Two years after Bette's death, Fast, still lonely, called Angela Foote, his fifty-two-year-old daughter's former Wellesley college friend, who lived only a few houses away. After Angela refused to date him, Howard told her, "All I want is someone interesting and intelligent to have dinner with." Some days after this conversation, Howard, though feeling somewhat uneasy about "breaking in on a party of women . . . with some lame excuse" about returning a book, arrived "unexpectedly" at Angela's Old Greenwich home during a reading group meeting.[36] And there among a dozen other women sat forty-seven-year-old Mercedes (Mimi) O'Connor. "Her eyes were not only wide and beautiful," Fast said, "they were luminous with grief." She looked like "a woman who had come to the end of her road." Indeed, Mimi was in the midst of nasty divorce proceedings, and although relieved that she'd soon be liberated from what she called an abusive relationship, she had only recently suffered a nervous breakdown.

Days later, after being invited to Angela's house to have coffee with Mimi, Howard, impressed by her resilience and interests nearly as broad as his own, asked her out to dinner. There were a number of mutually congenial and intellectually stimulating evenings, during one of which Mimi told Howard that he may have saved her life. Her husband, she said, had served her with divorce papers while she was hospitalized, and had left her with nothing but three boys and lots of bills. She confessed to having contemplated suicide until Howard came into her existence. This admission aroused suspicion among Fast's children and his seventeen-year-old granddaughter Molly. They thought that Mimi might be seeking no more than a meal ticket, but she insisted, as Howard did too, that there was "immediate good chemistry between them."[37]

Fast was soon inviting Mimi to his own home for coffee. Her first response, she said, was a promise to bring and make the coffee if Howard would do some writing for her. She wanted, Mimi said, to "see the great man at work." When she got to his house, Howard told her, "You know, I'm not really doing any writing now." Only half-jokingly, Mimi, arms folded across her chest, said, "No writing, no coffee." He relented.[38] In Howard's study, Mimi sat cross-legged on the floor, and the "great man," eyes straining, slowly began to "hunt and peck on his ancient Olympia upright." The page he typed, Mimi said, turned into the opening of *An Independent Woman,* published in 1997 as the sixth volume of *The Immigrants* series, the fifth and supposedly last of which had been issued twelve years earlier.[39]

Mimi could type and use the computer—an instrument Howard assiduously avoided—and she needed a job. "Successful enough . . . to afford her wages," Fast asked her to work with him. This decision, he said, confirming Mimi's account, gave him "an entirely new creative life." Mimi is "a well-read and remarkable woman," Fast wrote, "and within a week after the relationship began, I put aside gloom and began another book," which became the final volume "of the long series I had written about . . . the Lavette family."[40]

So "there it was," Fast said. "I was never going to write again, and I was writing, an old man past his eightieth year. . . . And the last thing in the world I had any intention of doing was falling in love." But Mimi, a devout Catholic who attended Mass regularly, was among those Howard called the "Innocents," people "incapable of hatred," who "move through the horrors of life with an unshakable faith in the goodness and decency of others. . . . This is Mimi," he said, "How could I not love her."[41] They began to live together near the end of 1996, she playing "muse" as well as first reader, editor, and supplier of information about contemporary mores, food, clothing, dinner parties, and the world of finance.

There is little doubt that Mimi influenced what went into *An Independent Woman*. There are a good many amiable meals described, vignettes about the rich and famous, and a discreet courtship with an ex–Jesuit priest that leads to a surprising marriage. But Bette, too, was on Fast's mind as he wrote. The fictive Barbara, like Bette, develops terminal colon cancer and dies, bringing the Lavette series to an end. Writing this book, Mimi said, "allowed Howard an intensely cathartic period, and even some closure," making it easier for him, though "still in love with Bette, to have a new and intimate relationship with me." They would often start the day with Mimi reading two or three newspapers to Howard over breakfast, followed by a discussion of the "issues." In their long and intense conversations, Mimi said, Howard confessed many things about his past, including his "self-doubt, fear, and defensive privacy." He regretted too, he told her, his early sharpness and aggressiveness.[42]

In addition to meditating together daily, the two frequently accompanied each other to Mass. "It is not easy to sit in a Catholic Church, filled with believers," Fast said, "and not be affected by a vibration of community and connectedness."[43] None of this, however, not his deeply felt love for Mimi, his new burst of creativity, his Buddhist practice, nor the connectedness he found at Mass, fully erased Fast's competiveness or envy of other writers. He would complain to Mimi and even to Bill Segal, his Zen "master," that "awards are always given to this one and that one for this or that other book, and I can write everyone of those winners under the table!" According to Mimi, Segal said, "How dare you complain, when you have won the ultimate prize, your soul?" Segal apparently recognized something in Fast that others did not. Neither his daughter nor his son, his ex-daughter-in-law, or his granddaughter ever saw Howard as a man at peace with himself.[44]

Fast continued, for example, to complain bitterly about the *New York Times* to anyone who would listen. He told Molly that the paper had been running a vendetta against him for decades. And during a radio interview in 1998 he told his host that the *Times* had failed to review, or even mention, his last three books. Yet reviews of eight of his last ten works, including *The Bridge Builder's Story,* and a mention of one other novel had appeared in the paper between 1984 and 1996.[45]

Just prior to his radio interview Fast was invited to speak at a February 1998 conference at Long Island University commemorating the one-hundredth anniversary of Paul Robeson's birthday. Fast was only one of dozens of speakers, but none, all of whom portrayed Robeson as a heroic man of great integrity and a tragic victim of anti-Communism and racism, was critical of the bigger-than-life icon of progressivism in any substantive way. No one, and certainly not Fast, who was guilty of all the same crimes committed by Robeson, spoke about Robeson's active support for denying civil liberties to Trotskyists, or about his angry attacks on black union leaders who fought for better pay and working conditions for their members during World War II, or about his immoral and irresponsible silence about antisemitism in the Soviet Union under Stalin. Attention to these subjects would have required an intellectual honesty and a political integrity among scholars and activists who were not yet ready to give up their cult-like worship of a talented, pro-Communist black man whose life and career were destroyed by McCarthyism.[46]

The conference was followed some months later by the release of a worshipful DVD documentary about Robeson, "Here I Stand," which also skirted the political and moral controversies surrounding him. But the producers could not escape touching on Robeson's life-long ardent and outspoken sympathy for the Communist Party and Stalin. The film actually showed the great singer-activist on his return from the Soviet Union in 1958, saying that Russia was still the very best "hope of the future." But it featured mostly positive reminiscences by old comrades, including Howard Fast, who said of Robeson, "We must revere him."[47]

Occasionally, Fast's self-righteousness, political dissent, and general irritability were channeled into his *Greenwich Time* columns about such things as American nonintervention (even in Kosovo), the soullessness of Bill Clinton, the violence in U.S. schools, the critical need for social spending over tax reduction, and the greed at the center of American energy policy. He had two letters in 1998 from Pete Seeger, an enthusiastic reader of Fast's columns, who proposed a possible fifty-year commemoration of the Peekskill concert. But mostly, the seventy-nine-year-old singer-activist, who had already "lost 90% of [his] voice," encouraged Fast to keep on writing his pieces. "Stay well, stick around!" he told Fast. "People like us have a job to do."[48]

Fast not only stuck around, he was writing fiction again, and "when I can write," he told his family, "I am much happier than when I can't." Grandpa "had . . . embrace[d] life" again, Molly said, and "he did what any rich, single octogenarian would do—he married his secretary a plucky young southern belle." Still suspicious of Mimi, Molly, with her trademark black humor, said, "Grandpa had 'lost' the prenuptial agreement," almost as quickly as he had signed it. But, even more darkly, she added, "I doubt" Mimi wanted to marry "grandpa for his money"; more likely she wanted to marry him "for the devastation and drama of his dying just a few years later."[49]

In any case in June 1999, Fast, a Jewish Buddhist Communist, up from poverty, now in his mid-eighties, married Mimi, a self-described "Irish-Catholic debutant from New Orleans" in her late forties. The wedding took place in Fast's home in Old Greenwich. And whatever Mimi's motives, she did shout, according to Jonathan, Rachel, and Molly, something like "I got him, I got him," and "He's mine, he's all mine," as soon as the ceremony was over. Rachel, using the mantra supplied by her psychoanalyst that very morning, "better her than me, better her than me," still cried quietly throughout. As she stood in the back of the room with Molly, Rachel and her niece were "rolling our eyeballs, making stupid faces at each other, trying not to throw up." And Jonathan was still trying to get over the age difference between his father and Mimi, and between Sterling Lord, Fast's octogenarian agent and wedding guest, and the forty-year-old "babe" he introduced as his wife.[50]

The reaction of his children notwithstanding, Fast was delighted and energized by his new wife. Before the year was out he published a new novel and had another in the works. Fast's protagonists in *Redemption* (1999) were drawn directly from his own recent experience. Ike Goldman, a widower and retired university professor, is like Fast a leftist veteran of earlier political wars; and Elizabeth (Liz) Hopper, thirty years Ike's junior, is like Mimi a depressed and abused former wife, who though a deeply religious, convent-raised Catholic, contemplates suicide.

Liz is talked out of jumping off a bridge by Ike, and both are "redeemed" by their new love. The novel, one of Fast's most hopeful, morphs into a swiftly moving murder mystery with a less than credible, but nonetheless satisfying, resolution, producing yet a different kind of "redemption." While Fast gives us another of his well-written entertainments, he spends too much time trying to make believable the relationship of a couple separated by a thirty-year age difference—as if he were defending his own second marriage.

Not widely reviewed—the *Times,* for example, took a pass—nor seen as anything more than "competent story-telling," *Redemption* filled the Fast's need for pumping out book-length work again, and *Greenwich* (2000), his sixty-fifth novel, counting the mysteries, soon followed. He told a writer from the *Times,* who took a positive view of *Greenwich,* that he credited his energy, good health, and happiness to "following his wife's careful diet" and daily exercise. He had turned his pen on his hometown, Fast said, because no other place "in Connecticut was as sharply divided in . . . political thinking" or class standing.[51]

In the novel, Fast returns to affairs in Latin America, where the imperialist role of the United States is clearest. The story features a former State Department official complicit in, but haunted by, the murder of nuns and Jesuit priests in El Salvador. In addition, a novelist, clearly modeled on Fast, is on the scene writing a book called *The Assassin,* similar to a mystery he had published in 1969 as E. V. Cunningham. Fast had hoped to attach a revised version of the older book as an appendix and fitting conclusion to *Greenwich.* That never came to pass, nor did another attempt at a memoir, "The Singularity of Being Jewish" ever get completed.[52]

16

Fall and Decline

$\mathcal{B}$y 2001, Howard Fast, at age eighty-seven, could no longer write. On vacation with Mimi in the Caribbean near the end of 2000, Fast fell and suffered a concussion. He told Jonathan it "seemed to be the beginning of his end." He also experienced a series of transient ischemic attacks, or "minor strokes," which resulted in slurred speech and "diminished functioning of the executive parts of the brain." Fast also developed congestive heart failure, which made it impossible for him to walk more than one hundred feet. Soon thereafter he became incontinent and began to suffer recurrent panic attacks.

Later, because he had started smoking cigars again in the late seventies when his books were best sellers, he developed emphysema. His doctor told Howard that with so little time left to him, he could continue to smoke. Mimi agreed. The emphysema was aggravated to a point Jonathan "found unbearable to watch." And sadly, Howard Fast, one of the twentieth century's most widely read writers, lost the ability to think abstractly. He denied this, but the condition was quite apparent to Jonathan when his father tried to discuss concepts or use metaphors.[1]

Still, at a dinner party only months before he died, Fast, looking frail and slurring his words, could respond with vigor to a question about whether director John Ford had "stolen" the structure and main character for his

1964 film *Cheyenne Autumn* from Howard's *The Last Frontier*. Fast shak-
ily poured himself some wine and said, "Yes, it's true." In the early fifties
"Ford came to me himself and said he wanted to make the movie with just
the dialogue from my book and 'no fucking screenwriter.'" But because of
"that son of a bitch J. Edgar Hoover," Fast claimed, Ford had to slip his book
to another writer after all.

Ford and his screenwriter, James R. Webb, actually did borrow important
material from *The Last Frontier*. And when Fast, after seeing previews of
Cheyenne Autumn, sued Warner Brothers, they had reason to worry. Attorney Martin Gang, best known for his battle against the Hollywood blacklist,
was contacted by the studio, and the rights to Mari Sandoz's book *Cheyenne
Autumn* (1954) were purchased for legal cover. Fast, especially in the face of
Warner Brothers' chicanery, was determined to have his due. "There was
an out of court settlement," Fast said with a grin of self-satisfaction; and with
telling this story he seemed "miraculously" self-restored.[2]

He took out a cigar. Mimi went to light it for him, but he did it on his own.
Now at his favorite place, the center of attention, Fast drank some more wine
and launched into his "Spartacus-Kirk Douglas-scum of the earth tale."
Then "spitting with rage and sarcasm" he lambasted "the cowardly actors
and producers who named names" and "didn't have the balls to stand up
to McCarthy."[3] It was Howard Fast's last hurrah. He died six weeks later.

During the funeral at Temple Sholom in Greenwich, where Rabbi Hillel Silverman officiated, Mimi's local priest also presided. Mimi, perhaps
because of the priest, didn't want many people "to know about the funeral,"
Jonathan said, and she "kept it quite secret." A priest was "particularly ap-
ropos," Fast's granddaughter Molly quipped later, "since we're all Jewish
and Grandpa loathed the Catholic Church" more than any other religious
institution.[4] Mimi had also had cards made up that looked, several said, distressingly like Catholic Mass cards. Howard's portrait was on the front, under which appeared the vaguely Buddhist and distinctly un-Jewish caption:
"He will live forever as a free man." On the back there was a well-intentioned
but botched quote of Hillel's, reading "Love one another, the rest is commentary," instead of "Do not unto others what is hateful to you. That is the
whole Torah, all the rest is commentary."[5]

In his early writing Fast made frequent use of the Jesus legend, but he had
almost always linked the prophet to his own sense of Jewishness—the secular messianic pursuit of social justice. Fast would often combine allusions

to the injunctions of Isaiah—never Hillel's—with a positive nod to Jesus, whom he saw as a Jew steeped in the same prophetic tradition, along with Amos and Micah. For Fast, these men were models who worked to fulfill the Jewish message of communal responsibility, freedom from tyranny, love, and the commitment to *tsedakah* inherent in Hebrew scripture. There must have been something deeply mystical, though not fully articulated, in Fast's consciousness that attracted him to prophetic Judaism, the Christ story, Communism, and later the practice of Zen Buddhism. But his funeral, presided over by priest and rabbi, and marred by a clumsy attempt to synthesize Hillel, Jesus, and Buddha, made a mockery of what was for Fast a serious, if for a long period dangerously distorted, commitment to the idea that there was in us, although often untapped, a universal quest for justice and dignity.[6]

Among family members there was considerable resentment over Mimi's role in the funeral arrangements and the cancelation later of a promised memorial. According to Rachel, the frazzled widow could not face "having to host a large crowd after whatever service she'd imagined."[7] There was also more than a little irritation about Howard's will. Fast had already given Mimi almost all of his money, leaving a small amount for Rachel and Jon to divide. What rankled, however, was Fast's having left to Mimi, a relative newcomer in Howard's long life, the literary rights to all his work—rights he had earlier promised to Rachel. And Molly got nothing. Although Howard had paid most of her tuition at Barnard, she was disappointed that her grandfather hadn't left things to his grandchildren, in particular his Emmy Award to Jonathan's son, who was studying film and TV at UCLA.[8] While Molly was put out and thought Mimi had been given much too much, and was "working hard not to be a footnote in all of this," in the end, Fast's granddaughter was resigned, as were Jonathan and Rachel, even about the literary rights. After all, Molly mused, "nobody else wanted to take care of grandpa."[9]

Grandpa Howie "was a left-wing hero," Molly said, "obsessed with the condition of the poor [and] the working classes." Indeed, she admitted, he had "*many* admirable beliefs, but none of them helped him to be nicer to his family."[10] His unkindness and tendency to be acerbic were generally acknowledged among Fast's intimates—his wife, brothers, nieces, nephews, and children—and these characteristics are not to be ignored or trivialized. But despite lingering wounds, Fast's son and daughter, by their own resilience and with the help of therapists, landed on their feet. Rachel and Jonathan each earned doctorates, and between them a half-dozen certifications and licenses, as they moved into successful careers in the helping professions of clinical psychology, psychoanalysis, and psychiatric social work. What Howard's wife Bette experienced because of her husband's infidelities, temper, and tendency to be controlling, we can only imagine.

Like a large part of his personal life, Fast's politics were often impulsive, outlandish, and frequently irresponsible. In the 1940s and '50s, Fast had descended into rigid, stifling Communist orthodoxy, and had become tightly attached to a party that gave him the all-embracing worldview and ego sustenance he desperately needed. Whenever confronted with evidence of the cpusa's duplicity, its servility to Moscow, or "tales" of the Soviet Union's unforgivable crimes against humanity, Fast consistently and disingenuously "refused to believe." "If the power of belief is great," he said, "then I can assure that the power of disbelief is equally great."[11]

This rationalization, however, is not credible for many, perhaps even most, Communists, and certainly not for Fast himself, despite his widely announced and dramatic resignation from the Communist Party in 1957. In the late sixties, Fast, at least privately, and like hundreds of other former Party members, returned to making excuses for the atrocious behavior of Stalin and the ussr. In the seventies and eighties, Fast dismissed the tyrannical autocracies of Cuba, China, Vietnam, and North Korea as inauthentic examples of socialism, all the while fantasizing about a Communist revolution he was sure would succeed "somewhere else."[12] When pressed, even as late as the nineties, it was not the "power of disbelief" Fast invoked. Instead, he told his son Jonathan that the "mistakes" of the Marxist-Leninists, while perhaps excessive, were the unfortunate collateral damage of historical necessity.[13]

In the year 2000, Fast said that his place on the political spectrum had never changed. "I'm a lefty," Fast asserted; "I was born one, and I'll die one."[14] As late as 2002 he would even wax enthusiastic about the former Soviet Union, especially Russia, just as he had in 1956 about the Soviet Union's accomplishments under Stalin. Russia, he said, "is not Tsar Nicholas or Stalin or Gorbachev or Putin . . .. Russia is [the] nation that gave the world Tolstoy, Rachmaninoff, [Dmitri] Mendeleev" (a brilliant chemist and engineer). Russia gave us "Chagall, the first satellite, and first cosmonaut."[15]

We need not forgive Howard Fast his political preferences, as controversial, dolefully consequential, and damaging as they were in his life and the lives of others, in order to recognize that he has earned a place in the American literary pantheon. In his first round as an authentic figure in the world of

American fiction, Fast between 1936 and 1946 wrote a total of seven novels, six full-length books for young adults, a short story collection, an edited anthology of Tom Paine's writings, and more than sixty articles in a variety of periodicals. This is a versatility that until now has been inadequately recognized. And by the late 1940s he added roles as a newspaper reporter, columnist, playwright, and screenwriter.

Perhaps this dispersion of energy in so many directions hampered his ability to achieve depth in any form. Even after he left the Communist Party in 1957 and devoted himself almost entirely to fiction, he produced so much, so fast, that in comparison with his pre-Party novels, much of his work suffered—in language, structure, fire, moral weight, and even to some extent in what he was best at, sheer storytelling prowess. Still in his "second career," from 1961 to 2000, Fast wrote two young adult classics, *April Morning* and *The Hessian,* and several commercially successful entertainments, including the six books in *The Immigrants* series, which were reissued beginning in 2004 and made available in several different editions, including Kindle in 2010.

"This huge force," Molly said of her grandfather, who had been "completely obsessed with getting and staying famous," the man who needed to be the only star in the family, "the one human, one person who got the air, food, and water," leaving none for others around him, "was left in the Jewish cemetery in Norwalk . . .. None of his books, none of his movies, none of the articles about him . . . were buried with him; Grandpa went alone into that dark night."[16] But Molly's bitterness, its astuteness and lyricism aside, misses a much larger point. "To remember me," her grandfather said in 1998, "will not accomplish a great deal, but I think to read the books I have written . . . these books have a power of their own. When I'm dead and the books are around, that's more than I could have ever dreamed."[17]

Howard Fast's books are indeed still "around," enough of them to make clear his considerable presence in American letters.[18] But as he himself said, he was not Saul Bellow, nor was he William Faulkner, Toni Morrison, Wallace Stegner, Philip Roth, John Updike, Cynthia Ozick, or dozens of others less well-known.[19] Fast, of course, is not in this league. He never aimed to be. He described himself accurately as a writer of stories and entertainments. As literary historian Gordon Hutner might put it, Fast wrote "the literature . . . not [of] the great, but of the pretty good."[20]

Fast was dismissive of what others deemed "great" contemporary fiction in each of the eight decades in which he produced his own books. By refusing to read, or failing to finish reading, the work of most living writers, Fast missed much illuminating and challenging literature, from William Styron, Nadine Gordimer, and Eudora Welty through Carlos Fuentes, Edna O'Brien, Cormac McCarthy, and Thomas Pynchon. The list is long. And to the end he insisted he could not or would not read modern writing.[21] Fair enough, perhaps. But had he even passing familiarity with post–WWII fiction he could not have said, "I find it absolutely ephemeral, filled with a phony mysticism."[22]

He was especially dismissive of the work of post-immigrant Jewish writers from plebian backgrounds, not so different from his own—such as Malamud, Bellow, and Roth—whose works were predominant in the second half of the twentieth century, and who represented the emergence of an important segment of Jews into the mainstream of American culture, even as they criticized it and exposed aspects of its underside. None of them, Fast said, inadvertently revealing further his ignorance of this literature, "writes about what is happening today."[23]

Nonetheless, a respectable number of Fast's books, most written before or after his Communist period, will likely endure. *The Last Frontier, Citizen Tom Paine, Freedom Road, April Morning,* and *The Hessian,* as well as *Spartacus* and *My Glorious Brothers,* not only merit recognition in literary history, they also appear to have influenced and continue to influence generations of young and not so young people in a politically progressive direction. What the demobilized soldier wrote to his friend James Oliver Brown at Little, Brown in 1946 gets at the heart of the matter and bears repeating:

> I've been feeding myself a concentrated literary diet of . . . Howard Fast—reading for the first time his FREEDOM ROAD and CONCEIVED IN LIBERTY, re-reading THE UNVANQUISHED and CITIZEN TOM PAINE. I don't know whether Fast is a great writer—who am I to say?—but I know he moves me as few writers have ever moved me, and makes me feel a very real and honest emotion. And a faith is restored to me . . . a faith in the essential dignity and integrity of man, a faith I thought I'd lost.[24]

Similarly, the many dozens of responses I received from an informal request on digital bulletin boards associated with Jewish studies and literary history, and in conversations I have had with colleagues, friends, and audience members at lectures I have given, were positive about Fast's early work; most indicated that reading him was a political awakening for them. The following responses are typical:

> "Thanks for letting me tell you how much *Freedom Road* still means to me. There must be millions of us out here. I came from a very conservative family. *Freedom Road* gave me a context that propelled me to action for civil rights."
>
> "*Freedom Road, The Unvanquished* and *Citizen Tom Paine*, had an enormous influence on me by presenting a view of history as a heroic struggle for justice. I would credit these books for my early and enduring commitment to political activism."[25]

For ideological single-mindedness and silence in the face of great crimes committed in the Soviet Union, Howard Fast stands guilty. This must remain central in assessing his life. But it is also necessary to recognize that he wrote a half-dozen books or more of lasting value, and gained the attention of tens of millions of readers, tens of thousands of whom may have been attracted to liberalism, or at the very least politically educated or entertained by him. This was no small feat. Many literary reputations have rested on much less, and Howard Fast's standing may yet grow again as new generations discover his best books and older ones reread them.

NOTES

INTRODUCTION

1. Tony Judt with Timothy Snyder, *Thinking the Twentieth Century* (New York: Penguin, 2012); Francis Fukuyama, "One Man's History," *New York Times Book Review*, February 5, 2012, 14; Judt, *Past Imperfect: French Intellectuals, 1944–1956* (New York: New York University Press, 2011), 122–134; Bernard Henri-Levy, *Left in the Dark: A Stand against the New Barbarism* (New York: Random House, 2008); David Caute, *The Fellow Travelers: Intellectual Friends of Communism* (New Haven: Yale University Press, 1988).

2. Lily Tuck, *Woman of Rome: A Life of Elsa Morante* (New York: Harper/HarperCollins, 2008), 220.

3. Freud in Clifford Yorke's review of *Anna Freud* by Elisabeth Young-Bruehl, *International Journal of Psycho-Analysis* 71 (1990): 527.

1. PARADISE POSTPONED

1. Fast to Maltz, July 20, 1948, box 16 (b16), folder 1 (f1), Maltz Papers (MP), Wisconsin State Historical Society (WSHS).

2. Claire Culleton and Karen Leick, *Modernism on File: Writers, Artists, and the Fbi, 1920–1950* (New York: Palgrave McMillan, 2008). That there were hundreds of FBI files on writers was a function of massive bureaucratic overkill fed by paranoia. Jeffrey Meyers, "Wanted by the FBI," *New York Review of Books* 30 (March 31, 1983): 17–20. Fast's FBI file numbers more than 1,600 pages. I retrieved it through the Freedom of Information Act; but it came to me in pieces over several years, and not without my having to harass the Justice Department, and finally get my congressman involved. The file is highly redacted, disorganized, and nonchronological, and documents are often untitled, unpaginated, and undated. The official number for Fast's

file is NY 100–61026. After the first reference, unless documents in the file are marked with useful finder's information, citations will take the form, "Fast FBI file."

3. "Meet the Authors," videotaped at Wilton, Conn., December 4, 2000.

4. "To Be an Artist," cited in an interview by Frank Campenni, April 12, 1968, box 8, folder 12, Fast Collection, University of Wisconsin-Milwaukee (UWM).

5. Rena to Howard, January 1, 1950, b1, f11, FC, UWM; Rachel Fast Ben-Avi (RFB), author interview, February 9, 2010. Words within quotes are Rena's.

6. Rena to Howard, January 1, 1950, b1, f11, FC, UWM; Barry Fast, author interview, October 22, 2007.

7. Barry Fast, author interview, October 22, 2007.

8. Fast, "Biography," unpublished ms., chap. 1, 7, b1, f8, FC, UWM.

9. Fast, "The Singularity of Being Jewish," unpublished ms., 65–67, Fast personal papers (FPP); Fast to Frank Campenni, November, 11, 1968, quoted in Campenni, "Citizen Howard Fast," Ph.D. dissertation, UWM, 1971, 164; Fast, "Biographical Sketch," in "Biography file," FPP.

10. Fast, "Something about My Life Briefly," unpublished ms., 1952, "Biography file," FPP; Rena to Howard, July 17, 1980, "F file," FPP; Barry Fast, author interview, October 22, 2007; "Singularity," 67.

11. Fast, "My Father," in The *Last Supper and Other Stories* (New York: Blue Heron Press, 1955), 206; "Biography," chap. 1, 8.

12. Fast, Campenni interview, April 12, 1968.

13. Fast, "Biography," chap. 1, 4, 10.

14. Ibid., 14.

15. Ibid.

16. Fast, "Biography," chap. 2, 1; Fast, Campenni interview, April 12, 1968; Fast, "Biography," chap. 1, 15.

17. Fast, Campenni interview, April 12, 1968. Fast made the connection between the lynchings in the South and in upper Manhattan clear: "The kids on my block had heard endless stories of the lynching of Negroes in the South, got hold of a . . . Negro boy and . . . lynched him, in order to participate vicariously in this American adult exercise." Fast, Campenni interview, December 1, 1967, b8, f11, FC, UWM.

18. Fast, *Being Red* (Boston: Houghton Mifflin, 1990), 34; Fast, *The Naked God* (New York: Frederick Praeger, 1957) 7.

19. Fast, Campenni interview, April, 12, 1968.

20. "Biography," chap. 2, 2.

21. Barry Fast, author interview, October 22, 2007.

22. "Biography," chap. 1, 16; Fast to Campenni, October 4, 1965, cited in Campenni, "Citizen Howard Fast," 48.

23. Barry Fast, author interview, October 22, 2007; *Being Red*, 39–40.

24. Film scholar Maury Klein cites *Little Caesar, The Public Enemy, City Streets,* and *Scarface* as good examples of the gangster genre and movies such as *The Front Page, Scandal Sheet, Lawyer Man, The Mouthpiece,* and *The Dark Horse* to illustrate the prevalent cynicism toward lawyers, politicians, and journalists. Audiences often identified with criminal strivers and experienced atonement for such guilty

pleasures when the would-be Caesars, little or large, paid for their sins in early death. At the movies they could forget their troubles for a couple of hours. Depression films, one left-wing critic maintained, were a modern form of bread and circuses, distracting Americans from their problems, reinforcing older values, and dampening political radicalism. But he also cogently argues that these films embodied a recurrent duality in American culture: the emphasis on individual effort and our society's abject failure to provide adequate relief, recovery, and reform prior to the New Deal. See Maury Klein, "Laughing through Tears: Hollywood Answers to the Depression," in *Hollywood's America: United States History through Its Films,* ed. Steven Mintz and Randy Roberts (St. James, N.Y.: Brandywine Press, 1993), 87–92. "Steve Fraser on the Crisis of Capitalism," at http://www.truthdig.com/arts_culture /print/20091105_steve_fraser_on_the_crisis_of_capitalism/.

25. *Being Red,* 47; *Naked God,* 10; Barry Fast, author interview, October 22, 2007. Julie's long affair with a librarian began in the late 1930s, and he took care of her when she got older. He writes about some of this in his entertaining autobiographical novel, *What Should We Do about Davey?* (New York: St. Martin's Press, 1988).

26. *Naked God,* 10.

27. "Biography," chap. 3, 15; Fast to Campenni, October 4, 1965; *Being Red,* 52–54.

28. *Being Red,* 47.

29. Barry Fast, author interview, October 22, 2007; *Being Red,* 47.

30. "Biography," chap. 2, 2.

31. *Being Red,* 49–51.

32. "Biography," chap. 3, 15. Joshua Kunitz expressed great excitement about the Soviet Union in 1930 and 1935. *New Masses,* November 1930, 14; *New Masses,* September 3, 1935, 21. Both Sarah and Joshua voluntarily left the Communist Party in 1939.

33. Koestler, *Arrow in the Blue* (New York: Collins, 1952), 278.

34. Fast to Campenni, October 4, 1965.

35. *Being Red,* 52–54.

36. "Biography," chap. 3, 4.

37. Ibid., 3–4; *Being Red,* 55–61.

38. There are names of manuscripts scattered throughout Fast's personal files from this period: *The Steer's Horn, Puppet Show, Annason,* and many others that were never published and have disappeared or were destroyed by Fast, which he admits to having done five or six times. There are also several letters of rejection, some of which will be cited in the text. Fast wrote that *The Children,* which he was working on from 1934 through 1935, followed "fourteen romances that had flowed out of my typewriter." This may be an exaggeration, but it is probably close to the correct number. "Biography," chap. 2, 11.

39. Jerry Fast to Howie, August 2, 1933, "F file," FPP.

40. Fast, Campenni interview, April 12, 1968.

41. There was a short, mostly favorable review in the *New York Times* (NYT): "Frontier America," *New York Times Book Review* (NYTBR), October 13, 1933, 9.

42. Fast to John G. Neihardt, July 26, 1937, "N file," FPP.

43. "Biography," chap. 1, 4.

44. Sarah Kunitz omitted Jack London, Mike Gold, Jack Conroy, and Nelson Algren, for example. The world that socially conscious novelists of the 1930s wrote about included inhabitants who had not been characterized realistically or at all in earlier fiction. For more on the proletarian writers see Michael Denning, *The Cultural Front: The Laboring of American Culture in the Twentieth Century* (New York: Verso, 2004); Alan Wald, *Trinity of Passion: The Literary Left and the Antifascist Crusade* (Chapel Hill: University of North Carolina Press, 2007).

45. Dos Passos, "'*The New Masses*' I'd Like," *New Masses* (*NM*) (June 1926): 20. Dos Passos's remark helped set off what cultural historian Daniel Aaron calls the literary wars within the 1930s left, inside and outside the Communist movement. Aaron, *Writers on the Left* (New York: Columbia University Press, 1992), 150–152.

46. Steven G. Kellman, *Redemption: A Life of Henry Roth* (New York: W. W. Norton, 2005); Gerald Sorin, "Was Henry Roth a Literary Gigolo?" http://www.jbooks.com/nonfiction/index/NF_Sorin_Kellman.htm; *Being Red,* 64.

47. *Being Red,* 64–65; Fast, "Author's Note," in *The Children* (New York: Duell, Sloan, and Pearce, 1947), vii.

48. "Biography," chap. 2, 11.

49. Buck to Fast, January 15, 1935, "B file," FPP.

50. Walsh to Fast, March 22, 1935, "W file," FPP.

51. Theodore Morrison to Fast, March 19, 1935, June 1, 1935, "M file"; Walsh to Fast, July 12, 1935, "W file," FPP.

52. Fast, Campenni interview, December 1, 1967, b8, f11, FC, UWM.

53. Fast to Campenni, October 4, 1965.

54. Fast, Campenni interview, April 12, 1968.

55. Howie to Bette, June 18 through July 6, 1936, b41, Fast Collection (FC), University of Pennsylvania (UP).

56. Howie to Bette, August 1, 1936, b41, FC, UP; "Stockade," *Ladies' Home Journal,* Dec. 1936, 14–15; Howie to Bette, August 10, 1936, b41, FC, UP.

57. Howie to Bette, August 1 through August 20, 1936, b41, FC, UP.

58. *Story* was founded in 1931 by Whit Burnett and Martha Foley and helped launch such writers as William Saroyan, Truman Capote, J. D. Salinger, Carson McCullers, and Richard Wright.

59. "Author's Note," *The Children,* vii.

60. *NYT,* March 19, 1937, 21; "Biography," chap. 2, 14.

61. *The Children,* 239.

62. Houseman to Fast, March 19, 1947, b40, FC, UP; Maltz to Fast, May 9, 1947, "Maltz file," FPP.

63. Fast, Campenni interview, December 1, 1967.

64. "Author's Note," *The Children,* vii.

65. Fast to Campenni, October 4, 1965.

66. Alfred Kazin, *NYTBR,* August 8, 1937, 8.

67. *Being Red,* 64–65; "Biography," chap. 2, 9.

68. Fast, Campenni interview, April 12, 1968.

69. Campenni, "Citizen Howard Fast," 25–40.

70. *Strange Yesterday* (New York: Dodd, Mead and Co., 1934), 3–7, 17, 201; *Two Valleys* (New York: Dial Press, 1933), 123, 278.

71. Despite the widespread dismissal of proletarian literature as art, there are many books and stories in this genre from which to derive aesthetic pleasure as well as insight into the 1930s. See for example the work of Jack Conroy, Josephine Herbst, and Tillie Olsen. And for a wide spectrum of opinion of this subject see Walter Rideout, *The Radical Novel in the U.S., 1900–1954* (New York: Hill and Wang, 1956); Aaron, *Writers on the Left;* Wald, *The Literary Left and the Ant-Fascist Crusade;* and Barbara Foley, *Radical Representations: Politics and Form in U.S. Proletarian Fiction, 1929–1941* (Raleigh, N.C.: Duke University Press, 1983).

72. "Author's Note," *The Children,* xi–xii.

73. "Biography," chap. 3, 15.

74. The struggle between Trotsky and Stalin was extraordinarily complex, and material about it would fill a mid-size library. Suffice it to say here that the differences between them, while ideological ("Socialism in one country," vs. "permanent world revolution," or centralized bureaucratic control vs. intraparty debate, for example) were more often arcane and personal, and the product of political intrigue, shifting alliances among the Bolsheviks, and paranoia, particularly Stalin's. The most definitive accounts are Robert Service's biographies *Stalin* (Cambridge, Mass.: Belknap Press, 2006), and *Trotsky* (Cambridge, Mass.: Belknap Press, 2009).

75. Maurice Isserman, *Which Side Were You On?* (Middletown, Conn.: Wesleyan, 1982), 25, 36, 123–24; *Being Red,* 68, 82.

76. Maltz, Victor Navasky interview, *Naming Names* (New York: Penguin Books, 1981), 296.

77. Fast, Campenni interview, December 1, 1967; *The Naked God,* 11.

78. *Being Red,* 2.

79. Alvah Bessie et al., eds., *Our Fight: Writings of the American Lincoln Brigade* (New York: Monthly Review Press, 1987); Janet Perez and Wendell Aycock, eds., *The Spanish Civil War in Literature* (Lubbock: Texas Tech University, 2007).

80. "Biography," chap. 4, 18–19.

81. Howie to Bette, Aug 24, 1936, b41, FC, UP.

82. *Being Red,* 69.

83. "Author's Note," *The Children,* vii; *Being Red,* 70.

84. *Being Red,* 2; Jonathan Fast, e-mail, January 20, 2009; *Being Red,* 70.

85. *Conceived in Liberty* sold 5,000 copies in the first six months after publication and went on to become Fast's first book to sell one million copies. *Washington Post,* March 14, 2003.

86. *NYTBR,* June 25, 1939, 4; *NYT,* June 26, 1939, 18. Fast unjustly accused the *Times,* almost from the very beginning of his writing career, of reviewing his books only negatively, or ignoring them altogether. Mimi Fast, author interview, August 8, 2008; Jonathan Fast, author interview, October 3, 2006.

87. *Conceived in Liberty,* in *The Call of Fife and Drum: Three Novels of the American Revolution* (Secaucus, N.J.: Citadel Press, 1987), 189

88. Ibid., 352.

89. Ibid., 215, 217, 225, 234.

90. Robert Crunden, *Ministers of Reform: The Progressives' Achievement in American Civilization, 1889–1920* (Urbana-Champlain: University of Illinois, 1985); Jonathan Frankel, *Prophecy and Politics: Socialism, Nationalism, and the Russian Jews, 1862–1917* (Cambridge: Cambridge University Press, 1984); Gerald Sorin, *The Prophetic Minority: American Jewish Immigrant Radicals, 1880–1920* (Bloomington: Indiana University Press, 1985); Aldon Morris, *The Origins of the Civil Rights Movement* (New York: Free Press, 1986).

91. Fast, Campenni interview, Dec 1, 1967.

92. "Biography," chap. 13, 17–18.

93. Fast, "Biographical Note," in *The Jews: Story of a People* (New York: Dell Press, 1968), 331–332; Mimi Fast, author interview, September 12, 2006.

94. "Biography," chap. 3, 17–18.

95. Fast to Werbel, August 4, 1942, FC, b64, UP.

96. Vestal to Fast, January 11, 1940; January 26, 1940, b3, f11, FC, UWM.

97. Fast, Campenni interview, April 15, 1968, b8, f13, FC, UWM.

98. Fast to Campenni, November 23, 1968, in Campenni, "Citizen Howard Fast," 164.

99. Campenni, "Citizen Howard Fast," 131–132; Jonathan Fast, author interview, October 3, 2006. Charles Pearce said the publishers "were astonished and delighted with the transformation." Pearce to Campenni, November 23, 1968, cited in "Citizen Howard Fast," 132.

100. *New York Herald Tribune,* July 4, 1941, IX, 3; *NYTBR,* July 27, 1941, 3; *NYT,* July 31, 1941, 15; La Farge, *Saturday Review of Literature* 24 (July 26, 1941): 5.

101. Orville Prescott, "A Handful of Rising Stars," *NYTBR,* March 21, 1943, 13.

102. *The Last Frontier* (New York: Duell, Sloan, and Pearce, 1941), 225–226; *Being Red,* 74; Hicks, "Howard Fast's One-Man Reformation," *College English* 7 (October 1945): 3.

103. "Foreword," *The Last Frontier* (New York: Reader's Club Edition, 1942).

104. Fast, Campenni interview, April 15, 1968.

105. *Being Red,* 2–5.

106. Fast, Campenni interview, April 15, 1968; *Being Red,* 74.

107. *A Picture-Book History of the Jews,* illustrated by Bette Fast (New York: Hebrew Publishing Company, 1942); *The Story of the Jews in the U.S.* (New York: Jewish Information Series, 1942); *Haym Solomon: Son of Liberty* (New York: Julian Messner, 1941); *Tall Hunter* (New York: Harper and Row, 1942); *Lord Baden-Powell of the Boy Scouts* (New York: Julian Messner, 1942); *Goethals and the Panama Canal* (New York: Julian Messner, 1942).

108. Fast to Campenni, October 4, 1965.

109. *New York Herald Tribune,* June 14, 1942, IX, 5; *Time* magazine, July 13, 1942, 88; *Nation,* August 14, 1942, 693; *New Republic,* August 17, 1942, 203.

110. Joshua Rubenstein, "Introduction," in *The Unknown Black Book,* ed. Ilya Altman (Bloomington: Indiana University Press, 2007); Timothy Snyder, *Bloodlands: Europe between Hitler and Stalin* (New York: Basic Books, 2010).

111. *The Unvanquished* (New York: Duell, Sloan, and Pearce, 1942), 140–141.

112. Ibid., 313.

113. In an "Afterword," Fast pays tribute to Rupert Hughes, scholar and author of *George Washington,* 3 vols. (New York: W. Morrow, 1926–1930), who generally lays out a deprecatory view of the worker and the farmer; also see letters between Carl Van Doren and Howard Fast in which Van Doren praises Fast for his historical accuracy. Fast to Van Doren, March 17, 1942, to July 1942, b16, f1, Charles Van Doren collection, Princeton University.

2. THE WAR AGAINST FASCISM

1. Flyer, box 3 (b3), folder 10 (f10), Fast Collection (FC), University of Wisconsin at Milwaukee (UWM).

2. Fast, Frank Campenni interview, April 16, 1968, b8, f14, FC, UWM.

3. Fast, "Biography," unpublished typescript, chap. 4, 11, b1, f8, FC, UWM.

4. *Being Red,* 4–7.

5. Fast, Campenni interview, April 16, 1968; Fast on CBS *Nightwatch,* December 7, 1990.

6. Fast, FBI file, NY 100–61026 (Fast FBI file)

7. "Biography," chap. 4, 13–14.

8. Likely based on an actual taxi drivers' strike in 1934, *Waiting for Lefty* brought audiences to their feet clamoring the final lines along with the actors, "Strike! Strike! Strike!" Ironically the bourgeois *Morning Telegraph* liked the play better than the Communist *Daily Worker* or *Der Morgen Freiheit,* both of which found the production insufficiently orthodox. Joseph Dorinson, "Breaking the Slump: 1930s American Popular Culture," unpublished ms., 4.

9. Selective Service card, 1943, Fast Personal Papers (FPP).

10. *Being Red,* 13–14.

11. *New York Herald Tribune Weekly Book Review,* April 4, 1943, 1; *NYTBR,* April 25, 1943, 1. Clifton Fadiman, reviewing *Paine,* called Fast one of America's most important historical novelists. "Books: 'Citizen Tom Paine,'" *New Yorker,* May 1, 1943, 70–74.

12. There were three printings in the first year, and another five by 1946, selling more than one million copies in hard back.

13. Paine, *Common Sense,* appendix, February 14, 1776 (reprint, Whitefish, Mont.: Kessinger Publishing, LLC, 2004).

14. *Citizen Tom Paine* (New York: Grove Press, 1983), 41.

15. Fast, "Who Was Tom Paine?" *New Masses* (NM), February 27, 1945, 23.

16. Whether or not Fast actually read the work of historians Carl Becker, Charles Beard, and Vernon Parrington, founders of the "progressive school" of historical interpretation, his novels on the Revolution employed several of the themes they made popular in the first half of the twentieth century, including the primacy of economic and geographical forces. But unlike these historians Fast did not, at least until 1944–45, see ideas or philosophical principles as merely instruments or masks for deeper realities. Becker, *History of Political Parties in the Province of New York, 1760–1776* (1909) (Madison: University of Wisconsin Press, 2007, e-book); Beard, *An Economic Interpretation of the Constitution of the United States* (1913) (New York: Free Press, 1986); Parrington, *Main Currents in American Thought,* 3 vols. (1927) (Norman: University of Oklahoma Press, 1987).

17. See Gordon Wood, *The Radicalism of the American Revolution* (New York: Knopf, 1992); Edmund Morgan, "The Other Founders," *New York Review of Books* 14 (September 22, 2005), at http://www.nybooks.com/issues/2005/sep/22/.

18. W. E. Woodward, *Tom Paine: America's Godfather, 1737–1789* (New York: Dutton, 1945); *NYTBR,* June 22, 1945, 23.

19. *Citizen Tom Paine,* 130, 186, 193, 198, 206, 256. For the Rumples, see 84–92.

20. Harvey Kaye, *Thomas Paine and the Promise of America* (New York: Hill and Wang, 2005).

21. Paine, quoted in Harvey Kaye, "Reclaiming Thomas Paine, Reviving Democracy and American Labor," at http://www.aflcio.org/mediacenter/speakout/harvey_kaye.cfm. Also see Kaye, *Thomas Paine and the Promise of America;* Craig Nelson, *Thomas Paine: Enlightenment, Revolution, and the Birth of Modern Nations* (New York: Viking, 2006). One of Paine's antislavery letters was published as a pamphlet called *African Slavery in America,* and got wide circulation.

22. *Being Red,* 16.

23. "Biography," chap. 4, 15–16.

24. Fast, edited and redacted manuscript, "Being Red," b52, FC, University of Pennsylvania (UP); *Being Red,* 17.

25. "Biography," chap. 4, 20.

26. Nancy Lynn Schwartz, *The Hollywood Writers' War,* completed by Sheila Schwartz (Backprint.Com, 2001), 15, 16, 21, 44.

27. Fast to Devery Freeman, August 14, 1943, b3, f12, FC, UWM; Fast, Campenni interview, August 12–19, 1977, b9, f2, FC, UWM.

28. Fast to Freeman, August 14, 1943; Schlesinger, *The Vital Center: The Politics of Freedom* (New York: Transaction Publishers, 1997), 125.

29. Fast to Freeman, August 14, 1943, b3, f12, FC, UWM; Fast, Campenni interview, August 12–19, 1977.

30. Fast, Campenni interview, December 1, 1967, b8, f11, FC, UWM.

31. *Being Red,* 79.

32. Martin Duberman, *Paul Robeson* (New York: Alfred A. Knopf, 1988).

33. Fast, Campenni interview, August 12–19, 1977.

34. Duberman, *Paul Robeson,* 90, 186.

35. "Biography," chap. 4, 24. Barry Finger, "Paul Robeson: A Flawed Martyr,"

New Politics 7 (Summer 1998), at http://www.wpunj.edu/~newpol/issue25/finger25
.htm.

36. Fast to Freeman, August 14, 1943, b3, f12, FC, UWM; "Biography," chap. 4,
24–25.

37. "Biography," chap. 4, 25; *Being Red,* 17.

38. *Being Red,* 19.

39. Glazer, *The Social Basis of American Communism* (New York: Harcourt Brace,
1961), 166.

40. *Being Red,* 95, 82.

41. Ibid., 82.

42. "Transcript of interview by Martin Agronsky," October 13, 1957, NBC television
network, published in *Progressive* 22 (March 1958): 35–38. Emphasis mine.

43. A secret protocol in the Nazi-Soviet pact known as the German-Soviet Boundary and Friendship Treaty stipulated, "Both parties will tolerate in their territories
no Polish agitation which affects the territories of the other party. They will suppress
in their territories all beginnings of such agitation and inform each other concerning
suitable measures for this purpose." At http://avalon.law.yale.edu/20th_century
/gsbound.asp.

44. Joshua Rubenstein and Vladimir P. Naumov, eds., *Stalin's Secret Pogrom: The
Postwar Inquisition of the Jewish Anti-Fascist Committee* (New Haven, Conn.: Yale
University Press, 2005), 8–10; Isserman, *Which Side Were You On?*, 159–160.

45. "How Erlich-Alter Case Affects U.S.-Soviet Relations," *PM,* March 18, 1943,
16–17; *New Republic,* March 15, 1943, 336; *Nation,* March 13, 1943, 11; *PM,* March 18,
1943.

46. "Biography," chap. 8, 20.

47. Ibid. Emphasis mine.

48. "A Conversation with Howard Fast, March 23, 1994," conducted by Alan Wald
and Alan Filreis, ed. Thomas J. Sugrue, *Prospects* 20 (1995): 511–523.

49. *Naked God,* 38.

50. *Being Red,* 42, 28.

51. In the early 1930s, Hitler's expansionist goals and rearmament program moved
Stalin to conclude that the Soviet Union and Communist parties in other countries
were at risk if they did not make coalitions with non-Communist political forces. In
1935 the Comintern called for joining the "Popular Front," a union of left and liberal groups against fascism that had emerged in the United States and elsewhere in
1933–34. The Popular Front got lots of support in the United States from New Dealers and other left-liberal groups in the Progressive and Farmer-Labor parties, from
the increasingly successful CIO and many other labor unions, as well as from artists,
entertainers, and intellectuals. These groups, with their enormous cultural creativity,
were not simply the "tools" of the Communist Party, as some have contended. The
Party did become the Popular Front's "institutional core" in America, yet it remained
largely dependent on the wider liberal antifascist coalition for its political influence
and moral authority. In the mid-to-late thirties (the height of the Popular Front's appeal as an antifascist force), when many leaders of democratic states seemed reluctant

to confront Hitler, Communists in the Popular Front alliance appeared to be the moral exemplar in the anti-Nazi battle. See Michael Denning, *The Cultural Front: The Laboring of American Culture* (New York: Verso, 1998), 4–50.

52. *Daily Worker* (DW), August 3, 1943, 1. Mark Naison, *Communists in Harlem during the Depression* (Urbana-Champagne: University of Illinois, 2004); James Edward Smethurst, *The New Red Negro* (New York: Oxford, 1999) 21–23. On the "women's question," male Communists usually responded with condescension, but there were few other organizations in the United States in which women could even challenge such attitudes. Moreover, the CPUSA helped increase employment opportunities for women and promoted equal pay within the union movement.

53. *Being Red,* 21–24.

54. Fast FBI file; flyer, "W" file, FPP; Robeson to Fast, January 4, 1943, "R file," FPP. "Communist front" is an inexact term, used loosely by the FBI and the attorney general's office. It would find its way, too, into newspapers, and other unofficial sources.

55. Letter of clearance, May 19, 1943, b7, f8, FC, UWM.

56. Local Board Permit for Departure from U.S., b7, f8, FC, UWM.

57. "Biography," chap. 4, 24; Fast, interviewed by Campenni, March 13–14, 1973, b9, f2, FC, UWM. Fast reiterated his claim that he wrote *Freedom Road* for Paul Robeson during a radio interview, on *Voices of Our World,* March 15, 1998, audiotape, FPP; http://movies.nytimes.com/movie/91991/For-Whom-the-Bell-Tolls/awards; Ed Krzemienski, "There's Something About Harry," *Bright Lights Film Journal* 25 (August 1999), at http://www.brightlightsfilm.com/25/tohave1.php.

58. Fast, Campenni interview, March 13–14, 1973.

59. William Edward Burghardt Du Bois, *Black Reconstruction in America* (1935) (reprint, New York: Free Press, 1998).

60. *Being Red,* 75–77.

61. *PM,* December 9, 1942, 12, 18–20.

62. Philip Bernstein, "The Jews of Europe: The Remnants of a People," *Nation,* January 2, 1943, at http://www.thenation.com/archive/jews-europe-i-remnants -people.

63. *PM,* August 27, 1943, 12–13.

64. *Being Red,* 75–77.

65. Glazer, *The Social Basis of American Communism,* 134–166.

66. Earl Ofari Hutchinson, *Blacks and Reds: Race and Class in Conflict, 1919–1990* (Lansing: Michigan State University, 1994), 61–68, 223–238; Junius Scales and Richard Nickson, *Cause at Heart: A Former Communist Remembers* (Athens: University of Georgia Press, 2005), 162–166, 210–211.

67. For much more on this see Alan M. Wald, *Trinity of Passion: The Literary Left and the Anti-Fascist Crusade* (Chapel Hill: University of North Carolina Press, 2007).

68. *Being Red,* 75–77.

69. Fast, *Freedom Road* (Armonk, N.Y.: M. E. Sharpe, 2005), 60.

70. Ibid., 104.

71. Eric Foner, *Reconstruction: The Unfinished Revolution* (New York: Harper Perennial Modern Classics, 2002).

72. "Howard Fast," in *Current Biography*, ed. Margaret Brooks (New York: H. W. Wilson, 1943), 200.

73. Russell Merritt, "Dixon, Griffith, and the Southern Legend," *Cinema Journal*, 12 (Autumn 1972): 26–45.

74. Ernest E. Leisy, *The American Historical Novel* (Norman: University of Oklahoma Press, 1950), 170–172, 188–189.

75. When David Levering Lewis interviewed Howard Fast in 1990 for his Pulitzer Prize–winning biography of Du Bois, the author of *Freedom Road* admitted that he had "relied heavily" and "proudly" on *Black Reconstruction in America*. Lewis, *W.E.B. Du Bois: The Fight for Equality and the American Century 1919–1963* (New York: Holt, 2001), 526. How heavily is evident from reading Du Bois's chapter on South Carolina. Fast did not technically plagiarize; but it is curious that in listing sources used in preparation of *Freedom Road*, Fast did not mention Du Bois's book.

76. Hammett to Hellman, March 1, 1945 in *The Selected Letters of Dashiell Hammett, 1921–1960*, ed. Richard Layman (Washington, D.C.: Counterpoint, 2001), 413.

77. "Fiction in Review," *Nation*, May 8, 1943, 676; *NYT*, August 16, 1944, 17.

78. George Mayberry, *New Republic*, August 14, 1994, 196; Edward Weeks, *Atlantic Monthly*, September 1944, 127.

79. *Being Red*, 84; *Newsweek*, August 21, 1944, 84.

80. Navasky, *Naming Names*, 239–246; Richard Wright, "I Tried to be a Communist," part 1, *Atlantic Monthly*, August 1944, 61–70; part 2, September 1944, 48–56.

81. Memo, Fast FBI File. Interestingly enough a Soviet critic thought *Freedom Road* an excellent book in which the author "by no means draws pessimistic conclusions." M. Urnov, "Howard Fast and America," *Soviet Literature*, November 11, 1948, 185–191.

82. Gerald Zahavi, "The 'Trial' of Lee Benson: Communism, White Chauvinism and the Foundations of the 'New Political History' in the United States," *History and Theory* 42 (October 2003): 332–362; Isserman, *Which Side Were You On?*, 107; Joseph C. Mouledous, "From Browderism to Peaceful Co-Existence: An Analysis of Developments in the Communist Position on the American Negro," *Phylon* 1 (1962) 79–90; *Naked God*, 139.

83. *Naked God*, 138. The Party was clearly adhering to a genre of art mandated by Stalin.

84. Ibid., 139. Emphasis mine. Several years later, in November 1952, Steve Nelson, an important veteran of the Spanish Civil War and major functionary of the Communist Party, wrote to Fast from prison that he had run into several of Howard's books "in the workhouse." A "large group of young Negroes read them," Nelson wrote. "Freedom Road was criticized (to my surprise) by a group of them. They dislike the dialect," he said. "I do not know if this is general. I never heard it among 'our people.' I just tell you for what it is worth." Nelson to Fast, November 5, 1952, b6, f4, FC, UWM.

85. *Being Red*, 141–142.

86. *Naked God*, 12.

87. For a persuasive exploration of this psycho-political process see Czeslaw Milosz, *The Captive Mind* (New York: Vintage, 1990).

3. THE LIFE OF THE PARTY

1. Hammett to Hellman, March 1, 1945, in *The Selected Letters of Dashiell Hammett*, 413.

2. Maltz to Fast, October 19, 1944, box 1, folder 22, Fast Collection (FC), University of Wisconsin at Milwaukee (UWM).

3. Stories as well as excerpts appeared in *Forward* (New York: Scott, Foresman, 1942); *Patterns for Living* (New York: MacMillan, 1943; *Adventures in Reading* (New York: Harcourt Brace, 1944); and *America in Literature* (New York: F. S. Crofts, 1944). Between 1942 and 1944, Fast wrote twenty-two stories for *Young America*. The announcement of the award appeared in *NYT*, October 10, 1944, 21.

4. For themes that would continue to engage Fast throughout his lifetime, see his early articles including "Proud to Be Black," *Negro Digest* 3 (March 1945): 6; "The Negro Finds His History," New Masses (*NM*), May 15, 1945, 17.

5. Fast, "Together with our Soviet Allies," *Soviet Russia Today,* November 1944, 7.

6. *Saturday Review,* February 20, 1943, 8.

7. Gitlin to Fast, November 26, 1943, b1, f8, FC, UWM.

8. "Howard Fast: Under Forty," *Contemporary Jewish Record* 7 (February 1944): 25–27.

9. Susan Schweik, *A Gulf So Deeply Cut: American Women's Poetry of the Second World War* (Madison: University of Wisconsin Press, 1991), 169–170. The poem eventually became part of the Jewish Reform and Reconstructionist liturgy.

10. Fast, "Under Forty," 25–27.

11. Fast, *Being Red,* 275.

12. *NM,* December 7, 1943, 1–2.

13. *NM,* January 11, 1944, 17.

14. Poets Eda Lou Walton, Lion Feuchtwanger, and Norman Rosten, while not as enthusiastic for a lynching as Maltz, thought Pound at least ought to be punished harshly for treason. Trial first, of course. *NM,* December 25, 1945, 6–7.

15. University of San Diego—Historical Monograph #4: "The KGB in San Francisco and Mexico City and the GRU in New York and Washington," at http://history.sandiego.edu/GEN/text/coldwar/venona4.html.

16. Michael Belknap, *Cold War Political Justice: The Smith Act, the Communist Party, and American Civil Liberties* (Westport, Conn.: Greenwood Press, 1977).

17. I. F. Stone, "The Case of the Trotskyists," *PM,* December 31, 1943, 2.

18. "The Disguised Nazism of the Trotskyites," *Daily Worker* (*DW*), July 12, 1941, 1.

19. Fast, interviewed by Natalie Robins, *Alien Ink: The Fbi's War on Freedom of Expression* (New York: William Morrow, 1992), 233–235.

20. "Agent Memo," June 27, 1946, Fast FBI file; Fast, in *Alien Ink,* 235.

21. *Tito and His People* (Winnipeg: Contemporary Publishers, 1944).

22. Memo, October 31, 1945, and other undated FBI memos in Fast's file.

23. "The New American Scholar," *Christian Register* 55 (February 1945): 124.

24. "Realism and the Soviet Novel," *NM*, December 11, 1945, 16.

25. Clearance papers in b7, f8, FC, UWM; page marked file number 100–18035, January 18, 1946, Fast FBI file.

26. "Agent Memo," June 27, 1946, 4, Fast FBI file; Fast, Official Photo ID, War Department, "file B," Fast Personal Papers (FPP).

27. Fast, "Biography," unpublished ms., chap. 5, 28, b8, f9, FC, UWM.

28. Ibid.

29. *Being Red,* 99.

30. Fast to Bette, June 14, 15, 1945, b1, f15, FC, UWM.

31. Fast to Bette, June n.d., June 19, 1945, b1, f15, FC, UWM.

32. Ibid.; *Being Red,* 105.

33. Fast to Bette, June 20, 1945, b1, f15, FC, UWM.

34. "Notes on India," 5, b9, f3, FC, UWM.

35. Fast to Bette, June 20, 1945, b1, f15, FC, UWM.

36. *Being Red,* 111–112; "Coca Cola," in Fast, *The Last Supper and Other Stories* (New York: Blue Heron Press, 1955), 63–73.

37. The Bengal is located in the northeast of South Asia, and today is mainly divided between the People's Republic of Bangladesh and the state of West Bengal in India.

38. *Being Red,* 123. Fast's bizarre story is rendered far less credible by Paul Greenough, *Prosperity and Misery in Modern Bengal: The Famine of 1943–44* (New York: Oxford University Press, 1982), 150; Amartya Sen, *Poverty and Famines: An Essay on Entitlement and Deprivation* (Oxford: Oxford University Press, 1981), 58–59, 70–83.

39. *Being Red,* 123.

40. Sumit Sarkar, *Modern India, 1885–1947* (New York: St. Martin's Press, 1989), 405–408.

41. "Notes on India," n.d., 1945, b9, f3, FC, UWM.

42. Fast to Bette, June 26, June 27, 1945, b1, f15, FC, UWM.

43. Bette to Howard, June 21, 1945, July 3, 1945, Rachel Fast Ben-Avi (RFB).

44. *Being Red,* 115.

45. "Notes on India," n.d., 1945, b9, f3, FC, UWM.

46. Fast to Bette, June 28, 1945, b1, f15, FC, UWM.

47. Ibid., part 2, b1, f15, FC, UWM; Fast, unpublished ms, "The Singularity of Being Jewish," 109, Fast personal papers (FPP).

48. Howard to Bette, June 29, 1945, b1, f15, FC, UWM.

49. Ibid.

50. Howard to Bette, June n.d., 1945, b1, f15, FC, UWM.

51. Bette to Howard, June 30 through July 17, 1945, RFB.

52. Fast, "Biography," chap. 6, 5, b8, f9, FC, UWM.

53. "Greetings to Foster," *Masses and Mainstream* (MM) (March 1951): 31–32.

54. Harvey Klehr, "Reflections of a Traditionalist Historian," *American Communist History* 4 (2005): 229. In Harvey Klehr, John Earl Haynes, and Kyrill M. Anderson, *Soviet World of American Communism* (New Haven, Conn.: Yale University

Press, 1998), documents 18, 19, and 20, at 101–105, demonstrate the wholly Soviet origins of the Duclos letter. Also see Isserman, *Which Side Were You On?* 219.

55. Arthur Schlesinger Jr. treats the Duclos article as evidence of a change in Soviet foreign policy in "Origins of the Cold War," *Foreign Affairs* 46 (October 1946): 22–52.

56. English translation in the theoretical journal of the CPUSA, *Political Affairs* 24 (July 1945): 656–672.

57. Isserman, *Which Side Were You On?* 217–220; Joseph Starobin, *American Communism in Crisis* (Cambridge, Mass.: Harvard University Press, 1972) 71–106.

58. James Barrett, *William Z. Foster and the Tragedy of American Radicalism* (Urbana: University of Illinois Press, 1998), 45, 249; William Foster, *Political Affairs* 24 (July 1945): 640–654, cited in Isserman, *Which Side Were You On?* 193. Emphasis mine.

59. "Greetings to Foster," 31–32.

60. "Biography," chap. 3, 4, b8, f9, FC, UWM.

61. Isserman, *Which Side Were You On?* 240–243; Starobin, *American Communism in Crisis,* 175–176; George Charney, *A Long Journey* (Chicago: Quadrangle Press, 1968), 218–222. Several writers and intellectuals, of the few still left in the Party, including Marc Blitzstein and a group of his friends, resigned, because Foster brought with him an increased anti-intellectual tendency.

62. Fast, "The Making of a Democrat," *NM,* May 15, 1945, 17. Also see Fast, "Not With Tears," *PM,* April 15, 1945, 8, and "Without Honor, Without Civilization: Fascism," *PM,* May 13, 1945, 2; Georg W. F. Hegel, *The Philosophy of History* (New York: Colonial Press, 1900), 30–31; Hegel, *The Philosophy of Right* (London: Oxford University Press, 1942), 245.

63. *Being Red,* 130–131.

64. Isserman, *Which Side Were You are On?* 215; clipping, *DW,* September 25, 1945, in FPP; Carl Van Doren to Fast, October 9, 1945, b2, f8, FC, UWM.

65. "Biography," chap. 6, 2.

66. Ibid., chap. 6, 3. Ronald Hayman, *Sartre: A Life* (New York: Simon and Schuster, 1987). See also Brian C. Anderson, "The Absolute Intellectual," *Policy Review,* February–March 2004, at http://www.hoover.org/publications/policyreview/3440601.html.

67. *Being Red,* 133–134.

68. Ibid.

69. William Deresiewicz, "Café Society," *Nation,* May 14, 2007, 47–50; Jonathan Judaken, *Jean-Paul Sartre and the Jewish Question: Antisemitism and the Politics of the French Intellectual* (Lincoln: University of Nebraska Press, 2009), 113–115.

70. Ian Birchall, *Sartre against Stalinism* (New York: Berghahn Books, 2004), 220.

71. Tony Judt, *Past Imperfect: French Intellectuals 1944–1956* (Berkeley: University of California Press, 1992), 122–134.

72. Ralph L. Collins to Fast, May 8, 1947, FPP. In a typescript of his biographical

information for Little Brown, January 23, 1948, Fast wrote: "I taught at four universities . . . and studied the Indian question at a fifth." Box 64, Fast Collection (FC), University of Pennsylvania (UP). This is another example of Fast's penchant for embellishment and mistruths. He did a workshop at Indiana in the summer of 1947, taught sporadically at the Jefferson School, not quite a university, and did a short stint of research at the library of the University of Oklahoma at Norman.

73. "The Current Scene," *DW*, April 3, 1956, at http://www.trussel.com/hf/incident .htm; *Being Red,* 53.

74. Maltz, "What Shall We Ask of Writers?" *NM*, February 12, 1946, 19–20.

75. Leon Trotsky, *Literature and Revolution,* ed. William Keach (Chicago: Haymarket Books, 2005), 154–176, 187–207.

76. Lee Bazandall and Stefan Morawski, eds., *Marx and Engels on Literature and Art* (New York: Telos Press, 1973), 88.

77. Maltz, "What Shall We Ask of Writers?"

78. Ibid.; Fast, "Art and Politics," *NM*, February 26, 1946, 6–8; Robins, *Alien Ink,* 97.

79. "Art and Politics," 8.

80. Fast, "Dreiser's Short Stories," *NM*, September 3, 1946, 11.

81. J. Hoberman, *An Army of Phantoms: American Movies and the Making of the Cold War* (New York: New Press, 2011), 23; Gerald Horne, *The Final Victim of the Blacklist: John Howard Lawson, Dean of the Hollywood Ten* (Berkeley: University of California Press, 2006), 5.

82. Atlas, in Victor Navasky, *Naming Names* (New York: Penguin Books, 1981), 291–292.

83. Stern to Maltz, February 18, 1946, and copy of Stern to Sillen, February 20, 1946, b15, Maltz Papers (MP), Wisconsin State Historical Society (WSHS). For a sampling of the articles beating up on Maltz see: Alvah Bessie, *NM*, March 12, 1946, 8; Michael Gold labeled Maltz a "vicious, voluble Trostkyite," helping "to establish an American Fascism as a prelude to an American conquest of the world [!]. *DW*, February 12, 23, March 2, 16, 1946. Even William Foster got around to throwing a punch, *NM*, April 23, 1946,

84. Navasky, *Naming Names,* 286–287.

85. Traube to Maltz, February 23, 1946, b15, MP, WSHS.

86. Ibid.

87. *NM*, April 9, 1946, 8–10, 21–22.

88. Educated at Columbia and the Yale School of Drama, Maltz published critically acclaimed novels and short stories including "The Happiest Man on Earth," which won the O. Henry Memorial Award as the best story in 1938. His script for *Moscow Strikes Back* (1942) won an Oscar for best documentary, and Maltz's work for *The House I Live In* won a special Academy Award in 1945. Much more on Maltz is available at http://www.imdb.com/name/nm0540816.

89. Maltz in Navasky, *Naming Names,* 297–299; Atlas in ibid., 231–232.

90. Lawson in Horne, *The Final Victim of the Blacklist,* 49, 5.

91. Navasky, *Naming Names,* 287–302.

92. "Agent memo," June 27, 1946, 3–4, Fast FBI file. Emphasis mine.

4. COLD WAR, HOT SEAT

1. Ellen Schrecker, *Many Are the Crimes: McCarthyism in America* (Boston: Little Brown, 1998); David Oshinsky, "In the Heart of the Heart of Conspiracy," *NYTBR,* January 27, 2008, last page. But also see John Y. Haynes, *Red Scare or Red Menace?* (Chicago: Ivan Dee, 1996.)

2. Fast, "Biography," unpublished ms., b8, f9, chap. 6, 5, Fast Collection (FC), University of Wisconsin-Milwaukee (UWM).

3. *NYT,* December 6, 1949, 8; Fast, letter to Renaud de Jouvenal, June 22, 1953, Fast Personal Papers (FPP).

4. Ibid., b8, f9, chap. 8, 23, FC, UWM. On "atomic diplomacy" see Gar Alperovitz, *The Decision to Use the Atomic Bomb* (New York: Alfred Knopf, 1995); Martin Sherwin, *A World Destroyed: Hiroshima and Its Legacies* (Stanford, Calif.: Stanford University Press, 2003).

5. Robert J. Goldstein, *American Blacklist: The Attorney General's List of Subversive Organizations* (Lawrence: University Press of Kansas, 2008). See especially 42–54.

6. Arthur McClure, *The Truman Administration and the Problem of Post-War Labor, 1945–1948* (Cranberry, N.J.: Associated University Press, 1969).

7. *New Masses* (NM), February 5, 1946, 6; *Daily Worker* (DW), January 18, 1946, 1, 3.

8. "Memo," February 27, 1946, 2, Fast FBI file. In November, Fast also made the long and somewhat dangerous trip to Columbia, South Carolina, to speak to the Southern Youth Legislature sponsored by the Southern Negro Youth Congress. Fast, "They're Marching up Freedom Road," *NM,* November 5, 1946, 20.

9. *NYT,* March 18, 1946, 4. The full text of Churchill's address at Fulton, Missouri, can be found at http://history1900s.about.com/library/weekly/aa082400a.htm.

10. "Confidential Report," April 26, 1946, 16, Fast FBI file.

11. *Being Red,* 138. Emphasis mine.

12. "Biography," b8, f9, chap. 6, 17–19, FC, UWM; "Proceeding against Dr. Edward K. Barsky and Others," HUAC, 79th Congress, 2nd Session, Report No. 1829, March 28, 1946, 1; Phillip Deery, "The AAUP, Academic Freedom and the Cold War," *AAUP Journal of Academic Freedom 1* (2010): 27–39.

13. *NYT,* March 29, 1946, 16; "Biography," b8, f9, chap. 6, 17–19, FC, UWM; "Proceeding against Dr. Edward K. Barsky and Others," 1; Deery, "The AAUP, Academic Freedom and the Cold War," 27–39.

14. For a full account of the anti-Communist assault on JAFRC see Phillip Deery, "'A Blot upon Liberty': McCarthyism, Dr. Barsky and the Joint Anti-Fascist Refugee Committee," *American Communist History* 8 (2009): 168–196.

15. United States Congress, House Committee on Un-American Activities, *Investigation of Un-American Propaganda Activities in the United States, Executive Board, Joint Anti-fascist Refugee Committee. Hearings before the Committee on Un-American*

Activities, House of Representatives, Seventy-ninth Congress, second session, on H. Res. 5 (Washington, D.C.: U.S. Government Printing Office, 1946), 17–26.

16. Robert G. McCloskey, *The Modern Supreme Court* (Cambridge, Mass.: Harvard University Press, 1972), 64–85; *NYT,* January 25, 1946, 5.

17. Because the term "collusion" (emphasis mine) was involved, a charge of conspiracy was added to the contempt citation. Members of the board would be charged on both counts at their trial in June 1947.

18. Schlesinger, "The U.S. Communist Party," *Life Magazine,* July 29, 1946, 84–86, 90.

19. Gregg Mitchell, *Tricky Dick and the Pink Lady: Sexual Politics and the Red Scare, 1950* (New York: Random House, 1998).

20. Celler, in *The Congressional Record,* April 16, 1946, quoted in *Being Red,* 155.

21. *NYT,* March 7, 1946, 11; April 17, 1946, 17; April 21, 1946, 84"; Biography," chap. 8, 9.

22. Joshua Rubenstein, *Tangled Loyalties: The Life and Times of Ilya Ehrenburg* (New York: Basic Books, 1996), 227.

23. *DW,* May 9, 1946, 1; "Memo," Fast FBI file; Joseph Brainin to Fast, May 6, 1946, "B file," FPP.

24. Ann Fagin Ginger and Eugene M. Tobin, eds., *The National Lawyers Guild: From Roosevelt to Reagan* (Philadelphia: Temple University Press, 1988), 3–10.

25. Goldstein, *American Blacklist,* 11–12; Harvey Klehr, *The Heyday of American Communism: The Depression Decade* (New York: Basic Books, 1984), 371–74, 385.

26. "Biography," chap. 6, 1.

27. *The American: A Middle Western Legend* (New York: Duell, Sloan and Pearce, 1946), 184, 154.

28. Ibid., 289.

29. Brown to Fast, August 9, 1946, "B file" FPP.

30. Daniel Bell, *The End of Ideology: On the Exhaustion of Political Ideas in the 1950s,* 2nd ed. (Cambridge, Mass.: Harvard University, 2000).

31. Commager, "The Eagle That Is Remembered," *New York Herald Tribune Weekly Book Review,* July 28, 1946, 4; Handlin, "Fake," *Commentary,* September 1946, 295–296; Trilling, "Fiction in Review," *Nation,* August 3, 1946, 134. *The American* received favorable notice in *Saturday Review of Literature,* July 20, 1946, 6.

32. *NYT,* November 27, 1946, 27; "Memorandum," Fast FBI file.

33. Donnelly to Fast, August 26, 1946, "D file," FPP.

34. Fast to Donnelly, September 1, 1946, FPP; Traube to Maltz, February 23, 1946, b15, Maltz Papers (MP), Wisconsin State Historical Society (WSHS).

35. Fast also makes a staunch defense of First Amendment rights in "The Way for a Nation," *Seventeen,* July 1946, 55–57.

36. Donnelly to Fast, September 3, 1946, FPP.

37. For more on the CPUSA's relationship with the Soviet Union and its connection to Stalinism see James R. Barrett, "The History of American Communism and Our Understanding of Stalinism," *American Communist History* 2, no. 2 (2003): 175–182.

38. *The Incredible Tito: Man of the Hour* (New York: Magazine House, 1944), 14. The sentence also appears in an edition prepared for publication in Canada, retitled *Tito and His People* (Winnepeg: Contemporary Publishers, 1944), at http://www .trussel.com/hf/editions/edit314.htm; *Being Red,* 153–154.

39. *NYT,* April 1, 1947, 30; April 4, 1947, 12.

40. *NM,* April 23, 1947, 3.

41. Fast, copy of telegram to Jose Ferrer, April 5, 1947, "F file," FPP; *DW,* April 26, 1947, 2.

42. Marx to Lincoln, November 1864, delivered February 1865, at http.www. marxist.org/history/interantional/wma/documents/1864/lincoln- letter.htmab. See William Harlan Hale, "When Karl Marx Worked For Horace Greeley," *American Heritage* 8, April 1957, at http://www.americanheritage.com/articles/magazine /ah/1957/3/1957_3_20.shtml.

43. Fast, "Marxism and Literature," unpublished notes, "M file," FPP; "Memorandum," Fast FBI file.

44. Lyman Bradley Testimony, HUAC, April 4, 1946, 79th Congress, 2nd session, 8; Thomas I. Emerson et al., *Political and Civil Rights in the U.S.,* 3rd ed. (Boston: Little, Brown, 1967), 1:355.

45. V. O. Key, *Public Opinion and American Democracy* (New York: Alfred A. Knopf, 1964), 352–353, 371; Gabriel Almond, *Americans and Foreign Policy* (New York: Frederick A. Praeger, 1960).

46. Peter Filene, "Cold War Culture Doesn't Say it All," in *Rethinking Cold War Culture,* ed. Peter J. Kuznick and James Gilbert (Washington, D.C.: Smithsonian, 2001), 157–174.

47. Ibid.; Alan Brinkley, "The Illusion of Unity in Cold War Culture," in *Rethinking Cold War Culture;* Dorothy B. Jones, "Communism and the Movies: A Study of Film Content," in John Cogley, *Report on Blacklisting,* vol. 1: *The Movies* (New York: Arno Press, 1972), 231; Nora Sayre, *Running Time: Films of the Cold War* (New York: Dial Press, 1982). The 1949 cycle of "Negro problem" pictures, *Home of the Brave, Pinky,* and *Lost Boundaries,* was also charged with stirring up "racial antagonisms." J. Hoberman, *An Army of Phantoms: American Movies and the Making of the Cold War* (New York: New Press, 2011), 50. For the FBI memo on *It's a Wonderful Life,* http://www.wisebread.com/FBIconsidereditsawonderful-life-communist. For excerpts of the DAR reviews see Murray Kempton's essay on the Hollywood Ten, "The Day of the Locust," in *Part of Our Time* (New York: NYRB Classics, 2004), 181–210.

48. David Rosenbloom, "Public Administration and Civil Liberties," *Public Administration Review* (1962): 58–60; David Caute, *The Great Fear: the Anti-Communist Purge under Truman and Eisenhower* (New York: Simon and Schuster, 1978) 85–87, 96, 147, 151; Ellen Schrecker, *Many Are the Crimes,* 210–212, 271–73; Goldstein, *American Blacklist,* 43–59, 145–147.

49. Rosenbloom, "Public Administration and Civil Liberties," 58–60; Goldstein, *American Blacklist,* 43–59, 145–147.

50. *NYT,* June 28, 1947, 1, 6; John Haynes and Harvey Klehr, *Venona: Decoding*

Soviet Espionage in America (New Haven, Conn.: Yale University Press, 2000), 192–194, 218–20.

51. *NYT*, July 17, 1947, 1.

52. Fast, Campenni interview, August 12–19, 1977, b9, f2, FC, UWM.

53. *NYT*, June 15, 1948, 1; "Obituary," *NYT*, June 7, 1979, D95.

54. Fast, Campenni interview, August 12–19, 1977.

55. Reprinted in Maltz, *The Citizen Writer: Essays in Defense of American Culture* (New York: International Publishers, 1950), 17–24.

56. Ibid., 24.

57. Fast, Campenni interview, December 1, 1967, b8, f11, FC, UWM.

58. *Clarkton* (New York: Duell, Sloan, and Pearce, 1947), 79. Fast told a different story to the audience attending the 67th national convention of the American Library Association in Atlantic City in June 1948. The publishers of *Clarkton,* he said disingenuously, "have responded to pressure and printed so few copies of the book that orders cannot be filled, an illustration of the devious methods of the censor." *ALA Bulletin* 42 (September 15, 1948): 75.

59. Fast, Campenni interview, December 1, 1967.

60. *NYTBR,* September 28, 1947, 4.

61. Jouvenal to Fast, January 21, 1948, "J file" FPP. Emphases mine.

62. Ignazio Silone, *Fontamara* (1931), and *Bread and Wine* (1937). Also, Fast could not have been unaware of Orwell's *Homage to Catalonia* (1938). There were, in addition, Koestler's essays in *The Yogi and the Commissar* (1944) devoted to persuading pro-Communists such as Sartre that the gulag was an actuality, that Communism in the USSR was an economic failure, and that Stalin was evil.

63. Fast to Jouvenal, February 10, 1948, FPP.

64. *Clarkton,* 207–209.

65. Many of these stories, originally published in *Masses and Mainstream,* appear in *The Last Supper and Other Stories* (New York: Blue Heron Press, 1955); see also "Who Is Jesus Christ?" *New Currents,* May 1944, 20. These stories are politicized, but they are not propaganda, which is more than one can say about Fast's novels of this period.

66. *Clarkton,* 87.

67. Mimi Fast, author interview, August 18, 2008.

68. Fast, Campenni interview, December 1, 1967. *NYT,* October 16, 1947, 5.

69. Glenora Brown and Deming Brown, *A Guide to Soviet Russian Translations of American Literature* (New York: King's Crown Press of Columbia University, 1954); Deming Brown, *Soviet Attitudes toward American Writing* (Princeton, N.J.: Princeton University Press, 1962), 281–282; Also see "Publication of Fiction in the USSR," *Soviet Literature,* no. 11 (1954): 209ff.; Maurice Friedberg, "Foreign Authors and Soviet Readers," *Russian Review* 13 (October 1954): 266–275.

70. For basic information on the settlement: *New York World Telegram,* January 13, 1948, 6, and *NYTBR,* January 25, 1948, 8.

71. *New York World Telegram,* July 14, 1946, 5.

72. What Fast did was in clear violation of his rash and unnecessary (for a novelist) public promise in 1941 to stick with only what was historically verifiable. Granville Hicks, "Howard Fast's One-Man Reformation," College English 7, no. 1 (October 1945): 1–6. More important is Fast's failure to credit Russell. For a more detailed but also more forgiving assessment of Fast on what looks like plagiarism, see Campenni, "Citizen Howard Fast: A Critical Biography," 141–147, 412–416.

73. Fast, Campenni interview, December 1, 1967.

5. BANNED, BARRED, AND BESIEGED

1. Fast, in Robins, *Alien Ink*, 235.

2. Rachel Fast, "Memoir," in *Red Diapers: Growing Up in the Communist Left*, ed. Judy Kaplan and Linn Shapiro (Chicago: University of Illinois, 1998), 127–129. Rachel Fast Ben-Avi (RFB), e-mail, August 27, 2008. Jonathan Fast also heard the assassination story many times and thinks "it may have been a strong wave of PARANOIA, to which my father was more than a little bit susceptible." E-mail, August 29, 2008. Capitals are in the originals.

3. Robins, *Alien Ink*, 232–233.

4. Herbert Mitgang, *Dangerous Dossiers* (New York: Donald I. Fine Books, 1988), 100.

5. Ibid., 280.

6. David Everitt, *A Shadow of Red: Communism and the Blacklist in Radio and Television* (Chicago: Ivan R. Dee, 2007); Rachael Kafrissen, "Mechanics of the Blacklist," lecture, Morris U. Schappes Centenary Series, New York City, November 7, 2007.

7. D. D. Guttenplan, "Red Harvest," *Nation*, May 25, 1909, 25–33. Even among the many Communists who participated in the Popular Front, there were some who saw their work not as a cynical stratagem, but as an authentic opportunity to work for a social democratic politics. Whatever the motives of the Party, Earl Browder did not merely accept the CPUSA line on the Popular Front; he liked the coalition and came genuinely to believe in it.

8. James R. Barrett, Steve Nelson, and Rob Ruck, *Steve Nelson: American Radical* (Pittsburgh, Pa.: University of Pittsburgh Press, 1981); James R. Barrett, *William Z. Foster and the Tragedy of American Radicalism* (Urbana: University of Illinois Press, 2001); Barrett, "The History of American Communism and Our Understanding of Stalinism," *American Communist History* 2 (2003): 175–182. "Although it served the Party's interest to present the 'witch-hunters' as indiscriminate smearers, in fact HUAC came to specialize in red-baiting reds and former reds. The real vice of HUAC was not that it bagged the wrong quarry but that it had no moral, political, or constitutionally legitimate hunting license in the first place." Navasky, *Naming Names*, 342.

9. Stephen Whitfield, *The Culture of the Cold War* (Baltimore: Johns Hopkins University Press, 1996), 3 and throughout.

10. Paul Buhle and David Wagner, *Hide in Plain Sight: The Hollywood Blacklistees in Film and Television, 1950–2002* (New York: Palgrave Macmillan, 2003), 250.

There were directly conscious suicides, too. Phil Loeb (husband "Jake," on the Molly Goldberg TV show), for example, whose "un-American" activities amounted to little more than his fight for black actors to have the same stage door as white actors, killed himself after being blacklisted.

11. Schlesinger, "Hollywood Hypocrisy," *New York Times Week in Review,* February 28, 1999, 19.

12. *NYT*, February 5, 1947, 26; *Journal of the Board of Education of the City of New York, 1947*, vol. 1, 489–493; *Citizen Tom Paine*, 22–23. By 1947 there had been eight printings of *Citizen Tom Paine* in hardcover, and a paperback was issued in 1946 that sold steadily in fourteen different languages. Fast wrote many pieces against censorship and in defense of civil liberties; two of the strongest are "No Man Can Be Silent," *New Masses* (*NM*), Mar 25, 1947, 12, and Fast, "One Man's Heritage," *NM*, September 30, 1947, 6–7.

13. *NYT*, February 20, 1947, 27.

14. Ibid.; Anne Lyon Haight, *Banned Books* (New York: R. R. Bowker, 1955), 111–112.

15. *Journal of the Board of Education,* 492–93.

16. Haight, *Banned Books,* 111–112.

17. AWA to Untermeyer, February 7, 1947, box 40, Fast Collection (FC), University of Pennsylvania (UP). Untermeyer had said he could not believe that the stated reason for the ban was anything but an excuse for political discrimination. *Daily Worker* (DW), February 6, 1947. The poet-anthologist read the full letter from AWA over the phone to Fast and subsequently sent it to him with a note saying that the whole thing "would be filthy if it were not so farcical." He promised his friend Howard a response that "should wither" the board of the AWA (FPP).

18. Maltz, "The Writer as the Conscience of the People," address delivered in a panel on literature at a conference on Thought Control in the United States, under the auspices of the Arts, Sciences, and Professions Council of the Progressive Citizens of America, Beverly Hills Hotel, Los Angeles, July 11, 1947, printed in *The Citizen Writer: Essays in Defense of American Culture* (New York: International Publishers, 1950), 17–19; *DW*, October 20, 1947; Report of "Confidential Informant T-51, of known reliability," Dossier 1953, 58–59, Fast FBI file.

19. *NYT*, February 5, 1947, 26; February 20, 1947, 27; February 26, 1947, 27; February 27, 1947, 18; March 12, 1947, 23.

20. "School Boards, Schoolbooks and Freedom to Learn," *Yale Law Journal* 59 (April 1950): 944–951, at http://www.jstor.org/stable/793219.

21. See chapter 3, note 3.

22. For examples of the kind of broadcasts Fast delivered see transcripts in box 7, folder 3, FC, UWM. By some technicality in the contract Columbia retained the title and produced a film called *The Last Frontier* in 1955, which had nothing to do with the Cheyenne Indians and their dramatic trek from Oklahoma to the Dakotas. Fast, letter to Bosley Crowther, December 13, 1955, FPP.

23. Fast, "The Railroad Men," *Masses and Mainstream* (MM), November 1948, 84–88.

24. Published by A. A. Knopf; Houghton Mifflin; D. Appleton-Century; Holt, Rinehart, and Winston, respectively.

25. Rukeyser to Untermeyer, June 25, 1940, Untermeyer Papers, University of Delaware. *Naked God,* 91.

26. Ralph L. Collins, chair, Department of English, University of Indiana, to Fast, May 8, 1947, FPP. Barry Fast, son of Jerry Fast, Howard's older brother, author interview, October 22, 27, 2007; Molly Jong-Fast, daughter of Jonathan Fast, and granddaughter of Howard, author interview, September 26, 2006.

27. Ellen Schrecker, *No Ivory Tower: McCarthyism and the Universities* (New York: Oxford University Press, 1986), 91.

28. Ibid.; *NYT,* December 11, 1947, 7.

29. *NYT,* December 18, 1927, 26. On the Bradley case and the quote by Pollock, see Phillip Deery, "Political Activism, Academic Freedom and the Cold War: An American Experience," *Labour History* 98 (May 2010): 183–205.

30. *NYT,* December 12, 1947, 36; December 13, 1947, 17; December 15, 1947, 24; December 18, 1947, 35; December 19, 1947, 52; *DW,* December 19, 1947.

31. *NYT,* December 20, 1947, 5; June 18, 1948, 10.

32. Buchman to Fast, March 26, 1948, "B file," FPP.

33. Fast to Buchman, April 1, 1948, "B file," FPP.

34. Information about *Rachel and the Stranger* is found at http://www.imdb.com/title/tt0040720/.

35. *Being Red,* 196–197.

36. *NYT,* April 17, 1948, 9. I am indebted to my good friend Dr. Helen Fein, author most recently of *Human Rights and Wrongs* (Boulder: Paradigm Publishers, 2007), for the phrase "universe of moral obligation."

37. Blitzstein discontinued his membership in the CPUSA in 1945 either because he considered his open homosexuality a liability to the Party or because after Foster replaced Browder as its chairman, an increased anti-intellectual tendency drove him and many of his artistic friends out. He remained in the movement, however, and was associated with many others on the left including Bertolt Brecht, Lillian Hellman, and Sean O'Casey. At http://www.marcblitzstein.com.

38. Marvin Gettleman, "'No Varsity Teams': New York's Jefferson School of Social Science, 1943–1956," *Science and Society* 66 (Fall 2002): 336–359. For Isabel Johnson go to: http://oasis.lib.harvard.edu/oasis/deliver/~sch00103. On the consensus that Johnson was beautiful see G. Edward White, *Alger Hiss's Looking-Glass Wars: The Covert Life of a Soviet Spy* (New York: Oxford University Press, 2004), 205–206. Also see *NYT,* July 1, 1948, 9.

39. *DW,* February 9, 1954.

40. Craig Thompson, "Here's Where our Commies Are Trained," *Saturday Evening Post,* March 12, 1949, 38.

41. *NYT,* May 3, 1948, 1.

42. Clippings from *Daily News,* May 4, 1948, and *DW,* May 10, 1948, Fast FBI File. Emphasis mine.

43. Vladimir Prostov, "The Ills of Limitation and the Evils of Disorientation: Perceptions of Post-WWII American Literature in the USSR/Russia," *American Studies International* 39 (October 2001): 41–50; Deming Brown, *Soviet Attitudes toward American Writing* (Princeton, N.J.: Princeton University Press, 1962); *NYT*, July 25, 1952, 10; Thomas Lahusen, *How Life Writes the Book: Real Socialism and Socialist Realism in Stalin's Russia* (Ithaca, N.Y.: Cornell University Press, 1997), 151–178; Ivan Khmarsky, letter to Fast, March 11, 1949, "K file," FPP; Victor Grossman and Mark Solomon, *Crossing the River: A Memoir of the American Left, the Cold War, and Life in East Germany* (Boston: University of Massachusetts Press, 2003), 67.

44. Gropper to Fast, October 12, 1947, b40, FC, UP.

45. Fast, to Thomas, March 19, 1948, April 25, 1948, "Thomas file," FPP.

46. Fast to Jouvenal, May 15, 1948, "J file," FPP.

47. Ibid.

48. Ibid. Emphasis mine.

49. Fast to editor, *New York Herald Tribune,* May 8, 1948; United States Congressional Record, 80th Congress, 2nd Session, 1948, 94, pt. 5, 6145–6149; Francis H. Thompson, *Frustration of Politics: Truman, Congress, and the Loyalty Issue, 1945–1953* (Madison, N.J.: Fairleigh Dickinson University Press, 1979), 79–85.

50. *NYT*, June 18, 1948, 10. Despite Fast's complaints about silence, many left-liberal groups and individuals voiced their dissent about the Supreme Court's decision. See for example "American Jewish Cultural Conference Resolutions," *Jewish Life,* August 1948, 29.

51. *NM* was discontinued in 1948 and merged with *Mainstream* to become *Masses and Mainstream,* the premiere literary journal of the CPUSA. See James Farrell's cutting farewell to the magazine in *NYTBR,* January 24 1948, 8.

52. Fast, "Open Letter," *MM*, July 1948, inside both covers. Emphasis Fast's.

53. *NYT*, June 18, 1948, 10.

54. Fast to Eleanor Roosevelt, June 25, 1948, "R file," FPP. Emphasis mine.

55. Fast to Jouvenal, May 15, 1948, "J file," FPP.

56. For the similarity between the views of Wright and Fast compare *Naked God* to Richard Wright's "I Tried to Be a Communist," part 1, *Atlantic Monthly,* August 1944, 61–70; part 2, September 1944, 48–56. For Wright's continued radicalism see Bill Mullen, "Discovering Postcolonialism," *American Quarterly* 54, no. 4 (2002): 701–708, and Mullen, *Richard Wright's Travel Writings: New Reflections* (Jackson: University Press of Mississippi, 2001).

57. Aragon to Fast, June 4, 1948, "A file," FPP. When Stalin died in 1953 Aragon was shattered. But by 1968, after the Soviet intervention in Czechoslovakia, he denounced Stalinism and even expressed a negative attitude toward socialist realism.

58. Fast to Maltz, June 30, 1948, box 16, folder 1, Maltz Collection (MP), Wisconsin State Historical Society (WSHS).

59. RFB, e-mail, February 19, 2010. Hannah apparently was temporarily incarcerated in a mental institution (only three years after being sprung from a concentration

camp in California), but years later the family got a card from her along with a picture of her husband and two children.

60. *NYT*, January 19, 1948, 1.

61. Even a small sample of Fast's activities during this period would fill several pages of footnotes. From mid-May to November 1948, he led demonstrations, picketed, circulated petitions, and spoke to audiences, large and small, more than two dozen times, often in concert with others, including Paul Robeson, Rockwell Kent, Elizabeth Gurley Flynn, John Howard Lawson, Alvah Bessie, and O. John Rogge. His doings were followed not only in the *DW*, *MM*, *PM*, and *Freiheit*, but also in the *New York Times*, *New York Sun*, and *New York World-Telegram*.

62. Fast to Little, Brown, January 23, 1948, b64, FC, UP. Emphases mine. Fast, *My Glorious Brothers* (New York: ibooks, 2003), vii–viii.

63. *My Glorious Brothers*, 17–18, 154–155.

64. Fast received a letter from Israeli editor Zvi Arad, who told him, "Without a trace of exaggeration, we can assert that MGB was one of the most widely read books in Israel in recent times." It "appeared at a time when many of our young people were in uniform, and could identify themselves in its pages." September 10, 1951, "I file," FPP.

65. John Cogley, *Report on Blacklisting*, vol. 1 ([New York]: Fund for the Republic, 1956), 121; Richard A. Schwartz, "How the Film and Television Blacklist Worked," *Film and History Annual For 1999* (CD ROM).

66. Schultz to Dear Friend, March 8, 1948, "S file," FPP.

67. Fast to Schultz, March 19, 1948, "S file," FPP.

68. Ibid.

69. Ibid.

70. Schultz to Dear Friend, March 8, 1948, FPP.

71. Schultz to Fast, March 30, 1948, FPP.

72. Thomas Lask, "Mr. Fast and the Maccabean Revolt," *NYTBR*, October 10, 1948, 4. The *Globe*'s reviewer found *My Glorious Brothers* "a stimulating tale from first page to last," and the *Tribune* characterized the novel as "vivid and vital," with characters "as real as the rocks and ravines from which the Jews fought for country and home." Blurbs from back cover of *My Glorious Brothers* (New York: ibooks, 2003). The advance sale was "close to 9,000. . . . While not exciting [it is] perfectly adequate to provide for stock on hand in the bookstores when the advertising begins." Angus Cameron to Fast, October 1, 1948, b64, FC, UP.

73. Fuller in Campenni, "Citizen Howard Fast," 311–312.

74. Milton Himmelfarb, "Fast and Loose," *Commentary*, December 1948, 584–585.

75. Morris Schappes, "Fast's Maccabees," *NM*, November 1948, 74–78.

76. *My Glorious Brothers*, 262.

77. Schappes, "Fast's Maccabees," 74.

78. Schappes denies the whole episode as recounted in *Being Red*. "Howard Fast Accuses Me," *Jewish Currents*, March 1991, 18–20. Only three months before *My*

Glorious Brothers was published Schappes had included Fast's arguably Jewish-centered and particularist short story, "Where Are Your Guns?" in his magazine *Jewish Life,* July 1948, 15–17. Earlier he included Fast's distinctly Jewish Story "An Epitaph for Sidney," but felt the need to say it was not a "great" story because the protagonist, although a radical, was not clearly enough against "bourgeois nationalism." "Commentary on 'An Epitaph for Sidney'" by Morris Schappes, *Jewish Life,* February 1947, 25–27.

79. Fast, Campenni interview, April 15, 1968, box 8, folder 13, Fast Collection (FC), University of Wisconsin–Milwaukee (UWM); "A Conversation with Howard Fast, March 23, 1994," conducted by Alan Wald and Alan Filreis, ed. Thomas J. Sugrue, *Prospects* 20 (1995): 511–523.

80. Hall, unpublished typescript, b64, FC, UP.

81. Fast to Little, Brown, January 23, 1948, b64, FC, UP.

82. See Fast's novels *Conceived in Liberty, Citizen Tom Paine,* and *Spartacus,* and his short stories "Who Is Jesus Christ?" *New Currents,* May 1944, 20; "Thirty Pieces of Silver," in *Departure and Other Stories* (Boston: Little, Brown, 1949); "Christ in Cuernavaca," "The Holy Child," and "The Last Supper," in *The Last Supper and Other Stories* (New York: Blue Heron Press, 1955).

83. Along with *Gentleman's Agreement,* and Saul Bellow's *The Victim* (1944), Arthur Miller's novel *Focus* (1945) was also part of the first wave of post-Holocaust books to address antisemitism in America. But like Sartre, Miller suggested that Jewish identity is constructed out of little more than persecution. No antisemitism, no Jews.

84. *The Naked God,* 141.

85. Bloor to Fast, October 27, 1948, "B file," FPP. Emphases Bloor's.

86. Fast and Heym were in correspondence from 1949 through 1960. Heym's letters to Fast are in "Stefan Heym," FPP. For the quotations in the text above see Heym, letters to Fast, November 23, 1953, April 7, 1954, FPP.

87. But among the few books, all smuggled in of course, that provided Russia's Jewish activists and "refuseniks" with spiritual nourishment in the 1960s and '70s were a Hebrew-language primer, a prerevolutionary volume of Jewish history, and two novels by American writers, Leon Uris's *Exodus* and Howard Fast's *My Glorious Brothers.*

88. Thomas to Fast, November 6, 1948, "Gwyn Thomas file," FPP. Emphasis mine. Also see n64.

89. Fast to Newman, January 27, 1949, b1, f5, FC, UWM; also Fast to Angus Cameron at Little, Brown, February 5, 1949, saying that Fast will avoid making a premature announcement, because there was some discussion by the JBC over the question of withdrawing the award on political grounds, b64, FC, UP.

90. Fast to Newman, January 27, 1949, b1, f5, FC, UWM.

91. Fast to Philip Goodman, February 10, 1949, b64, FC, UP; *NYT* carried a short piece on the award to Fast's *My Glorious Brothers* as "the best fiction work of Jewish interest published during the past year," April 8, 1949, 15.

92. Schappes to JBC, December 5, 1955, "S file," FPP. Wolfson was a philosopher

and historian at Harvard University, and the first to hold a chair of Judaic studies in the United States. His award winning book was *Philo: Foundations of Religious Philosophy in Judaism, Christianity and Islam* (Cambridge, Mass.: Harvard University Press, 1948).

93. Fast to Schappes, December 13, 1955, FPP; *Jewish Life* (April 1956): 37.

94. "Vast Majority of Cluster Headache Patients Are Initially Misdiagnosed, Dutch Researchers Report," World Headache Alliance, August 21, 2003, at http://www.wha.org/wha2/Newsite/resultsnav.asp?color=C2D9F2&idContentNews=595.

95. Karl Ekbom and Jurgen Lindahl, "Effect of Induced Rise of Blood Pressure on Pain in Cluster Headache," *Acta Neurologica Scandinavica* 46 (1970): 585–600, at http://www3.interscience.wiley.com/journal/121520609/abstract; Ruth Atkinson, "Physical Fitness and Headache," *Headache* 17 (November 1977): 189–191, at http://www3.interscience.wiley.com/journal/119625957/abstract; M. Gotkine et al, "Now Dear, I Have a Headache! Immediate Improvement of Cluster Headaches after Sexual Activity," *Journal of Neurology, Neurosurgery and Psychiatry* 77 (2006), at http://jnnp.bmj.com/cgi/content/extract/77/11/1296.

96. RFB, e-mail, November 12, 2006.

97. Wishengrad in Jeffrey Shandler, *Jews, God, and Videotape: Religion and Media in America* (New York: New York University Press, 2009), 77–78. Fast's story "The Price of Liberty" appeared in Fast, *Patrick Henry and the Frigate's Keel* (New York: Duell, Sloan and Pearce, 1945).

98. Fast, letter to Thomas, August 13, 1948, "Gwyn Thomas file," FPP.

99. John Gates, *The Story of an American Communist* (New York: Thomas and Nelson, 1958), 115.

100. Many of Macdonald's essays on culture and politics have been collected in anthologies not only because they are well written, but because they record and reflect the ferment of a generation of American intellectuals whose work spanned the Depression, the "radical" decade of the 1930s, the New Deal, World War II, the Cold War, and McCarthyism. Macdonald's *Henry Wallace: The Man and the Myth* (1948), argues, in effect, that the former VP did not earn the support of the American Left, primarily because of his professed admiration for Stalinist Russia.

101. For the full text of Truman's speech announcing the doctrine see: http://avalon.law.yale.edu/20th_century/trudoc.asp.

102. See John C. Culver and John Hyde, *American Dreamer: A Life of Henry A. Wallace* (New York: Norton, 2000), which tries to salvage Wallace's reputation, but also provides damaging evidence of his being "exploited" by the CPUSA.

103. *NYT*, October 16, 1947, 5.

104. *NYT*, December 6, 1949, 8. "Memo," Fast FBI file NY.

105. *Being Red*, 192–193, 303.

6. THE MYOPIA OF AMERICAN COMMUNISM

1. Fast did put together a book of short stories, *The Departure and Other Stories*, for Little, Brown in 1949, most of them previously published. Two of the stories

written in 1948 and 1949, "The Departure" and "Thirty Pieces of Silver," are among Fast's darker works, both dealing in different degrees with disillusionment and betrayal. See Fast's weekly column, "I Write As I Please," from August 1948 to June 13, 1956, for the *Daily Worker* (DW), which also appeared in *Seattle New World, Chicago Star,* and *San Francisco People's World.*

2. The literature on the Hiss case is monumental, contentious, and beyond the scope of this study. For a bibliography and further links see http://www.nndb.com /people/987/000055822/bibliography/.

3. Kathryn S. Olmsted, *Red Spy Queen: A Biography of Elizabeth Bentley* (Chapel Hill: University of North Carolina Press, 2002); Lauren Kessler, *Clever Girl: Elizabeth Bentley, the Spy Who Ushered in the McCarthy Era* (New York: Harper Perennial, 2003); *NYT,* July 30, 1948, 5; July 31, 1948, 4; August 4, 1948, 3; August 11, 1948, 1.

4. The Venona project, a secret collaboration between intelligence agencies of the United States and Great Britain, involved the cryptanalysis of messages sent by several intelligence agencies of the Soviet Union, mostly during WWII. The declassification of much of the information collected has led to a hornet's nest of contention over to what extent various individuals mentioned in the documents were actually involved with Soviet intelligence. A general consensus has emerged over the past dozen years that something like 200 or 300 people, including high-level leaders of the CPUSA such as Earl Browder and Eugene Dennis, were knowingly involved in spying in one form or another for the Soviet Union between the mid-1930s and the early 1950s. For a good sense of the complexity of all of this it is best to look at works on various sides of this issue, for example: John Earl Haynes and Harvey Klehr, *Venona: Decoding Soviet Espionage in America* (New Haven, Conn.: Yale University Press, 2000); Ellen Schrecker, *Cold War Triumphalism: The Misuse of History after the Fall of Communism* (New York: New Press, 2006). For more sources and links go to http://www .business.reachinformation.com/Venona_project.aspx.

5. D. D. Guttenplan, *American Radical: The Life and Times of I. F. Stone* (New York: Farrar, Straus, and Giroux, 2009), 244–248.

6. *NYT,* January 18, 1949, 1, 3, 8; January 17, 1949, 1; March 18, 1949, 3.

7. Michael Belknap, *Cold War Political Justice: The Smith Act, the Communist Party, and American Civil Liberties* (Westport, Conn.: Greenwood Press, 1977) 78 and chapter 3, passim; Martin Duberman, *Paul Robeson* (New York: Alfred Knopf, 1989), 338; *NYT,* January 18, 1949, 1; March 7, 1949, 3; March 8, 1949, 1.

8. Athan Theoharis, *Chasing Spies: How the Fbi Failed in Counterintelligence* (Chicago: Ivan R. Dee, 2002); Douglas M. Charles, *J. Edgar Hoover and the Anti-interventionists: Fbi Political Surveillance and the Rise of the Domestic Security State, 1939–1945* (Columbus: Ohio State University Press, 2007).

9. *NYT,* June 29, 1949, 4.

10. *NYT,* January 17, 1949, 9; Joseph Starobin, *American Communism in Crisis, 1943–1957* (Berkeley: University of California Press, 1975), 206–207.

11. See especially William Z. Foster, *Toward Soviet America* (New York:

Coward-McCann, 1932), 241–271. Once Foster adopted a revolutionary position he never changed it. James Barrett, *William Z. Foster and the Tragedy of American Radicalism* (Urbana: University of Illinois Press, 1998). Also see Maurice Isserman, *Which Side Were You On? The American Communist Party during The Second World War* (Middletown, Conn.: Wesleyan University Press, 1982), on Foster and Browder throughout.

12. John Haynes, *Red Scare or Red Menace?: American Communism and Anticommunism in the Cold War Era* (Chicago: Ivan R. Dee, 1996), 163–164.

13. Starobin, *American Communism in Crisis,* 206–207; David Shannon, *Socialism in America* (New York: MacMillan, 1955), 235–239.

14. "A Day at Foley Square with Howard Fast," *DW,* February 1, 1949; "Medina Suddenly Turns Sweet in Front of Jury Panel," *DW,* March 11, 1949; "Howard Fast Revisits Foley Square," *DW,* May 30, 1949. All at http://www.trussel.com/hf/articles .htm.

15. Alan Filreis, "Words with 'All the Effects of Force': Cold-War Interpretation," *American Quarterly* 39 (Summer 1987): 306–312; Peter Kenez, *The Birth of the Propaganda State: Soviet Methods of Mass Mobilization, 1917–1929* (Cambridge: Cambridge University Press, 1985), 22.

16. Fast in Robins, *Alien Ink,* 77.

17. See note 4.

18. Julia Allen, "'That Accursed Aesopian Language': Prosecutorial Framing of Linguistic Evidence in U.S. v. Foster, 1949," *Rhetoric and Public Affairs* 4 (Spring 2001): 109–134.

19. Filreis, "Words with 'All the Effects of Force,'" 306–312. For more on the implications of this kind of state behavior see Herbert Marcuse, *One-Dimensional Man* (Boston: Beacon Press, 1964), 94–98.

20. *NYT,* October 15, 1949, 14; October 16, 1949, sec. 4, 7.

21. *NYT,* June 8, 1949, 13.

22. Belknap, *Cold War Political Justice,* 78–79.

23. Ibid.

24. *NYT,* June 26, 1949, 35. The *Times* sub-header read simply and rather precisely: "U.S. Communists Favor Civil Liberties Only for Own Party." For Fast's behavior at the meeting I relied on Mimi Fast, who recounted conversations with Howard about the kind of behavior he regretted while a member of the CPUSA. Mimi Fast, author interview, September 12, 2006.

25. "Howard Fast Disputes Stone on Trotzkyists," *Daily Compass,* July 11, 1949, 9.

26. Starobin, *American Communism in Crisis,* 199–213.

27. Fast, Campenni interview, December 1, 1967, box 8, folder 11, Fast Collection (FC), University of Wisconsin-Milwaukee (UWM).

28. Fast, *Being Red,* 199, 202.

29. *NYT,* March 24, 1949, 4. Kaplan was joined in criticism of the conference by several notable rabbis ranging from the anti-Zionist William F. Rosenbaum to a celebrant of the "rebirth of the Israeli nation" in 1948, David Panitz, and from Louis

Gerstein of the Spanish and Portuguese Synagogue at Central Park West to Joseph Zeitlin of Temple Ansche Chesed on 100th Street and West End Avenue. *NYT,* March 27, 1949, 43.

30. William Barrett, "Culture Conference at the Waldorf," *Commentary,* May 1949, 491; Irving Howe, "The Culture Conference," *Partisan Review,* May 1949, 509–511.

31. Barrett, "Culture Conference at the Waldorf," 491; Howe, "The Culture Conference," 509–511.

32. Report of Confidential Informant, March 25, 1949 Fast FBI file, NY 100–61206; *NYT,* March 24, 1949, 12; March 25, 1949, 10; March 26, 1949, 6.

33. *Naked God,* 95.

34. Irving Howe, *Selected Writings: 1950–1990* (New York: Harcourt Brace Jovanovich, 1990), 344; *The Naked God,* 94–95; *Being Red,* 202.

35. *Being Red,* 202. For the Party's official position about the conference see, "Cultural Forces Rally against the Warmakers," *Political Affairs* 28 (May 1949): 29–38.

36. Howe, "The Culture Conference," 343.

37. Quoted in Peter Coleman, "The Brief Life of Liberal Anti-Communism," *National Review,* September 15, 1989, 35. Controversy about Shostakovich's role in the Stalinist system continues. He is seen as anything from a party hack to a kind of "secret dissident" struggling in his music against the enormous external forces that made him both "a celebrated hero and a shivering wreck." Edward Rothstein, "In a Subversive Key," *NYTBR,* May 8, 2011, 16–17; Wendy Lesser, *Music for Silenced Voices* (New Haven, Conn.: Yale University Press, 2011).

38. Michael O'Donnell, "Shostakovich's Ambivalence," *Nation,* May 9, 2011, 35–37; *NYT,* March 28, 1949, 1.

39. *The Naked God,* 94–95.

40. Fast said, "I feel certain that even if I were allowed to file an application for a passport, the State Department would fail to approve [it]." *NYT,* March 31, 1949, 4; Fast official papers, March 12, 1949, b1, f21, FC, UWM.

41. *Being Red,* 223, 216. In one version or another of the stories Fast told about Picasso, the Spanish master either kissed Howard, scribbled a dove on his napkin and autographed it, or signed, along with many other notables, the back of his conference identity card. Fast told his children that he had had the putative napkin framed, but that it disappeared in one of the family's many moves. Rachel Fast Ben-Avi (RFB), e-mail, January 8, 2011.

42. Translation courtesy of Mark Eisner, e-mail, December 14, 2009.

43. *Being Red,* 215–216, 221; *NYT,* April 25, 1949, 3.

44. *NYT,* April 25, 1949, 3.

45. Ibid., 21; Coleman, "The Brief Life of Liberal Anti-Communism," 36.

46. *Being Red,* 220–221.

47. Lily Phillips, "Howard Fast and the Refashioning of Postwar Protest," *Prospects* 27 (2002): 489–513.

48. *Being Red,* 217–219.

49. Fast to *NYTBR*, December 2, 1990, 82; Morris Schappes, "Fast, Isserman, Fadeyev, and Novick," *Jewish Currents*, April 1991, 19. One of the translators may have been P. Pavlenko, also of the SWU. He wrote to Fast thanking him for "the books you have presented me when [you] and I called on . . . Fadeev." Pavlenko, letter to Fast, September n.d., 1949, "P file," FPP. Pavlenko also visited Fast and his family in the United States in 1949.

50. Ibid.

51. The "creature of a slave state" was Irving Howe's description of Fadeyev at the Waldorf Conference.

52. For confirmation of Fast's account in *Being Red* of his encounter with Fadeyev in Paris, see succeeding editions of Ilya Ehrenburg's memoirs. In 1967, Ehrenburg was permitted by the Soviet authorities to relate how Fadeyev acknowledged that the questions of an unnamed writer "tormented" him. Almost a quarter century later more of Ehrenburg's text was restored, with Fadeyev acknowledging that it was Fast who had "tormented" him in Paris; see *Lyudi, Gody, Zhizn* [People, years, life], vol. 3 (Moscow, 1990), 122, cited in Joshua Rubenstein, ed., *Stalin's Secret Pogrom: The Postwar Inquisition of the Jewish Anti-Fascist Committee* (New Haven, Conn.: Yale University Press, 2001), 513n123. Much of this was confirmed by Rubenstein, phone call to author, April 19, 2007, and in face-to-face conversation with author, April 20, 2009. Rubenstein, the foremost biographer of Ehrenburg, says the Soviet writer's "memoirs are definitive." If Ehrenburg says the meeting took place, "it took place. He was in Paris, he knew Fast, he knew Fadeyev well." See also Rubenstein, *Tangled Loyalties: The Life and Times of Ilya Ehrenburg* (New York: Basic Books, 1996).

53. Novick to Fast, August 30, 1957; Fast, letter to Paul Novick, September 5, 1957, Novick Papers, YIVO; Schappes, "Fast, Isserman, Fadeyev, Novick," 16–19.

54. Joshua Rubenstein, "Some Were Poets, All Were Martyrs," *Forward*, August 9, 2002, 8.

55. Ibid.

56. Rubenstein, *Stalin's Secret Pogrom*, 55–64.

57. Fast to Novick, September 5, 1957, Novick Papers, YIVO; Novick, letter to Fast, August 30, 1957, Novick Papers, YIVO.

58. Fast to Novick, September 5, 1957; Novick to Fast, October 16, 1957, Novick Papers, YIVO; *Being Red*, 219.

59. *DW*, May 12, 1949, 7.

60. *Being Red*, 322–324, and a very revealing letter to Irving Adler, February n.d., 1953, which will be dealt with in a subsequent chapter. Also see Louis Rapoport, *Stalin's War against the Jews: The Doctors' Plot and the Soviet Solution* (New York: Free Press, 1990), and Rubenstein, *Stalin's Secret Pogrom*.

61. Most of what follows on Robeson is derived from Martin Duberman's sympathetic biography *Paul Robeson* (New York: Alfred Knopf, 1988), especially pages 350–355.

62. "Interview With Paul Robeson, Jnr." at http://www.gwu.edu/~nsarchiv/cold war/interviews episode6/robeson3.html.

63. Paul Robeson Jr., "How My Father Last Met Itzak Feffer," *Jewish Currents* (November 1981): 4–8; Robeson Jr., Letter to the Editor, *Jewish Currents,* February 1982, 25–28; Duberman, *Paul Robeson,* 354. Feffer and the other Jewish writers and members of the Jewish Anti-Fascist Committee were executed in 1952. The horrible irony in Robeson's claim about the safety of minorities in the USSR is that among the million or more civilians killed by the Stalin regime between 1937 and 1939, were some 250,000 people belonging to national minorities associated with states bordering the USSR. Ethnic cleansing was a major motive for Stalin's actions against his "enemies." Indeed, it was the Soviet leader, not Hitler, who initiated the first ethnic killing campaigns in interwar Europe. See Timothy Snyder, *Bloodlands: Europe between Hitler and Stalin* (New York: Basic Books, 2010), throughout.

64. Duberman, *Paul Robeson,* 21.

65. Rachel Fast, "Memoir," in *Red Diapers,* 129.

66. Duberman, *Paul Robeson,* 142–144, 151–155, 287, 294 and throughout. Robeson on art vs. family is quoted in the *Daily Herald,* July 11, 1930, and cited in Duberman, 613n35.

67. Jonathan Fast, e-mail, October 21, 2006.

68. Fast to Isabel Johnson Hiss, n.d., 1950; October 29, 1956; November 21, 1956, box 1, folder 12, Isabel Hiss collection, Schlesinger Library, Harvard University.

69. RFB, e-mail, May 30, 2007; Jonathan Fast, e-mail, May 30, 2007; RFB, e-mail, April 1, 2007; Barry Fast, son of Jerry Fast, Howard's older brother, interviewed by author, October 22, 2007; RFB, author interview, February 12, 2010.

70. Jonathan Fast, author interview, October 3, 2006; Memorandum, Special Agent in Charge (SAC) NY to Director, FBI May 25, 1949, Fast FBI file.

71. Bette to Howard, n.d.; September 1, 1949; September 15, 1949; "Bette letters file," FPP; RFB, e-mail, February 22, 2010.

72. Jonathan Fast, e-mail, October 21, 2006.

73. RFB, e-mail, September 19, 2006.

74. Jonathan Fast, author interview, October 3, 2006; RFB, e-mail, November 18, 2009.

75. Molly Jong-Fast, *Sex Doctors in the Basement* (New York: Villard Books, 2005), 20; Jong-Fast, author interview, September 26, 2006; Erica Jong, author interview, October 19, 2006.

76. Bette to Howard, September 1, 1949, FPP.

77. RFB, e-mail, February 22, 2010; *Being Red,* 226.

78. Bette to Howard, September 15, 20, 1949, FPP.

79. One of the few studies that looks at the riots from multiple perspectives is Joseph Walwik, *The Peekskill New York Anti-Communist Riots of 1949* (Lewiston, N.Y.: Edward Mellen, 2002).

80. Steve Courtney, "The Robeson Riots of 1949," *Reporter Dispatch,* September 5, 1982, at http://www.bencourtney.com/peekskillriots/

81. Associated Press version in Duberman, *Paul Robeson,* 342.

82. Randolph, quoted in Duberman, *Paul Robeson,* 342.

83. "Robeson Says U.S. Negroes Won't Fight against Russia," *Peekskill Evening Star,* April 21, 1949, 1; "Loves Soviet Best, Robeson Declares," *NYT,* June 20, 1949, 7.

84. Peter Filene, "Cold War Culture Doesn't Say It All," in *Rethinking Cold War Culture,* ed. Peter J. Kuznick and James Gilbert (Washington, D.C.: Smithsonian Institution Press, 2001), 157-174.

85. ACLU, *Violence in Peekskill* (New York: ACLU, 1949); James Rorty and Winifred Rauschenbush, "The Lessons of the Peekskill Riots," *Commentary,* October 1950, 309-323; Walwik, *The Peekskill New York Anti-Communist Riots,* 71-75.

86. Walwik, *The Peekskill New York Anti-Communist Riots,* 71-75.

87. Ibid.; *DW,* August 3, 1949, 3; Fast, *Peekskill, USA: A Personal Experience* (New York: Civil Rights Congress, 1951), 20-39.

88. *Eyewitness: Peekskill* (White Plains, N.Y.: Westchester Committee for a Fair Inquiry), 4; ACLU, *Violence in Peekskill; Westchester County Grand Jury Report* (June 1950), 1.

89. Rorty and Rauschenbush, "The Lessons of the Peekskill Riots," 316-319; Walwik, *The Peekskill New York Anti-Communist Riots,* 71-72.

90. Gerald Meyer, "Howard Fast: An American Leftist Reinterprets his Life," *Science and Society* 57 (Spring 1993): 86-91.

91. CRC flyer, in Thomas Dewey Papers, 5:22:35 Rush Rhees Library, University of Rochester; Walwik, *The Peekskill New York Anti-Communist Riots,* 88.

92. *NYT,* August 31, 1949, 16.

93. Duberman, *Paul Robeson,* 369; Fast, *Peekskill, USA,* 88; Fast, interviewed by Sam Roberts, February 24, 1998, DVD, NY News 1; and "Paul Robeson: Here I Stand," DVD, WNET, 1999.

94. Steve Courtney, "Peekskill's Days of Infamy: The Robeson Riots of 1949." For pictures of police trying to protect the victims of the mob violence see www.youtube.com/watch/?v=woo7xpFelNw.

95. T.C. Boyle, *World's End* (New York: Penguin Books, 1987), 406.

96. *NYT,* August 29, 1949, 16.

97. *DW,* August 29, 1949, 7; September 11, 1949, sec. 3, 1.

98. *Peekskill, USA,* 8, 36, 67-78.

99. Seeger interviewed at www.youtube.com/watch/?v=woo7xpFelNw, and quoted in Steve Courtney, "Peekskill's Days of Infamy." Fast, "Peekskill," *MM,* October 1949, 3-7.

100. Walwik, *The Peekskill New York Anti-Communist Riots,* iii.

101. Fast, "Peekskill," *MM.*

7. LITERATURE AND REALITY

1. *NYT,* May 30, 1950, 1.

2. Fast to Thomas, October 12, 1949, "Thomas file," Fast Personal Papers (FPP). *NYT,* December 6, 1949, 8.

3. Thomas to Fast, April 17, 1950, FPP.

4. *NYT,* April 2, 1950, 10. Matthiessen was not a Communist, nor, as a committed

Christian, a dogmatic Marxist. He lived a private homosexual life with painter Russell Cheney, who died in 1945, after which Matthiessen became increasingly distraught. Louis Hyde, ed., *Rat and the Devil: Journal Letters of F. O. Matthiessen and Russell Cheney* (New York: Alyson Books, 1988); Harry Levin, "The Private Life of F. O. Matthiessen," *New York Review of Books,* July 20, 1978, 42–46.

5. *NYT,* December 16, 1949, 21; May 24, 1950, 28.

6. *Literature and Reality* (New York: International Publishers, 1950), 3–5, 12–15, 22–36.

7. Ibid., 97. Ostrovsky (1904–36) was a Soviet socialist realist writer best known for his novel on the Russian Civil War, *How the Steel Was Tempered.* Sobolev was a novelist famous for his remark at a meeting of the Soviet Writer's Union that "the Party and the Government have given the writer everything and taken away from him only one thing—the right to write badly." *Encyclopedia of Soviet Writers,* at http://www.sovlit.com/bios/union.html.

8. P. Pavlenko to Fast, February n.d., 1950; March 30, 1951, "P file," FPP. Though critical, Pavlenko did have "something pleasant" to say. "'Freedom Road' had a great and deserved success here among our readers and critics," and Comrade Fadeyev asked that there be a continuing "exchange of opinions between us. Please give my hearty greetings to your wife and to those friends, whom I had the pleasure of meeting during my short stay in the USA. . . . The best wishes for strength and stoutness in your cause." *Literature and Reality* did get an abbreviated notice in the *Times* as an application of "party-line thinking to literature" that makes "monotonous reading." *NYT,* January 29, 1950, 170.

9. *Daily Worker* (DW), March 5, 1950, n.p.; *Masses and Mainstream* (MM), March 1950, 76–79.

10. Maltz to Fast, December 24, 1951, "Maltz file," FPP.

11. Fast, Campenni interview, December 1, 1967, b8, f11, Fast Collection (FC), University of Wisconsin-Milwaukee (UWM).

12. "American Literature and the Democratic Tradition," *College English,* March 1947, 279–284; "Culture and the Future," *New Masses* (NM), February 6, 1945, 11.

13. "American Literature and the Democratic Tradition," 282–283.

14. Ibid.

15. These paragraphs benefited from discussion with my friends and former colleagues in the English Department at SUNY, New Paltz, the prolific poets Richard Fein and Dennis Doherty.

16. "American Literature and the Democratic Tradition," 11.

17. Fast to P. Pavlenko, Oct 12, 1949, in Phillips, "Howard Fast and the Refashioning of Postwar Protest," 510; Fast to Boris Polevoy, September 19, 1956, in ibid., 492.

18. Government agencies, including the CIA, and private foundations, including the Congress of Cultural Freedom and its American section, the Committee for Cultural Freedom, and the Rockefeller foundation, did, beginning in 1950, play a role in promoting modern, even modernist, Western and American culture in riposte to the Soviet Cominform's "peace conferences" of the previous year. But the cultural shift

started well before any CIA involvement, and in the late 1940s and early 1950s, the agency was actually pleading for less overt anti-Communism. For a different view see Tobin Siebers, *Cold War Criticism and the Politics of Skepticism* (New York: Oxford, 1993) and Barbara Foley, "Renarrating the Thirties in the Forties and Fifties," *Prospects* 20 (1995): 455–66.

19. Samuel Sillen, "Better Politics and Better Art," *DW*, April 14, 1946, 21–22; Alfred Goldsmith, "Struggle for Survival," *NM*, May 21, 1946, 25–26; Wald, *Trinity of Passion*, 239–259.

20. *Literature and Reality*, 22. Somehow along the line Fast seemed to have missed what Picasso had said: "I am a Communist and my painting is Communist painting. . . . But if I were a shoemaker, Royalist or Communist or anything else, I would not necessarily hammer my shoes in a special way to show my politics." *Picasso on Art: A Selection of Views* (Cambridge, Mass.: Da Capo Press, 1988) 140; John Richardson, "How Political Was Picasso?" *New York Review of Books,* November 25, 2010, at http://www.nybooks.com/articles/archives/2010/nov/25/how-political-was-picasso.

21. Martha C. Nussbaum, *Poetic Justice: The Literary Imagination and Public Life* (Boston: Beacon, 1995), 45–68. For more on these social realists and many other writers and their work see Steven A. Reich, "The Great Migration and the Literary Imagination," *Journal of the Historical Society* 9, no. 1 (March 2009): 87–128.

22. "Deadline for Freedom" rallies were held in April on behalf of the Hollywood Ten and the board members of JAFRC in Manhattan, Brooklyn, and Queens. But only the usual suspects showed up to speak: several members of the Hollywood Ten, Paul Robeson, I. F. Stone, for example. *NYT*, April 12, 1950, 24.

23. David Alman to Fast, June 5, 1950, "A file," FPP; Fast to Hemingway, May 22, 1950, Ernest Hemingway Collection, John F. Kennedy Library.

24. O'Casey to Fast, April 18, 1950, "O file," FPP.

25. Muriel Rukeyser to Fast, April 17, 1950, "M file," FPP.

26. Rachel Fast, "Memoir," in *Red Diapers*, 126–127.

27. Jonathan Fast, author interview, October 3, 2006.

28. Rachel Fast, "Memoir," 125.

29. RFB, e-mail, February 21, 2011.

30. Bettina Aptheker, *Intimate Politics: How I Grew Up Red, Fought for Free Speech, and Became a Feminist Rebel* (New York: Seal Press, 2006), 54.

31. Josh Kornbluth, *Red Diaper Baby* (San Francisco: Mercury House, 1996), 4.

32. Rachel Fast, "Memoir," 125. Jonathan Fast, author interview, October 3, 2006, said that "really Rachel was the target of the indoctrination; by the time I was nine, my father was no longer in the Communist Party."

33. Rachel Fast, "Memoir," 125.

34. "We Have Kept the Faith," *MM*, July 1950, 23–28.

35. Fast, *Being Red*, 247.

36. *NYT*, June 8, 1950, 1; *DW*, June 5, 8, 1950, 1.

37. *Being Red*, 249.

38. Ibid., 250.

39. "Capital Punishment," *DW,* April 5, 1956, at http://www.trussel.com/hf/plots/t603.htm.

40. *Being Red,* 251.

41. Hammett in Lillian Hellman, *An Unfinished Woman* (Boston: Little, Brown, 1969), 263.

42. Alman to Fast, June 5, 1950, "A file," FPP.

43. Graham was introduced by Fast to Julian Messner, who published her first five books from 1944 to 1949. Messner had published three of Fast's books between 1941 and 1942. Also see David Levering Lewis, *W. E. B. Du Bois: The Fight for Equality and the American Century 1919–1963* (New York: Owl Books, 2001), 527.

44. Graham to Fast, June 11, 1950, Shirley Graham Du Bois Papers, series 3, folder 17.8–17.9, Arthur and Elizabeth Schlesinger Library, Harvard University.

45. Lewis, *W. E. B. Du Bois,* 526.

46. *NYT,* June 11, 1950, 28.

47. M. Sneh to Fast, July 24, 1950; clipping from *Al HaMishmar,* July 24, 1950; copy of cable to President Truman, all in "I file," in FPP.

48. Howard to Bette, June 14, 1950, b41, FC, University of Pennsylvania (UP).

49. *Being Red,* 253.

50. Howard to Bette, June 12, 1950, b41, FC, UP.

51. *NYT,* June 29, 1950, 18.

52. Howard to Bette, June 15 1950, b41, FC, UP; Maureen Crockett, "Doing Time on Kennison Mountain: Pocahontas County's Forgotten Prison," *Goldenseal* 11 (November 1985): 38.

53. Howard to Bette, June 15, 1950, b41, FC, UP.

54. *Being Red,* 264; Molly Jong-Fast, *Girl [Maladjusted]: True Stories from a Semi-celebrity Childhood* (New York: Random House, 2006), 22. My friend the poet Dennis Doherty said the poem "reads like Alan Ginsberg on a very bad day." Mark Eisner, a Neruda specialist, says it sounds like Neruda's work, but confirmed that it was never published. Eisner, e-mail, August 28, 2009. Neruda also included Fast in "Let the Wood-cutter Awake," the ninth canto in his *Canto General* (1950). The poet wrote about how the soldiers returning from WWII have "also found that Charlie Chaplin, the ultimate/father of the tenderness of the world,/must hide, and that the writers (Howard Fast, etc.),/the scholars and the artists/of your land/must sit down to be unjustified for un-american thoughts,/before a tribunal of merchants enriched by the war." Translation courtesy of Mark Eisner. Literary critic Ilan Stavans says that Neruda's poetry, especially in the late 1940s and 1950s, was often mere pamphleteering, "unbalanced" and "unconvincing." *Poetry of Pablo Neruda* (New York: Farrar, Straus, and Giroux, 2003), xxxvii–xxxvix; *Being Red,* 264.

55. Howard to Bette, June 8, 10 1950, b41, FC, UP.

56. Ibid., June 12, 19, 1950, b41, FC, UP.

57. Ibid., June 12, 15, 19, 25, 1950, b41, FC, UP.

58. Ibid., June 19, 1950, b41, FC, UP; Photograph, Fast and fellow mason, in *Being Red,* between pp. 184 and 185.

59. *Sunday Worker,* October 29, 1950, 4ff.

60. Fast, "introduction," ms., Yiddish edition of *Spartacus,* 1954; Fast, interviewed by Moses Schoenfeld, UN Press Section, "International Date Line," audiotape, n.d., 1990, FPP; Fast, interviewed by Keith Berwick, "At One," videotape, KNBC in Los Angeles, n.d., 1976, FPP.

61. Fast, interviewed by Amy Goodman, April 8, 1998, Pacifica Radio, transcript, FPP.

62. Howard to Bette, June 16, 8, 1950, b41, FC, UP.

63. Ibid., August 3, 1950, b41, FC, UP.

64. Ibid., July 27, 1950, b41, FC, UP. Fast also told Dr. Lee Kudrow his pain started in 1948. When "I was sent to prison. . . . the headaches became more painful," he said, but less frequent and "not unendurable." Fast to Kudrow, January 8, 1979, "K file," FPP.

65. Howard to Bette, August 8, 1950, b41, FC, UP.

66. Ibid., July 27, 1950, b41, FC, UP.

67. Arthur, "Resume of Contacts with Fast," handwritten pages dated and signed [signature redacted], October 11, 1950, with a note that he "had left quite a bit out." FBI Memo, November 11, 1950, Fast FBI file.

68. Ibid.

69. Julius Fast to Howard, June n.d., 1950, b1, f12, Fast Collection (FC), University of Wisconsin, Milwaukee (UWM).

70. Howard to Bette, June 19, 1950, b41, FC, UP; Bette to Howard, July 13, 26, 1950, b41, FC, UP.

71. Rachel Fast, "Memoir," 128–129. There are several reports by informants in Fast's FBI file concerning the couple's marital difficulties, including memos dated May 25, 1949; March 23, 1953; and November 5, 1953.

72. Bette to Howard, July 26, 1950, b41, FC, UP.

73. *Being Red,* 261.

74. Ibid.

75. Fast, Campenni interview, December 1, 1967.

76. Fast to Angus Cameron, September 9, 1948, "C file," FPP; Howard to Bette, June 19, 1950; August 8, 15, 1950, b41, FC, UP.

77. Howard to Bette, August 15, 1950, b41, FC, UP.

78. *Being Red,* 276.

79. Ibid., 256.

80. Fast, "The Singularity of Being Jewish," unpublished ms., 102, FPP.

81. Ibid.

82. Fast, Campenni interview, August 12–19, 1977, b9, f2, FC, UWM; Howard to Bette, August 8, 1950, b41, FC, UP.

83. Howard to Bette, June 29, 1950, b41, FC, UP.

84. Howard to Bette, August 3, 1950, b41, FC, UP.

85. Howard to Bette, August 20, 1950, b41, FC, UP.

86. Julius Fast to Howard, June 23, 1950, b1, f12, FC, UWM.

87. Jonathan Fast, author interview, October 3, 2006; "Son of a Writer," *New York Times Sunday Magazine,* July 29, 1984, 50.

88. "Son of a Writer," 50; Bette to Howard, July 3, 1945.

89. Jonathan Fast, author interview, October 3, 2006; Sue Shapiro, "All in the Family: Howard Fast," in *Only As Good As Your Word: Writing Lessons from My Favorite Literary Gurus,* author's ms., 65–79.

90. Jonathan Fast, "Son of a Writer."

91. RFB, e-mail, November 10, 2006.

92. Ibid., July 20, 2009.

93. Barry Fast, e-mail, July 24, 2009; Howard to Bette, August 20, 1950, b41, UP.

94. Rachel Fast, "Memoir," 131; Barry Fast, e-mail, July 23, 2009. For information on Paul Stewart, see http://www.imdb.com/name/nm0829717/.

95. Bette to Howard, August 17, 1950, b41, FC, UP. Emphasis mine.

96. Ibid. Emphasis mine.

97. Bette to Howard, August 23, 1950, FPP.

98. *DW,* September 1, 1950, 2; Howard to Bette, August 13, 20, 1950, b41, FC, UP.

8. FREE! BUT NOT AT LAST

1. Fast, Frank Campenni interview, December 1, 1967, box 8, folder 11, Fast Collection (FC), University of Wisconsin-Milwaukee (UWM); Fast, *Being Red,* 271–274; "A Conversation with Howard Fast, March 23, 1994," conducted by Alan Wald and Alan Filreis, ed. Thomas J. Sugrue, *Prospects* 20 (1995): 511–523; *Daily Worker* (DW), August 9, September 8, September 26, 1950. Quotes unless otherwise indicated are Fast's.

2. The Fasts had obviously not seen the notice in *DW* of August 9: "Earl Jones, the well-known Negro actor, will play one of the leading roles in *The Hammer*—a so-called 'white' part—in line with New Playwright's policy of anti-jimcrow [*sic*] casting according to ability."

3. *Being Red,* 271–274.

4. Fast, *The Naked God,* 21. Emphasis mine.

5. "A Conversation with Howard Fast," 518.

6. Lauter, "Fast's Play 'The Hammer' Presented by New Playwrights," *DW,* September 26, 1950, http://www.trussel.com/hf/plots/t645.htm. It was difficult to determine precisely the date of the play's closing. But everything points to a run of no more than a week or two.

7. Joseph Starobin, "More Comments on Howard Fast," *Masses and Mainstream* (MM), April 1957, 51–54.

8. *The Proud and the Free,* in *The Call of Fife and Drum: Three Novels of the American Revolution* (Secaucus, N.J.: Citadel Press, 1987).

9. *Naked God,* 146.

10. *NYT,* September 11, 1950, 12.

11. Fast, "Reply to Critics," *MM,* December 1950, 53–64.

12. "*The Proud and the Free:* Some Critical Observations," undated, in V. J. Jerome Papers, Ms #589, Yale University Manuscripts and Archives.

13. "Reply to Critics," 53–64.

14. Carl Van Doren, *Mutiny in January* (New York: Viking Press, 1943).

15. *New York Herald Tribune,* "Weekly Book Review," April 4, 1943, 1.

16. "Reply to Critics," 53–64.

17. Ibid.; Van Doren, *Mutiny in January.*

18. "Reply to Critics," 53.

19. Cameron to Fast, April 5, 1950, Fast Personal Papers (FPP).

20. A mixed review of *The Proud and the Free* appeared in the *Saturday Review,* a hostile one in the *New York Post.* On the silence that greeted this book, see Joseph North, *DW,* October 19, 1950, and Fast, *DW,* October 30, 1950.

21. *NYT,* November 8, 1950, 2; "Memo," October 25, 1951, Fast FBI file.

22. Fast, draft, undated,b7, f7, FC, UWM. Emphasis Fast's.

23. Ibid.

24. Stephen Whitfield, *The Culture of the Cold War* (Baltimore: Johns Hopkins University Press, 1996), 9–14.

25. "Hoover Planned Mass Jailing in 1950," *NYT,* December 23, 2007. There is no evidence that Truman or any other president approved any part of Hoover's proposal.

26. Punishment for being thought a "probable" conspirator, spy, or saboteur could be as much as a fine of $10,000 and ten years in jail. The law was never enforced.

27. Fast, *Never to Forget: The Story of the Warsaw Ghetto* (New York: Book League of Jewish Peoples Fraternal Order, I.W.O., 1946). The poem, published in a twenty-four-page pamphlet, elaborately illustrated by William Gropper, was one of the first literary treatments of the Holocaust in English.

28. Guttenplan, *American Radical,* 259.

29. A. Warren Littman, *Administration of the Internal Security Act of 1950: Prepared for the Subcommittee to Investigate the Administration of the Internal Security Act and Other . . . on the Judiciary, United States Senate* (United States Government Printing Office, 1975); Marc Patenaude, *The McCarran Internal Security Act, 1950–2005* (Germany: VDM Verlag Dr. Mueller e.K., 2008). Although sites for detention camps were prepared, no camps were actually built, and after Stalin's death in 1953, President Eisenhower decided they were unnecessary. The McCarran Act and its strengthened version, the Communist Control Act of 1954, were never enforced and are no longer operative.

30. Fast to Maltz, July 24 1951, b16, f5, Maltz Papers (MP), Wisconsin State Historical Society (WSHS).

31. See for example, Fast, "The Big Finger," *MM,* March 1950, 62–68.

32. James Reston, "Intellectual Left Silent in Campaign," *NYT,* November 2, 1950, 23.

33. Fast, *Crisis No. 1* (New York: Civil Rights Congress, 1951), 2; *NYT,* February 1, 1951, 11. "Never Again?" *Time,* June 25, 1956, 15.

34. *NYT,* November 21, 1950, 45; February 1, 1951, 11.

35. *New York World-Telegram,* December 2, 1950, editorial page.

36. *NYT,* December 15, 1950, 40.

37. *New York Post,* May 24 1950; "Brooklyn College Suspends Six Vanguard Editors: 50 Others on Staff of Undergraduate Paper Reprimanded," *Brooklyn Eagle,* May 21, 1950; both articles at http://www.ashp.cuny.edu/oralhistory/CLprimarydoc3 .html; Ida Selavan Schwarz, former president of the BC Folk and Square Dance Society, e-mail, December 19, 21, 2008.

38. Fast to Maltz, July 24, 1951, b16, f5, MP, WSHS.

39. This paragraph and the three that follow rely heavily on excellent studies by Philip Dray, *At the Hands of Persons Unknown* (New York: Random House, 2002) and Carol Anderson, *Eyes Off the Prize: The United Nations and the African American Struggle for Human Rights, 1944–1955* (Cambridge: Cambridge University Press, 2003). Also see: Peter Salwen, "A 'Northern Lynching,' 1949: Remembering the Trenton Six Case," at http://www.salwen.com/trenton6.html.

40. Dray, *At the Hands of Persons Unknown,* 405.

41. Communist involvement did not always mean negative results. The Scottsboro Case is a good example. See James R. Acker, *Scottsboro and Its Legacy: The Cases That Challenged American Legal and Social Justice* (New York: Praeger, 2007); Gerald Horne, *Powell v. Alabama: The Scottsboro Boys and American Justice* (New York: Franklin Watts, 1997).

42. Anderson, *Eyes on the Prize,* 175–183. For the most comprehensive study of the McGee trial see Alex Heard, *The Eyes of Willie McGee: A Tragedy of Race, Sex, and Secrets in the Jim Crow South* (New York: HarperCollins, 2010).

43. Fast, telegrams, signed "Howard Fast, Chairman, Writing Division, NCASP," in Fast FBI file.

44. Fast even wrote to Truman, a man he detested, and pleaded with him to use the "great moral and persuasive power of [his] office" to intervene in the Virginia case and prevent the executions. Fast to Truman, January 31, 1951, "T file," FPP.

45. Maltz to Fast, April 24, 1951, "Maltz file," FPP.

46. *Time,* February 12, 1951, http://www.time.com/time/magazine/article/0,9171,820649,00.html; "Agent Memo," Fast FBI file; *Daily Compass,* February 22, 1951, 10.

47. Gropper to Fast, February 19, 1951, FPP. Ten other leading artists contributed to the pamphlet, including Rockwell Kent and Phil Evergood. Fast to T. O. Thackerey, editor of the *Daily Compass,* March 16, 1951, "May Day file," FPP.

48. Fast to Kantorowicz, February 16, 1951, "K file," FPP. Emphasis mine.

49. Fast, "The Trenton Nightmare," DW, March 9, 1951, 8; DW, March 9, 1951, 5; DW, May 7, 1951, 3.

50. Joseph Blotner, *Faulkner: A Biography* (Oxford: University Press of Mississippi), 539.

51. "A Conversation with Howard Fast," 511–523; Note, 1951, Fast FBI file.

52. Fast, "Why We Could Not Save the Negro McGee," *Austrian People's Voice,* July 7, 1953, clipping in Fast FBI file. The *Austrian People's Voice* was the daily paper of the CP of Austria and had been printing a series of articles by Fast, since July 3, under the caption "American Diary." The FBI had these clipped and translated.

53. *NYT,* July 25, 1951, 12; Fast to Maltz, July 24, 1951, b16, f5, MP, WSHS.

54. Fast to Lerner, September 28, 1951; Lerner to Fast, October 4, 1951; October 9, 1951, FPP.

55. The CRC posted $176,000 for the other seventeen leaders arrested on June 20, but this bail was revoked when four of the 1949 arrestees became fugitives on July 2. Four of those arrested in June 1950 also went underground.

56. Robert Shaplen, "Scarsdale's Battle of the Books," *Commentary,* December 1950, 530–540; Fast to Simon and Schuster about the omission of his article on the 1937 Republic Steel Strike "massacre" from a projected anthology, November 28, 1948, box 64, FC, University of Pennsylvania. "Memorial Day Massacre" originally appeared in *New Masses,* June 3, 1947. Fast, letter to Bosley Crowther, December 13, 1955, saying he had thought he was on the blacklist since 1947, FPP.

57. Fast to Thomas, July 12, 1951, FPP.

58. Martin Duberman, *Paul Robeson* (New York: Alfred Knopf, 1989), 388.

59. Correspondence between Fast and Ruth Shipley, Chief, Passport Division, U.S. Department of State, 1951–1958, FPP. Ruth Shipley, who consistently turned down Fast's requests, was no ordinary bureaucrat. Her older brother, A. Bruce Bielski, had been the director of the FBI in the Wilson administration. Her younger brother, Frank Bielski, was the director of investigations at the OSS.

60. "A Conversation with Howard Fast," 511–523. Despite Truman's having sent the UN's Convention on the Prevention and Punishment of the Crime of Genocide to Congress with his full approval in June 1949, the United States did not sign on. Opponents feared the convention would be used by other nations as propaganda to protest racial conditions in America.

61. Dray, *At the Hands of Persons Unknown,* 408–411.

62. Shubin to Fast, December 8, 1956, "s file," FPP. J. Edgar Hoover believed that the play, not available in the United States, depicted "a Washington family broken up by a hunt for Communists and impugns the integrity of the FBI." Hoover to Legal Attache, London, 1951, Fast FBI file.

63. Fast to Fadayev, in Phillips, "Howard Fast and the Refashioning of Postwar Protest," 510; "A Conversation with Howard Fast," 511–523; *Naked God,* 137–158.

64. *Naked God,* 143.

65. Fast to Maltz, May 23, 1951, b15, f5, MP, WSHS.

66. Ibid.; *Being Red,* 245–246; Kent, "A Child is Lost," *This Week,* November 19, 1950, at http://www.trussel.com/hf/short.htm#T213. Fast got between fifteen hundred and two thousand dollars from *This Week.* But many other magazines picked up the story, and "suddenly it became a gold mine. Every day money was pouring in from this little thing." Fast, Campenni interview, August 19, 1974, b9, f1, FC, UWM. A secretary at Little, Brown may have been Confidential Informant T-50. Memorandum, Special Agent in Charge (SAC) to Director, FBI, December 20, 1951, Fast FBI file.

67. Fast, Campenni interview, August 19, 1974; *NYTBR* January 20, 1952, 16.

68. Fast to Maltz, May 23, 1951, b15, f5, MP, WSHS.

69. Maltz to Fast, December 24, 1951, "Maltz file." FPP.

70. Wald, *Trinity of Passion,* 1–11. Before the war Lacy was a member of the Communist-led League of American Writers, and afterward he was active in the Communist-influenced National Council of the Arts, Sciences and Professions.

71. Fast to Maltz, August 27, 1951, b16, f5, MP, WSHS.

72. Fast to Maltz, May 23, 1951, b15, f5, MP, WSHS.

73. Ibid.

74. Fast to Cameron, March 13, 1951, b64, FC, UP; Fast, *Naked God,* 147; Cameron, "Trade Report," June 27, 1951, FPP. Full report at www.trussel.com/hf/cameron1.htm.

75. *Counterattack,* no. 223, August 31, 1951; Campenni, *Citizen Howard Fast,* 366–67.

76. Cameron to Fast, June 27, 1951; September 25, 1951, b64, FC, UP.

77. Robins, *Alien Ink,* 242; *Being Red,* 288, 295–299.

78. Fast to Max Lerner, March 14, 1952, "L file," FPP. Foner, not named explicitly, is referred to only as a "small, liberal publisher."

79. Ibid.; Fast to Maltz, August 27, 1951, b16, f5, MP, WSHS.

80. Cameron, in Robins, *Alien Ink,* 242.

81. For an example see Fast to Burt Struthers, Oct 30, 1951 b16, f8, FC, UWM.

82. Memorandum, SAC, Boston to Director, FBI, December 29, 1951, Fast FBI file.

83. Fast to Isabel Johnson, n.d., 1951, b1, f12, Isabel Hiss Papers, Schlesinger Library, Harvard University.

84. Fast to "Dear Brother," May 16, 1952, b1, f5, FC, UWM.

85. Fast, *Spartacus* (Armonk, N.Y.: North Castle Books, 1996), vi.

86. Carl Hoffman, "The Evolution of a Gladiator: History, Representation, and Revision in *Spartacus,*" *Journal of American and Comparative Culture* 23 (Spring 2000): 63–71; Keith Bradley, *Slavery and Rebellion in the Ancient World, 140 B.C. to 70 B.C.* (Bloomington: Indiana University Press, 1989).

87. *Spartacus,* 132.

88. Ibid., 164.

89. "My God, My God, why hast thou forsaken me?"

90. Fast to Konstantin Siminov, editor of the *Literary Gazette,* Moscow, n.d., 1952, "S file," FPP. Emphasis mine.

91. Swados, "Epic in Technicolor," *Nation,* April 5, 1952, 331.

92. Many copies were also sold in England after it was published by Bodley Head, a development not unnoticed by the FBI's legal attaché at the U.S. Embassy in London. Memo from Attache to Director, September 3, 1952, Fast FBI file.

93. NYTBR, February 3, 1952, 22; *Nation,* April 5, 1952, 331.

94. *Worker,* February 17, 1952; MM, March 1952, 53–58. According to an FBI informant William Weiner, a financial director of the CPUSA, said that "FAST's recent writings, particularly 'Spartacus' have not been up to standards set by the Party and for that reason he is not considered a good Party writer. WEINER said there is no doubt about his loyalty to the Party but he had no grasp of 'Marxism' and is too much of an individualist in his writings." Memorandum, "Secret," July 3, 1953, 16, Fast FBI file.

95. Cameron to Fast, June 27, 1951, "C file," FPP.

96. *Naked God*, 153; Maltz to Fast, May 3, 1952, b1, f23, FC, UWM. Although John Howard Lawson praised the book, he found errors on "two very serious matters . . . psychological theory of history," and "serious weaknesses on the woman question." Lawson to Fast, February 4, 1952, "L file," FPP.

97. Fast to "Dear Librarian," December 27, 1951, b1, f6, FC, UWM; Fast to "Dear Friend," March 4, 1952, b1, f5, FC, UWM; Goldberg, letter to Fast, December 27, 1951, "G file," FPP.

98. Fast to Maltz, February 13, 1952, b16, f5, MP, WSHS.

99. *NYT*, September 23, 1992, C20.

100. Daniel Traister, "Noticing Howard Fast," *Prospects* 20 (1995): 525–541; L. Kislova, letter to P. A. Churikov, quoted in Phillips, "Howard Fast and the Refashioning of Postwar Protest," 505. Fast told the FBI that he was paid royalties by the Soviet Union and the East European countries until February 1957, and that he continued to receive payment from Poland even after that. "Interview," September 16, 1957, Fast FBI file. See also, for example, Moscow editor A. Chakovsky's 1955 letter to Fast, informing him "that the royalty for 'Lola Gregg' ($1,426.75) has been transferred to the New York address given by you." FPP.

101. Rossen Djagalov, "'I Don't Boast about it, but I'm the Most Widely Read Author of This Century," *Anthropology of East Europe Review* 27 (Fall 2009): 44.

102. Fast, unpublished ms. for "Foreword," *Spartacus,* Yiddish edition, 1954, "S file," FPP.

103. Fast, Campenni interview, 1977, b9, f2, FC, UWM; *NYT*, September 23, 1992, C20; Zvi Arad, Israeli publishers, *Sifriat Poalim,* to Fast, October, 1951, "I file," FPP; Fast to Nikolai Alexandreevich Michailov, Minister of Culture, Moscow, USSR, n.d., "M file," FPP.

104. In 1955, Fast told Albert Maltz that he had "laid out so much money" for Blue Heron, "that I cannot possibly go on as a publishing house." And to Gertrude Heym he wrote that the press has "left me triumphantly poor." Fast to Maltz, September 20, 1955; Fast to Heym, December 14, 1955, FPP; but see http://www.trussel.com/hf/blue heron.htm#11; Du Bois to Fast, October 21, 1953, "D file," FPP.

105. The FBI had its eye on Du Bois since 1942, when it characterized the African American historian and activist's writings as "socialist." Although indicted in 1951 for failing to register as a "foreign agent," Du Bois was soon acquitted for lack of evidence.

106. Fast, "On 'Oliver Twist,'" *MM*, September 1951, 20. The protest against the film was supported by the Anti-Defamation League of B'nai B'rith and the American Jewish Congress. For more on competing Jewish identities see: Deborah Dash Moore, "Reconsidering the Rosenbergs: Symbol and Substance in Second Generation American Jewish Consciousness," *Journal of American Ethnic History* 8 (Fall 1988): 21–37; Michael Staub, *Torn at the Roots: The Crisis of Jewish Liberalism in Postwar America* (New York: Columbia University Press, 2002), 19–44.

107. *NYT*, March 12, 1951, 22; *Daily Compass*, February 22, 1951, 10; *DW*, February 7, 1951, 3; *MM*, March 1951, 29; *DW*, March 9, 1951, 5; April 16, 1951, 4; April 30, 1951, 11; May 7, 1951, 3; Soviet Embassy to Howard and Bette Fast, May 17, 1951, b3, f19, FC, UWM; *DW*, July 2, 1951, 3; *NYT*, July 25, 1951, 12; *NYT*, August 15, 1951, 24; Fast, "On 'Oliver Twist'," 20; *DW*, October 30, 1951, 7; *Worker*, November 18, 1951, 8; Fast, "Labor on the Move: 2," *MM*, December 1951, 43–45.

108. Fast, "The Impenetrable Curtain of Lies," broadcast in Russia, reprinted in *Pravda* and contained in Memo, British Broadcast Company's "Summary of World Broadcasts," October 22, 1951, Fast FBI file; Fast, "Bulwark of Peace," in *We Pledge Peace: A Friendship Book* (San Francisco: Friendship Book, 1951), 43.

9. TRIALS AND TRIBULATIONS

1. Maltz to Fast, April 24, July 17, 1951, September 11, 1952, "Maltz file," FPP.

2. Cecil Eby, *Comrades and Commissars: The Lincoln Battalion in the Spanish Civil War* (Princeton, N.J.: Princeton University Press, 2006), 141–142, 184, 435; Steve Nelson, James R. Barrett, and Bob Ruck, *Steve Nelson, American Radical* (Pittsburgh: University of Pittsburgh Press, 1981). The FBI suspected that Nelson was also involved in atomic espionage in California and in direct contact with the NKVD.

3. *NYT*, January 17, 1952, 6.

4. "Report," January 28, 1952, Fast FBI file. *Pennsylvania v. Nelson* (1956) brought an end to state prosecutions for sedition. The Oyez Project, *Pennsylvania v. Nelson,* 350 U.S. 497 (1956), at http://oyez.org/cases/19501959/1955/1955_10.

5. Nelson would also soon be convicted and sentenced to five more years for violating the Smith Act. While ultimately acquitted on all counts, Nelson would spend close to two years either in prison awaiting bail or fighting his battles in court.

6. Fast to John S. Fine, July 21, 1952, b6, f4, Fast Collection (FC), University of Wisconsin-Milwaukee (UWM); Fast to Margaret Maltz, with the poem attached, which reads more like a resume; the last stanza, typical of the rest, reads: "Steel worker and commander of the Lincoln Brigade/Brave man and principled/Simple and humble/ Member of the Communist Party of the USA/and leader of our working class." Steve Nelson Papers, ALBA, b8, f8, Tamiment library.

7. *Daily Worker* (*DW*), July 13, 1952, 6; July 28, 1952, 8.

8. Fast, telegrams, n.d., b2, f16, FC, UWM.

9. Nelson to Fast, July 25, 1952, February 26, 1953; Fast to Aragon and Picasso, January 28, 1953, b6, f4, FC, UWM; Fast to William Patterson, February 21, 1953, b6, f4, FC, UWM. Nelson also told Fast that he "ran into some of your books in the workhouse—a large group of young Negroes read them. Freedom Road was criticized (to my surprise) by a group of them. They dislike the dialect. I do not know if this is general. I never heard it among 'our people.' I just tell you for what it is worth." Nelson to Fast, b6, f4, FC, UWM.

10. *NYT*, February 13, 1952, 23; "Confidential Report," February 11, 1953, 30, Fast FBI file.

11. *New Haven Register,* April 9, 1952; *Yale Daily News,* n.d., clippings, Fast FBI file.

12. For an all-too-typical example of this charge see the *DW,* December 7, 1947. The Feinberg Law was contested from its very inception; injunctions against enforcing it were issued, rescinded, issued again. There were innumerable court cases until the Supreme Court declared the Feinberg Law constitutional in 1952. There are nearly 200 articles in the *New York Times* about the law and the challenges to it from the beginning of 1949 through 1952. *Adler et al. v. Board of Education of the City of New York,* decided March 3, 1952. See http://law.jrank.org/pages/12531/Adler-et-al-v-Board-Education-City-NewYork.html#ixzz0hiYReZg. Also see James D. Folts, *History of the University of the State of New York and the State Education Department, 1784-1996* (Albany, N.Y.: State Education Department, 1996). The percentage of new teachers in New York City public schools who were Jewish increased steadily from 1920 onward, and as early as 1940, 56% of teachers entering the city school system were Jews. Deborah Dash Moore, *At Home in America: Second Generation New York Jews* (New York: Columbia University Press, 1981), 95-96.

13. *New Haven Register,* April 9, 1952, clipping, Fast FBI file.

14. Murray Friedman, *The Utopian Dilemma: New Political Directions for American Jews* (Washington, D.C.: Ethics and Public Policy Center, 1985), especially the chapter entitled "The Golden Age of American Jewry, 1945-1965." Moore, *At Home in America,* 201-242; Arthur Goren, *The Politics and Public Culture of American Jews* (Bloomington: Indiana University Press, 1990), 186-204.

15. The list could be expanded exponentially with names like Clement Greenberg, Isaac Rosenfeld, Lee Krasner, Jerome Robbins, Henry Youngman, Sid Caeser, Jules Feiffer, Jackie Mason, Paddy Chayefsky, Jerome Kern, Moss Hart, Groucho Marx, Paul Taylor, et al.

16. Jonathan Fast, author interview, October 3, 2006.

17. "Save the Rosenbergs," *Masses and Mainstream* (MM) (April 1952): 48-50; Moore, "Reconsidering the Rosenbergs," 21-37. Several paragraphs in this section are heavily indebted to Moore's incisive and illuminating article.

18. For another important example of diminishing radicalism in a Jewish community faced with "the Rosenberg problem," see the issues of the Jewish monthly *Commentary* from 1950 through 1954.

19. Michael Staub, *Torn at the Roots: The Crisis of Jewish Liberalism in Postwar America* (New York: Columbia University Press, 2002), 19-44; Moore, *At Home in America,* 201-230.

20. "Save the Rosenbergs," 48-50. Emphasis mine.

21. Ibid.

22. *New York Post,* June 19, 1952, 22.

23. William Reuben, "Truth about the Rosenbergs' Case," *Jewish Life,* November 1951, 4-7, and December 1951, 21-23; also see Louis Harap, "Anti-Semitism and the Rosenbergs," *Jewish Life,* January 1952, 24-26.

24. *DW,* February 28, 1952; Lucy Dawidowicz, "'Anti-Semitism' and the Rosenberg Case," *Commentary,* July 1952, 41-45.

25. Patterson in Dawidowicz, "'Anti-Semitism' and the Rosenberg Case," 43.

26. Igor Lukes, "The Rudolf Slansky Affair: New Evidence," *Slavic Review,* Spring 1999, 160–187; Ivan Margolius, *Reflections of Prague: Journeys through the 20th Century* (London: Wiley, 2006).

27. *Being Red,* 278; "The Rosenberg Case," November 14, 1952, translated and attached to message from Paris to J. Edgar Hoover, November 20, 1952, Fast FBI file; Ronald Radosh and Joyce Milton, *The Rosenberg File,* 2nd ed. (New Haven, Conn.: Yale University Press, 1997), 349–350.

28. No civilian had ever been executed in the United States for either espionage or treason, no less for "conspiracy to commit espionage." Even the five Americans convicted for treason for broadcasting propaganda for the enemy during the Second World War, including Tokyo Rose and Axis Sally, got prison sentences only. And soldiers who had deserted and went on to fight for America's enemies received life sentences when they were captured, not death.

29. *Jewish Life,* November 1951, 23, 24; January 1952, 17; February 1952, 20. While *Jewish Life* and other papers such as the *DW* and the *Morgen Freiheit* were defending Stalinism, major purges against Jews in positions of power or prominence were being conducted, and a half-dozen or more Yiddish writers and poets languished in Lubyanka Prison in Moscow.

30. Lukes, "The Rudolf Slansky Affair"; Stephen Whitfield, *The Culture of the Cold War,* 2nd edition (Baltimore: Johns Hopkins University Press, 1999), 32.

31. Fast to M. A. deJong, February 6, 1958, "D file," FPP.

32. *Tony and the Wonderful Door* (New York: Blue Heron Press, 1952). Wells's story entails both the rewards and risks of nostalgia for a lost time where the world is brighter and more harmonious. Fast was clearly inspired by it.

33. The editor in chief of *The Pioneer,* a magazine for children 10–14 years old, wrote Fast to tell him that the journal had received many letters from children "impressed and awed by *Tony.*" N. Ilyina, letter to Fast, n.d., "I file," FPP; in response to an informal 2008 questionnaire about Fast's influence on readers, I received several responses like this one: "I have a well-worn autographed copy of . . . *Tony and the Wonderful Door,* that was published in 1952 when I was 6. I must have read it ten times as a kid. I was even then a voracious reader and this was one of my favorite books." Susan Avery, e-mail, December 8, 2008. On this also see Eve Tal, "Tony and the Wonderful Door: A Forgotten Classic of American Children's Fantasy," *Lion and the Unicorn* 27, no. 1 (January 2003): 131–143.

34. Rachel Fast, "Memoir," in *Red Diapers,* 131.

35. Rachel Fast Ben-Avi (RFB), e-mail, March 15, 16, 17, 2010; "Memoir," 130–131; Fast, "We Have Kept the Faith," *MM,* July 1950, 23–28.

36. June 27, 1952, "S file," FPP.

37. *NYT,* April 16, 1952, 10; *DW,* April 18, 1952, 6; Fast, "The Man and the Books," in *Publisher on Trial: A Symposium. The Case of Alexander Trachtenberg* (New York: Committee to Defend Alexander Trachtenberg, 1952); David A. Lincove, "Radical Publishing to 'Reach the Million Masses': Alexander L. Trachtenberg and

International Publishers,1906–1966," *Left History,* Fall-Winter 2004, 85–124. After Trachtenberg spent three months in prison following his conviction on February 2, 1953, the decision was reversed when a government witness recanted his testimony.

38. Despite disappointments, Fast continued to speak out and to put himself front and center at many pro-Communist events. See for example *DW,* April 18, 1952, 6; April 21, 1952, 3; May 9, 1952, 1; *NYT,* April 16, 1952, 10; May 9, 1952, 21; May 17, 1952, 13.

39. RFB, author interview, February 7, 2010; Fast, *Being Red,* 302–303.

40. Isacson, obituary in *NYT,* September 25, 1996, B10, 1.

41. Fast told the editor of the *Daily Compass,* for example, that since "there is a four-way race here, I have a very good chance of being elected." September 15, 1952, b2, f7, FC, UWM.

42. Fast to Einstein, August 29, 1952, b2, f7, FC, UWM.

43. Letters to Fast, September 3, 4, 13, 15, 17, 1952, b2, f7, FC, UWM. Nothing relating to the endangerment of national security was ever proven about Lieber, or about Carnovsky, Da Silva, Schlamme, Robeson, Du Bois, Kahn, or Einstein. All had files in the offices of FBI, Einstein's amounting to 1,800 pages.

44. Fast to Truman, September 8, 1952, b2, f7, FC, UWM.

45. *NYT,* September 9, 1952, 19.

46. Fast to Shipley; Shipley to Fast, "S file," FPP.

47. Fast, campaign materials, b2, f7, FC, UWM.

48. Radio transcripts, b7, f3, FC, UWM. WMCA pre-screened all scripts.

49. RFB, e-mail, March 18, 2010; Rachel Fast, "Memoir," 132.

50. Fast sent a telegram to Truman, Eisenhower, Adlai Stevenson, Churchill, and Stalin calling for a cease-fire. September 18, 1952, b2, f7, FC, UWM.

51. Ibid; *NYT,* September 9, 1952, 19. Fast, campaign literature, b3, f13, FC, UWM; Fast to Impelliteri, September 12, 1952, and draft of a note to *DW,* September 19, 1952, b2, f7, FC, UWM.

52. In October Fast addressed a tribute dinner for Dr. Joseph Burg, newly appointed minister of health for Israel. "We who are Jews will take special pride in the strides the State of Israel makes in conquering problems of sickness [and] poverty, and pride in the leadership that Israel can and must give to the whole world on these questions." Text of speech, October 7, 1952, b2, f7, FC, UWM.

53. *NYT,* February 18, 2000, C2, 1.

54. Fast to Siminov, n.d., 1952, "S file," FPP.

55. Polner, e-mail, September 10, 2008; Polner, "Stalin's Secret Pogrom," at http://hnn.us/roundup/entries/17030.html.

56. On Stalin's paranoia see Simon Sebag Montefiore, *Stalin: The Court of the Red Tsar* (New York: Vintage, 2005), and *Young Stalin* (New York: Vintage, 2008). His murderousness is made abundantly clear in *Stalin's Secret Pogrom: The Postwar Inquisition of The Jewish Anti-Fascist Committee,* ed. and with introductions by Joshua Rubenstein and Vladimir P. Naumov, trans. Laura Esther Wolfson (New Haven, Conn.: Yale University Press, 2001).

57. "Vicious Spies and Killers under the Mask of Academic Physicians," *Pravda,* January 13, 1953, 1. An English translation of the article can be found at http://www .cyberUSSR.com/rus/vrach-ubijca-e.html.

58. Even Leonid Eitingon, the Jewish mastermind behind the assassination of Trotsky, about whom Stalin had said, "As long as I live, not a hair of his head shall be touched," was arrested. Mary-Kay Wilmers, *The Eitingons: A Twentieth Century Story* (New York: Verso, 2010).

59. Joshua Trachtenberg and Marc Saperstein, *The Devil and the Jews: The Medieval Conception of the Jew and Its Relation to Modern Antisemitism* 2nd international ed. (Philadelphia: Jewish Publications Society, 2007).

60. Quoted in Helen Rappaport, *Joseph Stalin: A Biographical Companion* (Westport, Conn.: ABC-CLIO, 1999), 297.

61. I use the word "apparently" because despite the impressionistic evidence, the memoirs, and the authoritative scholarly voices behind the claim, researchers since the opening of the Soviet archives in 1991 have found no trace of the paper trail that an operation of such dimension would have left behind.

62. Jonathan Brent and Vladimir Naumov, *Stalin's Last Crime: The Plot against Jewish Doctors* (New York: HarperCollins, 2003); Yakov Rapoport, *The Doctors' Plot of 1953: A Survivor's Memoir* (Cambridge, Mass.: Harvard University Press, 1991); Anastas I. Mikoyan, *Memoirs of Anastas Mikoyan: The Path of Struggle,* vol. 1, trans. Katherine T. O'Connor and Diana L. Burgin (Madison, Conn.: Sphinx Press, 1988). Mikoyan, a politically influential and loyal Stalinist, strongly suggests that the Jews were "at risk" of deportation.

63. Irving Adler to Fast, February 6, 1953, "N file," FPP.

64. Fast to NCASP, February 7, 1953, "N file," FPP.

65. Ibid.

66. Frankel to Fast, February 9, 1953, "F file," FPP. I. F. Stone, although missing the diversionary aspects of Communist behavior, said, in line with Frankel, "that the Rosenbergs were treated a good deal more fairly here, than Slansky and other Jewish victims of Stalin Justice," and that those who overlooked the Slansky case and the Doctors' Plot while at the same time carrying on for the Rosenbergs were a case for political psychiatry. See D. D. Guttenplan, *American Radical: The Life and Times of I. F. Stone* (New York: Farrar, Straus, and Giroux, 2009), 297.

67. NYT, February 19, 1953, 11. VOA and later the United States Information Agency were known as United States Information Service abroad.

68. Tydings in Richard M. Fried, *Nightmare in Red: The McCarthy Era in Perspective* (New York: Oxford University Press 1990), 124–125. See also 134–137.

69. See Chapter 2 for more on Fast's experience at the OWI.

70. NYT, February 14, 1953, 1; February 22, 1953, E1–E2.

71. Roy Cohn with Sidney Zion, *The Autobiography of Roy Cohn,* 3rd ed. (Secaucus, N.J.: Lyle Stuart, 1988), 57, 76–79. There are still great doubts about what Ethel did or did not do, likely almost nothing. But the evidence of Julius's guilt is incontrovertible; even his sons, who have long crusaded to reopen the case, had finally by

454 NOTES TO PAGES 266-271

2008 been convinced. *New York Times,* September 17, 2008, B1. Also see articles at http://cityroom.blogs.nytimes.com/2011/04/06/rosenberg-son-says-father-was-guilty-of-spy-charge/; http://www.weeklystandard.com/articles/sobell-confession_554817.html; http://www.tabletmag.com/news-and-politics/62998/cold-case/.

72. Testimony in the following paragraphs can be found in *Hearings before the Permanent Sub-Committee on Investigations of the Committee on Government Operations, United States Senate, Eighty Third Congress, First Session,* Pursuant to S Res 40 Part I and Part II (Washington, D.C.: United Sates Govt. Printing Office, 1953).

73. *NYT,* February 19, 1953, 1, 9.

74. Fast, "Why the Fifth Amendment?" *MM,* February 1954, 44–50; Rachel Fast "Memoir," 131. A snatch of the McCarthy-Fast confrontation can be seen on the DVD documentary *Seeing Red,* dir. Jim Klein and Julia Reichert (1983).

75. "Asked If He's a Commie, Fast Won't Tell Probers," *New York Daily News,* February 19, 1953, 2.

76. See, for example, "Dr. Compton Quits As Head of 'Voice': At Senate Inquiry into Agency, Howard Fast, Writer, Refuses to Say Whether He Is Red," *NYT,* February 19, 1953, 1, and "Voice Must Drop Works of Leftists: Agency Reveals Dulles Order and Declares Its Libraries Will Ban Books by Fast," *NYT,* February 20, 1953, 9.

10. MCCARTHYISM, STALINISM, AND THE WORLD ACCORDING TO FAST

1. The State Department memos were dated March 7, 1952, and February 3, 1953.

2. *NYT,* February 19, 1953, 11; February 22, 1953, E1.

3. *NYT,* February 22, 1953, E1; Campenni, "Citizen Howard Fast," 406.

4. Dulles had much earlier issued his own memo directing that books not be selected for overseas libraries by authors "whose ideology or views are questionable and controversial." Ellen Schrecker, *Many Are the Crimes: McCarthyism in America* (Boston: Little, Brown, 1998), 256–257; *NYT,* February 20, 1953, 9.

5. Ibid., 256–257. Ultimately, President Eisenhower was obliged to recognize the hullabaloo. During an address to the graduating class at Dartmouth College in June 1953, the president cautioned citizens against joining the "book burners." *NYT,* June 15, 1953.

6. Milton Bracker, "Books of 40 Authors Banned by U.S. in Overseas Libraries," *NYT,* June 22, 1953, 1. See also the *NYT,* June 4, 19; June 11, 1; June 19, 6; and June 22, 8; and Louise S. Robbins, *Censorship and the American Library Association's Responses to Threats to Intellectual Freedom, 1939–1969* (Westport, Conn.: Greenwood Press, 1996).

7. Fast, Campenni interview, December 1, 1967; Fast in Judy Waters Pasqualge, *International McCarthyism: The Case of Rhoda Miller De Silva* (Colombo, Sri Lanka: Social Scientists Association, 2008), 120.

8. Harry Schwartz, "Block to 'Cold War' Propaganda Seen in Directive Curbing Voice," *NYT,* February 26, 1953, 13.

9. Matthew T. Bolen, "The American Library Association, United States Government, and the Fight for Intellectual Freedom, 1939–1953," Master's degree paper, April 2006, at http://reference.kfupm.edu.sa/content/a/m/american_library

_association_history; David Oshinsky, *A Conspiracy So Immense: The World of Joe McCarthy* (New York: Free Press, 1985), 27–78; Richard Rovere, *Senator Joe McCarthy* (New York: Harper's, 1959), 199–205. What Schine and Cohn could not do was force European booksellers to remove Fast's works which were prominently displayed on the tables and in the windows of numerous bookshops in London, Paris, and Prague. *DW,* March 2, 1953.

10. David Oshinsky, "In the Heart of the Heart of Conspiracy," *NYTBR,* January 27, 2008, last page; Richard M. Fried, *Nightmare in Red: The McCarthy Era in Perspective* (New York: Oxford University Press, 1990).

11. Peter Filene, "Cold War Culture Doesn't Say it All," in *Rethinking Cold War Culture,* ed. Peter Juznick and James Burkhart Gilbert (Washington, D.C.: Smithsonian Institution Press, 2001), 157–174; Alan Brinkley, "The Illusion of Unity in Cold War Culture," in *Rethinking Cold War Culture,* 61–73.

12. Schrecker, *Many Are the Crimes;* Athan Theoharis, "The Rhetoric of Politics: Foreign Policy, Internal Security, and Domestic Politics in the Truman Era, 1945–1950," and "The Escalation of the Loyalty Program," in *Politics and Policies of the Truman Administration,* ed. Barton Bernstein (Chicago: Quadrangle, 1970), 196–242 and 242–268. For a sympathetic view that has Truman gamely handling unprecedented problems, see Robert Ferrell, *Harry S. Truman and the Cold War Revisionists* (Columbia: University of Missouri Press, 2006).

13. Norman Podhoretz, *Making It* (New York: Random House), 290–291. Many who considered themselves "liberals"—Sidney Hook, for a prime example—defended Communist conspiracy trials, rationalized intimidation of university administrations and faculties, and praised exposure of leftists by legislative committees. See Hook's article "Heresy, Yes—Conspiracy No," *New York Times Magazine,* July 9, 1950, 12, 38–39, which was distributed as a booklet by the American Committee for Cultural Freedom. For more on this see Ellen Schrecker, *No Ivory Tower: McCarthyism and the Universities* (New York: Oxford University Press, 1986).

14. Isserman, *Which Side Were You On?;* Irving Howe, *America and Socialism* (New York: Harcourt Brace Jovanovich, 1985).

15. By April 1954 Edward R. Murrow had shamed McCarthy on television; Smith Act trials had exposed no criminal acts or proof of conspiracy to commit violent acts against the United States in the future. More groups, including the Quakers and the Women's International League for Peace and Freedom, were taking public stands against McCarthyism.

16. A. H. Raskin, "7th Avenue's Little Kremlin: Behind the Anonymous Portal's of America's Communist Party," *New York Times Sunday Magazine,* August 23, 1953, 49.

17. Fast, Campenni interview, n.d., 1977, b9, f2, FC, UWM.

18. Montefiore, *Stalin: The Court of the Red Tsar;* Rubenstein, *Stalin's Secret Pogrom;* Rapoport, *Stalin's War against The Jews;* Snyder, *Bloodlands.*

19. Fast to Students for Democratic Action, March 18, 1953, b3, f11, FC, UWM.

20. Tibor Machan, *The Intellectual Portrait Series: A Conversation with Ernest van den Haag* (Indianapolis: Liberty Fund, 2000).

21. *DW,* April 17, 1953, 3.

22. *NYT,* March 22, 1953, 27. Fast also spoke at the important annual New England All-College Conference on "Censorship and the Arts." Fast to Jane Frizzell, April 17, 1953, b3, f11, FC, UWM.

23. Fast to Kirchwey, June 6, 1953; Carey McWilliams, managing editor of the *Nation,* to Fast, June 21, 1953, "N file," FPP.

24. Fast, "A Man and A Woman in Sing Sing Death House," in *DW,* June 14, 1953, 7; Radosh and Milton, *The Rosenberg File,* ix.

25. Fast to de Jouvenal, June 22, 1953, "J file," FPP. It is possible that the lives of the couple could have been saved had they talked, and perhaps Ethel would have gone free after a time to be a mother to her young children. To the Communists the Rosenbergs, guilty or innocent, were martyred heroes. To many others they were monsters who abandoned their children for a cause. And there is an extraordinary range of opinion in between these two extremes in the scholarship, journalism, and literature that has been generated about the case. Only Julius, about whose guilt there is no doubt, and Ethel, who was at worst a witness to Julius's espionage, knew why they refused to talk.

26. Sartre, translated and quoted in Pierre Rigoulot, "American Justice as a Pretext for Anti-Americanism," *Human Rights Review* 4, no. 3 (April-June 2003): 55-62. As to "killing innocents," Sartre, to what should have been his eternal shame, defended the PLO in 1972 when its assassins murdered Israeli athletes at the Munich Olympics. He argued, among other things, that the athletes were actually "soldiers" whose killings were therefore fully "justified." Susie Linfield, "Phantasms of Revolution," *Dissent,* Spring 2011, 87-91.

27. The ordeal of Sacco and Vanzetti from the very beginning generated and continues to produce a heated debate and an enormous literature about the case and trial. The titles of many of the books about the case give some idea of the spectrum of opinion; and it is on these that I have drawn for the discussion that follows: Herbert H. Ehrmann, *The Case That Will Not Die* (Boston: Little, Brown, 1969); Richard Newby, *Kill Now, Talk Forever: Debating Sacco and Vanzetti,* 8th ed. (Bloomington, Ind.: AuthorHouse, 2008); Francis Russell, *Sacco and Vanzetti: The Case Resolved* (New York: Harper and Row, 1986). But even the most thorough investigation of the case, Bruce Watson, *Sacco and Vanzetti: The Men, the Murders, and the Judgment of Mankind* (New York: Viking Adult, 2007), which devotes great attention to the haunting question of guilt or innocence, brings us no closer to a resolution than we were in the 1920s.

28. Fast to Kirchwey, June 6, 1953, "K file," FPP.

29. Fast to Jouvenal, February 4, 1954, "J file," FPP.

30. Watson, *Sacco and Vanzetti;* Robert K. Murray, *Red Scare: A Study in National Hysteria, 1919-1920* (Minneapolis: University of Minnesota Press, 1955).

31. Fast, Campenni interview, December 1, 1967. The careful reader will find similarities between the two works throughout. See especially pages 2-5 of Frankfurter's book and from page 51 on sporadic paragraphs of Fast's *Passion.* A great irony abounds here: Frankfurter himself cited and "quoted" scholarly sources in his book,

the texts of which he frequently changed. See Campenni, "Citizen Howard Fast," who has studied this knotty problem closely, 412–413, 451.

32. Fast to Jouvenal, February 4, 1954, "J file," FPP.

33. Ben Shahn, working between 1931 and 1932, had used the title *The Passion of Sacco and Vanzetti* for his painting of the two men in their coffins.

34. *The Passion of Sacco and Vanzetti: A New England Legend,* 2nd reprint (Westport, Conn.: Greenwood, 1972), 209.

35. *The Passion,* 103–104, 198, 230, 240, and passim. The trial transcript shows that Vanzetti himself was not above making this comparison. He expressed anger with one of his lawyers who, Vanzetti claimed, "sold me for a thirty golden money [*sic*] like Judas sold Jesus Christ." *Commonwealth v. Nicola Sacco and Bartolomeo Vanzetti* (1927), 4904–4905, at http://law2.umkc.edu/faculty/projects/ftrials/Sacco V/sacco255.html.

36. *The Passion,* 29.

37. Ibid., 15, 83, 222.

38. Ibid., 227.

39. Andrew Macdonald, *Howard Fast: A Critical Companion* (Westport, Conn.: Greenwood Press, 1996), 188; at http://www.bookrags.com/Howard_Fast.

40. Fast, Campenni interview, December 1, 1967.

41. *DW,* December 1, 1953, 7; Fast, letter to Izakov, March 9, 1955, b1, f23, FC, UWM.

42. Fast, clippings of "American Diary," from *Austrian People's Voice,* July 2, July 4, 1953, and photocopies of articles in the Harvard Crimson, April 8, 14, 15, 1953, Fast FBI file.

43. Fast, clippings of "American Diary," from *Austrian People's Voice,* July 4, 9, 1953, Fast FBI file.

44. Ibid., July 21, 1953. Emphasis mine.

45. RFB, e-mail, November 12, 2006.

46. Barry Fast, author interview, October 27, 2007; Judith (Fast) Zander, author interview, April 11, 2008; RFB and Jonathan Fast, author interviews, February 8, 2010, and October 3, 2006.

47. Kay Redfield Jamison, *Touched with Fire: Manic Depressive Illness and the Artistic Temperament* (New York: Free Press, 1996), 11–48, 109–116, 152–153, 261–270; John Gartner, *The Hypomanic Edge: The Link between (a Little) Craziness and (a Lot of) Success in America* (New York: Simon and Schuster, 2005), 4–6; Theodore Millon, *Disorders of Personality: DSM-IV and Beyond,* 2nd ed. (New York: Wiley, 1995), 393–429; Dr. Peter Kaplan, clinical psychologist, conversation with author, November 18, 2010; Jacqueline Brownstein, director, Mental Health America, Dutchess County, N.Y., conversation with author, November 20, 2010.

48. Erica Jong, e-mail, October 21, 2006; Molly Jong-Fast, author interview, September 26, 2006.

49. Barry Fast, author interview, October 27, 2007; Judith Zander, author interview, April 11, 2008; RFB and Jonathan Fast, author interviews, February 8, 2010, and October 3, 2006.

50. Rachel Fast, "Memoir," 125; Barry Fast, author interview, October 23, 27, 2007; Judith Zander, author interview, April 11, 2008; RFB and Jonathan Fast, author interviews, February 8, 2010, and October 3, 2006.

51. These stories would be published in *The Last Supper and Other Stories* in 1955.

52. Fast, "The Protest," *MM*, July 1954, 12-23.

53. "Report," April 26, 1956, Fast FBI file; *DW*, September 13, 1953; Fast, note, November 7, 1953, box 3, folder 9, FC, UWM; *DW*, December 11, 1953, 8; "Informant memo," December 5, 1953, Fast FBI file; Fast, clipping of "American Diary," from *Austrian People's Voice*, July 9, 1953, in FBI file NY.

54. *NYT*, September 24, 1953, 38; Fast, "On Receiving the Stalin Peace Award," *MM*, May 1954, 35-37.

55. "World Peace Award to American Novelist," *DW*, April 9, 1954, 9; *NYT*, December 21, 1953, 15; "On Receiving the Stalin Peace Award," *MM*, May 1954, 35-37.

56. *NYT*, December 29, 1953, 17; "Asked If He's a Commie, Fast Won't Tell Probers," *New York Daily News*, February 19, 1953, 2.

11. CULTURE AND THE COLD WAR

1. Robins, *Alien Ink,* 399.

2. Transcript of *See It Now,* March 9, 1954, at http://www.lib.berkeley.edu/MRC/murrowmccarthy.html. U.S. Congress, Senate, *Executive Sessions of the Senate Permanent Subcommittee on Investigations of the Committee on Government Operations* (McCarthy Hearings 1953-54), ed. Donald A. Ritchie and Elizabeth Bolling (Washington, D.C.: Government Printing Ooffice, 2003). S. Prt. 107-84; David M. Oshinsky, *A Conspiracy So Immense: The World of Joseph McCarthy* (New York: Macmillan, 1983).

3. Filene, "Cold War Culture Doesn't Say it All," 157-174; Brinkley, "The Illusion of Unity in Cold War Culture," 61-73.

4. Kazin and Charles Shapiro, "Introduction," in *The Stature of Theodore Dreiser* (Bloomington: Indiana University Press, 1965), 10, 12. That the concepts of alienation and uninvolvement can be reductionist is well illustrated in Rothko's case. In the 1930s, he was embedded in a community of Jewish expressionist artists ("The Ten") who protested the Whitney Museum's fierce emphasis on "literal painting." His statement that it does not matter what one paints as long as it is well executed earned him a label as an aesthetician, and he did try to keep his community of artists free of political "contamination" by disassociating it from leftist activity; but he also said that there is no such thing as good painting about nothing—and that the *only* subject matter with validity is tragic and timeless. "The picture must be . . . a revelation, an unexpected and unprecedented resolution of an eternally familiar need." See Anne Chave, *Mark Rothko, 1903-1970: A Retrospective* (New Haven, Conn.: Yale University Press, 1989); Mark Rothko, "The Individual and the Social," in *Art in Theory 1900-1990: An Anthology of Changing Ideas,* ed. Charles Harrison and Paul Wood (Malden, Mass.: Blackwell, 1993), 563-565.

5. Trilling, *The Liberal Imagination: Essays on Literature and Society* (1950) (reprint, New York: Harcourt, 1979); Howe, "This Age of Conformity," *Partisan Review* 21 (January–February 1954): 1–33.

6. Fast, Frank Campenni interview, April 16, 1968, box 8, folder 12, Fast Collection (FC), University of Wisconsin-Madison (UWM); Fast to A. Chakovsky, May 19, 1955, in Phillips, "Howard Fast and the Refashioning of Postwar Protest," 491. Emphasis mine.

7. Fast, in Robins, *Alien Ink,* 399.

8. Robins, *Alien Ink,* 399; Fast, Campenni interview, December 1, 1967, b8, f11, FC, UWM; *Being Red,* 243.

9. For "another kind of Modernism," see Barbara Foley, "Renarrating the Thirties in the Forties and Fifties," *Prospects* 20 (1995): 455–466.

10. Stephen Whitfield, *Cold War Culture* (Baltimore: Johns Hopkins University Press, 1996), 14; Thomas Sugrue, "Reassessing the History of Post-War America," *Prospects* 20 (1995): 493–509.

11. Ginsberg, "Howl," in *Howl,* at http://www.poetryfoundation.org/archive/poem.html?id=179381; Ferlinghetti, "Populist Manifesto No. 1," at http://www.poemhunter.com/poem/populistmanifesto-no-1.

12. Brinkley, "The Illusion of Unity in Cold War Culture," 61–73; Erik Barnouw, *Tube of Plenty: The Evolution of American Television,* 2nd ed. (1990); Mary A. Watson, *Defining Visions: Television and the American Experience since 1945* (Fort Worth, Tex.: Harcourt Brace, 1997).

13. Rachel Fast Ben-Avi (RFB), e-mail, October 10, 2009; Jonathan Fast, e-mail, October 11, 2009, June 13, 2010.

14. RFB, e-mail, October 10, 2009; Watson, *Defining Visions.*

15. Jeff Sharlet, *The Family: The Secret Fundamentalism at the Heart of American Power* (New York: Harper, 2008), 181; Mirisch, *I Thought We Were Making Movies, Not History* (Madison: University of Wisconsin Press, 2008), 39–40. For another take on some of this see: Nora Sayre, *Running Time: Films of the Cold War* (New York: Doubleday, 1982). Fast hated all the films mentioned above, but he liked *The Incredible Shrinking Man* (1957), perhaps because it indirectly deals with the effect of radiation poisoning and could be seen as an antiwar or antinuclear movie. Jonathan Fast, e-mail, October 11, 2009.

16. The established cultural, governmental, and economic institutions, however, with complex motives of their own, liked and encouraged, even subsidized, what they saw in the arts—the abstraction, the surreal, the dark, and the difficult. See Foley, "Renarrating the Thirties in the Forties and Fifties," 455–466.

17. *Lola Gregg* is loosely based on the actual experience of Communist Party leader Robert Thompson.

18. Fast to Boris Izakov, May 31, 1956, b1, f23, FC, UWM; Polevoy to Fast, March 1957, "Polevoy File," FPP; Alexander Shubin to Fast, Dec 8, 1956, "S file," FPP; A. Chakovsky to Fast, n.d., 1955, "C file," FPP.

19. Maltz to Fast, July 30, 1956, "Maltz file," FPP.

20. Brown, *Soviet Attitudes,* 289; Fast, *The Naked God,* 155–157.

21. Fast, Campenni interview, 1977, b9, f2, FC, UWM.

22. *NYT,* January 1, 1954, 22–23.

23. Fadeyev to Fast, January 7, 1954, "F file," FPP.

24. Fast to Maltz, February 26, 1954, b16, f5, Maltz Collection (MP), Wisconsin State Historical Society (WSHS); Maltz to Fast, April 13, 1954, January 14, 1955, b16, f5, MP, WSHS; Fast, "The Singularity of Being Jewish," unpublished ms., 133, FPP; RFB, e-mail, August 27, 2008.

25. *Daily Worker* (DW), May 9, 1954, 9; Fast, "On Receiving the Stalin Peace Award," April 22, 1953, at http://www.trussel.com/hf/plots/t90.htm. Stefan Heym wrote to Fast expressing his happiness about "the great reception you had. . . . You might not know the . . . prizes are paid out of Stalin's own [money]." And with no hint of facetiousness, Heym added, "Quite a man Stalin was." Heym to Fast, May 8, 1954, "Heym file," FPP.

26. "Singularity," 133.

27. RFB, e-mail, August 27, 2008; author interview, April 28, 2011; decoded cablegrams, Mexico City to State Department, June 9, 1954; Legation, Mexico to Director, FBI, July 21, 1954, Fast FBI file; "Singularity," 134.

28. RFB, e-mail, November 12, 2006; April 15, 2010.

29. Ibid.

30. Ibid.

31. Paul R. Haerle, "Constitutional Law, Federal Anti-Subversive Legislation, and the Communist Control Act of 1954," *Michigan Law Review* 53, no. 8 (1955): 1153–1165; Mary S. McAuliffe, "Liberals and the Communist Control Act of 1954," *Journal of American History* 63, no. 2 (1976): 351–367.

32. Rachel Fast, "Memoir," 132.

33. Ibid.; RFB, e-mail, September 19, October 5, 2006.

34. Fast to *Observer,* September 23, 1954, b1, f11, FC, UWM; *NYT,* October 11, 1954, 29.

35. RFB, e-mail, May 21, 2010.

36. See http://www.trussel.com/hf/blueheron.htm.

37. *NYTBR,* July 26, 1983, 20; Fast to "Dick," September 1956, b64, FC, University of Pennsylvania (UP).

38. Bette to Rachel, July 16, 1956. All letters between Rachel and her parents referred to here and throughout are in the possession of Rachel Fast Ben-Avi (RFB).

39. "Transcript," interview by Martin Agronsky, October 13, 1957, NBC television network, FPP, published in *Progressive* 22 (March 1958): 35–38.

40. *NYTBR,* July 26, 1983, 20; Fast, interviewed by Martin Agronsky. For other sources attesting to Fast's substantial royalties see L. Kislova to P. A. Churikov, January 6, 1952, in Phillips, "Howard Fast and the Refashioning of Postwar Protest," 505; Traister, "Noticing Howard Fast," 525–541; Fast to Nikolai A. Michailov, Minister of Culture, Moscow, 1953, "M file," FPP; Fast to Izakov, April 10, 1956, October 28, 1956, b1, f23, FC, UWM; Fast to Polevoy, May 28, 1956, b1, f25, FC, UWM.

41. Fast to Maltz, January 14, 1955, b16, f5 MP, WSHS.

42. Fast to A. Chakovsky, editor, *Inostrannaja Literatura,* August 15, 1955, "C file," FPP.

43. Fast to Izakov, February 6, 1956, "Izakov file," FPP.

44. Heym to Fast, December 12, 1955, "Heym file," FPP.

45. Rockwell Kent admired the stories enough to write Fast about them, August 29, 1955, b40, FC, UP. W. E. B. Du Bois also thought the stories "excellent." Letter to Fast, September 1, 1955, b40, FC, UP.

46. Fast to Polevoy, March 28, 1955, b1, f24, FC, UWM.

47. Ibid., April 29, 1955, in Phillips, "Howard Fast and the Refashioning of Postwar Protest," 503–504; Fast, to Boris Izakov, May 31, 1956, b1, f23, FC, UWM.

48. Fast to Lakovsky, May 9, 1955, "L file," FPP.

49. *Naked God,* 132–133; RFB, e-mail, May 22, 2010.

50. Fast to Polevoy, October 5, 1955, and December 20, 1955, b1, f25, FC, UWM.

51. Fast to Polevoy, December 20, 1955, b1, f25, FC, UWM.

52. RFB, author interview, February 8, 2010.

53. Fast to Polevoy, n.d., b1, f24, FC, UWM.

54. Fast to Maltz, February 7, 1956, "Maltz file," FPP; Fast, letter to Polevoy, January 5, 1956, "Polevoy file," FPP; Fast to Heym, January 10, 1956, "Heym file," FPP; Fast to Izakov, March 21, 1956, b1, f23, FC, UWM.

55. In the summer of 1955, HUAC returned to Foley Square in New York City to investigate Communist infiltration of Broadway theater. After four farcical days of hearings the committee was essentially laughed out of town. J. Hoberman, *An Army of Phantoms: American Movies and the Making of the Cold War* (New York: New Press, 2011), 9.

56. Fast, letter to Alfred Knopf, February 23, 1956, b1, folder 5, FC, UWM.

57. Full text of the speech at http://www.archive.org/details/ thecrimesoftheStalineraSpecialReporttothe20thCongress.

58. Peggy Dennis, *The Autobiography of an American Communist: A Personal View of a Political Life, 1925–1975* (Westport, Conn.: Lawrence Hill, 1977), 225.

59. Fast to Prudkov. March 5, 1956, "P file," FPP.

60. *NYT,* March 28, 1956, 1, 20; Fast, "Winds of Fear," *DW,* April 19, 1956, at http:// www.trussel.com/hf/articles.htm#T579.

61. Fast to Heym, April 11, 1956, "Heym File," FPP.

62. Howe, "Notes on the Russian Turn," *Dissent,* Summer 1956, 311; Rubenstein and Naumov, *Stalin's Secret Pogrom.*

63. Gates, *The Story of an American Communist,* 163.

64. Fast, "Justice and Death," *DW,* April 16, 1956, at http://www.trussel.com/hf /justice.htm.

65. See especially, "Capital Punishment," April 5; "Justice and Death," April 16; "Winds of Fear," April 19; "Cosmopolitanism," April 26; "What I Believe," May 7; "The Current Scene," May 9; "On Comparisons," May 10; "Freud and Science," May 14; "The Soviet Union," May 17; "The Tides of Tomorrow," May 24; "The Need to Believe," June 4; "Man's Hope," June 12. All at http://www.trussel.com/hf/articles.htm.

66. "The Soviet Union," *DW*, May 17, 1956.

67. "What I Believe," *DW*, May 7, 1956. Emphasis mine.

12. THINGS FALL APART; THE LEFT CANNOT HOLD

1. "Man's Hope," *Daily Worker* (*DW*), June 12, 1956, at http://www.trussel.com/hf/manshope.htm.

2. "Capital Punishment," *DW*, April 5, 1956, at http://www.trussel.com/hf/plots/t603.htm.

3. In a letter to Steve Nelson, May 26, 1955, Fast wrote that his "health is so bad that I don't dare [travel] even for a weekend." Nelson Papers, ALBA 8, b1, f48, Tamiment Library; letters to Polevoy, June 5, June 19, 1956, b1, f25, Fast Collection (*FC*), University of Wisconsin-Milwaukee (*UWM*).

4. Fast, "Man's Hope"; Lyons, "Open Letter to Howard Fast," *New Leader,* July 9, 1956, 6–8.

5. Lyons, "Open Letter to Howard Fast."

6. Fast, "Reply to Eugene Lyons," *DW*, July 27, 1956 and *Masses and Mainstream* (*MM*), August 1956, 54–59. Also available at http://www.trussel.com/hf/replyons.htm.

7. Ibid. Emphasis mine.

8. Ibid.

9. *New Leader,* July 30, 1956, 18–20.

10. Rachel Fast to parents, July 11, 1956; Fast to Rachel, July and August 1956. All correspondence between Rachel and her parents is in possession of Rachel Fast Ben-Avi (RFB). RFB, e-mail, June 1, 2010.

11. After Isabel was divorced from Hollywood screenwriter Lester Cole in 1956, she planned to return to New York. Fast wrote her saying, that he had "found a good relationship with my wife" and that it would be "unwise and hurtful to return to the past." But he also said, "We are each of us too precious . . . to the other to allow anything to interfere with our friendship." And "there is so much more that I would say that I cannot very well put in a letter. . . . When you come home, let's have a warm, good evening—and talk to each other." The "details will have to wait until I can buy you one of those oversized martinis at the St. Regis—you do remember. And I hope that won't be too long." He also informed her that he had taken a "little office in town" [47 West 63rd Street]. Letters to "Izzy," October 29, 1956; November 21, 1956, b1, f1, Isabel Hiss Papers, Schlesinger Library, Harvard University.

12. Fast to Rachel, July 6, 1956, July 16, 1956.

13. RFB, e-mail, June 1, 2010, October 5, 2006; author interview, February 7, 2010.

14. Ibid.; Fast, to Rachel, July 1953 to October 1978; RFB, e-mail, July 5, 2010.

15. RFB, e-mail, October 5, 2006, July 5, 2010.

16. Ibid., February 21, 2011.

17. Barrett, *William Z. Foster and the Tragedy of American Radicalism,* 251–277; David A. Shannon, *The Decline of American Communism; A History of the Communist Party of the U. S. since 1945* (New York: Harcourt Brace, 1959), 275–285, 309–310; Fast, *Being Red,* 343–353.

18. Leontyev to Fast, August 10, 1956, Fast Personal Papers (FPP).

19. Gates, *The Story of an American Communist,* 169.

20. Barrett, *William Z. Foster and the Tragedy of American Radicalism,* 251–277; Shannon, *The Decline of American Communism,* 275–285, 309–310; *Being Red,* 343–353; Peggy Dennis, *The Autobiography of An American Communist,* 225–227; Gates, *The Story of an American Communist,* 163–170; Klehr, Haynes, and Anderson, *The Soviet World of American Communism,* 351.

21. Heym to Fast, July 29, 1956, "Heym file," FPP.

22. Fast to Heym, August 20, 1956, "Heym file," FPP.

23. Heym to Fast, October 8, 1956, "Heym file," FPP; Fast to Heym, October 24, 1956, "Heym file," FPP.

24. Fast to Heym, October 24, 1956, "Heym file," FPP.

25. Charles Gati, *Failed Illusions: Moscow, Washington, Budapest, and the 1956 Hungarian Revolt* (Palo Alto, Calif.: Stanford University Press, 2006).

26. Shannon, *The Decline of American Communism,* 360.

27. Heym to Fast, November 9, 24, 1956; Fast to Heym, November 20, 1956; April 13, 1960. "Heym file," FPP.

28. Larner, author interview, June 19, 1997; Fast, "On the Role of the Critic," *Foreign Literature* 4 (1956): 2; Fast, "The Intellectual," *DW,* April 23, 1956,

29. Larner, author interview, June 19, 1997; Larner, "Remembering Irving Howe," *Dissent* 40 (Fall 1993): 539–41; Howe, *A Margin of Hope: An Intellectual Autobiography* (New York: Harcourt Brace, 1982), 189.

30. Daniel Seligman, "Dilemma in New York," *Fortune,* February 1957, 238.

31. *NYT,* February 1, 1957, 1, 4. For what Fast knew about antisemitism in the Soviet Union see chapters 6 and 9. Novick to Fast, August 30, 1957; Fast to Novick, September 5, 1957, Novick Papers, YIVO; Schappes, "Fast, Isserman, Fadeyev, Novick," *Jewish Currents,* April 1991, 19.

32. Ibid.; "Notes of Interview," February 5, 1957, unpublished typescript, "Miscellaneous file," FPP.

33. A. McGuire Gordon to Fast, February 1, 1957, b1, f9, FC, UWM; Edith Marzani to Fast, February 3, 1957, "M file," FPP. Fast even got a letter from James Farrell, whom Howard had defamed as a "Trotskyist" many times, and with whom he continued to be angry over the substitution of Farrell's introduction for Fast's in the 1956 reprint of a 1947 collection, *The Best Stories of Theodore Dreiser.* Farrell commended Fast for having condemned Stalin's crimes and publicly extended "congratulations and the hand of friendship." Upton Sinclair wrote to tell Fast "how happy I am over your recent statements about the Soviet horror. Now I can love you!" Fast, Campenni interview, December 1, 1967, b8, f11, FC, UWM; Joseph Griffin, "Howard Fast, James T. Farrell, and the Best Short Stories of Theodore Dreiser," *International Fiction Review* 14 (1987): 79–83; Sinclair to Fast, September 22, 1957, box 40, FC, University of Pennsylvania.

34. Fast, "My Decision," *MM,* March 1957, 29–38.

35. Ibid.

36. Ibid.

37. "Comment by the Editors," *MM*, March 1957, 39–42.

38. Harap, "More Comments on Howard Fast," *MM*, April 1957, 55–56; Aptheker, "More Comments," *MM*, April 1957, 42–47. Also see comments by Philip Bonovsky and Burt Cochran, *MM*, April 1957, 47–51, 54–55.

39. Starobin, "More Comments on Howard Fast," *MM*, April 1957, 51–54; Rossen Djagalov, "'I Don't Boast about It, but I'm the Most Widely Read Author of This Century,'" *Anthropology of East Europe Review* 27 (Fall 2009): 40–55.

40. Starobin, "More Comments on Howard Fast," 51–54.

41. Izakov to Fast, March 20, 1957, b1, f23, FC, UWM.

42. Polevoy to Fast, March 18, 1957, "Boris Polevoy file," FPP.

43. Fast to Polevoy, March 25, 1957, "Boris Polevoy file," FPP.

44. Polevoy to Fast, June 6, 1957; Harrison Salisbury, "Writers in the Shadow of Communism," *New York Times Magazine,* June 1957, 10.

45. Fast to Jouvenal, June 19, 1956, FPP.

46. Jouvenal to Fast, June 27, 1956, FPP. And this in a letter from Minna Edith Lieber to Bette Fast, from Warsaw, April 4, 1957: "The American Communists got the rudest shock of all, I guess, because they had the least idea of the facts of life—due to distance, due to the predominantly middle class composition of a large segment of the Party, and to what I can only call a typically American naïveté politically." "J file," FPP.

47. Jouvenal to Fast, June 27, 1956, FPP.

48. M. A. deJong to Fast, January 14, 1958; February 6, 1958, "D file," FPP.

49. Maltz to Fast, April 13, 1957, b1, f22, FC, UWM.

50. Fast to Heym, October 24, 1956, "Stefan Heym file," FPP.

51. Scott and Helen Nearing, to Fast, August 8, 1957, "N file," FPP.

52. *NYT*, August 25, 1957, 36; August 26, 1957, 8; Quotes from Brown, *Soviet Attitudes Toward American Writing,* 292.

53. "Transcript," *Today Show,* August 29, 1957, "G file," FPP.

54. Rachel Fast, "Memoir," 133; Fast to "Dearest collective sweethearts," May 5, 1961, RFB.

55. Robins, *Alien Ink,,* 239; Reports, August 30, September 4, and September 16, 1957, Fast FBI file.

56. Reports, September 4 and September 16, 1957, Fast FBI file.

57. Ibid.

58. Ibid.

59. Fast and Schwartz met several times over the course of the year, as had their families. Several letters were exchanged dealing with family matters, Schwartz's review of *The Naked God,* and future meetings. "S file," FPP.

60. "Transcript of NBC interview," October 13, 1957, FPP.

61. Ibid.

62. Hays to Fast, November 1957, "H file," FPP. Seeger too was something of a "Stalin worshipper." It wasn't until 1993 that he apologized "for following the party

line so slavishly, for not seeing that Stalin was a supremely cruel misleader." *NYT,* September 1, 2007, B7.

63. Report, September 4, 1957, FBI file.

64. "Howard Fast Balks on Queries on Reds," *NYT,* February 22, 1957, 2.

65. "Telegrams," to Fast, April, July 1957, "H file," FPP. In April, the FBI changed Fast's Security Index Card by deleting the phrase "key figure." His name, however, remained on file until 1971.

66. Fast to Praeger Publishers, February 22, 1957, "P file," FPP.

67. "The Writer and the Commissar," *Prospectus,* November 1957, 1–31; "On Leaving the Communist Party," *Saturday Review of Literature,* November 16, 1957, 5–17.

68. Reviews appeared in nearly all the leading magazines and newspapers in the United States including *Nation,* December 21, 1957; *New Republic,* December 16, 1957; *New York Times,* December 1, 1957; *New Leader,* February 3, 1958; *Reporter,* January 23, 1958; *Saturday Review,* December 14, 1957. In England reviews appeared in *Daily Mail, Daily Telegraph, Financial Times, Manchester Evening News, New Statesman, Times Literary Supplement, Sunday Times, Tribune, Oxford Mail. Newsweek* and *Saturday Evening Post* also wrote about the excerpts before the book was out. "Royalty reports," b1, f3, FC, UWM.

69. *Naked God,* 26, 39, 46, 58, 74, 99, 4–5.

70. Ibid., 154, 162–163.

71. Ibid., 21, 31.

72. *NYT,* February 1, 1957, 1, 4. Also see chapter 6 and 9.

73. Rubenstein, "Some Were Poets, All Were Martyrs," 8; *Naked God,* 128–129.

74. Richard Crossman, *The God That Failed* (New York: Columbia University Press, 2001).

75. Rachel Fast, *Memoir,* 133; *Naked God,* 18.

76. *Naked God,* 18–19.

77. Ibid., 177.

78. Wright, "I Tried to Be a Communist," part 2, 48–56.

79. Lawrence Janofsky, "Truth Has Not Made Him Free," *Reporter,* January 23, 1958, 11–15; Howe, *New Republic,* December 16, 1957, 18–19.

80. Fast to Rachel, July 13, 1957 RFB; Fast to Praeger Publishers, February 22, 1957, "P file," FPP; *Naked God,* 131.

81. *Naked God,* 197.

13. FAST FORWARD

1. Jackson (1914–2007), an African American Communist and civil rights activist, is best known for his role in founding and leading, along with his wife, Esther Cooper Jackson, the Southern Negro Youth Congress (1937–48). In 1951 he was indicted for conspiracy under the Smith Act and became a fugitive until 1956, when he was arrested. Jackson, one of six defendants whose convictions were unanimously reversed by a federal appeals court in 1958, served no time. The turnaround was based on *Yates v. United States,* the 1957 Supreme Court ruling that the mere teaching or advocacy

of an overthrow of the government did not constitute a "call to action." *Masses and Mainstream* chose not to publish Jackson's letter; but with the help of Professor Phillip Deery, 2011 scholar-in-residence at Tamiment Library, I found it in the Jackson Papers, TAM 347, b17, f21.

2. *General Washington and the Water Witch* (London: Bodley Head, 1956); *The Crossing*, unpublished ms., Fast Personal Papers (FPP); *NYT*, February 11, 1958, 34.

3. Brown, *Soviet Attitudes toward American Writing*, 292; *NYT*, January 31, 1958, 3.

4. Part of the proposed second volume appeared as a short story, "King of the Golden River," in *The Howard Fast Reader* (New York: Crown, 1960).

5. Fast, Frank Campenni interview, August 19, 1974, box 9, folder 1, Fast Collection (FC), University of Wisconsin-Milwaukee (UWM).

6. *NYT*, October 30, 1958, 3.

7. "A Matter of Validity," *Midstream* 4 (Spring 1958): 7–17.

8. Ibid.

9. "Cosmopolitanism," *Daily Worker* (DW), April 26, 1956, at http://www.trussel.com/hf/cosmopol.htm.

10. Fast, Campenni interview, December 1, 1967, b8, f9, FC, UWM.

11. *NYT*, September 5, 1959, 13.

12. James Charlesworth and Loren Johns, eds., *Hillel and Jesus* (Minneapolis: Frontier Press, 1997); Michael Walzer et al., *The Jewish Political Tradition*, vol. 1: *Authority* (New Haven, Conn.: Yale University Press, 2000).

13. *Agrippa's Daughter* (Garden City, N.Y.: Doubleday, 1964), 391.

14. Fast, Campenni interview, April 16, 1968, b8, f14, FC, UWM.

15. *NYTBR*, September 13, 1964, 52.

16. *NYTBR*, February 6, 1966, 22.

17. There are also Jewish characters in *Power* (1962), another of Fast's less successful books. Fast thought *Power* was "the only true novel . . . about the labor movement . . . ever . . . written." Fast, Campenni interview, December 1, 1967. More interesting than the book's Jewish quality, however, is that while its sympathy lies with the striking coal miners, *Power*'s main emphasis is on the corruption of the union leader Ben Holt and the danger of power when it became the instrument of a righteous cause— another example of Fast's public backing away from his Communist past.

18. *April Morning* (New York: Crown Publishers, 1961), 128–131.

19. Hoover, *Masters of Deceit* (New York: Henry Holt, 1958), 107, 118, 124.

20. *NYT* reviewed the book twice favorably: April 23, 1961, 438, and again by J. Donald Adams, who read the book through in one sitting and thought it would one day outstrip *The Red Badge of Courage* as an American classic, *NYTBR*, May 14, 1961, 2.

21. Fast's book was deservedly in good company. The list included James Baldwin's *Nobody Knows My Name*, *The Odyssey*, translated by Robert Fitzgerald, and *Dawn*, by Elie Wiesel. *NYT*, February 25, 1962, E8.

22. Campenni, "Citizen Howard Fast," 534; *The Howard Fast Reader*, an

anthology including the whole of *Freedom Road* and *The Children,* as well as twenty-one stories old and new, also appeared in 1960. Fast's science-fiction stories were republished in his collection, *Edge of Tomorrow* (New York: Bantam Books, 1961).

23. By 1958 the Supreme Court ruled that a passport could be denied only if a person had engaged in unlawful activity.

24. Fast, "Draft," n.d., 1958, b48, f12, Kirk Douglas Collection (KDC), Wisconsin State Historical Society (WSHS); Douglas, *The Ragman's Son* (New York: Simon and Schuster, 1988), 307; Fast, Campenni interview, March 14, 1973, b8, f16, FC, UWM; Fast, "Spartacus Revisited," unpublished ms., [1988?], 6, "Spartacus file," FPP.

25. Douglas, *The Ragman's Son,* 308–314; Fast, "Draft," n.d., 1958, b48, f13, KDC, WSHS; "Spartacus Revisited," 6.

26. "Spartacus Revisited," 6.

27. Fast, "The Singularity of Being Jewish," unpublished, ms., 158–160, "Biography file," FPP. The family lived in a "cottage" in Beverly Hills. RFB, e-mail, July 7, 2012.

28. NYT, February 23, 1960, 36; "Spartacus Revisited," 9. Nothing about Fast's writing role in the summer of 1959 appears in Douglas's latest memoir, *I Am Spartacus! Making a Film, Breaking the Blacklist* (New York: Open Road, 2012). But that Fast wrote a good part of the screenplay is attested to by his award from the screenwriters' guild for one of the Five Best Written American Dramas of 1960. Ken Englund, President of the Writers Guild of America, West, to Fast, February 20, 1961, FPP.

29. Fast, Campenni interview, 1977, b9, f2, FC, UWM.

30. "Spartacus: Bonus Material" DVD, companion disc to Stanley Kubrick's epic masterpiece includes, among other things, deleted scenes, vintage newsreel footage, cast interviews, including Douglas, Fast, Ustinov, et al. (from 1960 and 1992). Carl Hoffman, "The Evolution of a Gladiator: History, Representation, and Revision in Spartacus," *Journal of American and Comparative Cultures* 23 (Spring 2000): 63–70.

31. "Spartacus: Bonus Material" DVD; although in the novel, Fast does more than hint at sexual perversion and promiscuity among the patrician class, he says the "snails and oysters" scene, between handsomely masculine Olivier and pretty boy Tony Curtis, clearly suggestive of homosexuality (cut in original, restored in the "restoration") had nothing to do with the book, and had no place in the film. See also Richard Bernstein, "'Spartacus': A Classic Restored," NYT, April 18, 1991, C15; Janet Maslin, "The Two Messages of 'Spartacus,'" NYT, April 26, 1991, C6.

32. "Spartacus Revisited," 9–10.

33. "Singularity," 158–160. Fast, not knowing the full story, gives Douglas more credit than he deserves. See John Meroney and Sean Coons, "How Kirk Douglas Overstated His Role in Breaking the Hollywood Blacklist," *The Atlantic,* July 5, 2012. http://www.theatlantic.com/entertainment/archive/2012/07/how-kirk-douglas-over -stated-his-role-in-breaking-the-hollywood-blacklist/259111/#.T_WsHgNojAM.email.

34. Rachel Fast Ben-Avi (RFB), e-mail, May 12, 2010, July 5, 2010; Campenni, "Citizen Howard Fast," 535.

35. *NYTBR*, September 13. 1964, 52; Harvey Swados, "Epic in Technicolor," *Nation,* April 5, 1952, 331.

36. Fast, Campenni interview, 1977.

37. The material about Fast in Hollywood and all the quotations in the following paragraphs come from twenty-six letters Howard sent home from June 5 through June 28, 1961. RFB.

38. http://www.google.com/search?sourceid=navclient&aq=8h&oq=&ie=UTF-8 &rlz=1T4GGLG_enUS330US330&q=barbara+steele.

39. Jonathan Fast, author interview, October 3, 2006. Jon said that the affair with Steele came to his and Rachel's attention because it was impossible for their father to stay quiet about such a "conquest."

40. Ibid.; Fast to family, May 5, 1961, RFB.

41. Navasky, *Naming Names,* 268–73, 374–75. Fast to Rachel, March 16, 1963. All letters from Howard to Rachel are in the possession of Rachel Fast Ben-Avi (RFB).

42. *NYT,* April 24, 1988, H33; January 10, 2000, E6.

43. Fast to Bette, June 9, 1961, RFB.

44. Fast to Bette, June 23, 1961.

45. Fast to Bette, June 16, 1961.

46. RFB, e-mail, July 5, 2010; author interview, February 8, 2010; Molly Jong-Fast, author interview, September 26, 2006; Erica Jong, Fast's daughter-in-law for several years in the 1970s, reaffirmed this view in an interview with the author, October 18, 2006.

47. Fast, Campenni interview, 1977. In the 1960s Fast would "walk around the house singing . . . at the top of his lungs," the song "The Merry Minuet," made famous by the Kingston Trio, which included the verse "They're rioting in Africa," and some others either sung incorrectly by Howard or slightly misremembered by Jonathan: "But we can be grateful/And thankful and proud/That man's been endowed/ With a mushroom shaped cloud/And we know for certain/That some happy day/ Someone will set the spark off/And we will all be blown away." Jonathan Fast, e-mail, January 3, 2010.

48. *Sylvia* (1965), *Penelope* (1966), *The Face of Fear* (TV movie based on *Sally,* 1971), *What's a Nice Girl Like You . . .?* (TV movie based on *Shirley,* 1971).

49. There were also a number of "treatments" or written proposals that never came to fruition, including one on Leonardo da Vinci and another on Charlemagne. A film based on *Phyllis,* for which Fast was slated to be the scriptwriter and to function as an executive producer, also never came to pass. Fast to Rachel, January 18, 1963, March 18, 1963, and April 23, 1963.

50. Fast to Nearing, June 6, 1979, FPP.

51. "Singularity," 77–84.

52. Patricia Carrington to Fast, September 2, 1975; Fast to Carrington, October 2, 1975, FPP; Carrington, *Freedom in Meditation* (New York: Doubleday, 1977); *Fast, The Art of Zen Meditation* (Culver City, Calif.: Peace Press, 1977). Even this book, "the shortest . . . on meditation . . . ever . . . published," according to Fast, sold over 8,000 copies.

53. *The Hill* (Garden City, N.Y.: Doubleday, 1964), ix–x; Fast, Campenni interview, December 1, 1967.

54. Jonathan Fast, author interview, October 3, 2006.

55. Fast to Rachel, September 21, 27, 1962; Jonathan Fast, author interview, October 3, 2006; *NYT*, September 16, 1962, 139.

56. Fast to Rachel, September 19, October 2, 1962.

57. Fast to Rachel, November 11, 1962.

58. Fast to Rachel, February 21, 1963.

59. Fast to Rachel, November 4, 1962, February 12, 1963.

60. RFB, e-mail, November 12, 2006; Fast to Rachel, July 24, 1974. Howard's letter is misdated 1944, the year of Rachel's birth. Emphasis mine.

61. Jonathan Fast, author interview, October 3, 2006; e-mail, July 29, 2010. In 1966, Jon, eighteen years old, composed an opera with his father, who did the libretto. "There was not a lot of back and forth," Jon said, and the libretto took Howard "about 20 minutes; maybe 15." JF, *Alone: A monodrama,* unpublished ms., libretto by Howard Fast, 1966, photocopy at New York Public Library.

62. Fast to Rachel, May 5, 1963.

63. Jonathan Fast, author interview, October 3, 2006; RFB, e-mail, August 26, 2007.

64. Jonathan Fast, author interview, October 3, 2006; Jonathan Fast, e-mail, January 3, 2011. In the early sixties Dylan's songs divided America into moral factions, with munitions makers and arms dealers, crooked politicians, Southern racists, and the indifferent middle-class on one side and the young, the impoverished, the oppressed, and the folk-rock "protest" singers on the other.

65. RFB, e-mail, September 10, 2011.

66. Fast, Campenni interview, April 15, 1968, b8, f13; April 16, 1968; Fast to Russell, August 19, 1966, FPP.

67. Fast to Rabbi Arthur Gilbert, August 11, 1966, FPP.

68. Fast, Campenni interview, March 13–14, 1973. Fast also wrote sometime in the late nineties, "When the Fellowship of Reconciliation, a pacifist organization to which I have belonged for many years, asked me to put my name on their ballot for their Board, I replied that while I was apparently unshaken in my devotion to pacifism, were I living in Israel I might think differently. They printed my reply in their monthly leaflet, and a number of letters of outrage greeted it, all of them from Jews. Nevertheless, my thinking on the subject has not changed, and I do not consider pacifism an invitation to death by suicide bombers." "Singularity," 138.

69. Fast to James S. Best, editor, *Fellowship,* March 1969, FPP. Emphasis mine.

70. Fast, Campenni interview, March 13–14, 1973. Emphases mine.

71. "Negro and Jew: An Encounter in America," *Midstream,* December 1966, 17–18.

72. Ibid.

73. Fast, Campenni interview, December 1, 1967.

74. Fast, Campenni interview, April 12, 1968, b8, f12, FC, UWM.

75. See *The Partisan Review Anthology,* eds. William Phillips and Philip Rahv (New York: Holt Rinehart and Winston, 1962); Neil Jumonville, *Critical Crossings:*

The New York Intellectuals in Postwar America (Berkeley: University of California Press, 1991); Alan M. Wald, *The New York Intellectuals: The Rise and Decline of the Anti-Stalinist Left from the 1930s to the 1980s* (Chapel Hill: University of North Carolina Press, 1987); Irving Howe, *A Margin of Hope* (New York: Mariner, 1984), especially 27–29, 230–232. Among *PR*'s classic contributions are Saul Bellow's, "Two Morning Monologues"; two of T. S. Eliot's "Four Quartets"; George Orwell's "Such, Such Were the Joys"; Delmore Schwartz's "In Dreams Begin Responsibilities"; Isaac Bashevis Singer's "Gimpel the Fool" (translated by Saul Bellow); and Susan Sontag's "Notes on "'Camp.'"

76. Fast, Campenni interview, April 12, 1968.

77. Who could Fast have meant: Mike Gold, Abe Cahan, Daniel Fuchs, Anzia Yezierska (about whom he was likely unaware), Samuel Ornitz, or Saul Bellow with his *Dangling Man* (1944) or *Victim* (1947)? None of these writers fits Fast's description.

78. RFB, e-mail, January 13, 2011.

79. Fast, Campenni interview, April 16, 1968.

80. Mark Shechner, "Jewish Writers," in *Harvard Guide to Contemporary American Writing*, ed. Daniel Hoffman (Cambridge, Mass.: Harvard University Press, 1979), 190–207.

81. Ibid., 193.

82. It was not only the adulation Fast had had in the Soviet Union, but his influence on it that he may have missed. The Soviet Union relied heavily on Fast's advice in regard to American literature. Djagalov, "'I Don't Boast About it, but I'm the Most Widely Read Author of This Century," 48–51.

83. Fast's name was deleted from the FBI's Security Card Index as a "Key Figure" in 1957. Memoranda, Special Agent in Charge (SAC) New York to Director, FBI, April 13 and 24, 1957, Fast FBI file.

84. Jonathan Fast, author interview, October 6, 2006.

85. Ibid.; Jonathan Fast, e-mail, December 3, 2008; August 30, 2010; January 3, 2011. Fast's favorite lyrics from the anthem included "Be glorified, our fatherland, united and free!/ The sure bulwark of the friendship of the peoples!/ The Soviet banner is the flag of the people,/ Let it lead from victory to victory!"

86. Rabbi Jacob Pressman to Fast, March 9, 1976, FPP, full of effusive thanks for speaking at Temple Beth Am in Los Angeles is typical; Fast, interviewed on radio station KNBC by Keith Berwick, tape, n.d., 1976, FPP.

87. *NYT*, May 17, 1970, 103.

88. In 1971 Fast also had two of his teleplays broadcast as *The Face of Fear*, based on *Sally*, and *What's a Nice Girl Like You . . . ?* based on *Sylvia*.

89. Jonathan Fast, author interview, October 3, 2006.

90. Fast to Gilbert, August 11, 1966, FPP. Jonathan never understood why his father, himself a publicly announced pacifist, went through this charade for his son, who was also a publicly announced pacifist, and unlikely to have been denied CO status. Jonathan Fast, author interview, October 3, 2006.

91. Fast to Theodore Bayer, January 9, 1956, FPP; Fast interviewed by John F.

Baker, in *Publisher's Weekly,* April 1, 1983, 64–65; Jonathan Fast, author interview, October 3, 2006; *NYTBR,* September 10, 1972, 41.

92. Fast to Rachel, March 3, 1972.

93. Jonathan Fast, author interview, October 3, 2006; Fast, Campenni interview, March 13–14, 1973.

94. Fast, Campenni interview, March 13–14, 1973.

95. Fast to Rachel, April 29, 1974.

14. LIFE IN THE FAST LANE

1. Fast to Rachel, April 29, 1974, March 26, 1974.

2. Fast to Rachel, April 29, 1974.

3. Fast to Rachel, July 24, 1974.

4. RFB, author interview, February 8, 2010; e-mail, July 3, 2010; Fast to Rachel, July 24, 1974.

5. Fast to Rachel, July 24, 1974.

6. Ibid.; Campenni, "Citizen Howard Fast," 536. Although Campenni was out to see Fast once again for several days in 1977, the biography was never written. Campenni grew ill and could not complete the book; but he left behind reams of materials, including transcripts of interviews done with Fast over a twelve-year period.

7. *NYT,* November 21, 1974, 95; December 8, 1974, 199.

8. *The House* and *Sophie* for TV, and *Sam Houston* and *The Lions Club* written for the big screen.

9. Fast to Rachel, April 29, 1974.

10. Hughes to Fast, May 13, 1975, b40, FC, UP; Fast to Rachel, July 16, 1974.

11. Fast to Rachel, February 27, 1975; Jonathan Fast, e-mail, August 30, 2010.

12. Howard Fast and Edward Hume (Filmways Motion Pictures, 1976), based on the book *The Blood of Israel* by Serge Groussard.

13. "But He's Got Oranges in His Yard," *NYT,* June 8, 1977, 21.

14. Fast to Rachel, August 4, 1974.

15. Ibid., November 4, 1974.

16. "They Fell in Love at First Sight," *NYT,* February 14, 1981.

17. Jong, *Seducing the Demon: Writing for My Life* (New York: Tarcher, 2006), 197; Jong, author interview, October 19, 2006.

18. Martha Smilgris, "Howard Fast's Many Sides: A Born-Again Yankee, Black-listed Best-Seller," *People,* April 7, 1980, 119.

19. RFB, e-mail, July 14, 2010; Jonathan Fast, author interview, October 3, 2006.

20. Jong, *Seducing the Demon,* 197; Jong, author interview, October 19, 2006; Jonathan Fast, e-mail, September 6, 2010; RFB, e-mail, September 10, 2010.

21. Fast to Carole Losee, October 27, 1975, RFB; *NYT,* April 30, 1976, 54.

22. Fast, "Spartacus Revisited," unpublished ms., n.d., FPP.

23. Lord, author interview, March 30, 2007. *The Immigrants* (Boston: Houghton Mifflin,1977); *The Second Generation* (Boston: Houghton Mifflin,1978); *The Establishment* (Boston: Houghton Mifflin, 1979); *The Legacy* (Boston: Houghton

Mifflin,1981); *The Immigrant's Daughter* (Boston: Houghton Mifflin,1985); *An Independent Woman* (New York: Harcourt Brace,1997).

24. Lord, author interview, March 30, 2007; Fast to Rachel, February 28, 1975; Fast to Campenni, September 20, 1978, FPP. The Cunningham books written between 1977 and 1984 featured a male Japanese detective named Masao Masuto, who was first introduced in *Samantha* (1967). A Zen Buddhist like his creator, Masuto solves intricately plotted mysteries while he moves smoothly and wisely, and with a caustic wit, through the corrupt denizens of Beverly Hills and LA.

25. Frank Campenni, "Howard Fast: Phoenix from the Forties," unpublished ms., b8, f10, 1, FC, UWM; "Reds to Riches," *Time,* November 7, 1977, 120–122; JF, e-mail, December 4, 2008.

26. *The Immigrants,* 180, 214, 321.

27. *The Second Generation,* 187, 370, 443.

28. *The Immigrants,* 297.

29. *NYTBR,* October 2, 1977, 6.

30. "Howard Fast Speaks on a Half-Century of Writing," *Publisher's Weekly,* April 1, 1983, 64–65.

31. *People,* April 1980, 119; Susan Shapiro, *Only as Good as Your Word: Writing Lessons From My Favorite Literary Gurus,* author's proof, 71; Fast, talk at Wilton, Conn., High School, December 4, 2000, videotape, FPP. Not only does Fast do a great disservice to literary critics such as James Wood, Frank Kermode, Alfred Kazin, Edward Wilson, Harold Bloom, and Irving Howe, he neglects the fact that by the sixties or even earlier novelists were reviewing each other's novels.

32. "Howard Fast Speaks on a Half-Century of Writing," 64–65; Lord, author interview, March 30, 2007. Beginning in 2004 Fast's volumes in *The Immigrants* series began to appear in new paperback, audio, and Kindle editions.

33. Fast to Campenni, September 20, 1978, FPP. Fast in *Philadelphia Daily News,* October 19, 1981, 25.

34. O'Connor, "TV: 'The Immigrants,' Another Formula Series," *NYT,* November 20, 1978, C30.

35. Ibid.

36. Bette to Rachel, April 4, 13, 17, 1978; "Singularity," 150.

37. "Singularity," 155–156.

38. Fast, interviewed by Dorothy Whitcomb in "Self-Doubt Never Turned to Writer's Block," *Connecticut Today,* April 4, 1983.

39. *NYT,* October 28, 1979, D1, D33; October 29, 1979, C20.

40. Fast, to Eric Major, November 2, 1979, box 64, Fast Collection (FC), University of Pennsylvania (UP); *NYT,* June 8, 1977, 21; Don Swaim, CBS Radio Interview with Howard Fast (1984), in Ohio University's *Wired For Books,* at http://www.wiredfor books.org/howardfast/ (transcript at http://www.trussel.com/hf/swaim1.htm); *Philadelphia Daily News,* October 19, 1981, 25.

41. Jonathan Fast, e-mail, September 21, 2010; *Philadelphia Daily News,* October 19, 1981, 25; *Max* was published in 1982 and centered on a poor Jewish boy from the

slums of the Lower East Side, who, like Fast, with pluck and energy, fought his way to the top of his profession.

42. *Philadelphia Daily News,* October 19, 1981, 25; Shapiro, *Only As Good As Your Word,* 60.

43. *Philadelphia Daily News,* October 19, 1981, 25; *NYT,* September 7, 1988, C22. He also told his granddaughter Molly that he wanted to go on living forever. Author interview, September 26, 2006.

44. Rena Fast to Howard, July 17, 1980, December 3, 1980, May 4, 1981, FPP; "Receipt," Riverside Memorial Chapel, New York City, June 11, 1981, FPP.

45. Melissa Fast, letter to Howard, June 19 [?], FPP

46. Rachel Fast Ben-Avi (RFB), e-mail, March 10, 2007; Jonathan Fast, author interview, October 3, 2006; Fast, to Teddy Kolleck, May 6, 1978, b40, FC, UP. Howard had a penchant for moving to new apartments and houses. Rachel and Avrum estimated that there were more than twenty different residences for the Fasts from 1944 to 1980. E-mail, January 9, 2011. Jonathan also pointed out that his father was not only generous with money. He had also several times opened his home to friends and acquaintances in trouble. Most memorable, Jonathan said, was the night in the 1970s when noted sportswriter Roger Kahn's wife, Alice, had been victimized by one too many of her husband's physically abusive alcoholic rages. She "came to the door with the two kids," Jonathan said, "and Howard immediately took them in for at least several days, and lavished them with attention." Jonathan Fast, author interview, October 3, 2006.

47. Goldburg to Fast, December 27, 1951, FPP; and various pieces of correspondence concerning meetings, fundraising, benefit dinners, and demonstrations between Fast and Goldburg, "G file" FPP.

48. *The Outsider* (New York: Dell, 1984), 108.

49. CBS Radio Interview with Howard Fast (1984).

50. *The Outsider,* 142–143.

51. Ibid., 146, 161.

52. CBS Radio Interview with Howard Fast.

53. Ibid.; *Being Red,* 288.

54. Ibid. Fast's play *Triptych,* for which I could find no manuscript, was performed at the Cathedral of the St. John the Divine on the upper West Side of Manhattan on April 10, 1987. Fast introduced the play, which ran only one night, and read some of the poetry of Gabriel Garcia Marquez. *NYT,* April 10, 1987.

55. Citizen Tom Paine: A Play in Two Acts (Boston: Houghton Mifflin, 1985); *Philadelphia News,* January 26, 1987, 40; *Chicago Tribune,* April 23, 1987, 3; *Manhattan,* June–August, 1987, 61–64.

56. Corliss Lamont to Fast, September 25, 1987, b40, UP; *Manhattan,* June–August, 1987, 61–64.

57. *The Dinner Party* (New York: Dell Books, 1987), 234.

58. In 1988, too, *April Morning* was made into a TV movie that Fast thought was brought to the screen with reasonable care and intelligence. *NYT,* April 24, 1988, H33.

59. Janusz Bugajski, *Sandinista Communism and Rural Nicaragua* (Westport,

Conn.: Greenwood Press with the Center for Strategic and International Studies, Washington, D.C., 1990); Peter Dale Scott and Jonathan Marshall, *Cocaine Politics: Drugs, Armies, and the CIA in Central America,* updated ed. (Berkeley: University of California Press, 1998).

60. Bugajski, *Sandinista Communism and Rural Nicaragua.*

61. *The Confession of Joe Cullen* (New York: Dell Books, 1989), 301.

62. Fast, *Being Red,* 16, 79, 301.

63. Ibid., 195, 273–274, 323.

64. Ibid., 166–167.

65. Fast, *The Naked God,* 48; *Being Red,* 24, 82–83. Moreover, nothing was "plain" about WWII, for which the USSR was as equally responsible with Nazi Germany, nor was the Red Army nearly as noble as Fast portrays it. See Snyder, *Bloodlands.*

66. *Naked God,* 5–6.

67. *Being Red,* 72, 138.

68. Ibid., 329, 343. Barrett, *William Z. Foster and the Tragedy of American Radicalism;* Isserman, *Which Side Were You On?* on Foster and Browder throughout; Haynes and Klehr, *Venona,* 192–194, 218–220.

69. Fast, interviewed on *CBS Nightwatch,* December 7, 1990, audiotape, FPP; "A Conversation with Howard Fast, March 23, 1994," 511–523.

70. Jonathan Fast, author interview, October 3, 2006.

71. Ibid.; Ken Gross, "Howard Fast: A Former Communist and Lifelong Dissident Ends Up Rich and Beloved in Capitalist America," *People's Weekly,* January 28, 1991, 75–79.

72. Stefan Kanfer, "Fast Backward," *New Leader,* December 10–24, 1990, 21–23; Ronald Radosh "About Face," *Commentary,* March 1991, 62–64, at http://www.commentarymagazine.com/viewarticle.cfm/being-red—by-howard-fast-7817; *Washington Post,* March 14, 2007, B07; Maurice Isserman, "It Seemed a Good Idea at the Time," *NYTBR,* November 4, 1990, 14.

73. *Greenwich Time,* November 14, 1990, A1–A4. *Being Red* put Fast back in the news even more than what his children called his "recycled" literary career. His participation in a New York Public Library "Literary Lions" fundraising dinner after his political memoir was published drew an enormous audience and helped raise a million dollars for the library's book fund. Timothy Healy, president of the NYPL, in a letter to Fast said, "There would have been no crowd had it not been for you," and "Without you there would have been no . . . million dollars." December 12, 1990, b40, UP.

15. FAST AND LOOSE

1. Gross, "Howard Fast," 75–79.

2. Leslie Hanscom, "Non-notorious Howard Fast Still Leans Left," *Bridgeport Newsday,* March 15, 1987, clipping FPP.

3. Gross, "Howard Fast," 75–79.

4. Ibid., 79.

5. Ibid.

6. Molly Jong-Fast, author interview, September 26, 2006; Jong-Fast, *Sex Doctors in the Basement* (New York: Villard Books, 2005), 19–20.

7. Fast, interviewed by Moses Schoenfeld, United Nations Press Section, for *International Date Line,* audiotape, n.d., 1990, FPP.

8. Fast, interviewed on *The Bob McGonagle Show,* WGCH, audiotape, August [n.d.] 1992, FPP; Shapiro, *Only As Good As Your Word,* 71–74.

9. Shapiro, *Only As Good As Your Word,* 62.

10. Fast, *The Novelist: A Romantic Portrait of Jane Austen* (New York: Samuel French, 1992), 67.

11. *NYT,* October 23, 1991, C16. The *Village Voice* found the second act's "love over art" motif unconvincing. October 29, 1991, 100.

12. *NYT,* April 21, 1991, WC20.

13. See for example, *Courier-Journal* (Louisville, Ky.), August 6, 1992; *Providence Journal,* September 11, 1992; *Phoenix Gazette,* February 3, 1993; and *San Jose Evening News,* July 11, 1993, at http://www.trussel.com/hf/articles.htm#T700. Most of Fast's articles for the *Observer* are collected in *War and Peace: Observations of Our Times* (Armonk, N.Y.: M. E. Sharpe, 1993). A 1991 televised interview, with Richard D. Heffner, can be viewed at archive.org/details/openmind_ep423.

14. *Greenwich Time* and *Advocate,* clippings scrapbook, FPP.

15. Fast, interviewed Wisconsin Public Radio, October 18, 1993; Crown Publishers to Fast, August 29, 1994, b64, FC, University of Pennsylvania (UP).

16. *San Jose Mercury News,* July 11, 1993, 1C.

17. Peter Biskind, "Reconstructing Woody," *Vanity Fair,* December 2005, at http://www.vanityfair.com/culture/features/2005/12/woodyallen200512.

18. Allen, interviewed by Walter Isaacson, *Time,* August 31, 1992, at http://www.time.com/time/magazine/article/0,9171,976345-5,00.html; Fast, *Being Red,* 16.

19. RFB, e-mail, October 5, 2006. In the *San Jose Mercury News,* Fast wrote: "I don't know whether Woody Allen made improper advances to his small daughter. But I do know that millions of fathers and mothers have had their children crawl into warm beds with them and cuddle up to them."

20. Lord to Fast, August 19, 1993, b64, FC, UP.

21. Fast, "The Singularity of Being Jewish," unpublished ms., 162–163, FPP; Fast, untitled typescript, 1998, FPP.

22. Kirby F. Smith, "Symposium Examines Howard Fast's Life and Work. A Writer's Life in the Cold War: A Talk with Howard Fast and More," announcement of 1994 Symposium at the University of Pennsylvania, at http://www.trussel.com/hf/about.htm#T613.

23. Foley, "Renarrating the Thirties in the Forties and Fifties," 455–466; Alan Wald, "Marxist Literary Resistance to the Cold War," *Prospects* 20 (1995): 479–492; Sugrue, "Reassessing the History of Post-War America," 493–509.

24. Wald and Filreis, "A Conversation with Howard Fast, March 23, 1994," 511–523.

25. RFB, e-mail, April 27, 2008; Molly Jong-Fast, author interview, September 26, 2006.

26. "Singularity," 165.

27. Jonathan Fast, author interview, October 3, 2010; RFB, author interview, March 17, 2010.

28. "Singularity," 165–168.

29. *The Sculpture of Bette Fast,* foreword by Howard Fast (Armonk, N.Y.: M. E. Sharpe, 1995).

30. *The Bridge Builder's Story* (Armonk, N.Y.: M. E. Sharpe, 1995).

31. *Philadelphia Inquirer,* December 4, 1995, Local South Jersey section, SO1, at http://www.trussel.com/hf/age81.htm.

32. Erika K. Cardosa, "Crossing the Longest 'Bridge': The 65-year Career of Howard Fast," *Entertainment Weekly,* October 27, 1995, at http://www.ew.com/ew /article/0,,299245,00.html.

33. Ibid.

34. "Singularity," 167–168. By the time Fast died in 2003, the new "smaller" house was assessed at just under $2 million. http://www.realtor.com/ property-detail/55-TomacAve_Old-Greenwich_CT_06870_755c95.

35. *NYT,* August 4, 1996, 46; Shapiro, *Only As Good As Your Word,* 78.

36. "Singularity," 176–179.

37. Ibid., 173–176; author interviews with Mimi Fast, Molly Jong-Fast, Jonathan Fast, and Rachel Fast Ben-Avi, on September 12, 2006, September 26, 2006, October 6, 2010, February 8, 2010, respectively.

38. Mimi Fast, author interview, September 12, 2006.

39. Ibid.; Fast, unpublished ms., 1998, FPP.

40. Fast, unpublished ms., 1998, FPP; Singularity," 180.

41. "Singularity," 184.

42. Mimi Fast, author interview, September 12, 2006.

43. "Singularity," 184.

44. Ibid., 183; Mimi Fast, author interview, September 12, 2006.

45. Molly Jong-Fast, author interview, September 26, 2006; Fast, radio interview, on *Voices of Our World,* March 15, 1998, audio tape, FPP; *NYT,* March 27, 1985.

46. Joseph Dorinson, ed., "Paul Robeson (1898–1976): A Centennial Symposium," *Pennsylvania History* 66 (Winter 1999): 1–111.

47. *Paul Robeson: Here I Stand,* TV biography, DVD, 1999; *NYT,* February 24, 1999, E2, 2.

48. "Scrapbook," clippings, *Greenwich Time,* 1998–2000, FPP; Seeger to Fast, July 25, August 17, 1998, FPP.

49. Jong-Fast, *Sex Doctors,* 185, 24, 30–32; Jonathan Fast, e-mail, October 13, 2010.

50. RFB, author interview, February 9, 2010; e-mail, November 8, 2010, January 13, 2011; Jonathan Fast, author interview, October 3, 2006; Molly Jong-Fast, author interview, September 26, 2006; Jong-Fast, *Sex Doctors,* 30. The "babe" in question was also Jonathan Fast's editor on his 1988 novel, *Jade Stalk.*

51. *NYT,* July 9, 2000, CT4.

52. Ibid.; Fast remained interested in things Jewish. He worked on "Singularity"

until nearly his death, and in January 1998, he confirmed that he had published the three books under the name Boruch Behn—in Hebrew "Son of Barney": *In the Beginning: The Story of Abraham* (New York: Hebrew Publishing Company, 1958); *The Patriarchs: The Story of Abraham, Isaac and Jacob* (New York: Hebrew Publishing Company, 1959); *The Coat of Many Colors: The Story of Joseph* (New York: Hebrew Publishing Company, 1959).

16. FALL AND DECLINE

1. Jonathan Fast, e-mail, October 13, 2010, November 2, 2010.

2. Shapiro, *Only As Good As Your Word,* 80. Fast is listed as "uncredited" under the topic "writers" at http://www.imdb.com. Onscreen, the credits read that Ford's film was suggested by Mari Sandoz's book *Cheyenne Autumn* (1954). But when film historian Joseph McBride in the 1970s did the commentary for the DVD version of *Cheyenne Autumn,* the legal department at Warner Brothers removed all of his remarks about Fast and the novel-script controversy. McBride, e-mail December 11, 2010; McBride, *Searching for John Ford* (New York: Saint Martin's Press, 2001), 644, 646–647, 688–687; Bernard Smith, letter to Martin Gang, September 16, 1963, b3, f1; "Outline and Notes," b3, f2, "Final Script," b3, f6, Smith Papers, Wisconsin State Historical Society.

3. Shapiro, *Only As Good As Your Word,* 80.

4. Jonathan Fast, e-mail, February 20, 2011; Jong-Fast, *Sex Doctors,* 188.

5. Funeral card, in possession of author.

6. Fast, draft of "Communism and Morality," 1957, FPP; *Naked God,* 2.

7. RFB, e-mail, February 22, 2011.

8. Molly Jong-Fast, author interview, September 26, 2006; Erica Jong to Howard, July 22, 1997, FPP; Shapiro, *Only As Good As Your Word,* 86.

9. Jong-Fast, author interview, September 26, 2006.

10. Jong-Fast, *Sex Doctors,* 189.

11. *Naked God,* 127.

12. Ibid.

13. Jonathan Fast, author interview, October 3, 2006.

14. Fast, interviewed by Edward Morris, at http://www.trussel.com/hf/morris.htm.

15. *Moscow News,* March 2003, at http://www.trussel.com/hf/moscownews.htm.

16. Jong-Fast, *Sex Doctors,* 189.

17. Amy Goodman, "Transcript, Howard Fast interview," on Pacifica Radio's *Democracy Now,* April 8, 1998, FPP.

18. Traister, "Noticing Howard Fast," 525–541.

19. The list goes on; and while we might argue about an inclusion or exclusion here or there, a widespread consensus exists about which American writers during Fast's lifetime contributed works of literary value, including many more names than those listed above or in earlier chapters, e.g., George Eliot, Robert Penn Warren, Edna Ferber, James Baldwin.

20. Gordon Hutner, *What America Read: Taste, Class, and the Novel, 1920–1960* (Chapel Hill: University of North Carolina Press, 2008), 333.

21. Jonathan Fast, author interview, October 3, 2006; RFB, author interview, February 8, 2010.

22. Fast, interviewed by Edward Morris, at http://www.trussel.com/hf/morris .htm.

23. Ibid.

24. Brown to Fast, August 9, 1946, "B file" FPP.

25. When I, the son of Jewish working-class parents, read Fast as a teenager, especially *The Last Frontier, Citizen Tom Paine,* and *Freedom Road,* I moved from being a garden-variety liberal to several degrees left of center in my politics. When I revealed this story to my friend Larry Bush, a "red-diaper baby," and the editor of *Jewish Currents* (a secular progressive magazine, thoroughly de-Stalinized since 1956), he told me that after reading Fast's books, he, too moved to left-liberalism, but away from a middle-class family deeply entrenched in the Communist movement. Fast's historical novels written between 1941 and 1944, before he joined the CP, helped me discover that there was a lot more "wrong" with American life and behavior than I had been taught in school, and that the exercise of U.S. power in the world caused great damage as well as good. Larry, on the other hand, found in the pre-Communist writings of Fast a progressivism that could be recreated in the United States on the foundations of American history, values, and ideals—unconnected to Marxist-Leninism, or his own parents. Different starting points, different journeys, same destination.

BIBLIOGRAPHIC NOTE

The most important source for Howard Fast is the website created and maintained by Steve Trussel, http://www.trussel.com/hf/howfast.htm. Here you will find not only a listing of every book, article, essay, introduction, play, pamphlet, poem, edited anthology, and review written by Fast, and many of his newspaper pieces and columns, but also articles about him and reviews of almost all of his books. Many items are available for downloading at no cost. It is a remarkable feat to have put together this site, with its many links and ease of use. I owe Steve Trussel a deep debt of gratitude for providing this resource and for having saved me immeasurable amounts of time.

The main sources for Fast's papers are the Fast Collection at the University of Wisconsin at Milwaukee (UWM) and the Fast Collection at the University of Pennsylvania (UP). At UWM, in addition to reams of material including correspondence and manuscripts, are the transcripts of interviews of Fast by Frank Campenni conducted between 1965 and 1977. UP holds even more material relevant to Fast, including a significant number of letters between Howard and Bette Fast. I was fortunate also to have access to Fast's papers, letters, scrapbooks, and taped or videoed interviews still at his home in Old Greenwich, Connecticut, before they were sent to the University of Pennsylvania for cataloging and archiving, which at the time of this writing were still in process. In my acknowledgements and footnotes you will find other websites and archives that hold relevant materials on Fast and carry small numbers of his letters. Of particular importance is the Albert Maltz Collection at the Wisconsin State Historical Society.

Interviews and e-mail correspondence with Rachel Fast Ben-Avi and Jonathan Fast were critical. Other people interviewed who supplied valuable information and insight include Molly Jong-Fast, Erica Jong, Barry Fast, Judith (Fast) Zander, and Sterling Lord.

INDEX

Note: The abbreviation HF in subheadings refers to Howard Fast. Italic page numbers refer to photographs.

Aaron, Daniel, 410n45
Abbott, Berenice, 169
Abbott and Costello comedies, 123
Abraham Lincoln Battalion, 32
Abraham Lincoln Brigade, 70, 110
Abstract Expressionism, 286
Abzug, Bella, 226–227
Acheson, Dean, 229, 243, 259
Adams, J. Donald, 466n20
Adams, John Quincy, 366
Adamson, Ernest, 110, 119
AFL-CIO, 301
Agee, James, 23
Agronsky, Martin, 57, 327–328
Air Transport Corps (ATC), 79, 81
Akiva, Rabbi, 318
Algren, Nelson, 141, 410n44
Ali, Muhammad, 375
Alien and Sedition Laws of 1798, 224
Alien Registration Act of 1940, 76, 157
All Quiet on the Western Front (film), 18
All the King's Men (film), 95, 344

Allen, Hervey, 34–35
Allen, Woody, 390, 475n19
Allon, Yigal, 374
Alman, David, 64, 200
Alter, Victor, 58
Altgeld, John Peter, 114–117, 129
Amalgamated Clothing Workers, 158
Amann, Ernesto, 293–294
Amazing Stories, 20
Ambassador, The (teleplay), 376
American Business Consultants (ABC), 131, 132
American Civil Liberties Union, 137, 295
American Committee of Jewish Writers, Artists and Scientists (ACJWAS), 113–114
American Communist Party (CPUSA): and admiration for HF, 72–73; and art, 5, 6, 24, 70, 91–92, 417n83; and blacks, 5, 68–69, 70, 72, 217; and civil liberties, 76; and Cold War, 107; and Communist Control Act, 284, 295; and "Communist-front" organizations, 114; criticism of HF's writing, 219–222, 233, 234, 240, 291–292, 320, 327, 447n94; Cultural Section, 5,

55–56, 68, 72, 141, 177, 219–220, 230;
as destructive of own goals, 272; dogmatism of, 56, 59, 68, 72, 93–95, 157,
391; FBI arrests, 230; and Foley Square
Courthouse trial, 162, 163–168, 175;
HF as "disciplined Party member,"
178; HF as public face of, 1, 4, 136, 161;
and HF on free speech, 75, 76–77;
and HF's attacks on complexity in
literature, 78; HF's criticism of, 305,
312–314; and HF's identity, 6, 9, 86,
219, 222, 273, 296, 320, 325, 328; and
HF's Jewishness, 73–75, 80, 152, 358,
359; HF's joining of, 56; HF's loyalty
to, 231, 233, 244, 254, 272–273, 283,
291, 327–328, 331, 332–333, 383; HF's
motivation for joining, 2–4, 54, 55,
57–60, 71, 88–89; and HF's psychology of "true believer," 59, 272; and
HF's release from prison, 214–215, 216;
HF's renunciation of, 8, 145, 173, 179,
193, 233, 254, 316–325, 403; and HF's
speeches, 73; and HF's work for Office
of War Information (OWI), 45, 46, 49,
55–56, 63; and HF's writing, 5–7, 30–
31, 67, 117, 126, 127, 128, 151–152, 153,
154, 157, 333–334, 346, 425n65; and
Hollywood, 3, 51–52, 56, 57, 122–123;
and Hungarian revolution, 315; and
Israel, 149; Jews as Communists, 55,
58; and John Reed Club, 12, 21; and labor movement, 158–159; mass exodus
from, 307–308, 314, 332; and McGee,
229; members leaving in phases, 332;
middle class composition of, 464n46;
and Moscow Show Trials, 31, 305; and
Moscow-defined Party line, 3; and
Moscow's revolutionary outlook, 85,
86–87; national headquarters of, 272;
New York City members of, 60; place
in American life, 10; racial integration policy, 69; and Rosenberg case,
252–253; as secretive, 257, 272; and

Smith-Mundt Act, 143; Soviet spies
within, 166, 433n4; and Trotskyism,
76; and unofficial blacklists, 132; and
white chauvinism policy, 168, 217–218,
220; writers leaving, 68, 71, 94, 95,
145–146, 219
American Federation of Labor (AFL), 301
American Indians: in HF's novels, 2,
38–39; in magazine literature, 30
American Jewish Congress, 250, 259,
448n106
American Jewish League Against Communism (AJLAC), 149–150
American Labor Party (ALP), 112,
257–261
American League for Peace and Democracy, 114
American Legion, 132
American Library Association, 425n58
American literature: and Cold War,
194–195; HF on, 191–194, 285–286,
405; HF's place in, 10, 403–406; and
social writing, 284, 286, 287; and writ-
ers' political uninvolvement, 285–288.
See also proletarian literature; and
specific authors
American Mercury, 287
American Peace Crusade, 243
American Relief for Greek Democracy,
121
American Veterans Committee, 137
American Writers Association (AWA), 117,
134–135, 427n17
American Youth for Democracy, 77
Americans for Democratic Action, 137,
247
anarchism, 3
Anderson, Kyrill M., 419n54
Animal Farm (George Orwell), 127
Anna Christie (film), 18
Anthony Adverse (film), 35
Anthony Adverse (Hervey Allen), 34–35
anti-Communist sentiment: and

American Business Consultants, 131; and American literature, 286; and blacklists, 8, 51, 132–133, 149, 159, 214, 230, 231, 235, 256, 280, 297, 298, 427n10; and Cold War, 132, 284; decline in, 301; effects of, 132–133, 427n10; growth of, 56, 108; HF on, 190; and HUAC, 56, 76, 122, 124, 132; and loyalty boards, 123–124, 132; and New Deal, 109, 132; Peekskill, New York, anti-Communist riots, 7, 181–188, 190, 208; and social attitudes, 284–285; Trumbo as target of, 143. *See also* McCarthyism

Anti-Defamation League of B'nai B'rith, 250, 448n106

Anti-Fascist Refugee Committee, 120

antisemitism: Bellow on, 431n83; of black leaders, 354, 355; and Communism as "Jewish" invention, 31; and Great Depression, 55; in HF's childhood, 15–16; HF's encounters with, 64; HF's equating with fascism, 228, 247, 248; and HF's on Jewish identity, 74; Hobson on, 152, 431n83; and Peekskill, New York, anti-Communist riots, 183–184, 187; and Rosenberg case, 250, 252–253, 262; in Soviet Union, 57, 149, 174–179, 254, 262, 263–264, 272–273, 292, 304–305, 316–317, 318, 321–322, 327, 330–331, 337, 383; U.S. decline in, 249

Appeal to the World (Du Bois), 232

Appel, Benjamin, 64

April Morning (TV movie), 473n58

Aptheker, Bettina, 197

Aptheker, Herbert, 140–141, 197, 220, 230, 270, 302, 319

Arad, Zvi, 430n64

Aragon, Louis, 145–146, 154, 173, 191, 202, 246, 429n57

Armstrong, Louis, 23

Army-McCarthy Hearings of 1954, 269

Arrowsmith (film), 18

Artists, Writers, and Professionals Group, 89

Arts, Sciences, and Professions Council of the Progressive Citizens of America, 427n18

Arundel (Roberts), 34

Associated Veterans Council, 190

Atlas, Leopold, 93

atomic weapons, 107–108, 160, 189, 285

Attorney General's List of Subversive Organizations (AGLOSO), 51, 123, 133

Auslander, Jacob, 178, 198

Austen, Jane, 203, 210, 369, 388

Austrian People's Voice, 229, 279–281, 445n52

Authors Guild, 114

Babcock, Barbara, 368

Babel, Isaac, 330

Bad and the Beautiful, The (film), 214

Baden-Powell, Robert, 41

Baer, Ted, 292

Baldwin, James, 477n19

Ball, Lucille, 289

Ballad of the Sad Café, The (McCullers), 287

banned books: attempts to ban HF's novels, 130, 133–135, 427n17; banning of *Citizen Tom Paine,* 7, 133–136, 230, 340; Maltz on, 135, 427n18; and *Story* magazine, 27

Barbary Shore (Mailer), 381

Barnard, Harry Elmer, 128–129

Barnes, Joseph, 45

Barrett, William, 170

Barsky, Edward, 110–111, 112, 124

Barsky vs. U.S., 122

Baruch, Bernard, 242

Bass, Charlotta, 231

Bava, Mario, 343

Beard, Charles, 414n16

Beats, 288

Becker, Carl, 414n16

Behn, Boruch, 477n52

Being Red (Fast): and antisemitism of Soviet Communist Party, 174–175, 177–178, 383; and Bengal famine, 82; and Fadeyev, 176, 177, 178, 436n52; and free speech, 75; and *The Hammer,* 218; and HF's imprisonment, 199, 203, 205; HF's interviews about, 388–389; and Indiana University writing workshop, 91; and Marxism, 110; as memoir, 382–385, 474n73; and Progressive Party, 161; publishing of, 386; and Sartre, 89; and Schappes, 151, 430n78; and Waldorf World Peace Conference, 169, 171; and World War II, 474n65

Bell, Daniel, 116

Bellow, Saul: on antisemitism, 431n83; HF comparing himself to, 286, 404; Jewish characters of, 356, 357, 405; as Jewish writer, 249; and lack of political involvement, 285, 287; and *Literature and Reality,* 195; prohibition in Soviet Union, 142; relevance of, 290; subtlety of, 357

Ben-Avi, Avrum, 377, 392, 473n46

Bengal, famine of, 82, 419nn37–38

Ben-Gurion, David, 369

Benson, Elmer, 259

Bentley, Elizabeth, 163, 183, 331

Berg, Gertrude, 249

Bergelson, David, 171, 175, 254, 330

Beria, Lavrenti, 302, 305, 306, 322

Berle, Milton, 249

Berlin, Irving, 249

Berman, Lionel, 55–56, 216, 217

Bernstein, Leonard, 112, 169, 249

Bessie, Alvah, 93, 95, 214, 430n61

Best Untold, The (Biberman), 242

Best Years of Our Lives, The (film), 122, 195

Biberman, Edward, 242

Biberman, Herbert, 53, 54, 93, 293, 302

Bielski, A. Bruce, 446n59

Bielski, Frank, 446n59

Birth of a Nation (film), 66

Black Reconstruction in America (Du Bois), 62–63, 417n75

blacks: American Communist Party policy toward, 5, 68–69, 70, 72, 217; black troops, 68, 79; and HF on labor movement, 109; HF's research on integrating American armed forces, 62; Jews' interaction with, 63–65, 354; and lynchings, 15, 28, 408n17; in magazine literature, 30; and Popular Front, 60; reaction to *Freedom Road,* 417n84; segregation in prison, 204; and self-determination, 68–69; and Soviet Union, 182–183; and "Trenton 6," 182; and World War II, 183, 397. *See also* race and race relations; racial justice

Blitzstein, Marc, 23, 89, 140, 196, 293, 420n61, 428n37

Blob, The (film), 289

Bloch, Emanuel, 326

Bloom, Harold, 472n31

Bloor, Ella Reeve, 153–154

Blue Heron Publishing House, 241, 242, 297, 298, 308, 315, 448n104

Blum, Leon, 146

Bodley Head, 447n92

Body Language (Julius Fast), 213

Bolshevism, 31, 273, 411n74

Booklist Committee of the Independent School Education Board, 340, 466n21

Boston Herald, 67

Boston University, 280

Bowles, Chester, 116

Boyer, Robert, 264

Boyle, T. C., 186

Bradley, Lyman (Dick), 125, 138, 198, 204

Brandeis, Louis, 277

Brandeis University, 249, 315

Brando, Marlon, 169

Bread Loaf Writers' Conference, 25

Brecht, Bertolt, 202, 428n37

Bridgeport Newsday, 386

Bright, John, 51, 293

Britain, HF's attitude toward, 80, 82

Bronx Home News, 14

Brooklyn College, 137, 138, 225

Brooklyn Council of the Veterans of Foreign Wars, 283

Brooks, Van Wyck, 112

Brothers Ashkenazi, The (Singer), 373

Browder, Earl: on black self-determination, 69; calls for reinstatement of, 304; on free speech, 75; HF on, 86; ousted from American Communist Party leadership, 85, 87, 428n37; and Popular Front, 426n7; as Soviet spy, 433n4; and Voice of America libraries, 270; writings of, 165

Brown, James Oliver, 115–116, 405

Brown, John Mason, 25

Brown, Lloyd, 287

Brownell, Herbert, 283

Bryan, Helen R., 111–112, 113

Buchman, Sidney, 138–139

Buck, Pearl, 25

Buckley, William, Jr., 387

Buckmaster, Henrietta, 64

Buddenbrooks (Mann), 373

Budenz, Louis, 162, 165

Burg, Joseph, 452n52

Burnett, Whit, 410n58

Burns, George, 249

Bush, Larry, 478n25

Cabell, James Branch, 377

Caeser, Sid, 289, 450n15

Cahan, Abraham, 357

Caldwell, Erskine, 23, 121, 201

Call It Sleep (Henry Roth), 24, 28

Cameron, Angus, 205, 211, 233–236, 237, 238, 240–241, 431n89

Camp Jened, 14, 21–23, 26, 32, *98,* 203, 205

Campenni, Frank, 355–356, 358, 359, 362, 365–366, 471n6

Cannery Row (Steinbeck), 146

capital punishment, 199, 318, 338

capitalism: Hervey Allen on, 34; and art, 142; Foster on, 86; HF's fighting of, 90, 96, 107, 116; and inequality, 54; Koestler on, 20; Nazism compared to, 126; and North, 139; Odets's criticism of, 46; and proletarian literature, 23, 30; reform of, 57, 116; George Bernard Shaw on, 19; and Trotskyism, 76

Capote, Truman, 25, 410n58

Capra, Frank, 139

Carnovsky, Morris, 93, 258, 452n43

Carroll, Gladys Hasty, 25

Casanova, Laurent, 175

Catch 22 (Heller), 352

Catcher in the Rye (Salinger), 287

Catholic Church, 108, 157

Celler, Emanuel, 113

Center for Progressive Culture, 201

Central Intelligence Agency (CIA), 286, 439n18

Cerf, Bennett, 236, 277

Chakovsky, A., 291, 448n100

Chambers, Whittaker, 163, 183, 331

Chayefsky, Paddy, 289, 450n15

Cheney, Russell, 439n4

Cheyenne Autumn (film), 401, 477n2

Chicago Defender, 67

Chicago Peace Conference, 226

Chicago Tribune, 150

China: HF on United Nations' recognition of, 224; and Korean War, 223, 225, 246; and People's Liberation Army, 79, 174, 183

Christian Register, 73

Christianity, and HF, 36, 127, 210, 239, 318, 336, 355

Churchill, Winston, 109, 232

Citadel Press, 236, 241, 279

Citizen Kane (film), 46, 214

Citizen Tom Paine (Fast): banning of, 7, 133–136, 230, 340; characters of, 339; film rights to, 47, 50–51, 52, 54, 139, 342; and HF's love of country, 69, 115, 266; HF's writing of, 44, 45, 47, 62; in India, 83; and influence of HF's Communist colleagues, 49; Jesus in, 127, 278; legacy of, 405, 406; and McCarthy hearings, 266; "message" of, 48, 414n16, 478n25; and narrowness of HF's views, 96; paperback edition of, 342; as play, 369, 379; readers' reactions to, 117–119; reviews of, 47, 240, 413n11; and social class, 47–49; success of, 2, 8, 47, 50, 134, 135, 139, 241, 334, 413n12, 427n12

City College of New York (CCNY), 19, 21, 137–138, 274

City Streets (film), 408n24

Civil Rights Congress (CRC): and American Communist Party arrests, 446n55; American Communist Party involvement in, 114; and Foley Square Courthouse trial, 167–168, 227; HF's speeches for, 121, 242, 283; HF's support of, 297; and Martinsville Seven, 228; and McGee, 226–227, 229; and Peekskill, New York, anti-Communist riots, 128, 184–185, 186, 190; and Rosenberg case, 253; and Trenton Six, 226

Civil Service Commissions, 123–124, 132

Civil War, 21, 62

Clansman, The (Dixon), 66

Clark, Joseph, 330

Clark, Tom, 164

class. *See* social class

Cleveland, Grover, 115

Clinton, Bill, 397

Cobb, Lee J., 344

Cocteau, Jean, 254

Cohen, Isaac, 32–33

Cohn, Roy, 251, 265–266, 269, 270–271, 455n9

Cold War: and American Communist Party, 107; and American literature, 194–195; and anti-Communist sentiment, 132, 284; and Churchill's "Iron Curtain" speech, 109; easing of, 301–306; and Foley Square Courthouse trial, 164; HF on, 281; and HF's radicalism, 4, 107, 128, 141; and Jewish Anti-Fascist Committee, 176; Schlesinger on, 420n55; Shostakovich on, 172; and Stalin, 86; trials of, 245; and Truman, 123, 163; and U.S. civil liberties, 223

Cole, Lester, 51, 462n11

Columbia Pictures, 136, 139, 427n22

Columbia University, 53, 109, 137, 138, 140, 225, 261–262, 421n88

Commager, Henry Steele, 116–117

Commentary, 74, 150–151, 271

Committee for Cultural Freedom, 439n18

Committee of the Arts and Sciences for the Re-election of FDR, 77

Committee to Defend Trachtenberg, 256

Communism: anti-fascism equated with, 108; as economic failure in Soviet Union, 425n62; HF's association of Jewishness with, 149; HF's public denunciation of, 8; and Jewish identity, 250; and Nazism, 70; New Deal compared to, 31; and proletarian literature, 23; and Spanish Civil War, 3; and Twentieth Party Congress, 313; and utopianism, 3, 59, 115, 116. *See also* American Communist Party (CPUSA); anti-Communist sentiment

Communist Control Act of 1954, 284, 295, 444n29

Communist Party Training School, 109–110

Communist Political Association (CPA), 69, 77, 85, 304

"Communist-front" organizations: and

FBI, 61, 110, 114; HF as member of, 114, 117, 118; HF speaking for, 77, 243; list of, 123; and New Deal liberals, 132

Congress of Cultural Freedom, 439n18

Congress of Industrial Organizations (CIO), 301, 415n51

Conrad, Joseph, 121, 210

Conroy, Jack, 287, 410n44, 411n71

Contemporary Jewish Record, 74

Contemporary Writers, 117

Copland, Aaron, 23, 169

Coplon, Judith, 183

Coronet, 61, 77, 79, 81

Cosmopolitan magazine, 12

Coughlin, Charles, 31

Counterattack, 131, 236

Cowan, Louis, 60–61

Cowley, Malcolm, 42

Crane, Stephen, 29, 35, 194, 278, 339

Crawford, Joan, 18

Crossfire (film), 122

Crown Publishers, 336, 342

Cuban Missile Crisis, 349

Cultural and Scientific Conference for World Peace. *See* Waldorf World Peace Conference

Cultural Committee for Freedom, 286

Cunningham, E. V. (pseudonym), Fast's mysteries, 8, 343, 345, 346, 355, 359, 366, 367, 370, 379, 399, 472n24

Curtis, Tony, 467n31

Czechoslovakia, 159, 169, 231, 253, 254, 263, 297, 429n57

Da Silva, Howard, 258, 452n43

Daily Compass, 168, 452n41

Daily Worker: and Foley Square Courthouse trial, 168; and Gates, 32, 158, 304; and *The Hammer,* 218; HF writing for, 108–109, 117, 145, 147, 162, 203, 229, 246, 296, 298, 304–306, 307, 308–309, 312, 313, 449n6; and HF's election campaign, 260; and HF's Indiana

University experience, 91; and HF's release from prison, 215; and Hungarian revolution, 314–315; and Indian famine, 88; IRS raid on, 303–304; and *Literature and Reality,* 192, 195; and Odets, 413n8; on Peekskill, New York, anti-Communist riots, 187; and *The Proud and the Free,* 220; and Rosenberg case, 252–253; and Sillen, 77; and Starobin, 319–320

Dark Horse (film), 18, 408n24

Dark Stain, The (Appel), 64

Dark Sunday (film), 343

Daughters of the American Revolution, 123

Davis, Benjamin, Jr., 89, 134, 157, 163, 326

Davis, Bette, 345

Davis, Elmer, 45

Davis, Ossie, 375

Davis, Sammy, Jr., 348

Dayan, Moshe, 374

Debs, Eugene V., 115

Deep River (Buckmaster), 64

Deer Park, The (Mailer), 381

DeJong, M. A., 323

DeMille, Cecile B., 240

Democratic Party: and progressivism, 123, 158; and reforms of capitalism, 57; segregationist faction of, 157; successes of, 285; and U.S. Jewish community, 251. *See also* New Deal

Dennis, Eugene: and American Communist Party leadership, 85, 86, 304, 312, 313, 314, 319, 327, 332; arrest of, 157, 163; and contempt of Congress, 124, 168; and Foley Square Courthouse trial, 164, 165, 166, 168; HF's meeting with, 88; and HF's personal crisis, 312; and Khrushchev's speech, 303; as Soviet spy, 433n4

Dennis, Peggy, 303

Der Tog, 252

Dewey, John, 277, 331

Dial Press, 22

Disney, Walt, 18

Dixon, Thomas, Jr., 66

Dobbs, Farrell, 167

Doherty, Dennis, 441n54

Dollinger, Isidore, 261

Donne, John, 201

Donnelly, Clarence W., 117–119

Dos Passos, John: and American Writers Association, 134; HF on, 78, 93, 121; prohibition in Soviet Union, 142; and reality of Great Depression, 24, 410n45; on Spanish Civil War, 32; and Waldorf World Peace Conference, 170

Dostoevsky, Fyodor, 121

Doubleday, 236, 241

Douglas, Helen Gahagan, 113

Douglas, Kirk, 249, 340–342, 343, 369, 401, 467n28

Douglas, Paul, 116, 295

Douglas, William O., 277

Douglass, Frederick, 319

Dreier, Mary, 153

Dreiser, Theodore, 19, 29, 93, 193, 194, 278, 355

Du Bois, W. E. B.: Christmas party for Rosenberg sons, 255; and FBI, 448n105; and Freedom Road, 66, 417n75; and Shirley Graham, 200; HF protesting indictment of, 242; and HF's election campaign, 258; HF's publishing book of, 242; HF's relationship with, 7, 153; and HF's Stalin Prize, 293; and meeting between Stalin and Truman, 160; photograph of, 102; on Reconstruction, 62–63; as security risk, 452n43; and U.S. racial policy, 232

Duberman, Martin, 53, 179, 183, 186, 436n61

Dubinsky, David, 86

Duclos, Jacques, 85–86, 420nn54–55

Duell, Charles, 64

Duell, Sloan, and Pearce, 39, 126

Dulles, John Foster, 140, 270, 454n4

Duranty, Walter, 45

Dylan, Bob, 352, 469n64

Eagle Forgotten (Barnard), 129

Eban, Abba, 374

Ehrenburg, Ilya, 113, 436n52

Einikeit, 74

Einstein, Albert, 229, 258, 263, 452n43

Eisenhower, Dwight David, 261, 283, 284, 295, 444n29, 452n50, 454n5

Eisenstein, Sergei, 53

Eisner, Mark, 441n54

Eitingon, Leonid, 453n58

Eliot, George, 477n19

Eliot, T. S., 191

Elks magazine, 33

Ellison, Ralph, 287, 290

Ellul, Jacques, 237

Encyclopedia Judaica (EJ), 37

Engels, Friedrich, 92, 256

Ericson, Walter (pseudonym), 234

Erikson, Erik, 287

Erlich, Henryk, 58

Esquire, 61, 79, 81

Estonia, 58

Evans, Ray, 343

Evergood, Philip, 258, 445n47

Face of Fear, The (teleplay), 470n88

Fadeyev, Alexander: and antisemitism of Soviet Union, 171, 175–178; and Being Red, 176, 177, 178, 436n52; HF's relationship with, 174, 175–176, 262, 273, 292–293, 317, 337; Howe on, 171, 436n51; and Literature and Reality, 191, 439n8; and Waldorf World Peace Conference, 170, 172, 174

Fadiman, Clifton, 413n11

Farewell to Arms, A (film), 18

farm workers, 60

Farmer-Labor Party, 415n51

Farrell, James T.: HF's debate with, 280; and HF's imprisonment, 196; HF's meeting, 20; HF's opinion of, 91, 121, 463n33; HF's reading of, 19; proletarian literature of, 23; Soviet excommunication of, 320; and Waldorf World Peace Conference, 170

Farrow, Mia, 390

fascism: anti-fascism equated with Communism, 108, 119, 124, 126; Browder on, 75; HF linking Holocaust with, 247, 248, 251; HF on America as fascist state, 224, 274, 280, 285, 304; and HF on imprisonment, 198–199; and HF's characterization of Peekskill, New York, anti-Communist riots, 182, 186, 187, 188, 190; HF's commitment to fighting, 31, 42, 44, 46, 52, 53, 56, 57, 58, 61, 67, 88, 108, 143, 157, 188, 190, 227, 228; HF's equating with antisemitism, 228, 247, 248; HF's equating with racism, 227, 228, 229, 230, 232; and HF's novels, 42; and Popular Front, 415n51; progressivism versus, 32; Robeson's commitment to fighting, 54; and Smith-Mundt Act, 143–144; Soviet Union's antifascist military success, 4, 56–57; spread of, 31–32; and World War II, 47

Fast, Arthur, 12

Fast, Barbara, 213

Fast, Barnett (Barney), 12–14, 16, 17, 22, 41

Fast, Barry, 213, 281–282

Fast, Ben, 385

Fast, Bette Cohen: and American Communist Party, 60; art of, 33, 37, 367, 376, 387, 392; death of, 392–393; design work of, 297; health of, 390–391; and HF as war correspondent, 79, 81, 83–84, 207; HF's early relationship with, 25–26, 27, 31, 32–33; and HF's

headaches, 156; and HF's imprisonment, 197, 198, 201–204, 205, 207–208, 210, 211, 212–215; and HF's infidelity, 9, 34, 49, 84, 180–181, 203, 208, 256, 282, 343–344, 368–369, 376, 387, 388, 403; and HF's radical activism, 147; and HF's rejections by publishing houses, 233; Jewish sensibility of, 37; joining synagogue, 337; marriage of, 33–34, 50, 54, 84, 181, 182, 202–203, 207–208, 256, 311, 375–376, 387, 462n11; in Mexico, 293–294; miscarriage of, 41, 44; Paris trip of, 181–182, 198; photographs of, *100, 101, 102, 104, 105;* pregnancies of, 54, 60; and renunciation of American Communist Party, 325; and Sartre, 89; and Stalin portrait, 296; and Stalinism, 273; and television, 289; and World War II work for Signal Corps, 44–45, 49–51

Fast, David, 385

Fast, Dotty, 213

Fast, Edward, 14

Fast, Howard: on aging, 364, 365, 376; ambition of, 44, 52, 57, 62, 71, 88–89, 113, 139, 161, 244, 320, 333; on art and politics, 78, 92–93, 95–96, 191–196, 218–219, 235, 290; and attributions and plagiarism, 129, 130, 136, 256, 277, 279, 417n75, 426n72; on capitalism, 90, 96, 107, 116; childhood of, 1–2, 4, 12–17, 24, 29, 33, 55, 362; on Christianity, 36, 127, 210; and civil liberties, 75, 76–77, 118, 223, 224, 225, 231, 423n35, 427n12; and counterculture, 351–352; death of, 37, 401; education of, 2, 15, 16, 18, 19–20, 71, 109–110; and electoral politics, 8, 244, 257–261, 387, 452n41; embellishment of experiences of, 421n72; as father, 62, 255–256, 260, 280, 281–282, 288–289, 295–296, 300, 311–312, 344, 349–350, 360, 362, 470n90; financial condition of, 1–2, 8,

9, 12–18, 20, 33–34, 37, 38, 39–41, 52, 54–55, 139–140, 242, 266, 297–298, 328, 342, 370, 375, 386–387; health of, 12, 156, 205–206, 256, 257, 281, 293–294, 298, 299, 300, 308, 311, 345, 350, 355, 364, 365, 366, 399, 400, 442n64, 462n3; on Holocaust, 63, 224, 228, 444n27; and imprisonment, 7, 12, 75, 113, 124, 136, 142–143, 155, 162, 189, 196, 197–207, 209–216, 277, 284, 293, 295, 300; on Jewish-American literature, 357; Jewishness of, 2, 3, 9, 15–16, 37, 43, 73–75, 80, 84, 150, 152, 211; and Judaism, 36–38, 41, 127, 239, 318, 336, 338, 355, 402; on labor, 108–109, 138, 242–243; marriages of, 9, 33–34, 50, 54, 84, 181, 182, 202–203, 207–208, 256, 311, 375–376, 387, 462n11; and Marxism, 1, 4, 21, 35–36, 71, 96, 110, 126, 127; in Mexico, 293–294; and modernism, 286–287, 356, 405; photographs of, *97, 98, 99, 100, 101, 102, 103, 104, 106;* physical description of, 23; as playwright, 23, 211, 232–233, 335–336, 379, 388; and Progressive Party, 159–161, 257; and pseudonym use, 8, 234–235, 343, 477n52; on public activism, 28; and racial justice, 73, 90, 109, 226, 227, 242, 317, 354–355, 422n8; reading of, 2, 17, 18, 19, 21, 29, 203, 209–210; on religion, 37, 43, 63, 152, 153, 298–299, 318; as secularist, 3, 36, 37; and sexuality, 9, 18–19, 20, 137, 156, 180, 282, 311, 387–388; on Stalinism, 4, 93, 177, 273, 283, 333; and teaching, 91, 136–137, 140, 205, 206–207, 245, 282; temperament of, 26, 38–39, 50, 71, 149, 197, 402–403; as utopian, 59, 115, 116; on violence, 16, 65, 127, 152, 153, 239, 318, 338; will of, 402; and women, 34, 136–137, 140–141, 372, 383, 389–390; as writer, 2, 4, 5–9, 12, 17, 19–20, 22–30, 34, 37, 44,

244, 290, 324, 403–404, 409n38; on writing, 24–25, 27, 28–29, 30, 33, 37, 40, 52, 121, 128, 333, 355, 367, 368; on Zionism, 337

Fast, Howard, works of: *Agrippa's Daughter,* 338–339, 357; *Alice* (Cunningham), 345; *Amanda* (Cunningham), 367; *The Ambassador,* 366, 367, 376; *The American,* 6, 114–117, 126, 128–129, 131, 136, 174, 279, 290, 333; *April Morning,* 8, 339–340, 344, 359, 361, 393, 404, 405, 466n20, 473n58; "Art as a Weapon," 95; *The Assassin Who Gave Up His Gun,* 359; *The Battle,* 390; *The Bridge Builder's Story,* 393–394, 397; *The Children,* 15, 24, 25, 26, 27–28, 29, 30, 34, 409n38, 467n22; "Christ in Cuernavaca," 282, 299; *Clarkton,* 5–6, 126–128, 130, 278, 279, 290, 333, 425n58; *The Coat of Many Colors* (Behn), 477n52; *Conceived in Liberty,* 34, 35–36, 42, 43, 69, 115, 266, 278, 299, 405, 411n85; *The Confession of Joe Cullen,* 381–382, 388; *The Crossing,* 335–336, 344, 360; *Cynthia* (Cunningham), 359; *David and Paula,* 369; "The Departure," 433n1; *The Departure and Other Stories,* 137, 211, 432n1; "A Dialogue for Unity," 242; *The Dinner Party,* 379–380, 381, 382; *Edge of Tomorrow,* 467n22; "An Epigraph for Sidney," 431n78; *The Establishment,* 375; *Fallen Angel,* 234, 346; *The General Zapped an Angel,* 359; "The Gentle Virtue," 137; *George Washington and the Water Witch,* 335; *Goethals and the Panama Canal,* 41; *Green Goods* (Cunningham), 366; *Greenwich,* 399; *The Hammer,* 211–212, 215, 216–219, 233, 291, 443n2, 443n6; *Haym Solomon,* 41, 357; *Helen* (Cunningham), 346; *The Hessian,* 8, 359–361, 363, 366, 393, 404, 405;

The Hill, 348; "The Holy Child," 282, 299; *The Hunter*, 355; *The Immigrants*, 2, 8, 367, 370–374, 376, 380, 395, 404, 472n32; *The Immigrant's Daughter*, 378; "The Impenetrable Curtain of Lies," 243, 449n108; *In the Beginning* (Behn), 477n52; *The Incredible Tito*, 119–120; *An Independent Woman*, 395, 396; *The Jews*, 357–358; "The Large Ant," 340; *The Last Frontier*, 2, 38–41, 50, 67, 96, 136, 142, 150, 297, 334, 401, 405, 412n99, 478n25; "The Last Supper," 282, 299; *The Last Supper and Other Stories*, 245, 298; *The Legacy*, 376, 377; *Life and Literature in the Left Lane*, 2; *Literature and Reality*, 191–196, 211, 439n8; *Lola Gregg*, 6, 290–291, 298, 334, 459n17; *Lord Baden-Powell of the Boy Scouts*, 41; *Lydia* (Cunningham), 345; "Marxism and Literature," 121, 136; *Max*, 376; *Moses*, 8, 336–337, 338, 342, 357; "My Decision," 317–320, 335; *My Glorious Brothers*, 2, 6, 7, 148–156, 205, 241, 334, 337, 357, 374, 377, 405, 430n64, 430n72, 431n87, 431n89, 431n91; *The Naked God*, 18, 171, 174, 177, 329–333, 335, 336, 355, 383, 384, 385, 464n49, 465n68; "The New American Scholar," 78; "No Man Can Be Silent," 427n12; *The Novelist*, 369; "One Man's Heritage," 427n12; "Open Letter to the American People," 144; *The Outsider*, 377–379, 381; *Paper Moon*, 366; *The Passion of Sacco and Vanzetti*, 6, 244, 246, 276–279, 290, 334, 456n31; *The Patriarchs* (Behn), 477n52; *Peekskill, USA*, 188, 228, 297; *Phyllis* (Cunningham), 345, 346, 468n49; *Place in the City*, 29, 30, 33; *The Pledge*, 381, 382, 390; *Power*, 349, 466n17; "The Price of Liberty," 157; *The Proud and the Free*, 204, 211, 219–222, 233, 234, 290, 334, 366, 444n20; "Rachel," 139; *Redemption*, 398–399; *A Reveille for Writers*, 120; *The Romance of a People*, 37–38, 73, 357; *Sally* (Cunningham), 355, 470n88; *Samantha* (Cunningham), 346, 355, 379, 472n24; "Save the Rosenbergs," 250; *The Second Generation*, 370, 375; *Seven Days in June*, 393; *Shirley* (Cunningham), 345; *Silas Timberman*, 6, 245, 282, 290, 291, 292, 296, 334; "The Singularity of Being Jewish," 37, 293, 399, 476n52; "Stockade," 26–27; *Strange Yesterday*, 4, 22–23, 30; *Sylvia* (Cunningham), 343, 345, 390, 470n88; *The Tall Hunter*, 41; *Thirty Pieces of Silver*, 232–233, 291; "Thirty Pieces of Silver," 433n1; *Time and the Riddle*, 376; *Tito and His People*, 77; *Tony and the Wonderful Door*, 244, 254–255, 451n33; *Torquemada*, 338, 339, 357; *The Trap*, 355; *The Trial of Abigail Goodman*, 389; *Triptych*, 473n54; *21 Hours in Munich*, 367; *Two Valleys*, 4, 22–23, 30; *The Unvanquished*, 2, 41–43, 55, 69, 83, 115, 266, 334, 335, 339, 405, 406; "The Upraised Pinion," 298; "Walk Home," 298; "The Way for a Nation," 423n35; "What I Want for My Country in 1954," 292; "Where Are Your Guns?," 431n78; *The Winston Affair*, 8, 338, 346. See also *Being Red* (Fast); *Citizen Tom Paine* (Fast); *Freedom Road* (Fast); *Spartacus* (Fast)

Fast, Ida (Miller), 12–13, 14

Fast, Jenny, 14–15

Fast, Jerome (Jerry): caring for father, 41; death of, 364, 366; and HF's childhood, 1, 12, 13–19; and HF's imprisonment, 213; HF's visits with, 27, 281; and HF's writing, 22; jobs of, 19, 20; and television, 288

Fast, Jonathan: birth of, 147; childhood of, 282; on HF's Communism, 358; and HF's competitiveness, 350, 362; and HF's election campaign, 260; and HF's funeral, 401; and HF's generosity, 473n46; and HF's headaches, 156; and HF's health, 400; and HF's imprisonment, 197, 198, 208, 212; and HF's infidelity, 180, 343, 368, 468n39; HF's letters to, 280; and HF's paranoia, 131, 426n2; on HF's politics, 440n32; and HF's singing, 468n47, 470n85; in Mexico, 294; and molestation, 311; and music, 350–351, 469n61; opera composed with HF, 469n6; photograph of, *105;* relationship with HF as adult, 362–363, 369; and *Spartacus* filming, 341; and television, 288; and Vietnam War, 360; writing of, 367

Fast, Judith, 281, 282

Fast, Julius (Julie): in armed forces, 44, 46; autobiographical novel of, 409n25; birth of, 13; and HF's childhood, 16; and HF's infidelity, 180, 207, 213; HF's relationship with, 212, 213, 377; jobs of, 19; with maternal grandmother, 14; writing of, 212–213

Fast, Melissa, 377

Fast, Mercedes (Mimi) O'Connor: and *Clarkton,* 128; and Foley Square Courthouse trial, 434n24; and HF's literary rights, 402; HF's relationship with, 9, 395–399, 400, 401

Fast, Rena, 12, 13, 14, *103,* 377

Fast, Sam, 14, 23

Fast Ben-Avi, Rachel Ann: birth of, 62; childhood of, 255, 282, 390; and Jerry Fast's death, 364; on FBI investigations, 131, 197; on Heller, 352; and HF as war correspondent, 79; as HF's editor, 348; and HF's election campaign, 260; and HF's funeral, 402; and HF's gift of Stalin portrait, 295–296; on HF's headaches, 156, 281, 294, 311, 350; and HF's imprisonment, 197, 198, 204, 212, 213–214; and HF's infidelity, 180, 213, 468n39; and HF's interest in civil rights, 349; on HF's knowledge of Soviet Union, 331; HF's letters to, 280; and HF's politics, 197, 198, 440n32; and McCarthy hearings, 267; in Mexico, 293, 294; and mother's death, 392; on parents' marriage, 208; photographs of, *100, 102, 106;* on Polevoy, 300; relationship with HF as adult, 362–363, 365, 366, 369; on Robeson, 179–180, 310–311; and *Spartacus* filming, 341; and television, 288–289

Faulkner, William, 25, 121, 142, 146, 229, 304, 404

Federal Bureau of Investigation (FBI): and anti-Communist crusade, 108; and banning of *Citizen Tom Paine,* 135, 136; and Blitzstein, 293; and "Communist-front" organizations, 61, 110, 114; and destruction of social writing, 286; and Du Bois, 448n105; and Einstein, 452n43; extralegal operations of, 159; film investigations, 123; and *Freedom Road,* 165–166; and HF as Communist, 358, 470n83; and HF as security risk, 222, 247; HF questioned by, 325–327, 328, 340; and HF's association with Wallace, 78–79; and HF's blacklisting, 233, 237; and HF's denunciation of America, 69–70; HF's dossier, 12, 21, 61, 77, 109, 130, 164, 407n2, 445n52; and HF's imprisonment, 206; and HF's inability to obtain passport, 61; and HF's marriage, 208, 442n71; and HF's royalties, 448n100; and Jefferson School of Social Science, 141; and Little, Brown, 234, 236, 446n66; and Nelson, 449n2; and surveillance of HF, 77, 130–131, 197, 230, 447n92

Feffer, Itzak, 56, 171, 175–179, 254, 262, 330, 437n63
Feiffer, Jules, 450n15
Feinberg Law, 247–248, 450n12
Fellowship, 353
Fellowship of Reconciliation, 360, 469n68
Ferber, Edna, 477n19
Ferlinghetti, Lawrence, 288, 290
Ferrer, Jose, 111–112
Feuchtwanger, Lion, 418n14
Fiedler, Leslie, 249, 356–357
film noir, 287
Filreis, Alan, 391
Finland, 58
Fisk, Jim, 115
Fitzgerald, F. Scott, 8
Flexner, Eleanor, 140
Flynn, Elizabeth Gurley, 70, 430n61
Focus (Miller), 431n83
Foley, Martha, 410n58
Foley Square Courthouse trial: and American Communist Party, 162, 163–168, 175; HF's coverage of, 165, 167, 168, 434n24; jury for, 163–164; and Peekskill concert, 182
Folks-Stimme, 304, 316, 337
Fonda, Jane, 367
Foner, Philip, 140, 153, 236, 270, 447n78
Foote, Angela, 394, 395
For Whom the Bell Tolls (film), 62
Ford, John, 400–401
Fordham College, 225
Foreign Agents Registration Act, 242
Forrestal, James, 140
Fortune magazine, 316
Forward, 252
Foster, William: and American Communist Party leadership, 85, 86, 304, 313, 315, 319, 321, 326; anti-intellectualism of, 308, 420n61, 428n37; apology of, 312; arrest of, 157, 163; and Foley Square Courthouse trial, 165; HF's

admiration for, 70, 85, 86; and Maltz, 421n72; and revolutionary social change, 86, 165, 434n11; and Soviet Union, 302
Fountain, Lee, *106*, 392, 394
Franco, Francisco, 32, 110, 245
Frank, Jerome, 250
Frankel, Max, 264, 453n66
Frankfurter, Felix, 277, 279, 456n31
Franklin, Benjamin, 319
free speech: and anti-Communist sentiment, 132; and book banning, 135; and Foley Square Courthouse trial, 167, 168; HF on, 75, 76–77, 118, 247, 423n35, 427n12; and HF's speeches on college campuses, 137–138, 140, 225–226, 230; and Internal Security Act, 224; and McCarthyism, 75, 108; and Schlesinger, 133
Freedom Road (Fast): American Communist Party members' encouragement of HF's writing of, 63; American Communist Party's negative reaction to, 5, 68–69, 70, 72, 327; in anthology, 467n22; black dialect in, 70, 417n84; and black-Jewish vision, 64–65; and bravery, 279; FBI analysis of, 165–166; film rights to, 139, 342, 366; and Foley Square Courthouse trial, 165; Hammett on, 66–67, 72; and HF on violence, 65; and HF's use of Du Bois's work, 66, 417n75; and HF's view of America, 73, 115, 266; HF's writing for Robeson, 62, 416n57; HF's writing of, 44, 56, 62, 63; in India, 84; legacy of, 405; as moral fable, 290; Nelson on, 449n9; paperback edition of, 340; politics in, 406, 478n25; and racial justice, 63, 66, 67–70, 267; reviews of, 67, 68, 72, 240, 417n81; and Sartre, 89; and socialist ideal of human perfectibility, 65–66; success of, 2, 139, 174, 241, 439n8; television rights

for, 375; use of word "nigger" in, 5, 70, 220

Freeman, Devery, 21–22, 25–26, 51, 325, 343

French Communist Party, 85, 227, 253, 322–323

French resistance, Sartre's role in, 89, 90

Freud, Sigmund, 9, 192, 193, 234, 241, 305, 356

Front Page, The (film), 408n24

Frost, Robert, 25, 304

Fuentes, Carlos, 405

Fuller, Edmund, 150

Galbraith, John Kenneth, 287

Gallico, Paul, 162

Gandhi, Mohandis, 83

Gang, Martin, 401

Gannett, Lewis, 135

Garroway, Dave, 289, 324–325

Gates, John, 32, 158, 163, 167, 303–304, 312, 319

Gentleman's Agreement (film), 122, 152

Gentleman's Agreement (Hobson), 152, 431n83

German-Soviet Boundary and Friendship Treaty, 415n43

Germany, 31, 42. *See also* Hitler, Adolf; Nazism

Gershwin, George, 249

Gerstein, Louis, 434n29

Gide, André, 221

Gilbert, Arthur, 353

Gilbert, John, 392

Giles, Barbara, 136

Ginsberg, Alan, 288, 290, 441n54

Gitlin, Murray, 73

Gitlow, Benjamin, 149

Glamour, 140

Glazer, Nathan, 55

God That Failed, The, 331

Goethals, George Washington, 41

Gold, Michael, 94, 287, 357, 391, 410n44, 421n72

Goldburg, Robert E., 241, 377–378

Goldsborough (Heym), 242

Goldwyn, Samuel, 249

Gone with the Wind (film), 66

Gone with the Wind (Mitchell), 34, 66

Goodman, Benny, 249

Goodman, Robert (Bobby), 181, 282

Gordimer, Nadine, 405

Gordon, Leonovich, 177, 273

Gordon, Ruth, 112

Gorky, Maxim, 273, 291

Gould, Jay, 115

Grace, Barbara Aileen, 385

Graetz, Solomon, 37

Graham, Martha, 23

Graham, Shirley, *102,* 153, 200, 293, 441n43

Grapes of Wrath, The (Steinbeck), 146

Grapes of Wrath, The (film), 146

Great Depression: and antisemitism, 55; and Dos Passos, 24, 410n45; and fascism, 31; films of, 18, 409n24; and HF's childhood, 2, 4; and HF's reading, 35; and Hollywood lifestyle, 51; and Popular Front, 60; and proletarian literature, 23–24; public welfare compared to, 386; and socialism, 20

Greeley, Horace, 121

Green, Gil, 163, 257

Greenberg, Clement, 356, 450n15

Greenberg, Hank, 248–249

Greene, Grahame, 355

Greenwich Time, 393, 397

Grenough, Paul, 419n38

Gribachev, N., 336

Griffith, D. W., 66

Gropper, William, 23, 142, 143, 228, 270, 444n27

Guthrie, Woody, 184

Hall, Gus, 167, 257

Hall, Robert, 152, 153

Hammett, Dashiell: and Bette Fast, 181; and Foley Square Courthouse trial, 163; and *Freedom Road,* 66–67, 72; and HF's imprisonment, 200; HF's posting bail for, 242; and Jefferson School of Social Science, 140; prison sentence of, 231; private-eye tradition of, 346; and Voice of America libraries, 270; and Waldorf World Peace Conference, 169

Handlin, Oscar, 117

Harap, Louis, 319

Harper's Bazaar, 73

Hart, Moss, 450n15

Harvard University, 280

Hawthorne, Nathaniel, 27, 193, 194

Hayden, Tom, 367–368

Haym Solomon and the Revolution (Russell), 129, 426n72

Haymarket Riot of 1886, 114

Haynes, John Earl, 419n54

Hays, Lee, 328

Healy, Timothy, 474n73

Hebrew Publishing Company, 36–37, 38

Hegel, Georg, 87–88

Hellenic American Brotherhood of the International Workers Order, 170–171

Heller, Joseph, 352

Hellman, Lillian, 66–67, 72, 89, 169, 195, 236, 428n37

Hemingway, Ernest: classic works of, 361; films based on works of, 18, 62; HF on, 78, 121; and HF's imprisonment, 196, 201; Howe on, 304; prohibition in Soviet Union, 142; Soviet excommunication of, 320; on Spanish Civil War, 32

Herbst, Josephine, 23, 411n71

Hersey, John, 153, 196

Hessian, The (film), 8, 359–361

Heym, Gertrude, 448n104

Heym, Stefan: HF publishing novel of, 297; HF's relationship with, 7, 154, 242, 275, 304, 313–314, 315, 324, 431n86, 460n25; on HF's stories, 299

Hicks, Granville, 40

Hikmet, Nazim, 202

Hillman, Sidney, 86

Himes, Chester, 136, 195, 196

Himmelfarb, Milton, 150–151

Hindemith, Paul, 172

Hiss, Alger, 140, 163, 433n2

History of the Jews (Graetz), 37

Hitler, Adolf: and ethnic killing campaigns, 195, 437n63; expansionist goals of, 415n51; HF's comparison of American propaganda to, 158; HF's comparison of Feinberg Law to, 248; HF's comparison of IRS to, 304; HF's comparison of Smith-Mundt Act to, 144; HF's comparison of U.S. denial of rights to, 223, 229; and HF's comparison to Rosenberg case, 252, 253; Nuremberg laws of, 148; and pact with Stalin, 3, 57, 58, 69, 119, 305, 415n43; and Popular Front, 416n51; Stalin compared to, 309

Hobson, Laura, 152, 431n83

Hollywood: and American Communist Party, 3, 51–52, 56, 57, 122–123, 320; and anti-Communist films, 122; and *Citizen Tom Paine* as film, 50–51; HF's desire to work in, 62, 88, 146, 344–345; HF's income from, 25; and HF's work as screenwriter, 9; and U.S. Jewish community, 249

Hollywood blacklist: and Bright, 51; and *Spartacus,* 8, 342, 467n33

Hollywood Ten, 11, 51, 53, 95, 143, 157, 196, 440n22

Holmes, Oliver Wendell, Jr., 166

Holocaust: and *The Bridge Builder's Story,* 394; HF linking fascism with, 247, 248, 251; HF on, 63, 224, 228, 444n27; and Jewish Anti-Fascist Committee,

176; and Lemkin, 232; survivors of, 249

homosexuals and homosexuality: and American Communist Party, 428n37; and Blitzstein, 293; and loyalty boards, 123; and Matthiessen, 190, 439n4; and *Spartacus* film, 342, 467n31; and *The Winston Affair,* 338

Hook, Sidney, 331, 455n13

Hoover, J. Edgar: and American Communist Party members, 61; on ex-Communists, 340; and habeas corpus, 223, 444n25; and HF's dossier, 12, 130, 293; and HF's playwriting, 446n62; and HF's resignation from American Communist Party, 325–326, 327; and HF's screenwriting, 401; informants for, 206; and Little, Brown, 236; and Julius Rosenberg's arrest, 223; and television, 289

Horne, Lena, 23

Hostages (film), 51

Hourglass, The (Alman), 64

House Committee on Un-American Activities (HUAC): and American Communist Party, 76; and anti-Communist sentiment, 56, 76, 122, 124, 132; and Anti-Defamation League, 250; Broadway theater investigation, 461n55; Bryan's testimony, 112; and Cobb, 344; and "Communist-front" organizations, 114; and contempt citations, 112–113, 122, 124–125, 130, 136, 138, 139, 144, 156–157, 189, 423n17; decline of, 301; HF's fear of being recalled by, 293; HF's hearing postponed by, 329; HF's speeches against, 113, 121; HF's subpoena for, 7, 11, 110, 111; and HF's work on Tito, 119–120; HF's writing on, 120–121; Hollywood investigations of, 51; and investigation of higher education, 137, 138; and Joint Anti-Fascist Refugee Committee (JAFRC), 110–112, 113, 120, 122, 124–125, 143, 144–145, 156–157, 178, 189; and Maltz, 125; and red-baiting, 426n8; and reputation of Congress, 133; Rogge's attacks on, 124; rumors of new investigation of HF, 234; unconstitutional behavior of, 159

Houseman, John, 28, 45

Howe, Irving: as anti-Stalinist Socialist, 57, 170; on artists' lack of political involvement, 285; on Fadeyev, 171, 436n51; HF's presentation with, 315; on HF's style of thought, 333; as literary critic, 472n31; and socialism, 356; and Soviet extermination of Jews, 304; on Wallace, 160

Huckleberry Finn (Twain), 194

Hughes, Langston, 195

Hughes, Lawrence, 367

Hughes, Rupert, 134, 413n113

Humphrey, Hubert, 116, 295

Hungarian revolution, 8, 314–315, 318, 319, 326, 332

Hunter College, 138, 274

Hurston, Zora Neale, 134

Hutner, Gordon, 404

Hyman, Joe, 335

I Married a Communist (film), 122

Immigrants, The (television miniseries), 373–374

imperialism: and HF as war correspondent, 82; and HF's novels, 41; of Soviet Union, 58

Incredible Shrinking Man, The (film), 459n15

Independent, 77

Independent Citizens Committee of the Arts, Sciences, and Professions (ICC), 89, 94, 118

India, 79, 82–84, 85, 87, 88, 207

Indiana University, HF's writing workshop, 91, 136–137, 421n72

Inostrannaja literatura, 291, 300

Intelligent Woman's Guide to Socialism and Capitalism, The (George Bernard Shaw), 19

Internal Revenue Service (IRS), 303–304

International Ladies Garment Workers Union, 158

International Publishers, 77, 256

Invasion of the Body Snatchers, The (film), 289–290

Invisible Man (Ellison), 287

Iron Curtain (film), 122

Iron Heel (London), 19

Isacson, Leo, 258

Israel: and Kirk Douglas, 342; HF's advocacy of, 147, 258, 260, 337, 353–354, 452n52; and HF's imprisonment, 201; HF's visit to, 374; and Jewish Anti-Fascist Committee, 176; and *My Glorious Brothers,* 148–149, 150, 151–152, 154, 374, 430n64; and U.S. Jewish community, 249. *See also* Zionism

Italy, 31

It's a Wonderful Life (film), 123

Izakov, Boris, 279, 291, 292, 299–300, 301, 320–321, 324

J. P. Morgan and Company, 260

Jackson, Esther Cooper, 465n1

Jackson, Henry M., 265

Jackson, James, 335, 465n1

James, William, 121

Jamison, Hallie, 18

Japan, and fascism, 31, 42

Japanese-Americans, World War II incarceration of, 40, 79

Jefferson, Thomas, 310, 319

Jefferson School of Social Science (JSSS), 140–141, 242, 245, 282

Jens, Salome, 368

Jerome, Alice, 230

Jerome, V. J.: arrest of, 234; and Cultural Section of American Communist Party, 68, 141, 177, 219–220, 230; HF on, 391–392; HF's posting bail for, 231, 242; and status of Jews in Soviet Union, 178

Jesus: in *Citizen Tom Paine,* 127, 278; HF's view of, 36, 152, 209, 210, 238–239, 277, 278–279, 298–299, 310, 318, 336, 347–348, 358, 401–402

Jewish Anti-Fascist Committee (JAFC), 56, 58, 176–177, 178, 437n63

Jewish Book Council (JBC), 155–156, 431n89

Jewish Currents, 478n25

Jewish Foundation of Israel, 377

Jewish identity: and HF's Jewishness, 2, 3, 9, 15–16, 37, 43, 73–75, 80, 84, 150, 152, 211, 250, 336, 337–338, 353, 356–357, 358, 359, 393, 401; Marx on, 74–75; Miller on, 431n83; opposing versions of, 150; and radical activism, 10, 63, 150, 157, 250, 251; and Rosenberg case, 242

Jewish Life, 151, 156, 252, 319, 431n78

Jewish Peace Fellowship (JPF), 353, 360, 377

Jewish People's Fraternal Order, 250

Jewish Reform and Reconstructionist liturgy, 418n9

Jewish Socialist Bund, in Poland, 58

Jewish Theological Seminary (JTS), 157

Jewish Workmen's Circle, 218

Jewish Writers and Artists, 61, 73–74

Jews: blacks' interaction with, 63–65, 354; as Communists, 55, 58; divisions concerning Rosenberg case, 250; extermination during World War II, 42–43, 63, 148, 153, 248; Nazi extermination of, 63, 148, 153; Soviet extermination of, 304–305; as teachers, 248, 450n12; U.S. community of, 248–250, 450n15. *See also* antisemitism; Holocaust; Jewish identity; Judaism; Zionism

Jigsaw (film), 346
Jim Crow laws, 62
John Day, 25
John Reed Club, 12, 21, 28, 61, 121
Johnson, Arno, 138
Johnson, Isabel, HF's relationship with,
    140–141, 180–181, 202, 203, 207, 237,
    282, 311, 462n11
Johnson-Reed Act (1924), 15
Joint Anti-Fascist Refugee Committee
    (JAFRC): and "Deadline for Freedom"
    rallies, 440n22; HF's board member-
    ship, 7, 11–12, 110–111, 125; HF's resig-
    nation from, 205; and HUAC investiga-
    tion, 110–112, 113, 120, 122, 124–125,
    143, 144–145, 156–157, 178, 189; prison
    sentences of, 196, 198–199; and Walter
    B. Cannon Memorial Hospital, 174
Joint Distribution Committee, 176, 177,
    337
Joliot-Curie, Frederic, 154, 181
Joliot-Curie, Irene, 181
Jones, James Earl, 217, 218, 242, 443n2
Jong, Erica, *105*, 181, 282, 368, 369–370,
    385, 468n46
Jong-Fast, Molly: and *Being Red,* 385;
    The Establishment dedicated to, 375;
    on Bette Fast, 387; on Mimi Fast, 395,
    398; on Hammett, 181; HF on *New
    York Times,* 397; on HF's driving, 282;
    on HF's funeral, 401; on HF's legacy,
    404; on HF's will, 402; on Neruda,
    202; photograph of, *105*
Jouvenal, Renaud de, 126–127, 143,
    145–146, 173, 175, 275, 322–323
Joyce, James, 24, 49, 50, 121, 356
Judaism: and HF, 36–38, 41, 127, 239,
    318, 336, 338, 355, 402; in India, 84;
    and Jewish American Communists,
    63. *See also* Jews
Judt, Tony, 91

Kadar, Ján, 375

Kafka, Franz, 191
Kahlo, Frida, 254
Kahn, Albert, 231, 236
Kahn, Alice, 473n46
Kahn, Gordon, 259, 293, 452n43
Kahn, Roger, 473n46
Kandinsky, Wassily, 356
Kanin, Fay, 343
Kanin, Mike, 343
Kantor, MacKinlay, 195
Kantorowicz, Alfred, 229
Kaplan, Helen, 360
Kaplan, Judith, 197
Kaplan, Mordecai M., 169, 434n29
Karl Marx Society, 225
Kaufman, Irving, 242, 250, 251–252, 262,
    265, 277
Kautsky, Karl, 210
Kazan, Elia, 46, 52
Kazin, Alfred, 249, 285, 472n31
Kennedy, John F., 295, 349, 368
Kent, Rockwell, 7, 23, 160, 231, 258,
    430n61, 445n47, 461n45
Kent, Simon (pseudonym), 234
Kermode, Frank, 472n31
Kern, Jerome, 450n15
Khrushchev, Nikita: HF on, 306, 307,
    313, 316, 317, 322, 323, 324, 326; Ken-
    nedy's face-off with, 349; revealing
    Stalin's crimes, 179, 301–302, 303, 307,
    308–309, 332, 333; "secret" denuncia-
    tion of Stalin, 8
King, Martin Luther, Jr., 310
Kipling, Rudyard, 191
Kirchwey, Freda, 274
Kirdyanov, Vladimir, 385
Kirk, Grayson, 225
Kiss Me Deadly (film), 214
Klehr, Harvey, 419n54
Klein, Maury, 408n24
Koestler, Arthur, 6, 20, 93, 127, 331,
    425n62
Konrad, George, 7

Korean War: and anti-Communist sentiment, 163; and China, 223, 225, 246; Bette Fast on, 201; and HF's imprisonment, 198, 206, 208; and HF's McCarthy hearings, 267–268; HF's opposition to, 224, 229, 247, 260, 452n50; Kaufman linking Rosenberg case to, 251–252; and McCarthyism, 271; Robeson on, 231

Kornbluth, Josh, 197–198

Kornbluth, Paul, 197–198

Krasner, Lee, 450n15

Krivitsky, Walter, 331

Ku Klux Klan, 15, 65, 66, 133

Kubrick, Stanley, 340, 341, 342, 467n30

Kudrow, Lee, 442n64

Kunitz, Joshua, 20, 409n32

Kunitz, Sarah, 20–21, 23, 24, 28, 30, 56, 409n32, 410n44

Kvitko, Layb, 171, 175, 254, 321

La Farge, Oliver, 39

La nouvelle critique, 227

labor movement: and *The American,* 114–115; and American Communist Party, 158–159; and black/Jewish relationship, 64; and *Clarkton,* 126, 127, 128; consolidation of, 301; HF writing on, 108–109, 242–243; and HF's self-publishing of *Spartacus,* 238; and HF's speeches, 138; and Jefferson School of Social Science, 140; and McCarthyism, 284; and Nelson, 245; and Popular Front, 60, 415n51; and red-baiting, 162

Lacy, Ed, 234–235, 447n70

Ladies' Home Journal, 26–27, 29, 30, 33

Lakovsky, A. B., 300

Lamont, Corliss, 231, 260

Lardner, Ring, 32

Larner, Jeremy, 315

Lateshkey, Eugene, 273

Latvia, 58

Lauter, Bob, 218

Lawson, Jeffrey, 197

Lawson, John Howard: and American Communist Party, 95; HF's relationship with, 52, 391; and Hollywood Ten, 51, 95; on Maltz, 93; and proletarian literature, 68; radical activism of, 430n61; as screenwriter, 51, 52; as target of anti-Communist sentiment, 143

Lawyer Man (film), 408n24

Le Carre, John, 359

Le Figaro, 90, 181

Le Monde, 181, 322

Le Sueur, Meridel, 297

League of American Writers, 61, 447n70

Lemkin, Raphael, 232

Lenin, Vladimir, 165, 166, 191, 256

Leninism, 86

Leontyev, B., 312

Lerner, Max, 230

Les Lettres Francaises, 145, 323

Levin, Dan, 195

Lewin, Michael, 216

Lewis, David Levering, 200–201, 417n75

Lewis, Eddie, 341

Lewis, Fulton, Jr., 134

Lewis, Jerry, 249

Lewis, Sinclair, 18, 40, 121, 196, 201, 355

Lewisohn, Ludwig, 280

L'Humanité, 253

Liberal Party, 261

liberalism: and anti-Communist sentiment, 116, 123, 132, 133; and Communism, 230, 295; and Communist Control Act, 295; and Internal Security Act, 223; and Popular Front, 31; and U.S. Jewish community, 251; and Wishengrad, 157

Liberation, 275

Liberty Book Club, 241

Liberty magazine, 30, 33

Lieber, Maxim, 259, 293, 452n43

Limon, Jose, 169

Lincoln, Abraham, 121, 319

Lippmann, Walter, 277

Literary Gazette, 261, 303, 324, 336

Lithuania, 58

Little, Brown, 148, 205, 211, 233–236, 405

Little Caesar (film), 408n24

Loeb, Phil, 427n10

London, Jack: Communist thinking influencing, 355; HF's identification with, 193, 194; HF's reading of, 17, 19, 21, 49; as socially conscious novelist, 410n44; synthesizing naturalism and realism, 287

London Observer, 302

Long, Huey, 95

Lord, Sterling, 369–370, 398

Losee, Carole, 365, 377

Lowell, Robert, 171, 172, 195

Lowenfels, Walter, 242, 245, 281, 297

Luxemburg, Rosa, 75, 210

lynchings, 15, 28, 162, 408n17

Lyons, Eugene, 149, 308–309, 310, 329

MacArthur, Douglas, 229

Macdonald, Dwight, 116, 159, 171, 172, 432n100

Macmillan, 236

Mademoiselle, 73

Mailer, Norman: HF on early career of, 25; and Jewish characters, 152; as Jewish writer, 249; and *Literature and Reality,* 195; and McCarthyism, 381; and McGee, 229; prohibition in Soviet Union, 142; subtlety of, 357; and Waldorf World Peace Conference, 169–170

Mainstream, 135

Malamud, Bernard, 249, 356, 357, 405

Malraux, Andre, 127

Maltz, Albert: on art, 91, 92, 93, 94–95, 193, 391; attacks on, 93–96, 391, 421n72; on book banning, 135, 427n18; and civil liberties, 75–76, 418n14; on

Farrell, 91; on *Freedom Road,* 72; HF's correspondence with, 11, 28, 72, 93–94, 146, 206, 226, 227, 293, 298, 301, 323; and HF's election campaign, 258; HF's relationship with, 153, 173, 192, 209, 233, 234, 237, 241, 294; and HF's writing, 244, 291; and HUAC, 125; imprisonment of, 209, 211, 227; literary credentials of, 95, 421n88; on *Literature and Reality,* 192–193; and Mexico, 293; on Moscow Show Trials, 31; and Rossen, 95; as screenwriter, 51, 52, 92, 421n88; Soviet Union's response to, 128; and Traube, 118

Man in the Middle (film), 346

Mandelstam, Osip, 330

Mann, Arthur, 340

Mann, Thomas, 373

Mao Zedong, 183

Marcantonio, Vito, 112, 138

"March on Washington Movement," 68

March on Washington of 1963, 310

Marcuse, Herbert, 287

Markish, Peretz, 171, 175, 330

Marshall Plan, 123, 128, 160, 258

Martinsville Seven, 226, 227–228, 229, 256

Marx, Groucho, 289, 450n15

Marx, Karl: on artistic creativity, 92; HF alluding to, 239; HF on, 336; and HF on socialism, 310; HF on writing of, 121; on Jewish identity, 74–75; and modernists, 356; writings of, 165, 256

Marx brothers, 18

Marxism: and art, 95; and Browder, 85; and Du Bois, 63; and Foster, 86; Gribachev on, 336; and HF's education, 110; HF's initial impressions of, 21; HF's involvement in, 1, 4, 71, 96, 341; in HF's novels, 35–36, 126, 127; and Jefferson School of Social Science, 140; and utopia, 116; Zen Buddhism as substitute for HF, 347

Marxist-Leninism: and HF's apologetics, 331, 403; HF's progressivism contrasted with, 478n25; HF's rhetoric of, 191; and Nicaragua, 382; and Soviet Union, 307; Stalin's distortion of principles of, 302

Marzani, Carl, 124, 153, 162, 255, 317

Marzani, Edith, 317

Marzani, Riki, 255

Mason, Jackie, 450n15

Masses, The (journal), 45

Masses and Mainstream: as American Communist Party journal, 429n51; and HF's election campaign, 260; HF's writing for, 144–145, 242–243, 282, 298, 317–318, 335; and *Literature and Reality,* 192; and Peekskill, New York, anti-Communist riots, 187–188; and *The Proud and the Free,* 220

Masudo, Hannah, 79, 147, 429n59

Matthiessen, F. O., 190, 438n4

Mauriac, François, 146

May Day, 228, 242

Mayer, Louis, 249

McBride, Joseph, 477n2

McCarran, Pat, 223–224

McCarran Internal Security Act, 223–224, 247, 256, 260, 444n26, 444n29

McCarthy, Cormac, 405

McCarthy, Joseph: Army-McCarthy Hearings of 1954, 269, 285; backlash against, 285; and *Being Red,* 383; chilling effect of hearings, 284; on Communists in State Department, 223, 264; criticism of Hunter College, 274; and *The Crossing,* 335; decline of, 301; on Democratic Party, 295; HF's confrontation with, 8, 244, 257, 265–268, 401; and Murrow, 285, 455n15; rise of, 163, 250, 260, 264–265; and Voice of America, 265, 269–271

McCarthy, Mary, 171–172

McCarthyism: and anti-Communist sentiment, 284; decline of, 272, 455n15; and exaggeration of Communist threat, 271; and free speech, 75, 108; and HF's consideration of pseudonym, 234; in HF's novels, 381; Macdonald on, 432n100; and Robeson, 397; and Rosenberg case, 276; Schlesinger on, 247; and social attitudes, 284–285; and television, 289; and U.S. Jewish community, 251

McCullers, Carson, 196, 202, 287, 410n58

McGee, Willie, 226, 229–230, 256, 277

McKinley, William, 115

Medeiros, Celestino, 278

Medina, Harold, 163–164, 166–167

Meiklejohn, Alexander, 75

Meir, Golda, 176–177

Meisel, Nachman, 171

Melville, Herman, 193–194

Memoirs of My People, 73

Mencken, H. L., 160, 257, 277, 287

Meredith, James, 349

Messner, Julian, 441n43

Meyers, Gerald, 185

Middle of the Journey, The (Trilling), 381

Midstream, 337, 338

Mikhoels, Solomon, 56, 175–179

Miller, Arthur, 76, 169, 195, 241, 249, 431n83

Miller, Louis, 198

Mills, C. Wright, 287

Mirage (film), 346

Mirisch, Walter, 289–290

Mitchell, Margaret, 34, 35, 66, 134

Moby Dick (Melville), 193

Monroe, Marilyn, 241, 378

Montgomery, Harry, 245, 246

Morante, Elsa, 9

Moravia, Alberto, 9

Morgan, J. P., 115

Morgen Freiheit, 142, 175, 252, 260, 298, 303, 413n8

Morning Telegraph, 413n8

Morris, Robert, 328

Morrison, Toni, 404

Morse, Wayne, 295

Moscow Literary Gazette, 141

Moscow Show Trials, 3, 31, 57, 305

Moscow State Jewish Theatre, 56

Mother (Gorky), 291

Motley, Willard, 136, 195

Mouthpiece, The (film), 408n24

Mouthpiece, The (film), 18

Mr. Smith Goes to Washington (film), 139

Mundt, Karl, 113, 143, 144, 224

Murray, Philip, 86

Murrow, Edward R., 285, 289, 455n15

Myerson, Bess, 248

Myrdal, Gunnar, 68

Nabokov, Nicolas, 172

Nabokov, Vladimir, 172

Naked and the Dead, The (Mailer), 152, 169, 195

Nation, The 31, 58, 63, 167, 274, 303

National Academy of Design, 19

National Association for the Advancement of Colored People (NAACP), 232

National Committee of Arts and Sciences, 245

National Committee to Defeat the Mundt Bill, 144

National Committee to Secure Justice in the Rosenberg Case, 253

National Council of American-Soviet Friendship, 89

National Council of Jewish Women, 259

National Council of the Arts, Sciences and Professions, 141, 263, 447n70

National Guardian, 252

Nazism: and anti-German resistance in Poland, 58; atrocities of, 37, 42, 63, 293, 378; and *The Bridge Builder's Story,* 393; capitalism compared to, 126; and Communism, 70; and

extermination of Jews, 63, 148, 153; and French intellectuals, 144; HF linking Rosenberg case with, 251; HF on, 474n65; and Luxemburg, 210; Maltz's comparison of HUAC to, 125; pact with Soviets, 3, 57, 58, 69, 119, 305, 415n43; and Popular Front, 416n51; proto-Nazi associations, 31; and Reichstag fire of 1933, 61; Soviet antisemitism compared to, 263; spread of, 42; and Truman, 259; and Voice of America broadcasts, 45

Nazi–Soviet Pact, 3, 57, 58, 69, 119, 305, 415n43

Nearing, Helen, 153, 324

Nearing, Scott, 7, 153, 293, 324, 346

Nelson, Steve: HF's relationship with, 7, 417n84, 449n9; sedition case of, 244, 245–247, 256, 283, 301, 449n2, 449n5

Neruda, Pablo, 7, 173, 191, 201, 203–204, 441n54

Nevins, Alan, 41–42

New Criticism, 286

New Currents, 61, 73

New Deal: and anti-Communist sentiment, 109, 132; and antifascism, 57; Communism in Soviet Union compared to, 31; and Jerry Fast, 213; and Foster, 86; Macdonald on, 432n100; and Popular Front, 415n51; preservation of reforms, 285; progressivism of, 116; silence of supporters, 224; and Truman, 123; U.S. Jewish community's support of, 250, 251

New Masses: and banning of HF's novels, 135; financial condition of, 121; HF as contributing editor to, 108, 110; HF writing for, 73, 75, 77, 120, 145; and *Literature and Reality,* 195; and North, 55, 88; on Pound, 76

New Playwrights, 216–217, 443n2

New Republic, 31, 42, 58

New Times, 292

New York City Board of Education, 133–135

New York Daily News, 141, 268

New York Herald Tribune, 39, 45, 47, 67, 135, 218, 430n72

New York intellectuals: HF's introduction to, 20, 21; Howe's coining of, 356; Jewishness of, 358

New York Observer, 388

New York Post, 444n20

New York Times: on anti-fascism, 141–142; and Columbia University's barring of HF from speaking, 137; on Feinberg Law, 450n12; and Foley Square Courthouse trial, 434n24; and HF's exchange with Polevoy, 322, 329; and HF's renunciation of American Communist Party, 316–317, 324; and Khrushchev's speech, 302, 303; reviews of HF's work, 34, 35, 39, 47, 67, 126, 150, 234, 240, 338, 339, 361, 373, 379, 388, 397, 399, 411n86; and United Nations, 80; and World Congress of Peace, 174

New York University, 19, 20, 21, 125, 138, 225, 377

New York World Telegram, 129

New York World Telegram and Sun, 236

Newman, Lewis I., 155, 241

Newsweek, 67, 72

1984 (Orwell), 166

Nixon, Richard, 113, 143, 224

Normani, Nina, 216

Norris, Frank, 355

North, Joe, 55, 88, 94, 139, 153

North Africa, 60, 79–80, 207

North Atlantic Treaty, 128

Northwest Passage (Roberts), 34

Novick, Paul, 175, 177, 178, 302

nuclear weapons, 147

Nuremberg trials, 120, 124

O'Brien, Edna, 405

O'Casey, Sean, 7, 191, 196, 216, 428n37

Ocean Hill–Brownsville school crisis of 1968, 355

O'Connor, Flannery, 287

O'Connor, John J., 373–374

Odets, Clifford: HF on, 121; HF's relationship with, 46, 196, 202, 211; and progressive theater, 413n8; and Saxe, 216; and theater of social protest, 52; and Waldorf World Peace Conference, 169

Of Mice and Men (film), 146

Office of Strategic Services (oss), 124

Office of War Information (owi), HF's work for, 3, 45–47, 49, 55–56, 60, 61, 62, 63, 88, 89, 265, 266, 274, 320

Old Man and the Sea, The (Hemingway), 361

Oliver Twist (film), 242, 448n106

Olivier, Laurence, 341, 467n31

Olsen, Tillie, 411n71

O'Neill, Eugene, 18, 195

Ordroneux, Johnnie, 157

Orwell, George, 6, 66, 127, 166, 270, 425n62

Ostrovsky, N. A., 191, 439n7

Ozick, Cynthia, 404

pacifism: and *Agrippa's Daughter,* 338, 339; HF's commitment to, 9, 147, 152, 338, 339, 346–348, 352–354, 370, 374, 377, 469n68, 470n90; and Lowell, 171

Paine, Thomas, 47–48, 75, 117, 133–134, 369

Pakistan, 81

Palestine, 80–81, 147, 249

Paley, Grace, 249

Palmer, A. Mitchell, 276–277

Panitz, David, 434n29

Paramount Pictures, 343

Paris Peace Conference, 231

Parrington, Vernon, 414n16

Partisan Review, 170, 356, 357

Patterson, William, 77, 231, 232, 253
Pavlenko, P., 191–192, 194, 436n49, 439n8
Pearce, Charles, 412n99
Pearl Harbor, attack on, 42, 44
Peekskill, New York, anti-Communist riots, 7, 181–188, 190, 208
People from Heaven, The (Sanford), 64
People's Theatre, 216
People's Weekly, 386, 387
Permanent Subcommittee on Investigations of the Senate Government Operations Committee, 265. *See also* McCarthy, Joseph
Perry, Pettis, 233
Petry, Ann, 136, 195–196
Philadelphia Freedom of the Press Association, 246
Philbrick, Herbert, 289
Picasso, Pablo, 7, 173, 246, 254, 435n41, 440n20
Pioneer, The, 451n33
Pius XII (pope), 254
PM, 58, 63, 77
Podhoretz, Norman, 271
Poe, Edgar Allan, 193
Poland: conditions in, 332; and German-Soviet Boundary and Friendship Treaty, 415n43; HF's royalties from, 297; and Hitler, 119; Jewish Socialist Bund in, 58; Second World Peace Conference in, 222; slaughter in, 318; strikes in, 326
Polevoy, Boris, 7, 194, 291, 292, 299–300, 308, 320, 321–322, 324
Political Affairs (PA), 220
Politics, 171
Poll, Martin, 343
Pollock, Thomas, 138
Polner, Murray, 262
Popular Front: and black self-determination, 69; as coalition of liberals and Communists, 31, 87, 118, 158, 159, 415n51, 426n7; and Great Depression, 60; and nonrevolutionary period, 28
Portnoy's Complaint (Philip Roth), 356
Possessed (film), 18
Pound, Ezra, 76, 418n14
Praeger Publishers, 329
Pravda, 172, 262, 263, 321, 331
Prescott, Orville, 67
Pringle-Smith, Jo, 64
Pro Arte, 173
Progressive Citizens of America, 137, 147
Progressive Party: and American Communist Party, 159, 160, 161; and Benson, 259; and Einstein, 258; and HF, 159–161, 257; and Popular Front, 415n51; and Wallace, 158
progressivism: and anti-Communist sentiment, 132; and Cobb, 344; and Democratic Party, 123, 158; and experimental writing, 286–287; fascism versus, 32; HF's attraction to, 55, 152, 478n25; and HF's cause, 143; and historical interpretation, 414n16; and Robeson, 53, 54; and second-generation Jews, 55
proletarian literature: aesthetics of, 287, 391, 411n71; *Clarkton* as, 126; HF's contributions to, 30; Sarah Kunitz on, 23, 410n44; and Lawson, 68; and New York intellectuals, 21
Prospectus, 329
Proust, Marcel, 49, 50
Prudkov, O., 303
Public Enemy, The (film), 408n24
Pullman, George, 115
Putnam, Samuel, 210
Pynchon, Thomas, 405

Quakers, 455n15
Quill, Mike, 83

Rabble in Arms (Roberts), 34
race and race relations: and American

Communist Party, 70; and court cases, 226–227; Du Bois on, 62–63; and HF's childhood, 15; in HF's early literature, 30, 48; HF's encounters with racism, 64; and HF's interest in integration of American armed forces, 62; and HF's trip to the South, 22; and loyalty boards, 123; and Peekskill, New York, anti-Communist riots, 187; and Robeson, 54; and United Nations, 446n60; and U.S. Supreme Court, 301; and World War II, 67–68. *See also* blacks

Rachel and the Stranger (film), 139

racial justice: and American Communist Party, 60, 63, 69, 70, 72; and anti-Communist sentiment, 427n10; and civil rights, 301, 349, 354; Du Bois on, 62–63; and *Freedom Road,* 63, 66, 67–70, 267; HF's promotion of, 73, 90, 109, 226, 227, 242, 317, 354–355, 422n8; and HF's work at Office of War Information, 46; HF's writing on, 162

Radetzky March, The (Joseph Roth), 373

radical activism: and authors finding publishers, 136; and *Freedom Road,* 63; and HF's advocacy in Rosenberg case, 242, 251; and HF's cause, 142–143; and HF's Jewishness, 152, 153–154, 228; and HF's speeches, 147, 245, 430n61; and HF's writing, 4, 9, 63, 107, 147; and Jewish identity, 10, 63, 150, 157, 250, 251; and Spanish Civil War, 32

Radio Liberation, 336–337

Rahv, Philip, 20, 356

Rand, Ayn, 134

Randolph, A. Philip, 68, 183

Random House, 236

Rankin, John, 110, 112–113

Reader's Club, 40

Red Army, 58, 175

Red Badge of Courage (Crane), 339

Red Channels, 131

Red Menace, The (film), 122

Reisman, David, 287

Remarque, Erich Maria, 18, 35

"repairing the world" tradition, 2–3, 36, 60

Republican Party: and anti-Communist crusade, 108; and HF's election campaign, 261; and Joseph McCarthy, 264; successes of, 285; and Truman, 196

Reston, James, 224

Reynolds, Paul, 336

Rice, Elmer, 47

Rieff, Philip, 287

Ritt, Martin, 343

Rivera, Diego, 254, 294

RKO, 139

Robbins, Jerome, 450n15

Roberts, Kenneth, 34, 35

Robeson, Paul: and antisemitism in Soviet Union, 178–179, 330, 397; and "Deadline for Freedom" rallies, 440n22; entertainment career of, 53; and Foley Square Courthouse trial, 163, 168; health of, 308; HF as speaker at birthday anniversary, 397; and HF's election campaign, 258; HF's relationship with, 7, 53, 61, 62, 79, 89, 153, 231, 232, 375, 416n57; and HF's Stalin Prize, 293; and loyalty boards, 123; and McGee, 229; and minorities in Soviet Union, 179, 437n63; and Peekskill, New York, anti-Communist riots, 182–183, 184, 185–186, 187, 190; popularity in East Germany, 142; and radical activism, 430n61; as security risk, 452n43; and Stalin Prize, 283; and Wallace rally, 138; and World Congress of Peace, 173

Robinson, Edward G., 249

Rockefeller Foundation, 286, 439n18

Rockwell, Norman, 376

Rogge, O. John, 120, 124, 430n61

Romance, 29, 33

Roosevelt, Eleanor, 112, 145, 226, 267
Roosevelt, Franklin D.: American Communist Party support for, 158; and American Labor Party, 257–258; HF's endorsement of, 77; HF's obituary for, 87–88; and Wallace, 161; and War Relief Control Board, 110
Rose, Reginald, 289
Roseberg Defense Committee, 254
Rosen, Helen, 185–186
Rosen, Sam, 185–186
Rosenbaum, William F., 434n29
Rosenberg, Ethel: arrest of, 223, 252; charges against, 245, 252; conviction of, 250, 252; death of, 274; death penalty for, 250, 252, 253–254, 255, 261–262, 265, 274; Frankel on, 264, 453n66; and Frankfurter, 279; guilt of, 326, 453n71; HF's protesting death sentence, 242; HF's role in support of, 7–8, 244, 248, 251–252, 253, 256, 274, 275, 276, 277, 281; HF's speeches on, 261–262; HF's writing on, 251; as martyred hero, 456n25; and *The Outsider,* 378; Polevoy on, 322; Sacco and Vanzetti trial compared to, 276–277; and *Tony and the Wonderful Door,* 255; U.S. Jewish communities lack of support for, 251, 260
Rosenberg, Harold, 249
Rosenberg, Julius: arrest of, 223, 252; charges against, 245, 252; conviction of, 250, 252; death of, 274; death penalty for, 250, 252, 253–254, 255, 261–262, 265, 274; Frankel on, 264, 453n66; and Frankfurter, 279; guilt of, 326, 453n71, 456n25; HF's protesting death sentence, 242; HF's role in support of, 7–8, 244, 248, 251–252, 253, 256, 274, 275, 276, 277, 281; HF's speeches on, 261–262; HF's writing on, 251; as martyred hero, 456n25; and *The Outsider,* 378; Polevoy on, 322;

Sacco and Vanzetti trial compared to, 276–277; U.S. Jewish communities lack of support for, 251, 260
Rosenberg, Michael, 255, 275
Rosenberg, Robert, 255, 275
Rosenberg Defense Committee, 275
Rosenfeld, Isaac, 195, 356, 450n15
Rossen, Robert, 95, 219, 344
Rosten, Norman, 418n14
Roth, Henry, 24, 28
Roth, Joseph, 373
Roth, Philip, 356, 357, 404, 405
Rothko, Mark, 285, 458n4
Rowan, Carl, 226
Rubenstein, Joshua, 436n52
Rubin, Barney, 216, 217
Rubin, Ben, 212
Rukeyser, Muriel, 74, 136, 195, 196, 202, 249, 418n9
Russell, Bertrand, 352
Russell, Charles Edward, 129, 426n72

Sabatini, Rafael, 210
Sacco, Nicola, 246, 275–277, 278, 456n27
Sacks, Alan, 347
Salinger, J. D., 142, 287, 290, 410n58
Sandburg, Carl, 196
Sandoz, Mari, 401, 477n2
Sanford, John, 64
Saroyan, William, 410n58
Sartre, Jean Paul: and French resistance, 89, 90; HF's relationship with, 7, 89–90, 254; on Jewish identity, 74, 431n83; and Jouvenal, 146; and Koestler, 425n62; and Munich Olympics of 1972, 456n26; and Rosenberg case, 275, 276; and Soviet atrocities, 90, 91
Saturday Evening Post, 33, 141
Saturday Review, 72, 150, 329, 444n20
Saxe, Al, 216
Saxton, Alexander, 136
Saypol, Irving, 242, 251
Scandal Sheet (film), 18, 408n24

Scarface (film), 408n24

Schappes, Morris, 151, 155, 156, 270, 430n78

Schary, Dore, 47

Schechner, Mark, 357

Schine, G. David, 269, 270–271

Schlamme, Martha, 258, 452n43

Schlesinger, Arthur, Jr.: and Cold War, 420n55; HF's debate with, 247, 248, 250; and HF's speech at Harvard, 280; on Hollywood writers, 51–52; on HUAC, 133; on risk of American Communist Party, 112

Schoenberg, Arnold, 172

Schomburg Award in Race Relations, 67

Schulberg, Budd, 68, 196

Schulman, Arnold, 347

Schultz, Benjamin, 149–150, 153

Schwartz, Delmore, 356, 357

Schwartz, Harry, 303, 316–317, 321, 324, 327, 464n59

science fiction films, 289–290

Scope, 61–62, 77

Scottsboro Case, 445n41

Screen Writers Guild, 51

Second World Peace Conference, 222–223

Seeger, Pete, 7, 153, 184–185, 187, 328, 398, 464n62

Segal, William, 347, 396

Seize the Day (Bellow), 287

Senate Internal Security Subcommittee (SISS), 132, 133, 328

Serge, Victor, 331

Shahn, Ben, 23

Shapiro, Karl, 249

Shapiro, Linn, 197

Shapiro, Meyer, 356

Shapiro, Susan, 388, 394

Sharim, Bandar, 82

Shaw, David, 51

Shaw, George Bernard, 19, 21

Shaw, Irwin, 51, 152–153, 374

Shaw, Vivian, 50–51

Shaw, Warren, 385

Shipley, Ruth, 259, 446n59

Shostakovich, Dmitri, 171–172, 435n37

Shubin, Alexander, 291

Sillen, Samuel, 77, 94, 391

Sills, Beverly, 249

Silone, Ignazio, 7, 127, 331

Silverman, Hillel, 401

Siminov, Konstantin, 261

Simon, Neil, 249

Simon and Schuster, 38, 39, 236–237, 446n56

Sinatra, Frank, 23

Sinclair, Jo, 195, 196

Sinclair, Upton, 277, 463n33

Singer, I. J., 373

Siqueiros, David, 294

Slansky, Rudolf, 253, 254, 263, 264, 292, 453n66

Sloan, Sam, 39, 47, 56, 126

Smith, Lillian E., 64

Smith Act: and American Communist Party, 76, 157, 175, 230; and Foley Square Courthouse trial, 164, 167, 168; HF associating with fascism, 247; HF raising funds for children displaced by, 256; HF's advocating appeals of cases, 242, 244, 245, 256–257, 284; HF's calling for repeal of, 260, 292; ineffectiveness of, 455n15; and James Jackson, 465n1; and Nelson, 449n5; and Socialist Workers Party, 76

Smith-Mundt Act, 143–144

So Red the Rose (Young), 66

Sobell, Morton, 245

Sobolev, Leonid, 191, 439n7

social class: and *Citizen Tom Paine*, 47–49; and Duclos, 86; and HF on writing, 121, 287; and HF's involvement in American Communist Party, 86–87, 90, 108–109, 159; and HF's novels, 43

Social Democrats, 86, 112, 116, 117, 258, 319

social justice: HF's commitment to, 2, 251, 317, 319; and HF's work for Office of War Information, 46; and Hollywood, 52; and inequality, 285

Social Justice (journal), 31

socialism: and American exceptionalism, 86, 87; Duclos on, 85–86; and Eastern European Jewish immigrants, 55; HF's attraction to, 20, 59; HF's understanding of, 306, 310, 314, 328; and Robeson, 53–54; Soviet model of, 4, 20, 57, 72, 86–87, 306, 310, 321, 324, 330; and Steinbeck, 146

socialist realism: HF on, 191, 192, 196, 315; Pavlenko on, 192; philosophy of, 5, 70, 92–93, 417n83

Socialist Workers Party (SWP), 76, 167

Solomon, Haym, 41, 129

Sonnets of Love and Liberty (Lowenfels), 242

Souls of Black Folk, The (Du Bois), 242

Southern Youth Negro Conference, 422n8, 465n1

Soviet Communist Party, 7

Soviet Russia Today, 179

Soviet Union (USSR): and American Communist Party spies, 166, 433n4; and American public opinion, 122; antisemitism in, 57, 149, 174–179, 254, 262, 263–264, 272–273, 292, 304–305, 316–317, 318, 321–322, 327, 330–331, 337, 383; and art, 96, 141, 142; atrocities in, 58–59, 60, 90, 308, 403; and *Clarkton,* 128; confrontational policies of, 86; and cultural rebuilding, 142; and "Doctors' Plot," 262–264, 272, 292, 322, 337, 453n61, 453n66; German invasion of, 58, 69, 70, 119; gulags of, 3, 425n62; HF advocating peace with, 147, 160, 174; and HF awarded Stalin Prize, 244–245, 283, 293, 297, 317, 460n25; HF's apologetics for, 4, 58–59, 60, 90, 178, 188, 263, 272, 283,

299, 305–306, 309; HF's positive relationship with, 4, 56–59, 72, 142, 154, 170, 243, 244, 251, 265, 296, 307, 318, 358, 470n82; and HF's royalties, 241, 242, 296–297, 448n100; and Hungarian revolution, 8, 314–315, 318, 319, 326; and Israel, 149, 151, 154; Jews repressed in, 358–359; positive views of, 56; post-Stalin reforms in, 273, 301–303, 313–314, 316; and public-shame trials, 70; refugees of, 3; and Robeson, 53–54; socialist model of, 4, 20, 57, 72, 86–87, 306, 310, 312, 321, 324, 330; and Truman, 123; United States' relations with, 107–108, 123; and Waldorf World Peace Conference, 169, 170; and World War II, 42, 57, 58, 107

Soviet Writers Union, 7, 170, 174, 227, 291, 292, 324, 436n49

Soyer, Raphael, 141

Spanish Civil War: and Abraham Lincoln Battalion, 32; and Amann, 293; and Bessie, 93; and fascism, 31–32; and *The Immigrants,* 372; and Joint Anti-Fascist Refugee Committee, 11; and Nelson, 7, 417n84; and *The Proud and the Free,* 221; and Rubin, 216; and Trotskyism, 3; veterans of, 229

Spartacus (Fast): bravery in, 279; HF's self-publishing of, 237–238, 242, 297; legacy of, 405; literary quality of, 6, 334; in paperback, 340; political message of, 290; publishing of, 235–237; research on, 204; reviews of, 7, 240; success of, 2, 240, 241–242; translation of, 297; writing of, 210–211, 233, 235, 238–239, 240

Spartacus (film): and Kirk Douglas, 340–342, 401; HF writing screenplay for, 8, 340–341, 346, 467n28; and HF's desire for Hollywood work, 146; HF's opinion of, 341–342; homosexuality in, 342, 467n31; release of paperback book with, 340; Trumbo's work on screenplay, 8, 340, 341

Spellman, Francis, 162, 164

Spender, Stephen, 331

Spillane, Mickey, 235, 335, 346

Springsteen, Bruce, 352

St. Louis Post-Dispatch, 167

Stalin, Joseph: and American Communist Party, 119; antisemitism, of, 263; art mandated by, 94, 95–96, 417n83; and Cold War, 86; crimes of, 45, 59, 119, 179, 195, 262, 273, 301–302, 304, 322, 330, 331, 332, 403, 452n56, 464n62; cultural covert attacks on, 95; death of, 172, 272, 274, 429n57, 444n29; and ethnic cleansing, 437n63; and French intellectuals, 143; Great Terror purges, 3, 302, 330–331; HF quoting, 281; HF's admiration for, 296, 328; Hitler compared to, 309; Khrushchev compared to, 326; Khrushchev's "secret" denunciation of, 8; model of separation of ethnic groups, 68–69; and pact with Hitler, 3, 57, 58, 69, 119, 305, 415n43; and Popular Front, 416n51; and Sartre, 90; and Trotsky, 411n74; and Truman, 159–160; Wallace on, 78–79, 159–160, 432n100; writings of, 165, 256

Stalinism: and American left, 112; Aragon's denunciation of, 429n57; on art and politics, 3; atrocities of, 32, 253, 254, 272, 302–303, 318; HF's view of, 4, 93, 177, 273, 283, 333; and Hollywood, 133; and Hollywood Ten, 53; and Robeson, 179; and Trotsky's assassination, 76

Stanley, Edward, 79

Starobin, Joseph, 219, 319–320

Stars and Stripes, 80

Stavans, Ilan, 441n54

Steele, Barbara, 343, 468n39

Stegner, Wallace, 404

Steichen, Edward, 140

Steinbeck, John: HF on, 78, 93, 121, 146, 191, 201; Sarah Kunitz on, 23; prohibition in Soviet Union, 142; Soviet excommunication of, 320

Stern, Bernhard J., 93–94

Stern, Isaac, 169

Stevenson, Adlai, 261

Stewart, Paul, 214, 325, 343, 345

Stewart, Peggy, 214, 325, 343, 345

Stieglitz, Alfred, 140

Stone, I. F., 76, 168, 224, 440n22, 453n66

Story magazine, 27, 410n58

Stout, Rex, 346

Strange Fruit (Lillian Smith), 64

Stravinsky, Igor, 172, 356

Styron, William, 142, 405

Suller, Chaim, 175, 177, 178

Sunday Worker, 212

super-truth, 191

Swados, Harvey, 240, 287

Sylvia (film), 345

Taft-Hartley Law, 260

Tank, Herb, 216, 217

Taylor, Paul, 450n15

Teachers' Union, 135, 355

Teamsters Union, 76

Teheran Conference, 86

television, 288–289, 324–325, 327, 344, 374–375, 376

Tennyson, Alfred Lord, 191

Thayer, Webster, 277

This Gun for Hire (film), 51

This Week, 446n66

Thomas, Gwyn, 143, 154, 158, 189–190, 191, 203, 231

Thomas, J. Parnell, 113, 162

Thomas, Norman, 134

Thomas, Richard, 369

Thompson, Dorothy, 134

Thompson, Robert, 257, 459n17

Thought Control in the United States, 427n18

Thurmond, Strom, 157, 161, 187

Time magazine, 225

Tito, Josip Broz, 77, 119–120

Tolstoy, Leo, 121, 210, 372

Tortilla Flat (film), 146

Toynbee, Philip, 296

Trachtenberg, Alexander, 77, 256, 452n37

Transcendental Meditation, 347

Transportation Workers Union, 83

Traube, Shepard, 94, 118

Trenton Six, 226, 227, 277

Trilling, Diana, 67, 117

Trilling, Lionel, 285, 381

Trotsky, Leon: assassination of, 76, 294, 453n58; HF's reading of, 92; and Luxemburg, 210; and modernists, 356; and Stalin, 411n74

Trotskyism: charges of, 253; and Farrell, 91, 121, 463n33; and Foley Square Courthouse trial, 167, 168; HF on, 91–92, 117, 121, 191; and Moscow Show Trials, 31, 305; and Robeson, 397; and Smith Act, 76, 167, 168; and Spanish Civil War, 3

Truman, Harry S.: and atom bomb, 107, 189; and Cold War, 123, 163; and Foley Square Courthouse trial, 164, 167; HF on, 140, 189, 196, 223, 229, 280; and HF on Rosenberg case, 251, 252; and HF's imprisonment, 201; and HF's passport request, 259; and HF's pleading for Martinsville Seven, 445n44; and Hoover, 444n25; and integration, 157; and Internal Security Act, 224; and Korean War, 201, 224; and Stalin, 159–160; and United Nations, 446n60; and Wallace, 78–79, 159, 161

Truman Doctrine, 159, 160, 163

Trumbo, Dalton: and Communist ideas in films, 122–123; HF's relationship with, 341; and integration, 157; and Mexico, 293; and screenplay credits for *Spartacus,* 8, 340, 341; as target of anti-Communist sentiment, 143

Trupin, Julie, 257, 260

Tunney, Jack, 368

Tuttle, Frank, 51, 62

Twain, Mark, 17, 52, 193, 194, 328

Twelve O'Clock High (film), 214

21 Hours in Munich (TV docudrama), 367

Tydings, Millard, 265

Tydings Committee, 265

United Auto Workers, 158

United Mine Workers, 158

United Nations: and China, 224; Convention on the Prevention and Punishment of the Crime of Genocide, 232, 446n60; HF on, 80, 109; Human Rights Commission, 145, 168, 226; and loyalty boards, 123; Middle East arms embargo, 147; Soviet veto in, 160; Universal Declaration of Human Rights, 232

United Packinghouse Workers, 109

United States: and death penalty for espionage, 451n28; Jewish community of, 248–251, 450n15; loyalty to, 108, 123–124, 132; as postwar capitalist world power, 144; Soviet Union's relations with, 107–108, 123. *See also* American literature

Untermeyer, Louis, 45, 50, 134, 136, 153, 196, 368, 427n17

Updike, John, 404

Uris, Leon, 431n87

U.S. Army Signal Corps, 44–45, 49–51, 77, 266

U.S. Chamber of Commerce, 223

U.S. Civil Service Commission, 61

U.S. Justice Department: and Foley Square Courthouse trial, 165, 166; and HF's resignation from American

Communist Party, 325; and Trotsky-ism, 76

U.S. State Department: and anti-Com-munist sentiment, 124; and *Citizen Tom Paine*, 47; and HF's approved novels, 269–270; and HF's obtaining passport, 61, 78, 173, 222–223, 231–232, 259, 283, 435n40; and HF's work for Office of War Information, 46; and Isacson, 258

U.S. Supreme Court: and Bradley's con-viction for contempt of Congress, 125; on call to action, 465n1; and Feinberg law, 450n12; and Foley Square Court-house trial, 168; and HF's conviction for contempt of Congress, 11, 144, 156–157, 189; HF's opposing rejection of appeals, 242; and racial desegregation, 301, 310; and Rosenberg case, 254

U.S. War Department, 78, 79

USSR. *See* Soviet Union (USSR)

Ustinov, Peter, 341

Vallejo, Cesar, 202

van den Haag, Ernest, 274

Van Doren, Carl, 40, 221, 222, 413n113

Van Doren, Mark, 111

Vanzetti, Bartolomeo, 246, 275–277, 278, 456n27, 457n35

Venona project, 433n4

Vernon, Grenville, 22

Vestal, Stanley, 38–39

Veterans of the Abraham Lincoln Bri-gade (VALB), 114, 246

Victim, The (Bellow), 195, 431n83

Vietnam War, 352, 359, 360, 370, 372, 403

Viking, 236

Virginian, The (film), 18

Voice of America (VOA), 45–46, 60, 61, 265, 266, 269–270, 313

Voltaire, 75

Wald, Alan, 391

Waldorf World Peace Conference, 168–173, 174, 175, 434n29, 436n51

Wall, The (Hersey), 153

Wallace, Henry: American Communist Party support for, 158, 159, 160, 161, 163, 432n102; and HF's passport, 62, 78; HF's speeches for, 140, 147; HF's support for, 158, 160, 162, 256; Macdonald on, 432n100; and Mailer, 169; rally for, 138; and Truman, 78–79, 159, 161

Walsh, Richard, 25

Walter Reed Associates, 348

Walton, Edna Lou, 418n14

War Relief Control Board, 110

Warner Brothers, 401

Warren, Robert Penn, 195, 477n19

Washington, George, 34, 41–42, 43, 48

Washington Post, 167

Watchful at Night (Julius Fast), 212

We Charge Genocide, 231, 232

Weavers, 328

Webb, James R., 401

Weiner, William, 447n94

Weinstock, Louis, 153

Welles, Orson, 46

Wells, H. G., 255, 451n32

Welty, Eudora, 405

Werbel, Isadore, 36–37, 38

West, Benjamin, 376

Wharton, Edith, 355

What's a Nice Girl Like You . . . ? (tele-play), 470n88

Whitman, Walt, 193

Whitney Museum, 458n4

Williams, William Carlos, 196, 202

Wilson, Edmund, 277, 472n31

Winchell, Walter, 77

Winston, Harry, 167, 257

Wise, Stephen S., 63

Wise Blood (O'Connor), 287

Wishengrad, Morton, 157

Wolf, Benedict, 265, 266–267
Wolfson, Harry A., 155, 431n92
Woman's Day, 73
Women's Committee for Peace, 259
Women's International League for Peace
    and Freedom, 455n15
women's rights: and American Commu-
    nist Party, 416n52; HF on, 389–390;
    and Popular Front, 60; and Soviet
    Union, 172
Wood, James, 472n31
Wood, John, 110, 111, 119, 120
Woodhill (captain), 80–81, 211
Woodward, W. E., 48
World Congress of Peace, 169, 173–181
World Peace Conference, 130
World Publishers, 236
World War II: and American Com-
    munist Party, 70, 72; and *Being Red,*
    474n65; and blacks, 183, 397; espio-
    nage cases of, 451n28; extermination
    of Jews during, 42–43, 63, 148, 153,
    248; HF as war correspondent, 61,
    78–85; and HF's activism in civil
    rights, 73; and HF's novels, 42–43;
    HF's short stories on, 41; and *The Last
    Frontier,* 40; Macdonald on, 432n100;
    and Nazi–Soviet Pact, 3, 57, 58, 69,
    119, 305, 415n43; and race relations,
    67–68; and Soviet–United States alli-
    ance, 107; as war against fascism, 57
Wright, Richard: HF on, 93, 191; leaving

American Communist Party, 68,
    145–146, 331, 332; and *Literature and
    Reality,* 195; prohibition in Soviet
    Union, 142; publishing in *Story* maga-
    zine, 410n58
Wyeth, N. C., 19
Wynn-Ferber, Lori, 343–344, 363, 368

Yadin, Yigael, 374
Yale Political Union, 247
Yale University, 121
Yank, 80
*Yankee Doodle Stories of the Brave and
    the Free,* 131
Yates v. United States (1957), 465n1
Young, Stark, 66
Young America, 73, 418n3
Young Lions, The (Irwin Shaw), 152–153
Young Progressive Citizens of America,
    138, 225
Youngman, Henry, 450n15

Zen Buddhism, HF's practice of, 9, 346–
    348, 368, 369, 376, 396, 402, 468n52
Zinberg, Len, 234–235
Zionism: and anti-Communism senti-
    ment, 149; and Feffer, 176, 178; HF's
    respect for, 337; in Palestine, 151;
    and Robeson, 178; and Slansky, 253;
    Soviet anti-Zionism, 263–264; Soviet
    characterization of HF as Zionist, 314,
    336. *See also* Israel

GERALD SORIN

is Distinguished Professor Emeritus of American and Jewish Studies at the State University of New York at New Paltz. His most recent book, *Irving Howe: A Life of Passionate Dissent,* received the 2003 National Jewish Book Award in History. His other books include *The Prophetic Minority: American Jewish Immigrant Radicals, 1880–1920* (Indiana University Press, 1985).